MCAT® BIOLOGY REVIEW

MCAT® BIOLOGY REVIEW

The Staff of Kaplan

KAPLAN) PUBLISHING

New York

© 2010 by Kaplan, Inc.

Published by Kaplan Publishing, a division of Kaplan, Inc.
1 Liberty Plaza, 24th Floor
New York, NY 10006

Printed in the United States of America

10 9 8 7 6 5 4 3

ISBN: 978-1-60714-643-8

Kaplan Publishing books are available at special quantity discounts to use for sales promotions, employee premiums, or educational purposes. For more information or to purchase books, please call the Simon & Schuster special sales department at 866-506-1949.

Planet Friendly Publishing
✔ Made in the United States
✔ Printed on Recycled Paper
Learn more at www.greenedition.org

• Manufacturing books in the United States ensures compliance with strict environmental laws and eliminates the need for international freight shipping, a major contributor to global air pollution. Printing on recycled paper helps minimize our consumption of trees, water and fossil fuels.
• Trees Saved: 160 • Air Emissions Eliminated: 15,275 pounds
• Water Saved: 73,161 gallons • Solid Waste Eliminated: 4,458 pounds

Contents

KAPLAN'S EXPERT MCAT TEAM

Kaplan has been preparing premeds for the MCAT for more than 40 years. In the past 15 years alone, we've helped more than 400,000 students prepare for this important exam and improve their chances for medical school admission.

Marilyn Engle

MCAT Master Teacher; Teacher Trainer; Kaplan National Teacher of the Year, 2006; Westwood Teacher of the Year, 2007; Westwood Trainer of the Year, 2007; Encino Trainer of the Year, 2005

John Michael Linick

MCAT Teacher; Boulder Teacher of the Year, 2007; Summer Intensive Program Faculty Member

Dr. Glen Pearlstein

MCAT Master Teacher; Teacher Trainer; Westwood Teacher of the Year, 2006

Matthew B. Wilkinson

MCAT Teacher; Teacher Trainer; Lone Star Trainer of the Year, 2007

Thanks to Jason Baserman, Jessica Brookman, Da Chang, John Cummins, David Elson, Jeff Koetje, Alex Macnow, Andrew Molloy, Josh Rohrig, and Amjed Saffarini.

ABOUT SCIENTIFIC AMERICAN

As the world's premier science and technology magazine, and the oldest continuously published magazine in the United States, *Scientific American* is committed to bringing the most important developments in modern science, medicine, and technology to 3.5 million readers worldwide in an understandable, credible, and provocative format.

Founded in 1845 and on the "cutting edge" ever since, *Scientific American* boasts over 140 Nobel laureate authors, including Albert Einstein, Francis Crick, Stanley Prusiner, and Richard Axel. *Scientific American* is a forum where scientific theories and discoveries are explained to a broader audience.

Scientific American published its first foreign edition in 1890 and, in 1979, was the first Western magazine published in the People's Republic of China. Today, *Scientific American* is published in 17 foreign language editions with a total circulation of more than 1 million worldwide. *Scientific American* is also a leading online destination (www.ScientificAmerican.com), providing the latest science news and exclusive features to more than 2 million unique visitors monthly.

The knowledge that fills our pages has the power to inspire, to spark new ideas, paradigms, and visions for the future. As science races forward, *Scientific American* continues to cover the promising strides, inevitable setbacks and challenges, and new medical discoveries as they unfold.

How to Use this Book

Kaplan MCAT Biology, along with the other four books in our MCAT Review series, brings the Kaplan classroom experience to you—right in your home, at your convenience. This book offers the same Kaplan content review, strategies, and practice that make Kaplan the #1 choice for MCAT prep. All that's missing is the teacher.

To guide you through this complex content, we've consulted our best MCAT instructors to call out **Key Concept**, to offer **Bridge** to better understanding of the material, and **Mnemonic** devices to assist in learning retention. When you see these sidebars, you will know you're getting the same insight and knowledge that classroom students receive in person. Look for these as well as references to the **Real World** and **MCAT expertise** callouts throughout the book.

HIGH-YIELD MCAT REVIEW

Following the content sction, you will find a **High-Yield Questions** section. These questions tackle the most frequently tested topics found on the MCAT. For each type of problem, you will be provided with a stepwise technique for solving the question, as well as important directional points on how to solve it—specifically for the MCAT.

Our experts have again called out the **Key Concepts**, which show you which terms to review. Next, the **Takeaways** box offers a concise summary of the problem-solving approach best used. **Things to Watch Out For** points out any caveats to the approach discussed, which can lead to wrong answer choices. Finally, **Similar Questions** allows you to practice the stepwise technique on analogous, open-ended questions.

STAR RATING

The star rating is a Kaplan-exclusive system to help you focus your studies, using a 6-star scale. Two factors are considered when determining the rating for each topic: the "learnability" of the topic—or how easy it is to master—and the frequency with which it appears on the MCAT exam. For example, a topic that presents relatively little difficulty to master and appears with relatively high frequency on the MCAT would receive a higher star rating (e.g., 5 or 6 stars) than a topic which is very difficult to master and appears less frequently on the test. The combination of these two factors represented by the star rating will help you prioritize and direct your MCAT studies.

We're confident that this guide and our award-winning instructors can help you achieve your goals of MCAT success and admission to med school. Good luck!

Introduction to the MCAT

The Medical College Admission Test (MCAT) is different from any other test you've encountered in your academic career. It's not like the knowledge-based exams from high school and college, where emphasis was on memorizing and regurgitating information. Medical schools can assess your academic prowess by looking at your transcript. The MCAT isn't even like other standardized tests you may have taken, where the focus was on proving your general skills.

Medical schools use MCAT scores to assess whether you possess the foundation upon which to build a successful medical career. Though you certainly need to know the content to do well, the stress is on thought process, because the MCAT is above all else a critical thinking test. That's why it emphasizes reasoning, analytical thinking, reading comprehension, data analysis, writing, and problem-solving skills.

Though the MCAT places more weight on your thought process, you must have a strong grasp of the required core knowledge. The MCAT may not be a perfect gauge of your abilities, but it is a relatively objective way to compare you with students from different backgrounds and undergraduate institutions.

The MCAT's power comes from its use as an indicator of your abilities. Good scores can open doors. Your power comes from preparation and mindset because the key to MCAT success is knowing what you're up against. That's where this section of this book comes in. We'll explain the philosophy behind the test, review the sections one by one, show you sample questions, share some of Kaplan's proven methods, and clue you in to what the test makers are really after. You'll get a handle on the process, find a confident new perspective, and achieve your highest possible scores.

ABOUT THE MCAT

Information about the MCAT CBT is included below. For the latest information about the MCAT, visit www.kaptest.com/mcat.

MCAT CBT

Format	U.S.—All administrations on computer
	International—Most on computer with limited paper and pencil in a few isolated areas
Essay Grading	One human and one computer grader
Breaks	Optional break between each section
Length of MCAT Day	Approximately 5.5 hours
Test Dates	Multiple dates in January, April, May, June, July, August, and September
	Total of 24 administrations each year.
Delivery of Results	Within 30 days. If scores are delayed notification will be posted online at www.aamc.org/mcat
	Electronic and paper
Security	Government-issued ID
	Electronic thumbprint
	Electronic signature verification
Testing Centers	Small computer testing sites

Go online and sign up for a local Kaplan Pre-Med Edge event to get the latest information on the test.

PLANNING FOR THE TEST

As you look toward your preparation for the MCAT consider the following advice:

Complete your core course requirements as soon as possible. Take a strategic eye to your schedule and get core requirements out of the way now.

Take the MCAT once. The MCAT is a notoriously grueling standardized exam that requires extensive preparation. It is longer than the graduate admissions exams for business school (GMAT, 3½ hours), law school (LSAT, 3¼ hours), and graduate school (GRE, 2½ hours). You do not want to take it twice. Plan and prepare accordingly.

KAPLAN

THE ROLE OF THE MCAT IN ADMISSIONS

More and more people are applying to medical school and more and more people are taking the MCAT. It's important for you to recognize that while a high MCAT score is a critical component in getting admitted to top med schools, it's not the only factor. Medical school admissions officers weigh grades, interviews, MCAT scores, level of involvement in extracurricular activities, as well as personal essays.

In a Kaplan survey of 130 pre-med advisors, 84 percent called the interview a "very important" part of the admissions process, followed closely by college grades (83 percent) and MCAT scores (76 percent). Kaplan's college admissions consulting practice works with students on all these issues so they can position themselves as strongly as possible. In addition, the AAMC has made it clear that scores will continue to be valid for three years, and that the scoring of the computer-based MCAT will not differ from that of the paper and pencil version.

REGISTRATION

The only way to register for the MCAT is online. The registration site is: www.aamc.org/mcat.

You will be able to access the site approximately six months before your test date. Payment must be made by MasterCard or Visa.

Go to www.aamc.org/mcat/registration.htm and download *MCAT Essentials* for information about registration, fees, test administration, and preparation. For other questions, contact:

MCAT Care Team
Association of American Medical Colleges
Section for Applicant Assessment Services
2450 N. St., NW
Washington, DC 20037
www.aamc.org/mcat
Email: mcat@aamc.org

Keep in mind that you will need to take the MCAT in the year prior to your planned med school start date. Don't drag your feet gathering information. You'll need time not only to prepare and practice for the test, but also to get all your registration work done.

The MCAT should be viewed just like any other part of your application: as an opportunity to show the medical schools who you are and what you can do. Take control of your MCAT experience.

ANATOMY OF THE MCAT

Before mastering strategies, you need to know exactly what you're dealing with on the MCAT. Let's start with the basics: The MCAT is, among other things, an endurance test.

If you can't approach it with confidence and stamina, you'll quickly lose your composure. That's why it's so important that you take control of the test.

The MCAT consists of four timed sections: Physical Sciences, Verbal Reasoning, Writing Sample, and Biological Sciences. Later in this section we'll take an in-depth look at each MCAT section, including sample question types and specific test-smart hints, but here's a general overview, reflecting the order of the test sections and number of questions in each.

Physical Sciences

Time	70 minutes
Format	• 52 multiple-choice questions: approximately 7–9 passages with 4–8 questions each • approximately 10 stand-alone questions (not passage-based)
What it tests	basic general chemistry concepts, basic physics concepts, analytical reasoning, data interpretation

Verbal Reasoning

Time	60 minutes
Format	• 40 multiple-choice questions: approximately 7 passages with 5–7 questions each
What it tests	critical reading

Writing Sample

Time	60 minutes
Format	• 2 essay questions (30 minutes per essay)
What it tests	critical thinking, intellectual organization, written communication skills

Biological Sciences

Time	70 minutes
Format	• 52 multiple-choice questions: approximately 7–9 passages with 4–8 questions each • approximately 10 stand-alone questions (not passage-based)
What it tests	basic biology concepts, basic organic chemistry concepts, analytical reasoning, data interpretation

The sections of the test always appear in the same order:

Physical Sciences

[optional 10-minute break]

Verbal Reasoning

[optional 10-minute break]

Writing Sample

[optional 10-minute break]

Biological Sciences

SCORING

Each MCAT section receives its own score. Physical Sciences, Verbal Reasoning, and Biological Sciences are each scored on a scale ranging from 1–15, with 15 as the highest. The Writing Sample essays are scored alphabetically on a scale ranging from J to T, with T as the highest. The two essays are each evaluated by two official readers, so four critiques combine to make the alphabetical score.

The number of multiple-choice questions that you answer correctly per section is your "raw score." Your raw score will then be converted to yield the "scaled score"—the one that will fall somewhere in that 1–15 range. These scaled scores are what are reported to medical schools as your MCAT scores. All multiple-choice questions are worth the same amount—one raw point—and *there's no penalty for guessing*. That means that *you should always select an answer for every question, whether you get to that question or not!* This is an important piece of advice, so pay it heed. Never let time run out on any section without selecting an answer for every question.

The raw score of each administration is converted to a scaled score. The conversion varies with administrations. Hence, the same raw score will not always give you the same scaled score.

Your score report will tell you—and your potential medical schools—not only your scaled scores, but also the national mean score for each section, standard deviation, national scoring profile for each section, and your percentile ranking.

WHAT'S A GOOD SCORE?

There's no such thing as a cut-and-dry "good score." Much depends on the strength of the rest of your application (if your transcript is first rate, the pressure to strut your stuff on the MCAT isn't as intense) and on where you want to go to school (different schools have different score expectations). Here are a few interesting statistics:

For each MCAT administration, the average scaled scores are approximately 8s for Physical Sciences, Verbal Reasoning, and Biological Sciences, and N for the Writing Sample. You need scores of at least 10–11s to be considered competitive by most medical schools, and if you're aiming for the top you've got to do even better, and score 12s and above.

You don't have to be perfect to do well. For instance, on the AAMC's Practice Test 5R, you could get as many as 10 questions wrong in Verbal Reasoning, 17 in Physical Sciences, and 16 in Biological Sciences and still score in the 80th percentile. To score in the 90th percentile, you could get as many as 7 wrong in Verbal Reasoning, 12 in Physical Sciences, and 12 in Biological Sciences. Even students who receive perfect scaled scores usually get a handful of questions wrong.

It's important to maximize your performance on every question. Just a few questions one way or the other can make a big difference in your scaled score. Here's a look at recent score profiles so you can get an idea of the shape of a typical score distribution.

Physical Sciences				Verbal Reasoning		
Scaled Score	Percent Achieving Score	Percentile Rank Range		Scaled Score	Percent Achieving Score	Percentile Rank Range
15	0.1	99.9–99.9		15	0.1	99.9–99.9
14	1.2	98.7–99.8		14	0.2	99.7–99.8
13	2.5	96.2–98.6		13	1.8	97.9–99.6
12	5.1	91.1–96.1		12	3.6	94.3–97.8
11	7.2	83.9–91.0		11	10.5	83.8–94.2
10	12.1	71.8–83.8		10	15.6	68.2–83.7
9	12.9	58.9–71.1		9	17.2	51.0–68.1
8	16.5	42.4–58.5		8	15.4	35.6–50.9
7	16.7	25.7–42.3		7	10.3	25.3–35.5
6	13.0	12.7–25.6		6	10.9	14.4–25.2
5	7.9	04.8–12.6		5	6.9	07.5–14.3
4	3.3	01.5–04.7		4	3.9	03.6–07.4
3	1.3	00.2–01.4		3	2.0	01.6–03.5
2	0.1	00.1–00.1		2	0.5	00.1–01.5
1	0.0	00.0–00.0		1	0.0	00.0–00.0
Scaled Score Mean = 8.1 Standard Deviation = 2.32				Scaled Score Mean = 8.0 Standard Deviation = 2.43		

Writing Sample		
Scaled Score	Percent Achieving Score	Percentile Rank Range
T	0.5	99.9–99.9
S	2.8	94.7–99.8
R	7.2	96.0–99.3
Q	14.2	91.0–95.9
P	9.7	81.2–90.9
O	17.9	64.0–81.1
N	14.7	47.1–63.9
M	18.8	30.4–47.0
L	9.5	21.2–30.3
K	3.6	13.5–21.1
J	1.2	06.8–13.4
		02.9–06.7
		00.9–02.8
		00.2–00.8
		00.0–00.1

75th Percentile = Q
50th Percentile = O
25th Percentile = M

Biological Sciences		
Scaled Score	Percent Achieving Score	Percentile Rank Range
15	0.1	99.9–99.9
14	1.2	98.7–99.8
13	2.5	96.2–98.6
12	5.1	91.1–96.1
11	7.2	83.9–91.0
10	12.1	71.8–83.8
9	12.9	58.9–71.1
8	16.5	42.4–58.5
7	16.7	25.7–42.3
6	13.0	12.7–25.6
5	7.9	04.8–12.6
4	3.3	01.5–04.7
3	1.3	00.2–01.4
2	0.1	00.1–00.1
1	0.0	00.0–00.0

Scaled Score
Mean = 8.2
Standard Deviation = 2.39

WHAT THE MCAT REALLY TESTS

It's important to grasp not only the nuts and bolts of the MCAT, so you'll know *what* to do on Test Day, but also the underlying principles of the test so you'll know *why* you're doing what you're doing on Test Day. We'll cover the straightforward MCAT facts later. Now it's time to examine the heart and soul of the MCAT, to see what it's really about.

THE MYTH

Most people preparing for the MCAT fall prey to the myth that the MCAT is a straightforward science test. They think something like this:

> *"It covers the four years of science I had to take in school: biology, chemistry, physics, and organic chemistry. It even has equations. OK, so it has Verbal Reasoning and Writing, but those sections are just to see if we're literate, right? The important stuff is the science. After all, we're going to be doctors."*

Well, here's the little secret no one seems to want you to know: The MCAT is not just a science test; it's also a thinking test. This means that the test is designed to let you demonstrate your thought process, not only your thought content.

The implications are vast. Once you shift your test-taking paradigm to match the MCAT modus operandi, you'll find a new level of confidence and control over the test. You'll begin to work with the nature of the MCAT rather than against it. You'll be more efficient and insightful as you prepare for the test, and you'll be more relaxed on Test Day. In fact, you'll be able to see the MCAT for what it is rather than for what it's dressed up to be. We want your Test Day to feel like a visit with a familiar friend instead of an awkward blind date.

THE ZEN OF MCAT

Medical schools do not need to rely on the MCAT to see what you already know. Admission committees can measure your subject-area proficiency using your undergraduate coursework and grades. Schools are most interested in the potential of your mind.

In recent years, many medical schools have shifted pedagogic focus away from an information-heavy curriculum to a concept-based curriculum. There is currently more emphasis placed on problem solving, holistic thinking, and cross-disciplinary study. Be careful not to dismiss this important point, figuring you'll wait to worry about academic trends until you're actually in medical school. This trend affects you right now, because it's reflected in the MCAT. Every good tool matches its task. In this case the tool is the test, used to measure you and other candidates, and the task is to quantify how likely it is that you'll succeed in medical school.

Your intellectual potential—how skillfully you annex new territory into your mental boundaries, how quickly you build "thought highways" between ideas, how confidently and creatively you solve problems—is far more important to admission committees than your ability to recite Young's modulus for every material known to man. The schools assume they can expand your knowledge base. They choose applicants carefully because expansive knowledge is not enough to succeed in medical school or in the profession. There's something more. It's this "something more" that the MCAT is trying to measure.

Every section on the MCAT tests essentially the same higher-order thinking skills: analytical reasoning, abstract thinking, and problem solving. Most test takers get trapped into thinking they are being tested strictly about biology, chemistry, etc. Thus, they approach each section with a new outlook on what's expected. This constant mental gear-shifting can be exhausting, not to mention counterproductive. Instead of perceiving the test as parsed into radically different sections, you need to maintain your focus on the underlying nature of the test: It's designed to test your thinking skills, not your information-recall skills. Each test section presents a variation on the same theme.

WHAT ABOUT THE SCIENCE?

With this perspective, you may be left asking these questions: "What about the science? What about the content? Don't I need to know the basics?" The answer is a resounding "Yes!" You must be fluent in the different languages of the test. You cannot do well on the MCAT if you don't know the basics of physics, general chemistry, biology, and organic chemistry. We recommend that you take one year each of biology, general chemistry, organic chemistry, and physics before taking the MCAT, and that you review the content in this book thoroughly. Knowing these basics is just the beginning of doing well on the MCAT. That's a shock to most test takers. They presume that once they recall or relearn their undergraduate science, they are ready to do battle against the MCAT. Wrong! They merely have directions to the battlefield. They lack what they need to beat the test: a copy of the test maker's battle plan!

You won't be drilled on facts and formulas on the MCAT. You'll need to demonstrate ability to reason based on ideas and concepts. The science questions are painted with a broad brush, testing your general understanding.

TAKE CONTROL: THE MCAT MINDSET

In addition to being a thinking test, as we've stressed, the MCAT is a standardized test. As such, it has its own consistent patterns and idiosyncrasies that can actually work in your favor. This is the key to why test preparation works. You have the opportunity to familiarize yourself with those consistent peculiarities, to adopt the proper test-taking mindset.

The following are some overriding principles of the MCAT Mindset that will be covered in depth in the chapters to come:

- Read actively and critically.
- Translate prose into your own words.
- Save the toughest questions for last.
- Know the test and its components inside and out.
- Do MCAT-style problems in each topic area after you've reviewed it.
- Allow your confidence to build on itself.
- Take full-length practice tests a week or two before the test to break down the mystique of the real experience.
- Learn from your mistakes—get the most out of your practice tests.
- Look at the MCAT as a challenge, the first step in your medical career, rather than as an arbitrary obstacle.

That's what the MCAT Mindset boils down to: Taking control. Being proactive. Being on top of the testing experience so that you can get as many points as you can as quickly and as easily as possible. Keep this in mind as you read and work through the material in this book and, of course, as you face the challenge on Test Day.

Now that you have a better idea of what the MCAT is all about, let's take a tour of the individual test sections. Although the underlying skills being tested are similar, each MCAT section requires that you call into play a different domain of knowledge. So, though we encourage you to think of the MCAT as a holistic and unified test, we also recognize that the test is segmented by discipline and that there are characteristics unique to each section. In the overviews, we'll review sample questions and answers and discuss section-specific strategies. For each of the sections—Verbal Reasoning, Physical/Biological Sciences, and the Writing Sample—we'll present you with the following:

- **The Big Picture**
  You'll get a clear view of the section and familiarize yourself with what it's really evaluating.

- **A Closer Look**
  You'll explore the types of questions that will appear and master the strategies you'll need to deal with them successfully.

- **Highlights**
  The key approaches to each section are outlined, for reinforcement and quick review.

TEST EXPERTISE

The first year of medical school is a frenzied experience for most students. In order to meet the requirements of a rigorous work schedule, students either learn to prioritize and budget their time or else fall hopelessly behind. It's no surprise, then, that the MCAT, the test specifically designed to predict success in the first year of medical school, is a high-speed, time-intensive test. It demands excellent time-management skills as well as that sine qua non of the successful physician—grace under pressure.

It's one thing to answer a Verbal Reasoning question correctly; it's quite another to answer several correctly in a limited time frame. The same goes for Physical and Biological Sciences—it's a whole new ball game once you move from doing an individual passage at your leisure to handling a full section under actual timed conditions. You also need to budget your time for the Writing Sample, but this section isn't as time sensitive. Nevertheless when it comes to the multiple-choice sections, time pressure is a factor that affects virtually every test taker.

So when you're comfortable with the content of the test, your next challenge will be to take it to the next level—test expertise—which will enable you to manage the all-important time element of the test.

THE FIVE BASIC PRINCIPLES OF TEST EXPERTISE

On some tests, if a question seems particularly difficult you'll spend significantly more time on it, as you'll probably be given more points for correctly answering a hard question. Not so on the MCAT. Remember, every MCAT question, no matter how hard, is worth a single point. There's no partial credit or "A" for effort. Moreover because there are so many questions to do in so little time, you'd be a fool to spend 10 minutes getting a point for a hard question and then not have time to get a couple of quick points from three easy questions later in the section.

Given this combination—limited time, all questions equal in weight—you've got to develop a way of handling the test sections to make sure you get as many points as you can as quickly and easily as you can. Here are the principles that will help you do that:

1. FEEL FREE TO SKIP AROUND

One of the most valuable strategies to help you finish the sections in time is to learn to recognize and deal first with the questions that are easier and more familiar to you. That means you must temporarily skip those that promise to be difficult and time-consuming, if you feel comfortable doing so. You can always come back to these at the end, and if you run out of time, you're much better off not getting to questions you may have had difficulty with, rather than not getting to potentially feasible material. Of course, because there's no guessing penalty, always put an answer to every question on the test, whether you get to it or not. (It's not practical to skip passages, so do those in order.)

This strategy is difficult for most test takers; we're conditioned to do things in order. But give it a try when you practice. Remember, if you do the test in the exact order given, you're letting the test makers control you. But you control how you take this test. On the other hand, if skipping around goes against your moral fiber and makes you a nervous wreck—don't do it. Just be mindful of the clock, and don't get bogged down with the tough questions.

2. LEARN TO RECOGNIZE AND SEEK OUT QUESTIONS YOU CAN DO

Another thing to remember about managing the test sections is that MCAT questions and passages, unlike items on the SAT and other standardized tests, are not presented in order of difficulty. There's no rule that says you have to work through the sections in any particular order; in fact, the test makers scatter the easy and difficult questions throughout the section, in effect rewarding those who actually get to the end. Don't lose sight of what you're being tested for along with your reading and thinking skills: efficiency and cleverness.

Don't waste time on questions you can't do. We know that skipping a possibly tough question is easier said than done; we all have the natural instinct to plow through test sections in their given order. But it just doesn't pay off on the MCAT. The computer won't be impressed if you get the toughest question right. If you dig in your heels on a tough question, refusing to move on until you've cracked it, well, you're letting your ego get in the way of your test score. A test section (not to mention life itself) is too short to waste on lost causes.

3. USE A PROCESS OF ANSWER ELIMINATION

Using a process of elimination is another way to answer questions both quickly and effectively. There are two ways to get all the answers right on the MCAT. You either know all the right answers, or you know all the wrong answers. Because there are three times as many wrong answers, you should be able to eliminate some if not all of them. By doing so you either get to the correct response or increase your chances of guessing the correct response. You start out with a 25 percent chance of picking the right answer, and with each eliminated answer your odds go up. Eliminate one, and you'll have a $33\frac{1}{3}$ percent chance of picking the right one, eliminate two, and you'll have a 50 percent chance, and, of course, eliminate three, and you'll have a 100 percent chance. Increase your efficiency by actually crossing out the wrong choices on the screen using the strike-through feature. Remember to look for wrong-answer traps when you're eliminating. Some answers are designed to seduce you by distorting the correct answer.

4. REMAIN CALM

It's imperative that you remain calm and composed while working through a section. You can't allow yourself to become so rattled by one hard reading passage that it throws off your performance on the rest of the section. Expect to find at least one killer passage in every section, but remember, you won't be the only one to have trouble with it. The test is curved to take the tough material into account. Having trouble with a difficult question isn't going to ruin your score—but getting upset about it and letting it throw you off track will. When you understand that part of the test maker's goal is to reward those who keep their composure, you'll recognize the importance of not panicking when you run into challenging material.

5. KEEP TRACK OF TIME

Of course, the last thing you want to happen is to have time called on a particular section before you've gotten to half the questions. Therefore, it's essential that you pace yourself, keeping in mind the general guidelines for how long to spend on any individual question or passage. Have a sense of how long you have to do each question, so you know when you're exceeding the limit and should start to move faster.

So, when working on a section, always remember to keep track of time. Don't spend a wildly disproportionate amount of time on any one question or group of questions. Also, give yourself 30 seconds or so at the end of each section to fill in answers for any questions you haven't gotten to.

SECTION-SPECIFIC PACING

Let's now look at the section-specific timing requirements and some tips for meeting them. Keep in mind that the times per question or passage are only averages; there are bound to be some that take less time and some that take more. Try to stay balanced. Remember, too, that every question is of equal worth, so don't get hung up on any one. Think about it: If a question is so hard that it takes you a long time to answer it, chances are you may get it wrong anyway. In that case, you'd have nothing to show for your extra time but a lower score.

VERBAL REASONING

Allow yourself approximately eight to ten minutes per passage and respective questions. It may sound like a lot of time, but it goes quickly. Keep in mind that some passages are longer than others. On average, give yourself about three or four minutes to read and then four to six minutes for the questions.

PHYSICAL AND BIOLOGICAL SCIENCES

Averaging over each section, you'll have about one minute and 20 seconds per question. Some questions, of course, will take more time, some less. A science passage plus accompanying questions should take about eight to nine minutes, depending on how many questions there are. Stand-alone questions can take anywhere from a few seconds to a minute or more. Again, the rule is to do your best work first. Also, don't feel that you have to understand everything in a passage before you go on to the questions. You may not need that deep an understanding to answer questions, because a lot of information may be extraneous. You should overcome your perfectionism and use your time wisely.

WRITING SAMPLE

You have exactly 30 minutes for each essay. As mentioned in discussion of the 7-step approach to this section, you should allow approximately five minutes to prewrite the essay, 23 minutes to write the essay, and two minutes to proofread. It's important that you budget your time, so you don't get cut off.

COMPUTER-BASED TESTING STRATEGIES

ARRIVE AT THE TESTING CENTER EARLY

Get to the testing center early to jump-start your brain. However, if they allow you to begin your test early, decline.

USE THE MOUSE TO YOUR ADVANTAGE

If you are right-handed, practice using the mouse with your left hand for Test Day. This way, you'll increase speed by keeping the pencil in your right hand to write on your scratch paper. If you are left-handed, use your right hand for the mouse.

KNOW THE TUTORIAL BEFORE TEST DAY

You will save time on Test Day by knowing exactly how the test will work. Click through any tutorial pages and save time.

PRACTICE WITH SCRATCH PAPER

Going forward, always practice using scratch paper when solving questions because this is how you will do it on Test Day. Never write directly on a written test.

GET NEW SCRATCH PAPER

Between sections, get a new piece of scratch paper even if you only used part of the old one. This will maximize the available space for each section and minimize the likelihood of you running out of paper to write on.

REMEMBER YOU CAN ALWAYS GO BACK

Just because you finish a passage or move on, remember you can come back to questions about which you are uncertain. You have the "marking" option to your advantage. However, as a general rule minimize the amount of questions you mark or skip.

MARK INCOMPLETE WORK

If you need to go back to a question, clearly mark the work you've done on the scratch paper with the question number. This way, you will be able to find your work easily when you come back to tackle the question.

LOOK AWAY AT TIMES

Taking the test on computer leads to faster eye-muscle fatigue. Use the Kaplan strategy of looking at a distant object at regular intervals. This will keep you fresher at the end of the test.

PRACTICE ON THE COMPUTER

This is the most critical aspect of adapting to computer-based testing. Like anything else, in order to perform well on computer-based tests you must practice. Spend time reading passages and answering questions on the computer. You often will have to scroll when reading passages.

Part I
Review

The Cell

I can remember when I was in your shoes. The MCAT loomed large on my proverbial horizon. It was the first test that I can truly say that I was nervous to take before I even cracked a book (and might even have been a little more nervous after I saw how much I needed to learn). Some of you may be a little nervous right now. That's okay! It's perfectly natural to feel some anxiety. But we're here to help you reduce your anxiety and channel your energy into action that will lead to Test Day success. First, take a deep breath (breathing may be the most natural thing we do, yet in a moment of panic, breathing is usually the first thing that goes wrong) and relax. The next few paragraphs won't be tested. Rather, read them with an open and inquisitive mind. They will provide you with a basis to do well not only on the MCAT but also as a physician.

To start, I would like to provide you with a fundamental insight that led me to Test Day and medical school success.

Never be afraid to ask a question.

Sure. It sounds basic enough on the surface of it, but take a second to read it again and really get your synaptic connections firing (I'll wait). Those simple words carry a great deal of meaning. On a surface-level analysis, the MCAT is an exam based on questions: The test maker isn't afraid to ask you questions, and you shouldn't be afraid to ask questions, either!

To whom exactly should you be directing your questions? Everyone, including yourself. In a very literal sense, a question that you ask now might turn into a correct answer (and another point) on Test Day. The only person you hurt by not asking your questions is yourself.

And beyond the purpose of preparing for the MCAT, you should dig deeper in your thought process and learn to ask difficult questions for which answers are not always clear. I know that you aren't all philosophy majors and some of you may even dread liberal arts, but medicine as a field isn't only about science. It's not enough to know that iron is a critical prosthetic group in hemoglobin and that a deficiency could lead to anemia. Granted, there will be some nights during which you will be responsible for recalling large amounts of information on only a few hours of sleep, but that's just a means to an end, not "the end in and of itself," to crib Kant.

The practice of medicine requires a physician and patient working together to provide ideal treatment for a specific situation. It's not enough for you (the doctor) just to state, "Take two aspirin and call me in the morning," as the old saying goes. How do you arrive at the answers your patients (and you) seek? By asking questions. Believe it or not, many times patients are afraid to question their doctors. It's almost hard to imagine as professionals trained in the art of asking questions! Your patients will come to see you, pay you for your advice, but may be afraid to ask questions such as "why?" (which can be both profoundly simple and profoundly complex). Why this drug? Why this treatment? Why is this happening to me? The way you ask questions will be a model to your patients as you engage them as partners in the greater cause of seeking health and wellness.

To ask—and answer—these questions correctly, ethically, and fully in your future medical practice, you will need to make complete use of your *critical thinking* skills—which snaps you back to the MCAT and the next few months of your life.

The MCAT is designed to test your critical thinking. The test maker knows that in order for you to be a successful physician tomorrow, you need to learn how to ask questions today. In order to answer the questions your patients ask you, you must ask questions of them. Similarly, to answer the questions the MCAT asks you, you must ask questions of it. But learning to ask the right questions is only the first step in the critical thinking process. You also need to learn to assess the value and applicability of what you already know to what you will learn as you ask questions and gather information. In your medical practice, you will seek additional information from your patients, colleagues, lab tests, imaging studies, and journal articles. For example, you will be expected to be able to come up with a list of possible reasons for why your patient might have low iron (what's called the "differential diagnosis"), how to test for it, and how best to treat it. On the MCAT, you will gather information from the passages and question stems upon which the test is based and relate this information to what you already know and understand.

Kaplan's Review Notes and Test Day strategies are integral to the development of your critical thinking skills. The information contained in these pages is high-yield and essential for Test Day success. I assure you that we have done our homework in researching the topics that are included on the actual test. The topics included in this book are likely to appear on your MCAT with varying degrees of emphasis. Content areas not tested have been intentionally excluded from our discussions here so that we do not waste your time and energy. Pay attention not just to our discussion of content but also to our approach to solving MCAT problems. Learn and practice our methods until they become your methods. Upon the foundation of strong content understanding and time-proven methods, you will build your critical thinking skills. These are the skills that will allow you to reach the greatest heights of Test Day success.

So I encourage you to question yourself about your own knowledge and goals as we take this journey through biology together. Take caution as you study these notes. Beware of the extreme answer on practice questions. And don't question *everything*; I promise that biology is not a conspiracy theory. It is, after all, based on chemistry, which is based on physics. (And let me assure you now, in spite of how you may feel—and quite strongly too—physics itself is not a conspiracy theory!)

Our first chapter will introduce us to the cell. To get us going, let's look at a fun fact. There are approximately 10 trillion cells in our body (that's 10,000,000,000,000 to be exact) and approximately 100 trillion bacteria living in our gastrointestinal tract. Bacteria outnumber us in our own bodies by a cell ratio of 10:1. This, to say the least, gives new meaning to John Donne's famous saying that "No man is an island unto himself." As we figuratively digest that fact, we ought to begin to think about what we humans have in common with the lowly bacteria living in our gut. Although we are markedly different, we share some fundamental characteristics. The fundamental unit of the human body and of each of those bacteria is the cell. Our goal in this chapter will be to understand the basic structure and organization of the cell so that as we expand our focus to the larger organ systems, we will have a solid foundation for MCAT success.

Cell Theory

Consider that biology has always lagged behind physics and chemistry in terms of fundamental facts. Moreover, the majority of techniques that we now use to study cells required advancements in other fields, especially chemistry and physics. Biology doesn't stand on its own legs. Physics allows us to understand the fundamental laws of interaction in the universe; chemistry builds upon those laws by explaining how reactivity occurs; biology expands the discussion at a meta level to discuss how organisms interact. It wasn't until the development of microscopes in the 17th century that we were even able to look at our own components "beneath the surface," if you will, of visibility with the naked eye. Over time, and through repeated examination at the microscopic level, we came to recognize fundamental similarities among all living things. As with all good scientific models, we start with a theory. This is one of the MCAT's favorite topics, and we should take careful note of the basic tenets of the Cell Theory. The **Cell Theory** holds true for all organisms, whether they be unicellular or multicellular:

- All living things are composed of cells.
- The cell is the basic functional unit of life.
- Cells arise only from pre-existing cells.
- Cells carry genetic information in the form of **DNA**. This genetic material is passed on from parent to daughter cell.

The Cell Theory may seem pretty basic, but complex systems are built from these elementary rules. Consider that our own bodies (very sophisticated machines in their

MCAT Expertise

Know these points: The MCAT likes to test what sorts of systems could be considered "cells."

own right) are ultimately a collection of cells all living by these four rules! Pretty incredible and definitely test-worthy.

Methods and Tools

One of the primary obstacles that prevented early scientists from being able to study cells was their size. Ironically, we had lenses allowing us to peer into the depths of space and predict where planets were stationed, yet not until we turned these lenses inward did we begin to understand our own "inner space." Today, our primary techniques for examining the organism at the organ, tissue, cellular, or subcellular levels are **microscopy, autoradiography, and centrifugation**.

MICROSCOPY

Of all the items in the biologist's toolbox, the microscope is not only the one most commonly used but also the one most commonly tested on the MCAT. Two basic concepts that we should recall from the physics topic of light and optics are **magnification** and **resolution**. We're used to seeing these topics in the Physical Sciences section on MCAT, but as we previously noted, biology and physics are quite intertwined in real life! **Magnification** is the increase in the apparent size of an object; basically, "How much bigger does it look?" Imagine a tiny splinter painfully wedged into a friend's pinky finger. Many of us would search for a magnifying glass, because it enlarges the splinter's image. **Resolution** is the ability to differentiate two closely placed objects. Meaning, once we position our magnifying glass and have a tweezer ready to attack, we're going to want to make sure we pull out only the splinter—and not a layer of our friend's skin!

Compound Light Microscope

This is the most commonly used type of microscope. Similar to telescopes and other systems of lenses that we discuss in physics, a compound light microscope uses two lenses or a system of lenses to magnify the object. The total magnification power is the product of the two lenses: the eyepiece (often 10×) and the objective (4×, 10×, 20×, or 100×). In other words, the bacteria we might look at under a microscope may appear 100 times (or more) larger than their actual size. Such organisms are truly microscopic. While the MCAT isn't likely to test us on the specifics of compound microscopy, knowing the basic components can translate into easy points on Test Day when such questions do appear (see Figure 1.1).

1. The **diaphragm** controls the amount of light passing through the specimen, which is important for image contrast. Our cameras have diaphragms for the same reason. Imagine taking a photo with the sun in the background. The image doesn't develop clearly; rather, it appears washed out. The diaphragm can

be adjusted to change the amount of light allowed to pass through the lens. Without a diaphragm, it probably wouldn't show up at all.

2. The **coarse adjustment knob** roughly focuses the image. It does this by moving the stage (platform on which the slide sits) up and down.

3. The **fine adjustment knob** finely focuses the image. Its function is the same as the coarse knob's, but it works over a smaller range of focus.

By and large, compound light microscopes are for nonliving specimens. To increase contrast, samples are usually sliced into thin sections, prepared by using various chemical reagents, and then coverslipped. Sounds pretty brutal, huh? Not surprisingly, the organisms usually die sometime during that process. An example of a commonly used dye (which you don't need to memorize for the MCAT but will once you get to medical school) is hematoxylin, which will show nucleic acids (**DNA** and **RNA**) within the cell by binding to their negatively charged sugar-phosphate backbone moieties.

Phase Contrast Microscope

Although knowledge of the phase contrast microscope isn't commonly tested on the MCAT, we should know it for one major reason: It allows for the visualization of **living organisms**. Samples are not prepared as described above; rather, the microscope relies on differences in refractive indices among the different subcellular structures (We said that we'd see some physics!) This system provides a tradeoff: We are able to view the live organism conducting its cellular activities, but we aren't able to increase the contrast of certain structures specifically by using a dye or preparation technique.

Electron Microscope

The most powerful microscope available to the biologist is the **electron microscope**, which allows us to image down to the atomic level. Let's take a step back and consider how this process works. What is the limiting factor in the resolution of the light microscope, or any microscope for that matter? It is the medium that is used to transmit the image. For example, in a light microscope, the resolution of the image is limited by the wavelength of light, which is on the order of nanometers. Images cannot be resolved further, as light cannot distinctly transmit the information. An electron microscope uses a beam of electrons; thus, its resolution is at the atomic level on the order of picometers. Electron microscopy has paved the way for major advances in the understanding of subcellular structures: for example, the ability to visualize the interface between the inner and outer mitochondrial membrane. The major drawback is the preparation technique: Samples must be sliced very thinly and usually impregnated with heavy metals (often OsO_4) to allow for appropriate contrast. This requires the death of the organism.

MCAT Expertise

Don't overfocus on the physics here; concepts such as refraction are much more likely to be tested in the Physical Sciences section.

Bridge

We'll hear more about the mitochondrial membranes in Chapter 3 as we discuss cellular metabolism.

Figure 1.1

AUTORADIOGRAPHY

Another technique that relies on advances in chemistry and physics is autoradiography. Recall that radioactive compounds decay or transform into other compounds or elements through various processes such as alpha or beta decay. We harness this power in various medical technologies including x-rays, radioactive tracing, and nuclear medicine. For example, x-rays are capable of penetrating the body and generating an image. We've all had the routine visit to the dentist, during which images of our teeth are generated and used to identify cavities. We should note that x-rays (and electromagnetic energy in general) can be harmful. This is why it's necessary for us to wear a lead apron during the procedure: The heavy metal absorbs the high-energy rays and limits the exposure of our vital organs to radiation.

On a cellular level, we can use radioactive decay to follow the biochemical processes that occur in the cell. In a basic setup, cells are exposed to an essential compound (glucose, nucleotides, amino acids, etc.) that they need to survive. We manufacture these compounds such that they include radioactive atoms (e.g., tritium, an isotope of hydrogen). The cells are incubated for a given amount of time and then fixed and put onto glass slides for microscopy. Each slide is covered with a piece of photographic film and then kept in the dark to develop for a given amount of time depending on the material used. The appearance of an image on the photographic film shows the distribution of radioactive material within the cell and where the biochemical reactions of interest took place. The developed picture is a way to track processes of interest within the cell.

CENTRIFUGATION

Yet another common biological technique that relies on physical principles is **centrifugation**. Recall that a centrifuge, by spinning at very rapid speeds, is capable of increasing the apparent force on the object in the tubes. The contents of the sample settle toward the bottom of the tube at different rates depending on the shape and density of the particles (measured as the sedimentation coefficient). We discuss the relative strength of the centrifugation in relation to the force of gravity. Thus, a centrifuge that spins at $12,000\,g$ exerts a force on the sample that is 12,000 times greater than the force of gravity. If you think about the last time you were on a roller coaster, you can imagine the same forces in effect. When the roller coaster went through the upside-down loop, why didn't you fall out? Sure, the lap bar helped, but centrifugal force pushed you into your seat. (The centrifugal force, the apparent force equal to and opposite the centripetal force, is due to the object's inertia.)

Centrifugation is like a mini roller coaster for test tubes. It's a useful technique because it allows cells to be fractionated into their various components based on density. Why would this work? The force will have a greater effect on objects with a greater density (e.g., ribosomes) and pull them to the bottom of the tube while less dense objects (mitochondria and lysosomes) will remain closer to the tube's opening. These can then be carefully removed to study a specific set of subcellular organelles.

Prokaryotes versus Eukaryotes ★★★★☆

The first major biological distinction we can make between living organisms is whether they are **prokaryotes** or **eukaryotes**. (We'll discuss viruses later; they are in a class by themselves because they violate multiple tenets of the Cell Theory.)

MCAT Expertise
Although concepts such as these may seem complex, often a simple understanding is all that is necessary to result in higher scores on Test Day.

Key Concept
Remember that although viruses cannot replicate independently, they do contain a genome in the form of RNA or DNA.

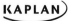

Now, are you ready to learn some Greek? Of course, there is no foreign language section on the MCAT, but a basic understanding of some word roots will give you quick hints on Test Day. The prokaryotic/eukaryotic distinction comes from the lack or presence of a nucleus, respectively. *Karyon* is Greek for "kernel" or "nucleus". *Pro–* means "before", and *eu–* means "true". Thus, prokaryotes existed before nuclei, and eukaryotes have true nuclei.

PROKARYOTES

Understanding prokaryotes won't just help you on the MCAT; they'll be part of your continuing education for the rest of your life as a physician—because many pathogens are prokaryotic! Prokaryotes are the simplest of all organisms (see Figure 1.2). They include all **bacteria** as well as blue-green algae. Their outer **cell wall** does not enclose any membrane-bound organelles (such as nuclei or endoplasmic reticulum). The genetic material of the organism is contained in a single circular molecule of DNA concentrated in an area of the cell called the **nucleoid** region. (We will discuss the reproduction of this genome in Chapter 4.)

Prokaryotes also have the interesting ability to carry other pieces of genetic information in small, circular pieces of DNA called **plasmids**. These are much smaller than the nuclear genome and often contain only a few genes. However, these genes are quite important. The difference between a bacterial strain that is susceptible to antibiotics and one that isn't may be due to a plasmid in the latter strain that confers resistance to a given antibiotic. These plasmids replicate independently of the nuclear genome, and copies of the plasmids can be transferred from one bacterial cell to another, which helps explain why bacteria are capable of passing resistance to other bacteria. It's a good bet that the bacteria you learn about in medical school will have evolved and changed a great deal by the time you attend your 20-year medical school reunion, thanks to plasmids.

ribosome
cell wall
cell membrane
flagellum
DNA (nucleoid region)

Figure 1.2

Most bacteria exist in one of two shapes. Spherical bacteria, known as cocci, include common pathogens like *Staphylococcus aureus* (see Figure 1.3a). Rod-shaped bacteria, like *Escherichia coli* (see Figure 1.3b), are also known as bacilli.

All bacteria contain a **cell membrane** and **cytoplasm**, and some have **flagella** (see Figure 1.4), which can also be found in eukaryotic cells (like sperm), where they

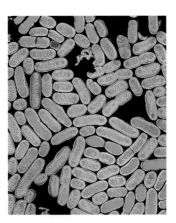

Figure 1.3a **Figure 1.3b**

give the cell motility. Since these structures are also found in eukaryotic cells, it is difficult to develop antibiotics that may target them. Instead, drugs tend to attack structures found specifically in bacteria. For instance, if you have ever taken azithromycin for an ear infection, you took a drug that specifically interfered with bacterial ribosomes, which are smaller than eukaryotic ribosomes. Before we move on, let's stress that not all bacteria are bad. In fact, our existence depends on some of them! We'll learn in a later chapter that bacteria in our large intestine help break down food. Others even produce vitamins for us.

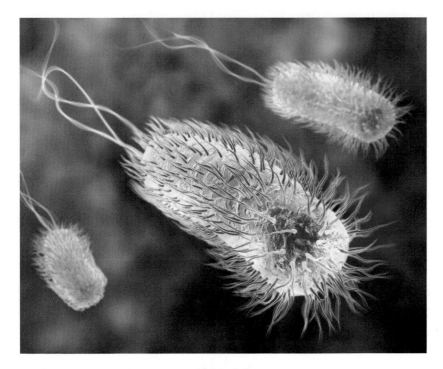

Figure 1.4

Key Concept

Prokaryotes	Eukaryotes
Bacteria	Protists, fungi, plants, animals
Cell wall present in all prokaryotes.	Cell wall present in fungi and plants only.
No nucleus	Nucleus
Ribosomes (subunits = 30S and 50S)	Ribosomes (subunits = 40S and 60S)
No membrane-bound organelles	Membrane-bound organelles
Unicellular	Unicellular or multicellular

MCAT Expertise

The fundamental differences between eukaryotic and prokaryotic cells will probably help us answer at least two questions on Test Day.

EUKARYOTES

Our second, and more test-worthy, set of organisms is the eukaryotes. As we discussed above, eukaryotes are made up of cells with true nuclei and membrane-bound organelles (see Figure 1.5). Remember that eukaryotes can be either unicellular or multicellular. We can think of the eukaryotic cell as a city. As we go through each of its structures, we can continue this analogy to help us remember key facts for the MCAT. Each cell has a cell membrane enclosing a semifluid **cytosol** in which the organelles are suspended. The cytosol is like the city air. It allows for the diffusion of molecules throughout the cell. Genetic material is encoded in DNA organized into linear strands known as **chromosomes**, which are found within the **nucleus**. There are some differences between different types of eukaryotes; for example, plants contain both a cell wall and **chloroplasts**, which are absent from animal cells. Let's discuss the organelles in more detail.

Figure 1.5

Eukaryotic Organelles ★★★★★★

Eukaryotic cells separate their biochemical reactions into distinct membrane-bound organelles, much as cities are divided into different districts and neighborhoods. These organelles are suspended within an aqueous cytosol that contains free proteins, nutrients, and other solutes.

If we continue to think about a eukaryotic cell as a city with distinct sections, we might better remember each of the parts. Every city needs a way to get from point

A to point B, a system of roads and highways. Just as cities have eight-lane highways as well as two-lane roads, so too does the cell. The cell has a **cytoskeleton**, which is made up of three types of proteins. From smallest to largest, they are **actin filaments, intermediate filaments**, and **microtubules**. These proteins form structures that allow materials to be moved around inside the cell. The cytoskeleton also provides a framework for anchoring other organelles within the cell.

The major organelles (or city structures) that we need to discuss for the MCAT are the nucleus, ribosomes, endoplasmic reticulum, Golgi apparatus, vesicles, vacuoles, lysosomes, microbodies, mitochondria, chloroplasts, and centrioles.

CELL MEMBRANE

The cell membrane is our city wall. It encloses our cell and selectively chooses who or what to let in and out. Just as a regular wall may be made of bricks, our wall is a **phospholipid bilayer** (see Figure 1.6). The theory that underlies this is known as the **fluid mosaic model**. The phospholipid bilayer is studded with proteins and lipid rafts that can control the movement of solutes in and out of the cell, much as a city gate controls the flow of traffic. These molecules are usually freely mobile within the membrane.

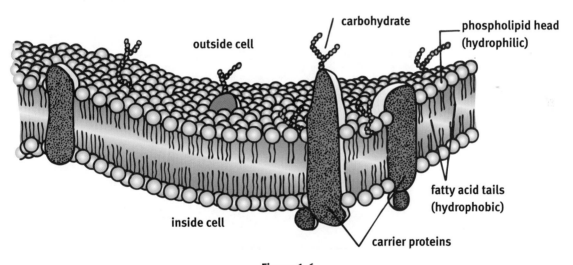

Figure 1.6

These phospholipids have a strongly hydrophobic tail (nonpolar) and a hydrophilic (polar) head. The hydrophilic regions face the interior and exterior of the cell, whereas the hydrophobic tails face each other along the intramembrane space. Cholesterol molecules also are found in the membrane; these help to regulate the fluidity or stiffness of the membrane. Cholesterol sometimes gets a bad reputation, owing to emphasis on its negative health effects, but cholesterol is important; our cells use cholesterol not only to help with membrane fluidity but also to generate all steroid hormones. Animal cells have the ability to produce cholesterol molecules for inclusion in cell membranes and steroid hormone production. We know, however,

Key Concept

The ability of different molecules to traverse a membrane is critical to cells. The cell must be able to allow nutrients and required compounds in while preventing bacteria, viruses, and harmful compounds from entering. This is a commonly tested MCAT topic.

that excessive dietary cholesterol is unhealthy. It has many deleterious health effects, such as atherosclerosis. Moderate dietary intake is key.

The proteins we discussed earlier may be visible on one or both sides of the membrane (see Figure 1.7). Moreover, they play a variety of roles within our cells. **Transport proteins**, which we can liken to border agents that control entry and exit into our city, allow polar molecules and ions to move in and out of the cell, whereas **cell adhesion molecules** (CAMs) are proteins that allow cells to recognize each other and contribute to proper cell differentiation and development.

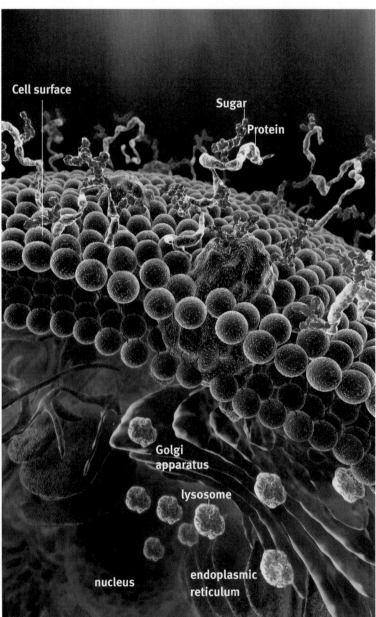

Figure 1.7

NUCLEUS

Continuing our voyage through our cellular city, we come to the nucleus, which we can think of as the city hall and the public library. The nucleus is the control center of the cell and functions much as a cellular city hall. The nucleus is the most commonly tested organelle on the MCAT, so we should focus on its intricacies. Moreover, it contains all of the genetic material necessary for replication of the cell; thus, it is also like the public library in that it serves as a repository for this information. The nucleus is surrounded by the **nuclear membrane** or **envelope**, a double membrane that maintains a nuclear environment separate and distinct from the cytoplasm. Of course, the nucleus cannot be completely isolated from the rest of the cell, so the nuclear membrane is punctured with **nuclear pores**, which allow for the selective two-way exchange of material into and out of the nucleus. The genetic material (DNA) is organized into coding regions called **genes**. The linear DNA is wound around organizing proteins known as **histones** and then further wound into linear strands called **chromosomes** (or **chromatids**), just as the books in a library are sorted based on subject and placed on shelves. Finally, there is a subsection of the nucleus known as the **nucleolus**, where the ribosomal RNA (**rRNA**) is synthesized.

Key Concept

The nucleus contains the cell's genetic material, DNA, which serves two main functions:
1. Directing protein synthesis
2. Serving as a genetic blueprint during cell replication

RIBOSOMES

Ribosomes (see Figure 1.8) are the factories of our city. They are responsible for protein production. Just as a factory takes an order and produces goods, so too do the ribosomes. They take orders from the nucleus (city hall) and produce goods (proteins) that are necessary for the survival of the cell. Ribosomes come in two varieties: free (traveling tradespeople) and bound (think of large factories that produce specific goods like cars). These central merchants all have the same shipping department, the **endoplasmic reticulum** (ER).

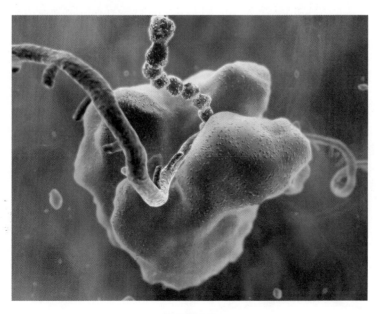

Figure 1.8

ENDOPLASMIC RETICULUM

Just outside the nucleus, the endoplasmic reticulum exists as a series of intercon-nected membrane-bound organelles. There are two varieties: **smooth** and **rough**. Rough ER's outer surface is ribosome studded, whereas smooth ER is ribosome-free.

By and large, the ER is responsible for the proper production (via bound ribosomes) and sorting of materials from the cell, especially those destined to be secreted. Think back to our analogy. The ER acts as a giant shipping center, taking the goods that were produced and sending them to the correct location. The smooth ER works to-ward lipid synthesis and detoxification of drugs and poisons, whereas the rough ER is more directly involved in the production of protein products.

GOLGI APPARATUS

Think about our shipping center. We know that it is going to be busy with getting goods out. Sometimes as the goods get shipped, they either reach the wrong destina-tion or have to be repackaged to make sure that they are correctly sorted. In much the same way, the Golgi apparatus is the way in which certain products in our cell get repackaged. The Golgi is a series of membrane-bound sacs; it receives materials from the smooth ER and then repackages them to send to the cell surface (see Figure 1.9). These products are often sent in **secretory vesicles** that release their contents to a cell's exterior in a process known as **exocytosis**. This is analogous to us sending a product to

Key Concept

The Golgi apparatus is Packaging Cen-tral. It directs materials within the cell.

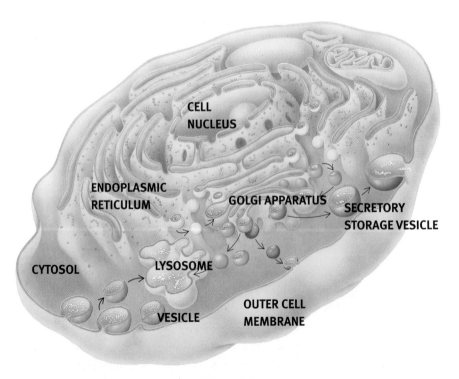

Figure 1.9

a different city. See how much fun our MCAT studying can be when we add in analogies? They may seem silly, but when it counts on Test Day, they will help us remember key facts and achieve a high score.

VESICLES AND VACUOLES

Vesicles and vacuoles are the wrapping we discussed in the previous paragraph. They are used to transport and store materials that are ingested, secreted, processed, or digested by the cell. Vacuoles are larger and more likely to be found in plant cells. Remember that there are many different types of eukaryotes we may be asked about on Test Day. Each of their organelles may be slightly different to fit the needs of that organism.

LYSOSOMES

Lysosomes are the garbage dumps of our cells. They take material brought in by endosomes (specialized vesicles that serve as garbage trucks) and, using hydrolytic enzymes at a lowered pH (5), they break down materials ingested by the cell. Just as we wouldn't want to live by a garbage dump, lysosomes are effectively able to sequester these hydrolytic enzymes from the remainder of the cell, which prevents them from damaging the cell through oxidized intermediates. Lysosomes are also important in the removal of old cellular components and replacement with newer ones, similar to the way buildings may be deconstructed and destroyed during the remodeling process. Finally, lysosomes serve an important purpose in that they can cause the death of the cell in a process known as **autolysis**. By selectively choosing when to release these enzymes, the cell can commit suicide if necessary (e.g., the DNA is damaged). In addition, lysosomes give us recycling properties in that some of the broken-down products can be reused in other cellular processes. You should be familiar with the key organelles (such as the nucleus), whose damage will cause the cell to go through apoptosis. This is great material for an MCAT discrete question.

MITOCHONDRIA

Mitochondria are the powerhouse of the cell or the power plant in our town. What kind of power plant is it? Well, of course, a nuclear one. Remember, we are dealing with eukaryotic cells. The mitochondrion contains two layers: the inner and outer membrane. Just as in a nuclear power plant, the outer membrane is like the walls. It allows in the appropriate materials for respiration, primarily based on size. The inner membrane is analogous to the reactor chamber of a nuclear power plant; it contains the molecules and enzymes necessary for the electron transport chain. The inner membrane contains numerous infoldings known as the **cristae**, which are highly convoluted structures that increase the surface area for the electron transport chain enzymes to sit within. The inner membrane encloses the **mitochondrial matrix**, which contains many other enzymes important in cellular respiration (see Chapter 3). Between the two membranes lies the **intermembrane space**.

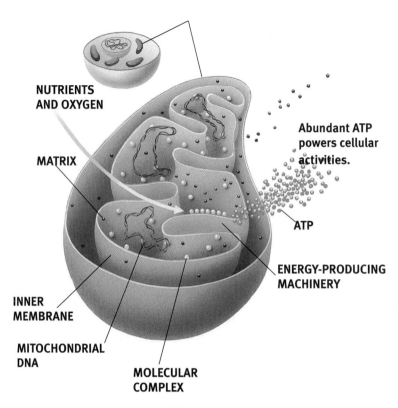

NUTRIENTS AND OXYGEN

MATRIX

Abundant ATP powers cellular activities.

ATP

ENERGY-PRODUCING MACHINERY

INNER MEMBRANE

MITOCHONDRIAL DNA

MOLECULAR COMPLEX

Figure 1.10

Mitochondria are different from other parts of the cell in that they are **semiautonomous**. They contain some of their own genes and replicate independently of the nucleus via binary fission. Mitochondria are thought to have evolved from one prokaryotic organism ingesting another in a symbiotic relationship (see Figure 1.11). Just as a nuclear power plant can have a meltdown incident (think Chernobyl), so too can the mitochondria. They can release some of the enzymes in the electron transport chain during the process of programmed cell death **(apoptosis)**.

MICROBODIES

Microbodies are specialized factories within our cellular city. They catalyze specific types of reactions by sequestering the necessary enzymes and substrates. Two specific microbodies are **peroxisomes** and **glyoxysomes**. Peroxisomes are responsible for the creation of hydrogen peroxide within a cell and are used to break down fats into usable molecules, as well as catalyze detoxification reactions in the liver. Glyoxysomes are important in germinating plants, where they convert fats to usable fuel (sugars) until the plant can make its own energy via photosynthesis. Remember that the MCAT may test you on some of the specific functions of organelles, so you should be filing these away as you study.

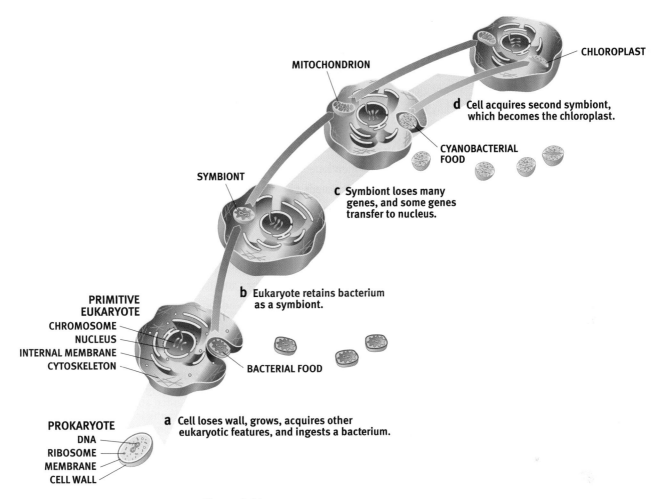

MITOCHONDRION

CHLOROPLAST

d Cell acquires second symbiont, which becomes the chloroplast.

CYANOBACTERIAL FOOD

SYMBIONT

c Symbiont loses many genes, and some genes transfer to nucleus.

b Eukaryote retains bacterium as a symbiont.

PRIMITIVE EUKARYOTE
CHROMOSOME
NUCLEUS
INTERNAL MEMBRANE
CYTOSKELETON

BACTERIAL FOOD

a Cell loses wall, grows, acquires other eukaryotic features, and ingests a bacterium.

PROKARYOTE
DNA
RIBOSOME
MEMBRANE
CELL WALL

Figure 1.11

CHLOROPLASTS

If the mitochondria are nuclear power plants, the chloroplasts are solar power plants. Chloroplasts are found in our more ecologically concerned organisms (plants and algae). They contain chlorophyll and are responsible for the generation of energy using water, carbon dioxide, and sunlight. They also contain their own DNA and may, like mitochondria, have evolved via symbiosis (see Figure 1.11).

CELL WALL

Sometimes the basic cell membrane (our city wall) isn't enough of a deterrent to foreign organisms. We need to reinforce it with stronger barriers and structural supports. Many eukaryotic cells are surrounded by a cell wall for both defense and increased stability. All plant cells have a cell wall composed of cellulose; fungi have walls made of chitin; animals do not have cell walls.

CENTRIOLES

Nothing more than a specialized type of microtubule, the centrioles are part of our highway system within the cell. They are important for spindle formation and are not membrane bound. Animal cells have a pair of centrioles that are oriented at right angles to one other. Plant cells do not have centrioles.

CYTOSKELETON

As we previously mentioned, the cytoskeleton is the highway system of our cell and provides a transport system as well as structural strength. There are three components: microfilaments, microtubules, and intermediate filaments (see Figure 1.12).

Microfilaments are made up of solid polymerized rods of **actin**. They are the smallest of our roads. Places of use include muscular contraction, where they interact with **myosin** (more on this in Chapter 6). They are also involved in movement of materials within the cellular membrane and amoeboid movement.

> **Key Concept**
>
> Not all cells have the same relative distribution of organelles. Form will follow function: Cells that require a lot of energy for locomotion (e.g., sperm cells) have lots of mitochondria; cells involved in secretion (e.g., pancreatic islet cells) have lots of Golgi bodies; and cells such as red blood cells, which primarily serve a transport function, have no organelles at all!

CELL SURFACE
NUCLEUS
CYTOSKELETON

CYTOSKELETON of a cell consists of microfilaments (*bottom left*), microtubules (*bottom center*), and intermediate filaments (*bottom right*), all of which are nanometers wide. The rounded shape near the center in each of these photographs is the cell nucleus. The three components interconnect to create the cytoskeletal lattice, which stretches from the cell surface to the nucleus (*top left*). The molecular structure of each component is shown above the corresponding photograph and is color coded to the top left illustration.

MICROFILAMENTS

MICROTUBULES

INTERMEDIATE FILAMENTS

Figure 1.12

Microtubules are hollow, unlike actin. They are polymers of **tubulin** proteins. Microtubules radiate throughout the cell, providing the largest roads (superhighways) for transport as well as structural support. They are involved in chromosomal separation during mitosis and meiosis; they are also the structural basis for **cilia** and flagella, which are structures involved in a variety of processes from trapping foreign matter (see Chapter 8) to providing motility for sperm (see Chapter 4).

Intermediate filaments are a collection of fibers that help maintain the overall integrity of the cytoskeleton.

Movement Across the Cell Membrane

Key Concept

Gradients rule! Be on the lookout throughout biology for examples where gradients drive physiological function:
- Oxygen–carbon dioxide exchange in tissues and lungs
- Urine formation in the kidneys
- Depolarization of neurons and conduction of the action potential
- Proton gradient in mitochondria
- Exchange of materials between the maternal and fetal blood across the placenta

Because cells spend much of their time and energy setting up membranes to control what passes in and out of the cell, they also need to regulate how substrates are capable of moving across that membrane. This is analogous to the border patrol we mentioned earlier, and we will take a look at these processes in turn. An important point to keep in mind is that all movement is based on concentration gradients, which are an MCAT favorite; knowing these will definitely net you points on Test Day. Regardless of what we are moving, the gradient will tell us whether this process will be passive or active.

SIMPLE DIFFUSION

The most basic of all processes, simple diffusion does not require energy; substrates move down their concentration gradient much as a ball would roll down a hill. There is potential energy (see—our MCAT physics is back in action) in a chemical gradient; each of these processes exploits that fact. **Osmosis** is a specific kind of simple diffusion that concerns water; water will move from a region of lower solute concentration to one of higher solute concentration. That is, it will move from a region of higher water concentration down its gradient to a region of lower water concentration. Osmosis is important in several places, notably where the solute itself is impermeable to a membrane. In such a case, water will move until the solute concentrations are equimolar (see Figure 1.13). If the concentration of solutes inside the cell is higher than the surrounding solution, the solution is said to be **hypotonic**; such a solution will cause a cell to swell, sometimes to the point of bursting. The opposite situation is known as a **hypertonic** solution. If the solutions inside and outside are equimolar, they are said to be **isotonic**. A key point here is that **isotonicity** does not prevent movement; rather, it prevents the net movement of particles. They still move; it's just a zero-sum game.

Mnemonic

Notice how the *O* in *hyp-O-tonic* looks like a swollen cell.

hypotonic solution | isotonic solution | hypertonic solution

Figure 1.13

MCAT Expertise

Hypertonicity and hypotonicity are commonly tested using an erythrocyte and the Na$^+$/K$^+$ ATPase pump, which can control the cell's volume when the cell is placed in a stressful environment.

Bridge

Diffusion is the biological version of a ball rolling down a hill—down its potential energy gradient. Active transport is the biological equivalent of pushing a ball up a hill; energy in the form of adenosine triphosphate must be expended, and work is performed.

Key Concept

Exocytosis and endocytosis allow the cell to compartmentalize certain functions, creating specific environments favorable to reactions such as digestion.

We can liken this process to the movement of people out of a city as it grows. As we have more and more people, some will move down the concentration gradient and out of our city. In real life, this principle can be demonstrated by placing a red blood cell in pure water. Because red blood cells have an osmolarity of 300 mOsm, versus 0 mOsm of pure water, we can determine that water will rush into the cell, causing it to burst.

FACILITATED DIFFUSION

Facilitated diffusion, also known as passive transport, is simple diffusion for molecules that need a little extra help. For molecules that are impermeable to the membrane (large, polar, and/or charged), the energy barrier (city wall) is too high to cross. Facilitated diffusion allows integral membrane proteins to serve as channels for these substrates to avoid the hydrophobic region of the phospholipid bilayer.

ACTIVE TRANSPORT

Active transport results in the net movement of a solute against its concentrations, just like rolling a ball uphill. Active transport always requires energy. Think about how your cells do this continually; it adds up to quite a Herculean task! This process is used throughout the body; for instance, in the nervous system to maintain the electric potential in neurons and in the kidneys to conserve useful solutes (e.g., glucose) from the filtrate.

Figure 1.14 shows simple diffusion, facilitated diffusion, and active transport. Table 1.1 summarizes these types of movement as well as osmosis.

ENDOCYTOSIS AND EXOCYTOSIS

Endocytosis is the process whereby the cellular membrane invaginates and engulfs material into the cell. The material is kept sequestered from the cytosol by virtue of being in a vesicle, which is important because cells will sometimes ingest toxic substances. **Pinocytosis** is the endocytosis of fluids and small particles, whereas

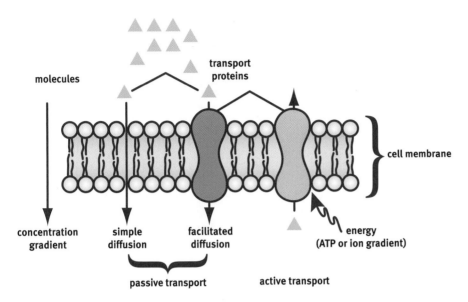

Figure 1.14

phagocytosis is the ingestion of large molecules. Often there will be a receptor to which substrates bind to induce ingestion, much as you might make airplane noises and move the spoon around when you try to make a baby ingest pureed carrots.

Exocytosis is the reverse process whereby substrates are released from the cell into the outside world. This becomes important in the nervous system and intracellular signaling.

Figure 1.15 shows endocytosis and exocytosis.

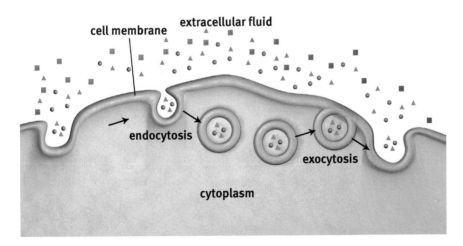

Figure 1.15

Table 1.1. Movement across the Cellular Membrane

	Simple Diffusion	Osmosis	Facilitated Diffusion	Active Transport
Concentration Gradient	High ⟶ Low	High ⟶ Low	High ⟶ Low	Low ⟶ High
Membrane Protein Required	No	No	Yes	Yes
Energy Required	NO—this is a PASSIVE process.	NO—this is a PASSIVE process.	NO—this is a PASSIVE process.	YES—this is an ACTIVE process; requires ATP.
Type of Molecule(s) Transported	Small, nonpolar (O_2, CO_2, etc.)	H_2O	Large, nonpolar (e.g., glucose)	Polar molecules or ions (e.g., Na^+, Cl^-, K^+, etc.)

Tissues

In multicellular organisms, cells may organize into discrete tissues that carry out different functions. To continue our analogy, if cells are like cities, tissues are the states into which they organize themselves. We will be discussing each of the organ systems in turn; several are MCAT favorites, including the circulatory, excretory, and nervous system.

EPITHELIAL TISSUE

These tissues cover the body and line the cavities; they provide a means for protection against invasion, and desiccation. Epithelium is also involved in absorption, secretion, and sensation.

CONNECTIVE TISSUE

Connective tissue supports the body and provides a framework for higher-level interactions. Bone, cartilage, tendons, ligaments, adipose tissue, and blood are all connective tissues.

NERVOUS TISSUE

Neurons are the primary cells in nervous tissue. They make use of electrochemical gradients to allow for cellular signaling and the coordinated control of multiple tissues, organs, and organ systems.

MUSCLE TISSUE

There are three types of muscle tissue: **skeletal**, **smooth**, **and cardiac**. Whereas each serves a specific function (which we will discuss in Chapter 6), they all exhibit great contractile ability and strength.

Viruses

If we remember back to the beginning of the chapter when we discussed the Cell Theory, we noted that viruses don't fit the definition of a living thing. By definition, viruses are acellular structures composed of nucleic acids surrounded by a protein coat. They may be as small as 20 nm or as large as 300 nm. For reference, prokaryotes are 1–10 μm, and eukaryotes are an order of magnitude larger (see Figure 1.16).

[size limits]

Tiny Aliens
The smallest bacteria have a diameter of about 200 nanometers. Autonomous organisms on our tree of life cannot be much smaller because they must contain protein-building cellular structures called ribosomes, which are each about 20 to 30 nanometers across. But if alien microbes could function without ribosomes, they could be comparable in size to the smallest viruses, which are only 20 nanometers wide. (Viruses do not need ribosomes, because they appropriate the machinery of infected cells to reproduce.)

Virus

20 nm

Bacterium

1 μm

Figure 1.16

The nuclear information may be circular or linear, single or double stranded, and DNA or RNA. The protein coat is known as a **capsid**. Since they cannot reproduce independently, viruses are known as **obligate intracellular parasites**. They must express and replicate their genetic information within a cell because they lack the necessary machinery to do it themselves. After hijacking a cell's machinery, a virus will replicate and turn out new copies of itself known as **virions**, which can be released to infect new cells. **Bacteriophages** are viruses that specifically target bacteria (see Figure 1.17). They do not actually enter bacteria; rather, they simply inject their genetic material, leaving the remaining structures outside the infected cell. Viruses can be likened to spies that hijack our factories and alter orders from the city hall (nucleus) to make their own nefarious products.

Bridge

Consider that viruses evade the immune system differently than bacteria do. Most bacteria never enter a cell, whereas viruses must do so in order to replicate. This has immune system implications that will be discussed later.

Real World

Diseases caused solely by viruses include the common cold, measles, mumps, chicken pox, croup, polio, influenza, hepatitis, and AIDS. It's trickier to use drugs against viruses than against bacteria, because viruses actually live inside host cells and have no organelles of their own (recall that many antibiotics work by targeting specific prokaryotic organelles). To date, the few antiviral medications that exist work by interfering with enzymatic reactions involved in viral replication. More success in combating viruses has been achieved through vaccination. Of the diseases listed above, vaccines currently exist for measles, mumps, chicken pox, polio, influenza, and hepatitis.

Figure 1.17

Conclusion

Our first chapter introduced the basis of all biology: the Cell Theory. We then introduced some of the techniques used in biology, and it's important for us to know how and when to apply these techniques. This sort of critical thinking is important to doing well on the MCAT. The eukaryotic versus prokaryotic distinction was our next topic of discussion. Eukaryotes will be the primary focus on the MCAT, but a few key facts about prokaryotes will net you a couple of points on Test Day. The subcellular organelles were discussed in detail; learn these well. Finally, we took a quick look at viruses and how they violate parts of the Cell Theory. We will now turn our attention to enzymes, which allow cells to carry out the basic chemical reactions necessary to support life.

CONCEPTS TO REMEMBER

☐ The Cell Theory defines what a cell is. Moreover, it gives us a basis for determining what sorts of organisms fit the biological definition of life.

☐ A variety of tools exist for biologists to study living organisms. Keep in mind that the basis for these techniques is physics and chemistry, and they may be tested that way.

☐ Prokaryotes are organisms that lack a nucleus and membrane-bound organelles.

☐ Eukaryotes contain both a nucleus and membrane-bound organelles, although those organelles may differ based on the organism and its ecological niche (e.g., plants have chloroplasts whereas animal cells do not).

☐ Membrane-bound organelles provide a mechanism for eukaryotic organisms to separate biological reactions and functions into discrete compartments. Know the function of each of these compartments.

☐ Passive transport (simple diffusion, facilitated diffusion, and osmosis) transfers solutes down their concentration gradients. No energy input is required. The energy has already been stored in the chemical gradient.

☐ Active transport requires energy and moves solutes against their concentration gradients.

☐ Endocytosis and exocytosis provide a mechanism whereby a cell can either engulf or excrete substrates. Moreover, they provide a way to isolate these compounds from the cytosol.

☐ Cells of similar type will organize together into tissues that can carry out higher-level functions.

☐ Viruses are obligate intracellular parasites that violate several tenets of the Cell Theory and are not considered to be alive.

Practice Questions

1. All of the following are components of the Cell Theory EXCEPT

   A. all living things are composed of cells.
   B. all living things possess mitochondria.
   C. cooperation among cells allows for complex functioning in living things.
   D. all cells arise from pre-existing cells.

2. Upon bacteriophage infection, the host cell is directed to synthesize viral protein. A scientist wishing to study the location of this process in the cell might use

   A. centrifugation.
   B. autoradiography.
   C. electrophoresis.
   D. phase contrast microscopy.

3. A student is trying to determine the type of membrane transport occurring in a cell. She finds that the molecule to be transported is very large and polar and when transported across the membrane, no ATP is used. Which of the following is the most likely mechanism of transport?

   A. Active transport
   B. Simple diffusion
   C. Facilitated diffusion
   D. Exocytosis

4. Which of the following is NOT a type of tissue found in the human body?

   A. Connective tissue
   B. Nervous tissue
   C. Adipose tissue
   D. Cytoplasmic tissue

5. Which of the following types of nucleic acid will never be found in a virus?

   A. Single-stranded DNA
   B. Double-stranded DNA
   C. Single- and double-stranded RNA
   D. All of these can be found in a virus.

6. Which of the following activities occurs in the Golgi apparatus?

   A. Synthesis of proteins
   B. Modification and packaging of proteins
   C. Breakdown of lipids and carbohydrates
   D. Photosynthesis

7. Mitochondrial DNA

   A. is circular.
   B. is self-replicating.
   C. is important in the synthesis of mitochondrial ribosomes.
   D. both (A) and (B).

8. Which of the following is NOT a function of the smooth endoplasmic reticulum?

A. Lipid synthesis
B. Poison detoxification
C. Protein synthesis
D. Transport of proteins

9. What is the main function of the nucleolus?

A. Ribosomal RNA synthesis
B. DNA synthesis
C. Cell division
D. Chromosome assembly

10. In which of the following organelles is pH the lowest?

A. Lysosomes
B. Mitochondria
C. Rough ER
D. Chloroplasts

11. Which of the following is NOT a difference that would allow one to distinguish between a prokaryotic and a eukaryotic cell?

A. Ribosomal subunit weight
B. Presence or absence of the nucleus
C. Presence or absence of the cell wall
D. Membrane-bound versus no membrane-bound organelles

12. A researcher treats a solution containing animal cells with ouabain, a poisonous substance that interferes with the Na^+/K^+-ATPase embedded in the cell membrane, and causes the cell to lyse. Which of the following statements best explains ouabain's mechanism of action?

A. Treatment with ouabain results in high levels of extracellular Ca^{2+}
B. Treatment with ouabain results in high levels of extracellular K^+ and Na^+
C. Treatment with ouabain increases intracellular concentrations of Na^+
D. Treatment with ouabain decreases intracellular concentrations of Na^+

13. Which of the following is NOT involved in cell movement?

A. Cilia
B. Flagella
C. Actin
D. Centrioles

Small Group Questions

1. Can glucose freely diffuse through the cell membrane? Why or why not?

2. Explain why mitochondria and chloroplasts possess similar characteristics.

3. Cystic fibrosis is a genetic disease characterized by thick mucus secretions that block air passages in the lungs. This disease results from faulty chloride channels that allow Cl^- and Na^+ to remain in the cells that line the airways. How does this cause the mucus in the airways to become thick?

4. Most biologists consider viruses to be nonliving because they are unable to replicate independently. How might you argue against this position? What characteristics do viruses have that make them lifelike?

Explanations to Practice Questions

1. B

The Cell Theory can be summarized by four main ideas: (1) all living things are composed of cells, (2) the cell is the basic functional unit of life, (3) cells arise only from pre-existing cells, and (4) cells carry genetic information in the form of DNA. From the given choices, all of them are components of the Cell Theory, with the exception of (B). The presence or absence of mitochondria is not a component of the Cell Theory, making (B) the correct answer.

2. B

The best way to identify the location of synthesis of viral proteins is to label amino acids with radioactive isotopes. This technique is used in autoradiography, which utilizes radioactive molecules to trace and identify cell structures and localize biochemical activity. Autoradiography, (B), is therefore the correct answer.

3. C

We are asked to identify the type of transport that would allow a large, polar molecule to cross the membrane without any energy requirement. This scenario describes facilitated diffusion, which uses a transport protein (or channel) to facilitate the movement of large, polar molecules across the nonpolar, hydrophobic membrane. Facilitated diffusion, like simple diffusion, does not require any energy, which explains why no ATP was consumed during this transport process. (C) is therefore the correct answer.

4. D

The four basic types of tissue found in the human body are epithelial (skin), connective (bone, cartilage, tendons, ligaments, adipose tissue, and blood), nervous (neurons), and muscle (skeletal, cardiac, and smooth). There is no such thing as cytoplasmic tissue, making (D) the correct answer.

5. D

In a virus, the nucleic acid can be either linear or circular and is found in four varieties: single-stranded DNA, double-stranded DNA, single-stranded RNA, and double-stranded RNA. Thus, all types of nucleic acid can be found in a virus, making (D) the correct answer.

6. B

The Golgi apparatus consists of a stack of membrane-enclosed sacs. It receives vesicles and their contents from the smooth ER, modifies them (e.g., glycosylation), repackages them into vesicles, and distributes them. Therefore, from the given choices, only (B) matches the function of the Golgi apparatus.

7. D

Mitochondrial DNA, or mDNA, is circular and self-replicating, which allows the mitochondria to be semi-autonomous. Mitochondria are capable of synthesizing some of their own proteins and can replicate via binary fission. However, mitochondria are not entirely independent from the rest of the cell, as many of their components (e.g., ribosomes) are produced in the nucleolus of the cell, along with the other ribosomes. (D) is therefore the correct answer.

8. C

The smooth endoplasmic reticulum is involved in the transport of materials throughout the cell, in lipid synthesis, and in the detoxification of drugs and poisons. Proteins can cross into the smooth ER, where they are secreted into cytoplasmic vesicles and transported to the Golgi apparatus. Thus, from the given choices, protein synthesis is not a function of the smooth ER but rather of the ribosomes associated with the rough ER. (C) is therefore the correct answer.

9. A

The nucleolus (not to be confused with the nucleus) is a dense structure in the nucleus where ribosomal RNA (rRNA) is synthesized. Ribosomal RNA is the main component of the ribosomal subunits. (A) is therefore the correct answer.

10. A

A low pH indicates an acidic environment. From the given choices, only lysosomes maintain an acidic environment since they contain hydrolytic enzymes involved in intracellular digestion. These enzymes are maximally effective at a pH of 5 and need to be enclosed within the lysosome—in an environment that is distinct from the neutral pH of the cytosol—to prevent them from digesting the cell itself. When a cell is injured, it can commit suicide by rupturing the lysosomal membrane and releasing hydrolytic enzymes into the cell. (A) is therefore the correct answer.

11. C

The main differences between prokaryotes and eukaryotes are these: prokaryotes do not have a nucleus, while eukaryotes do; prokaryotes have ribosomal subunits of 30s and 50s, while eukaryotes have ribosomal subunits of 40s and 60s; and prokaryotes do not have membrane-bound organelles, whereas eukaryotes do. Lastly, it is important to note that while a cell wall is present in most prokaryotes, fungi and plants are the only eukaryotes that have cell walls. Therefore, the presence or absence of a cell wall does not definitively differentiate between prokaryotes and eukaryotes, making (C) the correct answer.

12. C

This question requires an understanding of osmosis and the action of Na^+/K^+-ATPase. When a cell is placed in a hypertonic solution (a solution having a higher solute concentration than the cell), fluid will diffuse out of the cell into the solution, resulting in cell shrinkage. When a cell is placed in a hypotonic solution (a solution having a lower solute concentration than the cell), fluid will diffuse from the solution into the cell, causing the cell to expand and possibly lyse. The Na^+/K^+-ATPase moves three sodium ions out for every two potassium ions it lets into the cell. Therefore, inhibition of the Na^+/K^+-ATPase by ouabain will cause a net increase in the Na^+ concentration inside the cell and water will diffuse in, down its concentration gradient, causing the cell to swell and then lyse. Thus (C) is the correct answer.

13. D

From the given choices, all of them are involved in cell movement with the exception of (D). Centrioles are composed of microtubules and direct the separation of chromosomes during cell division. Therefore, they are not involved in cell motility, making (D) the correct answer.

Enzymes

Introduction

Tune into the national news on any given night, and you are likely to hear a report on hypertension—what causes it, how we can avoid it, and most urgently, what we can do to treat it. The risk of hypertension, or high blood pressure, is especially high in individuals whose weight and body fat percentage classify them as obese, which means that as the obesity epidemic becomes more widespread, hypertension does as well. Increased sodium intake and pregnancy can also lead to hypertension, but luckily, neither of these risk factors are permanent.

Millions of Americans are told each year to alter their diet, add exercise to their daily regimen, or even take prescription drugs to control their hypertension. Many of these medications fall under a category called ACE inhibitors. ACE, short for angiotensin-converting enzyme, converts a peptide called angiotensin I to angiotensin II. Angiotensin II goes on to stimulate a hormone that raises blood pressure. Let's back up a little bit. In response to a drop in blood pressure, specialized cells in the kidney, known as juxtaglomerular cells, release an enzyme called renin. Renin converts the dormant precursor angiotensinogen into angiotensin I, which is cleaved by ACE to angiotensin II. Angiotensin II stimulates aldosterone, a steroid hormone that allows the kidney to reabsorb more sodium, and because water generally follows sodium, water re-enters blood as well. The blood's volume increases, thus the hydrostatic pressure against blood vessels also increases. Another name for hydrostatic pressure against blood vessels? Blood pressure. So without ACE, angiotensin II can't stimulate aldosterone, and blood pressure stays low. This is how ACE inhibitors work.

So there are natural enzymes and hormones that actually raise blood pressure? Doesn't that contribute to the problem? Well, it's not supposed to. The human body must always remain in a very delicate stable state known as homeostasis. If that balance is tipped even a little bit, chemical messengers rush to correct it. In other words, when we're dehydrated or injured, we'd be goners without ACE. Enzymes are crucial proteins that dramatically increase the rate of chemical reactions. They're used to regulate homeostatic mechanisms in every organ system, and they are regulated by inhibitors themselves, like the ACE inhibitors used to treat hypertension. They're kept safe and ready to go in inactive forms, like angiotensinogen, and are sent on their way when needed. In this chapter, we'll learn all about how enzymes work and how different conditions influence their activity. We'll also see how enzymes are regulated, which will help us tie concepts together in every organ system we learn for the MCAT.

Thermodynamics and Kinetics ★★★★☆

Recall that thermodynamics relates the relative energy states of a reaction in terms of its products and reactants. An **endothermic** reaction is one that requires energy input, whereas an **exothermic** reaction is one in which energy is given off. Remember that *endo–* means "in" and *exo–* means "out", so endothermic reactions take energy in to go forward, whereas exothermic reactions release energy out as they go forward. We can look at a reaction diagram to see this demonstrated more clearly.

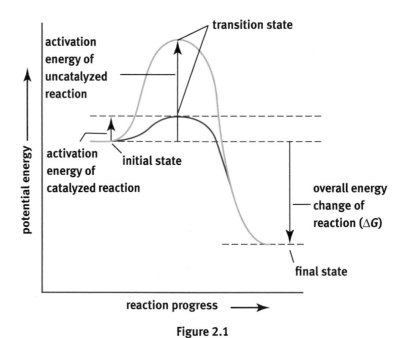

Figure 2.1

The reaction shown in Figure 2.1 is exothermic. Note that the ΔH for this reaction is negative. A very important characteristic of enzymes is that they do not alter the overall enthalpy change for a reaction, nor do they change the equilibrium of a reaction. Rather, they affect the rate (kinetics) at which a reaction occurs; thus, they can affect how quickly a reaction gets to equilibrium but not the actual equilibrium state itself. Recall that enzymes, as catalysts, themselves are unchanged by the reaction. What is the functional consequence of this? Far fewer enzymes are required relative to the overall amount of substrate. Think back to general chemistry and recall how catalysts exert their effect. They lower the activation energy; in other words, they make it easier for the substrate to reach the transition state. Imagine having to walk to the other side of a tall hill. The only way to get there is to climb to the top of the hill and then walk down the other side. Wouldn't it be easier if something could bore a tunnel through the center of that hill so you wouldn't have to climb as high? That's exactly what enzymes (and all catalysts) do for chemical reactions.

Most reactions catalyzed by enzymes are technically reversible, although that reversal may be energetically unfavorable and therefore unrealistic.

Enzyme Specificity

Enzymes are picky; they tend to catalyze a single reaction or class of reactions. For example, urease catalyzes the breakdown of only urea. Chymotrypsin, on the other hand, can cleave peptide bonds around the amino acids phenylalanine, tryptophan, and tyrosine in a variety of polypeptides. Although those amino acids aren't identical, they all contain an aromatic ring, which makes chymotrypsin specific for a class of molecules.

NORMAL ACTIVITY OF ENZYME

ACTIVE SITE OF ENZYME

ACTIVE SITE OF ENZYME

Figure 2.2

Most enzymes end in the prefix *–ase*. The molecule upon which an enzyme acts is known as its **substrate**. Biochemists cleverly named the complex between the enzyme and substrate the **enzyme-substrate complex**. The **active site** is the location within the enzyme where the substrate is held during the chemical reaction (see Figure 2.2). Two competing theories explain how enzymes and substrates interact, but one of those two is generally more accepted than the other.

THE LOCK AND KEY THEORY

This theory is aptly named. It suggests that the enzyme's active site (lock) is already in the appropriate confirmation for the substrate (key) to bind. No alteration of the tertiary or quaternary structure is necessary upon binding of the substrate (see Figure 2.3).

Bridge

Consider that enzymes often break down or create molecules (H_2O_2, OCl–) that would be damaging to the cell if they were released into the cytoplasm. Think back to the last chapter's discussion on how cells deal with these oxidants and/or reactive oxygen species, which are necessary for certain reactions.

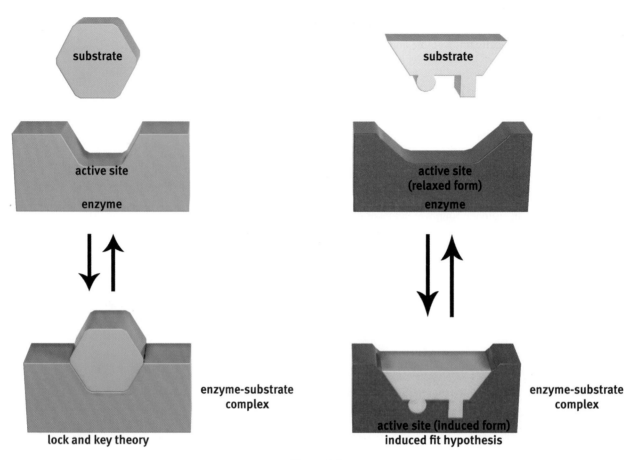

Figure 2.3

THE INDUCED FIT THEORY

The more scientifically accepted theory is the induced fit theory, and this is the one we are more likely to see on Test Day (see Figure 2.3). Imagine this: The enzyme is a foam stress ball, and the substrate is a frustrated MCAT student's hand. What's the desired interaction? The student wants to release some stress and relax. As his hand squeezes the ball, both change conformation. The ball is no longer spherical and his hand is no longer flat because they adjust to fit each other well. Ball squeezing takes energy, and therefore, this part of the reaction is endothermic. Once the student lets go of the stress ball, we have our desired product: a relaxed, more confident test taker. Letting go of the stress ball is pretty easy and doesn't require extra energy. This part of the reaction is exothermic. Just like enzymes, foam stress balls return to their original shape once their crunchers (substrates) let go of them.

What would happen if we tried to cure an earache using a stress ball? Well, unfortunately, inner ears don't really have any ability to grab stress balls. Try holding a stress ball up to your ear; it's a good bet that nothing would change shape. Similarly, a substrate of the wrong type will not cause the appropriate conformational shift in the protein, which allows for exposure of the active site. No reaction occurs.

Table 2.1 summarizes the key points to remember about enzymes.

Table 2.1. Key Features of Enzymes

1. Lower the activation energy.
2. Increase the rate of the reaction.
3. Do not alter the equilibrium constant.
4. Are not changed or consumed in the reaction. (This means that they will appear in both the reactants and products.)
5. Are pH and temperature sensitive, with optimal activity at specific pH ranges and temperatures.
6. Do not affect the overall ΔG of the reaction.
7. Are specific for a particular reaction or class of reactions.

Cofactors

Many enzymes require nonprotein molecules called **cofactors** to be effective. Enzymes without their cofactors are called **apoenzymes**, whereas those containing them are **holoenzymes**. Cofactors are attached in a variety of ways, ranging from weak noncovalent interactions to strong ones. These tightly bound factors are known as **prosthetic groups**. Cofactors are a topic that we are likely to see on Test Day, so we should know they are essential.

Two important types of cofactors are small metal ions and small organic groups. The latter organic cofactors are actually called **coenzymes**. If we think back to the introduction of the previous chapter and recall all the bacteria living in our gut, this turns out to be a good thing, because some of these bacteria make biotin, a necessary human cofactor. The vast majority of these coenzymes are vitamins.

Enzyme Kinetics

Enzyme kinetics is a high-yield topic that can score us several points on Test Day. Just as the relief our student derives from squeezing a stress ball depends on a number of factors, such as size or shape of the ball, enzyme kinetics are dependent on conditions such as temperature, pH, and concentrations of substrate and/or enzyme.

EFFECTS OF CONCENTRATION

The concentration of the substrate [S] and enzyme [E] greatly affects how quickly a reaction will occur. Let's say that we have 100 stress balls (enzymes) and only 10 frustrated students (substrates) to squeeze them (high enzyme concentration relative to substrate). We will quickly reach equilibrium (students letting go and feeling relaxed) as there are many active sites available. As we slowly add more substrate (students), the rate of the reaction will increase, and more people will be happy in the same amount of time because we have plenty of available stress balls for them to squeeze. However, as we add more and more people (approaching 100), we begin to level off and reach a maximal rate of relaxation. There are fewer and fewer available stress balls until all sites are occupied. Unlike before, inviting more students to the room will not change the rate of the reaction. It cannot go any faster once it has reached **saturation**. At this rate, the enzyme is working at **maximum velocity**, denoted by V_{max}. If you don't yet understand this, keep reading and look at Figure 2.4. This concept is essential for Test Day.

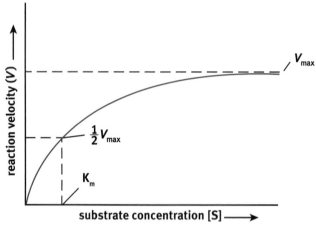

Figure 2.4

The Michaelis-Menten equation proposed in 1913 suggests the following. Enzyme-substrate complexes form at a rate k_1. The ES complex can either dissociate at a rate k_2 or turn into E + P at a rate k_3. Note that in either case, the enzyme is again available.

$$E + S \underset{k_2}{\overset{k_1}{\rightleftharpoons}} ES \overset{k_3}{\Rightarrow} E + P$$

Some important and Test Day–relevant math can be derived from this equation. When the reaction rate is equal to $\frac{1}{2} V_{max}$, $K_m = [S]$ and can be understood to be the point at which half of the enzyme's active sites are full (half the stress balls are in use). When [S] is less than K_m, changes in [S] will greatly affect the reaction rate. In contrast, at high [S] (many students), [S] exceeds K_m and approaches V_{max}.

Key Concept

We can assess an enzyme's affinity for a substrate by noting the K_m. A low K_m reflects a high affinity for the substrate (low [S] required for 50% enzyme saturation). Conversely, a high K_m reflects a low affinity of the enzyme for the substrate.

EFFECTS OF TEMPERATURE

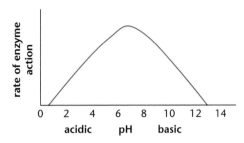

Figure 2.5

Enzyme-catalyzed reactions tend to double in rate for every 10°C increase in temperature until the optimum temperature is reached; for the human body, this is 37°C. After this, activity falls off sharply, as the enzyme will denature at higher temperatures (see Figure 2.5). Some enzymes that are overheated may regain their function if cooled. A real-life example of temperature dependence occurs in Siamese cats. Siamese cats are dark on their faces, ears, tails, and feet but white elsewhere. Why? The enzyme responsible for pigmentation, tyrosinase, is mutated in Siamese cats. It is ineffective at body temperature but at cooler temperatures becomes active. Thus, the tail, feet, ears, and face (cooled by air passing through the nose and mouth) have an active form of the enzyme and are dark.

> **Key Concept**
>
> Consider how the human body uses this. What part of the human body might require enzymes that work at a lower temperature? The answer will appear in Chapter 4.

EFFECTS OF pH

Most enzymes also depend on pH in order to function properly. For enzymes that circulate and function in human blood, this optimal pH is 7.4 (see Figure 2.5). This means that a pH of 7.3 in human blood is termed acidosis, even though it's more basic than chemically neutral 7.0. The MCAT assumes that we know this, so let's commit it to memory now. Where might exceptions to this occur? Both are in our digestive tract. Pepsin, which works in the stomach, has maximal activity around pH 2, whereas pancreatic enzymes, which work in the small intestine, work best around pH 8.5. We will discuss the pH levels in the stomach and intestine in Chapter 7.

Regulation of Enzymatic Activity

Although enzymes are useful, we want to be able to control when they work. This may be accomplished in a variety of ways; two test-worthy ones are **allosteric effects** and **inhibition**.

> **Bridge**
>
> Consider that digestive enzymes chew up fats, proteins, and carbohydrates—the very same compounds of which our body is made. How do these enzymes know to digest your food but not your body? Simply put, they don't! So we regulate their activity in a coordinated manner using feedback mechanisms and other substances.

ALLOSTERIC EFFECTS

Enzymes that are allosteric have multiple binding sites. The active site is present, as well as at least one other site that can regulate the availability of the active site. These are known as **allosteric sites**. **Allosteric enzymes** alternate between an active and an inactive form. The inactive form is incapable of carrying out the enzymatic reaction. Binding in the allosteric site may consist of either **allosteric activators** or **allosteric inhibitors**. Binding of either causes a conformational shift in the protein. The effect is what differs. An activator will result in a shift that makes the active site more available for binding to the substrate. An inhibitor will make it less available. In addition to being able to alter the conformation of the protein, binding of activators or repressors may alter the affinity of the enzyme for its substrate. For example, the binding of one molecule of oxygen to hemoglobin shifts the entire molecule such that there is an increased affinity of the remaining subunits for oxygen.

INHIBITION

The activity of an enzyme may be regulated by one of its products (feedback inhibition) or other molecules that can bind to the enzyme (reversible and irreversible inhibition).

Feedback Inhibition

A large number of biological reactions are regulated through feedback inhibition. Once we have enough of a product, why create more? In feedback inhibition, the product may bind to an enzyme or enzymes that acted earlier in its biosynthetic pathway, thereby making the enzyme unavailable for other substrates to use. This is schematically represented in Figure 2.6, as we see product D feeding back to inhibit the first enzyme in the pathway. Let's be sure we have a good handle on this concept before we move on, because it appears often in endocrine pathways (Chapter 12) and is commonly tested on the MCAT.

Figure 2.6

Reversible Inhibition

There are three types of reversible inhibition: competitive, noncompetitive, and uncompetitive. **Competitive inhibition** simply involves occupancy of the active site. Substrates cannot access enzymatic binding sites if there is an inhibitor in the way. Competitive inhibition can be overcome by adding more substrate so that the substrate-to-inhibitor ratio is higher. If more molecules of substrate are available than molecules of inhibitor, then the enzyme will be more likely to bind substrate than inhibitor (assuming the enzyme has equal affinity for both molecules). What about noncompetitive inhibition? This term describes inhibitor binding to an allosteric site instead of the active site, which induces a change in enzyme conformation. Since the two molecules do not compete for the same spot, inhibition is *noncompetitive* and cannot be overcome by adding more substrate. Once the enzyme's conformation is altered, no amount of extra substrate will be conducive to forming an enzyme-substrate complex.

Irreversible Inhibition

In this type of inhibition, the active site is made permanently unavailable, or the enzyme is permanently altered. A real-world example is aspirin. Acetylsalicylic acid (aspirin) irreversibly acetylates cyclooxygenase. The enzyme can no longer make its products (prostaglandins), which are involved in modulating pain and inflammatory responses. To make more prostaglandins, new cyclooxygenase will have to be synthesized through transcription and translation.

Inactive Enzymes

Certain enzymes are particularly dangerous if they are not tightly controlled. These include the digestive enzymes (e.g., trypsin), which if released from the pancreas in an uncontrolled manner, would digest the organ itself. To avoid this danger, these enzymes and others are secreted as inactive **zymogens** (e.g., trypsinogen for trypsin). Zymogens contain a catalytic (active) domain and regulatory domain. The regulatory domain must be either removed or altered to expose the active site. Apoptotic enzymes (caspases) exhibit similar regulation.

Conclusion

Our current study focused on the way in which cells are able to carry out the reactions necessary for life. We began with a thermodynamics and kinetics review in relation to enzymes, which are biological catalysts. We went on to discuss the factors that may affect enzyme activity, including substrate concentration (think Michaelis-Menton kinetics), cofactors, temperature, and pH. All of these are likely to appear on Test Day. Enzymes need to be regulated; we analyzed the basics of inhibition, primarily mediated via negative feedback. Finally we talked about inhibitors of enzymes that may be reversible or irreversible. The difference between competitive and noncompetitive inhibition is a key Test Day concept. Let's move on now to discuss cellular respiration, a series of chemical reactions designed to generate energy for the cell. These reactions depend on the assistance of enzymes.

Key Concept

Reversible Inhibition

Competitive Inhibitor	Noncompetitive Inhibitor
Binds to active site.	Binds to site other than active site.
Can be overcome by adding more substrate.	Cannot be overcome by adding more substrate.
$\uparrow K_m$	K_m remains unchanged but $V_{max} \downarrow$

Real World

The concept of competitive inhibition has relevance in the clinical setting. For example, methanol (wood alcohol), if ingested, is enzymatically converted to toxic metabolites, which can cause blindness and even death. Administration of intravenous ethanol is the treatment of choice for a patient suffering from methanol poisoning. Ethanol works by competing with methanol for the active sites of the enzymes involved.

CONCEPTS TO REMEMBER

☐ Enzymes are biological catalysts that lower the activation energy necessary for biological reactions.

☐ Enzymes do not alter the enthalpy change (ΔH) that accompanies the reaction; rather, they change the rate (kinetics) at which equilibrium is reached.

☐ Enzymes have an active site, which is where the relevant chemistry occurs.

☐ Each enzyme catalyzes a single reaction or type of reaction with fairly high specificity.

☐ Some enzymes require cofactors to be active. These tend to be either metal cations or small organic molecules.

☐ Temperature and pH can both affect the enzyme's activity. Temperature and pH can result in denaturing of the enzyme and loss of activity owing to loss of secondary, tertiary, and, if present, quaternary structure.

☐ Feedback inhibition provides a way for an enzyme to slow its activity. If product builds up, the enzyme has completed its task and can stop working rapidly. Often it is the product that binds to an allosteric site of the enzyme to cause this change.

☐ Reversible inhibition can be competitive or noncompetitive. Competitive inhibition may be overcome by increasing the amount of substrate.

☐ Irreversible inhibition alters the enzyme in such a way that it is no longer available and never will be. New enzyme molecules must be synthesized from scratch.

☐ Some enzymes that could be harmful to the parent organism (e.g., digestive enzymes such as trypsin) are secreted in inactive forms (zymogens) to prevent their unintended activity.

Practice Questions

1. Consider a biochemical reaction A → B, which is catalyzed by A–B dehydrogenase. Which of the following statements is true?

   A. The reaction will proceed until the enzyme concentration decreases.
   B. The reaction will be more favorable at 0°C.
   C. A component of the enzyme is transferred from A to B.
   D. The free energy change (ΔG) of the catalyzed reaction is the same as for the uncatalyzed reaction.

2. Consider the following enzyme pathway.

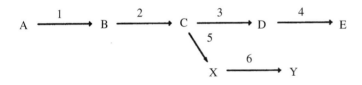

   An increase in [E] leads to the inhibition of enzyme 3. All of the following are results of the process EXCEPT

   A. an increase in [B].
   B. an increase in [Y].
   C. decreased activity of enzyme 4.
   D. increased activity of enzyme 6.

3. Which of the following statements about enzyme kinetics is FALSE?

   A. An increase in the substrate concentration (at constant enzyme concentration) leads to proportional increases in the rate of the reaction.
   B. Most enzymes operating in the human body work best at a temperature of 37°C.
   C. An enzyme-substrate complex can either form a product or dissociate back into the enzyme and substrate.
   D. Maximal activity of many human enzymes occurs around pH 7.2.

4. At which pH would pancreatic enzymes work at maximum activity?

   A. 5.3
   B. 6.7
   C. 7.2
   D. 8.5

5. Some enzymes require the presence of a nonprotein molecule to behave catalytically. An enzyme devoid of this molecule is called a(n)

   A. holoenzyme.
   B. apoenzyme.
   C. coenzyme.
   D. zymoenzyme.

6. Which of the following factors determine an enzyme's specificity?

   A. The three-dimensional shape of the active site
   B. The Michaelis constant
   C. The type of cofactor required for the enzyme to be active
   D. The prosthetic group on the enzyme

7. Enzymes increase the rate of a reaction by

   A. decreasing the activation energy.
   B. increasing the overall free energy of the reaction.
   C. both (A) and (B).
   D. None of the above

8. Bonding between atoms within an enzyme such as trypsin is best described as

   A. peptide.
   B. saccharide.
   C. ionic.
   D. van der Waals.

9. In the equation below, substrate C is an allosteric inhibitor to enzyme 1. Which of the following is another mechanism caused by substrate C?

$$A \rightarrow \text{enzyme } 1 \rightarrow B \rightarrow \text{enzyme } 2 \rightarrow C$$

   A. Competitive inhibition
   B. Irreversible inhibition
   C. Feedback enhancement
   D. Negative feedback

10. When lactase hydrolyzes its substrate, lactose, which of the following occurs?

   A. Lactase retains its structure after the reaction.
   B. Lactose retains its structure after the reaction.
   C. Lactase increases the activation energy of the reaction.
   D. Lactose decreases the activation energy of the reaction.

Small Group Questions

1. Why do enzymes function at specific pH and temperature ranges?

2. Describe the kinetic effects of increasing substrate concentration while enzyme concentration remains constant.

3. Explain the significance of K_m in enzyme-catalyzed reactions.

Explanations to Practice Questions

1. D

In an enzyme-catalyzed reaction, the rate of a reaction is increased by a decrease in the activation energy. Furthermore, enzymes are not changed or consumed during the course of the reaction. Also, the overall free energy change of the reaction, ΔG, remains unchanged in the presence of an enzyme. This implies that (D) is the correct answer.

2. A

Looking at the enzyme pathway, we notice that if enzyme 3 is inhibited, everything that is controlled by it will decrease in concentration and activity. That is, the concentration of D and E will eventually decrease. The activity of enzyme 4 will also decrease, because it will be acting on a decreased amount of substrate. In addition, if enzyme 3 is inhibited, more of C will be converted to X through enzyme 5. As such, the concentration of X and Y is expected to increase, as is the activity of enzyme 6. Anything before the enzyme 3 should remain unaffected. Therefore, the concentration of B will remain the same, making (A) the correct answer.

3. A

Most enzymes in the human body operate at maximal activity around a temperature of 37°C and a pH of 7.2, which is the pH of most body fluids. In addition, as characterized by the Michaelis-Menten model, enzymes form an enzyme-substrate complex, which can either dissociate back into the enzyme and substrate or proceed to form a product. So far, we can eliminate (B), (C), and (D), so let's check choice (A). An increase in the substrate concentration, while maintaining a constant enzyme concentration, leads to a proportional increase in the rate of the reaction only initially. However, once most of the active sites are occupied, the reaction rate levels off, regardless of further increases in substrate concentration. At high concentrations of substrate, the reaction rate approaches its maximal velocity and is no longer changed by further increases in substrate concentration. Therefore, the statement in (A) is not entirely true.

4. D

Pancreatic enzymes work optimally in the alkaline conditions of the small intestine. It is not necessary to know the exact pH at which these enzymes work because the only very basic pH is seen in (D).

5. B

An enzyme devoid of its necessary cofactor is called an apoenzyme and is catalytically inactive. (B) is therefore the correct answer.

6. A

An enzyme's specificity is determined by the three-dimensional shape of its active site. Regardless of which theory of enzyme specificity we are discussing (lock and key or induced fit), the active site determines which substrate the enzyme will react with. (A) is therefore the correct answer.

7. A

Enzymes increase the rate of a reaction by decreasing the activation energy. They do not affect the overall free energy, ΔG, of the reaction. (A) is therefore the correct answer.

8. A

(A) is correct because enzymes are proteins. Proteins are composed of amino acids linked together by peptide bonds. The other choices are not bonds that would be found in proteins. (B) is a type of bond found in polysaccharides. (C) is a chemical bond formed through electrostatic interaction between positive and negative ions. (D) may be formed between secondary or tertiary structures but is not as good an option as (A).

9. D

By limiting the activity of enzyme 1, the rest of the pathway is slowed, which is the definition of negative feedback. (A) is incorrect because there is no competition for the active site with allosteric interactions. There is not enough information for (B) to be correct because we aren't told whether the inhibition is reversible. In general, allosteric interactions are temporary. (C) is incorrect because it is the opposite of what occurs when enzyme 1 activity is reduced.

10. A

(A) is the correct answer because, by definition, an enzyme remains unchanged by the reaction that it catalyzes. (B) is incorrect because a substrate is changed by an enzymatic reaction. (C) is not true, as an enzyme would decrease the activation energy. (D) is also incorrect since a substrate does not affect the activation energy.

3

Cellular Metabolism

What do vitamin C, omega-3 fatty acids, papaya enzymes, iron, turmeric, Saint John's wort, calcium, and coenzyme Q_{10} (CoQ_{10}) have in common? They are all found in over-the-counter dietary supplements. Some of them have proven benefits, whereas others seem to provide the most for those who believe in them. CoQ_{10} is of special interest in disorders that seem to decrease its natural levels in the body. According to some, these disorders range from Parkinson's disease to Alzheimer's disease to cancer. It's most commonly used to ward off cancer or in patients who suffer from heart disease.

So what does CoQ_{10} actually do? It's naturally found in the inner mitochondrial membrane of the cell and helps make adenosine triphosphate (ATP). Decreased levels of CoQ_{10} translate to decreased levels of ATP, and increasing CoQ_{10} does the opposite. Increased levels of ATP drive protein production, muscle contraction, and innumerable other biochemical processes, including those involved in immune function. In addition, as an antioxidant, CoQ_{10} counters the harmful effects of free radicals, which we most often hear about in anti-aging face cream commercials. But free radicals aren't just aesthetic obstacles; rather, they are implicated in a number of disorders including cancer, Parkinson's disease, and Alzheimer's disease (sound familiar?).

The truth is, it's not totally proven that CoQ_{10} is a miracle vitamin. In some cases, it works; in others, it doesn't. For some cancers, it helps; for others, not so much. Part of the problem is that controlled studies in humans either have not been run or have not confirmed the effects of CoQ_{10} on the progress of these disorders. In many cases, CoQ_{10} cannot be advised positively or negatively, and it's really up to the patient to try it, if so desired. It *is* advised, however, that all supplements be reported to the managing physician so that potential ill interactions can be avoided.

In this chapter, we'll observe CoQ_{10}'s antioxidant powers in the electron transport chain. We'll also learn about the other processes that harvest high-energy electrons—namely, glycolysis, pyruvate decarboxylation, and the Krebs cycle. Furthermore, we'll look at how some cells metabolize glucose without an electron transport chain. Finally, we'll analyze the energy potential in noncarbohydrate sources.

Transfer of Energy

THE FLOW OF ENERGY

All energy for living organisms is ultimately derived from the sun. **Autotrophs** are organisms that are capable of using the sun's energy to create organic molecules (e.g., glucose) that can store that energy in their bonds. By and large, plants carry out most of earth's autotrophic functions through the anabolic process of **photosynthesis**. These organisms do not require an exogenous source of organic compounds. **Heterotrophic** organisms, on the other hand, derive their energy by breaking down the organic molecules made by plants, and harnessing the power held in the bonds of the molecules (see Figure 3.1). Thus, as humans, we are catabolic in our energy generation.

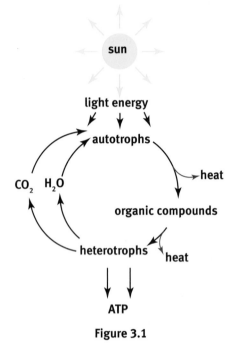

Figure 3.1

Glucose ($C_6H_{12}O_6$) is a central mediator in this process. Like many other six-carbon monosaccharides, it is capable of forming a ring structure, known as a pyranose, in either an α or β configuration.

The formation of glucose by autotrophs involves the breaking of C–O bonds in CO_2 and O–H bonds in H_2O. These atoms are then rearranged into glucose while storing energy in the chemical bonds that are being formed. Because the sun's energy powers photosynthetic reactions, it is considered to be an endothermic process.

$$6\ CO_2 + 6\ H_2O + \text{Energy} \Rightarrow C_6H_{12}O_6 + 6\ O_2$$

Heterotrophic organisms liberate this energy by breaking these bonds and coupling the energy release to perform useful work. The cellular respiration equation is simply the photosynthesis equation in reverse.

$$C_6H_{12}O_6 + 6\ O_2 \Rightarrow 6\ CO_2 + 6\ H_2O + \text{Energy}$$

No machine is perfect, however; some energy must be lost along the way. Our biological systems are no exception. Energy is lost in the form of heat for each of the relevant reactions.

ENERGY CARRIERS

The energy that is released during glucose catabolism must be harnessed to provide any useful value. To do so, our cells use intermediates, such as **ATP** and the coenzymes **NAD⁺** and **FAD**. These molecules serve as high-energy electron shuttles between the cytoplasm and mitochondria.

ATP

Adenosine triphosphate is the primary energy currency of the cell. Its rapid formation and degradation allow for energy to be stored and released as needed. Whereas we might equate fat with an IRA or glycogen with a certificate of deposit, ATP is the dollar bill in your wallet. You can use it immediately.

Adenosine triphosphate is generated during glucose catabolism. It consists of the nitrogenous base adenine, the sugar ribose, and three phosphate groups. Can you recall how to tell if the sugar is ribose or deoxyribose? Ribose's 2′ carbon is bound to a hydroxyl group, whereas deoxyribose's 2′ carbon is bound only to a hydrogen. The actual energy is stored in the high-energy phosphate bonds (see Figure 3.2). Let's think back to our chemistry lessons: Why would these bonds be high-energy? Because it is energetically unfavorable to have so many negative charges (such as those found in phosphate groups) in close proximity to one another. To do so requires strong covalent bonding, which, when broken, releases usable energy.

Figure 3.2

Adenosine triphosphate may be broken down into adenosine diphosphate (ADP) and inorganic phosphate (P_i) or adenosine monophosphate (AMP) and pyrophosphate (PP_i). In both cases, the release of energy is approximately 7 kcal/mol.

$$ATP \Rightarrow ADP + P_i + 7 \text{ kcal/mol}$$
$$ATP \Rightarrow AMP + PP_i + 7 \text{ kcal/mol}$$

Processes that require energy, such as muscular contraction or active transport, will be coupled to the energy release from ATP breakdown. Alternatively, glucose catabolism provides the energy necessary to reverse this process and regenerate the high-energy currency.

$$ADP + P_i + 7 \text{ kcal/mol} \Rightarrow ATP$$

NAD⁺ and FAD

Nicotinamide adenine dinucleotide (NAD^+) and flavin adenine dinucleotide (FAD) are coenzymes capable of accepting high-energy electrons during glucose oxidation. These electrons usually come in the form of hydride ions, denoted as $H:^-$. They do not provide energy themselves; rather, they are a means to an end. By passing through the **electron transport chain**, ATP can be generated by using their captured stored energy. It's like returning a shirt that you bought so that you can get the money back (ATP). The unworn shirt is worth a certain amount of money and holds that value until you return it.

Redox reactions are often tested in the chemistry sections, but by no means are they absent from biology. Recall that reduction results in a lowering of oxidation state and oxidation results in an increase in oxidation state. Can we imagine how this will come into play in cellular respiration?

Cellular respiration is just one big series of redox reactions. When NAD^+ and FAD accept hydride ions during glycolysis and the Krebs cycle, they are **reduced** to NADH and $FADH_2$, respectively (see Figure 3.3). The hydride electrons are carried to the electron transport chain on the inner mitochondrial membrane, where they are liberated to produce ATP. That liberation reverses (i.e., **oxidizes**) NADH and $FADH_2$ to their original forms.

oxidized form		reduced form
NAD⁺	$\xrightarrow{\text{H:}}$	NADH
FAD	$\xrightarrow{\text{2H}}$	$FADH_2$

Figure 3.3

Bridge

Hydride ions are very strong reducing agents. Two reagents we'll often see are $LiAlH_4$, lithium aluminum hydride, and $NaBH_4$, sodium borohydride.

Key Concept

These redox reactions do not directly produce usable energy. Rather, they transport high-energy electrons to a final electron acceptor (oxygen), which is coupled to ATP generation.

Glucose Catabolism

At last, we have arrived at the meat of this chapter. Heterotrophic cells require glucose as their primary source of fuel. The energy they contain is liberated through two distinct processes: **glycolysis** and **cellular respiration**. As we start examining these processes, recall from earlier chapters that we emphasized the ability of the eukaryote to separate different chemical reactions into different subcellular organelles. We will see that principle in action throughout this chapter.

GLYCOLYSIS

Glycolysis is a series of reactions that break down glucose into two smaller organic molecules. Before we become too worried about the various steps and intermediates, however, let's remember that the MCAT is more interested in our overall understanding of the concepts. We don't need to know a series of reactions. In fact, for our purposes, we can consider all of glycolysis to be one smooth reaction. All we need to know are net inputs and outputs for that "one reaction." We'll guide you through the relevant information in the next few pages.

Glycolytic Pathway

Glycolysis occurs in the cytoplasm, in the presence or absence of oxygen. The pathway is outlined for us in Figure 3.4, but we'll learn just enough to focus on the inputs and outputs. First, let's glance at the products of step 4. **Dihydroxyacetone phosphate** isomerizes into a second molecule of **glyceraldehyde 3-phosphate (PGAL)**. Takeaway? Since we now have twice as many PGALs as glucoses, steps five through nine will all be occurring twice as many times as steps one through four, per molecule of glucose. Starting with organic molecules, let's count our inputs and outputs. Our input is six-carbon glucose, and our output is two molecules of three-carbon **pyruvate**. Next, let's look at our ATP inputs and outputs. Steps 1 and 3 each consume one molecule of ATP. Steps 6 and 9 each produce one ATP and occur twice—a total of four, a net of two. The direct generation of ATP from ADP and P_i is known as **substrate-level phosphorylation**. What about electron carriers? NAD^+ is reduced to NADH twice, so we start with two molecules of NAD^+ and finish with two molecules of NADH.

Step 1

Step 2

Step 3

Step 4

Step 5

Step 6

Step 7

Step 8

Step 9

*NOTE: Steps 5–9 occur twice per molecule of glucose (see text).

Figure 3.4

The net reaction for glycolysis is this:

$$\text{Glucose} + 2\text{ ADP} + 2\text{ P}_i + 2\text{ NAD}^+ \Rightarrow 2\text{ Pyruvate} + 2\text{ ATP} + 2\text{ NADH} + 2\text{ H}^+ + 2\text{ H}_2\text{O}$$

This process doesn't give us much bang for our buck. Indeed, most of the chemical energy extracted from the sun is still stored in pyruvate's bonds. Pyruvate has two potential fates based on the character of the cell's environment. It's kind of like a choose-your-own-ending novel. In aerobic organisms (those that use oxygen to survive and thrive), pyruvate undergoes further oxidation through the mitochondrial electron transport chain. In anaerobic organisms (those that function without oxygen), pyruvate undergoes an oxygen-free process called fermentation. Some cells are obligate aerobes or anaerobes, meaning that they require that designated environment. Others are facultative; they prefer one environment over the other but can survive in either.

Fermentation

Take a quick glance back at our glycolysis equation. NAD$^+$ is a necessary reagent and must be present for glycolysis to occur. At the end of glycolysis, the coenzyme is present only in its reduced form, NADH. One way to regenerate NAD^+ is through oxidation in the electron transport chain, but anaerobic organisms wouldn't participate in that. So another method is used: fermentation. Fermentation reduces pyruvate to either **ethanol** or **lactic acid**. Recall that redox reactions always occur in pairs. So if we reduce pyruvate, what are we doing to NADH? Oxidizing it back to NAD^+ so that we can recycle it for further rounds of glycolysis.

The term *fermentation* actually refers to all the steps of glycolysis plus the reduction of pyruvate. The postglycolytic reduction does not produce any new ATP, only NAD^+. This means that anaerobic organisms cash out a total of two ATP dollars. Not bad, but the payout would be much larger in the presence of oxygen.

Alcohol Fermentation

This process occurs in yeast and some bacteria; in fact, after acing the MCAT, we might want to celebrate with beverages made through this process! Pyruvate is first decarboxylated to acetaldehyde, which is then reduced by NADH to ethanol, thereby regenerating the NAD^+.

$$\text{Pyruvate (3C)} \Rightarrow CO_2 + \text{Acetaldehyde (2C)}$$
$$\text{Acetaldehyde} + \text{NADH} + H^+ \Rightarrow \text{Ethanol (2C)} + NAD^+$$

Lactic Acid Fermentation

This process occurs in some fungi and bacteria, as well as in our own mammalian muscles when oxygen demand exceeds supply. Basically, many glucose molecules are put through glycolysis, yielding twice as many molecules of pyruvate and NADH. Not all of the pyruvate can be immediately put through cellular respiration, so it builds up. Concurrently, NADH builds up, depleting cells' supply of NAD^+. To keep muscles working, pyruvate is reduced to lactic acid (3C), and NADH is oxidized back to NAD^+. Lactic acid decreases the local pH, which we feel as the burn and fatigue effects of strenuous exercise. Once oxygen supply catches up to demand, the lactic acid may be converted back to pyruvate in a process known as the **Cori cycle**. The amount of oxygen necessary to do this is known as the **oxygen debt**.

$$\text{Pyruvate (3C)} + \text{NADH} + H^+ \Rightarrow \text{Lactic Acid} + NAD^+$$

CELLULAR RESPIRATION

Whereas glycolysis seems to impart little bang for our proverbial buck (glucose), cellular respiration definitely knows how to maximize it. Indeed, it is the most efficient means of glucose catabolism, generating approximately 36 to 38 ATP per

Bridge

The conversion of acetaldehyde to ethanol is a typical reduction reaction of an aldehyde to an alcohol in organic chemistry.

Key Concept

Remember that the prefix *acet*– refers to two-carbon molecules.

molecule of glucose (in other words, $36 to $38 output for a $2 input). Respiration is aptly named; it is an aerobic process using an electron transport chain, with oxygen being the final electron acceptor. We noticed that glycolysis took place in the cytoplasm; we'll see a bit more action in the cytoplasm and then a move over to the mitochondria.

There are three key phases for us to cover: **pyruvate decarboxylation**, the **citric acid cycle**, and the **electron transport chain**. A productive way to keep track of these reactions will be to follow the carbons (again, the inputs and outputs). Recall that glucose has six and our two pyruvates have three each. Thus, we haven't lost any yet… but we will. As we go through the next three processes, note where carbons are split up and how many are lost. Organizing our facts this way helps us organize the intricate details for Test Day success.

Pyruvate Decarboxylation

The first step in aerobic respiration is pyruvate decarboxylation. This step itself does not require oxygen, but it only occurs once the cell commits to aerobic respiration—and that commitment is made only in the presence of oxygen. Pyruvate is transported from the cytoplasm into the mitochondrial matrix, where it is decarboxylated (i.e., loses a CO_2). The remaining acetyl (2C) group is bound to a **coenzyme A** molecule to form **acetyl-CoA**. One NAD^+ is reduced to NADH per pyruvate; in other words, two NAD^+ molecules are reduced per molecule of glucose. Acetyl-CoA is a key intermediate in the utilization of fat, protein, and other carbohydrate energy reserves. Let's keep track of our carbons. We started with six, three in each pyruvate. We are left with two acetyl-CoA molecules that have two carbons each, and we release the other two as carbon dioxide molecules.

$$2 \text{ Pyruvate (3C)} + 2 \text{ CoA} + 2 \text{ NAD}^+ \rightarrow 2 \text{ NADH} + 2 \text{ Acetyl-CoA (2C)} + 2 \text{ CO}_2 \text{ (1C)}$$

Citric Acid Cycle

The citric acid cycle goes by other names: the **Krebs cycle,** after the man who described it, and the **tricarboxylic acid cycle (TCA)**, as many of its intermediates are tricarboxylic acids. Regardless of what we call it, the MCAT wants us to know it (see Figure 3.5). The cycle starts with the combination of acetyl-CoA (2C) and oxaloacetate (4C) to generate citrate (6C). Through a series of eight reactions, two CO_2 molecules are released, and oxaloacetate is regenerated. As we've mentioned before, we should know the inputs and outputs of the cycle, but the individual steps and intermediates are not particularly test-worthy.

Key Concept

Remember that glucose has six carbons. Two of the original six carbons are lost during pyruvate decarboxylation as CO_2.

Key Concept

Energy checkpoint:
2ATP (from glycolysis)
2NADH (from glycolysis)
2NADH (from decarboxylation of pyruvate)

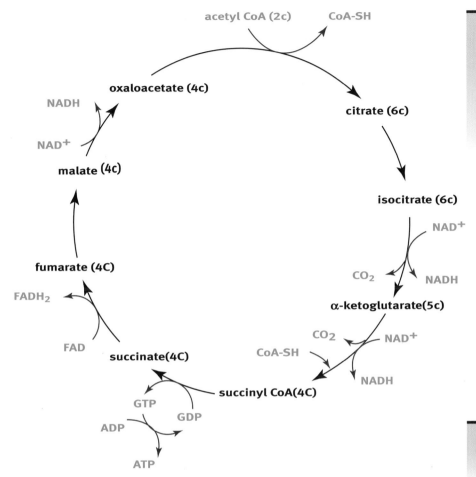

MCAT Expertise

We do not need to know the eight intermediates of the TCA cycle. We should know that the major purpose of this cycle is to generate high-energy intermediates that can be used to make ATP. Note that some ATP is generated from GTP directly through substrate-level phosphorylation.

Figure 3.5

The citric acid cycle doesn't directly generate much energy. Each turn of the cycle generates one ATP via substrate-level phosphorylation and a GTP intermediate, for a total of "two dollars" per glucose molecule. Add that to our total from before, and we have "four dollars" from substrate-level phosphorylation. The value of the citric acid cycle is its ability to generate high-energy electrons that are carried by NADH and $FADH_2$. For each molecule of acetyl-CoA that enters the cycle, three NADH and one $FADH_2$ are produced. Let's summarize our Krebs cycle outputs. We'll multiply all our products by two to account for the fact that the cycle turns twice per molecule of glucose.

$$2 \times 3 \text{ NADH} \Rightarrow 6 \text{ NADH}$$
$$2 \times 1 \text{ FADH}_2 \Rightarrow 2 \text{ FADH}_2$$
$$2 \times 1 \text{ GTP (ATP)} \Rightarrow 2 \text{ ATP}$$

These coenzymes then transport the electrons to the electron transport chain on the inner mitochondrial membrane, where more ATP is produced via **oxidative**

Key Concept

This ATP is actually made in the form of GTP, which is energetically equivalent.

Key Concept

Energy checkpoint:
2ATP (from glycolysis)
2NADH (from glycolysis)
2NADH (from decarboxylation of pyruvate)
6NADH (TCA cycle)
2FADH$_2$ (TCA cycle)
2ATP (TCA cycle)

phosphorylation. At the end of the citric acid cycle, oxaloacetate is regenerated in anticipation of the next round.

The overall reaction is as follows:

$$2 \text{ Acetyl CoA} + 6 \text{ NAD}^+ + 2 \text{ FAD} + 2 \text{ GDP} + 2 \text{ P}_i + 4 \text{ H}_2\text{O} \Rightarrow$$
$$4 \text{ CO}_2 + 6 \text{ NADH} + 2 \text{ FADH}_2 + 2 \text{ ATP} + 4 \text{ H}^+ + 2\text{CoA}$$

Let's account for carbon inputs and outputs. We had a carbon input of four, two in each acetyl-CoA. Our output is four carbon dioxide molecules (two per turn). No useful organic products are left over.

Electron Transport Chain

Electron Transfer

The phases of glucose catabolism that we have reviewed to this point (glycolysis, pyruvate decarboxylation, and the TCA cycle) have reduced several high-energy electron carriers, but we have not yet been able to use that harnessed energy. In other words, we have a lot of valuable goods but have not yet sold them for cash. The electron transport chain allows us to do so. Oxidative phosphorylation is the process by which electrons from NADH and FADH$_2$ are passed along an assembly line of carriers that release free energy with each transfer. That free energy is put toward ATP production. Most of these carriers are enzymes known as **cytochromes**. They resemble hemoglobin in that they each contain a central iron atom that can undergo reversible redox reactions as electrons bind and release. Like many other transition metals, iron can be present in more than one oxidation state, which makes it a likely candidate to participate in redox reactions.

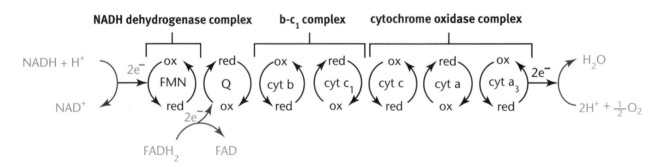

Figure 3.6

These cytochromes are best organized into three major complexes. Take a look at Figure 3.6. The first complex is called **NADH dehydrogenase (complex I)**, next is the **b-c$_1$ complex (complex III)**, and the last is **cytochrome oxidase (complex IV)**. You'll probably notice that we've left out two things: complex II and carrier Q. Let's get into a bit more detail.

First, NADH gives its electrons directly to **FMN (flavin mononucleotide)**, which is part of complex I. Those electrons are then passed to **carrier Q (ubiquinone)**. Carrier Q is a small hydrophobic molecule, not an enzyme (protein) like its neighbors. It's as important as the others but just isn't named the same way. Carrier Q passes the electrons on to complex III, which donates them to complex IV. Oxygen takes the electrons from **cytochrome a$_3$**, a protein in complex IV, along with two protons to make water. The energy from each NADH generates three ATP molecules (see Figure 3.7).

The FADH$_2$ molecules each generate only two ATP molecules. Why? Their electrons don't start with complex I. They're actually given directly to **complex II**, **succinate-Q oxidoreductase**. Complex II gives those electrons to carrier Q, and the rest of the pathway is the same as NADH's. Let's visualize complex II directly above carrier Q in the membrane. FADH$_2$'s high-energy electrons travel a shorter distance to get to oxygen, and therefore, less energy is extracted from them.

$$2\,H^+ + 2\,e^- + \tfrac{1}{2}\,O_2 \Rightarrow H_2O$$

Figure 3.7

When will the electron transport chain not be a viable method of regenerating NAD$^+$ and FAD? We've already discussed that fermentation occurs concurrently with oxygen debt. In addition, certain poisons can inhibit the system. **Cyanide** blocks the final transfer of electrons to O$_2$, and **dinitrophenol (DNP)** destroys the mitochondrion's ability to generate a useful proton gradient that is necessary for effective ATP generation.

ATP Generation and the Proton Pump

The actual production of energy relies on coupling the energy drops to the phosphorylation of ADP. A **proton gradient** across the inner mitochondrial membrane links the oxidation of NADH and FADH$_2$ to ADP phosphorylation. How is this gradient created? As the reduced carriers give up electrons, free protons are passed into the mitochondrial matrix, where they accumulate. The electron transport chain then pumps these ions out of the matrix into the intermembrane space at each of the major protein complexes. The accumulation of H^+ in the intermembrane space makes it both positively charged and acidic. In Chapter 1, we learned that such a concentration differential is a form of stored energy. Here, the electrochemical gradient drives H^+ passively back across the inner mitochondrial membrane into the mitochondrial matrix. This is known as the **proton-motive force**. How does this happen? We should also recall from Chapter 1 that charged species are particularly impermeable to membranes because the energetic barrier is simply too high for a charged species to navigate a large nonpolar region. Instead, we used channels: here, enzyme complexes called **ATP synthases** (see Figure 3.8). As the H^+ ions pass through these specialized channels back into the matrix, the energy released allows for the phosphorylation of ADP back to ATP. This is the process known as **oxidative phosphorylation**.

MCAT Expertise

Our cell compartmentalizes the glycolytic pathway in a location separate from pyruvate decarboxylation, the TCA cycle, and electron transport chain. The locations where these processes occur are a perennial MCAT favorite.

Figure 3.8

REVIEW OF GLUCOSE CATABOLISM

The overall generation of energy in glucose catabolism (see Figure 3.9) comes from two sources: substrate-level phosphorylation and oxidative phosphorylation (based on the generation of high-energy intermediates). The total amount of ATP generated depends on these two processes and how much of each occurs. We should be familiar with the relative amount of energy produced by each for Test Day success.

Figure 3.9

Substrate-Level Phosphorylation

Degradation of one molecule of glucose will yield a net of four ATP: two net ATP from glycolysis and one ATP per turn of the TCA cycle (it turns twice, once for each acetyl-CoA).

Oxidative Phosphorylation

Follow Table 3.1 as we walk through the steps. First, we will count high-energy intermediates; then we will calculate the total ATP. Pyruvate decarboxylation yields two NADH (one for each pyruvate). Each turn of the TCA cycle gives us three NADH and one $FADH_2$; this means a total of six NADH and two $FADH_2$, because we have two acetyl-CoA molecules that enter the cycle per molecule of glucose. Each NADH can generate three ATP per molecule, except for the two from glycolysis. Those two cannot traverse the inner mitochondrial membrane and instead give their electrons directly to carrier Q. Thus, they only generate two ATP each. So the total ATP extracted from NADH is four from glycolysis (2×2), six from pyruvate decarboxylation (2×3), and 18 from the TCA cycle (6×3). This leads to a subtotal of 28 ATP from NADH ($4 + 6 + 18$). What about $FADH_2$? There are two total $FADH_2$ molecules generated, and at two ATP each, we get a

Key Concept

Event	Location
Glycolysis	Cytoplasm
Fermentation	Cytoplasm
Pyruvate to acetyl CoA	Mitochondrial matrix
TCA cycle	Mitochondrial matrix
Electron transport chain	Inner mitochondrial membrane

Key Concept

NADH $\Rightarrow$ 3 ATP. (The only exception is NADH generated in cytoplasm: It will generate only two ATP per molecule of NADH.) $FADH_2 \Rightarrow$ 2ATP.

Key Concept

In an *anaerobic* environment, eukaryotic cells can generate only 2 net ATP; in an *aerobic* environment, these cells can generate a net of 36 ATP!

total of four from $FADH_2$. When we add the four ATP generated by substrate-level phosphorylation, we have a grand total of 36. Can you imagine investing $2 and cashing out $36? These aerobic cells are great financial planners! Prokaryotes are even more successful, they're capable of generating 38 total ATP. Can we figure out why? What is the key difference between prokaryotes and eukaryotes? Nuclei and membrane-bound organelles. Since the NADH molecules from glycolysis don't have a prokaryotic mitochondrial membrane to traverse, they save two ATP (one per NADH).

Table 3.1. Eukaryotic ATP Production per Glucose Molecule

Glycolysis		
2 ATP invested	−2	ATP
4 ATP generated	+4	ATP (substrate)
2 NADH × 2 ATP/NADH	+4	ATP (oxidative)
Pyruvate Decarboxylation		
2 NADH × 3 ATP/NADH	+ 6	ATP (oxidative)
Citric Acid Cycle		
6 NADH × 3 ATP/NADH	+18	ATP (oxidative)
2 $FADH_2$ × 2 ATP/$FADH_2$	+ 4	ATP (oxidative)
2 GTP × 1 ATP/GTP	+ 2	ATP (substrate)
Total	**+36**	**ATP**

Alternate Energy Sources

Certainly there will be times when our glucose stores run low. During those times, we can rely on other sources of energy, which will be able to feed into the glycolytic and TCA pathways. These molecules fall into three large categories: carbohydrates, proteins, and fats. We will discuss the ingestion and digestion of these molecules in Chapter 7.

CARBOHYDRATES

Glucose is a monosaccharide. Sugar polymers (carbohydrates) can be broken down during digestion and then stored in the liver for later use in a polysaccharide form known as glycogen. The glycogen will be converted to glucose-6-phosphate, a glycolytic intermediate, when needed.

FATS

Fats are stored in adipose tissue in the form of triglycerides (aka triacylglycerol). Three long-chain fatty acids are esterified to a glycerol (three-carbon) molecule for long-term storage. Glycerol can be converted to PGAL, which is a glycolytic intermediate; however, the real energy of fats is stored in the fatty acids. Fatty acids will first be activated in the cytoplasm in a process requiring two ATP. They will then be transported to the mitochondrial matrix to undergo sequential rounds of **beta-oxidation**, whereby acetyl-CoA (input for the TCA cycle) will be generated. Each round of oxidation results in creation of one NADH and one $FADH_2$. Triglycerides are usually three fatty acids (16C each) bound to glycerol. Thus, they have 48 total carbons. Because we remove 2 at a time, we can undergo 24 total rounds of beta-oxidation, generating 24 NADH and 24 $FADH_2$. Close to 100 ATP can be generated by one fat molecule. It is an amazingly efficient form of energy storage. In an average adult human, fat stores are sufficient for one month's worth of energy needs.

PROTEINS

Proteins are polypeptides, which are themselves made up of amino acids. They are used as energy sources only when carbohydrates are insufficient. The removal of the amine moiety from amino acids by **transaminases** results in molecules known as α-keto acids. The vast majority of these acids can be converted into acetyl-CoA or are intermediates of the TCA cycle and can enter into it directly.

Key Concept

The ability of the body to use a variety of energy sources is the basis for several fad diets. Regardless of the intake, however, the same three types of molecules (carbohydrates, proteins, and fats) are used to run the body.

Metabolic Map

The relationship of the three major energy sources is diagrammed in Figure 3.10.

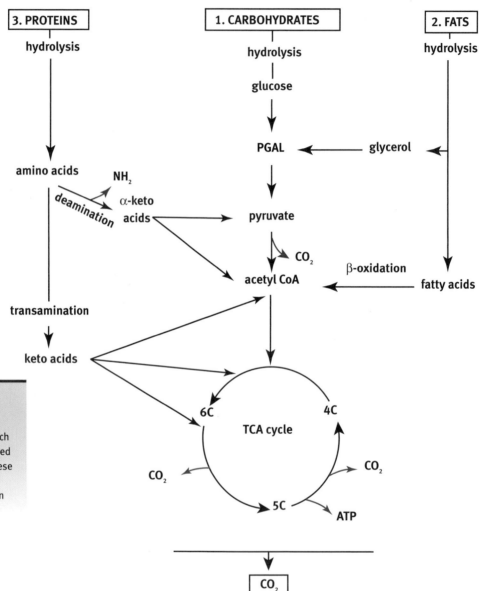

Figure 3.10

Key Concept

Remember to follow the carbons. Glucose is a six-carbon molecule; each of these carbons is eventually removed from the body in the form of CO_2. These carbon dioxide molecules are generated during pyruvate decarboxylation and the TCA cycle.

Conclusion

Cellular metabolism is a complex and intricate topic on heavy rotation on the MCAT playlist. We started by discussing energy generation from a stratospheric view, separating heterotrophs from autotrophs. We then moved on to discuss the basic energy currency of the cell, ATP, likening it to the dollar bill in our wallet. We also took time to examine the high-energy intermediates that may be used to generate ATP. Glucose catabolism made up the meat of this chapter. At a first glance, we discussed catabolism, which provided little net energy for the input; we noted that the vast majority of the energy was still stored in the high-energy bonds of pyruvate. We then went on to examine how this energy could be liberated by going through pyruvate decarboxylation, the TCA cycle, and the electron transport chain. Recall that 18 times as many ATP could be generated from aerobic processes as could be from glycolysis alone. Finally, we noted that because glucose is not our only food intake, there must be metabolic mechanisms to handle other carbohydrates, fats, and proteins. A large amount of detail was presented in this chapter; it's important to identify those points that are critical for MCAT success. As we mentioned several times, it's most important to focus on the inputs and the outputs. Let's move on to reproduction (Chapter 4), where we'll focus on a different eukaryotic organelle: the nucleus.

CONCEPTS TO REMEMBER

☐ Organisms may be broadly divided into heterotrophs and autotrophs; the MCAT is primarily concerned with heterotrophs.

☐ ATP is the primary energy currency of the cell. NAD^+ and FAD are coenzymes that may be reduced to carry high-energy electrons, which can generate ATP.

☐ Glycolysis results in the generation of two pyruvate and two net ATP. It can be carried out by all organisms.

☐ Eukaryotic organisms separate the different catabolic processes (glycolysis, oxidative phosphorylation, etc.) into different organelles to compartmentalize enzymes and prevent energy loss.

☐ Fermentation (ethanol or lactic acid production) provides a means to regenerate NAD^+ in anaerobic organisms or aerobic organisms with oxygen debt. NAD^+ must be regenerated for glycolysis to continue in the absence of O_2.

☐ Pyruvate decarboxylation and the TCA cycle generate some ATP but are primarily responsible for capturing high-energy electrons for use in the ETC.

☐ Molecular oxygen is the final electron acceptor and results in the formation of water molecules.

☐ ATP production depends on the generation of a proton gradient across the inner mitochondrial membrane.

☐ The sum total of ATP generated by glucose catabolism is 36 ATP (38 in prokaryotes). The vast majority of this is due to the processes other than glycolysis.

☐ The interplay of carbohydrates, proteins, and fats occurs at the level of cellular metabolism; specifically, each of these molecules may be converted into glucose, one of its derivatives, or processing intermediates.

Practice Questions

1. Which of the following INCORRECTLY pairs a metabolic process with its site of occurrence?

   A. Glycolysis—cytosol
   B. Citric acid cycle—mitochondrial membrane
   C. ATP phosphorylation—cytosol and mitochondria
   D. Electron transport chain—inner mitochondrial membrane

2. Which of the following processes has a net reaction of

   $2\text{Acetyl CoA} + 6\text{NAD}^+ + 2\text{FAD} + 2\text{GDP} + 2\text{P}_i + 4\text{H}_2\text{O} \rightarrow 4\text{CO}_2 + 6\text{ NADH} + 2\text{FADH}_2 + 2\text{GTP} + 4\text{H}^+ + 2\text{CoA}$

   A. Glycolysis
   B. Fermentation
   C. Tricarboxylic acid cycle
   D. Electron transport chain

3. In glucose degradation under aerobic conditions

   A. oxygen is the final electron acceptor.
   B. oxygen is necessary for ATP synthesis.
   C. water is produced.
   D. both (A) and (C).

4. Fatty acids enter the catabolic pathway in the form of

   A. glycerol.
   B. adipose tissue.
   C. acetyl CoA.
   D. keto acids.

5. In which of the following reactions is the reactant oxidized?

   A. $\text{FAD} \rightarrow \text{FADH}_2$
   B. $\text{NAD}^+ \rightarrow \text{NADH}$
   C. $\text{NADPH} \rightarrow \text{NADP}^+$
   D. $\text{ADP} \rightarrow \text{ATP}$

6. Which of the following statements correctly identifies the purpose of fermentation?

   A. To use up excess pyruvate formed as a result of glycolysis
   B. To produce NAD^+ in order to continue glycolysis
   C. To produce NADH in order to continue glycolysis
   D. To prevent further increases in oxygen debt

7. In which part of the cell would you expect to find cytochrome c?

   A. Mitochondrial matrix
   B. Outer mitochondrial membrane
   C. Inner mitochondrial membrane
   D. Cytosol

8. Which of the following is LEAST likely to occur during oxygen debt?

   A. Buildup of lactic acid
   B. Buildup of pyruvate
   C. Decrease in pH
   D. Fatigue

9. Autotrophic organisms, as compared to heterotrophs, convert sunlight into bond energy through photosynthesis. Which of the following best describes the type of process that photosynthesis is?

A. Anabolic
B. Catabolic
C. Glycolytic
D. Fermentation

10. In the course of glycolysis

A. NADH is reduced to NAD^+.
B. NAD^+ is oxidized to NADH.
C. glucose is degraded into two molecules of pyruvate.
D. both (A) and (B).

11. Which of the following correctly describes the amount of ATP produced from the high-energy carrier coenzymes?

A. $1 \text{ FADH}_2 \rightarrow 1 \text{ ATP}$
B. $1 \text{ FADH}_2 \rightarrow 3 \text{ ATP}$
C. $1 \text{ NADH} \rightarrow 1 \text{ ATP}$
D. $1 \text{ NADH} \rightarrow 3 \text{ ATP}$

12. What is the total amount of ATP yielded by the catabolism of one glucose molecule via the Krebs cycle?

A. 6 ATPs
B. 12 ATPs
C. 24 ATPs
D. 36 ATPs

Small Group Questions

1. Oxidation-reduction reactions can involve a variety of molecules. Why are those involving hydrogen and oxygen of such importance in biological systems?

2. If a hole is created in a mitochondrion, can it still perform oxidative respiration? Can mitochondrial fragments perform oxidative respiration?

Explanations to Practice Questions

1. B

To answer this question, we have to look at each answer choice in turn. Glycolysis does indeed occur in the cytosol, so we can eliminate (A). The citric acid cycle (also known as the TCA or Krebs cycle) occurs in the mitochondrial matrix, which means that (B) incorrectly pairs the metabolic process with its site. Glancing at (C) and (D), we can confirm that they are true. Therefore, the correct answer is (B).

2. C

It is not necessary to have all the net reactions memorized for each metabolic process. All we need to answer this question correctly is to identify a few key reactants and products. In this case, we start with acetyl CoA and end with CoA. We also notice that in this reaction, NAD^+ and FAD are reduced to NADH and $FADH_2$ and that CO_2 is formed. The only metabolic process in which all of the above reactions would occur is the TCA cycle, also referred to as the Krebs or citric acid cycle. (C) is therefore the correct answer.

3. D

This question is testing our general knowledge of cellular respiration. Notice that all types of cellular respiration (aerobic and anaerobic) start with the degradation of glucose. In aerobic respiration, oxygen is the final electron acceptor, and water is therefore produced at the end of the electron transport chain. While oxygen is needed for aerobic respiration in order to produce 36 molecules of ATP, it is not necessary for ATP synthesis in general (e.g., ATP is also produced via substrate-level phosphorylation); ATP can also be produced via anaerobic processes, even though it will be made in smaller quantities. From the given answers, (D) is the correct response.

4. C

Fat molecules stored in adipose tissue can be hydrolyzed by lipases to fatty acids and glycerol. While glycerol can be converted into PGAL, a glycolytic intermediate, a fatty acid must first be activated in the cytoplasm by cleaving an ATP into cAMP. Once activated, the fatty acid is then taken to the mitochondrion where, through a series of oxidation reactions, it is converted to acetyl CoA. Thus, fatty acids are converted into acetyl CoA, which enters the TCA cycle, making (C) the correct answer.

5. C

To answer this question, we must remember that *reduction* is a reduction in charge through the gain of electrons, while *oxidation* is an increase in charge through the loss of electrons. In the case of the energy-storing molecules of cellular respiration, the high-potential electrons generally come from hydride ions ($H:^-$). Since the question is asking us to determine in which reaction the reactant gets oxidized, our task is to select the equation in which the reactant loses one hydride ion. From the given choices, the only one that matches our prediction is (C). Another way to look at it is to notice that $NADP^+$ has a +1 charge, which represents an increase from the zero charge of NADPH, suggesting that the reactant was oxidized to yield the product.

6. B

Fermentation (either alcohol fermentation or lactic acid fermentation) occurs during anaerobic conditions. To ensure that cells have a minimum amount of energy (in the form of ATP), even during periods of oxygen deprivation, fermentation works to make sure that glycolysis continues its course. As a result of glycolysis (an anaerobic process), two molecules of ATP are formed. While this is a modest amount of energy, it is sufficient to maintain some metabolic processes for a limited amount of time. During this process, NAD$^+$ is reduced to NADH. For glycolysis to continue, however, the cells have to oxidize NADH so as to form NAD$^+$. Without NAD$^+$, glycolysis would stop, and the cells would quickly run out of energy. The purpose of fermentation, therefore, is to produce the NAD$^+$ necessary for glycolysis by oxidizing NADH. (B) matches our prediction and is thus the correct answer.

7. C

While you are not expected to know every last detail of cellular respiration, you should recognize the word *cytochrome* as being part of the cytochrome oxidase complex, which participates in the last part of the electron transport chain. Our task then becomes identifying where in the cell the ETC takes place. (C), the inner mitochondrial membrane, correctly identifies the location of the electron transport chain and is thus the correct answer.

8. B

Oxygen debt refers to the amount of oxygen that would be needed to convert the lactic acid formed through fermentation back to pyruvate. In a way, it is a measure of how far behind on oxygen the cell is. During anaerobic conditions, when the cell is deprived of oxygen, lactic acid fermentation occurs, which results in an increase in the amount of lactic acid and, consequently, a decrease in the pH of the cytoplasm. This, paired with the limited amount of energy (ATP) that the cell can produce in anaerobic conditions (through glycolysis), also leads to fatigue. Thus, the least likely to occur during oxygen debt is a buildup of pyruvate. Pyruvate is used up in lactic acid fermentation in order to produce the NAD$^+$ required to maintain glycolysis. (B) is therefore the correct answer.

9. A

Autotrophic organisms (e.g., green plants) convert sunlight into bond energy, which is stored in organic compounds (mainly glucose). This is achieved through the anabolic process of photosynthesis, during which carbon dioxide, water, and energy from the sun are processed to produce glucose and oxygen. Since photosynthesis is an energy-requiring

process involving the biosynthesis of complex organic compounds from simpler molecules, we refer to it as anabolic. (A) is therefore the correct answer.

10. C

During glycolysis, one molecule of glucose is degraded to form two molecules of pyruvate. In this process, NAD$^+$ is reduced to form NADH, and two molecules of ATP are formed in the net reaction. The only choice that correctly describes glycolysis is (C).

11. D

During oxidative phosphorylation, energy is harvested from the carrier coenzymes FADH$_2$ and NADH in order to form ATP. As such, one molecule of FADH$_2$ will be oxidized to produce two molecules of ATP. Similarly, one molecule of NADH will be oxidized to produce either two or three molecules of ATP (depending on where the NADH was generated) in the electron transport chain. The only answer that correctly illustrates the amount of ATP generated from one of the high-energy carrier coenzymes is (D).

12. C

You are asked to calculate the amount of ATP produced per glucose molecule. First, calculate the total amount of ATP produced per acetyl CoA molecule: 3×3(from NADH) + 2(FADH$_2$) + 1(GTP) = 12. Next, since each glucose molecule produces two acetyl CoA molecules, multiply the answer by 2: $2 \times 12 = 24$. The final number is therefore 24, making (C) the correct answer.

Reproduction

All mammals share certain characteristics: milk-producing mammary glands, three bones in the middle ear and one in the lower jaw, fur or hair, heterodont dentition (different kinds of teeth), and both sebaceous (oil-producing) and sudoriferous (sweat) glands. Those all make sense, right? We can all identify with those traits. What about the presence of a placenta during embryonic development? Sure, that's characteristic of eutherians such as humans and bats and whales. But there are two groups of mammals that birth their young a bit differently: prototherians and metatherians.

We've probably all seen illustrations of friendly-looking koalas and kangaroos, our metatherian (marsupial) friends from Australia that appear to carry their young in their pockets. A typical metatherian fetus (joey) undergoes some development in his mother's uterus, then climbs his way out of the birth canal and into her marsupium, or pouch. The pouch protects her nipples so that her joey can have full, safe access to her nourishing milk until he is ready to survive on his own.

What about prototherians? As the word's root should indicate, prototherians are probably more primitive than metatherians and eutherians. And in fact, they share more characteristics with ancestral reptiles (who evolved over 100 million years earlier) than do the other two younger groups of mammals. Reptiles encase their developing embryos within hard-shelled amniotic eggs and lay them to be hatched. This method of development is referred to as *oviparity*. Prototherians (monotremes), though more advanced than reptiles, are also oviparous. They hold onto their eggs longer than reptiles but do eventually lay them for hatching. More evidence? Also like reptiles, monotremes reproduce, urinate, and defecate all through the same orifice: the cloaca. In addition, their legs are on the sides of their bodies (think lizard) rather than underneath them (think dog).

Hard to imagine a mammal laying eggs, huh? Keep in mind that to be classified as mammals, the two living monotreme species (platypus and echidna) had to share only those specific characteristics that we already discussed with kangaroos, eared seals, and your pet cat. It might seem a little strange that something as essential as reproduction could be so different in other mammals, but the truth is, there is a wide variety of reproductive mechanisms in nature. Many organisms reproduce without a sexual partner. Others are versatile and can reproduce sexually or asexually, depending on environmental conditions. In this chapter, we'll examine some different methods of reproduction and discuss the advantages and disadvantages of each. We'll also get into the fine details of sexual reproduction, at both the cellular and tissue levels.

Cell Division

In the simplest sense, organisms must find a way to create more of the cells they are composed of. Babies certainly don't have as many cells as adults. Where do those

Key Concept

It's hard to believe but true—all the nucleated cells of our body, regardless of their structure and function, have exactly the same chromosomes. The only exceptions are the sex cells, which have only half as many chromosomes as somatic cells. Thus, different cell types have distinct structures and functions not because their DNA is different but because the *expression* of what's coded in the DNA is unique to that cell type. We will discuss this in much greater detail in Chapter 5.

extra cells come from? Cell division is the process whereby a cell replicates its DNA, doubles its organelles and cytoplasm, and then splits into two daughter cells. These cells will be identical in that they have the same genetic complement (much as identical twins have the same DNA). This is a key MCAT point to which we will return later. Cell division results in different fates for prokaryotes and eukaryotes. For prokaryotes (which are all unicellular), cell division provides a mechanism of reproduction. The same goes for unicellular eukaryotes, but for multicellular eukaryotes, cell division also replaces cells that are ready to retire.

First, let's talk about prokaryotes. These organisms divide via **binary fission**, a type of asexual reproduction (more on this shortly). Because prokaryotes have no organelles, the single DNA molecule attaches itself to the cell membrane and duplicates itself while the cell itself grows in size. The cell membrane then invaginates, or pinches inward, to create two identical daughter cells.

Eukaryotic cell division is a bit more complex. That's not a bad thing for us, because it simply means more possible points on Test Day. Since there are multiple chromosomes per cell, organisms must properly segregate these chromosomes during duplication. Moreover, we must also make new cytoplasm and organelles. Eukaryotic **autosomal** cells contain the **diploid ($2n$)** number of chromosomes. **Haploid**, or germ cells contain the n number of chromosomes. For humans, these numbers are 46 and 23, respectively; we inherit 23 of these chromosomes from each parent. Eukaryotic autosomal cells reproduce by a process known as the cell cycle.

THE CELL CYCLE

The cell cycle is a perennial MCAT favorite, so let's get those synaptic connections firing as we work our way through its phases: G_1, S, G_2, and **M** (see Figure 4.1). Mitosis is the stage in which the cells actually divide. The other three phases are collectively known as interphase.

Interphase

This is the longest part of the cell cycle. Cells that divide may spend as much as 90 percent of their time in this phase. On the other hand, cells that enter terminal differentiation (e.g., muscle and nerve cells) spend all of their time in an offshoot of G_1 called G_0.

G_1 Stage (Presynthetic Gap)

During this phase, cells create organelles for energy and protein production (mitochondria, ribosomes, and endoplasmic reticulum) while also doubling in size. In addition, the passage into S (synthesis) phase is governed by a **restriction point**. Certain criteria must be met for the cell to pass the restriction point and enter the synthesis phase. Think of it this way: Would we want to go to

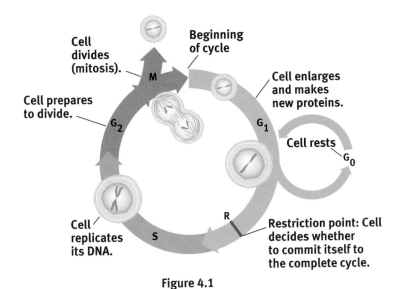

Figure 4.1

the Olympics without a proper trainer and a nutritious diet? Similarly, the cell makes sure all the necessary equipment is available and ready for S phase.

S Stage (Synthesis)

During this phase, the cell replicates, or synthesizes, its genetic material so that each daughter cell will have identical copies. After replication, each chromosome consists of two identical **chromatids**, which are bound together at a specialized region known as the **centromere** (see Figure 4.2). Note that the ploidy of the cell does not change, even though the number of chromatids has doubled (in humans, 46 chromosomes and 92 chromatids). Cells entering G_2 contain twice as much DNA as cells in G_1.

Figure 4.2

G_2 Stage (Postsynthetic Gap)

This is the final stage before actual cell division; think of it as quality control. We have already duplicated the DNA, and now we are just making sure that we have enough organelles and cytoplasm to make two daughter cells.

M Stage (Mitosis)

The mitotic stage consists of mitosis itself along with cytokinesis. Mitosis is divided into four phases: prophase, metaphase, anaphase, and telophase (see Figure 4.3). Cytokinesis is the splitting of the cytoplasm and organelles into the daughter cells.

> **Key Concept**
>
> In autosomal cells, division results in two genetically identical daughter cells. In germline cells, the daughters are *not* equivalent.

Key Concept

Each chromatid is composed of a complete, double-stranded molecule of DNA. Sister chromatids are identical copies of each other. The term *chromosome* may be used to refer to either the single chromatid or the pair of chromatids attached at the centromere.

Key Concept

Mitosis

Prophase: Chromosomes condense; spindles form.

Metaphase: Chromosomes align.

Anaphase: Sister chromatids separate.

Telophase: New nuclear membranes form.

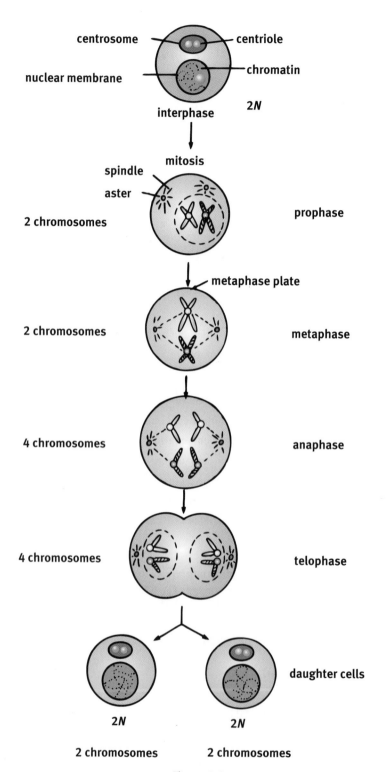

Figure 4.3

During interphase, individual chromosomes are not visible with light microscopy. They are in a less condensed form known as **chromatin**. Why would this be? During interphase, the DNA must be open so that we can transcribe genes from it and replicate it prior to cell division. During mitosis, however, it's preferable for the DNA to be tightly bound into chromosomes so that we don't lose any material during division.

The proper movement of our chromosomes depends on specialized subcellular organelles known as **centrioles** (see Figure 4.4). These paired cylindrical organelles, located outside the nucleus in a region known as the **centrosome**, are responsible for the correct division of the DNA. During prophase, the centrioles migrate to opposite poles of the cell and begin to form the **spindle fibers**, which are made from microtubules. Each of the fibers radiates outward from the centrioles, giving the chromosomes an attachment point for later separation during anaphase. These attachment points are known as **asters**. The asters extend toward the center of the cell to form a spindle apparatus. Subsequent shortening of this apparatus results in separation of sister chromatids.

Figure 4.4

Mitosis can be studied in four discrete phases, although the process itself is continuous. Indeed, we can watch certain types of quickly dividing cells undergo the entire mitotic process in about 20 minutes using nothing more than a light microscope. For the purposes of the MCAT, learn these phases and the major events in each, as they are definitely test-worthy.

Prophase

The chromosomes condense, the centriole pairs separate and move toward opposite poles of the cell, and the spindle apparatus forms between them. The nuclear membrane dissolves, allowing spindle fibers to enter the nucleus, while the nucleoli become less distinct or disappear. Kinetochores, with attached kinetochore fibers, appear at the chromosome centromere.

Metaphase

The centriole pairs are now at opposite poles of the cell. The kinetochore fibers interact with the fibers of the spindle apparatus to align the chromosomes at the metaphase plate (equatorial plate), which is equidistant to the two poles of the spindle fibers.

Anaphase

The centromeres split so that each chromatid has its own distinct centromere, thus allowing the sister chromatids to separate. The telomeres are the last part of the chromatids to separate. The sister chromatids are pulled toward the opposite poles of the cell by the shortening of the kinetochore fibers.

Telophase and Cytokinesis

The spindle apparatus disappears. A nuclear membrane re-forms around each set of chromosomes, and the nucleoli reappear. The chromosomes uncoil, resuming their interphase form. Each of the two new nuclei has received a complete copy of the genome identical to the original genome and to each other. Cytokinesis occurs.

Cytokinesis

At the end of telophase, cytokinesis allows us to separate the cytoplasm and organelles so that each daughter cell has what it needs to survive on its own. Each cell undergoes a finite number of divisions before programmed death; for human somatic cells, this is usually between 20 and 50. After that, the cell can no longer divide without incorporating errors and will probably die without being replaced.

Some cells never undergo division (muscle and nerve), whereas others, such as cancer cells, escape this cycle and divide continuously. Indeed, unregulated cell division is one of the hallmarks of cancer.

Asexual Reproduction

Asexual reproduction is the production of offspring from the genetic material of a single parent. It is similar to mitosis in eukaryotic cells in that the daughter cells will be genetically identical to their parents (other than random mutations that may arise during the process). We will briefly examine four different forms of asexual reproduction: **binary fission, budding, regeneration,** and **parthenogenesis.**

BINARY FISSION

cell wall
cell membrane
circular chromosome

replication

invagination

daughter cells

Figure 4.5

This is a simple form of reproduction seen in prokaryotes (think bacteria). The circular chromosome attaches to the cell wall and replicates while the cell continues to grow in size. Eventually the plasma membrane and cell wall will begin to grow inward along the midline of the cell to produce two equal daughter cells (see Figure 4.5). This process also occurs in some simple eukaryotic cells. This process is simple, so it can proceed rapidly; indeed, some strains of *Escherichia coli* can replicate every 20 minutes under ideal growth conditions. Some bacteria have plasmids of additional DNA that contribute to genetic diversity; however, this is an evolved adaptation and not the basis of binary fission.

BUDDING

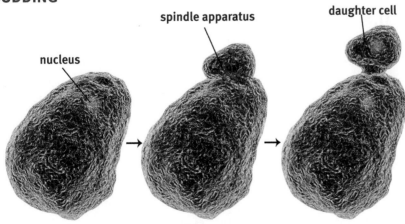

spindle apparatus

daughter cell

nucleus

Figure 4.6

Budding is *equal* replication followed by *unequal* cytokinesis. In other words, the daughter cell receives DNA identical to her parent's but far less cytoplasm (see Figure 4.6). The daughter cell may immediately break off or stay attached to the parent until it grows to full size. Budding takes place in several organisms, including hydra and yeast (both eukaryotes).

REGENERATION

One of the most fascinating topics in the entire animal kingdom is regeneration, in which an entire body part can be regrown. Lizards that lose their tails when threatened may regrow them, and annelid worms can regenerate anterior head segments. Regeneration primarily occurs in lower organisms and is accomplished by mitosis. Some animals have extensive capabilities; in fact, sea stars may reproduce their bodies from just an arm, as long as an area known as the central disk is intact. Higher organisms have more difficulty with this process, primarily due to nerve damage, as central nervous system nerves do not regenerate. There are always exceptions; in humans for example, the liver exhibits extensive regenerative properties. In fact, it is now possible to perform liver transplants in which a piece of a living donor's liver is transplanted into a recipient. Both livers (or liver pieces) will grow back to the appropriate size, no worse for the wear!

PARTHENOGENESIS

Parthenogenesis is the process whereby an adult organism develops from an unfertilized egg. Many social insects (bees and ants) produce males via parthenogenesis. This process does not occur naturally in higher organisms, although it has been induced in the laboratory in rabbits. What does this mean in terms of the number of chromosomes that will be found in each cell? They will be haploid in number because only one parent contributed genetic material. The ability to think through key concepts such as this will help us when presented with new information on the MCAT.

Sexual Reproduction ★★★★☆

The key difference in sexual reproduction that we are likely to be tested on for the MCAT is that the offspring are genetically unique. Each parent contributes one-half of the offspring's genetic material. The specialized sex cells that contribute to this process are known as **gametes**, and they are produced through a process known as **meiosis**. Meiosis shares some similarities with mitosis. In both processes, for instance, genetic material must be duplicated. The differences between the two processes, however, are MCAT favorites. Mitosis results in two identical diploid ($2n$) daughter cells, whereas meiosis yields four different haploid (n) gametes; somatic cells undergo mitosis, whereas **gametocytes** undergo meiosis.

> ## Key Concept
>
> Binary fission results in two cells of equal size, whereas budding results in cells of unequal size. Both methods however, give rise to genetically identical cells.

> ## Key Concept
>
> The MCAT loves to test on the differences between mitosis and meiosis. Remember, the diploid number is maintained throughout mitosis, whereas the process of meiosis results in haploid cells.

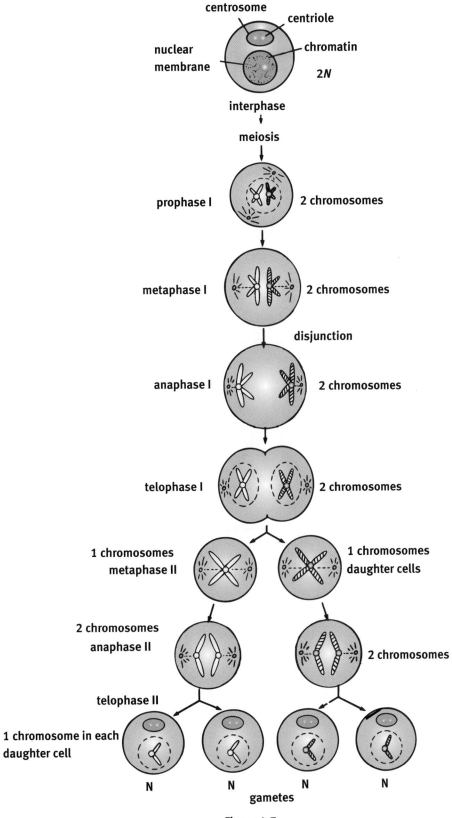

Figure 4.7

MEIOSIS

Whereas mitosis consists of one round of replication and division each, meiosis is composed of one round of replication followed by two rounds of division. Meiosis I (the first division) results in homologous chromosomes being separated, generating haploid daughter cells; this is known as the **reductional division**. Meiosis II (the second division) is similar to mitosis in that it results in the separation of sister chromatids, and is also known as the **equational division**. The result is four genetically unique haploid cells (see Figure 4.7).

MEIOSIS I

Prophase I

Although we begin the discussion with prophase, it's important for us to know that an interphase similar to that of mitosis duplicates homologous chromosomes in preparation for division. Homologous chromosomes code for the same genes; one is inherited from each parent. During prophase, the chromatin condenses into chromosomes, the spindle apparatus forms, and the nucleoli and nuclear membrane disappear. The first major difference between meiosis and mitosis occurs at this point. Homologous chromosomes come together and intertwine in a process called **synapsis**.

Figure 4.8

At this stage, each chromosome consists of two sister chromatids, so each synaptic pair of homologous chromosomes contains four chromatids and is, therefore, referred to as a tetrad. Chromatids of homologous chromosomes may break at the point of synapsis (**chiasma**; pl: **chiasmata**) and exchange equivalent pieces of DNA; this process is called **crossing over** (see Figure 4.8). Note that crossing over occurs between homologous chromosomes and not between sister chromatids of the same chromosome. (The latter are identical, so crossing over would not produce any change.) Those chromatids involved are left with an altered but structurally complete set of genes. Sister chromatids are no longer identical. Such genetic recombination can unlink linked genes, thereby increasing the variety of genetic combinations that can be produced via gametogenesis. Recombination among chromosomes results in increased genetic diversity within a species.

Metaphase I

Homologous pairs (tetrads) align at the metaphase plate, and each pair attaches to a separate spindle fiber by its kinetochore. Metaphase is the easiest to identify pictorially because the chromosomes are all neatly lined up on the metaphase plate. If you see a problem on the MCAT that asks you to identify stages of mitosis or meiosis, try to start with metaphase.

Anaphase I

Homologous pairs separate and are pulled to opposite poles of the cell. This process is called disjunction, and it accounts for a fundamental Mendelian law. During disjunction, each chromosome of paternal origin separates (or disjoins) from its homologue of maternal origin, and either chromosome can end up in either daughter cell. Thus, the distribution of homologous chromosomes to the two intermediate daughter cells is random with respect to parental origin. Each daughter cell will have a unique pool of alleles (genes coding for alternative forms of a given trait; e.g., yellow flowers versus purple flowers) from a random mixture of maternal and paternal origin.

Telophase I

A nuclear membrane forms around each new nucleus. At this point, each chromosome still consists of sister chromatids joined at the centromere. Are the cells haploid or diploid at this point? They are haploid; once homologous chromosomes separate, only the n number of chromosomes is left (23 in humans). There are still 46 chromatids: 2 per chromosome. Each chromatid within a pair, however, has the same origin (save for genetic recombination). The cell divides (by cytokinesis) into 2 daughter cells. Between cell divisions, there may be a short rest period, or interkinesis, during which the chromosomes partially uncoil.

Meiosis II

This second division is very similar to mitosis. Thus, we only need to learn the few salient differences between the two, and we'll have a good grasp on both. We shouldn't do more work than is necessary for Test Day; instead, we should study efficiently, and this is a perfect example of how to do just that. First of all, meiosis II is not preceded by chromosomal replication. Let's go through the steps of meiosis II as a quick review. We'll see a couple more differences along the way.

Prophase II

The centrioles migrate to opposite poles, and the spindle apparatus forms.

Metaphase II

The chromosomes line up along the metaphase plate. The centromeres divide, separating the chromosomes into pairs of sister chromatids.

Anaphase II

Sister chromatids are pulled to opposite poles by the spindle fibers.

Telophase II

A nuclear membrane forms around each new (haploid) nucleus. Cytokinesis follows, and two daughter cells are formed. Thus, by the completion of

---

Key Concept

It is critical to understand how meiosis I is different from mitosis. The chromosome number is halved (reductional division) in meiosis I. The daughter cells have the haploid number of chromosomes (23 in humans). Meiosis II is similar to mitosis in that sister chromatids are separated from one another; therefore, no change in ploidy is observed.

Key Concept

Mitosis	Meiosis
$2n \rightarrow 2n$	$2n \rightarrow n$
Occurs in all dividing cells.	Occurs in sex cells only.
Homologous chromosomes don't pair.	Homologous chromosomes pair up at metaphase plate, forming tetrads.
No crossing over.	Crossing over can occur.

meiosis II, four haploid daughter cells are produced per gametocyte. (In females, only one of these becomes a functional gamete.)

The random distribution of chromosomes in meiosis, coupled with crossing over in prophase I, enables an individual to produce gametes with many different genetic combinations. Thus, as opposed to asexual reproduction, which produces identical offspring, sexual reproduction provides the advantage of great genetic variability, which is believed to increase the capability of a species to evolve and adapt to a changing environment.

HUMAN SEXUAL REPRODUCTION

The haploid **sperm** and **ovum** fuse during fertilization to form a single-celled zygote in the **fallopian tubes**. These cells are produced by the **gonads**, which in both males and females are derived from the same embryological structure.

Male Reproductive Anatomy

In males, the primitive gonads develop into the **testes**. The testes have two functional components: the **seminiferous tubules** and the **interstitial cells (cells of Leydig)**. Sperm are produced in the highly coiled seminiferous tubules, where they

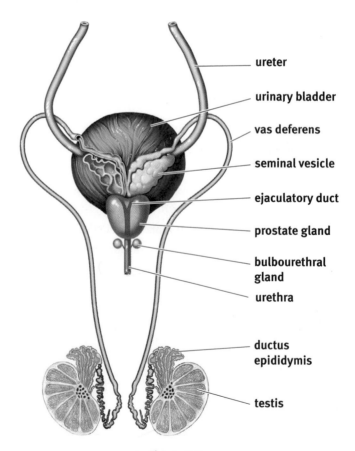

Figure 4.9

are nourished by **Sertoli cells**. The cells of Leydig secrete **testosterone** and other male sex hormones **(androgens)**. The testes are located in the **scrotum**, which is an external pouch that hangs below the **penis** and maintains a temperature 2° to 4°C lower than the body. This temperature differential is essential to proper sperm production; if we think back to our chapter on enzymes, what might be true of enzymes that are testes-specific? Perhaps these enzymes function only at that lower temperature. This sort of critical thinking is exactly what we need on Test Day.

As sperm mature, they are passed to the **epididymis**. They gain motility in the form of a flagellum and are then stored until **ejaculation**. The maturation process of a sperm takes approximately 72 days from origination until ready for ejaculation. During ejaculation, sperm travel through the **ejaculatory duct** and **urethra**, and exit the body through the penis (see Figure 4.9). In males, the reproductive and urinary systems share a common pathway; this is not the case in females.

As sperm passes through the reproductive tract, it is mixed with **seminal fluid**, which is produced through a joint effort by the **seminal vesicles**, **prostate gland**, and **bulbourethral gland**. The combination of sperm and seminal fluid is known as **semen**. The seminal vesicles contribute fructose to nourish sperm, and the prostate gland gives the fluid mildly alkaline properties so it will be able to survive the relative acidity of the female reproductive tract.

Spermatogenesis

Spermatogenesis, the formation of haploid sperm through meiosis, occurs in the seminiferous tubules. The diploid stem cells in males are known as **spermatogonia** (sing: **spermatogonium**). In the process of differentiation, they replicate their genetic material and develop into diploid **primary spermatocytes**.

Mnemonic:

To remember the pathway of sperm from creation to ejaculation, think SEVEN UP:

Seminiferous tubules

Epididymis

Vas deferens

Ejaculatory duct

(Nothing)

Urethra

Penis

Real World

Enlarged prostate glands are a common problem in older males. Because the prostate surrounds the urethra, classic symptoms of the condition are urinary frequency and urgency.

plasma membrane
acrosome
nucleus
sperm head
midpiece
tail

Figure 4.10

Key Concept

spermatogonia (2*n*)
↓
1° spermatocytes (2*n*)
↓meiosis I
2° spermatocytes (*n*)
↓meiosis II
spermatids (*n*)
↓
spermatozoa (*n*)

The first meiotic division will result in haploid **secondary spermatocytes**, which then undergo meiosis II to generate haploid spermatids. The spermatids undergo maturation, to become **spermatozoa**. Spermatogenesis creates four functional sperm for each spermatogonium. A mature sperm is very compact. It consists of a head (containing the genetic material), a midpiece (to generate energy from fructose for motility), and a tail (for motility) (see Figure 4.10). What sort of organelles would we expect an abundance of in the midpiece? Since we're looking to create ATP, mitochondria would be our best bet. Each sperm head is covered by a cap known as an **acrosome**. This structure is derived from the Golgi apparatus and is necessary to penetrate the **ovum**. Once a male reaches sexual maturity (puberty), approximately 3 million sperm are produced per day.

Female Reproductive Anatomy

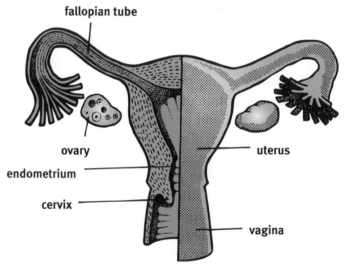

Figure 4.11

All of the female reproductive organs are internal, as opposed to external in the male (see Figure 4.11). The gonads, known as **ovaries**, produce estrogen and progesterone (much more on this when we discuss the endocrine system in chapter 12). The ovaries are located below the digestive system in the pelvic cavity; each consists of thousands of **follicles**, which are multilayered sacs that contain, nourish, and protect immature ova. Between puberty and menopause, one egg per month will be released into the peritoneal sac, which lines the abdominal cavity. It then moves into the fallopian **tube**, or **oviduct**, which is lined with cilia to usher it along. The fallopian tubes are connected to the muscular **uterus**, which is the site of fetal development. The lower end of the uterus known as the **cervix** connects to the **vaginal canal**, where sperm is deposited during intercourse. The vagina is also the passageway through which childbirth occurs. The external female anatomy is known collectively as the **vulva**. As we mentioned earlier, unlike males, females have separate excretory and reproductive tracts.

Oogenesis

The production of female gametes is known as oogenesis. Although gametocytes undergo the same meiotic process in both females and males, there are some test-worthy differences to keep track of. First, there is no unending supply of stem cells analogous to spermatogonia in females. All the oogonia a woman will ever have are formed during fetal development. At birth, females have predifferenti-ated cells known as **primary oocytes**. These cells are $2n$ (like primary spermato-cytes) and are actually frozen in prophase I. Once a woman reaches menarche, one primary oocyte per month will complete meiosis I, producing a **secondary oocyte** and a polar body. The division is characterized by unequal cytokinesis, which doles ample cytoplasm to one daughter (the secondary oocyte) and nearly none to the other (polar body). The polar body does not divide any further and never produces functional gametes. The secondary oocyte remains frozen in metaphase II and does not complete the remainder of meiosis II, unless fertilization occurs.

Two cell layers surround oocytes: the **zona pellucida** and the **corona radiata**. Meiosis II is triggered when a sperm penetrates these layers with the help of acro-somal enzymes. The secondary oocyte undergoes the second division to split into a mature ovum and another polar body, which will eventually die. With respect to the scheme of meiosis we learned earlier, are four haploid daughter cells formed through oogenesis? Sort of. If the first polar body underwent equational divi-sion, we'd have three polar bodies and one ovum as our final products. Although the ovum is the only functional gamete, all four would carry the haploid genetic material prescribed by theoretical meiosis. But, simply put, because its daugh-ters would not be functional anyway, there is no productive reason for the first polar body to divide again. A mature ovum is a very large cell consisting of large amounts of cytoplasm and organelles.

Until menopause (usually between ages 45 and 55), women ovulate one second-ary oocyte approximately every 28 days. After menopause, the ovaries become less sensitive to their stimulating hormones (follicle-stimulating hormone [FSH] and luteinizing hormone [LH]) and eventually atrophy. So, if the ovaries contrib-ute to a negative feedback loop and are not responding to FSH and LH, what do we think will happen to the levels of these hormones? They will shoot sky-high because they have no estrogen and progesterone feedback (both of which are secreted by the ovaries). Profound physical and physiological changes usually accompany this process. (We will discuss the complete interplay of FSH, LH, estrogen, and progesterone in Chapter 12.)

Fertilization

Secondary oocytes are capable of being fertilized within 24 hours of ovulation. Sperm will usually survive for one to two days after ejaculation if the environ-ment (uterine, in this case) is suitable. The fusion of these haploid cells, usually in

---

Key Concept

Remember that spermatogenesis in males is a 1:4 division, whereas in females, oogenesis is 1:1.

Key Concept

1° oocyte ($2n$)

↓meiosis I

2° oocyte (n)

↓fertilization

↓meiosis II

ovum (n)

---

the widest part of the fallopian tube, results in restoration of the diploid chromosome number and a cell known as a **zygote**.

sperm

egg

Figure 4.12

How does fusion occur? Sperm cells secrete acrosomal enzymes to digest the corona radiata and penetrate the zona pellucida (see Figure 4.12). Once the first sperm comes into direct contact with the secondary oocyte's cell membrane, it forms a tubelike structure known as the **acrosomal apparatus**, which extends to and penetrates the cell membrane. Its nucleus may then freely enter the ovum (no longer a secondary oocyte). After this process, the ovum undergoes a **cortical reaction**. Ca^{2+} ions are released into the cytoplasm, which in turn leads to the formation of the **fertilization membrane**. This membrane is impenetrable to other sperm—can we figure out why? To prevent multiple fertilizations. The release of Ca^{2+} also greatly increases the metabolic rate of the ovum and soon-to-be zygote.

Multiple Births

Monozygotic (Identical) Twins

Monozygotic twins develop when a single zygote splits into two. Because the genetic material is all the same, so too will be the offspring. If division is incomplete, conjoined twins may result in which the two offspring are physically attached at some point. Genetically identical offspring share the same genome and blood type.

Dizygotic (Fraternal Twins)

If two eggs are released in the same cycle, they may both be fertilized. Each zygote will implant in the uterine wall individually and develop a separate placenta, chorion, and amnion (although the placentas may fuse if the zygotes implant close to one another). Fraternal twins are no more genetically similar than any other pair of siblings.

Conclusion

We have taken a look at how cells produce more of themselves: one of the key tenets of the Cell Theory from Chapter 1. We first examined mitosis, which results in genetically identical daughter cells. We then moved on to asexual reproduction, which similarly results in genetically identical offspring. A variety of processes exist for asexual reproduction, including binary fission, budding, parthenogenesis, and regeneration. Sexual reproduction gives rise to genetically unique offspring and requires specialized cells known as gametes. Their fusion results in a zygote, whose development will be discussed in Chapter 5. The generation of these cells requires a process known as meiosis, which is similar to mitosis but has several test-worthy differences. Finally, we discussed the anatomy of the male and female reproductive tracts. We will revisit these topics when we discuss the endocrine system, as well as in the next chapter, when we discuss fetal development.

CONCEPTS TO REMEMBER

☐ Reproduction is necessary for propagation of a species.

☐ Mitosis involves one round of DNA replication and one round of cellular division. Daughter cells are genetically identical.

☐ Asexual reproduction results in organisms that are genetically identical, thus severely limiting diversity in the species.

☐ Asexual reproduction is primarily used by lower organisms, such as prokaryotes, yeasts, and hydra, and in certain circumstances by some animals.

☐ Sexual reproduction provides for the combination of two genomes, resulting in genetically unique offspring.

☐ The generation of specialized sex cells for sexual reproduction is known as gametogenesis.

☐ Meiosis is a process similar to mitosis but consists of one round of replication followed by two rounds of division. Thus, the daughter cells are unique and haploid.

☐ The male reproductive and excretory tracts share some common structures.

☐ Females are born with all their gametes already existing as primary oocytes.

☐ Twinning can occur and result in monozygotic (genetically identical) or dizygotic (fraternal; genetically distinct) twins.

Practice Questions

1. Which of the following is the correct sequence of the development of a mature sperm cell?

   A. 1° spermatocyte → spermatid → 2° spermatocyte → spermatozoan

   B. 1° spermatocyte → 2° spermatocyte → spermatid → spermatozoan

   C. Spermatogonium → 1° spermatocyte → 2° spermatocyte → spermatozoan

   D. 1° spermatocyte → 2° spermatocyte → spermatogonium → spermatid

2. Which of the following correctly pairs the stage of development of an egg cell with the different periods in its life cycle?

   A. From birth to ovulation—prophase II

   B. At ovulation—meiosis I

   C. At ovulation—meiosis II

   D. At fertilization—meiosis I

3. Some studies suggest that in patients with Alzheimer's disease, there is a defect in the way the spindle apparatus attaches to the kinetochore fibers. At which stage of mitotic division would you expect to see this problem?

   A. Prophase

   B. Metaphase

   C. Anaphase

   D. Telophase

4. If you wanted to incorporate a fluorescently labeled adenine into one of the two daughter cells that would arise as a result of mitosis, at which stage of cell development should you add in the nucleotide?

   A. G_1

   B. G_2

   C. M

   D. S

5. According to the endosymbiont hypothesis, mitochondria are bacterial descendants because they formed as a result of a eukaryotic cell engulfing a prokaryotic cell. Based on this, what type of division would you expect to see in mitochondria?

   A. Binary fission

   B. Mitosis

   C. Budding

   D. Regeneration

6. Upon ovulation, the oocyte is released into the

   A. fallopian tube.

   B. follicle.

   C. abdominal cavity.

   D. uterus.

7. Cancer cells are cells in which mitosis has gone wild. If a cure were found that could target only cancer cells without affecting normal cells, at which point in the cell cycle would the treatment effectively prevent cancer cell division?

   A. During the S stage

   B. During prophase

   C. During metaphase

   D. All of the above could work.

8. Which of the following INCORRECTLY pairs the term with its definition?

A. Scrotum—location of the testes

B. Epididymis—site of sperm maturation

C. Vas deferens—tube connecting the epididymis to the prostate

D. Semen—composed of seminal fluid and sperm

9. During which phase of the meiotic cycle does the cell have a diploid number of chromosomes?

A. In the beginning of prophase I

B. At the end of anaphase I

C. At the end of telophase II

D. Both (A) and (B)

10. Which of the following does NOT contribute to genetic variability?

A. Random fertilization of a sperm and an egg

B. Independent assortment of homologous chromosomes

C. Crossing over between homologous chromosomes during meiosis

D. The interkinesis that occurs during telophase I

11. Which of the following statements correctly identifies a key difference between mitosis and meiosis?

A. In metaphase of mitosis and metaphase of meiosis I, replicated chromosomes line up in single file.

B. During anaphase of mitosis and anaphase of meiosis I, homologous chromosomes separate, but sister chromatids remain attached.

C. At the end of telophase of mitosis and the end of telophase of meiosis I, the daughter cells are identical to the parent cell.

D. During metaphase of meiosis I, homologous pairs of replicated chromosomes line up.

12. The chromosome number of an offspring produced via parthenogenesis would be

A. diploid.

B. haploid.

C. 2*N*.

D. both (A) and (C).

13. Which of the following is true regarding prophase?

A. The chromosomes separate and move to opposite poles of the cell.

B. The spindle apparatus disappears.

C. The chromosomes uncoil.

D. The nucleoli disappear.

14. Which of the following INCORRECTLY pairs the term with its definition?

A. Seminal vesicles—secrete sperm

B. Urethra—the tube through which sperm is expelled from the body

C. Seminiferous tubules—initial site of sperm formation

D. Interstitial cells—produce testosterone and other androgens

Small Group Questions

1. Colchicine binds to tubulin and prevents its assembly into microtubules, while cytochalasins bind to the ends of actin filaments and prevent their elongation. What effect would these substances have on cell division in animal cells?

2. In terms of biological diversity, would mitosis or meiosis be more important?

3. The evolutionary success of organisms depends on reproduction. Some organisms reproduce asexually, while others reproduce sexually. What environmental conditions would favor sexual reproduction? What environmental conditions would favor asexual reproduction?

Explanations to Practice Questions

1. B

Diploid cells called spermatogonia differentiate into primary spermatocytes, which undergo the first meiotic division to yield two haploid secondary spermatocytes. These undergo a second meiotic division to become immature spermatids. The spermatids then undergo a series of changes leading to the production of mature sperm, or spermatozoa. The only answer that correctly identifies the sequence of development of a mature sperm cell is seen in (B).

2. B

From the time of birth until a few hours before ovulation, all egg cells are arrested at the prophase stage of meiosis I. These cells are referred to as primary oocytes. At ovulation, the egg cell has completed meiosis I and is now a haploid cell called a secondary oocyte. When a sperm penetrates the outer layers of the secondary oocyte, it undergoes meiosis II to become a mature ovum. The nucleus of the ovum fuses with the sperm to form a diploid zygote; if fertilization does not occur, the secondary oocyte will not undergo meiosis II. (B) is therefore the correct answer.

3. B

The spindle apparatus interacts with the kinetochore fibers in order to align the chromosomes on the equatorial plate during metaphase. (B) is therefore the correct answer.

4. D

To ensure that the labeled adenine will be incorporated into the DNA of one of the daughter cells, we have to insert the nucleotide when the DNA of the parent cell replicates. As such, when each chromosome is replicated, one of the chromatids will include the labeled nucleotide. When the cell undergoes mitosis, only one of the daughter cells will contain the labeled adenine. The chromosomes are replicated during the S stage, where the *S* stands for *synthesis*. After replication, the chromosomes consist of two identical sister chromatids held together at a central region called the centromere. However, in our case, because we only added one labeled nucleotide, only one of the chromatids will contain it. Therefore, although the DNA sequence will be identical and the two chromatids will behave the same, we can easily distinguish one from the other. (D) correctly identifies the developmental stage at which we should include the labeled adenine to transfer it to only one of the new daughter cells.

5. A

Since mitochondria are bacterial descendents and possess their own DNA, we would expect them to divide in the same fashion as any other prokaryote. As such, we would expect mitochondria to divide through binary fission, a simple form of asexual reproduction. In binary fission, the chromosome replicates, and a new plasma membrane grows inward along the midline of the cell, dividing it into two equally sized cells, each containing a duplicate of the parent chromosome. (A) is therefore the correct answer.

6. C

This subtle point about ovulation eludes most students and remains hard to believe until the organs are examined in anatomy class in medical school. The ruptured ovarian follicle releases an oocyte into the abdominal cavity, close to the entrance of the fallopian tube. With the aid of beating cilia, the oocyte is drawn into the fallopian tube, through which it travels until it reaches the uterus. If it is fertilized (in the fallopian tube), it will implant in the uterine wall. If fertilization does not occur, it will be expelled along with the uterine lining during menstruation. (C) is therefore the correct answer.

7. D

The question is asking us to determine at which point in the cell cycle we can prevent or at least lower the number of cells undergoing mitosis. One idea would be to prevent DNA synthesis during the S stage of the cell cycle. Without the DNA being replicated, the daughter cells would not be identical, with half having a normal diploid number of chromosomes and half having zero DNA (nonviable daughter cells). Another idea would be preventing the mitotic cycle from occurring altogether in prophase by preventing spindle apparatus formation, preventing the nuclear membrane from dissolving, etc. Similarly, a treatment that would act on cells in the metaphase stage of the cell cycle would also interfere with the mitotic cycle. Therefore, any of the three solutions presented in the answer choices would be a viable option, making (D) the correct answer.

8. C

The surest way to answer this question is to go through each answer choice and determine which one is false. Glancing at the answer choices, we notice that (A), (B), and (D) all correctly pair the terms with their respective definitions. In (C), however, there is an error. The vas deferens is the tube that connects the epididymis to the ejaculatory duct. The prostate, on the other hand, secretes a milky fluid that protects the sperm from the acidic environment of the female reproductive tract. Sperm first mix with this alkaline fluid before reaching the epididymis. (C) is therefore the correct answer.

9. D

Although this concept is sometimes difficult to grasp, it is important to be aware of each stage of the meiotic cycle. The first part of meiosis, meiosis I, begins with prophase I where crossing over occurs. Homologous pairs are lined up in metaphase I and pulled apart, leaving the sister chromatids intact in anaphase I. This concept is easily missed—each daughter cell at the end of telophase I thus contains two sister chromatids in each chromosome, but it is considered to be haploid because these cells do not contain a full genetic complement but rather two copies of half a complement. These sister chromatids are then pulled apart during meiosis II. Therefore, during both prophase and anaphase I, the cell will be diploid. It is not until after telophase I that the cell becomes haploid. At any stage after telophase I, the cell is haploid. At the end of telophase II, four distinct daughter cells, each containing n number of chromosomes, are present. The correct answer therefore is (D).

10. D

To safest way to answer this question correctly is to go through each answer choice and eliminate the ones that contribute to genetic variability. The random fertilization of a sperm and an egg, the independent assortment of homologous chromosomes, and crossing over between homologous chromosomes during meiosis all contribute to genetic variability during sexual reproduction. Interkinesis refers to the fact that, during telophase I, chromosomes partially uncoil before entering meiosis II. It has no impact on genetic variability, making (D) the correct answer.

11. D

Glancing at the answer choices, we notice that they all mention metaphase, anaphase, or telophase of either mitosis or meiosis I, so let's quickly review the major differences between these two cell division cycles. In metaphase of mitosis, replicated chromosomes line up in single file; during anaphase, sister chromatids separate and move to opposite poles of the cell; finally, at the end of telophase, the two daughter cells are identical to each other and the parent cell. In metaphase I of meiosis, homologous pairs of replicated chromosomes line up; during anaphase I, the homologous chromosomes separate, but sister chromatids remain attached; at the end of telophase I, the two daughter cells are distinct from each other and the parent cell because crossing over occurred during prophase I. From the given choices, only (D) correctly identifies a key difference between mitosis and meiosis.

12. B

Parthenogenesis is the development of an unfertilized egg into an adult organism. Because the organism develops from a haploid egg, all of its cells will be haploid. This process occurs naturally in certain lower organisms, such as bees, ants, and salamanders. (B) is therefore the correct answer.

13. D

In prophase, the chromatin condense into chromosomes, the spindle apparatus forms, and the nucleoli and nuclear membrane disappear. (D) matches a process that occurs during prophase and is thus the correct answer.

14. A

The safest way to answer this question correctly is to go through each answer choice and determine which one gives an incorrect definition of the respective term. Starting with (A), we notice an error right away: The seminal vesicles produce and secrete seminal fluid, not sperm. Sperm are produced by the seminiferous tubules, as stated in (C). The seminal vesicles secrete a fructose-rich fluid, which serves as an energy source for the highly active sperm. (A) is therefore the correct answer.

Embryology

"Is it a boy or a girl?" is one of the most common questions asked of pregnant women, probably second only to "When are you due?" The suspense of the baby's sex never fails to excite family and friends, although only half of all bets are won. For centuries, members of the elder generations have offered advice and suggestions on how to predict the outcome, or even plan it. "Dangle a needle over your belly by a thread. Does it swing side to side or in circles?"

For the modern mom-to-be, needle dangling doesn't carry the same credibility as technological advances like ultrasonography. Ultrasonography is performed by placing a probe that emits high-frequency sound waves near the tissue to be examined. Early pregnancies are often better detected through transvaginal ultrasounds, in which a probe is safely placed inside the birth canal. Older, larger pregnancies are easily viewable by transabdominal sonography. The probe transduces a photo onto a computer screen, which can be measured to determine gestational age, screen for multiple pregnancies or anomalies, or used to determine the baby's sex. Obstetricians look for three to four parallel lines to indicate an early vulva and labial folds in female fetuses and the presence of a developing scrotal sac in males.

So how early can eager grandparents place their bets? All embryos are female by default—that is, for a male fetus to develop, it must undergo not only masculinization but also defeminization. These processes occur (or don't) around six to eight weeks postfertilization. Don't expect any answers before 16 to 17 weeks, though, because ultrasonography equipment is not yet advanced enough to give immediate answers. Human childbirth has existed for a couple of million years, whereas these techniques don't date back even a hundred. We'll stay tuned, though; who knows what will be possible in another century?

In this chapter, we'll follow the development of a unicellular, dependent zygote in to an autonomously breathing baby. We'll examine how its cells divide and the way they differentiate. How the fetus connects to its mother is of great importance to us, and we'll discuss that along with giving an overview of the stages of pregnancy and childbirth.

Early Developmental Stages   ★★★★☆☆

CLEAVAGE

The zygote takes a whirlwind ride within its first few days of existence. After fertilization in the fallopian tubes, the newly formed, single-celled entity must change both its name and address to continue to develop. In the process of moving to the uterus for implantation, it undergoes rapid mitotic cell divisions in a process called **cleavage**. The first cleavage officially creates an embryo, as it nullifies one of the zygote's defining characteristics, unicellularity. Although several rounds of mitosis occur, the total size of the embryo remains unchanged during the first few divisions. Imagine wanting to make a nice steak dinner for a couple of study buddies. Using a kitchen cleaver, we could cut up a few pieces. Does this mean we now have more steak? No, we have more pieces but the same total amount of steak. Similarly, by dividing into progressively smaller cells (remember, these divisions are rapid, so there really isn't time for enlargement in between), the cells increase two ratios: the nuclear to cytoplasmic ratio and the surface area to volume ratio. Thus, the cells achieve increased area for gas and nutrient diffusion relative to overall volume. There are two types of cleavage: **indeterminate** and **determinate**. Indeterminate cleavage results in cells that can still develop into complete organisms.

Bridge

Monozygotic twins have identical genomes because they both originate from indeterminately cleaved cells of the same embryo.

Figure 5.1

Determinate cleavage results in cells whose fates are, as they sound, determined; in other words, they are committed to **differentiating** into a certain type of cell. Think back to that steak dinner. After one cut, the beef is still versatile and can give us more than one kind of steak. But after several cuts, we begin to determine the final platter, be it filet mignon or New York strip.

For the MCAT, we should be aware of a few key time points in our embryo's development. The first, second, and third cleavages occur at 32, 60, and 72 hours postfertilization, respectively. At this point, our eight-celled embryo has completed its journey to the uterus (see Figure 5.1).

Figure 5.2

Several divisions later, the embryo becomes a solid mass of cells knows as a **morula** (see Figure 5.2). That name is derived from the Latin word for *mulberry*, which might help us grasp what an embryo at this stage looks like. Next up is **blastulation**, which forms the similarly named **blastula**. Blastulas are characterized by the presence of a hollow, fluid-filled inner cavity known as a **blastocoel** (see Figure 5.3). The mammalian blastula is known as a **blastocyst** and consists of two noteworthy cell groups: the **trophoblast** and **inner cell mass**. The trophoblast cells surround the blastocoel and give rise to the chorion, and later the placenta, whereas the inner cell mass protrudes into the blastocoel and gives rise to the organism itself.

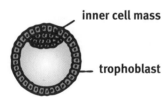

Figure 5.3

IMPLANTATION

Everything we've talked about so far happened as our zygote (and then embryo) free-wheeled its way down the fallopian tube and into the uterus. For development to continue, the blastocyst must settle down in its new home—the uterine wall. During blastulation (five to eight days postfertilization), the blastocyst implants in the **endometrium**, which has been prepared in anticipation. Specifically, the steroid hormone **progesterone** promotes proliferation of the (endometrial) mucosal layer to help the embryo implant. In addition, embryonic cells secrete enzymes that strategically burrow into the endometrial lining to allow for implantation. This is a key step, as it forms a connection to maternal circulation for nutrient and gas exchange. Implantation is like planting a tree. As we plant a seed (embryo) into the ground (endometrium), we'll want to make sure that the soil is fertile, as progesterone does to the endometrium. We'll also need a shovel to plant the seed in the ground, the same way that proteolytic enzymes allow the embryo to settle into the uterine wall. As the tree grows, it generates roots (like the **placenta**) that allow for gas and nutrient exchange with the soil (endometrium).

Mnemonic

Remember that an embryo with a "blasted-out" cavity is a blastula.

Real World

Sometimes, the blastula implants itself outside of the uterus, a situation referred to as an ectopic pregnancy. Over 95 percent of ectopic pregnancies occur in the fallopian tube (also known as the oviduct). Ectopic pregnancies are generally inviable because the narrow fallopian tube is not an environment in which an embryo can properly grow. If the embryo does not spontaneously abort, the tube may rupture, and a considerable amount of hemorrhaging may occur.

GASTRULATION

Once the cell mass implants, it can begin further developmental processes such as **gastrulation**, the generation of three distinct cell layers. Much of our developmental knowledge comes from the study of other organisms. In sea urchins, gastrulation begins with a small invagination in the blastula. Cells continue moving toward the invagination, resulting in elimination of the blastocoel. Imagine blowing up a beach ball but leaving the seal open. Now, as we begin to push down on a specific point, it will begin to form a two-layered cup just like our newly formed **gastrula**. The air escaping the beach ball can be likened to the loss of the blastocoel. The inner cell layer (inside of the cup and the spot to which we applied pressure) is known as the **endoderm**. The outer cell layer (and outside of the beach ball) is the **ectoderm**. The cavity created by the deep invagination is known as the **archenteron**, which later develops into the gut. The opening of the archenteron is called the **blastopore** (see Figure 5.4). In **deuterostomes**, such as humans, the blastopore develops into the anus. In **protostomes**, it develops into the mouth.

Mnemonic

How can we remember the blastopore's fate in protostomes versus deuterostomes? Let's think about any time we have been around toddlers or babies. When asked about their bodily habits, parents will often describe them euphemistically in terms of "number one" or "number two." Deuterostomes starts with *deu*, which sounds like *duo*, meaning *two*. Thus, in deuterostomes, the blastopore develops into the anus, associated with "number two." *Proto–* means *before*, so what comes way before the anus in the alimentary tract? The mouth.

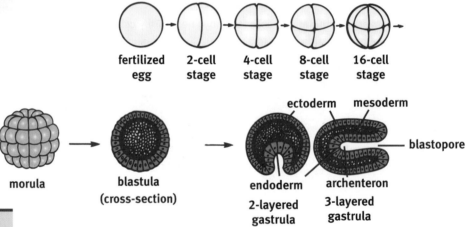

Figure 5.4

Mnemonic

How can we keep track of our three germ layers? The ectoderm is the "attracto"-derm. These are systems and organs that attract us to other people: their looks, their eyes, and their smarts. The mesoderm is the "means"-o-derm. This is how we get from place to place in the world, and how constituents get from place to place in the body. Bone, muscle, heart, and blood vessels all allow us to do this. Finally, the endoderm is easy to remember because it gives rise to the "endernal" organs; these include parts of the long tube that runs from the mouth to the anus (digestive tract) and the organs attached to it (accessory organs of digestion). The endodermal layer also gives rise to the lungs.

Eventually some cells will also migrate into the area between the ectoderm and endoderm, generating a third cell layer known as the **mesoderm**. These primary germ layers are one of the most commonly tested MCAT topics. Knowing the structures to which they give rise will almost certainly translate into a point or two on Test Day. From the outermost to the innermost embryonic layer, they develop into the following:

Ectoderm—integument (including the epidermis, hair, nails, epithelium of the nose, mouth, and anal canal), lens of the eye, and the nervous system

Mesoderm—musculoskeletal system, circulatory system, excretory system, gonads, muscular and connective tissue coats of the digestive and respiratory systems

Endoderm—epithelial linings of digestive and respiratory tracts (lungs, too) and parts of the liver, pancreas, thyroid, bladder, and distal urinary and reproductive tracts

WHAT ARE EMBRYONIC STEM CELLS?

Embryonic stem (ES) cells are derived from the portion of a very early stage embryo that would eventually give rise to an entire body. Because ES cells originate in this primordial stage, they retain the "pluripotent" ability to form any cell type in the body.

CELL FATE

Less than a week after a human egg is fertilized, the developing embryo contains about 100 to 150 cells that have yet to differentiate. The embryo is a hollow ball, called a blastocyst, consisting only of an outer cell mass, which in a pregnancy would later form the placenta, and an inner cell mass (ICM), which would become the fetus. Inside a womb, these cells would continue multiplying, beginning to specialize by the third week. The embryo, called a gastrula at this stage, would contain three distinctive germ layers whose descendants would ultimately form hundreds of different tissue types in the human body.

FERTILIZED EGG
(1 day)

Outer cell mass
Inner cell mass

BLASTOCYST
(5 to 6 days)

GASTRULA
(14 TO 16 DAYS)

EMBRYONIC GERM LAYERS AND SOME OF THE TISSUES IN THEIR LINEAGES

ENDODERM
(internal layer)

Pancreas
Liver
Thyroid
Lung
Bladder
Urethra

MESODERM
(middle layer)

Bone marrow
Skeletal, smooth, and cardiac muscle
Heart and blood vessels
Kidney tubules

ECTODERM
(external layer)

Skin
Neurons
Pituitary gland
Eyes
Ears

MAKING EMBRYONIC STEM CELLS

To create ES cell lines, scientists remove the inner cell mass from a blastocyst created in the laboratory, usually left over from an attempt at in vitro fertilization. The ICM is placed on a plate containing feeder cells, to which it soon attaches. In a few days, new cells grow out of the ICM and form colonies (above). These cells are formally called embryonic stem cells only if they meet two criteria: They display markers known to characterize ES cells, and they undergo several generations of cell division, or passages, demonstrating that they constitute a stable, or immortalized, cell line.

Figure 5.5

MCAT Expertise

The MCAT likes to test us on development of the adrenal glands. The adrenal cortex is derived from the mesoderm, but the adrenal medulla is derived from the ectoderm (since it contains some nervous tissue).

Real World

In development of the eyes, lateral outpocketings from the brain (optic vesicles) grow out and touch the overlying ectoderm. The optic vesicle induces the ectoderm to form the lens placode. The lens placode in turn induces the optic vesicle to create the optic cup. The optic cup then induces the lens placode to develop into the cornea and lens. Experiments with frog embryos show that if this ectoderm is transplanted to the trunk (after the optic vesicles have grown out), a lens will develop in the trunk. If, however, the ectoderm is transplanted before the outgrowth of the optic vesicles, it will not form a lens.

You may wonder why the kidneys derive from mesodermal cells if they are contained in the abdomen. Aren't they internal organs? Well, yes, but they're not really in the abdomen. They're completely external to the gut sac (also known as the peritoneum), making them retroperitoneal organs. We won't need such detail until we get to medical school, so let's just remember "different cavity, different germ layer."

In Chapter 4, we noted that all somatic cells in an organism contain the same DNA. They all have the same genome, so how can they differentiate to carry distinct functions? Primarily, it is by selective transcription of the genome; in other words, only the genes necessary in the eye are turned on in the eye. Imagine our seventh-grade school binder. It had five tabbed subjects: Algebra, English, Science, History, and Spanish. When we went to history class, we used only the History portion of our binder. In Spanish class, we only used the Spanish section. It's not that the other sections disappeared but rather that we didn't need our algebra notes to conjugate reflexive verbs.

Selective transcription is often related to the concept of induction, which is the ability of a certain group of cells to influence the fate of other nearby cells. This process is mediated by chemical substances called inducers, which are passed from the organizing cells to the responsive cells. These chemicals are responsible for processes such as the guidance of neuronal axons (which is no easy feat considering that some go from the spinal cord all the way to our pinky toes). The tabs we used to organize our seventh-grade binders were similar to inducers, because they told us where to file papers from each class.

NEURULATION

Once the three germ layers are formed, **neurulation**, or development of the nervous system, can begin. Remember that the nervous system is derived from the ectoderm. How, then, do cells originating on the outer part of the embryo (ectoderm) end up inside the final organism? Recalling what we learned in the previous paragraph, cells are induced to migrate inward. First, a rod of mesodermal cells known as the **notochord** forms along the long axis of the organism (just as our spinal cord runs up and down our back). These cells induce a group of ectodermal cells to slide inward to form **neural folds**, which surround a **neural groove** (imagine a valley running between two mountains). The neural folds grow toward one another until they fuse into a **neural tube**, which gives rise to the central nervous system (see Figure 5.6). At the tip of each neural fold are **neural crest cells**. These cells migrate outward to form the peripheral nervous system, including the sensory ganglia, autonomic ganglia, adrenal medulla, and Schwann cells. Finally, ectodermal cells will migrate over the neural tube and crests to cover the rudimentary nervous system.

Figure 5.6

Fetal Respiration ★★★★☆☆

We've mentioned that nutrient and gas exchange with maternal circulation is an important and necessary part of fetal development. This is taken care of by two specialized structures: the **placenta** and the **umbilical cord**, which develop in the weeks after fertilization. The placenta is primarily formed from an extra-embryonic membrane called the **chorion**, which, as we mentioned earlier, develops from tro-phoblast cells. Just like the umbilicus cord that connects astronauts to their space shuttles and provides them with oxygen, the human umbilical cord and vessels provide attachment to the chorion and nutrition for the fetus. The other three extra-embryonic membranes that we should be aware of are the **allantois**, **amnion**, and **yolk sac**. The allantois is surrounded by the amnion, which is a thin, tough mem-brane filled with **amniotic fluid** that serves as a shock absorber during pregnancy and labor (the same way our car's airbags lessen the impact of a collision). Moving outward, we come to the yolk sac, the site of early blood vessel development. Finally, the outermost embryonic layer is the chorion, which completely surrounds the other membranes, providing an added level of protection. **Chorionic villi** eventually grow into the placenta and support maternal-fetal gas exchange. Last but not least, the umbilical cord is surrounded by a jellylike matrix and is the initial connection of the fetus to the mother (see Figure 5.7).

Key Concept

Although the fetus obtains its nutrients and oxygen from the mother, there is no actual mixing of the blood. Instead, the placenta allows for the close proximity of the fetal and maternal bloodstreams so that diffusion can occur between them.

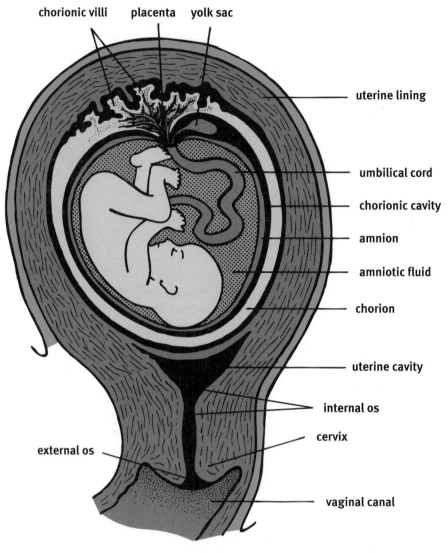

chorionic villi   placenta   yolk sac

uterine lining

umbilical cord

chorionic cavity

amnion

amniotic fluid

chorion

uterine cavity

internal os

cervix

external os

vaginal canal

Figure 5.7

Key Concept

Remember, gas exchange in the fetus occurs across the placenta. Fetal lungs do not function until birth.

Now that we have discussed the structural features of the organs of fetal development, we can examine how they function. The placenta is the organ where nutrient, gas, and waste exchanges occur (see Figure 5.8). It is crucial that there be no mixing of maternal and fetal blood, as they may have different blood types. The simplest way to move nutrients and waste products would be diffusion; in fact, this is how water, glucose, amino acids, and inorganic salts are transferred. We should recall, though, that diffusion requires a gradient. So for oxygen to diffuse from mother to fetus, there must be a higher P_{oxygen} in maternal blood than in fetal blood. In addition to an oxygen gradient, fetal blood cells are equipped with **fetal hemoglobin (Hb-F)**, which exhibits a greater affinity for oxygen than does maternal (adult) hemoglobin, known as Hb-A. Fetal hemoglobin's increased affinity makes it even more favorable for oxygen to diffuse away from maternal hemoglobin. Waste materials and carbon dioxide move in the opposite direction.

Figure 5.8

Key Concept

Consider what the fetal Hb–O$_2$ dissociation curve would look like compared with an adult's. For fetal Hb to "steal" oxygen from the maternal/adult Hb, it must demonstrate a higher affinity for O$_2$, which shifts the curve left (see Chapter 9).

The placental barrier also serves another function: immune protection. Remember that the fetus is immunologically naïve because it lacks both experience and exposure, defense-strengthening tools on which immune systems depend. Many foreign particles and bacteria are too large to cross the placental barrier by diffusion, but unfortunately, viruses (e.g., HIV, rubella), alcohol, and toxins (e.g., cocaine and other illicit drugs) are not. In addition, the placenta qualifies as an endocrine organ because it produces progesterone, estrogen, and human chorionic gonadotropin (hCG), all of which are essential for maintaining pregnancy.

Fetal Circulation ★★★★★☆

Several key differences between fetal and adult circulation serve important functional roles in the developing organism. First, let's discuss two important organs that are underdeveloped in the fetus and must rely on the placenta to carry out their functions: the lungs and liver. In adult circulation, blood is sent from the heart to the lungs for oxygenation. That just won't work in fetal circulation, because the lungs are not yet able to oxygenate circulating blood. In addition, since fetuses are suspended in aqueous amniotic fluid, there is no air for the lungs to take in. Oxygen must come from maternal circulation and, therefore, diffuse through placental vessels.

How do we keep blood away from the lungs? Two fetal shunts reroute blood within the heart. The first, called the **foramen ovale**, connects the right and left atria, with the intent that blood entering the right atrium from the superior vena cava will flow into the left atrium instead of the right ventricle so that it can eventually be pumped out of the aorta into systemic circulation. Now, there must be some incentive for the blood to travel from the right atrium to the left, and in this case, it's a pressure differential. Where is the pressure higher? The right atrium, because blood will travel spontaneously down the pressure gradient. This gradient is reversed in adults, so the foramen ovale must be shut after birth for the adult heart to function properly. We must remember, though, that the valve separating the right atrium and ventricle isn't closed shut, so not all blood will be immediately sent to the left side. The **ductus arteriosus** is present to shunt leftover blood from the pulmonary artery to the aorta. It works for the same reason that the foramen ovale does: The pressure in the right fetal heart is higher than that in the left.

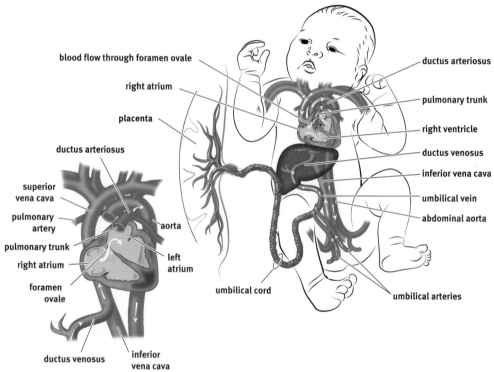

Figure 5.9

The liver is also underdeveloped and is not fully able to carry out its adult tasks in utero (detoxification, sugar storage, and balance, etc.). Actually, the liver's to-do list is long, which means that any blood supply that travels toward it would be put toward completing those various tasks. Since the placenta is plenty capable of pitching in during gestation, blood returning from the placenta via the umbilical vein is rerouted to the inferior vena cava via the **ductus venosus**. It's not that the fetal liver doesn't need oxygen; in fact, it needs a lot. But to prevent it from stealing oxygen designated for the rest of the body, the liver has its own reserves from arteries leaving the heart.

Speaking of shunts and vessels, we should be clear on what kind of blood the umbilical arteries and veins carry. Just like all other arteries that take blood *away* from the heart, the umbilical arteries carry blood *away* from the fetus. And just like all other veins that carry blood *toward* the heart, the umbilical veins carry blood *toward* the fetus. The best way to remember which kind of blood each carries is to recall which way the blood travels in each vessel and to use that pathway to deduce what kind of blood is flowing. The fetus would return blood to the placenta only if all the oxygen in it were used up. Thus, the umbilical arteries carry deoxygenated blood. Similarly, the only kind of blood that the fetus wants from the placenta is oxygenated blood, so it must be the case that the umbilical veins carry oxygenated blood.

Gestation

Human pregnancy lasts an estimated 266 days, which are divided into three trimesters. As a general rule, the larger the animal, the longer the gestational period and the fewer the offspring. For example, elephants usually have one calf and gestate for 22 months (almost two years). Mice have 10 to 12 offspring per litter and gestate for only 20 days—quite a difference! Maybe their seemingly unparalleled fertility led to the old wives' tale that elephants are afraid of mice.

Although we don't need to know every detail of gestation for the MCAT (the way we will have to in medical school), there are some key developmental events with which we should be familiar.

FIRST TRIMESTER

During the first weeks, the major organs begin to develop. The heart begins to beat at approximately 22 days, and soon afterward the eyes, gonads, limbs, and liver start to form. By five weeks, the embryo is 10 mm in length and by week six, it has grown to 15 mm. The cartilaginous skeleton begins to harden into bone by the seventh week (see Chapter 6). By the end of eight weeks, most of the organs have formed, the brain is fairly developed, and the embryo is referred to as a fetus. At the end of the third month, the fetus is about 9 cm long.

SECOND TRIMESTER

During the second trimester, the fetus undergoes a tremendous amount of growth. It begins to move around in the amniotic fluid, its face appears human, and its toes and fingers elongate. By the end of the sixth month, the fetus measures 30 to 36 cm long.

THIRD TRIMESTER

The seventh and eighth months are characterized by continued rapid growth and further brain development. During the ninth month, antibodies are transported by highly selective active transport from the mother to the fetus for protection against

Real World

Advances in medicine have allowed babies to be born as early as 24 weeks, which is far short of a normal 39. There is a chance that these neonates may survive, although there are often severe complications, as fetal development is not complete at 24 weeks. These problems are most apparent in the respiratory system due to insufficient surfactant production; more on this in Chapter 8.

foreign matter, in preparation for life outside the womb. The growth rate slows, and the fetus becomes less active, as it has less room to move about.

Birth

Vaginal childbirth is accomplished by rhythmic contractions of uterine smooth muscle, coordinated by prostaglandins and the peptide hormone oxytocin. Birth consists of three basic phases. First, the cervix thins out, and the amniotic sac ruptures, which is commonly known as the *water breaking*. Next, strong uterine contractions result in the birth of the fetus. Finally, the placenta and umbilical cord are expelled. These are often referred to as *afterbirth*.

Conclusion

Our chapter has taken us through the rapid development of a single-celled zygote to the birth of a full-fledged baby. What normally takes nine months, we have accomplished in only a few pages!

Adult structures that arise from embryonic germ layers are of special importance to us because they are commonly tested on the MCAT. How about the rest of it? From the first cleavage to the last uterine contraction, we should simply extract the main structures and highlights of embryonic development in addition to the differences between fetal and adult physiology. Now that we are familiar with prenatal development, we'll move on to discuss adult organ systems in the next few chapters. Keep an eye out for Chapters 8 and 9 (adult circulatory and respiratory systems), which we can use as reference points for studying fetal physiology.

CONCEPTS TO REMEMBER

- ☐ The zygote undergoes several rapid divisions, which ultimately result in determinate cleavage.

- ☐ Indeterminate cleavage allows for the generation of identical twins.

- ☐ Implantation of the embryo into the endometrium is necessary for proper and successful growth.

- ☐ Gastrulation is the generation of three primary germ layers: ectoderm, endoderm, and mesoderm.

- ☐ Each of the primary germ layers gives rise to specific organs and structures. This is an exceedingly important topic to be familiar with for Test Day success.

- ☐ The development of the nervous system is known as neurulation and occurs during gastrulation.

- ☐ Fetal respiration is carried out at the placenta and not in the developing lungs.

- ☐ Fetal circulation contains three shunts: the ductus venosus, the foramen ovale, and the ductus arteriosus, which serve to bypass blood from the liver and lungs.

- ☐ Gestation consists of three trimesters of three months each; certain key developmental milestones are reached during each trimester.

- ☐ Vaginal childbirth is accomplished by coordinated and rhythmic contractions of uterine smooth muscle.

Practice Questions

1. Which of the following developmental stages has the greatest nuclear-to-cytoplasmic material ratio?

   A. Eight-cell zygote
   B. Morula
   C. Blastula
   D. Archenteron

2. Which of the following associations is INCORRECT?

   A. Endoderm—thyroid
   B. Endoderm—lens of the eye
   C. Ectoderm—nails
   D. Mesoderm—kidneys

3. Which of the following changes does NOT occur immediately after birth?

   A. The infant begins to produce adult hemoglobin.
   B. Resistance in the pulmonary arteries decreases.
   C. Pressure in the left atrium increases.
   D. Pressure in both the inferior vena cava and the right atrium increases.

4. During which period is a teratogen most likely to affect brain development during gestation?

   A. First trimester
   B. Second trimester
   C. Third trimester
   D. At birth

5. From which of the following germ layers does the notochord form?

   A. Ectoderm
   B. Mesoderm
   C. Endoderm
   D. Archenteron

6. The influence of a specific group of cells on the differentiation of another group of cells is referred to as

   A. neurulation.
   B. indeterminate cleavage.
   C. determinate cleavage.
   D. induction.

7. Which of the following structures is NOT formed from the endoderm?

   A. Pancreas
   B. Lining of the respiratory tract
   C. Circulatory system
   D. Liver

8. Which of the following is true regarding fetal hemoglobin?

   A. It continues to be produced for a few months after birth.
   B. It can be found in small quantities in the mother's blood during pregnancy.
   C. It has a greater affinity for oxygen than adult hemoglobin.
   D. It can help transport vitamins across the maternal capillaries to fetal blood.

9. Which of the following may be found in the mother's bloodstream?

A. hCG
B. Fetal white blood cells
C. CO_2 produced by fetal cells
D. Two of the above

10. Which of the following INCORRECTLY pairs the fetal circulation shunt with its function?

A. Ductus venosus—bypasses the liver
B. Ductus venosus—bypasses the pulmonary veins
C. Ductus arteriosus—directs blood from the pulmonary artery to the aorta
D. Ductus arteriosus—prevents blood from entering the lungs

11. Which of the following blood vessels do NOT contain deoxygenated blood?

A. Fetal umbilical artery
B. Adult pulmonary arteries
C. Fetal umbilical vein
D. Superior vena cava

12. Which of the following statements is FALSE?

A. In fetal circulation, blood is oxygenated in the placenta.
B. A small amount of blood reaches the fetal lungs.
C. After birth, the blood pressure in the right atrium decreases.
D. In fetal circulation, the blood delivered via the aorta has a higher partial pressure of oxygen than the blood that was delivered to the lungs.

13. Which of the following changes to fetal circulation occurs after birth?

A. Increased left atrial pressure coupled with decreased right atrial pressure causes the foramen ovale to close.
B. The ductus venosus degenerates over time, completely closing three months after birth.
C. The infant starts to produce adult hemoglobin.
D. All of the above.

14. The placenta releases all of the following hormones EXCEPT

A. progesterone.
B. LH.
C. hCG.
D. estrogen.

Small Group Questions

1. What would happen if a mammalian embryo failed to produce sufficient amounts of human chorionic gonadotropin (hCG) in early pregnancy?

2. Compare and contrast fetal and adult circulation.

3. Why can the allantois be considered an adaptation to terrestrial life?

Explanations to Practice Questions

1. C

The question is asking us to determine the developmental stage with the greatest nuclear-to-cytoplasmic material ratio. During the series of rapid mitotic divisions known as cleavage, the number of cells increases dramatically without a corresponding increase in the amount of cytoplasm. As such, a high ratio of nuclear-to-cytoplasmic material will be found at the stage with the greatest amount of cells. From the given choices, the stage with the greatest number of cells is the blastula. (C) is therefore the correct answer.

2. B

To answer this question, it could be useful to review quickly the embryonic layers. The ectoderm gives rise to the integument (the epidermis, hair, nails, and epithelium of the nose, mouth, and anal canal), the lens of the eye, and the nervous system. The endoderm gives rise to the epithelial linings of the digestive and respiratory tracts and parts of the liver, pancreas, thyroid, and bladder. Finally, from the mesoderm arise the musculoskeletal system, the circulatory system, the excretory system, and the gonads. Therefore, the only incorrect association can be found in (B), since the lens of the eye is derived from the ectoderm.

3. D

The safest way to answer this question is to review all the answer choices and eliminate the ones that do occur immediately after birth. When a baby is born, she can finally breathe air and thus no longer needs fetal hemoglobin to extract oxygen from her mother's blood. Right away, the infant begins to produce adult hemoglobin. Because she starts breathing, resistance in the pulmonary vessels decreases, which causes an increase in blood flow through the lungs. Along with it, as normal blood circulation begins, the foramen ovale snaps closed, the ductus arteriosus and ductus venosus constrict, and the pressure in the left atrium increases. So far, we can eliminate (A), (B), and (C). However, when blood flow through the umbilical cord stops, the blood pressure in the inferior vena cava decreases, causing a decrease in the pressure in the right atrium. (D) states the exact opposite of this, making (D) the correct answer.

4. A

The question is basically asking us when during human pregnancy the brain develops. During the first weeks of gestation, the major organs begin to develop, among them the brain. This explains why it is so dangerous when women who do not know they are pregnant consume alcoholic drinks; even a small amount of alcohol in the first trimester can harm the embryo's brain development, possibly leading to fetal alcohol syndrome. (A), first trimester, is thus the correct answer.

5. B

A rod of mesodermal cells, called the notochord, develops along the longitudinal axis just under the dorsal layer of ectoderm. Through inductive effects from the notochord, the overlying ectoderm starts bending inward and forms a groove on the dorsal surface of the embryo. The dorsal ectoderm will eventually pinch off and develop into the spinal cord and brain. (B) is therefore the correct answer.

6. D

The influence of a specific group of cells on the differentiation of another group of cells is termed *induction*. For example, the eyes are formed through a constant back-and-forth game of induction from the brain on the ectoderm and the ectoderm on the brain, each one influencing the other at different stages of development, until, little by little, all the parts of the eye are formed. (D) is therefore the correct answer.

7. C

Before looking at the answer choices, let's quickly review the different structures that arise from the endoderm. The endoderm is responsible for the differential development of the epithelial linings of the digestive and respiratory tracts (including the lungs), parts of the liver, pancreas, thyroid, and bladder. From the answer choices, the only structure that is not formed from the endoderm is the circulatory system. In fact, the circulatory system is formed from the mesoderm, making (C) the correct answer.

8. C

The main points to remember about fetal hemoglobin are that it has a higher affinity for oxygen than adult hemoglobin and it stops being produced at birth, when the infant can breathe on its own and is capable of making adult hemoglobin. Therefore, the correct answer is (C).

9. D

The bloodstreams of the mother and fetus are not directly connected. Large macromolecules and cells cannot cross the placental barrier. However, smaller molecules, such as ethanol, drugs, and hormones, can cross the placenta. Thus, the mother may have detectable hCG in her blood, but fetal white blood cells should not be found in her bloodstream. CO_2 released during fetal respiration diffuses through the placenta into maternal circulation, so fetal CO_2 would also be found in maternal blood. (D) is therefore the correct answer.

10. B

Glancing at the answer choices, we notice that they can be divided into two groups: half mention the ductus venosus, while the others mention the ductus arteriosus. Let's quickly review the function of each of these shunts in fetal circulation. Since the liver is not yet formed and not yet ready to break down toxins, blood must be shunted away from it. This is accomplished via the ductus venosus,

allowing blood to bypass the liver before converging with the inferior vena cava. In addition, because the fetus obtains oxygen from the mother's blood, a shunt exists to divert blood away from the undeveloped fetal lungs. The ductus arteriosus directs blood from the pulmonary artery to the aorta, in this way preventing blood from entering the lungs. Therefore, (A), (C), and (D) correctly pair the shunt with its respective function. Only (B) is false and, therefore, the answer we are looking for.

11. C

Let's begin by looking at the two adult blood vessels and deciding what type of blood they carry, since adult circulation can seem more familiar than fetal circulation. The pulmonary arteries carry blood from the right ventricle to the lungs, taking deoxygenated blood from the body to the lungs where it can be oxygenated. Similarly, the superior vena cava brings blood from the upper body, such as the head and the brain, and thus contains deoxygenated blood. This leaves choices (A) and (C). In fetal circulation, the umbilical artery carries blood from the infant's body to the placenta, which means that the blood is deoxygenated. By contrast, the umbilical vein carries blood from the placenta to the fetus and, therefore, contains oxygenated blood. (C) is thus the correct answer.

12. D

Let's attack this question by going through each answer choice and eliminating the ones that are true. (A) states that in fetal circulation, blood is oxygenated in the placenta. This is a true statement. In the fetus, the lungs do not oxygenate blood as they do in adult circulation. However, a small amount of blood must and does reach the pulmonary circulation to nourish the developing lungs. Therefore, we can eliminate (B). Next, (C) states that at birth, the blood pressure in the right atrium decreases. Indeed, when the umbilical blood flow stops, the blood pressure in the inferior vena cava decreases, causing a decrease in the pressure in the right atrium. We are left with (D). In fetal circulation, the blood delivered via the aorta will have a lower partial pressure of oxygen than the blood delivered to the lungs. This is because oxygenated and deoxygenated blood mix in the heart through the foramen ovale. Also, the deoxygenated blood bypasses the lungs through the ductus arteriosus, which allows blood to pass from the pulmonary arteries to the aorta. Thus, the blood in the aorta will have a lower oxygen content than the blood delivered to the lungs. (D) contains a false statement and is therefore the correct answer.

13. D

Let's answer this question by reviewing each answer choice and determining whether it is true. If we find two true statements, (D) must be the correct answer, and we no longer have to read the third statement. Similarly, if we find one false statement, then (D) must be incorrect. (A) states that increased left atrial pressure coupled with decreased right atrial pressure causes the foramen ovale to close. This statement is true and important in the healthy development of an infant. If the foramen ovale, ductus arteriosus, and ductus venosus do not close soon after birth, this poses a problem that needs to be fixed through surgery or medication for the infant to thrive. Indeed, (B) must also be a true statement based on the previous explanation. The ductus venosus degenerates over time and, in most infants, is completely closed after three months. (D) must therefore be the correct answer, but let's quickly take a look at (C). The infant starts producing adult hemoglobin soon after birth, and by the end of the first year, very little fetal hemoglobin can be detected in blood. (D) is thus the correct answer.

14. B

During gestation, the placenta functions as an endocrine gland, producing the hormones progesterone, estrogen, and human chorionic gonadotropin (hCG), all of which are essential for maintaining a pregnancy. From the given choices, the only hormone that is not released by the placenta is luteinizing hormone (LH), which is secreted during the normal menstrual cycle by the anterior pituitary to stimulate ovulation. (B) is therefore the correct answer.

6

The Musculoskeletal System

Populations affected by large disasters or traumatic events like wars or earthquakes often serve as fodder for unique medical discoveries. These discoveries may result from conditions of a disaster itself or from the subsequent recovery period. Furthermore, those conditions may be instantaneous (e.g., painful injury) or created over several years (e.g., a change in diet due to famine). During World War II, Nazi Germany bombed London for 57 consecutive days in the beginning of what came to be known as the *Blitzkrieg*, or eight-month Lightning War. Victims of the Blitz, as it is known in London, included those afflicted with a specific set of symptoms: pain and swelling, with accompanying effects of depleted blood volume (shock, weakness, low blood pressure, and decreased urine output). Less obvious was acute kidney failure, which can lead quickly to death when untreated.

What caused the Blitz victims to suffer from these symptoms? Extreme physical trauma to muscles—namely, compression—destroys skeletal muscle tissue. This condition is called rhabdomyolysis (*rhabdo*– refers to the skeleton, *myo*– to muscle, and –*lysis* to breakdown). There are other causes of this extremely painful disorder, such as electric shock, alcohol withdrawal, tetanus, or even extreme physical exercise. The symptoms alert physicians to pinpoint myocardial infarction (heart attack) as the culprit, but if any injuries are documented, rhabdomyolysis is the next suspect.

The products of skeletal muscle dissolution, some of which are toxic, circulate in the blood until they are filtered out. Creatine kinase is one of these products; in fact, rhabdomyolysis is defined as a creatine kinase level five times the normal upper limit. Myoglobin is another. Much like hemoglobin, myoglobin uses heme to carry oxygen. It is not, however, housed within a red blood cell. Thus, an erythrocyte-free urine sample that tests positive for heme points compellingly toward rhabdomyolysis. Myoglobin oxygen reserves are just one of the specialized features of muscles, as we will see in this chapter. Muscles also have unique endoplasmic reticula (called sarcoplasmic reticula) and specialized cell membranes (sarcolemmas). Some muscle cells can even contract without nervous input. In the next few pages, we'll learn all about muscles and their interactions with the body, starting with the skeletal system.

Skeletal System ★★★★☆☆

From Chapter 5, we should recall that the skeleton is derived from the mesoderm (or "means-o-derm"). Two types of skeletons exist: **exoskeletons** and **endoskeletons**. Exoskeletons encase whole organisms and are commonly found in arthropods (e.g., shellfish and insects).

Mnemonic

Endo– means "within" (endoderm, endocytosis). *Exo*– means "outside of" (exocrine, exocytosis). We will see these roots in other chapters and should be sure to remember them for Test Day.

Vertebrates like us have **endoskeletons**. We should take a minute to think about the relative advantages of these systems. What would we like about exoskeletons? Like suits of armor, they protect entire organisms because they surround them completely. However, we can identify one major drawback. Organism growth requires shedding of the exoskeleton (picture lobsters and crabs). Our endoskeletons, on the other hand, are internal; thus, they don't protect our surfaces and organs as well as exoskeletons, but we don't need to shed them as we grow, either.

Figure 6.1

The components of our skeletal system are divided into **axial** and **appendicular** sections (see Figure 6.1). The axial skeleton consists of the skull, vertebral column, and ribcage; it provides the basic central framework for the body. The appendicular skeleton consists of the arms, legs, and pelvic and pectoral girdles that are attached to the axial skeleton for stability. Our skeleton is built much like a skyscraper. The axial skeleton represents the steel beams that make up the basic core of the building and provide the overall shape. The appendicular skeleton includes the smaller beams and concrete, which also provide some structure but ultimately depend on the larger beams for attachment. Both skeleton types are eventually covered by other structures (muscle, connective tissue, and vasculature); similarly, our skyscraper would be fitted with carpets, windows, and lights that go over the steel.

The skeleton is created from two major components: **cartilage** and **bone**.

Cartilage

Back at summer camp, we probably often used pipe cleaners to make some of our arts and crafts projects. Cartilage is similar in that it is softer and more flexible than bone, which we might liken to a strong beam of wood. Cartilage consists of a firm (but elastic) matrix called **chondrin** that is secreted by cells called **chondrocytes**.

From our last chapter, we should recall that much of the fetal skeleton is made up of cartilage. This is highly advantageous, because fetuses need to grow in a cramped environment as well as pass lithely through the birth canal. During development (both pre- and postnatal), much of this cartilage will calcify into bone. Adults have cartilage only in body parts that need a little extra flexibility (external ear, nose, walls of the larynx and trachea, and joints). Degradation of this cartilage, usually in old age, can lead to medical issues like arthritis. Arthritis is painful because a lack of cartilage in joints leads bones to rub directly against one another. One last point we should keep in mind is that cartilage is relatively avascular (without blood and lymphatic vessels) and is not innervated. That's not to say it wouldn't hurt if a heated debate over endosymbiosis led to a punch in the nose! The pain would be transmitted through receptors in the skin and underlying tissue.

Bone

Like our cartilage, bone is also comprised of connective tissue derived from embryonic mesoderm. Bone is much harder than cartilage, which is important because it must support our entire bodies. Although it is quite strong, it is also relatively lightweight. Consider that an average human femur is about 40 times as strong as concrete.

MACROSCOPIC BONE STRUCTURE

Bone's characteristic strength is derived from **compact bone**. It lives up to its name, as it is both strong and compact. The other type of bone structure is **spongy** or **cancellous** bone. Spongy bone is also well named because it looks just like a kitchen sponge. Its lattice structure is visible under microscopy and consists of bony spicules (points) known as **trabeculae**. If we can imagine a honeycomb, then we know exactly

Mnemonic

Simply remembering that the root *chondro–* relates to cartilage will clue us into both the material and the cells that make it up.

Real World

Nonarticular cartilage can grow and repair throughout life. This is why the noses and ears of many older individuals seem larger than the other features on the face.

Real World

An adult human has 206 bones. Over 100 of these are in the feet and hands.

what trabeculae look like. These cavities are filled with **bone marrow**, which may be either **red** or **yellow**. Red marrow is filled with hematopoietic stem cells, which are responsible for generation of all the cells in our blood (see Chapter 9); yellow marrow is composed primarily of fat and is relatively inactive. When patients undergo bone marrow transplants, where do those transplanted cells come from? From a generous donor whose hip marrow was extracted using an extra long needle. Ouch!

Figure 6.2

Bones in the appendicular skeleton are typical **long bones** (see Figure 6.2), which are characterized by cylindrical shafts called **diaphyses** (singular: **diaphysis**) and dilated ends called **epiphyses** (singular: **epiphysis**). The peripheries of the epiphyses and diaphyses are both composed of compact bone, whereas their internal cores differ. Long bone diaphyses are full of marrow. The epiphyses, on the other hand, have a spongy bone core inside their compact bone sheath for more effective dispersion of force at the joints. Separating the epiphysis and diaphysis in each bone is an **epiphyseal plate**, which is a cartilaginous structure and the site of longitudinal growth. Finally, a fibrous sheath called the **periosteum** surrounds the long bone to protect it as well as serve as a site for muscle attachment. Some periosteum cells are capable of differentiating into bone-forming cells; a healthy periosteum is necessary for bone growth and repair.

MICROSCOPIC BONE STRUCTURE

In our last two sections, we mentioned that compact bone is strong but didn't yet discuss where that strength comes from. It comes from the **bone matrix**, which has both organic and inorganic components. The organic components include collagen, glycoproteins, and other peptides. The inorganic components include calcium, phosphate, and hydroxide ions, which harden together to form hydroxyapatite crystals. Minerals such as sodium, magnesium, and potassium are also stored in bone.

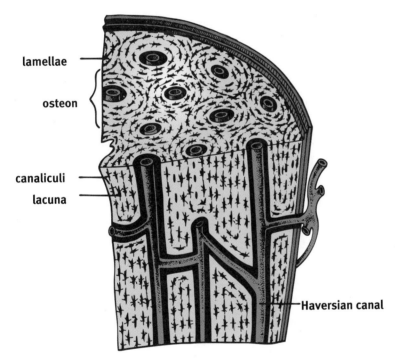

Figure 6.3

Strong bones require uniform distribution of inorganic material. The bony matrix is similarly ordered into structural units known as **osteons** or **Haversian systems** (see Figure 6.3). Each of these osteons encircles a central microscopic channel known as a **Haversian canal**, surrounded by concentric circles of bony matrix called **lamellae**. Remember that tree stump next to your cabin at summer camp? The one on which you and your three-legged race partner engraved your undying love? The Haversian system is the center of the tree stump and the rings are the lamellae that surround it. These canals contain the blood vessels, nerve fibers, and lymph that keep the bone in peak condition. The rings in a tree are not touching; rather, they are

> ### Key Concept
>
> Bone appears to be rigid and static, but it is actually quite dynamic. It is both vascular and innervated, which is why it hurts so much to break one. In addition, bone remains in a vigorous equilibrium between construction and destruction, known as bone remodeling.

> ### Mnemonic
>
> Just as all things cartilage start with *chondro–*, all things bone start with *osteo-*.

spaced out a bit. So, too, are the lamellae in our bone. Interspersed within the matrix are spaces called **lacunae**, which house mature bone cells known as **osteocytes**.

These osteocytes are involved in bone maintenance. Each of the lacunae is interconnected by **canaliculi**, which are little canals that allow for exchange of nutrients and wastes between them and the Haversian canals.

BONE FORMATION (OSSIFICATION)

We mentioned previously that most of the bones in the body are created by the hardening of cartilage. This process is known as **endochondral ossification** (*endo-* means "within", *chondro-* means "cartilage"), and it is responsible for the formation of most of the long bones in the body. Bones may also be formed through **intra-membranous ossification**, in which undifferentiated embryonic connective tissue (**mesenchymal tissue**) is transformed into, and replaced by, bone.

BONE REMODELING

We now can introduce our last two players on the scene: **osteoclasts** and **osteoblasts**. Let's head back to summer camp one more time. On rainy days, we were stuck inside with building blocks. We'd build a large castle, only to have it knocked down by another, less imaginative child who wanted to use the same blocks to build a fortress. We could knock the fortress down and rebuild a slightly different castle, but it would just get knocked down again by someone else. The construction and destruction would continue in a never-ending cycle. Similarly, osteoblasts *build* bone, and osteo-clasts *resorb* bone. These processes together contribute to the constant maintenance of bone. During **bone reformation**, essential ingredients like calcium and phosphate are obtained from the blood. During bone resorption (breakdown), these ions are released into the bloodstream. Endocrine hormones like parathyroid hormone and calcitonin are involved in the remodeling process, as well as other compounds such as vitamin D. The old adage, "Use it or lose it," has its place here, because bone remodeling is affected by exercise and use.

Key Concept

Osteo*blasts* build bone; osteo*clasts* destroy or resorb bone.

Real World

Osteoporosis is the most common bone disease in the United States. It is thought to be the result of increased osteoclast resorption and some concomitant slowing of bone formation, both of which lead to loss of bone mass. Estrogen is believed to help prevent osteoporosis by stimulating osteoblast activity.

DEGRADATION: Osteoclasts release enzymes that dissolve bone, releasing calcium into the bloodstream.

REFORMATION: Osteoblasts build new bone using both organic and inorganic materials.

Figure 6.4

Joints

Before we leave the skeletal system, we need to discuss how the 206 bones in the adult body articulate with one another. Like bone and cartilage, joints are also made of connective tissue and come in two major varieties: **movable and immovable**. Movable joints (see Figure 6.5) work like door hinges and allow for bones to shift relative to one another (think knees and elbows). These joints are strengthened by **ligaments**, which are pieces of fibrous tissue that connect bones to one another, and consist of a **synovial capsule**, which encloses the actual **joint cavity (articular cavity)**. Since all of these structures are solid, we use **synovial fluid** to ease the movement of one structure over the other. Synovial fluid is a lubricant and works just like the oil with which we grease our car's pistons. The **articular cartilage** that we mentioned previously also contributes to the joint by coating the articular surfaces of the bones so that impact is restricted to the lubricated joint cartilage, rather than to the bones. Immovable joints (e.g., in the skull) consist of bones that we would not want to move relative to one another; imagine a brace that we use to join two pieces of wood so that they are held in fixed positions. We definitely want our skull to be fixed in place, as it is protects our brain, the repository of all our Test Day knowledge!

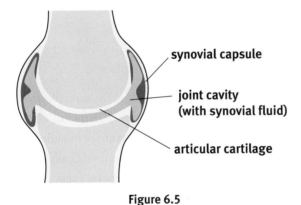

synovial capsule

joint cavity (with synovial fluid)

articular cartilage

Figure 6.5

Now that we have introduced the basic structure of our skyscraper (skeleton), we want to start filling the floors of our building. Let's begin with muscles, which exist in three varieties: **skeletal**, **smooth**, and **cardiac**.

Skeletal Muscle

A great way to relieve some MCAT stress is to take a leisurely walk outside in the sunshine. This is achieved by skeletal muscle, which is innervated by the **somatic** nervous system. Muscles are intricate in their design but are ultimately made up of repeating units (like a polymer in chemistry). We'll start small and build up to a whole muscle.

The basic contractile unit of a muscle is the **sarcomere**. These sarcomeres are then put together end to end to build **myofibrils** (see Figure 6.6).

Figure 6.6

Myofibrils are surrounded by a covering known as the **sarcoplasmic reticulum** (SR; a modified endoplasmic reticulum that contains a great deal of Ca^{2+}). Outside the sarcoplasmic reticulum, we arrive at the **sarcoplasm**, the modified cytoplasm in these cells. As we reach the cell membrane **(sarcolemma)**, we finally have a complete cell. Many myofibrils can be contained within each **myocyte** (muscle cell). Most cells are multinucleate due to the fusion of several embryonic uninucleate cells. These nuclei are usually found at the cell periphery. What we refer to as a "muscle" is simply a parallel arrangement of many of these myocytes. The sarcolemma is capable of propagating an action potential. A system of **T-tubules** is connected to the sarcolemma and oriented perpendicularly to the myofibrils, allowing for ions to flow.

When skeletal muscle is viewed microscopically, it is striated, appearing as if it has stripes. This is due to the alignment of Z-lines (which we'll discuss in a second) and their increased density relative to other structures. Skeletal muscle consists of **red** and **white** fibers. Red muscle fibers (also known as slow twitch) have a high **myoglobin** content and primarily derive their energy aerobically. Myoglobin is a protein similar to hemoglobin, but it consists of a single polypeptide chain. It binds oxygen more tightly than hemoglobin. We will discuss the functional consequence of this in Chapter 9. White fibers (fast twitch) are anaerobic and have much less myoglobin. Based on what we learned in Chapter 3 and the way in which these cells derive their energy, which cells would we expect to be mitochondria-rich and which poor in mitochondria? Red fibers are mitochondria-rich because they derive energy aerobically, and white fibers are mitochondria-poor because they do not use an electron transport chain. White fibers can contract more rapidly but are also easier to fatigue.

The Sarcomere ★★★★☆

STRUCTURE

Before we move into the actual contraction of muscles, let's take a moment to dissect the sarcomere, which we should recall is the basic unit of the muscle fiber. Sarcomeres are made up of **thick** and **thin** filaments. The thick filaments are organized bundles of **myosin**, whereas the thin filaments are made up of **actin** along with two other proteins, **troponin** and **tropomyosin**.

Figure 6.7

Mnemonic

Myosin, the "thicker" word, is composed of thick filament. *Actin*, the "thinner" word, is composed of thin filament. We can also remember that *troponin* and *tropomyosin*, both of which start with *t*, are associated with *acTin*, rather than myosin.

Let's return to our biologist's toolbox (which is getting large at this point) and pull out our handy-dandy electron microscope to visualize some muscular microanatomy (see Figure 6.7). **Z-lines** define the boundaries of each sarcomere (and are responsible for the striated nature of skeletal and cardiac muscles). The **M-line** runs down the center of the sarcomere. The **I-band** is the region containing exclusively thin filaments, whereas the **H-zone** exclusively contains thick filaments. Much as we used *thick* and *thin* to remember the association with myosin and actin, respectively, we can note that the letter *I* is thinner and the letter *H* thicker to help us remember which filament type each refers to (actin or myosin) on Test Day. The **A-band** contains the thick filaments in their entirety, including any overlap with thin filaments. During contraction, the H-zone, I-band, and distance between Z-lines all become smaller, whereas the A-band's size remains constant.

Key Concept

Z-lines, I-band, and H-zone—all of these get smaller or closer together during contraction because they are defined relative to one another. The A-band remains constant because it is defined as the total length of the thick fibers ("A"ll of the thick fibers), regardless of state of contraction.

CONTRACTION

Contraction of muscle requires a series of coordinated steps that are repeated to induce further shortening. As we examine each step, let's keep the key players in mind, one of which we saw in previous chapters and will continue to see: ATP.

Initiation

A good MCAT study session should involve a midnight ice cream break. When do we decide we're ready for it? Hunger pangs from our stomach are a pretty good message that we need a snack. The nervous system will send this signal via a **motor neuron**. This signal will travel down the neuron until it reaches the **nerve terminal (synaptic bouton)**, where the release of neurotransmitter (e.g., acetylcholine) into the **synapse** results in contraction of the muscle due to binding of the neurotransmitter to its receptor on the muscle. This connection point between nerve and muscle is aptly named the **neuromuscular junction**. If enough acetylcholine binds to the muscle cell, the muscle will be depolarized (action potential generation), and the sarcolemma's permeability will increase.

Shortening of the Sarcomere

Now that our muscle has its signal, how do we get it to contract in a coordinated fashion? The action potential generated at the neuromuscular junction will be conducted along the sarcolemma and T-system and then transmitted into the muscle fiber itself. If we recall that the sarcoplasmic reticulum is full of Ca^{2+} and electrically responsive to depolarization, we can predict that this will result in the massive release of calcium ions from the SR. Calcium will bind to troponin, causing tropomyosin to shift and exposing the **myosin-binding sites** on actin (see Figure 6.8). Muscle cells need calcium the same way that we need a ticket to board an airplane. With our calcium ticket, we're allowed to pass through security (tropomyosin shift), exposing the gates (myosin binding sites), which allow us to get to our destination (actin and myosin binding that result in movement).

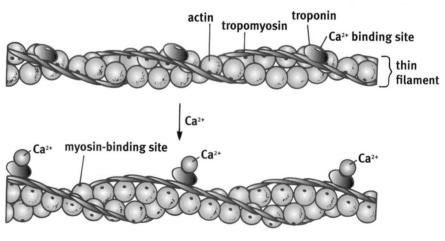

Figure 6.8

The free globular heads of the myosin molecules move toward and bind the exposed sites on actin. The newly formed actin–myosin cross bridges then allow actin to pull on myosin, which draws the thin filaments to the center of the H-zone and shortens the sarcomere (see Figure 6.9).

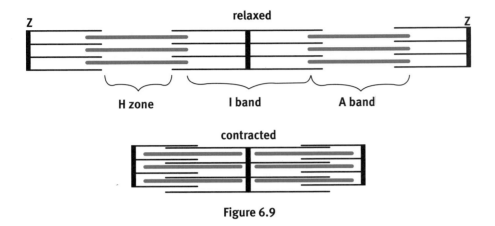

Figure 6.9

ATPase activity in the myosin heads provides the energy for the power stroke and results in dissociation of actin from myosin. The myosin then resets itself by binding another molecule of ATP and is free to bind another actin molecule.

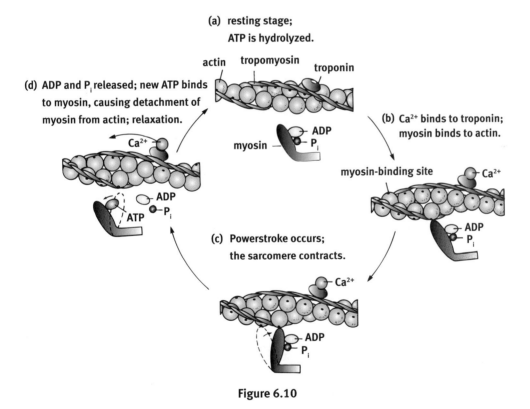

Figure 6.10

Relaxation

Once the SR's receptors are no longer stimulated, calcium levels will fall. The SR tightly controls intracellular calcium so that muscles are contracted only when necessary. The products of ATP hydrolysis that were released from the myosin head during the power stroke leave room for a new ATP molecule to bind, allowing for dissociation of myosin from the thin filament. Once the myosin and actin disconnect, the sarcomere can return to its original width. Without calcium, the myosin-binding sites will be covered by tropomyosin and prevent contraction. After death, ATP is no longer produced. Myosin heads cannot detach from actin, making it impossible for muscles to relax. This is known as rigor mortis.

STIMULUS AND MUSCLE RESPONSE

With any luck, we all have study buddies who won't actually throw a punch if we disagree on endosymbiosis. Could that punch break a nose? Power is directly related to how much force we generate from the muscle. Let's take a quick look at how stimulation is coupled to muscle response.

Stimulus Intensity

Muscle cells (like nerves with action potentials) exhibit what is known as an **all-or-none** response; either they respond completely or not at all. For muscle cells to respond, stimuli must reach a **threshold value**. For example, imagine a long car trip with an annoying sister. It might be fun (maybe just to see what happens) to poke her in the arm. At first nothing will happen; she'll just ignore it. After several pokes, an annoyance threshold will be attained, and she'll turn around and retaliate (complete response).

The strength of this individual response by a muscle fiber cannot be adjusted, because the only options are all or nothing. Rather, muscles control overall force by the number of fibers they recruit to respond. Maximal response occurs when all fibers are stimulated to contract simultaneously. Instead of a single punch (one contraction or simple twitch), perhaps this sister is so annoyed that she ends up initiating a no-holds-barred throwdown once the car is stopped (maximal response).

Tonus refers to muscles in a constant state of low-level contraction. It is essential for some voluntary and involuntary muscles.

Simple Twitch

A simple twitch is the response of a single muscle fiber to a brief stimulus at or above the threshold. It consists of a **latent period, contraction period, and relaxation period**. The latent period is the time between reaching threshold (enough pokes) and onset of contraction (getting punched). It is during this time that the action potential spreads along the muscle and allows for Ca^{2+} to be released from the SR. After this period, the muscle will be unresponsive to stimuli. This is known as the **refractory period** of which there are two types: **absolute** and **relative**. During the absolute refractory period, no amount of stimulus (sister poking) will generate a response because the muscle is restoring its resting potential. During the relative period, the muscle can still be activated, but a higher than normal stimulus is required.

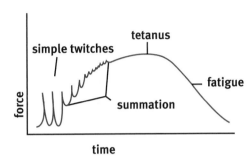

simple twitch (single fiber)

summation and tetanus (whole muscle)

Figure 6.11

Summation and Tetanus

If we expose our muscle fibers to frequent and prolonged stimulation, they will have insufficient time to relax. The contractions will begin to combine, becoming stronger and more prolonged. This is known as **frequency summation** (see Figure 6.11). If we continue to poke our sister often, her punches back will come closer and closer together and become stronger. Eventually, the contractions may become so frequent that there is no time for the muscle to relax. This is known as **tetanus** and is stronger than a simple muscle fiber twitch. Prolonged tetanus will result in muscle fatigue.

Smooth Muscle ★★★☆☆

Smooth muscle is responsible for involuntary action and is controlled by the **autonomic nervous system**. It is found in the digestive tract, bladder, uterus, blood vessel walls, and many other locations. Smooth muscle cells have single centrally placed nuclei. Just like skeletal muscle, they contain actin and myosin, but those fibers are not organized in a striated fashion. Smooth and skeletal muscles also contract in the same way. However, smooth muscle is capable of longer and more sustained contractions. Moreover, it can contract without nervous system input in what is known as **myogenic activity**.

Cardiac Muscle ★★★☆☆

Our last type of muscle is **cardiac muscle**. This is the hydraulic lift that allows the elevators and transport systems to travel up and down inside the skyscraper (which we will learn more about in Chapter 9). Cardiac fibers' characteristics are a conglomerate of the properties of smooth and skeletal muscle. They are primarily uninucleate

Key Concept

Skeletal Muscle
- Striated
- Voluntary
- Somatic innervation
- Many nuclei per cell
- Ca^{2+} required for contraction

Cardiac Muscle
- Striated
- Involuntary
- Autonomic innervation
- 1–2 nuclei per cell
- Ca^{2+} required for contraction

Smooth Muscle
- Nonstriated
- Involuntary
- Autonomic innervation
- One nucleus per cell
- Ca^{2+} required for contraction

and involuntary like smooth muscle, but they are striated like skeletal muscle. Like both other types of muscle, calcium is required for contraction. Cardiac muscle may also exhibit myogenic activity. Knowing the basic differences between muscle types may translate into quick points on Test Day. Table 6.1 summarizes these differences.

Table 6.1. Muscle Types

Smooth Muscle	Cardiac Muscle	Skeletal Muscle
• Nonstriated	• Striated	• Striated
• 1 nucleus per cell	• 1–2 nuclei per cell	• Multinucleated cells
• Involuntary/Autonomic nervous system	• Involuntary/Autonomic nervous system	• Voluntary/Somatic nervous system
• Smooth continuous contractions	• Strong forceful contractions	• Strong forceful contractions

Energy Reserves

CREATINE PHOSPHATE

Muscles require energy in order to function. Muscles can generate ATP from several sources: fatty acids, glycogen, and glucose (recall Chapter 3 and see Chapter 7). In addition, energy can be derived from a high-energy compound known as **creatine phosphate**. During times of plenty, we store away creatine phosphate by transferring a phosphate from ATP to creatine. This process can be reversed during muscle use to rapidly generate ATP from ADP. It is advantageous to have creatine phosphate reserves, because they allow for immediate creation of ATP that would otherwise need to be formed from glycolysis or the TCA cycle.

$$\text{Creatine} + \text{ATP} \leftrightarrow \text{creatine phosphate} + \text{ADP}$$

MYOGLOBIN

If we think back to Chapter 3, we learned that we could generate more energy by aerobic rather than anaerobic metabolism. However, what was absolutely required? Oxygen. Myoglobin, which is found in muscle and similar in function to hemoglobin, binds oxygen and holds on to it (more tightly than hemoglobin). As exercising muscles run out of oxygen, we can use myoglobin's reserves to keep aerobic metabolism going. Once we exhaust these reserves, we'll have to ferment the remaining pyruvate to regenerate NAD^+ and start glycolysis again.

Bridge

Remember that the lactic acid from fermentation can be converted back into energy-producing intermediates once sufficient levels of oxygen become available. This process occurs in the liver and is known as the Cori cycle (Chapter 3).

Connective Tissue

Connective tissue is rightly named in that its purpose is to bind and support other tissues. Much as we might use nails and glue and screws to bind the floors of our skyscraper together, connective tissue holds the body together.

Connective tissue is composed of a sparsely scattered population of cells contained in an amorphous ground substance that may be liquid, jellylike, or solid. Loose connective tissue is found throughout the body. It attaches epithelium to underlying tissues and is the packing material that holds organs in place. It contains proteinaceous fibers of three types: **collagenous fibers**, which are composed of collagen and have great tensile strength (think nails and screws); **elastic fibers**, which are composed of elastin and endow connective tissue with resilience (think of glue, which can expand and contract in building joints); and **reticular fibers**, which are branched, tightly woven fibers that join connective tissue to adjoining tissue. There are two major cell types in loose connective tissue: **fibroblasts**, which secrete substances that are components of extracellular fibers, and **macrophages**, which engulf bacteria and dead cells via phagocytosis (recall Chapter 1).

Dense connective tissue is connective tissue with a high proportion of collagenous fibers. The fibers are organized into parallel bundles that give the fibers great tensile strength, just like the woven steel cable bundles, which hold up the Golden Gate Bridge in San Francisco. Dense connective tissue forms **tendons**, which attach muscle to bone, and **ligaments**, which hold bones together at the joints.

> **Mnemonic**
>
> We have already seen the root *lig–* in ligaments, which connect bone to bone. We also see it in DNA *ligase*, which joins parts of the sugar phosphate backbone in DNA. Again, word roots will help us with unfamiliar vocabulary on the MCAT.

Muscle-Bone Interactions

Just as the multiple systems in our skyscraper must interact, locomotion depends on interactions between the skeletal and muscular systems. If a given muscle (including associated joints) is attached to two bones, contraction of the muscle will cause only one of the two bones to move. The end of the muscle attached to the stationary bone is called the **origin**; in limb muscles, it corresponds to the **proximal** end. The end of the muscle attached to the bone that moves during contraction is called the **insertion**; in limb muscles, the insertion corresponds to the **distal** end.

Often, our muscles work in antagonistic pairs; one relaxes while the other contracts. Such is the case in the arm, where the biceps and triceps work antagonistically. When we move our hand toward our shoulder, the biceps contract and the triceps relax; when we move our hand down again, the biceps relax and the triceps contract (see Figure 6.12). We should take a moment to discuss why this antagonism occurs. We spent a good bit of time discussing muscle contraction, but haven't yet mentioned muscle elongation. It's because muscles don't have an elongation function; the contraction of the antagonistic muscle will lengthen the paired muscle (e.g., biceps contracts, triceps elongates). Note that elongation is different from relaxation. All muscles can relax when the myosin heads and actin are unbound. There are also **synergistic** muscles, which assist the principal muscles during movement.

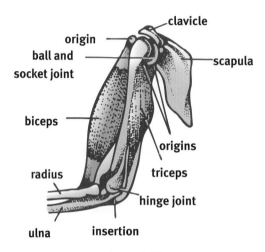

Figure 6.12

Muscles also may be classified by the type of movements they coordinate. A **flexor** muscle will contract to decrease the angle of a joint (e.g., the biceps will flex the elbow joint), whereas an **extensor** muscle will contract to straighten the joint (e.g., the action of the triceps on the elbow). An **abductor** moves a part of the body away from the body's midline; an **adductor** moves a part of the body toward the midline.

Conclusion

This chapter introduced us to two organ systems that work in close concert with one another. We began our discussion with the skeletal system, focusing on bone's properties and functions. A brief foray into joints led us to discuss the muscular system in greater detail. Striated muscles (skeletal and cardiac) have defined sarcomeres, whereas smooth muscle does not. Cardiac and smooth muscles are under involuntary control, whereas skeletal muscle usage is voluntary. Muscle contraction depends on the presence of ATP and calcium, and multiple energy reserves are available to replenish muscles when necessary. We concluded our chapter with a discussion on the interactions between muscle and bone, as they work together to allow us movement.

CONCEPTS TO REMEMBER

- [ ] Cartilage, bone, ligaments, and tendons are all connective tissues. Muscle is contractile tissue.

- [ ] Cartilage is made by chondrocytes and serves as a flexible building medium.

- [ ] Bones may be either compact or spongy. The type depends on the location and specific purpose of the bone.

- [ ] Compact bone is filled with bone marrow, which may be red or yellow. Red marrow is important for hematopoeisis.

- [ ] Bones consist of both organic and inorganic components. Complex microscopic anatomical structures (e.g., Haversian canals) allow for bones to receive nutrients for the organic components.

- [ ] Joints are the juxtaposition of two or more bones. They may be movable or immovable and are often associated with a cartilaginous lining.

- [ ] Muscles may be divided into three major categories: skeletal, cardiac, and smooth.

- [ ] The sarcomere is the basic functional unit of all muscle.

- [ ] Contraction of muscle occurs in an all-or-none fashion analogous to the action potential of a neuron. Increased force is due to increased muscle fiber recruitment, not the increase of force of any one individual fiber's contraction.

- [ ] The interaction of muscles and bones is what allows for locomotion. Muscles are often paired antagonistically such that one lengthens while the other contracts.

Practice Questions

Questions 1, 2, and 3 are based on the following diagram.

1. During muscle contraction, which of the following regions decrease(s) in length?

  A. 2 only
  B. 3 only
  C. 4 only
  D. 2, 3, and 4

2. Region 1 refers to

  A. the thick filaments only.
  B. the thin filaments only.
  C. the A band.
  D. the I band.

3. Which region represents one sarcomere?

  A. 1
  B. 2
  C. 3
  D. 4

4. With which of the following molecules does Ca^{2+} released from the sarcoplasmic reticulum bind?

  A. Myosin
  B. Actin
  C. Troponin
  D. Tropomyosin

5. Which of the following cells is correctly coupled with its definition?

  A. Osteoblasts—bone cells involved in the secretion of bone matrix
  B. Osteoclasts—immature bone cells
  C. Osteocytes—multinucleate cells actively involved in bone resorption
  D. Chondrocytes—undifferentiated bone marrow cells

6. You are looking at a right leg X-ray of a child whose right femur has slowed its growth and is below the average length for a child of this age. To which region of the bone should you pay particular attention to see if there are any abnormalities?

  A. Diaphysis
  B. Epiphyses
  C. Epiphyseal plate
  D. Periosteum

7. Which of the following INCORRECTLY pairs the type of fiber with its definition?

  A. Red fibers—slow-twitching
  B. Red fibers—high levels of myoglobin
  C. White fibers—fast-twitching
  D. White fibers—high levels of myoglobin

8. When the knee moves back and forth as a person walks, what keeps the surfaces of the leg bones from rubbing against each other?

  A. The articular cartilage
  B. The epiphyses
  C. The periosteum
  D. A sheath of smooth muscle

9. When a muscle fiber is subjected to very frequent stimuli,

    A. an oxygen debt is incurred.
    B. a muscle tonus is generated.
    C. the contractions combine in a process known as summation.
    D. the threshold value is reached.

10. To facilitate the process of birth, the infant's head is somewhat flexible. This flexibility is given in part by the two fontanelles, which are soft spots of connective tissue on the infant's skull. With time, these fontanelles will ossify through a process known as

    A. endochondral ossification.
    B. intramembranous ossification.
    C. resorption.
    D. longitudinal growth.

11. When a muscle is attached to two bones, usually only one of the bones moves. The part of the muscle attached to the stationary bone is referred to as

    A. origin.
    B. proximal.
    C. distal.
    D. insertion.

12. Which type of muscle is always multinucleated?

    I. Cardiac muscle
    II. Skeletal muscle
    III. Smooth muscle

    A. I only
    B. II only
    C. III only
    D. I and II only

13. Which type of muscle has myogenic activity?

    I. Cardiac muscle
    II. Skeletal muscle
    III. Smooth muscle

    A. I only
    B. II only
    C. III only
    D. I and III only

14. Red bone marrow is involved in erythrocyte function, whereas yellow bone marrow

    A. is involved in leukocyte formation.
    B. is involved in draining lymph.
    C. is involved in spicule formation.
    D. contains adipose tissue.

15. Which of the following statements regarding the periosteum is INCORRECT?

    A. The periosteum serves as the site of attachment of bone to muscle.
    B. Cells of the periosteum differentiate into osteoblasts.
    C. The periosteum is a fibrous sheath that surrounds long bones.
    D. None of the above

Small Group Questions

1. Contrast the ways by which chondrocytes and osteocytes are nourished.

2. Explain how rigor mortis occurs.

Explanations to Practice Questions

1. D

We are given a diagram of a sarcomere and asked to determine which regions shorten during muscle contraction. Glancing at the answer choices, we notice that we are only interested in regions 2, 3, and 4. Region 2 refers to the I band, formed only of thin actin filaments. During muscle contraction, the I band reduces in size as the thick filaments overlap the thin filaments. Region 3 refers to the H zone, formed only of thick myosin filaments. During contraction, this region also decreases in length as the thin filaments overlap the thick filaments. Finally, region 4 on the diagram refers to the area between the Z lines, which defines the boundary of a single sarcomere. During muscle contraction, as the sarcomere shortens, the Z lines come closer together, so region 4 also decreases in length. As such, all of these three regions decrease in length during muscle contraction, making (D) the correct answer.

2. C

Looking at the diagram, we notice that region 1 contains both thick and thin filaments overlapping one over the other. This region refers to the A band and is measured from one end to the other of the thick filaments. This is also the only portion of the sarcomere that does not change length during muscle contraction. (C) is the correct answer.

3. D

One sarcomere is represented by the area between two vertical lines, referred to as the Z lines. In addition, the Z lines anchor the thin filaments. In the diagram, a sarcomere is therefore defined by region 4, making (D) the correct answer. The sarcomere is also the contractile unit in striated muscle cells.

4. C

Calcium is released from the sarcoplasmic reticulum into the sarcoplasm. It binds the troponin molecules on the thin filaments, causing the strands of tropomyosin to shift, thereby exposing the myosin-binding sites on the filaments. Thus, (C) is the correct answer.

5. A

Let's quickly define each one of the four cells discussed in the answer choices. Osteoblasts are bone cells involved in the secretion of bone matrix, as (A) states. Osteoclasts are large, multinucleated cells involved in bone resorption. Osteocytes are mature osteoblasts that eventually became surrounded by their matrix and whose primary role is bone maintenance. Finally, chondrocytes are cells that secrete chondrin, an elastic matrix that makes up cartilage. Only (A) couples the type of cell with its definition and is therefore the correct answer.

6. C

This question is basically asking us where exactly longitudinal growth occurs in bones. The most likely site of abnormalities in this child's femur is the epiphyseal plate, a disk of cartilaginous cells separating the diaphysis from the epiphysis. The epiphyseal plate is the site of longitudinal growth. (C) is thus the correct answer.

7. D

Glancing at the answer choices, we realize that our task is to characterize the two types of fibers, red and white. Red fibers are slow-twitching fibers that have high levels of myoglobin and many mitochondria. They derive their energy from aerobic respiration and are capable of sustained vigorous activity. In general, marathon runners have more red fibers. White fibers, on the other hand, are fast-twitching fibers and contain lower levels of myoglobin and fewer mitochondria. Because of their composition, they derive more of their energy anaerobically and fatigue more easily. Short distance runners usually have more white fibers. From the given choices, the only one that incorrectly pairs the type of fiber with its characteristic is (D).

8.   A

The articular surfaces of the bones are covered with a layer of smooth articular cartilage. In addition, the joints contain a clear, viscous liquid called synovial fluid, which lubricates the surfaces that glide past each other, preventing the bones from rubbing. (A) is therefore the correct answer.

9.   C

When a muscle fiber is subjected to very frequent stimuli, the muscle cannot fully relax. The contractions begin to combine, becoming stronger and more prolonged. This is known as frequency summation. (C) therefore is the correct answer.

10.   B

The question is basically asking us for the name of the ossification process that occurs in the skull. This is known as intramembranous ossification, where mesenchymal cells directly create bone matrix, as stated in (B).

11.   A

The part of the muscle that is attached to the stationary bone is referred to as the origin, as (A) indicates. In limb muscles, the origin corresponds to the proximal end. The part of the muscle that is attached to the bone that moves during contraction is called the insertion. In limb muscles, this corresponds to the distal end.

12.   B

The only type of muscle that is always multinucleate is skeletal muscle, making (B) the correct answer. Cardiac muscle may contain one or two centrally located nuclei, so statement I is incorrect. Smooth muscle, on the other hand, only has one centrally located nucleus.

13.   D

Myogenic activity refers to the ability of a muscle to contract reflexively without nervous stimulation. Smooth and cardiac muscle both possess myogenic activity. (D) is therefore the correct answer.

14.   D

Yellow marrow is inactive and largely infiltrated by adipose tissue, making (D) the correct answer.

15.   D

The periosteum, a fibrous sheath that surrounds long bones, is the site of attachment to muscle tissue. Some periosteum cells are capable of differentiating into bone-forming cells called osteoblasts. Choices (A), (B), and (C) are therefore true statements about the periosteum and can be eliminated. Thus, (D) is the correct answer.

Digestion

In the connoisseurial world of coffee consumers, no coffee is rarer or more prized than Kopi Luwak, also known as Civet coffee. Only one thousand pounds of this exquisite bean are released into the world's coffee market each year. It sells for an astonishing $160 to $600 per pound! High-end cafés that are able to procure a small quantity for their customers may charge between $50 and $100 per cup of this luxurious brew. You might be wondering what could possibly be so special about these beans to justify (or at least explain) the breathtaking prices. We can assure you that it is nothing close to what you might be thinking. No, it's not the variety of the bean itself, or the growing conditions, or anything related to the process of roasting or brewing the beans. Brace yourself, and hold your nose, because you're about to go where you would have least expected.

In the native language of Indonesia, where this coffee originates, *kopi* means "coffee" and *luwak* is the local name given to the Asian palm civet, a cat-sized mammal native to southeast Asia and southern China. Its diet consists of fruits such as mango and rambutan, palm flower sap, small insects, and even small mammals. It also happens to enjoy perfectly ripe red coffee cherries (berries). The civets eat the cherries, and as the fruits pass through their digestive tracts, the flesh surrounding the coffee beans is digested but the beans themselves are not, because civets lack the enzymes necessary for digesting the hard beans. Since the beans are not digested, they pass through the intestinal tract and are defecated. At this point, we are forced to acknowledge the truth of the saying, "One's trash is another's treasure," for the defecated beans are collected, washed (thank goodness for small things!), and lightly roasted, at which point they are ready for market.

Those who drink Civet coffee insist that it is not for mere shock value that they do so; rather, they claim that the digestive enzymes in the civet's gut penetrate into the hard bean and break down the proteins that are responsible for the bitter flavor normally present in coffee. As a result of these enzymatic activities, they claim, the "processed" beans yield a brew that is sweeter, richer, and altogether unique—and worth every dollar spent. We don't know about you, but we will stick to our large half-caf, low-fat, no-foam soy vanilla lattés, thank you very much.

As we continue our survey of organ systems, we come to the digestive system. Although this chapter is brief, it is jam-packed with information we can use to our advantage on Test Day. As with our previous reviews of other organ systems, we will start with a basic anatomical overview of the organs of digestion (including accessory organs) and then move on to discuss how these organs function to provide overall nutrition to the organism. This structure-function approach will keep us focused on the most important information for Test Day. The digestive system allows us to take in complex compounds in the foods that we eat and drink and reduce them to smaller, simpler compounds that can be absorbed from the gut; transported to the tissues by the circulatory system; and used by the cells for energy, growth, development, maintenance, and other essential activities.

We have already imagined the system of beams and concrete in a skyscraper as analogous to the musculoskeletal system of the human body. Let's continue with this imagery by considering the manner in which bulk supplies are brought into a city office building and subsequently broken down into smaller units for distribution and use. Many large buildings have a loading dock where pallets of supplies are received. Certainly, this office building will receive deliveries of supplies such as pens, pencils, and paper in bulk, but no one office worker is going to need 100 pens or 5,000 sheets of paper in a single day. Instead, the distribution center (which we might consider the digestive system of this building) will break these large bulk shipments down into the amounts that can be used by the people working inside the building. Indeed, once broken down into the smaller units, the pens and paper and toner for the copiers will even be transported from the loading dock and distribution center (the building's gut) to all the different offices, departments, and building inhabitants through the elevators, hallways, and staircases, which we might characterize as the building's circulatory system.

The foodstuffs that we eat, and from which we derive nutrition, are made of carbohydrates, proteins, and fats along with vitamins, minerals, and water. The large organic molecules are the bulk shipments we receive into our body, but these must be broken down into smaller units in our digestive system for the cells of our body to use and benefit from the energy stored in our food. For example, the glucose molecules that are the substrate of cellular respiration (see Chapter 3) originate from the carbohydrates in our diet. These carbohydrates (called *polysaccharides*) must first be digested into monomeric forms (called *monosaccharides*) and then absorbed from the digestive system into the circulatory system by which they are delivered to the tissues and cells of the body.

Anatomical Considerations

The sort of digestion that we considered in Chapter 3, such as glucose breakdown, and the digestion of compounds within lysosomes is a form of **intracellular digestion**. We are now concerned with **extracellular digestion**, which occurs outside the cells' borders. In humans, digestion occurs within the lumen of the **alimentary canal**, as it does for all mammals. This canal is actually "outside" the body in that the space contained within it is outside cell borders: Between the mouth and anus is one long continuous tube, sectioned off by sphincters. One could argue that the difference between humans and cannoli is minimal, except, of course, that cannoli are much more delicious.

The human digestive tract, as alluded to earlier, has specialized sections with different functional roles. The most basic functional distinction is that between **digestion** and **absorption**. Digestion involves the breakdown of food into its constituent organic molecules: lipids (fats) into free fatty acids, starches (carbohydrates) into monosaccharides, and proteins into amino acids. Digestion can be subdivided into mechanical and chemical processes. Mechanical digestion is the physical breakdown of large food particles into smaller food particles but does not involve the breakage of chemical bonds. Chemical digestion is the enzymatic cleavage of chemical bonds (e.g., the peptide bond of proteins or the glycosidic bond of starches). Absorption involves the transport of products of digestion from the digestive tract into the circulatory system for distribution to the body's tissues and cells. Our digestive tract begins with the **oral cavity**, followed by the **pharynx**, **esophagus**, **stomach**, **small intestine**, and **large intestine**. In addition, there are the salivary glands and accessory organs such as the **pancreas**, **liver**, and **gall bladder**.

Epithelium

If we were to look at our own body (using the microscope from the biologist's toolbox), we could see that our exterior surfaces (e.g., skin, tongue, inner eyelids, nasal cavities) as well as the interior surfaces we can't visualize directly (lungs, and gastrointestinal and urinary tracts) are covered with continuous sheets of epithelial cells. These constitute a first border and primary protection against the outside world. For this purpose, these cells are tightly joined and may also be ciliated. We will see examples of this ciliation in both this chapter and Chapter 8, when we discuss the respiratory system. In most of our body cavities (e.g., nasal cavities, inner eyelids, mouth, gastrointestinal tract), these epithelia are known as **mucous membranes**. Our skin and other epithelial linings help us by preventing fluid loss as well as by allowing for selective absorption of materials that our bodies require, especially in the digestive tract. Because we want to be sure that our epithelium doesn't escape from us (think cartoon characters being literally scared out of their skin), it is bound to a connective tissue layer known as the **basement membrane**. This sort of structure is analogous to the foundation a house is built on to give it stability. In the digestive tract, the epithelium that is attached to the basement membrane is replaced every few days, due to the harsh conditions (e.g., corrosive environments or extreme temperatures) to which the epithelium is exposed.

We can classify different epithelia according to the number of layers they have and the shape of their cells. You shouldn't worry too much about remembering all the types for the MCAT, as that will be a medical school focus. Instead, you should know that there are different types and that they can serve different purposes. Let's start with layers. **Simple** refers to one layer, **stratified** means multiple layers, **and**

Key Concept

Although all of these tissue types have epithelium, we should be careful not to confuse this with their embryological origin. In adults, epithelia are developed from all three germ layers. The epithelium of the skin is derived from ectoderm; the epithelium of blood vessels is derived from mesoderm; the epithelium of the GI tract is derived from endoderm.

pseudostratified means that it looks like multiple layers due to differences in cell height but is really just one.

Turning to shape, cells may be **cuboidal**, **columnar**, and **squamous**. We can think of the first two using the root of the word. Cuboidal cells look like the sugar cubes we might put in our coffee (one lump or two?), whereas columnar cells look like the columns of buildings. Squamous cells are scalelike, much as we might see on a snake or lizard. In fact, Squamata is the name of the order of scaled reptiles that includes snakes and lizards. Now that we have the basic definitions out of the way and know the names of the structures in digestion, let's examine Figure 7.1 and take a walkthrough of the digestive system. As we do, if we ever get lost, we can just glance back at our figure to become reoriented. One critical point that we should consider with each organ in this system is its role in digestion.

Figure 7.1

Oral Cavity ★★★★☆☆

It all starts here. We might think of the mouth as being the loading dock in our office building where boxes of supplies are taken in. The mouth can carry out both **mechanical** and **chemical digestion**. Mechanical digestion in the mouth, in a process called **mastication**, involves the breaking up of large food particles into smaller particles by using the teeth, tongue, and lips—much as workers on the loading dock will begin to unpack the larger boxes from the truck. This is an important first step in the digestion process. What would be the advantage in doing this, since the chemical bonds in the food are not broken? For a hint, think back to our discussion of the early stages of embryology when the cell divides rapidly after fertilization. The cells increase their surface area to volume ratio to allow for greater gas and nutrient exchange across the cell membrane. The results of mastication are similar: Mechanical digestion increases the surface area of the food particles for more efficient chemical digestion.

Chemical digestion through enzymatic activity (those enzymes from Chapter 2 keep making an appearance) allows for breakage of the chemical bonds that store the actual food energy (remember ATP?). The salivary glands in our mouth secrete saliva, which aids mechanical digestion by moistening and lubricating the food. If you have ever swallowed a cracker or tortilla chip too fast, and experienced painful scratching as it moved down your esophagus, you know that saliva is important. In addition, saliva (secreted from the salivary glands in response to nervous system signals that sense the presence of food in the oral cavity) contains **salivary amylase**, also known as **ptyalin**, and **lipase**. Ptyalin is capable of hydrolyzing starch into smaller sugars (maltose and dextrin), whereas lipase catalyzes the hydrolysis of lipids. The amount of chemical digestion that occurs in the mouth is minimal, though, because the food does not stay in the mouth for long. Our muscular **tongue** forms the food into a **bolus**, which is forced back to the pharynx and swallowed.

Pharynx ★★☆☆☆☆

The pharynx is the cavity that leads from the mouth and nose to the esophagus. You might also recognize that the pharynx has a connection to the larynx, which is a part of the respiratory tract. How can we prevent food from getting into the respiratory tract? We make use of our **epiglottis**, which folds down and covers the trachea during swallowing (see also Chapter 8). Failure of this mechanism can lead to choking.

Key Concept

The chemical digestion of carbohydrates is initiated in the mouth but is completed in the small intestine. Salivary amylase (active in the mouth) and pancreatic amylase (active in the small intestine) have the same function.

Real World

If you chew on a plain cracker long enough without swallowing, the cracker will start to taste sweet, as salivary amylase begins to hydrolyze the complex carbohydrates (starches) in the cracker into disaccharides such as maltose. These compounds interact with receptors on our taste buds, leading to the sensation of sweetness. The next time you take an MCAT study break, you should feel free to try this experiment, not only to provide you with brain power in the form of maltose and dextrin that your cells can convert to glucose but also to drive home an MCAT concept: Digestion . . . sweet!

Esophagus

The esophagus serves as the connection from the mouth to the stomach, much as there might be a conveyer system to move supplies around the loading dock in our office building. The esophagus is a muscular tube that starts out with striated muscle and transitions into smooth muscle in the thorax. What does this mean in terms of control? The majority of the esophagus (and most of the rest of the gastrointestinal tract, for that matter) is under involuntary control through the autonomic nervous system. Only the upper third of the esophagus, with its striated skeletal muscle, is under voluntary motor control. You can initiate a swallow, but the continuation of that muscular contraction in the form of **peristalsis** is involuntary. At no point is the involuntary nature of peristalsis more evident than when the direction of contraction reverses. Try as you might, there is no stopping a digestive system that insists on expelling its contents through the same oral cavity by which those contents entered the system.

The swallow initiated in the muscles of the oropharynx continues into the smooth muscles of the esophagus as the progressive contractions known as peristalsis. These contractions form waves that continue throughout the gastrointestinal tract and push the food through the tube. The bolus doesn't just fall down the esophagus with a passive reliance on gravity; rather, it is actively pushed, propelled, and squeezed from one region of the digestive tract to the next. This is most evidenced by the fact that if you eat or drink something while hanging upside down, the food or drink are moved against gravity into your stomach rather than falling or flowing out of your mouth and/or nose. As the bolus approaches the stomach, a muscular ring known as the **lower esophageal sphincter (cardiac sphincter)** opens to allow the passage of food.

> **Real World**
>
> Weakness in the lower esophageal sphincter can lead to classic heartburn after eating. As food and acid reflux into the lower esophagus, irritating the less protected mucosa, pain receptors are stimulated. The location of the sphincter, right behind the heart, leads to this common misnomer.

Stomach

Recall from Chapter 3 that we have three main energy sources: carbohydrates, proteins, and fats. The chemical digestion of carbohydrates and fats is initiated in the mouth. No mechanical or chemical digestion takes place in the esophagus (except for the continued enzymatic activity initiated in the mouth by the salivary enzymes). Now we come to our first major site of digestion. Let's turn to the stomach and see what it can do.

We might not think of our stomach as a storage organ, but it has a capacity of about two liters (think of that bottle of soda you might drink while studying for the MCAT) and is muscular. In humans, the stomach is located on the left side of the upper abdomen under the diaphragm (see Chapter 8). You are probably already aware that the stomach uses acid and enzymes to digest food in a fairly harsh environment.

So what would we expect of the mucosa here? It is quite thick, to protect the stomach from autodigestion.

The stomach mucosa contains the **gastric glands** and the **pyloric glands**. The gastric glands respond to signals from the brain, which are activated by the sight, taste, and smell of food. Just as our mouth waters when we see a meal, so too do our gastric glands. These glands are composed of three cell types: **mucous cells**, **chief cells**, and **parietal cells**. The function of the mucous cells is simple to remember: They produce the mucus that protects the muscular wall from the harshly acidic (pH 2) and proteolytic environment of the stomach (which, as muscle, is made of protein).

Gastric juice is the combination of secretions from the other two cell types in the gastric glands. The chief cells, which are the "chiefs" of digestion in the stomach, secrete **pepsinogen**, which is the zymogen form of the proteolytic enzyme **pepsin** (recall zymogens from Chapter 2). Pepsin digests proteins by cleaving peptide bonds near aromatic amino acids, resulting in short polypeptide fragments. Parietal cells secrete **hydrochloric acid (HCl)**, a strong acid that serves many purposes. We know that zymogens must be activated, and HCl does that for pepsin. Pepsin, which is most active at pH 2 (maintained by the HCl concentration), is unique among human enzymes, most of which are active in neutral to slightly basic pH ranges (i.e., the pH of blood). The acid also kills most harmful bacteria (with the exception of *Helicobacter pylori*, whose infection is usually asymptomatic but can cause inflammation and ulcers) and breaks down the intracellular glue that holds food together.

Now let's turn our attention to the pyloric glands. These glands secrete **gastrin**, which is a hormone. Gastrin induces our stomach to secrete more HCl and to mix the contents of the stomach. This produces an acidic, semifluid mixture known as **chyme**. The combined mechanical and chemical digestive activities of the stomach result in a significant increase in the surface area of the food particles (now unrecognizable as food) so that when the chyme reaches the intestines, the absorption of nutrients from it can be maximized.

You should remember for Test Day that *the stomach is primarily a site of digestion, not absorption*. Certain substances (e.g., alcohol, aspirin) can be directly absorbed, but for our purposes, we should think of the stomach as a digestive site.

Key Concept

The stomach secretes 6 products:
1. H^+ (kills microbes, denatures proteins, converts pepsinogen into pepsin)
2. Pepsinogen (pepsin partially digests proteins)
3. Mucus (protects mucosa)
4. Bicarbonate (protects mucosa)
5. Water (dissolves and dilutes ingested material)
6. Intrinsic Factor (required for normal absorption of vitamin B12)

Real World

Zöllinger-Ellison syndrome is a rare disease resulting from a gastrin-secreting tumor (gastrinoma). Typically, this tumor is found in the pancreas. As we would suspect, the excess gastrin leads to excessive HCl production. Not surprisingly, one of the most common reports of Zöllinger-Ellison syndrome is the presence of intractable ulcer disease.

Small Intestine

Food leaves the stomach through the **pyloric sphincter**, entering the duodenum of the small intestine. Now we come to the exciting part. The bulk supplies received at the loading dock have been partially broken down but are still not ready for distribution throughout the building (circulatory system). More digestion (breaking down) must take place. Indeed, the bulk of chemical digestion, as well as most absorption, occurs in the small intestine. Let's see how.

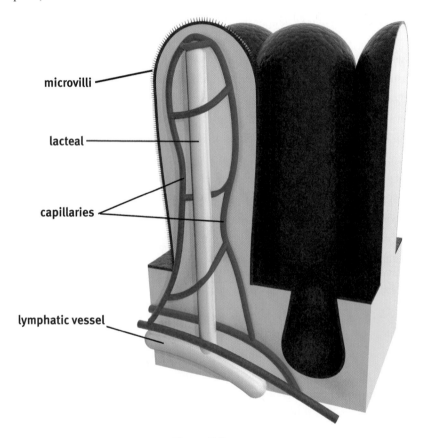

microvilli

lacteal

capillaries

lymphatic vessel

Figure 7.2

The small intestine is divided into three sections: **duodenum**, **jejunum**, and **ileum**. The small intestine is quite long (six meters), and to further maximize the surface area available for absorption, a specialized microanatomy is in place (see Figure 7.2). The surface of the inner wall of the small intestine is covered in projections called **villi** (from the Latin for *shaggy hair*), each of which is covered in its own set of **microvilli**. This has the overall effect of increasing the relative surface area to over 300 square meters, thereby dramatically increasing the absorptive capabilities of the small intestine. Bacteria reside throughout the small intestine and assist with its digestive and absorptive functions. In Figure 7.3, we see bacteria (green) lining the duodenum wall. Over 400 species of bacteria reside in the gut!

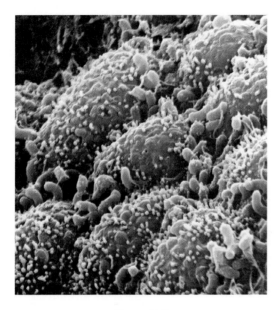

Figure 7.3

DIGESTIVE FUNCTIONS

Simple to remember for the MCAT, most *d*igestion occurs in the *d*uodenum; note that both start with a *d*. At this point, the accessory organs of digestion become necessary, because the enzymes and other compounds secreted by the accessory organs (liver, gall bladder, and pancreas) are key to successful digestion. As chyme enters the duodenum, it triggers the release of hormones that lead to secretions from the small intestine itself, as well as from the accessory organs of digestion.

Pancreatic juice is a complex mixture of several enzymes in a bicarbonate (basic) solution. As we mentioned in Chapter 2, this bicarbonate helps to neutralize acidic chyme, as well as provide an ideal working environment for each of the digestive enzymes. The enzymes produced by the pancreas are most active around pH 8.5. Pancreatic juice contains enzymes that can digest all three types of nutrients: carbohydrates, fats, and proteins. Pancreatic amylase, which breaks down large polysaccharides into small disaccharides, is responsible for carbohydrate digestion. The pancreatic peptidases (**trypsinogen**, **chymotrypsinogen**, **elastinogen**, and **carboxypeptidase**) are released in their zymogen form but, once activated, are responsible for protein digestion. Enterokinase, produced by the small intestine, is the master switch. It activates trypsinogen to trypsin, which can then activate the other zymogens. Finally, the pancreas secretes **lipase**, which is capable of breaking down fats to free fatty acids.

Bile is a complex fluid made up of bile salts, bile pigments, and cholesterol. It is produced by the liver and stored in the gall bladder. The gall bladder releases bile into the duodenum by way of the bile duct in response to the hormone **cholecystokinin (CCK)**, which is released by the small intestine in response to the movement of chyme

> ### Key Concept
>
> Intestinal and pancreatic enzymes are key to proper digestion and absorption. Only the monomeric form of the organic compounds (i.e., monosaccharides, monopeptides, and free fatty acids) can be absorbed by the gut. Without the pancreatic and intestinal enzymes, the compounds in the chyme couldn't be further broken down, which would prevent their absorption in the small intestine. They would pass through to the large intestine, where they would be digested by the bacterial flora (e.g., lactose used as substrate for cellular respiration in *E. coli*) or expelled by the body in the feces.

Bridge

Just as we saw that cholesterol served a positive function in mediating membrane fluidity, here again we see a good effect of cholesterol: serving as the substrate to make bile salts.

Real World

Although the gall bladder stores bile, it isn't completely necessary for life. High-fat diets commonly result in formation of stones or sludge within the gall bladder or cystic duct. If this blockage cannot be cleared, the gall bladder may have to be removed. This is known as a cholecystectomy. The bile will now no longer be stored in the gall bladder, but will be released from the liver directly into the duodenum. This may present problems if a person ingests a high-fat meal and the liver cannot keep up with demand for bile.

out of the stomach and into the intestines. The pH of bile is between 7.5 and 8.8; like the pancreatic juice, it is alkaline to help neutralize the acidity from the stomach.

Bile salts, made from cholesterol, are not enzymes and therefore do not directly impact chemical digestion (the enzymatic cleavage of chemical bonds). However, they serve an important role in the mechanical digestion of fats and ultimately facilitate the chemical digestion of lipids. If we think back to Chapter 1, where we learned about the phospholipid bilayer, we can understand how bile salts work. Like phospholipids, bile salts have a hydrophobic and hydrophilic region. This allows them to serve as a bridge between aqueous and lipid environments. In fact, bile salts are much like the common soaps and detergents we use to wash our hands, clothes, and dishes. In the small intestine, they serve a key function by allowing fat to be emulsified. An emulsification is a mixture of two immiscible liquids. Because chyme is aqueous, without bile, fats would spontaneously separate out of the mixture, forming two layers (aqueous and lipid), just as oil and vinegar salad dressing separate into two layers. Without bile to **emulsify** the dietary fats and cholesterol into **micelles**, we would be unable to keep it in solution (where the water-soluble pancreatic lipase is found). In addition, these micelles expose more of the surface of the fats to the actions of lipase. The bottom line is that we need both bile and lipase. Bile gets the fats into the solution and increases the surface area by placing them in micelles (mechanical digestion). Then, lipase can come in to hydrolyze the ester bonds holding the lipids together (chemical digestion). A common trend is emerging: Systems throughout the body use increased surface area to increase the efficiency of different processes.

We now understand the importance of the accessory organs through their production of enzymes and compounds essential for both mechanical and chemical digestion in the small intestine. But what about the small intestine itself? Chyme in the duodenum causes the small intestine to release disaccharidases (**maltase**, **lactase**, and **sucrase**), **peptidases** (including **dipeptidases**), **enterokinase**, **secretin**, and **CCK**. The first three are enzymes that can digest disaccharides (e.g., lactase breaks down lactose into a galactose and a glucose). Peptidases break down proteins (or peptides, as the name implies). Dipeptidases cleave the peptide bond of dipeptides to release monopeptides (free amino acids). **Secretin** is a hormone that causes pancreatic juice to be exuded from the pancreas. Finally, **CCK**, also a hormone, stimulates the release of both pancreatic juice and bile. We can see that the small intestine itself is capable of digesting carbohydrates and proteins. In fact, the enzymes secreted by the small intestine are collectively called the brush border enzymes, because they act upon their dimeric substrates at the brush border where the monomeric products will be absorbed. If you are having trouble remembering all these compounds when studying for Test Day, refer to Table 7.1 at the end of the chapter.

As with all organ systems, there are mechanisms of control in the digestive system. For example, bile release is tied to the level of fat ingested. If you have a very fatty meal (say, a double burger with cheese and a large order of french fries), the duodenum will release the hormone **enterogastrone** to slow the movement of the chyme and allow a greater time to digest the fat. Furthermore, the autonomic nervous system can exert control over the digestive system. The parasympathetic division is involved in stimulation (rest and digest) and the sympathetic is involved in inhibition (fight or flight) of digestive activities. The fact that so often we feel sleepy and lethargic (as many people call it, "food coma") after eating a big meal is due, in part, to parasympathetic activity. On the other hand, if your lovely picnic in the woods were disrupted by a large grizzly bear, your sympathetic division would kick into high gear, and suddenly digesting that cookie you had just eaten wouldn't be at the top of your body's priority list. Your sympathetic system would decrease blood flow to the digestive organs and decrease their activity.

ABSORPTIVE FUNCTIONS

Up to this point, we have only discussed the breakdown (digestion) of the food. We haven't discussed how the nutrients (i.e., the organic molecules, vitamins, and minerals) are taken up by the body for use. The absorptive processes mostly occur in the jejunum and ileum. Let's examine the absorption of each class of nutrients separately.

We'll start with carbohydrates and amino acids. Simple sugars (e.g., glucose, galactose) and amino acids are absorbed by active transport and facilitated diffusion into the epithelial cells lining the gut. Then, they move across the epithelial cell into the intestinal capillaries. Because blood is constantly passing by the epithelial cells in the capillaries, carrying the carbohydrate and amino acid molecules away from them, a concentration gradient is established such that the capillary blood has a lower concentration of these molecules than the epithelial cells. Thus, the simple carbohydrates and amino acids diffuse from the epithelial cells into the capillaries. The absorbed molecules then go to the liver via the **hepatic portal circulation**.

What about fats? Small fatty acids will follow the same process as carbohydrates and amino acids by diffusing directly into the intestinal capillaries. Let's stop and think for a minute: Why don't they need transporters? They are nonpolar, so they can easily traverse the cellular membrane. Larger fats, glycerol, and cholesterol move separately into the intestinal cells but then re-form into triglycerides (think back to Chapter 3). The triglycerides and esterified cholesterol molecules are packaged into insoluble **chylomicrons**, and rather than entering the bloodstream, they enter the lymphatic circulation through **lacteals**, small vessels that form the beginning of the lymphatic system. These lacteals converge and enter the venous circulation through the lymphatic duct in the neck region (the thoracic duct).

Chylomicrons are processed directly in the bloodstream into low-density lipoprotein (LDL), the so-called "bad" cholesterol. Because this occurs right in the bloodstream,

> **Key Concept**
>
> Most fat bypasses the liver. This means it directly enters the circulation without first-pass metabolism. The liver has moderate control over the levels of sugar and protein in the blood because the absorbed carbohydrates and amino acids are first directed to hepatic portal circulation before being released to the rest of the body. Fats aren't subject to such restrictions.

LDL in excess can lead to atherosclerosis. LDL molecules are taken up by the liver, where they can be repackaged into high-density lipoprotein (HDL, "good" cholesterol), very low-density lipoprotein (VLDL), or more LDL.

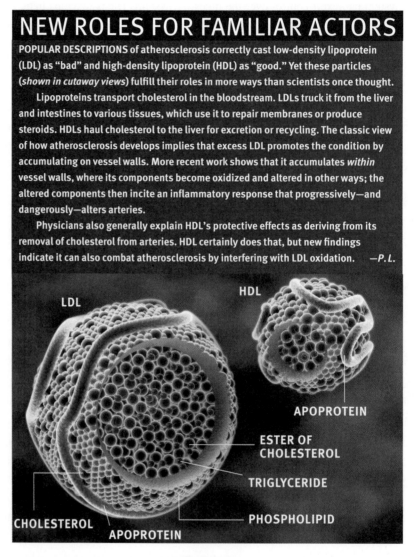

NEW ROLES FOR FAMILIAR ACTORS

POPULAR DESCRIPTIONS of atherosclerosis correctly cast low-density lipoprotein (LDL) as "bad" and high-density lipoprotein (HDL) as "good." Yet these particles (*shown in cutaway views*) fulfill their roles in more ways than scientists once thought.

Lipoproteins transport cholesterol in the bloodstream. LDLs truck it from the liver and intestines to various tissues, which use it to repair membranes or produce steroids. HDLs haul cholesterol to the liver for excretion or recycling. The classic view of how atherosclerosis develops implies that excess LDL promotes the condition by accumulating on vessel walls. More recent work shows that it accumulates *within* vessel walls, where its components become oxidized and altered in other ways; the altered components then incite an inflammatory response that progressively—and dangerously—alters arteries.

Physicians also generally explain HDL's protective effects as deriving from its removal of cholesterol from arteries. HDL certainly does that, but new findings indicate it can also combat atherosclerosis by interfering with LDL oxidation.   —*P. L.*

Figure 7.4

You do need to know for Test Day the different mechanisms of vitamin absorption. We can categorize vitamins as either fat- or water-soluble. Because there are only four fat-soluble vitamins (A, D, E, and K), we can memorize them, knowing that anything else we might come across on Test Day (e.g., B vitamins or vitamin C) must be water-soluble. Failure to digest fat properly, which would subsequently inhibit its proper absorption, may lead to a deficiency of the fat-soluble vitamins, which are normally absorbed alongside the fats. The water-soluble vitamins are absorbed, along with water, amino acids, and carbohydrates, across the endothelial cells and pass directly into the plasma of the blood.

Large Intestine

The final part of the gastrointestinal tract is the large intestine. It is primarily involved in water absorption, although the overall water balance in the body is controlled by the kidneys. The large intestine is, well, larger than the small intestine in terms of diameter. However, it is only 1.5 meters long and, therefore, shorter than the small intestine in overall length. The large intestine is divided into three major sections: the **cecum**, **colon**, and **rectum**. The cecum is simply a pocket with no outlet that connects the small and large intestines and contains the **appendix**. The appendix is a tiny structure that was once thought to be **vestigial**, although recent evidence has suggested that it may have a role in warding off certain bacterial infections. Inflammation of the appendix (appendicitis) is a medical emergency; in fact, it is the most common reason for an unscheduled surgery in the United States.

Table 7.1. Digestive Enzymes

Nutrient	Enzyme	Site of Production	Site of Function	Function
Carbohydrates	Salivary amylase (ptyalin)	Salivary glands	Mouth	Hydrolyzes starch to maltose.
	Pancreatic amylase	Pancreas	Small intestine	Hydrolyzes starch to maltose.
	Maltase	Intestinal glands	Small intestine	Hydrolyzes maltose to two glucose molecules.
	Sucrase	Intestinal glands	Small intestine	Hydrolyzes sucrose to glucose and fructose.
	Lactase	Intestinal glands	Small intestine	Hydrolyzes lactose to glucose and galactose.
Proteins	Pepsin (secreted as pepsinogen)	Gastric glands	Stomach	Hydrolyzes specific peptide bonds.
	Trypsin (secreted as trypsinogen)	Pancreas	Small intestine	Hydrolyzes specific peptide bonds. Converts chymotrypsinogen to chymotrypsin.
	Chymotrypsin (secreted as chymotrypsinogen)	Pancreas	Small intestine	Hydrolyzes specific peptide bonds.
	Carboxypeptidase	Pancreas	Small intestine	Hydrolyzes terminal peptide bond at carboxyl end.
	Aminopeptidase	Intestinal glands	Small intestine	Hydrolyzes terminal peptide bond at amino end.
	Dipeptidases	Intestinal glands	Small intestine	Hydrolyzes pairs of amino acids.
	Enterokinase	Intestinal glands	Small intestine	Converts trypsinogen to trypsin.
Lipids	Bile*	Liver	Small intestine	Emulsifies fat.
	Lipase	Pancreas	Small intestine	Hydrolyzes lipids.

*Note that bile is *not* an enzyme.

> **Key Concept**
>
> Although the large intestine reabsorbs massive amounts of water, it is the kidneys that actually regulate total body water.

The colon is responsible for absorbing water and salts (e.g., sodium chloride) in the undigested material from the small intestines. The colon acts as a recycling system, sifting through the processed food and pulling those last little bits of nutrients out of the remaining waste products. Too little or too much water absorption can cause diarrhea or constipation, respectively.

Finally, the rectum serves as a storage site for **feces**, much as the office workers would temporarily store trash and waste before it is removed from the office building. Feces consist of indigestible material, water, bacteria (*E. coli*, etc.), and certain digestive secretions that aren't reabsorbed (enzymes and bile). The **anus** is the opening through which wastes are eliminated and consists of two sphincters: the **internal** and **external** anal sphincters. The external sphincter is under voluntary control (somatic), but the internal sphincter is under involuntary control (autonomic). Do you remember which embryonic structure gives rise to the anus in humans? It's the blastopore (see Chapter 5 for more details).

Conclusion

In this chapter, we have reviewed a lot of information about the digestive system that we can use to our advantage on Test Day. We began with an overview of the anatomy, keeping in mind that the system is designed to carry out extracellular digestion. Considering all our foodstuffs are made up of fats, proteins, and carbohydrates, these compounds have to be broken down to their simplest molecular forms before they can be absorbed and distributed to the tissues and cells of the body. As we moved through the gastrointestinal tract, we discussed whether each organ was a site of absorption, digestion, or both. We spent a good bit of time discussing each of the enzymes involved in digestion and its specific purpose. Absorption primarily occurs in the jejunum and ileum, where transport across the epithelial cells is slightly different depending on the compound. Finally, we discussed the large intestine and its three sections and its role in water and salt absorption, as well as its role in the temporary storage of waste products. Although the amount of information about the digestive system may seem overwhelming, these concepts are relatively simple and a systematic approach (think charts, tables, or flash cards) to managing this information will spell Test Day success for you.

CONCEPTS TO REMEMBER

- ☐ Digestion consists of two processes: mechanical and chemical. Mechanical breaks the food into smaller pieces, whereas chemical breaks the actual bonds in food molecules.

- ☐ The mammalian digestive tract is a one-way system that begins with the mouth and ends at the anus. Several accessory organs of digestion are attached.

- ☐ The stomach is responsible for digestion through the use of enzymes and HCl that is secreted by the parietal cells.

- ☐ The epithelium of the stomach is protected from damage by mucous that is secreted from mucous cells.

- ☐ Pancreatic juice contains bicarbonate that helps neutralize the acidic chyme after it leaves the stomach. Bile also contributes to this effect.

- ☐ The enzymes in pancreatic juice and from the duodenum are capable of digesting all three classes of foods: carbohydrates, proteins, and fats.

- ☐ Bile is required for the proper digestion and absorption of fats, as they must be emulsified for these processes to occur.

- ☐ Vitamins are also absorbed. They may be either fat- or water-soluble. The fat-soluble vitamins are A, D, E, and K.

- ☐ The large intestine consists of three sections: the cecum, colon, and rectum.

- ☐ Although the large intestine reabsorbs water, its primary function is not to regulate total body water. Rather, it absorbs water so that feces are semisolid by the time they reach the rectum. Salts and some vitamins (e.g., vitamin K, which is produced by bacteria in the large intestine) may also be absorbed.

Practice Questions

1. Which of the following associations between the type of gastric cell or gland and its secretions is correct?

   A. Mucous cells—HCl
   B. Chief cells—pepsinogen
   C. Parietal cells—mucus
   D. Pyloric glands—gastric juice

2. Which of the following is NOT part of the small intestine?

   A. Ileum
   B. Cecum
   C. Jejunum
   D. Duodenum

3. In an experiment, enterokinase secretion was blocked. As a direct result, levels of all of the following enzymes were affected EXCEPT

   A. trypsin.
   B. aminopeptidase.
   C. chymotrypsin.
   D. carboxypeptidase.

4. Which of the following INCORRECTLY pairs the digestive hormone with its function?

   A. Trypsin—hydrolyzes specific peptide bonds
   B. Lactase—hydrolyzes lactose to glucose and galactose
   C. Pancreatic amylase—hydrolyzes starch to maltose
   D. Lipase—emulsifies fats

5. Where are proteins digested?

   A. Mouth and stomach
   B. Stomach and large intestine
   C. Stomach and small intestine
   D. Small intestine and large intestine

6. Which of the following choices INCORRECTLY pairs a digestive enzyme with its site of secretion?

   A. Sucrase—salivary glands
   B. Carboxypeptidase—pancreas
   C. Trypsin—pancreas
   D. Lactase—intestinal glands

7. You are looking at a CT scan of the abdomen of a child who presented to you with various symptoms, including projectile vomiting. You notice a constriction in the digestive system that prevents food from reaching the small intestine. Which structure is the most likely site of the problem?

   A. Cardiac sphincter
   B. Pyloric sphincter
   C. Cecum
   D. Rectum

8. All of the following processes occur in the mouth EXCEPT

   A. moistening of food.
   B. bolus formation.
   C. chemical digestion of starch.
   D. chemical digestion of proteins.

9. The two graphs below show the relative activities of two enzymes in solutions of varying pH. Which of the following choices correctly identifies the two enzymes?

1.

2.

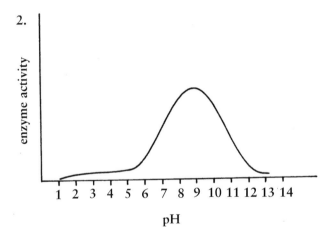

A. 1—chymotrypsin; 2—pepsin
B. 1—pepsin; 2—chymotrypsin
C. 1—bile; 2—lactase
D. 1—carboxypeptidase; 2—enterokinase

10. Which of the following choices correctly illustrates the course that a piece of bread takes through the digestive tract?

A. Mouth → trachea → esophagus → cardiac sphincter → stomach → pyloric sphincter → small intestine → large intestine → rectum → anus

B. Mouth → pharynx → esophagus → cardiac sphincter → stomach → pyloric sphincter → small intestine → large intestine → rectum → anus

C. Mouth → pharynx → esophagus → pyloric sphincter → stomach → cardiac sphincter → small intestine → large intestine → rectum → anus

D. Mouth → pharynx → esophagus → cardiac sphincter → stomach → pyloric sphincter → small intestine → large intestine → anus → rectum

11. The epiglottis is to the trachea as the lower esophageal (cardiac) sphincter is to the

A. stomach.
B. heart.
C. small intestine.
D. liver.

12. Which of the following choices correctly pairs the nutrient with its site of absorption?

A. Chylomicrons—lacteals
B. Amino acids—large intestine
C. Vitamins A and E—stomach
D. Cholesterol—ascending colon

13. Starch is hydrolyzed into maltose by

A. salivary amylase.
B. maltase.
C. pancreatic amylase.
D. both (A) and (C).

14. The intestinal capillaries transport nutrients from the intestines to the

A. large intestine.
B. liver.
C. kidney.
D. heart.

15. Which of the following choices INCORRECTLY pairs a digestive enzyme with its site of secretion?

A. Pancreatic amylase—pancreas
B. Aminopeptidase—stomach
C. Enterokinase—intestinal glands
D. Maltase—intestinal glands

16. Which of the following INCORRECTLY pairs a digestive enzyme with its function?

A. Sucrase—hydrolyzes sucrose to glucose and fructose
B. Carboxypeptidase—hydrolyzes the terminal peptide bond at the amino end
C. Trypsin—hydrolyzes some peptide bonds and converts chymotrypsinogen to chymotrypsin
D. Lactase—hydrolyzes lactose to glucose and galactose

Small Group Questions

1. Why do you suppose the monosaccharide glucose is circulated in the blood of humans rather than a disaccharide, such as sucrose, which is the transport sugar found in plants?

2. How does the stomach protect itself from its own acidic environment?

3. In the digestive system, some enzymes are secreted as inactive precursors, which are later converted to their active forms. Why might this occur?

Explanations to Practice Questions

1. B

The surest way to answer this question correctly is to analyze each answer choice. (A) is false because mucous cells secrete mucus. (B) is true, because chief cells do indeed secrete pepsinogen, the zymogen of the protein-hydrolyzing enzyme pepsin. (C) and (D) are false, since parietal cells secrete hydrochloric acid, whereas the pyloric glands secrete gastrin. (B) is therefore the correct answer.

2. B

The small intestine is divided into three sections: the duodenum, the jejunum, and the ileum. Thus, the correct answer is (B); the cecum is part of the large intestine.

3. B

Let's take a look at each of the listed enzymes and eliminate the ones that are affected by enterokinase. Trypsin is the active form of trypsinogen, a zymogen activated by enterokinase, so we can eliminate (A). Aminopeptidase does not interact with enterokinase in any way and, therefore, would not be affected by a blockage in enterokinase secretion. We can now select (B). For the sake of completion, let's take a look at the last two choices. Chymotrypsin is the active form of chymotrypsinogen, another pancreatic enzyme activated by enterokinase. Finally, carboxypeptidase is secreted as a zymogen and activated by trypsin, which, in turn, requires enterokinase to be activated from its zymogen form, trypsinogen. (B) is therefore the correct answer.

4. D

The best way to answer this question is to look at each answer choice and determine if the association is false. Looking at (A), we can decide right away that it is a correct association, because trypsin does indeed hydrolyze specific peptide bonds. (B) is also true: Lactase hydrolyzes lactose to glucose and galactose. Next, we can eliminate (C), because it is true that pancreatic amylase hydrolyzes starch to maltose. We are left with (D), which must be false. The function of lipase is to hydrolyze lipids; bile salts emulsify fats. (D) is therefore the correct answer.

5. C

Protein digestion begins in the stomach, where pepsin (secreted as pepsinogen) hydrolyzes specific peptide bonds. Protein digestion continues in the small intestine as trypsin (secreted as trypsinogen), chymotrypsin (secreted as chymotrypsinogen), carboxypeptidase, aminopeptidase, and dipeptidase hydrolyze specific parts of the peptide. (C) is therefore the correct answer.

6. A

Let's take a look at each choice in part and determine which one contains a false association. Starting with (A), we notice a mistake right away. Sucrase is secreted by the intestinal glands, not the salivary glands. Its function is to hydrolyze glucose to fructose. Glancing at the other choices, we confirm once more that (A) is the correct answer.

7. B

The question is basically asking us to identify the structure that would prevent food from reaching the small intestine. Because the child presents with projectile vomiting, we can assume that food reached the stomach but cannot continue its course to the intestine. The structure that regulates the passage of chyme from the stomach to the small intestine is called the pyloric sphincter, and this is the most likely site of the patient's problem. (B) is thus the correct answer.

8. D

The mouth has an important role in digestion, because it is the first part of the digestive tract to interact with food. Several things happen in the mouth as we eat. First, the mouth (the teeth and tongue, specifically) churns the food into small pieces, a process called mechanical digestion. The salivary glands produce saliva, which helps moisten the food. With the help of the tongue, a bolus is formed, which will then be swallowed and sent through the esophagus to the stomach. Primarily one type of chemical digestion occurs in the mouth: the chemical digestion of starch to maltose, a process initiated by salivary amylase (ptyalin). Although lingual lipases are present, very little fat digestion actually takes place. (D) is therefore the correct answer as the chemical digestion of protein begins in the stomach.

9. B

The question gives us two graphs and asks us to identify the type of enzyme that each one represents based on how the enzyme's activity changes as a function of pH. Looking at the first graph, we notice that the enzyme has maximal activity at a relatively low pH (3–4). It must be an enzyme that functions in an acidic environment, most likely in the stomach. The second graph portrays an enzyme whose optimal activity occurs at a high pH (9.5). It must correlate to an enzyme that works in a basic environment, such as the small intestine. Our task now is to select the answer choice that pairs the first graph to a gastric enzyme, and the second graph to a small intestinal enzyme. (B) matches our prediction and is, therefore, the correct answer. Pepsin is secreted in the stomach and works best in an acidic pH, whereas chymotrypsin acts in the small intestine at a basic pH.

10. B

In the mouth, teeth chew the bread into smaller particles, and salivary amylase digests some of the starch (the major component of bread) into maltose. The bread bolus is then propelled through the pharynx and esophagus, entering the stomach through the cardiac sphincter. There is no chemical digestion of starch in the stomach, so after a couple of hours,

the chyme will pass through the pyloric sphincter and enter the small intestine. In the small intestine, pancreatic amylase hydrolyzes starch into maltose, whereas maltase, sucrase, and lactase hydrolyze various disaccharides into their respective monosaccharides. Most of the monosaccharides (i.e., glucose, fructose, and galactose) are absorbed into the circulatory system through the intestinal wall. Finally, the piece of bread will finish its course through the large intestine and the rectum and will eventually be expelled through the anus. The only choice that correctly identifies all of the segments of the digestive tract is (B).

11. A

The epiglottis is a small flap that covers the trachea during swallowing; in a way, it is a switch that ensures food and air travel through different passageways. The lower esophageal (cardiac) sphincter controls the passage of food into the stomach and prevents anything from getting out of the stomach. The correct answer therefore is (A).

12. A

Glancing at each choice, we realize that only chylomicrons are correctly paired with their site of absorption. Large fatty acids and glycerol, which combine to form triglycerides, along with phosphoglycerides and cholesterol, are packaged into protein-coated droplets called chylomicrons. The chylomicrons are then absorbed into tiny lymph vessels within the villi called lacteals, which lead to the lymphatic system. (A) is therefore the correct answer.

13. D

Starch is hydrolyzed to maltose by two enzymes: salivary amylase (secreted by the salivary glands) in the mouth and pancreatic amylase (secreted by the pancreas) in the small intestine. (D) is therefore the correct answer

14. B

The intestinal capillaries transport nutrients from the intestines to the liver, where they get processed, repackaged, and distributed. (B) is therefore the correct answer.

15. B

Let's take a look at each choice to determine which one contains a false association. (A) can be eliminated because pancreatic amylase is indeed secreted by the pancreas (as the name indicates). (B) is a red flag; aminopeptidase is secreted by the intestinal glands. Although this means that (B) is the correct answer, for the sake of completion, let's check the last two choices. It is true that both enterokinase and maltase are secreted by the intestinal glands, so (C) and (D) can be eliminated.

16. B

Let's quickly analyze each choice and determine which one contains a false association. Sucrase does indeed hydrolyze sucrose to glucose and fructose, a process that occurs in the small intestine; we can eliminate (A). Carboxypeptidase, on the other hand, is an enzyme that hydrolyzes a terminal peptide bond at the carboxy terminal, as the name indicates. (B) is therefore false and the correct answer. Glancing at the other two answers, we confirm that (C) and (D) are indeed true associations.

Respiration

Coughing. Fever. Shortness of breath. Hypoxia. All are symptoms of a type of hypersensitivity pneumonitis, also known as extrinsic allergic alveolitis (EAA). More specifically, they're symptoms of hot tub lung.

The first two names refer to alveolar inflammation caused by the inhalation of some substance that was not properly filtered out by nasal hairs and mucus. Hot tub lung is a specific form of EAA caused by the gram-positive *Mycobacterium avium*. That genus name might sound somewhat familiar; in fact, *M. avium*'s cousin is none other than *M. tuberculosis*! Although hot tub lung seems contagious by its mechanism of infection, it's not easily transmitted from one human to the next, the way tuberculosis is.

So what exactly *is* its mechanism of infection? Many of us see hot environments as inhospitable for bacterial growth, but let's remember that the number of bacterial *species* outnumbers animal species at least by the millions (even billions might be an underestimate). Surely there exist species that can survive in every environment on earth! Including those at 102°F; that is, the temperature at which most hot tubs are set. It just so happens that *M. avium* flourishes at this temperature. Bubbles at the hot water's surface burst, releasing nice warm mist into the air. That warm mist, unfortunately, might be full of *M. avium* waiting to make you their new home. The happy, relaxed bathers who breathe these bacteria might be in for a long road of respiratory troubles.

Not all cases of hot tub lung are severe, but certainly none are enjoyable. They're often misdiagnosed as asthma or bronchitis, and they're sometimes treated with steroids. As mentioned earlier, hot tub lung falls in a category of hypersensitivities, which can potentially go away by themselves. As a result, antibiotic therapy is not always recommended. The best way to avoid hot tub lung is to make sure that the tub is being cleaned properly and routinely before entering it.

Hot tub lung is as aptly named, as are some other types of hypersensitivity pneumonitis: mushroom-worker's lung, cheese-washer's lung, and wine-grower's lung. The lesson here isn't to avoid hot tubs, mushrooms, cheese, and wine. It's that the lungs are essential, sensitive organs with delicate membranes that must be protected. Many types of stressors (pathogens, particles, or chemicals) can irritate them and cause respiratory distress. In this chapter, we'll look at the structure of the lungs and their precious membranes, along with the microanatomy of respiration. We'll also talk about respiratory volumes and how pulmonologists assess proper lung function. Last but not least, we'll preview gas exchange to prepare us for a discussion of gas transport in the next chapter.

Anatomy ★★★☆☆

Gas exchange occurs at the **lungs** (see Figure 6.1). Air enters the respiratory tract through the **external nares** of the nose and then passes through the nasal cavity, where it is filtered through mucous membranes and nasal hairs. Just as the air that is brought into a building may be passed through a filtration system for cleaning, numerous cilia in the nasal pathway trap particulate matter (such as dust) so that we don't breathe it into our lungs.

Next, air passes into the pharynx and the **larynx**. The pharynx serves as a tunnel between the mouth and esophagus through which food travels (Chapter 7), whereas the larynx is only a pathway for air. To keep food out of the respiratory tract, the opening of the larynx (glottis) is covered by the **epiglottis** during swallowing. From the larynx,

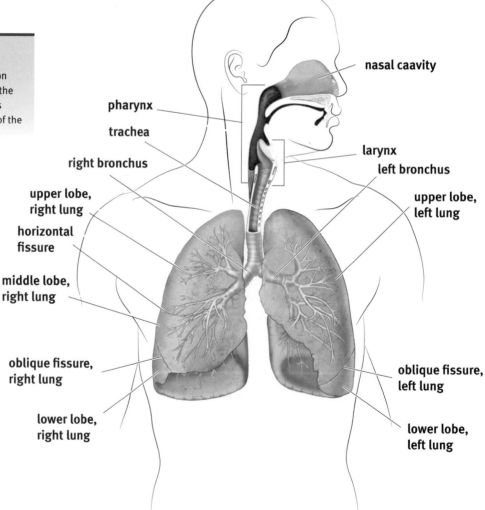

Figure 8.1

air passes into the cartilaginous **trachea** and then into the mainstem **bronchi** (one per side). These bronchi continue to divide into smaller structures known as **bronchioles** until they are tiny structures in which gas exchange occurs (the **alveoli**). This is analogous to a building's ventilation system, which will continue to divide into smaller and smaller tubes and pipes until we reach the vent in each individual room.

The bronchi and trachea also contain ciliated epithelial cells to catch material that may have made it past the initial check in the nose. Each alveolus is coated with **surfactant**, a detergent that lowers surface tension and prevents the alveolus from collapsing on itself. A network of capillaries surrounds each alveolus to carry oxygen and carbon dioxide. The branching and minute size of the alveoli allow for an exceptionally large surface area for gas exchange—approximately 100 m^2.

Ventilation ★★★★☆

The lungs themselves are contained in the **thoracic cavity**, which, as we will see in the next chapter, also contains the heart. They are separated from the organs of digestion by a muscle known as the **diaphragm**, which is necessary for **inspiration**. Although breathing is controlled autonomically, the diaphragm is actually composed of skeletal muscle and is, therefore, under somatic control.

The chest wall forms one side of the thoracic cavity. Membranes known as **pleurae** (sing.: **pleura**) surround each lung. The pleurae are a closed sac against which the lung grows. The surface adjacent to the lung is **visceral**, and all other parts of the sac are **parietal** (see Figure 8.2). Imagine that we have a large, partially deflated balloon. Now, let's take our fist and push it against the balloon so that the balloon comes up and surrounds our hand. This is analogous to a lung and its pleurae. Our fist is the lung, and the balloon represents both pleural layers. The side directly touching our fist is the visceral pleura, and the outer layer is the parietal pleura, which is

Bridge

The digestive system uses villi and microvilli to generate a similar advantage.

Real World

Pneumothorax is a common result of a penetrating injury to the chest. Air enters the intrapleural space, thereby increasing the intrapleural pressure and collapsing the lung. Pneumothorax is treated by inserting a needle and withdrawing air from the intrapleural space.

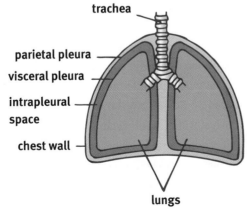

Figure 8.2

associated with the chest wall in real life. The space within the sac is referred to as the **intrapleural space**, which in our bodies contains a thin layer of fluid (imagine pouring a bit of water into the balloon before blowing it up). This fluid helps lubricate the two pleural surfaces. In addition, there is a pressure differential between the intrapleural space and the lungs. This difference is critical for proper respiration.

STAGES OF VENTILATION

Let's turn to the mechanics of ventilation. This might sound a lot like physics, and the process of ventilation is, in fact, grounded in physics. We can use pressure to do useful work in a system. Here, we are going to use pressure differentials between the lungs and intrapleural space to drive air into the lungs.

Inhalation

Inhalation is an active process. We use our diaphragm as well as the **external intercostal muscles** (layer of muscles between the ribs) to expand the thoracic cavity. As the cavity enlarges, the diaphragm flattens down, and the chest wall moves out (see Figure 8.3). Intrapleural volume increases. Can we predict what will happen to intrapleural pressure? From our understanding of Boyle's law, an increase in intrapleural volume leads to a decrease in intrapleural pressure.

Now we have low pressure in the intrapleural space. What about inside the lungs? The gas in the lungs is at atmospheric pressure, which is now higher than the pressure in the intrapleural space. We can see, then, that the lungs will expand as air is sucked in from a higher-pressure environment. What environment is this? The outside world. This mechanism is referred to as **negative-pressure breathing**, because the driving force is the lower (relatively negative) pressure in the intrapleural space compared with the lungs (alveoli). If we were curious, we would also predict that this pressure differential would affect how the heart fills, since it's also in the thoracic cavity (which we don't need to know for the MCAT but will learn plenty about in medical school).

Exhalation

Luckily, exhalation does not have to be an active process. Simple relaxation will reverse the processes we discussed in the last paragraph (see Figure 8.3). Let's see how. As the diaphragm and external intercostals relax, the chest cavity decreases in size (volume). What will happen to pressure in the intrapleural space? It will go up, again explained by Boyle's law. Now, pressure in the intrapleural space is higher than in the lungs, which is still at atmospheric level. So air will be pushed out, resulting in exhalation. During highly active tasks, we can speed this process up by using the **internal intercostal muscles**, which oppose the externals and pull the rib cage down, actively decreasing the volume of the thoracic cavity. Finally, we should recall that surfactant prevents the complete collapse of our alveoli during exhalation by reducing surface tension at the alveolar surface.

Bridge

Boyle's law says that the pressure and volume of gases are inversely related. This is the principle underlying negative-pressure breathing.

Real World

Emphysema is a disease characterized by the destruction of alveolar walls. This results in reduced elastic recoil of the lungs, making the process of exhalation extremely difficult. Most cases of emphysema are caused by cigarette smoking.

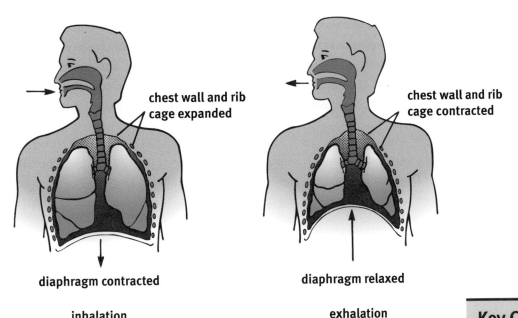

chest wall and rib cage expanded

chest wall and rib cage contracted

diaphragm contracted

diaphragm relaxed

inhalation

exhalation

Figure 8.3

CONTROL OF VENTILATION

Breathing requires input from our nervous control center, which we will examine in much more detail in Chapter 13. Let's just briefly mention a few controls that are relevant to this discussion. Our ventilation is primarily regulated by neurons (**ventilation centers**) in the medulla oblongata that rhythmically fire to cause regular contraction of respiratory muscles. These neurons are primarily sensitive to carbon dioxide concentration. As the partial pressure of carbon dioxide rises, the respiratory rate will increase to counter it. How is carbon dioxide concentration measured? **Chemoreceptors** on the neurons' surfaces monitor changes in the blood's pH. Let's say that pH is decreased (increased proton concentration). Can we predict what will happen? The answer to this is a critically important MCAT concept that will be covered in great detail in Chapter 9.

We can, to a limited extent, control our breathing through the cerebrum. We can choose to breathe more rapidly or slowly; however, extended periods of hypoventilation would lead to increased carbon dioxide levels and an override by the medulla oblongata (which would jump-start breathing). The opposite process (hyperventilation) would blow off too much carbon dioxide and inhibit ventilation (hopefully before we pass out!)

Lung Capacities and Volumes ★★★★☆☆

Certainly we can't pop our lungs out to measure air volumes, but pulmonologists (doctors who deal with the lungs and respiration) need to assess lung capacities

> **Key Concept**
>
> Inhalation and exhalation are different processes in terms of energy expenditure. Muscle contraction is required to create the negative pressure in the thoracic cavity that forces air in during inspiration. Expiration during calm states is entirely due to elastic recoil of the lungs and musculature. Of course, during more active states, the muscles can be used to force air out and speed the process of ventilation.

> **Key Concept**
>
> Although oxygen is necessary for life, it is primarily a response to rising CO_2 that drives ventilation. Not until oxygen falls to a very low level does hypoxia drive the ventilatory response.

somehow. One instrument used is a **spirometer**, which can measure the amount of air normally present in the lungs and the rate at which ventilation occurs. Note that we do not breathe all that rapidly when oxygen is abundant; a normal respiration rate is around 12 breaths per minute. On top of Mount Everest, where there is only one third as much oxygen as at sea level, ventilation may increase to 80 to 90 times per minute!

Let's start with the largest measure and work our way down. **Total lung capacity (TLC)** in healthy human beings is about six to seven liters. Graphically, we can imagine two three-liter bottles: one for each lung. If we breathe in as much as possible, the total amount of air in our lungs at this point is the TLC.

Now let's say we breathe out until we cannot breathe out any more (i.e., we force out all air using our musculature). The total amount we forced out was the **vital capacity (VC)**. This makes sense, as it is the amount that we can actually (or vitally) use. The amount left over is the **residual volume (RV)**. There will always be some air left over, because expelling it all would require lung collapse, which we definitely want to avoid. Now, if we were to add the VC and RV, what would we get as our answer? The TLC.

Of course, we don't always work at the extremes, which is what TLC, VC, and RV represent. Instead, we shallowly breathe only what we need, which may be a liter or so with each breath. This is known as the **tidal volume (TV)**. It is analogous to the difference in level between the ocean's high tide (breathe in) and low tide (breathe out). The TV is not like the VC, which we had to force out. TV is the air that naturally comes out with exhalation. If we use respiratory muscles to push air out, the last bit of air that exits is the **expiratory reserve volume (ERV)**. Because there is an expiratory reserve volume, there must also be an **inspiratory reserve volume (IRV)**, which is the amount of extra air we can take in after a tidal breath. One last formula: What should the TV, ERV, and IRV sum to? The vital capacity, which is the total amount of gas that can be moved.

Key Concept

Remember that TLC = RV + VC and that VC = TV + ERV + IRV.

Let's take a look at Figure 8.4 to see these represented graphically.

Figure 8.4

Gas Exchange ★★★★★★

Our last item for this chapter is the actual movement of gas in the lungs, which is, after all, their primary function. As we already mentioned, a network of pulmonary capillaries surrounds each alveolus. The capillaries bring deoxygenated blood from the pulmonary arteries, which stem from the right ventricle. As they approach, the single-celled alveolar layers allow for diffusion of carbon dioxide from the blood into the lungs and oxygen in the opposite direction. The oxygenated blood returns to the heart via the pulmonary veins (see Figure 8.5).

The driving force is the pressure differential of the gases. Since blood is deoxygenated as it enters, it has a relatively low partial pressure of oxygen and a relatively high pressure of carbon dioxide, facilitating the transfer of each down its respective concentration gradient. Since the gradient between the blood and air in the lungs is already present as the blood enters the lungs, no energy is required for gas transfer. Although we will discuss this further in Chapter 9, it's worth mentioning that oxygen travels through the body using hemoglobin as its transporter.

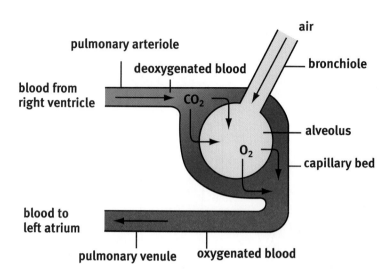

Figure 8.5

Now that we have mastered the respiratory system, let's take a break from MCAT studying and go skiing. How would our respiratory systems adjust on the slopes as we move to higher altitudes where less oxygen is available? First, we can breathe more rapidly to try and increase gas exchange; second, we could make more red cells to carry the oxygen (polycythemia; see Chapter 9). In the long term, we could develop more blood vessels (vascularization), which would facilitate the distribution of a lower amount of oxygen to tissues. Finally, we can alter the binding dynamics of hemoglobin to oxygen. This will be a major point of discussion in Chapter 9. Now, let's exhale and get ready for the next chapter.

Conclusion

The functional unit of the lung is the alveolus, just as the basic unit of muscle was the sarcomere. We learned that gas exchange across the lungs is a result of passive diffusion of carbon dioxide and oxygen down their concentration gradients. This diffusion is accomplished in the alveoli, which, when laid out, have an area of 100 m²! The actual process of breathing in and out is controlled by chemoreceptors in the ventilatory centers of the brain stem. Although we can voluntarily influence our breathing rate to a certain degree, our nervous system takes care of ventilation and gas concentrations in the body. Pressure gradients between the intrapleural space and lung provide the physical basis for ventilation. We literally suck air in from the atmosphere, because the pressure in the thoracic cavity during inspiration is lower than that in the outside world. Boyle's law is a key to understanding this process. The binding of oxygen to hemoglobin in the lungs is a concept that will be expanded on in the next chapter, as well as how altitude, pH, and chemicals may affect this binding.

CONCEPTS TO REMEMBER

- ☐ The alveolus is the basic unit of the lung and the site of gas exchange.

- ☐ The external nares and nasal cavity provide a method to both remove contaminants from air as well as humidify it before it reaches the lungs.

- ☐ The epiglottis provides a mechanism to prevent large material from entering the larynx and bronchi.

- ☐ The diaphragm and intercostal muscles are responsible for generating the negative pressure differential between each intrapleural space and its associated lung.

- ☐ Negative-pressure breathing is explained by Boyle's law and results in air literally being sucked into the lungs during inspiration.

- ☐ pH-sensitive chemoreceptors in the medulla oblongata control respiration rate.

- ☐ Measurement of lung volumes can be accomplished by using a spirometer. Deviations from standard values may indicate pathological conditions (e.g., increased TLC in emphysema).

- ☐ Total lung capacity is the sum of residual volume and vital capacity.

- ☐ Vital capacity is the sum of inspiratory reserve volume, tidal volume, and expiratory reserve volume.

- ☐ Gas exchange in the lungs is a passive process resulting from the large, pre-existing concentration gradients of oxygen and carbon dioxide.

Practice Questions

1. All of the following facilitate gas exchange in the lungs EXCEPT

   A. thin alveolar surfaces.
   B. moist alveolar surfaces.
   C. differences in the partial pressures of O_2 and CO_2.
   D. active transport.

2. Which of the following associations between the two stages of respiration and the contraction of muscles is correct?

   A. Inhalation—diaphragm relaxes
   B. Inhalation—external intercostal muscles relax
   C. Exhalation—diaphragm contracts
   D. Exhalation—external intercostal muscles relax

3. What does negative-pressure breathing refer to?

   A. Breathing in low-oxygen conditions
   B. Breathing in low-pressure conditions
   C. Inhalation
   D. Breathing with use of a ventilator

4. The intrapleural space in the lungs is bounded by the

   A. visceral pleura and the parietal pleura.
   B. visceral pleura and the diaphragm.
   C. parietal pleura and the alveolar pleura.
   D. parietal pleura and the lungs.

5. Which of the following best describes the residual volume of the lungs?

   A. The amount of air normally inhaled and exhaled with each breath
   B. The maximum amount of air that can be forcibly inhaled and exhaled from the lungs
   C. The volume of air that can still be forcibly exhaled following a normal exhalation
   D. The volume of air that always remains in the lungs

6. The lungs can collapse from

   A. insufficient surfactant production.
   B. rupture of the parietal pleura.
   C. overproduction of surfactant.
   D. Both (A) and (B)

7. Which of the following mechanisms exists in the respiratory system to ensure that inhalation occurs rapidly and safely?

   A. The epiglottis covers the glottis to ensure that food does not enter the trachea during swallowing.
   B. The trachea and bronchi are lined by ciliated epithelial cells.
   C. The large surface area of the alveoli facilitates gas exchange.
   D. All of the above

8. Which is the correct sequence of passageways through which air travels during inhalation?

   A. Pharynx → trachea → bronchioles → bronchi → alveoli
   B. Pharynx → trachea → lungs → bronchi → alveoli
   C. Larynx → pharynx → trachea → bronchi → alveoli
   D. Pharynx → larynx → trachea → bronchi → alveoli

9. Which of the following is generally a passive process?

   A. Inhalation
   B. Exhalation
   C. Gas exchange
   D. Both (B) and (C)

10. Total lung capacity is equal to the vital capacity plus the

   A. tidal volume.
   B. expiratory reserve volume.
   C. residual volume.
   D. inspiratory reserve volume.

Small Group Questions

1. Why are there more pulmonary veins than pulmonary arteries?

2. Would you expect the vital capacity of mountain dwellers to be greater or less than the vital capacity of people residing at sea level? What other physiological adaptations would you expect to observe in mountain dwellers?

Explanations to Practice Questions

1. D

Gas exchange in the lungs relies on passive diffusion of oxygen and carbon dioxide. This is accomplished easily because there is always a difference in the partial pressures of these two gases. In addition, the thin and moist alveolar surfaces allow for fast diffusion and gas exchange across their membranes. Therefore, (A), (B), and (C) can be eliminated. (D) is indeed the correct answer, since active transport is not needed in the gas exchange process in the lungs.

2. D

The muscles involved in ventilation are the diaphragm (which separates the thoracic cavity from the abdominal cavity) and the intercostal muscles of the rib cage. During inhalation, the diaphragm contracts and flattens, while the external intercostal muscles contract, pushing the rib cage up and out. These actions cause an overall increase in the size of the thoracic cavity. During exhalation, both the diaphragm and the external intercostals relax, causing a decrease in the size of the thoracic cavity. Thus, the only correct association from the given answers is (D).

3. C

During inhalation, as the diaphragm and external intercostal muscles contract, the rib cage and chest wall are pushed up and out, and the thoracic cavity increases in volume. This volume increase, in turn, reduces the intrapleural pressure, causing the lungs to expand and fill with air. This process is referred to as negative-pressure breathing because air is drawn into the lungs by a vacuum. In contrast, positive-pressure breathing, as in a patient on a ventilator, occurs when air is forced into the lungs because the pressure is greater in the ventilator than in the lungs. (C) is therefore the correct answer.

4. A

The lungs are surrounded by two membranes: the visceral pleura and the parietal pleura. The parietal pleura surrounds the visceral pleura. The space between the pleurae is referred to as the intrapleural space and contains a thin layer of serous fluid. (A) is therefore the correct answer.

5. D

The residual volume is the volume of air that always remains in the lungs and cannot be forcibly exhaled. (D) is thus the correct answer. (A) refers to the tidal volume, (B) defines the vital capacity, and (C) describes the expiratory reserve volume.

6. D

There are two major mechanisms in place to prevent the lungs from collapsing. First, the pleurae (visceral and parietal) surround and protect the lungs. An injury to the chest in which the parietal pleura is ruptured results in air getting into the intrapleural space, which can quickly cause the lungs to collapse, a condition known as pneumothorax. In addition, the alveoli are coated with a thin layer of surfactant, which reduces the high surface tension of the fluid lining the alveoli and prevents the lungs from collapsing during exhalation. As such, (A) and (B) are both true, making (D) the correct answer.

7. D

Several mechanisms exist to ensure that inhalation is rapid and poses no danger to the body. First, to prevent food particles from reaching the lungs, a flap of epiglottis covers the entrance to the trachea, called the glottis, during swallowing. Second, the trachea and bronchi are lined with ciliated epithelial cells, which filter and trap particles inhaled along with the air. Third, at the level of the alveoli, several mechanisms exist to ensure rapid inhalation: Thin, moist alveolar surfaces facilitate gas exchange, while lining of the alveoli with surfactant prevents lung collapse and facilitates gas exchange. Based on this, (D) is the correct answer.

8. D

Air enters the respiratory tract through the external nares (nostrils) and travels through the nasal cavities. It then passes through the pharynx and into a second chamber called the larynx. Ingested food also passes through the pharynx on its way to the esophagus; to ensure that food does not accidentally enter the larynx, the epiglottis covers the larynx during swallowing. After the larynx, air goes to the trachea, which eventually divides into two bronchi, one for each lung. The bronchi branch into smaller and smaller bronchi, the terminal branches of which are referred to as bronchioles. The bronchioles are surrounded by clusters of alveoli. From the given sequences, only (D) correctly describes the sequence of the passages through which air travels.

9. D

Exhalation is generally a passive process involving elastic recoil of the lungs and relaxation of both the diaphragm and the external intercostal muscles. (However, during vigorous exercise or forced expiration, active muscular contraction assists in expiration.) Gas exchange is also a passive process; the gases diffuse down their partial pressure gradients. Inhalation, however, is an active process requiring contraction of the diaphragm and the external intercostals. (D) is thus the correct answer.

10. C

Total lung capacity is equal to the vital capacity (the maximum amount of air that can be forcibly inhaled and exhaled from the lungs) plus the residual volume (the air that always remains in the lungs, preventing the alveoli from collapsing). (C) is therefore the correct answer.

The Cardiovascular System

As late as the 19th century, physicians adhered to the principle of health known as *humouralism*. No, this was not some strange hybrid of medicine and stand-up comedy. Humouralism was a theory of the makeup and functioning of the human body developed by Greek and Roman physicians and philosophers and adopted by Islamic physicians. It was dominant in medical thought and practice until it was ultimately displaced by modern medical research in the 1800s.

The humoral theory holds that the human body is composed of four fluids or substances called humors. These are black bile, yellow bile, phlegm, and blood. In the state of health, these four humors are in balance, but excess or deficiency of any one of them causes illness, disease, and even maladaptive personality characteristics. Over the course of a lifetime, the levels of each of the four humors would rise and fall in accordance with diet and activity, resulting in maladies reflective of the imbalance. Treatments were intended to restore the balance.

Furthermore, personalities came to be associated with each of the humors. Those who had an excess of phlegm were phlegmatic, which was associated with winter and characterized as wet and cold. Phlegmatic people were said to be calm, unemotional, and shy. Those who had an excess of blood were sanguine, which was associated with spring and characterized as wet and hot; they were said to be fun loving, spontaneous, and gregarious but also prone to arrogance, indulgence, and even mania.

Perhaps one of the most well-known medical treatments associated with humouralism is the practice of bloodletting. Since many diseases were associated with an excess of blood, physicians (for nearly 2,000 years, mind you!) would rely on the withdrawal of significant amounts of blood from their patients to restore balance to the four humors. Methods for bloodletting were many, and some were dramatic, including drawing blood from major veins in the arm or neck and puncturing arteries. Devices known as scarificators were developed to cut through to the superficial vessels. Most famously, leeches were used, especially in the early 19th century, to draw out the excess blood. In fact, in the early decades of the 1800s, hundreds of millions of leeches were used by European physicians; in the 1830s, France alone imported about 40 million leeches per year for medical treatments.

Now, before you start feeling superior to these "primitive" doctors and their "barbaric" medical practices, you should be aware that although the humoral theory has been completely discredited by modern medical research, some practices associated with humouralism are still being used, albeit based on very different medical understanding and for very different purposes. For example, new research has shown that medicinal leeches can be used effectively in microsurgery, where they help prevent blood coagulation, and in reconstructive surgery, where they help stimulate circulation to the reattached organ.

One of the most commonly tested MCAT topics is the cardiovascular system, which serves a variety of functions, including the movement of respiratory gases, nutrients, and wastes. We will review the structures and functional anatomy of the cardiovascular system and then discuss blood and its functional components. Electrically excitable cells, whose connections we will outline, initiate and spread contractions throughout the heart. A quick recap of genetics and inheritance will help us understand ABO and Rh antigens, whose functional consequences we will also discuss. In addition, the ability of oxygen and carbon dioxide to bind to hemoglobin will be detailed, including a discussion of the factors that may affect this binding.

Anatomy of the Cardiovascular System

The cardiovascular system consists of a muscular four-chambered **heart**, **blood vessels**, and **blood.** In casual observation, we usually think and speak of the heart as a single pump, but actually it is two pumps connected in series (analogous to a circuit with two batteries in series). The right pump (the right heart) accepts deoxygenated blood returning from the body and moves it to the lungs by way of the pulmonary arteries for oxygenation. The left pump (the left heart) receives oxygenated blood from the lungs by way of the pulmonary veins and forces it out to the body through the aorta. The connections of the left and right heart to the systemic and pulmonary circulations, respectively, are commonly tested and easily learned MCAT topics. Each side of the heart is made up of two chambers: an **atrium** (pl. *atria*) and a **ventricle**. The atria are thin walled, and you can think of them as the lobbies or waiting rooms for each side of the heart: Blood is received (from the body or from the lungs) in the atria before it is moved to the ventricles, which are more muscular because they do the actual work of pumping the blood out of the heart (to the body or the lungs).

We can follow the path of blood through the left and right sides of the closed cardiovascular circuit by picking any place within the circuit as our starting point (see Figure 9.1). If we begin, say, in the left atrium with oxygenated blood, then we can follow the blood as it moves to the left ventricle and then into the **aorta**, the largest artery in the body. Major arteries, such as the coronary, common carotid, and renal arteries, divide the blood flow from the aorta toward the different peripheral tissues. Arteries branch into **arterioles**, and these ultimately lead to **capillaries**, which perfuse the tissues. On the venous side of a capillary network, the capillaries join together into **venules**, which join into **veins**. The deoxygenated blood travels through the veins into the inferior and superior **vena cavae** (IVC and SVC), the largest veins in the body, which carry the blood to the right atrium. Blood then moves into the right ventricle, which pumps the blood to the lungs via the pulmonary arteries for gas exchange. Finally, blood leaves the lungs through the pulmonary veins and goes to the left atrium, where we started. Written out in shorthand, the pathway appears like this:

Left atrium → left ventricle → aorta → arteries → arterioles → capillaries → venules → veins → IVC and SVC → right atrium → right ventricle → pulmonary arteries → lungs → pulmonary veins → left atrium

In some cases, blood actually passes through two capillary beds, which are connected by venules, before being returned to the heart. Each of these networks has a special purpose and is referred to as a **portal system**. A hepatic portal system (see Chapter 7) connects the vasculatures of the intestines and the liver, and a hypophyseal portal system in the brain connects the vasculatures of the hypothalamus and the pituitary gland (see Chapter 12). Both are test-worthy topics that you should review and understand.

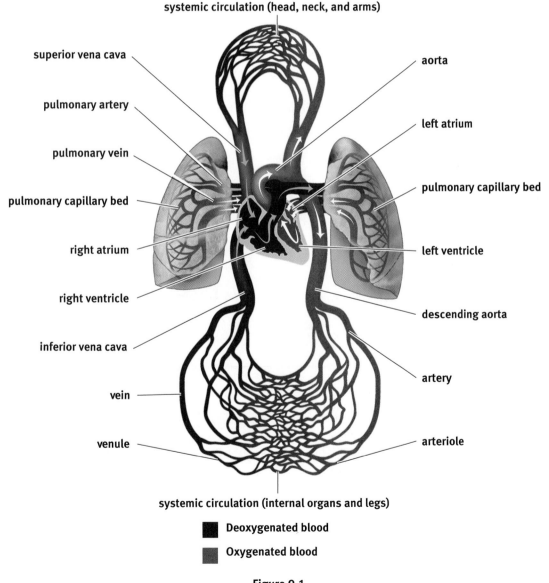

Figure 9.1

Real World

Oxygen and nutrients are supplied to the heart muscle by the coronary arteries. A delicate balance exists between the supply of oxygen to the heart (coronary blood flow) and the myocardial oxygen demand. Deprivation of oxygen and nutrients to the heart is called myocardial ischemia. The most common clinical manifestation of this condition is a type of chest pain called *angina*. If this ischemia goes on unchecked, parts of the heart muscle may become irreversibly damaged. This is called myocardial infarction (heart attack). Although there are many possible causes for decreased coronary blood flow, the most common by far is atherosclerosis of the coronary arteries (the formation of a plaque composed primarily of cholesterol).

THE HEART

Alas, the human heart is not the lacy pink object associated with Valentine's Day. (Can you imagine the utter shock of the cardiothoracic surgeon who finds, upon opening up a patient's chest cavity, a heart-shaped box of chocolates?) Nor is the human heart merely a square four-room apartment with two entrances, two exits, and two sets of French doors connecting the anterior and posterior room—although for simplicity and clarity, the heart is usually drawn like the floor plan of said apartment: a box divided into four square chambers. The heart is a muscular organ a little larger than your fist, weighing between 7 and 15 ounces. Located between the lungs, it lies behind and a little to the left of the sternum, and it is tilted ever so slightly so that the exterior wall of the right ventricle forms the base of the heart. The walls of the heart are composed of cardiac muscle of varying thickness. It may seem to be an obvious point, but we've known students to make this mistake, so let's be as clear as possible: Cardiac muscle is found only in the heart, and no other muscle type composes the muscle tissue of the heart.

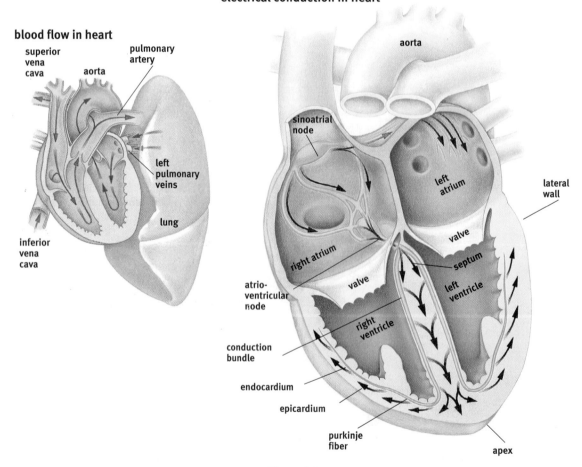

Figure 9.2

Can we make an MCAT-worthy prediction concerning whether the left or right heart will be more muscular? Let's think about which side works at higher pressures and has to pump the blood farther. The left heart is responsible for pumping blood to all the tissues of the body by way of the systemic circulation. To do so, it must be able to generate high pressures. The right heart, on the other hand, is responsible for pumping blood to the lungs via the pulmonary circulation. It can do so at lower pressures (because there's little resistance to the blood flow through the pulmonary circulation). Therefore, the left heart must be more muscular, since it has to generate higher pressures to pump the blood over greater distances. In fact, the wall of the left ventricle is the thickest in the heart, at about half an inch. You may have heard that there is a difference in the volumes of arterial blood and venous blood; indeed, that is true. Nevertheless, because the right and left sides of the heart are in series with each other, the total volumes of blood passing through the two sides (about 5 liters per minute) are the same.

Valves

As we discussed, the heart moves blood through the systemic and pulmonary vasculatures by generating pressures through contraction. It is critical for blood to move in a single direction (forward) in the system. Different valves in the heart and in veins ensure that the blood will flow only in one direction. The heart contains four valves. Between each of the atria and ventricles are the aptly named **atrioventricular (AV) valves**. These valves also have colloquial names, which you should know for Test Day. The right AV valve is also called the **tricuspid** valve because it has three leaflets; the left AV valve has only two leaflets and is also known as the **bicuspid** or **mitral** valve. When the heart beats by ventricular contraction, the blood must move forward into the pulmonary arteries and aorta. These two valves prevent backflow into the right and left atria, respectively.

There are also valves that prevent backflow into the ventricles. Each ventricle is protected by a **semilunar valve** with three cusps. The right semilunar valve is called the **pulmonary** valve, because it sits between the right ventricle and pulmonary arteries; the one on the left is the **aortic** valve, as it separates the left ventricle from the aorta. They prevent backflow of blood from the pulmonary arteries and aorta into the ventricles during ventricular relaxation (**diastole**), whereas the AV valves prevent backflow from ventricles into atria during contraction (**systole**).

Contraction

Phases

The heart is a muscle that must contract in order to move blood. Each heartbeat is composed of two phases known as systole and diastole. During systole, ventricular contraction and closure of the AV valves occur, and blood is pumped out of the ventricles. During diastole, the heart is relaxed, semilunar valves are closed, and blood from the atria is filling the ventricles. Contraction of the ventricular muscles generates the higher pressures of systole, whereas their relaxation during diastole causes the pressure to decrease. The elasticity of the walls of the large arteries, which stretch out to receive the volume of blood from the heart, allows the vessels to maintain sufficient pressure while the ventricular muscles are relaxed. In fact, if it weren't for the elasticity of the large arteries, your diastolic blood pressure (which is a gauge pressure) would plummet to zero and you wouldn't survive for very long: *die*-astolic indeed!

A measure we should be aware of is the **cardiac output**, the total blood volume pumped by the ventricle in a minute. Does it matter which ventricle we choose? No. The two pumps are connected in series, so the volumes of blood passing through each side are the same. This sort of critical thinking is exactly what we need on Test Day. Cardiac output is the product of **heart rate** (beats per minute) and **stroke volume** (volume of blood pumped per beat). For humans, cardiac output is about 5 L/min. Incidentally, the average total volume of blood in a human is about 5 liters. Cardiac output will depend on size and age of person, as well as cardiovascular and systemic health of the individual. During periods of rest or exercise, the autonomic nervous system will decrease (parasympathetic) or increase (sympathetic) cardiac output, respectively.

Mechanism and Control

The autonomic nervous system regulates cardiac output by increasing or decreasing the heart rate, similar to the way in which it regulates breathing (see Chapter 8). However, cardiac muscle, like smooth muscle, demonstrates myogenic activity (see Chapter 6). In other words, neural signals can modulate the rate at which the heart beats, but the heart will continue to function even without input from the nervous system. We might even say that the heart marches to the beat of its own drummer.

The coordinated, rhythmic contraction of cardiac muscle originates in an electrical impulse generated by and traveling through a pathway formed by four electrically excitable structures (see Figure 9.2 and 9.3). This commonly tested pathway consists of, in order, the **sinoatrial (SA) node**, the **atrioventricular (AV) node**, the **bundle of His (AV bundle)**, and the **Purkinje fibers**. **Impulse** initiation occurs at the SA node, which generates 60–100 signals per minute without any neural input. This small collection of cells is located in the wall of the right atrium. As the depolarization wave spreads from the SA node, it causes the two atria to contract simultaneously. Atrial systole (contraction) results in an increase in atrial pressure and more blood pumped into the ventricles. This additional volume of blood forced from the atria into the ventricles is called the atrial kick and accounts for about 5–30 percent of the cardiac output. Next, the signal reaches the AV node, which sits at the junction of the atria and ventricles. The signal may be delayed here to allow for the ventricles to fill completely before they contract. It then travels down the bundle of His, embedded in the interventricular septum (wall), and to the Purkinje fibers, which distribute the electrical signal through the ventricular muscle, causing ventricular contraction.

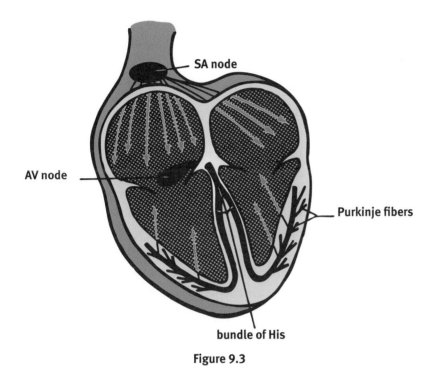

Figure 9.3

The SA node has an intrinsic rhythm of 60–100 signals per minute, so the normal human heart rate is 60–100 beats per minute. Highly conditioned athletes (most famously, triathletes) may have heart rates significantly lower than 60, in the range of 40–50 beats per minute. Stress, exercise, excitement, surprise, or danger can cause the heart rate to rise significantly above 100. We wouldn't advise doing so, but you could test this by suddenly clapping and yelling very loudly in the middle of the MCAT testing session and then immediately measuring the heart rate of the other test takers. We guarantee that you would observe tachycardia (elevated heart rate) in every person. Granted, you might not survive the violence directed toward you long enough to collect the data for your little Test Day experiment.

So what part of the nervous system influences cardiac contractions? The autonomic division, which consists of **parasympathetic** ("rest and digest") and **sympathetic** ("fight or flight") branches, controls the heart. Parasympathetic neurotransmitters slow the heart via the **vagus nerve** (more on this in Chapter 12), whereas sympathetic neurotransmitters speed it up. Quick review: Which system would jump into action when we're in the woods, running away from an angry bear? The sympathetic branch of the autonomic division. We exploit this autonomic control of heart rate in medicine all the time. For example, after suffering a heart attack, a patient will often be given a drug called a β-blocker, which blocks sympathetic β-receptors. The β-blocker reduces the heart rate and blood pressure, thereby reducing the cardiac workload and reducing the heart's need for oxygen. It is thought that by preventing the heart from overworking after a heart attack, the risk of death and of future heart attacks can be reduced.

Blood Vessels

We have considered how the heart acts as a pump to move blood through systemic and pulmonary circulation, and we have even compared the two sides of the heart to low- and high-voltage batteries connected in series. Now let's consider the conductive pathway of this vascular circuit by examining the vessels through which the blood flows. The three major types of vessels are arteries, veins, and capillaries. Arteries are strong, thick-walled structures that always carry blood *away* from the heart (*ar*teries = *a*way) to the lungs and all other parts of the body, like our brain (which will need a lot of nourishment for critical thinking on Test Day!). Most arteries contain oxygenated blood. Only the pulmonary arteries and (fetal) umbilical arteries carry deoxygenated blood. Veins are thin-walled and inelastic vessels that transport blood *to* the heart (*v*eins con*v*erge near the heart). Except for the pulmonary and umbilical vessels, all veins carry deoxygenated blood. Take a look at Figure 9.4. Notice that arteries and veins share the same components, simply in different proportions. Don't worry about the names of all the different layers. Simply be able to recognize that the same types of cells comprise both types of vessels and that arteries have much more smooth muscle than veins.

Due to their high elasticity, arteries offer high resistance to the flow of blood, which is why the left ventricle must generate the higher pressures. After they are filled with blood, the elastic recoil from their walls maintains a high pressure and forces blood forward. Conversely, veins are capacitive and can carry large amounts of blood owing to their thin, inelastic walls, which stretch out easily and do not recoil. Indeed, three-fourths of our total blood volume may be in venous circulation at any given moment.

Given that the heart is located in the chest, the blood flow in most veins is upward from the lower body back to the heart, against gravity. In the inferior vena cava, this translates into a lot of blood in a large column. As you might imagine, the pressure at the bottom of this venous column in, say, the large veins of the legs can be quite high. In fact, it can exceed systolic pressure (120 mmHg), going as high as 200 mmHg or more. In light of this, two questions must be answered: How do veins prevent backflow in the venous circulation? And how do veins move blood forward toward the heart, given the inelasticity and the thinner or absent layer of smooth muscle in

Figure 9.4

a. Lumen
b. Tunica intima
c. Tunica media
d. Tunica externa
e. Endothelium
f. Smooth muscle

their walls? First, the larger veins have one-way valves to prevent backflow. Blood flowing forward pushes the valves open, but if blood begins to move backward, the valves are pushed shut. Failure of the venous valves results in the formation of varicose veins, which are distended where the blood has pooled. Pregnant women are especially susceptible to the formation of varicose veins because the total blood volume increases dramatically during pregnancy, resulting in increased venous pressure, especially in the lower body due to the fetus compressing the IVC.

The second question is answered by considering the relationship between the large veins and skeletal muscles. Most large veins are surrounded by skeletal muscle, which squeezes the veins as muscles contract, forcing the blood up against gravity in much the same way that squeezing the bottom of a tube of toothpaste causes the contents to be expelled onto your toothbrush. This is why sitting motionless for long periods of time, such as in a cramped middle seat on a long transatlantic flight, can increase the risk of pulmonary embolism. Blood pools in the lower extremities; sluggish blood coagulates more easily. If a blood clot forms in the vein and becomes dislodged, it may be carried through the heart into the pulmonary vasculature, where it may get stuck in a small vessel.

The third and final type of blood vessel is the capillary. Capillaries are vessels with a single endothelial cell layer, which allows for exchange of nutrients and gases. Capillaries can be quite delicate. The punch that you so rudely received from your sibling in Chapter 6 probably left a bruise, an area in which broken capillaries allowed erythrocytes to escape into the interstitial space. Capillaries are usually so small that blood cells must traverse them single file.

BLOOD PRESSURE

The voltage or potential difference between two points in a circuit is analogous to blood pressure: The pressure gradient from left to right is the fundamental determinant of the movement of blood through the closed vascular circuit, just as the electric potential difference between two points causes charge to move between them. Blood pressure is a measure of the force per unit area that is exerted on the wall of the blood vessels. This is exactly how we define pressure when discussing any fluid or solid: force per unit area. The device used to measure blood pressure is called a **sphygmomanometer** (and is quite a mouthful!). Sphygmomanometers measure the gauge pressure in the systemic circulation, which is the pressure above atmospheric pressure (760 mmHg at sea level). Blood pressure is expressed as a ratio of the systolic (ventricular contraction) to diastolic (ventricular relaxation) pressures. Pressure gradually drops from the arterial to venous circulation, although the largest drop is across the arterioles (see Figure 9.5).

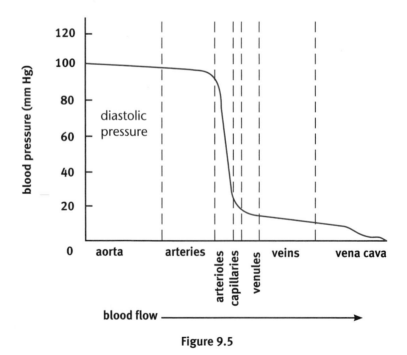

Figure 9.5

Blood ★★★★☆

Now that we have examined the pump and the pipes, let's talk about the fluid that travels through them.

COMPOSITION

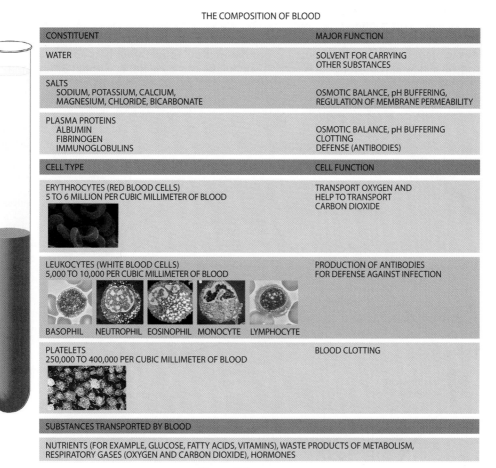

Figure 9.6

We learn from those pesky paper cuts that blood is a bright red substance and that it's never a good idea to run the edge of paper over your skin, even on a dare. To learn more about blood, we'll need some help from our MCAT biologist's toolbox. First, using a centrifuge, we can spin blood down to separate its components by density. Doing so separates the blood into two compartments: By volume, blood is 55% liquid and 45% cells, as seen in Figure 9.6. **Plasma** is the liquid portion of blood, an aqueous mixture of nutrients, salts, respiratory gases, hormones, and blood proteins. Finally, if we pull out our handy-dandy microscope, we can examine the components of the cell compartment, which fall into three major categories: **erythrocytes**, **leukocytes**, and **platelets**. All blood cells are formed from the same hematopoietic stem cells, which originate in the bone marrow. See Figure 9.7 for a schematic of how blood cells are all ancestrally related.

HIERARCHY IN BLOOD-FORMING CELLS

Stem cells in the blood-forming, or hematopoietic, system illustrate principles governing the activity of stem cells in other tissues as well. A small population of hematopoietic stem cells (HSC) in the bone marrow is the source of most of the different blood and immune cell types that circulate in the human body. HSCs reside in an environmental niche, surrounded by stromal cells that provide important regulatory signals to the stem cell. When new blood or immune cells are needed, an HSC divides to produce one daughter cell, which remains in the niche and retains the long-term HSC identity, and another short-lived daughter termed a multipotent progenitor cell (MPP). The MPP, in turn, divides to produce progenitors committed to generating cells in the myeloid (blood) or lymphoid (immune) lineages. As the descendants of progenitors become increasingly specialized, they experience a programmed decline in their ability to proliferate until they stop dividing and are said to be terminally differentiated. Only the stem cell retains unlimited proliferative potential through its ability to renew itself indefinitely by dividing without differentiating.

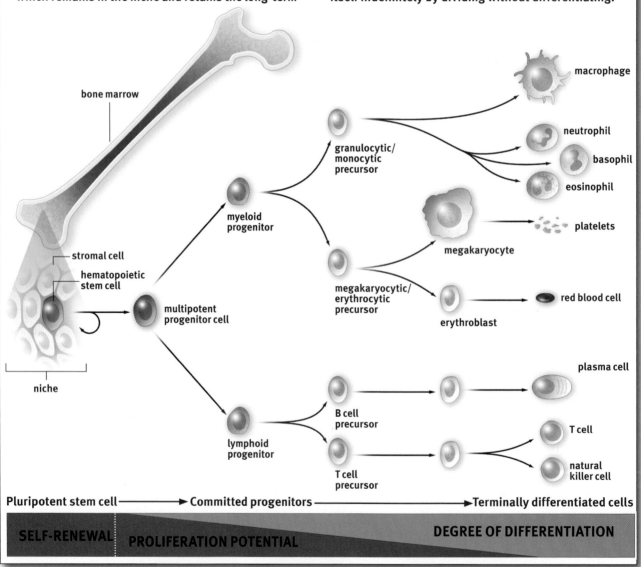

Figure 9.7

Erythrocytes (Red Blood Cells)

In the body, oxygen and nutrients are delivered to the peripheral tissues, and carbon dioxide and other wastes (e.g., hydrogen ions, ammonia) are picked up from the peripheral tissues and delivered to the organs of waste management—the lungs, liver, and kidneys. The erythrocyte is a specialized cell designed for oxygen transport. Red blood cells are like couriers who travel up and down elevators all day, delivering goods and picking up packages. Oxygen is not simply dissolved in the cytoplasm of the red blood cell. (Remember, molecular oxygen is nonpolar and therefore has low solubility in aqueous environments.) Rather, each erythrocyte contains about 250 million molecules of **hemoglobin** protein, and each hemoglobin can bind four molecules of oxygen. That's 1 billion molecules of oxygen per cell! Red blood cells are unique in other ways, as well, and the modifications reflect their special role in the human body. On the surface, they look different from other cells: They have a biconcave disk shape that serves a dual purpose. First, this shape assists them in traveling through tiny capillaries. Second, it increases the cell's surface area, which allows for greater gas exchange.

However, beauty isn't only skin deep; when we peer beneath the cell membrane of the erythrocyte, we discover many more fascinating characteristics—fascinating more for what is not there than what is. As red blood cells mature, they lose their nuclei, mitochondria, and other membranous organelles. (You'll recall from our discussion in Chapter 6 that red blood cells form and mature in the bone marrow before they are released into the circulation.) The loss of membrane-bound organelles is a dramatic modification, to say the least. What purpose does this serve? It essentially clears some room, which allows the cell to carry a maximal amount of hemoglobin for gas exchange. Additionally, since no mitochondria are present to enable aerobic respiration, none of the transported oxygen will be used up for cellular respiration. Of course, this means that red blood cells must rely on fermentation (lactic acid, not ethanol—human cells are not microbreweries!) for ATP production. Furthermore, without nuclei, erythrocytes cannot divide. They live for about 120 days in the bloodstream, getting knocked about, dented, and dinged, before cells in the spleen and liver phagocytize them for recycled parts. There are about 5 million erythrocytes per milliliter of blood. This translates into a total of about 25 billion red blood cells that can carry up to 100 billion oxygen molecules in the total blood volume!

Leukocytes (White Blood Cells)

Like erythrocytes, leukocytes, or white blood cells, form in the bone marrow. Leukocytes usually comprise less than 1 percent of total blood volume. This translates into about 500–1,000 leukocytes per milliliter of blood, which is a small number relative to the erythrocyte concentration. This number can massively increase under certain conditions when we need supplemental white blood cells, most notably during infection. White blood cells are a crucial part of the immune system, acting as our defenders against pathogens, foreign cells, and other materials not recognized as self. Let's briefly discuss five basic types of leukocytes, which are all categorized into two classes: granulocytes and agranulocytes.

The granular leukocytes (**neutrophils, eosinophils**, and **basophils**) are so named because cytoplasmic granules are visible under microscopy. These granules are like miniature bombs containing a variety of compounds that are toxic to invading microbes. (Remember how we mentioned viral and bacterial infections as invaders and spies in Chapter 1.) Granular leukocytes are involved in inflammatory reactions, allergies, pus formation, and destruction of bacteria and parasites.

The agranulocytes, which do not contain granules, consist of **lymphocytes** and **monocytes**. Lymphocytes are important in the **specific immune response**, the body's targeted fight against particular pathogens such as viruses and bacteria. Some lymphocytes are involved in the immediate fight against an infection, while others function to maintain a long-term memory bank of pathogen recognition. These cells, in a very real sense, help our body learn from experience and are prepared to mount a lightning-fast response to repeated exposure to familiar pathogens. For example, most children in the United States receive vaccines to help build their immune systems. One such vaccine is the chickenpox vaccine, which includes a live but weaker strain of the virus (varicella) that causes chickenpox. When the vaccine is administered, the virus is recognized as foreign, and an immune response is activated. In the process, certain immune cells develop that maintain a memory of the virus; our body learns what it looks like and prepares itself to ward off the virus later in life.

Lymphocyte maturation takes place in one of three locations. Those lymphocytes that mature in the spleen or lymph nodes are referred to as B-cells, and those that mature in the thymus are called T-cells. B-cells are responsible for antibody generation, whereas T-cells kill virally infected cells and activate other immune cells.

The other agranulocytes are monocytes, which phagocytize foreign matter such as bacteria. They are renamed to **"macrophages"** once they leave the marrow, travel through the bloodstream, and move into tissue outside the vascular system. In the brain, they are called **microglia**.

Platelets

Platelets are actually cell fragments derived from the breakup of cells known as **megakaryocytes** in the marrow. Their function is to clot blood. They are present in concentrations of 200,000–500,000 per milliliter. The enzymatic reactions involved in the formation of a clot (the clotting cascade) will be discussed shortly.

Real World

Human immunodeficiency virus (HIV) causes a loss of a certain subset of T-cells known as helper T-cells (CD4⁺). Although the loss of helper T-cells alone is not fatal, the destruction of these lymphocytes prevents the generation of immune responses against opportunistic infections. This is why people infected with HIV (often referred to as *immunocompromised*) are more susceptible to a variety of diseases against which an intact immune system would normally defend.

BLOOD ANTIGENS

How do we know who we are? Existential questions of self, identity, being, and purpose are beyond the scope of the MCAT. (But we would certainly encourage you to think about these questions when you're not studying for the MCAT!) In part, we each define ourselves based on an outward projection, an image or representation of an interior sense of self. Our mannerisms, speech patterns, style of dress, and political or religious activities, to name but a few outward expressions of interior processes, help us recognize ourselves as self and distinguish ourselves from others. Cells operate in similar ways to identify themselves and recognize each other. Cells put on a style of dress or a manner of acting reflective of the processes going on deep inside the cell. For example, a direct way of identifying cell type is to examine the proteins expressed on the extracellular surface of the cell membrane. Since surface proteins expressed by a cell may initiate an organism's immune system, we call these proteins *antigens*. The two major antigen families that we need to discuss relative to blood groups are the **ABO antigens** and the **Rh factor** protein.

ABO Group

First up is the ABO classification. Take a look at Table 9.1, and we will discuss it below.

Table 9.1. ABO Blood Types

Blood Type	Antigen in Red Blood Cell	Antibodies Produced
A	A	anti-B
B	B	anti-A
AB (universal recipient)	A and B	none
O (universal donor)	none	anti-A and anti-B

Now that we know what we are looking at, let's fill in the details. The ABO system is based on the existence of three alleles for blood type. But, as we will discuss in Chapter 14 (and we may already know), the human genome is diploid; for each gene, there will be two alleles, one of maternal and the other of paternal origin. For this particular class of erythrocyte cell-surface protein, the A and B alleles are codominant. This is to say, if the allele for A is present (I^A), it will be expressed; if the allele for B is present (I^B), it will be expressed; and if we have an allele for each, both will be expressed. O is recessive to both. People with type O blood don't express either variant of this protein (antigen). For the type O blood phenotype, the genotype is ii. The naming system of blood types based on the presence or absence of these protein variants doesn't refer to the alleles themselves but to the proteins, and the four blood types are A, B, AB, and O. Be aware that there are two possible genotypes each for

MCAT Expertise

You are almost guaranteed to see at least one question on blood groups on Test Day. It is critical that you learn how the system works (A/B codominant).

Key Concept

Antigens are the stimulus for B-cells to make antibodies. After exposure of a B-cell to its specific antigen, the cell transforms into a factory that makes many antibodies.

Real World

When an Rh⁻ woman is pregnant with an Rh⁺ fetus, the risk of erythroblastosis fetalis in subsequent Rh-mismatched pregnancies can usually be avoided by giving the Rh⁻ mother Rh-immune globulin during pregnancy and immediately after delivery. Administration of immune globulin (which is a type of passive immunization; see Chapter 10) will suppress the development of the mother's active immunity, preventing the production of anti-Rh antibodies.

type A and type B blood. The possible genotypes for type A blood are I^AI^A or I^Ai and for type B blood, the possible genotypes are I^BI^B or I^Bi.

Why are we making such a big deal about this? Because the MCAT makes a big deal about this. "And why is that?" you might be asking. Because the ABO classification has such important implications for medical practice. For example, it is critical to match blood types for transfusions. It's no exaggeration to say that blood type matching is a life and death matter, given the severe hemolysis that can result if the donor blood antigen is recognized as foreign by the recipient's immune system. The foreign antigens are recognized by antibodies. For example, a person with type A blood will recognize the type A protein variant as self but the type B variant protein as foreign and will make antibodies to type B. Since type O blood cells express neither antigen variant, they will not initiate any immune response, regardless of the recipient's actual blood type. However, a recipient who is type O, and whose immune system does not recognize either protein variant as self, will produce both anti-A *and* anti-B antibodies. This leads to our recognition of **universal recipients and donors**. People with type AB blood (universal recipients) can receive from all blood types. No blood antigen is foreign to AB blood group members, so no adverse reactions will occur upon transfusion. People with type O blood can donate to all groups (universal donor), as their blood cells have no ABO antigens on the surface for anti-A or anti-B antibodies to recognize.

Rh Factor

The Rh factor (so named because it was first described in Rhesus monkeys) is also a surface protein expressed on red blood cells. Although at one time it was thought to be a single antigen, it has since been found to exist as several variants. However, there is one predominant variant whose presence or absence is indicated by a plus or minus superscript on the ABO blood type (e.g. O⁺, AB⁻). Rh⁺ individuals express the Rh protein on their erythrocytes, and Rh⁻ individuals do not. The presence of the Rh factor is a dominant condition; one positive allele is enough for the protein to be expressed.

The Rh factor status is particularly important in maternal-fetal medicine. During childbirth, women are often exposed to fetal blood. If a woman is Rh⁻ and her fetus is Rh⁺, she will become sensitized to the Rh factor, and her immune system will begin making antibodies against it. This is not a problem during first pregnancies because sensitization and antibody production begin only at the time of delivery. However, any subsequent pregnancy in which the fetus is Rh⁺ will present a problem because maternal anti-Rh antibodies can cross the placenta and attack the fetal blood cells, resulting in hemolysis of the fetal cells. This condition is known as **erythroblastosis fetalis**, which can be fatal to the fetus. Today, we can use medicine to prevent this condition (see the sidebar). There is less concern with ABO mismatching between mother and fetus, because these maternal antibodies do not readily cross the placenta (they are a different subclass of antibody). ABO and Rh typing often appear as discrete MCAT questions.

Functions of the Cardiovascular System

We have fully discussed the anatomical components of the cardiovascular system—the heart, blood vessels, and blood—and we are now ready to discuss the overarching purpose of the system. The cardiovascular system transports many compounds, including gases, nutrients, and waste products, to and from the body's tissues through the red blood cells and plasma. Furthermore, it serves an important role in immunity through the production of the different types of leukocytes and delivery of those immune cells to fight against localized or systemic pathogens. Finally, through the activity of platelets and clot formation, the system has a built-in mechanism for repairing damaged vessels. Let's start with gas transport.

TRANSPORT OF GASES

Two major gases are transported in the blood: oxygen and carbon dioxide. Oxygen is delivered from the lungs to the tissues and carbon dioxide is removed from the tissues for transport to the lungs. We will investigate each one separately.

Oxygen is primarily carried by hemoglobin in the blood. We should recall that hemoglobin is a protein made up of four separate but interacting chains, each of which has a prosthetic heme group to bind an oxygen molecule. The actual binding of oxygen is accomplished by the heme group's central iron atom, which can undergo changes in its oxidation state. The binding or releasing of oxygen to or from the iron atom in the heme group is a redox reaction.

As the first oxygen binds to a heme group, it induces a conformational shift in the shape of hemoglobin from taut to relaxed. This shift results in an increase in hemoglobin's affinity for oxygen, making it easier for subsequent molecules of oxygen to bind to the other unoccupied heme groups. Once hemoglobin is full, the removal of one molecule of oxygen also results in a conformational shift. This shift results in a decrease in hemoglobin's affinity for oxygen, making it easier for the other molecules of oxygen to leave the heme groups. This phenomenon is referred to as cooperative binding and results in the classic sigmoidal (*S*-shaped) hemoglobin-binding curve. From our discussion of enzymes in Chapter 2, you should recognize this pattern of binding as an allosteric effect (due to the quaternary structure of the hemoglobin protein).

Key Concept

Remember that hemoglobin is composed of four subunits (i.e., hemoglobin protein has quaternary structure). The interaction among the four subunits (allosteric effect) results in a change in hemoglobin's binding affinity for oxygen and gives the classic sigmoidal binding curve. Myoglobin, the globular protein responsible for transferring oxygen from hemoglobin to the muscle cells, is composed of only one subunit and lacks quaternary structure. Its curve is not sigmoidal but shows rapid saturation at low P_{O_2}.

To make sure that we fully understand this important concept, let's draw a second curve to the right of the normal one in Figure 9.8. Notice that at the same partial pressure of O_2 (e.g., 60 mmHg), the O_2 saturation level will be lower on the right curve than on the normal one. The oxygen saturation is lower because the hemoglobin is more readily giving up its oxygen.

MCAT Expertise

The hemoglobin-oxygen dissociation curve is not static—it can shift to the right or left depending on the circumstances. A shift to the right means that for a given partial pressure of O_2, less O_2 will be bound to hemoglobin (more oxygen has been unloaded, and the hemoglobin has a lower percent saturation) due to a decrease in affinity. Several conditions produce a right shift, including an increase in the partial pressure of CO_2, a decrease in pH, and an increase in temperature. These seemingly disparate conditions are associated with periods of increased metabolic rate and signal a need for more oxygen, such as during exercise. For example, we would predict that rapidly and repeatedly contracting muscles would have higher pCO_2 (increased metabolism), lower pH (because of increased pCO_2 and lactic acid buildup), and higher temperature (increased thermal energy release). Conversely, a shift to the left means that for a given partial pressure of O_2, more O_2 will be bound to hemoglobin (the hemoglobin has a higher percent saturation) due to an increase in affinity. Fetal hemoglobin, which has a higher affinity for O_2 than adult hemoglobin, has a left-shifted curve.

Figure 9.8

Delivering oxygen to tissues is only part of the job of transporting respiratory gases; removing CO_2 (the primary waste product of cellular respiration) is also important. Carbon dioxide gas, like oxygen gas, is essentially nonpolar and therefore has low solubility in the aqueous plasma; only a small percentage of the total CO_2 being transported in the blood to the lungs is dissolved in the plasma. Carbon dioxide can be directly carried by hemoglobin, but hemoglobin has a much lower affinity for carbon dioxide than for oxygen. The vast majority of CO_2 exists in the blood in a disguised form, as the bicarbonate ion (HCO_3^-). How does that happen? When CO_2 enters a red blood cell, it encounters the enzyme carbonic anhydrase, which catalyzes the combination reaction between CO_2 and H_2O to form carbonic acid (H_2CO_3). Carbonic acid, as a weak acid, will then dissociate into a proton and the bicarbonate anion. The hydrogen ion (proton) and bicarbonate ion both have high solubilities in water and, thus, provide a much more effective means of transporting cellular respiration's waste product to the lungs for excretion. We hear your silent protest, "But we breathe out CO_2 gas, not hydrogen ions and bicarbonate ions!" And you are absolutely correct: The same reactions that led to the formation of the ions can be reversed once the blood reaches the alveolar capillaries in the lungs. Carbon dioxide gas is rapidly reformed by the reverse action of carbonic anhydrase in the lungs and is breathed out.

$$CO_2\ (g) + H_2O\ (l) \xleftrightarrow[\text{carbonic anhydrase}]{} H_2CO_3\ (aq) \leftrightarrow H^+\ (aq) + HCO_3^-\ (aq)$$

This chemical reaction is important not only because it provides an effective means of ridding the body's tissues of carbon dioxide gas but also because the concentration of free protons in the blood affects pH; the pH, in turn, can have allosteric effects on the hemoglobin-oxygen dissociation curve. Increased proton concentration (lowered pH) shifts the curve to the right; this is known as the **Bohr effect**. When will a right shift occur? When we have high energy demands (such as running a race), which require an increased rate of cellular respiration and a concomitant increase in oxygen supply. Higher rates of cellular metabolism will yield greater P_{CO_2} and accumulation of lactic acid, both of which will decrease the pH, signaling to the hemoglobin that the tissue needs more oxygen. Consequently, hemoglobin will experience a reduced affinity for oxygen (the allosteric effect of the hydrogen ion) and will be able to give off (or dump) more oxygen to the metabolically active tissue. If we believe that it is a *downright* shame to not have enough oxygen to finish the race, then we'll remember which way the curve shifts.

Equally important is the link between blood pH homeostasis and the respiratory and renal systems. You'll recall from general chemistry that a solution containing a weak acid and its conjugate base in roughly equal concentrations is called a buffer. The presence of the weak acid–conjugate base pair in solution helps to minimize dramatic shifts in pH. We might characterize a buffer as an acid-base sponge, soaking up excess hydrogen ions or hydroxide ions to keep the solution's pH relatively steady. The carbonic acid–bicarbonate ion pair is the most important buffer system for the blood. The pH of blood must be maintained within a narrow range around 7.4, slightly alkaline. Metabolic or respiratory disturbances can cause the pH to shift down (acidosis) or up (alkalosis), giving rise to potentially dangerous and life-threatening conditions in which other systems malfunction and proteins become denatured. In response to changing blood pH, the respiratory rate may rise or fall to increase or decrease the amount of carbon dioxide gas excreted, and the kidneys can increase or decrease the amount of bicarbonate ion secreted into the nephron filtrate. For example, in response to a metabolic acidosis (decreased pH), the respiratory rate will increase to reduce the systemic P_{CO_2} so as to shift the reversible system to the left, resulting in a decrease in hydrogen ion concentration (and an increase in the pH).

> **Key Concept**
>
> Only a small percentage of carbon dioxide is actually bound directly to hemoglobin (as carboxyhemoglobin); most of the CO_2 is dissolved in plasma and lives as HCO_3^-.

TRANSPORT OF NUTRIENTS AND WASTES

The blood serves as a way to mobilize nutrients, vitamins, minerals, and other compounds necessary for proper cell and tissue functions. Let's quickly review how each of our major nutrients enters the blood.

Carbohydrates and Amino Acids

These are absorbed in the small intestine capillaries, and enter systemic circulation via the hepatic portal system.

Fats

Fats are absorbed into lacteals in the small intestine. They bypass the hepatic portal circulation and enter systemic circulation via the thoracic duct. Once in the bloodstream, fats are packaged in lipoproteins, which are water-soluble.

Wastes

Wastes, such as carbon dioxide (see previous discussion), ammonia, and urea, enter the bloodstream throughout the body as they travel down their concentration gradients from the tissues into the capillaries. The blood eventually passes through the excretory organs, where these waste products are filtered or secreted for removal from the body (see Chapter 7), just as the building maintenance staff might remove waste products from the office building.

Gradients

An essential concept that has come up again and again is the movement of compounds and molecules along the gradients, which may be electrical, chemical, pressure, or a combination of these. This should indicate how important understanding the roles of gradients is to your performance on the MCAT, in both the Physical Sciences and the Biological Sciences sections. In the bloodstream, two pressure gradients are essential for maintaining a proper balance of fluid volume and solute concentrations in the interstitium. These are the opposing but related **hydrostatic and oncotic (osmotic) pressures**. Let's take a look at Figure 9.9 and figure out why.

Key Concept

Hydrostatic pressure *pushes* fluid *out* of vessels (dependent on blood pressure driven by the heart). Osmotic pressure *pulls* fluid black *into* vessels (dependent on the number of particles dissolved in the plasma).

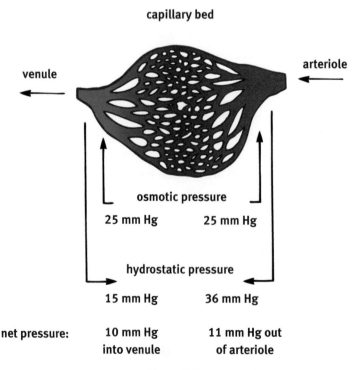

Figure 9.9

At the arteriole end of the capillary, hydrostatic pressure (generated by the contraction of the heart and the elasticity of the arteries; measured upstream in the large arteries as blood pressure) is relatively high. Hydrostatic pressure is the force per unit area that the blood exerts against the vessel walls. Capillaries are leaky by design, so fluid will be forced out of the bloodstream into the interstitial space of the tissues, carrying with it some of the nutrients. As fluid moves out of the vessels, the hydrostatic pressure drops significantly. At the venule end of the capillary bed, the hydrostatic pressure has dropped below the oncotic pressure, which is the osmotic pressure generated by the concentration of particles in the plasma compartment. Because the primary determinant of plasma osmotic pressure is the concentration of plasma proteins, it is called oncotic pressure. The osmotic/oncotic pressure is essentially constant along the capillary, as nutrients filter out and wastes filter in at a relatively equal rate. Unlike hydrostatic pressure, oncotic pressure exerts an inward force and draws fluid, nutrients, and wastes out of the tissues into the bloodstream.

The balance of these opposing pressures, which are also called the Starling forces, is essential for maintaining the proper fluid volumes and solute concentrations inside and outside the vasculature. Imbalance of these pressures can result in too much or too little fluid in the tissues. For example, accumulation of excess fluid in the interstitium results in a condition called edema. We should note that some interstitial fluid is also taken up by the lymphatic system, which is another venous circulatory system that runs parallel to the venous central circulatory system. Lymphatic fluid (lymph) returns to the central circulatory system by way of a channel called the thoracic duct. Blockage of lymph nodes by infection or surgical invasion can also result in edema. Although you do not need to learn or memorize the Starling equation, which quantifies the net filtration rate between two fluid compartments, you should understand that the movement of solutes and fluid at the capillary level is governed by pressure differentials, just like the movement of carbon dioxide and oxygen in the lungs.

CLOTTING

We have now covered most of the functions of red blood cells and the plasma. Let's turn to platelets. As we have already discussed, platelets protect the vascular system in the event of damage to a vessel by forming a clot, which prevents (or at least minimizes) the pathological loss of blood through vascular damage or injury. Recall from Chapter 6 that connective tissue underlies most of our other tissues and is partly composed of collagen. When platelets come into contact with exposed collagen, they sense this as evidence of injury. In response, they release their contents and begin to aggregate, or clump together. One of the important chemicals they release is a clotting factor known as **thromboplastin**. Thromboplastin converts **prothrombin** into **thrombin** with some help from its enzymatic cofactors, calcium and vitamin K. Thrombin then converts **fibrinogen** into **fibrin**. Fibrin is a protein that functions just

Key Concept

Note how much lower hydrostatic pressure is in the capillaries than in the arteries (normal arterial pressure is 120 mmHg during systole and 80 mmHg during diastole). Recall that this pressure drop occurs across the arterioles and is necessary because the delicate capillaries cannot handle such high pressure. Capillary walls are only a single cell thick, so water flow and nutrient and waste exchanges can occur quickly and efficiently.

as its name suggests. It makes little fibers that aggregate into a woven structure, like a net, which captures red blood cells and other platelets, forming a clot (a plug) over the area of damage (see Figure 9.10). If the clot forms on a surface vessel that has been cut (e.g., a paper cut), we call the clot a scab.

THROMBUS FORMATION, or blood clotting, occurs when blood vessels are injured. The process begins as small cells called platelets attach to the matrix that becomes exposed when the endothelial cells lining blood vessels are disrupted. This attachment then activates quiescent αIIbβ3 integrin molecules, causing them to adhere to circulating proteins—including fibrinogen, which forms bridges to additional platelets. Together the cells and proteins ultimately form a network of cells and fibers dense enough to plug the injury and prevent blood loss until the wound can be repaired.

PLATELETS AGGREGATE

Figure 9.10

Certain genetic diseases, such as hemophilia, cause malfunctions in the cascade of clotting reactions and increase the risk of life-threatening blood loss from even relatively minor injuries. Hemophilia, which is a recessive disorder, has run surprisingly commonly through some branches of European royal families, leading to all sorts of scandalous court gossip and innuendos. We will take a closer look at the inheritance patterns of these diseases and other traits in Chapter 14.

IMMUNOLOGICAL REACTIONS

As we discussed before, the body has the ability to differentiate between self and foreign by identifying cell-surface antigens. The development of immunity and the roles and activities of the different cell types in the immune system are discussed in more detail in Chapter 10.

Conclusion

The cardiovascular system is one of the most commonly tested MCAT topics. You should be familiar with its basic structure: a system with two pumps in series, which we have compared with two batteries in series in a circuit. We discussed the basic anatomy of the heart and its connection to the systemic and pulmonary circulations. We discussed the myogenic activity of cardiac muscle and the pathway that electricity follows in the heart through the SA node, AV node, bundle of His, and Purkinje fibers. The movement of blood through the vascular system is a function of the heart's pumping to generate pressure. Blood pressure is a measure of the blood's force per unit area on the vessel walls and is recorded as a gauge pressure (pressure above atmospheric pressure). We discussed the differences among arteries, veins, and capillaries and how these anatomical differences are reflective of the different functions. We then took a look at the composition of blood and discussed the three major cell types. Red blood cells and platelets were discussed in detail. We examined the ABO and Rh antigen systems, which commonly appear on the MCAT due to their widespread clinical relevance. Hemoglobin's ability to carry oxygen and carbon dioxide was also described; recall that carbon dioxide is primarily carried as bicarbonate ion in the blood. The conversion of carbon dioxide to and from this ion is accomplished by the enzyme carbonic anhydrase. We will revisit white blood cells when we discuss the immune system in Chapter 10.

CONCEPTS TO REMEMBER

- ☐ The electrical signal travels from the SA node to the AV node to the bundle of His and down the Purkinje fibers. Thus, the heart can fire without descending input from the nervous system. This is known as myogenic activity.

- ☐ During the contraction phase (systole), blood is pumped from the heart and through the vasculature. During the relaxation phase (diastole), the heart fills with blood.

- ☐ The pipes of the circulatory system are the arteries, veins, and capillaries. Whereas arteries have intrinsic smooth musculature that is used to regulate capacity, veins rely on adjacent skeletal muscles to squeeze venous blood progressively back to the heart.

- ☐ Capillaries are a single cell-layer thick to allow for efficient gas and nutrient exchange.

- ☐ Blood pressure is a gauge pressure. It is highest in the arterial side of the circulation.

- ☐ Leukocytes have two classes: granulocytes and agranulocytes. Each of these cell types is involved in different parts of the immune response.

- ☐ Blood can be classified by the set of surface antigens that are expressed on RBCs. The ABO classification is based on the codominant expression patterns of the I^A and I^B alleles. Blood can also be Rh^+ or Rh^-.

- ☐ Oxygen (and carbon dioxide, to a lesser degree) is carried by hemoglobin. The relative affinity of oxygen for hemoglobin is depicted by a sigmoidal curve and may be affected by temperature, pH, altitude, and CO_2.

- ☐ Carbon dioxide is primarily carried as bicarbonate ion. The formation of the ion is catalyzed by carbonic anhydrase.

- ☐ Platelets are involved in forming clots. Deficiency will result in bleeding disorders.

Practice Questions

1. Which of the following is a FALSE statement regarding erythrocytes?

    A. They contain hemoglobin.
    B. They are anaerobic.
    C. Their nuclei are located in the middle of the cells' disklike depressions.
    D. They are phagocytized in the spleen and liver after a certain period of time.

2. Which is the correct sequence of a cardiac impulse?

    A. SA node → AV node → Purkinje fibers → bundle of His → ventricles
    B. AV node → bundle of His → Purkinje fibers → SA node → ventricles → atria
    C. SA node → atria → AV node → bundle of His → Purkinje fibers → ventricles
    D. SA node → AV node → atria → bundle of His → Purkinje fibers → ventricles

3. Hemoglobin's affinity for O_2

    A. increases in exercising muscle tissue.
    B. decreases as blood pH increases.
    C. decreases as blood pH decreases.
    D. is higher in maternal blood than in fetal blood.

4. Which of the following correctly traces the circulatory pathway?

    A. Superior vena cava → right atrium → right ventricle → pulmonary artery → lungs → pulmonary veins → left atrium → left ventricle → aorta
    B. Superior vena cava → left atrium → left ventricle → pulmonary artery → lungs → pulmonary veins right atrium → right ventricle → aorta
    C. Aorta → right atrium → right ventricle → pulmonary artery → lungs → pulmonary veins → left atrium → left ventricle → superior vena cava
    D. Superior vena cava → right atrium → right ventricle → pulmonary veins → lungs → pulmonary artery → left atrium → left ventricle → aorta

5. The tricuspid valve prevents backflow of blood from the

    A. left ventricle into the left atrium.
    B. aorta into the left ventricle.
    C. pulmonary artery into the right ventricle.
    D. right ventricle into the right atrium.

6. At the venous end of a capillary bed, the osmotic pressure

    A. is greater than the hydrostatic pressure.
    B. results in a net outflow of fluid.
    C. results in a net reabsorption of fluid into the blood.
    D. both (A) and (C).

7. A patient's chart reveals that he has a cardiac output of 7,500 mL/min and a stroke volume of 50 mL. What is his pulse (in beats per minute)?

    A. 50 beats/min

    B. 100 beats/min

    C. 150 beats/min

    D. 400 beats/min

8. An unconscious patient is rushed into the emergency room and needs a fast blood transfusion. Because there is no time to check her medical history or determine her blood type, which type of blood should you, as her doctor, give her?

    A. A^-

    B. AB^+

    C. O^+

    D. O^-

9. Which of the following is true regarding arteries and veins?

    A. Arteries are thin walled, muscular, and elastic, whereas veins are thick walled and inelastic.

    B. Arteries always conduct oxygenated blood, whereas veins always carry deoxygenated blood.

    C. The blood pressure in the aorta is always higher than the pressure in the superior vena cava.

    D. Arteries facilitate blood transport by using skeletal muscle contractions, whereas veins make use of the pumping of the heart to push blood.

10. At any given time, there is more blood in the venous system than the arterial system. Which of the following features of a vein allows this?

    A. Relative lack of smooth muscle in the wall

    B. Presence of valves

    C. Proximity of veins to lymphatic vessels

    D. Thin endothelial lining

11. Which of the following is involved in the body's primary blood-buffering mechanism?

    A. Fluid intake

    B. Absorption of nutrients in the gastrointestinal system

    C. Carbon dioxide produced from metabolism

    D. Reabsorption in the kidney

Small Group Questions

1. Why does O^- blood not elicit an immune response when transferred to an individual with AB blood?

2. In which direction does the dissociation curve for fetal hemoglobin shift compared with adult hemoglobin? Explain.

3. How does the pH of arterial blood affect the rate of ventilation?

4. Erthryocytes are anaerobic. Why is this advantageous for the organism?

Explanations to Practice Questions

1. C

Erythrocytes, or red blood cells, are produced in the red bone marrow and circulate in the blood for about 120 days, after which they are phagocytized in the spleen and the liver. Red blood cells have a disklike shape and lose their membranous organelles (like mitochondria and nuclei) during maturation. Erythrocytes thus cannot multiply on their own and are anaerobic. Their main role is the transport of oxygen to the tissues and of the carbon dioxide to the lungs; this task is accomplished through the use of hemoglobin, which carries oxygen and a limited amount of carbon dioxide. Choice (C) is false and, therefore, the correct answer to this question.

2. C

An ordinary cardiac contraction originates in, and is regulated by, the sinoatrial (SA) node. The impulses travel through both atria, stimulating them to contract simultaneously. The impulse then arrives at the atrioventricular (AV) node, which momentarily slows conduction, allowing for completion of atrial contraction and ventricular filling. The impulse is then carried by the bundle of His, which branches into the right and left bundle branches and through the Purkinje fibers in the walls of both ventricles, generating a strong contraction. The only choice that correctly depicts this sequence is (C).

3. C

Let's quickly review how hemoglobin's affinity for O_2 changes. According to the Bohr effect, decreasing the pH in the blood decreases hemoglobin's affinity for O_2. A decrease in the pH of the blood generally occurs during heavy exercise, when the muscles produce a lot of lactic acid. This decreased affinity for O_2 facilitates the unloading of O_2 to tissues in need. Based on this, (C) is the correct

answer. (A) and (B) state the opposite. (D) is incorrect, because hemoglobin's affinity for O_2 is higher in fetal blood than in adult blood.

4. A

Blood drains from the superior vena cava into the right atrium. It passes through the tricuspid valve and into the right ventricle, and then through the pulmonary valve into the pulmonary artery, which leads to the lungs. Oxygenated blood returns to the left atrium via the pulmonary veins. It flows through the mitral valve into the left ventricle. From the left ventricle, it is pumped through the aortic valve into the aorta for distribution throughout the body. The only choice that correctly illustrates this path is (A).

5. D

The atrioventricular valves are located between the atria and the ventricles on both sides of the heart. Their role is to prevent backflow of blood into the atria. The valve on the right side of the heart has three cusps and is called the tricuspid valve. As such, it prevents backflow of blood from the right ventricle into the right atrium, making (D) the correct answer. The valve on the left side of the heart has two cusps and is called the bicuspid or mitral valve (early anatomists thought this valve looked like a miter, the hat traditionally worn by bishops). The mitral valve prevents backflow from the left ventricle into the left atrium.

6. D

The exchange of materials is greatly influenced by the relative balance between the hydrostatic and osmotic pressures of blood and tissue fluids. The osmotic pressure of the surrounding tissue remains constant; however, the hydrostatic pressure at the arterial end is greater than the hydrostatic pressure at the venous end. As a result, fluid moves out of the capillaries at the arterial end and back in at the venous end. Fluid is reabsorbed at the venous end because the osmotic pressure exceeds the hydrostatic pressure. (D) is thus the correct answer.

7. C

The first step in solving this problem is to define cardiac output:

$$\text{cardiac output} = \text{heart rate} \times \text{stroke volume}$$

We are given the stroke volume and the cardiac output, so we can calculate the heart rate, or pulse, according to the following equation:

$$\text{heart rate} = \text{cardiac output/stroke volume}$$
$$\text{heart rate} = (7{,}500 \text{ mL/min})/(50 \text{ mL})$$
$$\text{heart rate} = 150 \text{ beats/min}$$

The patient thus has a pulse of 150 beats/min; (C) is the correct answer.

8. D

Without knowing a patient's blood type, the only type of transfusion that we can safely give is O⁻. People with O⁻ blood are considered universal donors because their blood cells contain no surface antigens. Therefore, O⁻ blood can be given to anyone without causing potentially life-threatening consequences. (D) is the correct answer.

9. C

The only answer choice that correctly describes arteries and veins is (C); the pressure in the aorta is usually about 120 or 80 mmHg, depending on whether the heart is in systole or diastole, whereas the pressure in the superior vena cava is extremely low. (A) is wrong because arteries are thick walled and veins are thin walled. (B) is also incorrect; this relationship is reversed in pulmonary circulation. (D) is an opposite answer choice. Arteries make use of the pumping of the heart and the "snapping back" of their elastic walls to transport blood, whereas venous blood is "pumped" by skeletal muscle contractions.

10. A

The relative lack of smooth muscle in venous walls allows stretching to store most of the blood in the body. Valves in the veins allow for one-way flow of blood toward the heart. Both arteries and veins are close to lymphatic vessels, which has no bearing on their relative difference in volume. Both arteries and veins have a thin endothelial lining.

11. C

Carbon dioxide is a by-product of metabolism in cells, which later combines with water to form bicarbonate in a reaction catalyzed by carbonic anhydrase. This system is blood plasma's most important buffer system. Food and fluid absorption are not significant sources of buffering.

The Immune System

Within the past decade or so, the public's imagination has been captured by alarming reports of "flesh-eating" bacteria and diseases. Descriptions and images that seem to have been lifted directly from the neural synapses of Wes Craven suggest a bacterial entity, large and ravenous, capable of consuming a person in one pustulant gulp. In fact, flesh-eating bacteria do not actually eat flesh, but that doesn't make them any less dangerous. The pathological and life-threatening impact of necrotizing fasciitis, caused by many different types of bacteria, including group A streptococcus, *Clostridium perfringens*, and methicillin-resistant *Staphylococcus aureus* (MRSA), is a massive destruction of skin, muscle, and connective tissue by the release of bacterial toxins called superantigens. These proteins cause the immune system to become nonspecifically overactivated, resulting in the overproduction of cytokines, a set of chemical messengers that are important for activation and regulation of the immune system. Overproduction of cytokines, sometimes called a cytokine storm, consists of a positive feedback loop between cytokines and immune cells and results in destruction of host tissues and organs as well as a systemic inflammatory response, which can severely impact cardiovascular and respiratory functions. Necrotizing fasciitis is a serious disease that requires aggressive medical and surgical treatment, including intravenous antibiotics and surgical debridement (removal) of the necrotic tissue—sometimes even amputation. Mortality rates have been recorded as high as 73 percent.

In Chapter 1, we introduced bacteria and viruses as invaders and spies. Our immune system is the counterespionage force (think Homeland Security) that attempts to neutralize these threats. We will consider both specific and nonspecific defenses. Nonspecific defenses, such as the skin, are the initial barriers against infection. If microbes breach them, we then rely on the activities of specific defense, which are mediated by the leukocytes that we introduced in Chapter 9. We will also discuss advances in medical techniques, which allow us to manipulate and control the immune system to our advantage, such as immunizations, which can prevent us from ever having to suffer a debilitating disease (e.g., hepatitis vaccination). By examining each of these topics, we will be ready to search and destroy any questions related to the immune system on Test Day.

Anatomy

The immune system is not housed in a single organ. The structures and components that serve as nonspecific defenses (discussed next) often serve functions in other organ systems. Leukocytes, which are vital for specific immunity, are born in the bone marrow and may contribute to either **innate immunity** or **adaptive immunity**. We introduced the two major classes of leukocytes in Chapter 9. **Granulocytes** include neutrophils, eosinophils, and basophils. **Agranulocytes** include the **lymphocytes**, which are responsible for antibody production, immune system modulation, and

Key Concept

Organs of the immune system:
- **Lymph Nodes** (filter lymph and help attack bacteria & viruses)
- **Bone Marrow** (immune cell production)
- **Thymus** (secretes thymosin—a hormone that stimulates pre-T cells to mature)
- **Spleen** (storage area for blood; filters blood & lymph)

targeted killing of infected cells. Finally, **monocytes** (primarily macrophages) are also agranulocytes and serve as nonspecific sanitation workers that travel the body picking up debris, both foreign (invaders) and domestic (our own). The lymphocytes that contribute to adaptive immunity are B-cells and T-cells, so named because of their site of maturation: T-cells mature in the thymus, and B-cells mature in the spleen (in birds, the B-cells mature in an organ called the bursa of Fabricius, from which these leukocytes originally derived their moniker).

THE DIVISIONS OF THE IMMUNE SYSTEM

The mammalian immune system has two overarching divisions. The innate part (*left side*) acts near entry points into the body and is always at the ready. If it fails to contain a pathogen, the adaptive division (*right side*) kicks in, mounting a later but highly targeted attack against the specific invader.

INNATE IMMUNE SYSTEM
This system includes, among other components, antimicrobial molecules and various phagocytes (cells that ingest and destroy pathogens). These cells, such as dendritic cells and macrophages, also activate an inflammatory response, secreting proteins called cytokines that trigger an influx of defensive cells from the blood. Among the recruits are more phagocytes—notably monocytes (which can mature into macrophages) and neutrophils.

ADAPTIVE IMMUNE SYSTEM
This system "stars" B-cells and T-cells. Activated B-cells secrete antibody molecules that bind to antigens—specific components unique to a given invader—and destroy the invader directly or mark it for attack by others. T-cells recognize antigens displayed on cells. Some T-cells help to activate B-cells and other T-cells (*not shown*); other T-cells directly attack infected cells. T- and B-cells spawn "memory" cells that promptly eliminate invaders encountered before.

Figure 10.1

Innate immunity refers to the responses cells can carry out without learning; for this reason, it is also known as the **nonspecific immune response**. Conversely, adaptive immunity is developed as immune cells learn to recognize and respond to particular antigens, and is often aptly referred to as the **specific immune response**. We can also parse the specific immune system into **humoral immunity** (driven by B-cells and antibodies) and **cell-mediated immunity** (provided by T-cells). Figure 10.1 shows the components of innate and adaptive immunity.

How do these defense mechanisms know to destroy microbial targets and not attack our own cells? Remember that antigens are proteins and carbohydrates present on the outer membranes of most cells. They allow our immune systems to distinguish between self and nonself (or foreign) and to recognize our self-antigens and antigen-presenting cells as nonthreatening. Antigens that the immune cells learn to recognize as foreign will cause activation of the immune response. When the immune system fails to learn the distinction between self and foreign, it may attack self-antigens as if they were foreign, a condition termed **autoimmunity**. Note that autoimmunity is only one potential problem with immune functioning; another problem arises when the immune system misidentifies a foreign antigen as dangerous when, in fact, it is not. Pet dander, pollen, and peanuts are not inherently threatening to human life, yet some people's immune systems are hypersensitive to these antigens and become overactivated (to varying degrees) when these antigens are encountered. **Allergies** and autoimmunity are part of a family of immune disorders classified as hypersensitivity reactions.

Real World

One form of diabetes (type I) results from pancreatic β-cells being attacked by the immune system. The loss of these cells results in an insulin deficiency; such patients must receive insulin replacement therapy for the remainder of their lives.

Nonspecific Defense Mechanisms

Our first line of defense is the skin (integument). In the next chapter, we will discuss its homeostatic functions, but for now, let's focus on how it keeps us protected. By providing a physical barrier between the outside world and our internal organs, the skin keeps microbes at bay. Additionally, sweat contains an enzyme that attacks bacterial cell walls and, therefore, serves an antibacterial purpose in addition to its better-known role in thermoregulation. A cut or abrasion on the skin provides an entry point for pathogens into the body, and the deeper the wound is, the deeper the pathogens can gain initial entry. This is why painful puncture wounds from nails or playful bites from kittens can lead to serious infections.

We outlined another mechanism of defense in the respiratory chapter. The respiratory passages, which are mucous membranes, are lined with cilia to trap particulate matter and push it up toward the oropharynx, where it is swallowed. We definitely don't want to breathe in smoke and dirt, but we *really* want to prevent the bacteria and viruses that may be hitching a ride on the particulate matter suspended in the air from reaching deep lung tissue, where they may set up serious infection. Several other mucous membranes, including around the eye and in the oral cavity, produce a nonspecific bactericidal enzyme (lysozyme), which is secreted in the tears and saliva, respectively.

If foreign particles do make it past the skin, macrophages will phagocytize them. Macrophages may be called to a site of **inflammation** by chemicals such as

THE PLAYERS

The immune system consists of innate cells, which form a first line of defense against pathogens, and members of the adaptive system, which targets invaders with greater specificity.

INNATE

MACROPHAGE
This immune defender engulfs and consumes pathogen invaders.

MAST CELL
This cell releases histamine and other chemicals that promote inflammation.

GRANULOCYTE
Three cell types with tiny granules in their interior—the neutrophil, eosinophil, and basophil—participate in the inflammatory response.

DENDRITIC CELL
It presents antigens—fragments of protein or other molecules from pathogens or cancer cells—to adaptive immune cells, inducing the cells to attack bearers of the displayed antigens.

NATURAL KILLER CELL
This cell destroys the body's own cells that have become infected with pathogens; it also goes after cancer cells.

ADAPTIVE

B-CELL
Antigens stimulate this cell to divide and produce antibodies that neutralize invaders or tag them for killing.

T-CELL
A killer T-cell destroys an infected cell in which it detects the presence of antigens. Other T-cells—such as helper and regulatory types—coordinate the immune response.

histamine, which causes vasodilation and allows macrophages to move out of the bloodstream and into the tissue. The granulocytes, especially neutrophils, may be called out in a similar manner. This process works well against pathogens that are extracellular, like bacteria. But how do we contain viruses, which are obligate intracellular pathogens? Immune cells and cells that have been infected with viral particles may produce **interferon**, a protein that prevents viral replication and dispersion. Note that interferon is directed against viruses but not against specific viruses, so it is considered a nonspecific defense.

Each of these mechanisms is a part of the innate immune system. Interferon, for example, doesn't have to be previously exposed to a virus to know how to defeat it. The protein is produced upon infection and is immediately effective against the viral particle. Innate immunity is useful because it can begin to fight disease immediately. However, its major drawback is that, as a defense mechanism, it is not adaptive. Organisms cannot make their innate defense mechanisms more effective over time. This is of particular interest when dealing with quickly mutating viruses that evolve the ability to overcome interferon. Whereas the innate, nonspecific immune defenses form an important first barrier system, this system has its limitations. As a more sophisticated defense mechanism, the adaptive immune system works by forming **immunological memory**, which improves the effectiveness and alacrity of the immune response.

Humoral Immunity ★★★★☆☆

When we are exposed to a pathogen, it may take a few days for the physical symptoms to be relieved. This occurs because the adaptive immune response takes time to get geared up. **Humoral immunity**, which involves the production of antibodies, may take as long as a week to become fully effective. These antibodies are specific to the antigens of the invading microbe. Antibodies are produced by B-cells, which are lymphocytes that originated in the bone marrow and matured in the spleen and lymph nodes.

Antibodies (also called **immunoglobulins [Ig]**) can carry out many different jobs in the body. Once they bind to their specific antigens, they may attract other leukocytes to phagocytize those antigens immediately, or they may clump together (agglutinate) with the antigens to form large insoluble complexes that can be phagocytized. Antibodies are *Y*-shaped molecules (see Figures 10.2 and 10.3) that are made up of two identical **heavy chains** and two identical **light chains**. Disulfide linkages and noncovalent interactions hold the heavy and light chains together. Each antibody has an **antigen-binding region** at the two top tips of the *Y*. Within this region, there are specific polypeptide sequences that will bind one, and only one, specific antigenic sequence. Each B-cell makes one antibody, but we have many B-cells, so our immune system can recognize many antigens. The remaining part of the antibody molecule is known as the **constant region**, which is involved in recruitment and binding of other immune modulators (e.g., macrophages).

Figure 10.2

Not all B-cells that are generated actively or constantly produce antibodies. Why wouldn't we want all of our B-cells to be active? Antibody production is an energetically expensive process; there is no reason to expend energy producing antibodies we don't need. Instead, B-cells wait in the lymph nodes for their particular antigens to come along. Upon exposure to the correct antigen, a B-cell will proliferate and produce two types of daughter cells. **Plasma cells** produce large amounts of antibody, whereas **memory cells** stay in the lymph nodes for use upon being re-exposed to the same antigen. This initial activation takes approximately seven to ten days and is known as the **primary response**. The plasma cells will eventually die, but the memory cells may last the lifetime of the organism. If the same microbe is ever encountered again, the memory cells jump into action and produce the antibodies specific to that pathogen. This immune response, called the **secondary response**, will be more rapid and robust. The development of these lasting memory cells is the basis of the efficacy of **vaccinations**.

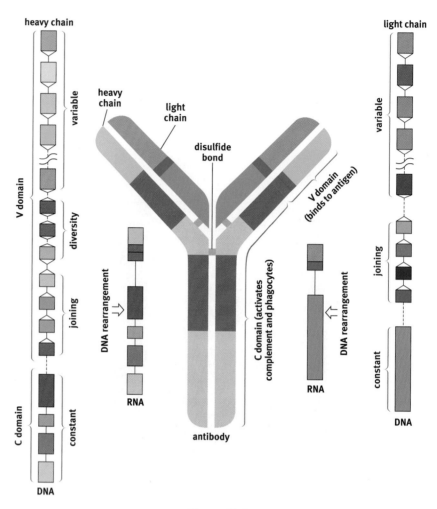

Figure 10.3

Bridge

Viruses must occupy a host cell in order to replicate; thus, they can often evade the body's defenses. One way that the immune system deals with this problem is by using cytotoxic T-cells to kill virally infected cells.

Cell-Mediated Immunity ★★★★☆☆

Whereas humoral immunity is based on the activity of B-lymphocytes, cell-mediated immunity involves the T-lymphocytes. Although both B-cells and T-cells originate from the same set of stem cells in the bone marrow, T-cells mature in the thymus, unlike the B-cells, which mature in the spleen and lymph nodes. There are three major types of T-cells: **helper T-cells**, **suppressor T-cells**, and **killer (cytotoxic) T-cells**. Helper T-cells, also called T4 cells because they express the CD4 cell-surface protein, coordinate the immune response by secreting chemicals known as **lymphokines**. These molecules are capable of recruiting other immune cells (e.g., plasma cells, cytotoxic T-cells, macrophages) and increasing their activity. The loss of these cells prevents the immune system from mounting an adequate response to infection. HIV destroys T4 cells, essentially immobilizing the host immune system and paving the way for opportunistic infections. Cytotoxic T-cells, also called T8 cells because of their expression of the CD8 surface protein, are capable of directly killing virally infected cells by secreting toxic chemicals. Suppressor T-cells, another group of T8 cells, help to tone down the immune response once infection has been adequately contained. T-cells may also form memory cells so that the next exposure to the same antigen will result in a more robust response. T-cells bind to antigens presented by major histocompatibility (MHC) class I molecules at a cell's surface. Figure 10.4 shows the process by which antigens are produced, incorporated into MHC I molecules, and then transported to the cell surface via the secretory pathway.

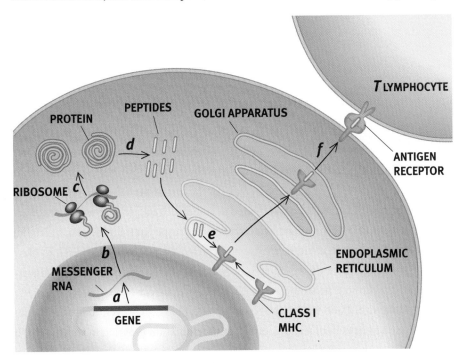

Figure 10.4

Chapter 4 referred to the transplantation of a liver from a donor to a patient in need. However, the donated liver would have antigens native to the donor that would be recognized as foreign in the recipient. Rejection will occur as the cytotoxic T-cells, having identified the transplanted liver cells as foreign, try to destroy it. Organ transplantation requires the use of **immunosuppressants**, which are drugs that can prevent activation of the immune system. Autoimmunity, mentioned before, can be treated in a similar manner.

Refer to Figure 10.5 for an overview of lymphocyte differentiation and the cell types involved in each branch of specific immunity.

Real World

The distinction between the role of B-cells and T-cells can be appreciated by studying immunodeficiency states that affect one lymphocyte class but not the other. Bruton's agammaglobulinemia is an X-linked genetic disease expressed only in male infants and characterized by the absence of B-cells. Typically, the child becomes ill at eight to nine months of age, once he is deprived of the passive immunity conferred by the placental transfer of maternal immunoglobulins. The lack of B-cells results in the absence of circulating antibodies, leading to recurrent bacterial infections. Defenses against viral and fungal disorders are normal because those microorganisms are generally handled by the T-cells. In contrast, DiGeorge's syndrome is a selective T-cell disorder resulting from the underdevelopment or absence of the thymus gland. Circulating antibody levels are normal, but these children have impaired defenses against viral and fungal infections.

Figure 10.5

Immunization

Often, diseases can have significant, long-term consequences. Infection with the poliovirus, for example, can leave a person disabled for the remainder of his or her life. The former president of the United States, Franklin Roosevelt, contracted polio in the summer of 1921 and was paralyzed for the rest of his life. So concerned was he that the paralysis would be interpreted as political weakness, he went to extraordinary lengths to hide it. In fact, he commissioned a special train car into which the presidential limousine could be driven and carried from Washington, D.C. to New York City, where the train would stop in a special station underneath the Waldorf-Astoria Hotel so that he would never have to leave his car and expose his malady to the public eye. Polio used to be a widespread illness; however, today we hardly hear about it as a result of a highly effective **vaccinization** program, which led to the virtual eradication of polio in this country.

Immunization can be achieved in an active or passive fashion. In active immunity, the immune system is stimulated to produce antibodies against a specific pathogen. The means by which we are exposed to this pathogen may either be natural or artificial. Through natural exposure, antibodies are generated by B-cells once an individual becomes infected. Artificial vaccination also results in the production of antibodies; however, the individual never experiences true infection. Instead, he receives an injection containing an antigen that will activate B-cells to produce antibodies to fight the specific infection. The antigen may be a weakened or killed form of the microbe, or it may be a part of the microbe's protein structure. A recent example is the vaccination against chicken pox, which became available in 1995 in the United States. Once exposed to chicken pox, people usually are immune to it and do not become infected again. Prior to 1995, immunity was achieved by natural means; individuals became infected and were protected from future bouts of the disease. In fact, some parents were known to expose their children intentionally to the virus to ensure infection at a young age (when the virus results in a milder form of illness). After 1995, inoculation began with a live but weakened (attenuated) form of the virus (artificial active immunization). This allowed for B-cells and antibodies to be generated but did not result in the normal course of infection.

Immunization may also be achieved passively. Passive immunity results from the transfer of antibodies to an individual. The immunity is transient as only the antibodies, and not the B-cells that produce them, are given to the immunized individual. Natural examples are the transfer of antibodies across the placenta during pregnancy to protect the fetus and the transfer of antibodies from a mother to her nursing infant through breast milk. An artificial example is the administration of RhoGAM to an Rh⁻ woman (see Chapter 9) to prevent sensitization to her Rh⁺ fetus's blood.

See Figure 10.6 to see how DNA vaccines incite an immune response. You'll notice that the primary response to the vaccine is no different than a primary response to any other antigen.

Real World

Sometimes the organisms that cause different diseases are so alike in structure that the immune system can be fooled—even for our benefit. When Edward Jenner was trying to find a treatment for smallpox, he inoculated his son with infectious particles from a different, but related disease, cowpox. His experience with cowpox immunized him to smallpox, thanks to the similarity of the two diseases!

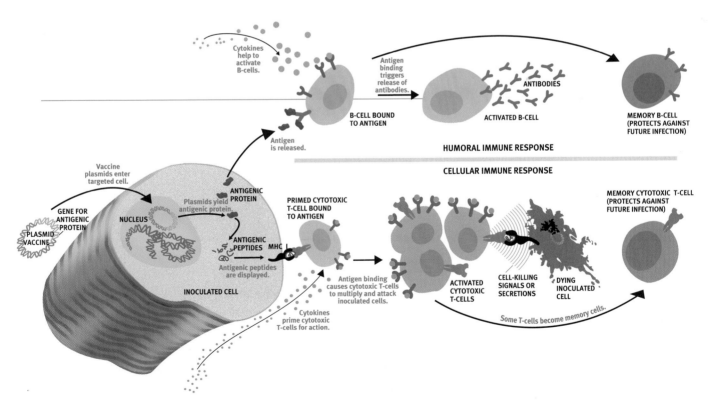

Figure 10.6

Lymphatic System

The lymphatic system, along with the cardiovascular system, is a type of circulatory system (see Figure 10.7). It is made up of one-way vessels that become larger as they move toward the center of the body (toward the heart). Hence, the lymphatic system is a venous system. These vessels carry lymphatic fluid and join to comprise a large thoracic duct in the chest, which then delivers the fluid into the left subclavian vein (near the heart).

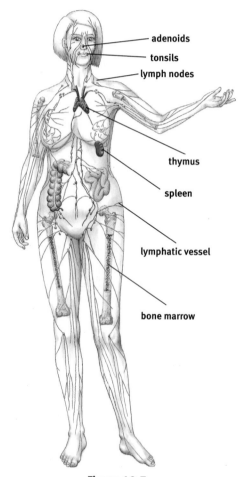

Figure 10.7

We mentioned in Chapter 9 that at the capillary level, not all the fluid is reabsorbed from the interstitial space; the excess fluid is collected by the lymphatic vessels and then returned to cardiovascular circulation. We also saw in Chapter 7 that the smallest lymphatic vessels **(lacteals)** collect fats in the form of chylomicrons from the villi in the small intestine and deliver them into the bloodstream, bypassing the liver. Along the lymphatic vessels are swellings **(lymph nodes)** that contain immune cells (primarily B-cells). These areas provide a place for antigens from microbes to first interact with the adaptive immune system and allow its activation. You can think of lymph nodes as security checkpoints for fluid that is being returned from the peripheral tissues to the central circulation. It makes sense that this fluid should be checked for pathogens only before being returned to the systemic highway system. In fact, physicians often discover underlying disease by the presence of enlarged or hardened lymph nodes during a physical exam.

Conclusion

The ability to fend off microbial invasion is critical to our survival. The immune system is housed in many locations in the body and involves many different organs and cell types. Nonspecific mechanisms, such as intact skin, mucous membranes, interferon, and lysozyme, constitute a first line of defense; these mechanisms also make up part of the innate immune system, which is capable of an immediate response but cannot learn from experience. The adaptive immune system, comprised of T- and B-lymphocytes, allows for our immune system to learn from past exposure. Thus, once we are infected with a certain strain of virus, activation of specific immunity confers long-term protection against that particular virus. Immunization is a type of adaptive immunity. In active immunization, our immune cells are stimulated in response, resulting in long-term immunity. Passive immunization results from the transfer of antibodies alone; therefore, the protection it provides is transient.

CONCEPTS TO REMEMBER

- ☐ Leukocytes are the functional cells of the immune system. They consist of granulocytes (neutrophils, eosinophils, and basophils) and agranulocytes (lymphocytes and monocytes).

- ☐ Nonspecific defenses are activated immediately upon infection; however, they cannot learn from past exposure.

- ☐ Humoral immunity is mediated by B-cells. B-cells proliferate to make plasma cells and memory cells. Antibodies are made by the plasma cells.

- ☐ Humoral immunity is more effective at combating bacterial infections, whereas cell-mediated immunity fights viral and fungal infections.

- ☐ Antibodies fight infection by binding to foreign antigens, thereby allowing other immune cells (e.g., macrophages) to phagocytize them.

- ☐ Cell-mediated immunity requires T-cells. The three major classes are helper T-cells, suppressor T-cells, and killer (cytotoxic) T-cells.

- ☐ Immunizations may be active or passive. Active immunization results in a sustained immune response mediated by B-cells, whereas the effects of passive immunization are short-lived.

- ☐ Immunizations may be natural or artificial. Natural immunization is the result of exposure to the antigen in nature or transfer of antibodies from mother to fetus. Artificial active immunization uses weakened or dead forms of microbes to generate an immune response without causing active infection.

- ☐ The lymphatic system is a secondary circulation system that removes excess fluid from the interstitial space. It also transports fat molecules from the intestinal epithelial cells to the bloodstream and serves as a conduit for the movement of immune cells.

Practice Questions

1. If a virus, such as HIV, destroys the body's T-lymphocytes, to which type of diseases would the patient be most susceptible?

   A. Viral infections
   B. Bacterial infections
   C. Autoimmune diseases
   D. Immunoglobulin deficiencies

2. Which of the following is NOT involved in cell-mediated immunity?

   A. Memory cells
   B. Plasma cells
   C. Cytotoxic cells
   D. Suppressor cells

3. The lymphatic system

   A. transports hormones throughout the body.
   B. transports absorbed chylomicrons to the circulatory system.
   C. filters the blood.
   D. both (A) and (B).

4. Which of the following is involved in antibody production?

   A. Plasma cells
   B. Memory cells
   C. Helper cells
   D. Cytotoxic cells

5. Which of the following is *true* regarding passive and active immunity?

   A. Active immunity requires weeks to build, whereas passive immunity is acquired immediately.
   B. Active immunity is short-lived, whereas passive immunity is long-lived.
   C. Active immunity may be acquired during pregnancy through the placenta.
   D. Passive immunity may be acquired through vaccination.

6. Which of the following is NOT an example of a nonspecific defense mechanism?

   A. Skin provides a physical barrier against invasion.
   B. Macrophages engulf and destroy foreign particles.
   C. An inflammatory response is initiated in response to physical damage.
   D. Cytotoxic T-cells destroy foreign antigens.

Small Group Questions

1. Explain the basis of autoimmunity.

2. Under what conditions is there a risk for erythroblastosis fetalis? Explain why subsequent pregnancies are at greater risk than the first.

Explanations to Practice Questions

1. A

T-lymphocytes act primarily against the body's own cells that are infected by a fungus or virus. Therefore, a patient who lacks T-cells would be prone to viral and fungal infections, as choice (A) indicates.

2. B

The lymphocytes involved in cell-mediated immunity are the T-lymphocytes, or T-cells. There are four types of T-cells, each playing a different role in cell-mediated immunity: cytotoxic T-cells, helper T-cells, memory T-cells, and suppressor T-cells. Thus, from the answer choices, the only cells not involved in cell-mediated immunity are the plasma cells, which are differentiated immunoglobulin-secreting B-lymphocytes involved in humoral immunity. Choice (B) is therefore the correct answer.

3. B

The main function of the lymphatic system is to collect excess interstitial fluid and return it to the circulatory system, maintaining the balance of body fluids. However, this is not one of the answer choices. In addition, the lymphatic system absorbs chylomicrons from the small intestine and delivers them to the cardiovascular circulation. Transport of hormones and filtration of blood are not functions of the lymphatic system, so (A), (C), and (D) are incorrect. Thus, (B) is the correct answer.

4. A

Humoral immunity is involved in the production of antibodies following exposure to an antigen. Antibodies are produced by plasma cells derived from B-lymphocytes. Antibodies recognize and bind to specific antigens, marking them so they can be recognized by specific cells called phagocytes. Antibodies may also cause the antigens

to agglutinate and form insoluble complexes, facilitating their removal. (A) is therefore the correct answer.

5. A

Active immunity refers to the production of antibodies during an immune response. Active immunity may be conferred by vaccination, such as when an individual is injected with a weakened, inactive, or related form of a particular antigen, which stimulates the immune system to produce antibodies. Active immunity may require weeks to build. Passive immunity, on the other hand, involves the transfer of antibodies either passively or by injection. An example would be during pregnancy, when some maternal antibodies cross the placenta and enter fetal circulation, conferring passive immunity upon the fetus. Although passive immunity is acquired immediately, it is very short-lived, lasting only as long as the antibodies circulate in blood. (A) is therefore the correct answer.

6. D

The body employs a number of nonspecific defense mechanisms against foreign invasion. The epithelium provides a physical barrier against bacterial invasion. In addition, sweat contains an enzyme that attacks bacterial cell walls. Certain passages, such as the respiratory tract, are lined with ciliated mucus-coated epithelia, which filter and trap foreign particles. Macrophages engulf and destroy foreign particles. The inflammatory response is initiated in response to physical damage. The only choice that is not a nonspecific defense mechanism is (D), the correct answer. Cytotoxic T-cells are involved in cell-mediated immunity.

Homeostasis

Have a headache? Pop an ibuprofen. Backache? Works for that, too. Swollen foot? Sure, why not? It's easy enough. Ibuprofen, which has been around for over 40 years, is an inexpensive, over-the-counter, nonsteroidal anti-inflammatory drug (NSAID). Because of its ability to relieve pain, it's also known as an analgesic. It's often said to be safer than aspirin, and it usually proves successful with minimal side effects. Many people use it as a cure-all for aches and pains throughout the body, and when used in moderation, it seems to work just fine.

The problem arises when people take multiple doses every day for several years. Usually the drug is taken orally, which means that it circulates to the affected location and to all other organs, too. These other organs include the kidneys, which are sensitive to overuse of analgesics. They are especially sensitive to combination analgesics (e.g., acetaminophen + codeine). Years of analgesic use (usually self-therapy) can lead to kidney failure, known as analgesic nephropathy. If untreated, kidney failure is fatal. If caught, however, dialysis and perhaps a kidney transplant can save the patient's life. All over-the-counter painkillers will have to be discontinued, and other methods, such as counseling or behavior modifications, will need to be employed to control pain.

This isn't an issue for people who have a headache once a week. This is an issue for people who suffer from chronic pain due to injury, lifestyle (job demands, etc.), or simply as a side effect from another condition. Chronic pain afflicts millions of Americans each year. The subset of this group that suffers from analgesic nephropathy is primarily composed of females over 30 years of age who have some sort of chronic pain (head or backaches, severe menstrual pain), often emotional or behavioral changes, and sometimes a history of tobacco or alcohol use. Luckily, the painkiller most associated with analgesic nephropathy (phenacetin) is no longer on the market, and combination analgesics usually need to be prescribed by a clinician. It is currently estimated that analgesic nephropathy affects 0.004 percent of the population.

How does dialysis save an analgesic nephropathy patient experiencing kidney failure? Dialyzing fluid has many of the same solutes as blood (in strategic concentrations), and it is separated from blood by a semipermeable membrane. As blood is filtered through the dialysis machine, fluid and solutes diffuse down their concentration gradients, limited only by size. The dialysis machine therefore performs filtration, a crucial step in which healthy kidneys would participate to purify the blood and excrete wastes. In this chapter, we'll learn more about filtration and the major processes that accompany it, reabsorption and secretion. These processes are collectively involved in osmoregulation. Osmoregulation is just one mechanism that the body uses to stabilize its fluids and tissues. In this chapter, we'll also discuss other organs, such as the liver, large intestine, and skin, all of which play a role in upholding a constant internal environment. Together, these processes contribute to a necessary stable state known as homeostasis.

Key Concept

Maintenance of an internal environment wouldn't really be that hard if the external environment were static. However, we know that in the real world, it does change. Thus, homeostasis becomes an absolutely critical adaptation to life.

The Kidneys

The kidneys are located behind the abdomen at the level of the bottom rib. Cleverly enough, they are shaped like kidney beans. The functional unit of the kidney is the **nephron**, of which each kidney has approximately 1 million.

STRUCTURE

Each kidney is subdivided into the **cortex** and the **medulla**, as shown in Figure 11.1. The definitions for these areas hold constant for all organs to which they apply. The kidney's cortex is the outermost layer, much like the brain's. Also like the brain, the medulla of the kidney sits beneath the cortex (see Chapter 13). Each kidney also has a renal pelvis, which is its deepest layer. The renal pelvis is so named because its shape appears similar to the pelvic bone structure. The **renal artery**, **renal vein**, and **ureter** enter and exit the kidneys through the renal pelvis.

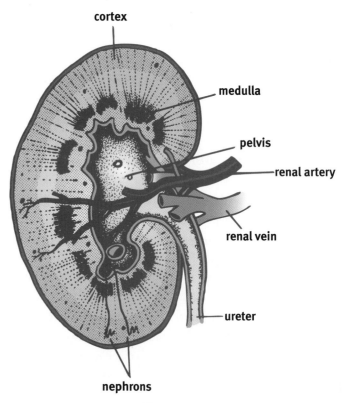

Figure 11.1

As we mentioned in Chapter 9, the kidney has one of the few **portal systems** in the body. Remember that a portal system consists of two sets of capillaries in series through which blood must travel before returning to the heart. The renal artery branches out much like the limbs of a tree and travels through the medulla and into the cortex as **afferent arterioles**. The capillaries that are derived from these afferent arterioles are known as **glomeruli** (sing.: **glomerulus**) and together form a highly convoluted structure. After blood passes through the glomerulus, the **efferent arterioles** lead blood away from it.

As is the case in portal systems, the glomerular capillaries lead to a second set of arterioles (the efferents) rather than venules. Like most arterioles, the efferent arterioles also lead to a set of capillaries. This second set of capillaries is known as the **vasa recta**.

Nephrons are the functional units of the kidney. Figure 11.2 will help us understand their microanatomy.

Key Concept

The kidneys have two sets of arterioles: afferent and efferent. The afferent arterioles lead into capillaries, and the efferent arterioles branch out from them. How can we remember this distinction on Test Day? *A* comes before *E* in the alphabet, with *C* in between, just as the *A*fferent arterioles come before the *E*fferent ones, with the *C*apillaries in between.

Bridge

Our discussion of nerves (Chapter 13) uses some of the same terms as do the blood vessels when we describe their organization. Afferent nerves carry sensory information toward the brain much as afferent arterioles carry blood toward the glomeruli. Efferent nerves relay signals away from the brain toward muscle just as efferent arterioles carry blood away from the glomerulus.

Figure 11.2

We will begin with the glomerulus. Our complex net of capillaries will be surrounded by a cuplike structure known as **Bowman's capsule**. Bowman's capsule leads to a long tubule with many distinct areas; in order, they are the **proximal convoluted tubule**, **descending** and **ascending limbs of the loop of Henle**, the **distal convoluted tubule**, and the **collecting duct**. Although we may think of these distinctions as trivial, the kidney's ability to excrete waste is intricately tied to the proper order and placement of these structures. When building a skyscraper, for instance, it is important that the plumbing be properly installed. We want the restrooms and water fountains and tap water to be connected in the right fashion. This requires the coordinated integration of many pipes, just as in our kidneys.

OSMOREGULATION BASICS

Now that we are experts on kidney structure (both macroscopic and microscopic), we can analyze function. Similar to the way we divided parts of the digestive system into digestive or absorptive roles, we can use **filtration**, **secretion**, and **reabsorption** to categorize each kidney structure. The three processes work together to ensure appropriate salt and water balance (osmoregulation) .

Filtration

The nephron's first step is filtration. Many of the offices inside that skyscraper filter what they throw away. Some items can be reused (such as paper), whereas others are useless and can only be discarded (the banana peel from lunch). Now, imagine that this filtering goes on in a special room right off the elevators in the basement. This is basically how the glomerulus is set up.

In the kidneys, approximately 20 percent of the blood that passes through the glomerulus is filtered into Bowman's space. The collected fluid is known as the filtrate. It is similar in composition to blood but does not contain cells or proteins due to the filter's ability to select based on size. In other words, molecules or cells that are larger than glomerular pores will remain in the blood. Where does that blood go next? On to the efferent arterioles and then through a second capillary network, the vasa recta. The filtrate is isotonic (Chapter 1) to blood so that neither the capsule nor the capillaries swell. Our kidneys filter about 180 liters a day, which is approximately 36 times our blood volume. This means that our entire blood volume is filtered about 36 times per day—truly impressive!

Secretion

In addition to their ability to filter blood, the nephrons are able to secrete salts, acids, bases, and urea directly into the tubule by both active and passive transport. We might liken this to being able to add specific items to the pile in our trash room in the skyscraper basement due to their relative excess in the building (e.g., if we received a duplicate shipment of light bulbs and had no room to store them, we might choose to discard the excess). Similarly, our kidneys can get rid of ions or other substances when they are present in relative excess in the blood. Secretion is also a mechanism for excreting wastes that are simply too large to pass through glomerular pores.

Reabsorption

The kidneys are firm believers in "Waste not, want not." Some compounds that are filtered and/or secreted may be taken back up for use. Certain substances are always reabsorbed, like glucose and amino acids. Imagine realizing that you threw away a lot of paper that could actually be reused in the copy machines. Sorting through the trash to find that paper would be similar to reabsorption in the kidney (without the *ick* factor, of course!).

NEPHRON FUNCTION

If our last few paragraphs had you wondering how the kidney could possibly stay on top of its to-do list, don't worry. The kidneys make use of selective permeability and osmolarity gradients to support all of their tasks. These gradients allow the kidney to reabsorb water, salt, and nutrients from the filtrate while selectively excreting waste products. As we have probably noticed by now, a solid understanding of gradients will help us make the grade on Test Day!

Selective Permeability

In the same way that molecules must be able to cross the cell membrane to enter a cell, compounds that we want to reabsorb and keep must be able to leave the filtrate (by crossing the plasma membranes of the cells lining the tubule). Remember that failure to leave the tubule will result in excretion from the body. Where does reabsorption occur? The proximal and distal tubules are capable of reabsorbing most substances (including water). The ascending and descending limbs of the loop of Henle and the collecting duct are a bit more selective. The descending limb is permeable to water but not salt, whereas the ascending limb is permeable to salt but not water. The collecting duct almost always reabsorbs water, but the amount is variable. When the body is very well hydrated, the collecting duct will be fairly impermeable to salt and water. When in conservation mode (imagine walking on a hot day with no water bottle), antidiuretic hormone and aldosterone will each act to increase the permeability of the collecting duct, allowing for greater water reabsorption and more concentrated urine output. We will discuss these hormones shortly. Figure 11.3 depicts reabsorption in the kidneys.

Osmolarity Gradient

The kidney is capable of altering the osmolarity of the interstitium (the tissue surrounding the tubule). This creates a gradient that, coupled with the selective permeability mentioned above, will allow us to reabsorb and excrete compounds as needed. Together, they work as a **countercurrent multiplier system**. In the normal physiological state, the osmolarity in the cortex is approximately the same

Real World

In certain conditions (e.g., congestive heart failure), the body tends to accumulate excess water as fluid in the lungs or peripheral tissues (edema). The judicious use of a diuretic drug can help the body get rid of excess fluids. Diuretics typically inhibit the reabsorption of sodium in one or more regions of the nephron, thereby increasing sodium excretion. Sodium, as an osmotically active particle, will pull water with it, thereby relieving the body of some of its excess fluid.

Figure 11.3

as that in the blood and remains at that level. As we descend deeper into the medulla, the osmolarity in the interstitium can range from isotonic with blood (when trying to excrete water) to four times as concentrated (when trying to conserve water). Water will move out of the tubule, into the interstitium, and eventually back into the blood if the concentration of solute is very high in the surrounding tissue, thereby conserving the water. If the concentration is the same in the tubule and in the interstitium, there is no driving force (gradient), and the water will be lost in urine. The solute movements that set up the countercurrent gradients are going to be major concepts for us to learn in medical school; however, for the MCAT, we just want to know that altering the osmolarity of the interstitium and selective permeability of the tubule are what allow this system to work.

Flow of Filtrate

Following the anatomical path we described before and integrating the two characteristics we just discussed, let's follow the filtrate through the nephron. In the proximal convoluted tubule, glucose, amino acids, soluble vitamins, and the majority of

Bridge

The entire system under which the kidney operates is based on membrane transport and gradients (Chapter 1). Both active and passive transport are used, and the extent of each depends on the specific section of the nephron in question. The takeaway is that membrane permeability is absolutely necessary for the kidneys to work.

salts are reabsorbed along with water. Almost 70 percent of filtered sodium will be reabsorbed here, but the filtrate remains isotonic to the interstitium. The descending limb of the loop of Henle is only permeable to water. As we travel down it, the concentration of the surrounding tissue will increase (we could also say it's hypertonic), which will drive water out of the tubule. Water loss increases the filtrate's osmolarity to roughly the same level as the interstitium's. The ascending limb is permeable only to salt. As the filtrate moves back up the loop toward the cortex, the concentration in the area surrounding the tubule drops and salt will be actively pumped out. Again, the filtrate is isotonic to the interstitium. The distal convoluted tubule maintains the same concentration as the cortex by reabsorbing salt and water in roughly equal proportions. The final concentration of urine will depend on the permeability of the collecting duct. As permeability increases, so does water removal, which concentrates the urine. Ultimately, the duct itself works under the directions of antidiuretic hormone (ADH) and aldosterone. Let's examine these hormones in a bit more detail.

HORMONAL REGULATION

We've mentioned ADH and aldosterone several times now because of their influence on renal function, but we haven't yet discussed how they exert their effects. Both are hormones (Chapter 12) that alter the permeability of the collecting duct in different ways. We will look at each in turn briefly and discuss their regulation by the endocrine system in the next chapter.

Aldosterone

Aldosterone is a steroid hormone that is secreted by the adrenal cortex in response to decreased blood volume. A decreased blood volume means we have less fluid in our "pipes," which would lead to low blood pressure (hypotension). Aldosterone is released from the adrenal glands in response to an increase in angiotensin, which itself is positively regulated by renin (see Chapter 12).

Aldosterone works by altering the ability of the collecting duct to reabsorb sodium. Remember that water doesn't move on its own; it travels down the osmolarity gradient. If we reabsorb more sodium, water will follow it. This has the net effect of increasing blood volume and therefore blood pressure. Aldosterone will also increase potassium excretion. We exploit this often in medicine for people with high blood pressure (hypertension). By giving a drug that blocks aldosterone's receptor, we can prevent its activity. If aldosterone doesn't bind its receptor because of the drug, less sodium (and therefore less water) are reabsorbed. Less water means less blood volume and a lower blood pressure!

ADH

Antidiuretic hormone (also known as vasopressin) is a peptide hormone that directly alters the permeability of the collecting duct. It allows more water to be reabsorbed by making the cell junctions of the duct leaky. Increased concentration

Key Concept

Water is not reabsorbed alone. In fact, water is not usually pumped at all. The kidney moves ions (primarily Na^+ and Cl^-) to create gradients that water will follow by osmosis.

Bridge

As a quick flashback to Chapter 5, we can quiz ourselves on which embryonic germ layer the adrenal cortex arises from (...the mesoderm). Also, recall that the adrenal medulla is generated from the ectodermal cell layer.

in the interstitium (i.e., hypertonic to the filtrate) will then cause the reuptake of water from the tubule. ADH is made in the hypothalamus, stored in the posterior pituitary, and secreted when blood osmolarity is high. Alcohol and caffeine both inhibit ADH and lead to the frequent excretion of dilute urine.

EXCRETION

Anything that doesn't leave the tubule will be excreted. The collecting duct is essentially the point of no return. After that, there are no further transporters for reuptake. As the filtrate leaves the tubule, it collects in the renal pelvis. The fluid, which carries mostly urea, uric acid, and excess ions (e.g., sodium, potassium, magnesium, calcium), flows through the ureter to the bladder, where it is stored until voiding. Urine is excreted through the urethra (see Figure 11.4).

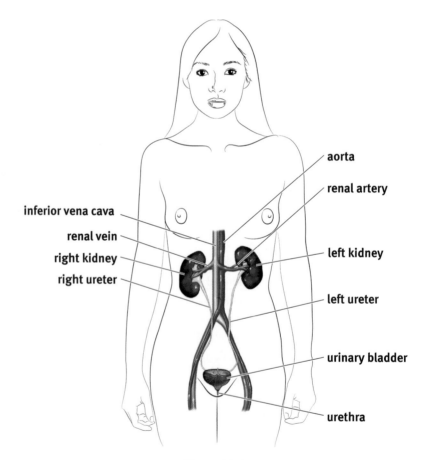

Figure 11.4

Three compounds that should always be absent from healthy urine are blood, protein, and glucose. Their presence indicates kidney pathology. Erythrocytes are too large to filter, so their appearance in urine usually indicates a problem with the glomerulus; glucose, amino acids, and small proteins are freely filtered but should be fully reabsorbed.

The Liver ★★★★☆

We have already discussed the function of the liver in digestion. It produces bile, which aids in the absorption of fats by solubilizing them. The liver is also responsible for assisting with blood glucose regulation and the elimination of nitrogen waste through urea. We previously learned that the nutrients absorbed during digestion are delivered to the liver through the **hepatic portal vein** (Chapter 7).

In times of plenty (like just after a meal), the liver will combine circulating glucose molecules into glycogen, a polymerized storage form. During times of famine (the early morning hours before we wake up and the later morning if we skip breakfast), this glycogen can be broken back down into glucose and released into the bloodstream. Additionally, the liver can make new glucose from a variety of precursors through **gluconeogenesis**.

The liver simply serves as a storage depot for glucose; we will see how this process is controlled in the next chapter.

In addition to glucose regulation, the liver also has the responsibility of dealing with nitrogenous waste products. Proteins are composed of amino acids, which contain amino groups. When there is a shortage of glucose, amino acids are used for vital processes such as cellular respiration. They must first undergo deamination (removal of the amino group), which would normally result in the formation of toxic ammonia. To prevent an ammonia buildup, the liver combines it with carbon dioxide to create urea—which we already learned can be excreted by the kidneys. The liver has several other functions, including the following:

- Detoxification
- Storage of vitamins and cofactors (iron and B_{12})
- Destruction of old erythrocytes
- Synthesis of bile
- Synthesis of various blood proteins
- Defense against antigens
- Beta-oxidation of fatty acids to ketones
- Interconversion of carbohydrates, fats, and amino acids

The Large Intestine ★★☆☆☆

We already saw in Chapter 7 that the large intestine is capable of reabsorbing salt and water (but not directing overall fluid balance). This organ can also excrete certain salts, such as calcium and iron.

Mnemonic

We have seen several word roots in previous chapters that can help us on Test Day. The liver is no different. *Hepato–* refers to the liver and its processes. In fact, we can remember this on the MCAT by thinking of hepatitis, which is an inflammation of the liver resulting from bacterial or viral infection.

Mnemonic

The name says it all: *gluco–* for "glucose", neo– for "new", and genesis for "creation"; thus, gluconeogenesis creates new glucose.

Key Concept

When we discussed eukaryotic cells in Chapter 1, we learned that organelle compartmentalization helped cells carry out fairly dangerous reactions without damaging themselves. Here again in the liver, we see the compartmentalization of a damaging molecule (ammonia) and its conversion to a nontoxic intermediate (urea) that can be safely excreted.

The Skin

STRUCTURE

By both weight and size, the skin (integument) is the largest organ in our bodies. It makes up about 16% of total body weight, on average. Just as we might cover our building in panels to keep heat in and soot-filled air out, skin protects us from the elements and disease (as we saw in Chapter 10). In fact, our skyscraper may have multiple layers of exterior paneling, and the same goes for the skin. Starting from the outside and working in, these layers are the **epidermis**, **dermis**, and **hypodermis** (subcutaneous layer) (see Figure 11.5). Remember that the skin is derived from the ectodermal germ layer.

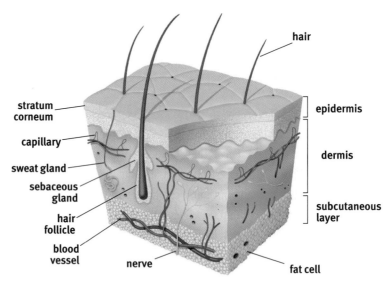

Figure 11.5

The epidermis is also subdivided into layers (strata). From the skin surface inward, these are the **stratum corneum, stratum lucidum, stratum granulosum, stratum spinosum, and stratum basalis**. The deepest layer is responsible for further proliferation. The outer layers are formed from cells that have pushed up from the stratum basalis. As these cells reach the outermost layer, they die and lose their nuclei, forming the scales (squames) of keratin that we mentioned way back in Chapter 1. The tight packing of these cells serves an immune function (as we discussed in the previous chapter) and helps to prevent loss of fluids and salt. Hair projects above the skin, and there are openings for sweat glands.

The dermis also consists of multiple layers. The upper layer (right below the epidermis) is the **papillary layer**, which consists of loose connective tissue. Below the

Mnemonic

Squamata is the name of the order of scaly reptiles that includes snakes and lizards.

papillary layer is the denser **reticular layer**. In addition to the three major layers of skin in Figure 11.5, we can also see the sweat glands, sense organs for touch and temperature, blood vessels, and hair follicles in the dermis.

Finally, we reach the hypodermis, which is the layer of connective tissue that connects our skin to our bodies. Imagine the walls in a house. The deepest layer is the drywall; this is analogous to the hypodermis. We then add paint and wallpaper and hang pictures from the drywall, the same way that the dermis and epidermis are layered on top of the hypodermis. We can't get attachment for our dermis and epidermis (paint, wallpaper, and pictures) without the hypodermis (drywall) connecting the skin to the body.

FUNCTION

We have already mentioned that skin is capable of protecting us from the elements and microbes. It also has other functions, including ultraviolet protection, thermoregulation in **endotherms**, and transduction of sensory information from the outside world. When we go to celebrate our excellent MCAT scores on the beach, we will need full use of our **melanocytes**. These epidermal cells secrete the pigment **melanin**, which helps keep us safe from ultraviolet light and its consequent DNA damage.

The skin can also serve as a receptor for touch and temperature. Thermoregulation is achieved by vasodilation, vasoconstriction, and sweating. Sweating, while it may seem unsightly, is actually an excellent cooling mechanism. By using the heat of our bodies as the heat of vaporization (a significant energy barrier), sweat helps us keep cool.

Heat loss is prevented in a variety of ways. Pads of subcutaneous fat provide insulation. Hair also contributes by trapping heat close to the skin's surface. Shivering in the cold is a result of involuntary muscle contraction and relaxation, a by-product of which is heat. Fat, as we mentioned in Chapter 3, also serves as a storage depot for excess energy, generating close to 100 ATP per molecule of triacylglycerol. We will see in the next chapter how epinephrine can alter the metabolic rate, affecting how rapidly this fat is stored and utilized.

Although we are all mammals, dogs rid themselves of excess heat a bit differently than we do: they pant. The basic concept is the same: Evaporation of warmth results in a cooling effect, but they evaporate warm air from the respiratory passages rather than warm water from skin. Moreover, all mammals, by definition, have hair. In some (especially our canine friends), it is quite thick and is called **fur**. Their fur serves the same function as the hair we already discussed but does so much more effectively. Animals that maintain a constant temperature are known

Real World

People who have albinism suffer from a genetic metabolic disorder characterized by the inability to synthesize melanin. Typically, albinism is inherited in an autosomal recessive fashion. As would be expected, patients with albinism are exquisitely sensitive to the harmful effects of the sun. A more common pigmentation disorder is vitiligo. Vitiligo is caused by the loss of epidermal melanocytes. Vitiligo is easily diagnosed, as there are usually well-defined zones of pigment loss. It is now believed that vitiligo is primarily an autoimmune disorder (homemade antibodies against self-melanocytes cause the depigmentation).

Bridge

The skin is also involved in the production of vitamin D with the aid of sunlight. Recall that vitamin D is critical in bone maintenance.

as **endotherms** or homeotherms, whereas those whose temperature depends on the external environment (e.g., snakes) are called **ectotherms** (previously, we may have heard these animals called cold-blooded or poikilotherms).

Finally, some animals may choose to enter a state of decreased arousal **(torpor)** during periods of excessive heat or cold. During the warm months, some desert animals may choose to **aestivate** (*aestas* is Latin for "summer"). During the winter months, the analogous process is called **hibernation**. In both cases, metabolic rate, heart rate, and respiration are far below normal. The benefit of these modes is the minimal expenditure of energy in an inhospitable environment.

Bridge

Homeostatic mechanisms are largely maintained involuntarily by the autonomic nervous system. The endocrine system plays a significant role, which we'll review in the next chapter.

Conclusion

This chapter introduced us to a new organ system (renal) and shed a different light on some organs we've already discussed (liver, large intestine, and skin). Each of these plays an integral role in maintaining a constant internal environment. For their small size, the kidneys have the immense task of filtering the blood and regulating water balance. The liver is a jack-of-all-trades; it acts as a storage depot, waste handler, and detoxifier in addition to several other roles. We've seen the skin play a role in immunity, and now we've also seen it serve in the regulation of temperature and sense perception. Now that we know how these systems work, let's move on to Chapter 12 to discuss how they are controlled.

CONCEPTS TO REMEMBER

☐ Homeostasis is the ability to maintain a constant internal environment despite a changing external environment.

☐ The kidneys use selective permeability and osmolarity gradients to maintain the body's water and salt balance.

☐ The functional unit of the kidney is the nephron, which has five basic sections: glomerulus, proximal convoluted tubule, distal convoluted tubule, loop of Henle (ascending and descending), and the collecting duct.

☐ Aldosterone is a steroid hormone that increases the amount of reabsorbed salt (directly) and thereby water (indirectly). It is secreted as part of a hormone cascade in response to low blood pressure.

☐ ADH is a peptide hormone that increases the ability of water to flow out of the collecting duct. It is secreted in response to an increase in blood osmolarity.

☐ The liver allows for excretion of excess nitrogenous waste by coupling ammonia to carbon dioxide, thereby creating the relatively nontoxic compound urea.

☐ The large intestine is capable of directly secreting ions and metals into solid waste.

☐ Thermoregulation in the skin is accomplished by vasodilation and vasoconstriction of surface blood vessels. Vasodilation of surface vessels allows more blood to run close to the skin's surface; heat is carried away by convection. Vasoconstriction of these same vessels prevents convection by minimizing the amount of blood at the skin's surface.

☐ Melanocytes in the epidermis secrete melanin, giving skin its pigmentation and protecting it from ultraviolet damage.

☐ Hibernation and aestivation are states of decreased metabolic activity and awareness. They serve to conserve resources in a time of scarcity.

Practice Questions

1. Which of the following would most likely be filtered through the glomerulus into Bowman's capsule?

  A. Erythrocytes
  B. Monosaccharides
  C. Platelets
  D. Proteins

2. In which of the following segments is sodium NOT actively transported out of the nephron?

  A. Proximal convoluted tubule
  B. The thin segments of the loop of Henle
  C. Distal convoluted tubule
  D. Sodium is always actively transported out of the nephron.

3. Which region of the kidney has the lowest solute concentration?

  A. Nephron
  B. Cortex
  C. Medulla
  D. Pelvis

4. Which of the following sequences correctly shows the passage of blood flow through the vessels of the kidney?

  A. Renal artery → afferent arterioles → glomerulus → efferent arterioles → vasa recta → renal vein
  B. Afferent arterioles → renal artery → glomerulus → vasa recta → renal vein → efferent arterioles
  C. Glomerulus → renal artery → afferent arterioles → efferent arterioles → renal vein → vasa recta
  D. Renal vein → efferent arterioles → glomerulus → afferent arterioles → vasa recta → renal artery

5. Which of the following statements is FALSE?

  A. ADH increases water reabsorption in the kidney.
  B. Aldosterone indirectly increases water reabsorption in the kidney.
  C. ADH acts directly on the proximal convoluted tubule.
  D. Aldosterone stimulates reabsorption of sodium from the collecting duct.

6. In the nephron, amino acids enter the vasa recta via the process of

  A. filtration.
  B. secretion.
  C. excretion.
  D. reabsorption.

7. On a very cold day, a man waits for over an hour at the bus stop. Which of the following structures helps his body set and maintain a normal body temperature?

  A. Hypothalamus
  B. Kidneys
  C. Heart
  D. Brain stem

8. Glucose reabsorption in the nephron occurs in the

  A. loop of Henle.
  B. distal convoluted tubule.
  C. proximal convoluted tubule.
  D. collecting duct.

9. All of the following are functions of the liver EXCEPT

    A. destruction of erythrocytes.

    B. storage of bile.

    C. detoxification of toxins.

    D. β-oxidation of fatty acids.

10. The primary function of the nephron is to create urine that is

    A. hypertonic to the blood.

    B. hypotonic to the blood.

    C. hypertonic to the filtrate.

    D. hypotonic to the vasa recta.

11. The liver

    A. decreases blood glucose levels.

    B. increases blood glucose levels.

    C. synthesizes glucose.

    D. All of the above are functions of the liver.

Small Group Questions

1. The kidneys of desert animals have modified nephrons, which help them survive long periods without water. What modifications would you expect to see in such a desert animal?

2. The glomeruli filter out a tremendous amount of water and molecules needed by the body, which must later be reabsorbed by an energy-requiring process. The Malpighian tubules of insects might seem to function more logically, secreting molecules and ions that need to be excreted. What advantages might a filtration-reabsorption process provide over a strictly secretion method of elimination?

3. You are planning to travel to a hot and arid desert region where little water is available. What kind of modifications to your epithelium would you expect to occur?

Explanations to Practice Questions

1. B

The glomerulus functions like a sieve; small molecules dissolved in the fluid will pass through the glomerulus (e.g., glucose, which is later reabsorbed), whereas large molecules, such as proteins and blood cells, will not. Some proteins can be filtered if they are small enough, but (B), monosaccharides, is always true and therefore the correct answer.

2. B

Sodium is actively transported out of the nephron in the proximal and distal convoluted tubules, where the concentration of sodium outside of the nephron is higher than inside; thus, energy is required to transport the sodium molecules against their concentration gradient. In the inner medulla, however, sodium and other ions (such as chloride) diffuse passively down their concentration gradient. The thin segments of the loop of Henle are the only structures that dip into the inner medulla, making (B) the correct answer.

3. B

The region of the kidney that has the lowest solute concentration is the cortex, where the proximal convoluted tubule and a part of the distal convoluted tubule are found. (B) is thus the correct answer.

4. A

Blood enters the kidney through the renal artery, which divides into many afferent arterioles that run through the medulla and into the cortex. Each afferent arteriole branches into a convoluted network of capillaries called a glomerulus. Rather than converging directly into a vein, the capillaries converge into an efferent arteriole, which divides into a fine capillary network known as the vasa recta. The vasa recta capillaries enmesh the nephron tubule, where they reabsorb various ions, and then converge into the renal vein. This arrangement of tandem capillary beds is known as a portal system. (A) correctly describes the passage of blood through the kidney.

5. C

Glancing at the answer choices, we notice right away that they all test us on our knowledge about ADH and aldosterone. These two hormones ultimately act to increase water reabsorption in the kidney; their respective mechanisms of action, however, are different. ADH increases water reabsorption by increasing the permeability of the collecting duct to water, whereas aldosterone stimulates reabsorption of sodium from the DCT. Using this knowledge, we can now attack the answer choices. (A), (B), and (D) are all true statements, while (C) is false; ADH does not act on the proximal convoluted tubule. (C) is thus the correct answer.

6. D

Essential substances, such as glucose, salts, amino acids, and water, are reabsorbed from the filtrate and returned to the blood in the vasa recta. This results in the formation of concentrated urine, which is hypertonic to the blood. (D) correctly identifies the process through which amino acids enter the vasa recta. By knowing that the body does not want to lose any proteins, and thus amino acids, we could eliminate (A), (B), and (C).

7. A

The hypothalamus functions as a thermostat that regulates body temperature. When it's cold outside, nervous stimulation to the blood vessels in the skin is increased, causing the vessels to constrict. This constriction diminishes blood flow to the skin surface and prevents heat loss. Sweat glands are turned off to prevent heat loss through evaporation.

Skeletal muscles are stimulated to shiver (rapidly contract), which increases the metabolic rate and produces heat. Furthermore, the cerebrum stimulates warmth-seeking behaviors, such as foot stamping. If the cold stress becomes severe, the hypothalamus will stimulate the secretion of thyroid and adrenal hormones, which will provide additional heat by further increasing the metabolic rate. Since the hypothalamus is the main structure involved in maintaining body temperature, (A) is correct.

8. C

The filtrate enters Bowman's capsule and then flows into the proximal convoluted tubule, where virtually all glucose, amino acids, and other important organic molecules are reabsorbed via active transport. (C) is thus the correct answer.

9. B

The liver is a complex organ and plays many crucial roles in the maintenance of homeostasis. Among the main functions, we can enumerate the conversion of glucose into glycogen, the destruction of erythrocytes, the detoxification of toxins, and the β-oxidation of fatty acids. From the given choices, the only function that cannot be attributed to the liver is (B). Although bile is produced in the liver, it is stored in the gallbladder. (B) is therefore the correct answer.

10. A

The kidneys function to eliminate wastes such as urea, while reabsorbing various important substances such as glucose and amino acids for reuse by the body. Generation of a solute concentration gradient from the cortex to medulla allows a considerable amount of water to be reabsorbed. Excretion of concentrated urine serves to limit water losses from the body and helps to preserve blood volume. Thus, the primary function of the nephron is to create urine that is hypertonic to the blood, making (A) the correct answer.

11. D

The liver helps regulate blood glucose levels through three main mechanisms: conversion of glucose to glycogen, conversion of glycogen to glucose, and gluconeogenesis (synthesis of glucose from noncarbohydrate precursors). Thus, (A), (B), and (C) all identify functions of the liver, making (D) the correct answer to this question.

The Endocrine System

In medicine, certain terms have onomatopoeic qualities: the *lub-dub* of the heart sounds, the *rhonchi* of respiratory illnesses. Although ovulation, the rupture of the follicle and release of the oocyte from the surface of the ovary, is a silent event, the pain that some women experience in the hours around ovulation is described by a term that possesses the sensory equivalent of onomatopoeia: *mittelschmerz*. It just *sounds* unpleasant, doesn't it? German for "middle pain", *mittelschmerz* is experienced by about 20 percent of ovulating women. Ranging from dull to sharp, typically located in the lower abdomen and pelvis, the pain may last anywhere from a few hours to a couple of days. In some women, the pain is so localized that they can tell from which ovary the egg was released, and because ovulation occurs randomly from each ovary every month, the pain may switch sides month to month. Analgesics (pain relievers) may be used in cases of moderate to severe discomfort. The source of the pain may be related to irritation of the abdominal cavity wall by the fluid and blood released from the ruptured ovarian follicle.

Ovulation is a key event in the cycle of female fertility. Highly controlled by a complex system of positive and negative feedback loops involving chemical messengers called hormones, the menstrual cycle is the example par excellence of endocrine system activity. The MCAT will test your general understanding of the endocrine system, which is a complex association of many different organs and tissues working together to control the activity of other organs and maintain homeostasis. Although the menstrual cycle is a primary focus for the MCAT, you must also be sure to understand endocrine regulation of blood glucose concentration, renal function and osmoregulation, and thyroid function as it relates to thermoregulation, to name but a few aspects of the overall concept of homeostasis.

Although the hypothalamus is one of the major regulators of the endocrine system, there is no single control center. Glands throughout the organism contribute to endocrine effects. We will briefly examine the anatomy of the endocrine glands and then jump into the functional products, hormones. The hypothalamus and pituitary will get special attention because they are involved in many disparate functions, including menstrual regulation, the stress response, and tissue growth and development. Hormones can appear in antagonistic pairs, in a way analogous to the antagonistic pairing of muscles. We will see examples of hormone antagonist pairs that control blood glucose and calcium concentrations. The effects of hormones are mediated through their receptors, so we will close with a discussion of the chemical classes of hormones. Table 12.1 at the end of the chapter will be an important study resource for you. As we discuss each hormone, we will draw your attention to the source of each hormone, its general structure, its receptor location, and its effect on the target cell.

Key Concept

Unlike the other organ systems that we have discussed thus far, the basis of the endocrine system is action at a distance. Each organ has a local effect that can be passed through the bloodstream to affect the entire organism. Furthermore, the endocrine system regulates activities that require duration rather than speed.

Anatomy

★★☆☆☆

Endocrine organs exert their influence, sometimes over long distances, upon other areas in the body to provide both feedback and stimulation. Depending on the distance between the endocrine organ and the intended site of action of its hormone, signaling may be described as **autocrine**, **paracrine,** or **endocrine**. In autocrine signaling, the same cell is stimulated. For example, some T-cells (see Chapter 10) will release interleukin-2. This cytokine can then bind to the same T-cells to increase their immune functionality. Paracrine signaling occurs between cells that are placed close to one another; we can use two neurons signaling between the hypothalamus and pituitary as an example. Finally, endocrine signaling involves our classic action at a distance. We can think of follicle-stimulating hormone (FSH), which is released by the anterior pituitary but exerts its effects at the level of the gonads. We need to be mindful of the involvement of the different hormones in the various types of signaling (autocrine, paracrine, and endocrine). Table 12.1 at the end of the chapter will help guide us.

Endocrine Glands

★★★★☆

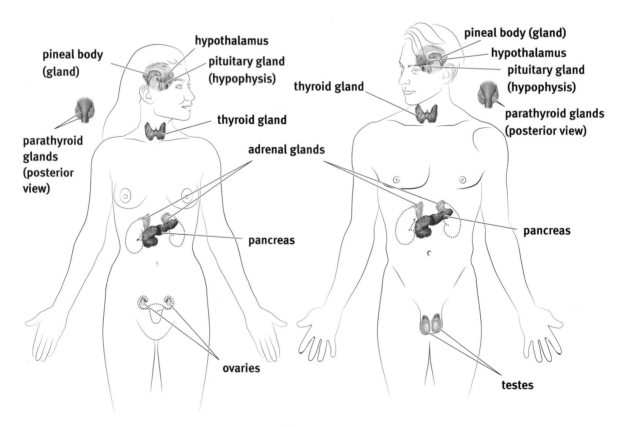

Figure 12.1

Many organs in the body have endocrine capabilities, and we have mentioned several of them already! This group includes the **hypothalamus**, the **pituitary**, the **testes** and **ovaries**, the **pineal gland**, the **kidneys**, the **gastrointestinal glands**, the **heart**, and the **thymus** (see figure 12.1). Each of these organs is capable of synthesizing and secreting one or more hormones. Furthermore, we may identify collections of cells within organs that serve important endocrine roles. Perhaps the most well-known collection of cells having endocrine activity are the pancreatic islets of Langerhans, which are primarily responsible for glucose homeostasis. Hormones come in two varieties: **peptide** and **steroid**. We will discuss the physiological consequences of this shortly, but in either case, hormones must bind to their receptors to be effective. Thus, we can say that hormone activity is controlled not only by the release of hormone but also by the presence of receptors on target organs.

HYPOTHALAMUS

We will start with the hypothalamus, the master control gland in the brain. If the endocrine system was a complex political organization, we might characterize the hypothalamus as the president. By regulating the pituitary (see below), the hypothalamus is capable of having organism-wide effects. The hypothalamus is located in the forebrain (see Chapter 13), directly above the pituitary gland and below the thalamus (hence, *hypo*thalamus). Since the hypothalamus and the pituitary are close to each other, the hypothalamic control of the pituitary is by paracrine release of

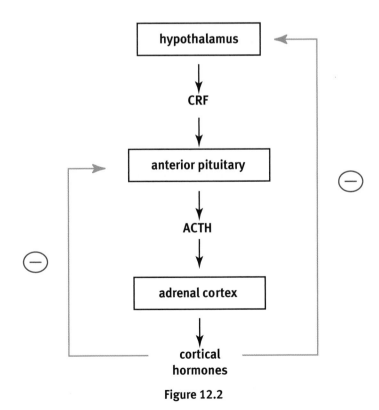

Figure 12.2

Bridge

Enzymes are often regulated via feedback inhibition. The endocrine system is regulated in a similar manner. As shown in Figure 12.2, as concentrations of the final effector molecule rise (e.g., cortisol), negative feedback to the hypothalamus and pituitary decreases their release of the upstream signaling molecules (e.g., CRF and ACTH, respectively).

hormones into a portal system that directly connects the two organs. The hypothalamus receives input from a wide variety of neural sources; for example, a part of the hypothalamus called the suprachiasmatic nucleus (which we don't need to remember for Test Day) receives some of the light input from the retinas and helps control sleep-wake cycles. The release of hormones by the hypothalamus is also regulated by negative feedback (recall Chapter 2 and control of enzymatic activity). As part of our discussion of the hypothalamus, we should note that the pituitary has an **anterior** and **posterior** component. The different roles of each will be examined shortly. The hypothalamus controls both parts but in different ways.

Interactions with the Anterior Pituitary

The hypothalamus secretes compounds into the **hypophyseal portal system** (see Chapters 7 and 9), which is shown in Figure 12.3. Although the name may sound funny, **hypophysis** is just the medical name for the pituitary (remember, *hypo*– means *below*; the pituitary is below the hypothalamus). Hormones are released from the hypothalamus into this portal bloodstream. They then travel down the pituitary stalk and bind to receptors in the anterior pituitary, where they stimulate the release of other hormones.

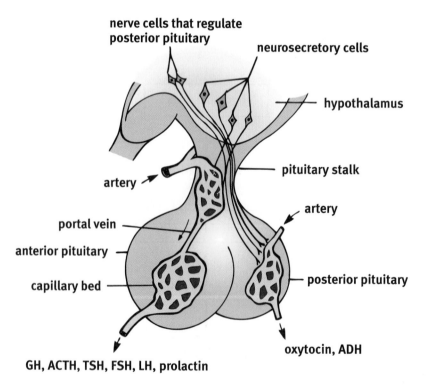

Figure 12.3

Tuning In

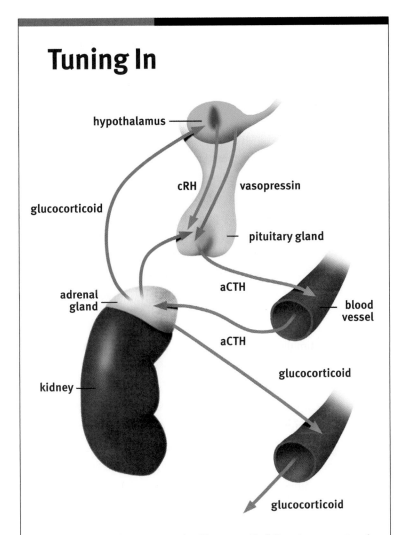

The hypothalamus runs the "long arm" of the stress system by secreting the hormone CRH. CRH flows through veins (*green arrow*) to the pituitary, which in turn releases the hormone ACTH into the blood. ACTH stimulates the adrenal glands to produce glucocorticoid hormones, which put the body on alert. In acute stress, the hypothalamus secretes vasopressin as well to further activate the adrenals. The system regulates itself down after a threat is over via a negative feedback loop (*blue arrows*), in which glucocorticoids bathe both the hypothalamus to suppress CRH secretion and the pituitary to suppress ACTH. But daily stress may endlessly activate the system.

Figure 12.4

For each of the next pairs of hormones, the first is the hypothalamic hormone, whose binding in the anterior pituitary causes the release of the second hormone:

- **Gonadotropin-releasing hormone (GnRH)** with **follicle-stimulating hormone (FSH)** and **luteinizing hormone (LH)**

Mnemonic

To remember the seven products of the anterior pituitary, think FLAT PEG:

FSH

LH

ACTH

TSH

Prolactin

Endorphins

GH

- **Growth hormone-releasing hormone (GHRH)** with **growth hormone (GH)**
- **Prolactin inhibitory factor (PIF)** with **prolactin**
- **Thyroid-releasing hormone (TRH)** with **thyroid-stimulating hormone (TSH)**
- **Corticotropin-releasing factor (CRF)** with **adrenocorticotropic hormone (ACTH)**

Each of the hypothalamic–anterior pituitary hormone pairs, with one exception, operates in the same manner: Increased release from the hypothalamus will cause increased release of the corresponding hormone from the anterior pituitary. The oddball in the bunch is PIF/prolactin. Prolactin is constitutively released from the anterior pituitary and is *inhibited* by prolactin inhibitory factor.

Excessive levels of hormones can be detrimental. To keep the amounts within a healthy range, the hypothalamus and pituitary are both subject to feedback inhibition. Let's take a look at an example of this (diagrammed in Figure 12.2).

Release of CRF (also known as CRH, cortisol-releasing hormone) from the hypothalamus will stimulate the anterior pituitary to generate ACTH. ACTH will then cause the adrenals to increase the level of **cortisol** being secreted into the blood. However, we wouldn't want cortisol levels to rise too high (we will see why shortly). To prevent excess cortisol secretion, cortisol can inhibit the hypothalamus and anterior pituitary from releasing CRF and ACTH, respectively. This makes sense, as CRF and ACTH have now had their desired effect: namely, getting more cortisol into the blood. What does this mean in terms of receptors in the hypothalamus and pituitary? They must contain receptors for cortisol; otherwise, they wouldn't be able to recognize that cortisol levels had increased.

Interactions with the Posterior Pituitary

Connection between the hypothalamus and the posterior lobe of the pituitary is not by way of the hypophyseal portal system. Rather, neurons in the hypothalamus send their axons (see Chapter 13) down the pituitary stalk and into the posterior pituitary, where they can release **oxytocin** and **anti-diuretic hormone (ADH)**. ADH, also called vasopressin, is a hormone we have discussed already in the context of renal function; oxytocin is new to us but will be described in detail in the next section.

PITUITARY

We have already introduced the anatomical divisions in the pituitary, the anterior and posterior lobes, which are also functionally distinct. We will consider each in turn.

ANTERIOR PITUITARY

One distinction that can help us organize the anterior pituitary hormones is categorizing them into **direct** or **tropic** roles. Direct hormones will bind to receptors on their target organs and have a direct effect (i.e., no intermediate is needed).

Tropic hormones also bind to receptors on organs, but rather than resulting in immediate changes, they cause the release of effector hormones (i.e., they act as an intermediate). Both are important mechanisms. The FLAT PEG mnemonic helps us not only to remember the hormones but also to separate them according to their direct versus tropic effects.

Direct Hormones

Growth hormone is named for what it does: It promotes the growth of bone and muscle. This sort of growth is energetically expensive (think of how much hungrier you were and how much you ate during puberty). Growth hormone prevents glucose uptake in certain tissues (nongrowing ones) and stimulates the breakdown of fatty acids. We can see that this will increase the availability of glucose overall, allowing the muscle and bone to use it. If we think back to the hypothalamus, we know that the release of GH is tied to GHRH stimulation.

We mentioned in Chapter 6 that growth occurs at the epiphyseal plates of the long bones; these plates seal during puberty. An excess of GH released in childhood (before this closure) can cause **gigantism**. A deficit results in **dwarfism**. In adults, the situation is slightly different. Because the long bones are sealed, GH still has an effect, but it is in the smaller bones. Bone remodeling occurs throughout life, and an excess of GH in adulthood will affect smaller bones disproportionately. The medical condition is known as **acromegaly**. The bones most commonly affected are those in the hands, feet, and head. Patients will present because they have had to buy larger shoes, they cannot wear their rings, and they can no longer fit into their hats.

The other two direct hormones are prolactin and the endorphins. Prolactin is more important in females than in males, where it stimulates milk production in the **mammary glands**. Milk production in the male is pathologic, as stated previously.

Finally, endorphins have a direct effect on pain modulation by decreasing the perception of pain. Many pharmaceutical agents, such as morphine, mimic the effect of these naturally occurring painkillers. A real-life example of this occurs in runners. After completing a marathon, many people will say they are on an endorphin "high" or "rush." Endorphins mask the pain from just having run 26.2 miles and induce a sense of euphoria. People who eat very spicy food claim a similar sensation in response to capsaicin, the compound found in peppers.

Tropic Hormones

We are going to mention the tropic hormones only briefly here. They work by causing the release of another hormone at the organ level. We will discuss those effector hormones with each organ system. ACTH is regulated by CRF. It induces the adrenal cortex to release glucocorticoids. As we might expect with a root like *gluco–*, glucocorticoids can affect sugar balance in the body. TSH is released in response to TRH stimulation. TSH is appropriately named, as it stimulates the thyroid to take up iodine and release **thyroid hormone**. Both LH and FSH are secreted when GnRH levels rise. They affect the ovaries and testes. The specific effects of each hormone with which we want to be familiar for the MCAT will be discussed later.

POSTERIOR PITUITARY

The posterior pituitary contains the nerve terminals of neurons whose bodies are in the hypothalamus. The posterior pituitary receives and stores two hormones produced by the hypothalamus, ADH and oxytocin. These hormones are released into the bloodstream by the posterior pituitary. Oxytocin is secreted during childbirth and allows for coordinated contraction of uterine smooth muscle. Its secretion may also be stimulated by suckling, which in turn will lead to increased milk production.

We already examined the details of ADH in Chapter 11, but as a quick review, we will highlight key points. ADH is secreted in response to increased blood osmolarity (sensed by **osmoreceptors**) or low blood volume (sensed by **baroreceptors**). Its action is at the level of the collecting duct, where it increases the permeability of the duct to water. The net effect is a greater reabsorbtion of water from the nephron filtrate, resulting in greater retention of water and expansion (and dilution) of the vascular compartment.

THYROID GLAND

The thyroid is controlled by the pituitary (TSH) and the hypothalamus (TRH). The human thyroid is on the front surface of the trachea; if you put your fingers gently on the front of your windpipe, you can feel it as the organ that moves up and down with swallowing. The thyroid has two major functions: setting basal metabolic rate and calcium homeostasis. It mediates the first effect by releasing **thyroxine** and **triiodothyronine (the thyroid hormones)**, whereas calcium levels are controlled by **calcitonin**.

Thyroid Hormones (Thyroxine and Triiodothyronine)

Thyroxine (T_4) and triiodothyronine (T_3) are both produced by the iodination of the amino acid tyrosine in the follicular cells of the thyroid. The numbers 3 and 4 refer to the number of iodine atoms attached. Thyroid hormones are capable of resetting the basal metabolic rate of the body by making energy production more or less efficient, as well as altering the utilization of glucose and fatty acids. Increased amounts of T_3 and T_4 will lead to increased cellular respiration. They will also cause a greater amount of protein and fatty acid turnover by speeding up both synthesis and degradation of these compounds. High plasma levels of thyroid hormones will lead to decreased TSH and TRH synthesis; we expect this negative feedback so that T_3 and T_4 levels don't become excessive.

A deficiency of iodine or an inflammation of the thyroid may result in **hypothyroidism**, in which thyroid hormones are secreted in insufficient amounts or not at all. The condition is characterized by lethargy, decreased body temperature, slowed respiratory and heart rate, cold intolerance, and weight gain. Thyroid hormones are required for appropriate neurological and physical development in children. Most children are tested at birth for appropriate levels because a deficiency will result in mental retardation and developmental delay **(cretinism)**. An excess of thyroid hormones, which may result from a tumor or thyroid over-stimulation, may lead to **hyperthyroidism**. We can predict its clinical course by considering the opposite of each of the effects seen in hypothyroidism: heightened activity level, increased body temperature, increased respiratory and heart rate, heat intolerance, and weight loss.

In both hyperthyroidism and hypothyroidism, the organ itself may enlarge and become visible by external examination. This is known as a **goiter**.

Calcitonin

If we were to examine thyroid tissue under a light microscope, we would see two distinct cell populations within the gland. Follicular cells produce thyroid hormones, and C-cells produce **calcitonin**. Calcitonin acts to decrease plasma calcium levels in three ways: increase excretion from the kidneys, decrease absorption from the gut, and increase storage in the bone. High levels of calcium in the blood stimulate secretion of calcitonin from the C-cells.

PARATHYROID GLANDS

The hormone produced by the parathyroid glands is aptly, if unimaginatively, named **parathyroid hormone (PTH)**. The parathyroids are four small pea-shaped structures that sit on the surface of the thyroid. PTH serves as an antagonistic hormone to calcitonin. It functions to increase plasma levels of calcium by reversing the effects of calcitonin; namely, it decreases excretion of calcium through the kidneys, increases absorption of calcium in the gut, and increases bone resorption, thereby freeing up calcium. PTH also activates vitamin D to its active form, which is required for the absorption of calcium in the gut. Like the hormones we have already seen, PTH is also subject to feedback inhibition. As levels of plasma calcium rise, PTH secretion is decreased.

ADRENAL GLANDS

The adrenal glands are the next endocrine organ we will examine as we continue our whirlwind journey through the body. The adrenals are located on top of the kidneys, one on each side (adrenal, meaning near or next to the kidney). As we mentioned in Chapter 11, they consist of a cortex and a medulla. The distinction is more than anatomical; each part of the gland is responsible for secretion of a different hormone. Let's take a look.

Key Concept

Calcium is an exceptionally important ion. If you've been reading this book carefully, you've already noted several critically important functions of calcium:

- Principal component of bone
- Regulator of muscle contraction
- Cofactor for normal blood clotting

In addition, calcium also plays a role in cell movement, exocytosis, and neurotransmitter release.

Mnemonic

Just like insulin and glucagon, PTH and calcitonin are antagonistic to one another. We should think of them as a pair whose primary function is to regulate calcium levels in the blood. PTH increases Ca^{2+} levels, whereas calcitonin decreases Ca^{2+} levels. (Calcitonin "tones down" Ca^{2+}).

Bridge

Yet another good function of cholesterol is its role as a precursor for steroid hormones.

Adrenal Cortex

The adrenal cortex secretes a set of hormones called the **corticosteroids**. These compounds are secreted in response to ACTH stimulation from the anterior pituitary, which itself responds to CRF from the hypothalamus. All of the corticosteroids are steroid hormones (derived from cholesterol); they may be divided into three functional classes: **glucocorticoids**, **mineralocorticoids**, and **cortical sex hormones**. One way to remember the corticosteroids is to think of the three *s*'s of the adrenal cortex: sugar, salt, and sex. A medical school professor once said that we should no longer have any problem remembering these, given how much of our waking (and dreaming) hours are spent fantasizing about or actually pursuing each of them.

Glucocorticoids

The name of this class of hormones gives us an insight to their function. The prefix *gluco–* gives us the clue that they help regulate glucose levels. In addition, they affect protein metabolism. Two glucocorticoids we should be familiar with for Test Day are **cortisol** and **cortisone**. How might these compounds raise blood glucose? They increase gluconeogenesis (see Chapter 11) and decrease protein synthesis. Cortisol and cortisone can also decrease inflammation and immunological responses. When we see football players receiving steroid shots to cut down on inflammation in their knee joints, glucocorticoids are being used. Cortisol is often known as the stress hormone, as it is released in response to physical or emotional stress. As we can see in Figure 12.5, stress affects several parts of the body, so it should make sense that it stimulates an endocrine release.

Mineralocorticoids

Considering the name of this class of hormones, we can predict that mineralocorticoids will help us to keep a healthy mineral balance. And they do, in fact, control salt balance in coordination with the kidneys. You should recall the mineralocorticoid that we discussed in Chapter 11: **Aldosterone** causes increased reabsorption of sodium and thereby water. The increased sodium and water leads to expansion of the blood volume and a higher blood pressure. Aldosterone can also affect the levels of potassium and hydrogen ions. It enhances the secretion of these two atoms into the tubule. What will be the net result of this movement? Potassium and hydrogen will be excreted from the body in the urine.

The secretion of aldosterone is under the control of the **renin-angiotensin-aldosterone** system. Decreased blood volume causes the juxtaglomerular cells of the kidney to secrete renin, which cleaves an inactive plasma protein **angiotensinogen** to its active form, **angiotensin I**. Angiotensin I is then

THE GOOD AND BAD EFFECTS OF STRESS

The human body is superb at responding to the acute stress of a physical challenge, such as chasing down prey or escaping a predator. The circulatory, nervous, and immune systems are mobilized, while the digestive and reproductive processes are suppressed. If the stress becomes chronic, though, the continual repetition of these responses can cause major damage.

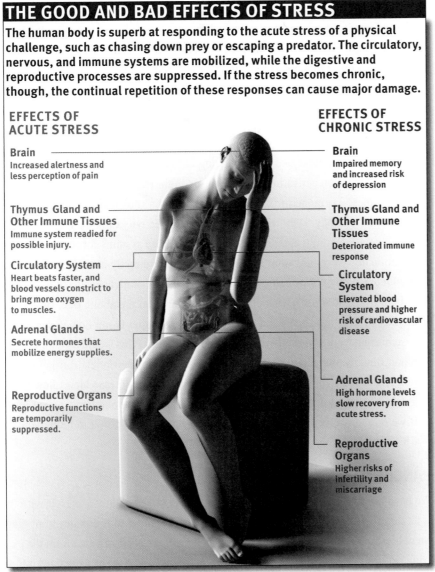

EFFECTS OF ACUTE STRESS

Brain
Increased alertness and less perception of pain

Thymus Gland and Other Immune Tissues
Immune system readied for possible injury.

Circulatory System
Heart beats faster, and blood vessels constrict to bring more oxygen to muscles.

Adrenal Glands
Secrete hormones that mobilize energy supplies.

Reproductive Organs
Reproductive functions are temporarily suppressed.

EFFECTS OF CHRONIC STRESS

Brain
Impaired memory and increased risk of depression

Thymus Gland and Other Immune Tissues
Deteriorated immune response

Circulatory System
Elevated blood pressure and higher risk of cardiovascular disease

Adrenal Glands
High hormone levels slow recovery from acute stress.

Reproductive Organs
Higher risks of infertility and miscarriage

Figure 12.5

converted to **angiotensin II** (see the sidebar), which will stimulate the adrenal cortex to secrete aldosterone. Once fluid volume is restored, there is a decreased drive to stimulate renin release, thus serving as the negative feedback mechanism for this system.

Cortical Sex Hormones

The adrenals are also capable of making male sex hormones **(androgens)**. Because normal males make much larger amounts of androgens in the testes, the hormones secreted from the adrenals are relatively unimportant. In females, however, the lower baseline of androgens is subject to greater perturbation. An increase in adrenal sex hormones may have masculinizing effects, such as excess hair growth and an increase in other male secondary sex characteristics.

Real World

In addition to stimulating the secretion of aldosterone, which increases blood volume and hence blood pressure, angiotensin II also increases blood pressure directly by a powerful vasoconstrictive effect. Angiotensin converting enzyme (ACE) inhibitors block the conversion of angiotensin I to angiotensin II, inhibiting vasoconstriction and actually producing vasodilation. Therefore, ACE inhibitors frequently are prescribed for the treatment of high blood pressure and congestive heart failure. (In the latter case, vasodilation helps reduce the resistance against which the failing heart must pump.)

Adrenal Medulla

Nestled inside the adrenal cortex is the adrenal medulla. A derivative of the nervous system, it is responsible for the production of the flight-or-fight sympathetic hormones **epinephrine** and **norepinephrine**. The specialized nerve cells in the medulla are capable of secreting these compounds directly into the circulatory system. Both epinephrine and norepinephrine are peptide hormones that belong to a larger class of molecules known as **catecholamines**.

If we ever found ourselves actually being chased by a bear, our survival would, in part, depend on activation of the fight-or-flight response. As a part of this response, these hormones from the adrenal medulla modulate a wide variety of systems in the body. They will act to increase the activity of body systems necessary for fight-or-flight and decrease activity to those systems for rest-and-digest. Additionally, we would want to make energy more directly available in the form of glucose. Epinephrine can increase the conversion of glycogen back to glucose in both liver and muscle, as well as increase the basal metabolic rate. Both compounds will increase heart and respiratory rate and alter blood flow to supply the systems that would be used in a sympathetic response. This would mean increased blood flow by vasodilation of the arteries leading to the skeletal muscle, heart, lungs, and brain. In addition, vasoconstriction would decrease blood flow to the gut, kidneys, and skin. After all, we won't need to worry about digesting our lunch if we don't escape! We will discuss the fight-or-flight response in more detail in Chapter 13.

PANCREAS

We have already seen the exocrine function of the pancreas in Chapter 7, with the cells that secrete digestive enzymes into the ducts leading to the duodenum. Now, we will examine the *endocrine* function. Small groups of cells distinct from the exocrine ones are known as **islets of Langerhans**. If we look at these areas microscopically, we will see three distinct types of cells: **alpha**, **beta**, and **delta** cells. The alpha cells secrete **glucagon**, the beta cells are responsible for the production of **insulin**, and delta cells make **somatostatin**.

Glucagon

Glucagon is a hormone whose actions are antagonistic to those of insulin. It is secreted during times of famine (the word *famine* might sound a bit harsh, so perhaps we'll imagine the hunger we feel before breakfast!). When glucose levels run low, the following are stimulated: degradation of protein and fat, conversion of glycogen to glucose, and production of new glucose via gluconeogenesis. In addition to being secreted by low blood glucose, certain gastrointestinal hormones (e.g., CCK and gastrin; see Chapter 7) increase glucagon release from the alpha cells. In times of feast, or high glucose levels, secretion will be inhibited.

Bridge

The secretions of the exocrine pancreas are components of the pancreatic juice that enters into the duodenum:

- Amylase (carbohydrate digestion)
- Lipase (lipid digestion)
- Trypsin, chymotrypsin, and carboxy-peptidase (protein digestion)

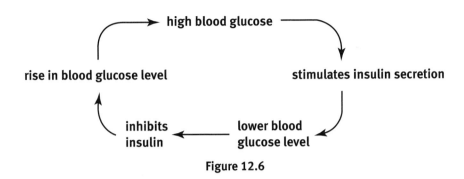

Figure 12.6

Mnemonic

We can remember when glucagon levels are high because it is secreted when glucose is *gone*.

Insulin

If insulin is antagonistic to glucagon, when would we expect it to be secreted? Insulin levels in plasma rise in conjunction with blood glucose levels (see Figure 12.6). Insulin induces muscle and liver cells to take up glucose and store it as glycogen for later use. In addition, since it is active when glucose levels are high, insulin stimulates anabolic processes such as fat and protein synthesis.

In excess, insulin will cause **hypoglycemia**, which is characterized by low blood glucose. Underproduction, insufficient secretion, or insensitivity to insulin all can result in **diabetes mellitus**, which is clinically characterized by **hyperglycemia**, excess glucose in the blood. As we saw in Chapter 11, excessive glucose in the filtrate will result in its presence in the urine. Since it is an osmotically active particle, its (abnormal) presence in the filtrate leads to excess excretion of water and expansion, sometimes dramatic, of the urine volume. Diabetics often report **polyuria**, increased frequency of urination, and **polydipsia**, increased thirst. There are two types of diabetes. **Type I** (insulin-dependent diabetes mellitus) is caused by autoimmune destruction of the beta cells of the pancreas; these individuals produce little to no insulin, as the majority of beta cells have been destroyed. Type I diabetics require regular injections of insulin to prevent hyperglycemia. **Type II** (non-insulin-dependent diabetes mellitus) is a result of the body resisting the effects of insulin at its receptor. It is partially inherited and partially due to high-sugar diets. Certain pharmaceutical agents can be taken orally to help the body more effectively use the insulin it produces. These individuals require insulin only when their body cannot naturally control glucose levels, even when aided by these other medications.

Key Concept

Insulin decreases plasma glucose. Glucagon increases plasma glucose. Don't forget that growth hormone, the glucocorticoids, and epinephrine are also capable of increasing plasma glucose.

Somatostatin

Somatostatin is an inhibitor of both insulin and glucagon. High blood glucose and amino acid concentrations stimulate its secretion.

TESTES

The testes, present only in the male, are the site of spermatogenesis (Chapter 4). To carry out this function properly, there is a delicate interplay of FSH and LH stimulation on two structures in the testes. FSH stimulates the Sertoli cells and is necessary for sperm maturation, whereas LH causes the interstitial cells to produce **testosterone**, the major androgen in the male. In addition to being important for spermatogenesis, testosterone is necessary for male embryonic differentiation, male sexual development at puberty, and maintenance of secondary sex characteristics (e.g., axillary and pubic hair). It provides negative feedback to FSH, LH, and GnRH. If the receptors for testosterone are absent from an individual, it cannot exert its effects. The result is a condition called **androgen insensitivity syndrome**, in which a genetic male (XY) has secondary female sexual characteristics.

OVARIES

The ovaries, which are derived from the same embryonic structure as the testes, are found only in females. They are also under the control of FSH and LH secreted from the anterior pituitary, which itself is directed by GnRH release from the hypothalamus. The ovaries produce both **estrogens** and **progesterone**.

Hormones

Estrogens

Estrogens, which are secreted in response to elevated FSH and LH, are responsible for the development and maintenance of secondary female sexual characteristics. They also lead to thickening of the **endometrium** each month in preparation for implantation of a zygote. In the embryo, they stimulate development of the female reproductive tract. Estrogens are secreted by the ovarian follicles and the **corpus luteum**.

Progesterone

Progesterone is secreted in response to LH stimulation from the anterior pituitary. It is released from the corpus luteum (the remnant follicle on the ovary surface) and is responsible for the development and maintenance (but not generation) of the endometrium. By the end of the first trimester of a pregnancy, progesterone is supplied by the placenta, and the corpus luteum ceases functioning.

The Menstrual Cycle

Each month after the onset of puberty and until menopause, the endometrial lining will grow and shed in a cyclical manner. This is known as the **menstrual cycle**. It is controlled by the relative levels of estrogen and progesterone. The menstrual cycle may be divided into four phases: the **follicular phase**, **ovulation**, the **luteal phase**, and **menstruation**. As we describe each phase, follow along with Figure 12.7 to see how the hormone levels change.

Follicular Phase

The follicular phase begins when the **menstrual flow**, which sheds the uterine lining of the previous cycle, stops. GnRH secretion from the hypothalamus increases in response to the lower levels of estrogen and progesterone, whose concentrations fall off toward the end of each cycle. The higher concentrations of GnRH cause increased secretions of both FSH and LH. These two hormones work in concert to develop several ovarian follicles. The follicles begin to produce estrogen primarily, which at this point has a negative feedback effect and causes the GnRH, LH, and FSH concentrations to level off. Estrogen works to regrow the endometrial lining, stimulating vascularization and glandularization of the **decidua**.

Figure 12.7

Ovulation

Estrogen is interesting in that it can have both negative and positive feedback effects. Late in the follicular phase, the developing follicles secrete more and more estrogen. Eventually, estrogen concentrations reach a level that paradoxically results in positive feedback, and GnRH, LH, and FSH levels spike. The **surge** in LH is important; it induces **ovulation**, the release of the ovum from the ovary into the abdominal cavity.

Luteal Phase

After ovulation, LH causes the ruptured follicle to form the corpus luteum. The corpus luteum secretes progesterone. From above, we know that although estrogen helps regenerate the uterine lining, it is progesterone that maintains it for implantation. Progesterone levels now begin to rise, while estrogen levels remain high. The very high levels of estrogen and progesterone cause negative feedback on GnRH, FSH, and LH. What is the purpose? To prevent the development of multiple ova in the same cycle; after all, we don't want to put all our eggs in one basket (*ba da bum!*).

Menstruation

If implantation does not occur, human chorionic gonadotropin (hCG, an LH analog; see Chapter 4) will not be made. Without hCG to stimulate the corpus luteum, progesterone levels decline, and the uterine lining is sloughed off. The loss of high levels of estrogen and progesterone removes the block on GnRH so that the next cycle can begin.

Pregnancy

If fertilization has occurred, the corpus luteum will be maintained by the presence of hCG, which is secreted by the blastocyst, and the developing placenta. During the first trimester of development, it is the estrogen and progesterone secreted by the corpus luteum that keep the uterine lining in place. By the second trimester, hCG levels decline, but progesterone and estrogen rise since they are now secreted by the placenta itself. The high levels of estrogen and progesterone serve as negative feedback mechanisms and prevent further GnRH secretion.

Menopause

Menopause, which usually occurs between the ages of 45 and 55, results from decreased responsiveness of the ovaries to FSH and LH. Fewer follicles will begin to develop each month, and some may fail to rupture. The decreased response to FSH and LH results in decreased levels of estrogen and progesterone. FSH and LH lose their feedback inhibition, so their plasma concentrations are usually increased in postmenopausal women. Many women report flushing, hot flashes, bloating, headaches, and irritability during menopause as a result of these fluctuating hormone concentrations.

PINEAL GLAND

The pineal gland is located deep within the brain, where it secretes the hormone **melatonin**. The actual function of this hormone is unclear, although it is hypothesized that it may be involved in **circadian rhythms**. The evidence for this is projection of visual information from the eyes to this area of the brain, but the pineal gland is not directly involved in vision.

OTHER ENDOCRINE GLANDS

A brief mention of a few remaining organs with endocrine functionality will put us in good stead for Test Day. In the gastrointestinal tract, glandular tissue can be found in both the stomach and intestine. Many gastrointestinal peptides have been identified, and important ones include secretin, gastrin, and cholecystokinin (see Chapter 7). As we might expect for an organ system whose primary goal is to take food and break it down into its constituent components, the stimulation for release of most of these peptides is food intake.

In Chapter 11, we described the kidney's role in water balance. The renin-angiotensin-aldosterone system was mentioned as a way to increase salt and water reabsorption. The kidney also produces **erythropoietin**, which stimulates bone marrow to increase production of erythrocytes. It is secreted in response to low oxygen levels in the blood.

Two final organs that display endocrine function are the heart and the thymus. The heart releases **atrial natriuretic peptide (ANP)** to help regulate salt and water balance. The thymus, located directly behind the breastbone, releases **thymosin**, which is important for proper T-cell development and differentiation (Chapter 10). The thymus atrophies by adulthood. A full list of hormones and their actions can be found at the end of the chapter in Table 12.1.

Real World

Patients with chronic kidney disease can become anemic as a result of impaired erythropoietin production, causing inadequate red cell production from the bone marrow. Recently, genetically engineered erythropoietin has been employed to stimulate the bone marrow to produce more red blood cells in such patients.

Mechanisms of Hormone Action ★★★★★★

Although we have described a number of hormones and their actions, we have not actually described the mechanism by which they effect those actions. Hormones are classified into three major groups: **peptide hormones**, **steroid hormones**, or **amino acid-derived hormones**. These distinctions are based on their chemical structure.

PEPTIDES

Peptide hormones are made up of amino acids. They range in size from quite small (ADH) to relatively large (insulin). They are all derived from larger precursor polypeptides that are cleaved by posttranslational modifications (see Chapter 14). These smaller units are transported to the Golgi, which, we know from Chapter 1, is the site of modification. These modifications activate the hormone and direct it to the correct location in the cell. Such hormones are released by exocytosis after having been packaged into vesicles.

Peptide hormones are charged, so they cannot cross the phospholipid cell membrane and instead bind to receptors on the exterior cell surface. They act as **first messengers**. Upon binding to their receptors, they stimulate the production of **second messengers**, such as cyclic AMP (cAMP). This conversion is catalyzed by the enzyme **adenylate cyclase**. cAMP can then bind to intracellular targets, such as proteins or DNA, to exert the hormone's ultimate effect. The connection between the hormone at the surface and the effect brought about by cAMP within the cell is known as a **signaling cascade**. At each step, there is the possibility of **amplification**. One hormone molecule may bind to multiple receptor molecules before it is degraded. Each receptor may activate several adenylate cyclases, each of which will make much cAMP. Thus, there is more signal after each step. The actions of cAMP are terminated by **phosphodiesterase**.

The effects of peptide hormones are usually shorter lived, because they work through transient second messenger systems. It is quicker to turn them on and off, compared with steroid hormones, but their effects do not last without relatively constant stimulation.

STEROIDS

How Estrogen Acts in Cells

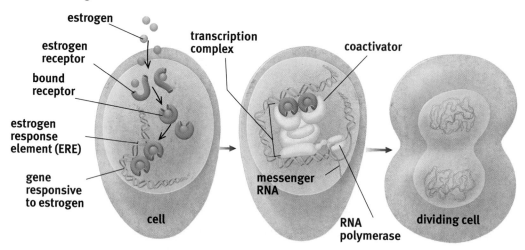

1. Estrogen binds to its receptor, which then binds to certain genes.
2. A transcription complex forms and activates gene transcription.
3. Cell behavior changes.

Figure 12.8

As we have pointed out many times already, all steroid hormones (e.g., aldosterone, estrogen) are derived from cholesterol. Since they are derived from a nonpolar molecule, steroid hormones can easily cross the cell membrane. In fact, their receptors are usually intracellular or intranuclear. Upon binding to the receptor, they dimerize (pair up with another receptor-hormone complex). This dimer can then bind directly to DNA and alter its transcription (see Chapter 14), either increasing or decreasing transcription depending on the hormone and gene in question. The effects of steroid hormones are longer lived, as they alter the amount of mRNA and protein present in a cell; however, it takes longer to see the effect of steroid hormones, as the processes of transcription and translation are not immediate.

AMINO ACID DERIVATIVES

These hormones are less common than peptide and steroid hormones, but they include some of the most important compounds that we mentioned in this chapter, including epinephrine, norepinephrine, and thyroxine. They are derived from one or two amino acids, usually with a few additional modifications. For example, thyroid hormone is made from tyrosine and includes the addition of several iodine atoms. Depending on the polarity of the molecule, they may either work through second

> ### Key Concept
>
> **Peptide hormones:**
> - Surface receptors
> - Generally act via secondary messengers.
>
> **Steroid hormones:**
> - Intracellular receptors
> - Hormone-receptor binding to DNA promotes transcription of specific genes.

messenger systems the way peptide hormones do (epinephrine falls in this category), or they may actually enter the cell and act like steroid hormones (thyroxine).

Table 12.1 Principal Hormones in Humans

Hormone	Source	Action
Growth hormone	Anterior pituitary	Stimulates bone and muscle growth
Prolactin	Anterior pituitary	Stimulates milk production and secretion
Adrenocorticotropic hormone (ACTH)	Anterior pituitary	Stimulates the adrenal cortex to synthesize and secrete glucocorticoids
Thyroid-stimulating hormone (TSH)	Anterior pituitary	Stimulates the thyroid to produce thyroid hormones
Luteinizing hormone (LH)	Anterior pituitary	Stimulates ovulation in females; testosterone synthesis in males
Follicle-stimulating hormone (FSH)	Anterior pituitary	Stimulates follicle maturation in females; spermatogenesis in males
Oxytocin	Hypothalamus; stored in posterior pituitary	Stimulates uterine contractions during labor, and milk secretion during lactation
Vasopressin (ADH)	Hypothalamus; stored in posterior pituitary	Stimulates water reabsorption in kidneys
Thyroid hormone	Thyroid	Stimulates metabolic activity
Calcitonin	Thyroid	Decreases the blood calcium level
Parathyroid hormone	Parathyroid	Increases the blood calcium level
Glucocorticoids	Adrenal cortex	Increase blood glucose level and decrease protein synthesis
Mineralocorticoids	Adrenal cortex	Increase water reabsorption in the kidneys
Epinephrine and Norepinephrine	Adrenal medulla	Increase blood glucose level and heart rate
Glucagon	Pancreas	Stimulates conversion of glycogen to glucose in the liver; increases blood glucose
Insulin	Pancreas	Lowers blood glucose and increases storage of glycogen
Somatostatin	Pancreas	Suppresses secretion of glucagon and insulin
Testosterone	Testis	Maintains male secondary sexual characteristics
Estrogen	Ovary/placenta	Maintains female secondary sexual characteristics
Progesterone	Ovary/placenta	Promotes growth/maintenance of endometrium
Melatonin	Pineal	Unclear in humans
Erythropoietin	Kidney	Stimulates bone marrow to increase production of erythrocytes
Atrial natriuretic hormone	Heart	Involved in osmoregulation
Thymosin	Thymus	Stimulates T lymphocyte development

Conclusion

Our chapter contains a bevy of useful information. We have nearly completed our study of the organ systems; only the nervous system remains. The endocrine system is unique in that it is not a single organ or housed in a single location. Hormones that are made in a variety of localities can have wide-reaching effects throughout the entire organism. We need to be familiar with several points about each hormone for Test Day: name, effect, regulated by and regulator of, and chemical precursor. Table 12.1 should be our guide. The endocrine system allows for integration and execution of the homeostatic parameters that we saw in the previous chapter. For example, we learned that calcium is maintained within a narrow concentration range in the plasma by the antagonistic actions of calcitonin and parathyroid hormone. To do this, these hormones affected absorption, excretion, and bone remodeling. Vitamin D even became important when we discussed parathyroid hormone. The takeaway message for each of these hormones is that, although they have specific effects (e.g., decreasing blood glucose for insulin), they lead to manipulations that change the steady state of the whole organism. As we turn to the nervous system, we will also see how higher-level control can lead to systemwide coordination.

CONCEPTS TO REMEMBER

☐ The endocrine system is made up of organs throughout the body. They are defined by their ability to exert action at a distance.

☐ Hormones will be ineffective at sites where their receptors are absent.

☐ The hypothalamus is the master control gland. It directs the release of hormones from the anterior pituitary.

☐ The anterior pituitary's hormones may be classified as direct (prolactin, endorphins, and growth hormone) or tropic (FSH, LH, ACTH, and TSH). Direct hormones exert their effects immediately, whereas the binding of tropic hormones to their receptors causes the release of another hormone (e.g., cortisol is released from the adrenal cortex by ACTH stimulation).

☐ The adrenal medulla makes epinephrine and norepinephrine, which are responsible for mediating the flight-or-fight sympathetic response (e.g., increased heart rate, greater blood flow to skeletal muscle).

☐ Parathyroid hormone and calcitonin are antagonistic hormones that control blood calcium levels. The former is secreted by the parathyroid glands, whereas the thyroid makes calcitonin. They alter absorption, excretion, and mobilization of calcium from bone.

☐ Insulin and glucagon are antagonistic hormones secreted by the islets of Langerhans that control blood glucose concentration.

☐ Estrogen exhibits both positive and negative feedback during the menstrual cycle.

☐ The presence of hCG maintains the corpus luteum, which is necessary for progesterone production during the first trimester of pregnancy.

☐ Hormones fall into one of three structural classes: steroid hormones (derived from cholesterol), peptide hormones (made up of amino acids), or amino acid derivatives (constituted of one or two amino acids with modifications).

Practice Questions

1. Which of the following associations between the hormone and its classification is FALSE?

   A. Cortisol—glucocorticoid
   B. Aldosterone—mineralcorticoid
   C. ADH—mineralcorticoid
   D. Androgens—cortical sex hormones

2. Which of the following hormones directly stimulates its target organ?

   A. ACTH
   B. TSH
   C. LH
   D. GH

3. Increased activity of the parathyroid gland leads to

   A. an increase in blood Ca^{2+} concentration.
   B. a decrease in the rate of bone resorption.
   C. a decrease in metabolic rate.
   D. a decrease in blood glucose levels.

4. Which of the following statements concerning growth hormone is NOT true?

   A. Overproduction of growth hormone in adults results in acromegaly.
   B. It promotes growth of bone and muscle.
   C. It is secreted by the hypothalamus.
   D. A deficiency in growth hormone results in dwarfism.

5. At which two points of the menstrual cycle are the levels of estrogen highest?

   A. Immediately before and after ovulation
   B. At ovulation and during the menstrual flow
   C. During the menstrual flow and pregnancy
   D. During pregnancy and after menopause

6. Iodine deficiency may result in

   A. acromegaly.
   B. cretinism.
   C. gigantism.
   D. hyperthyroidism.

7. Which of the following would NOT be seen during pregnancy?

   A. High levels of HCG in the first trimester
   B. High levels of estrogen and progesterone throughout the pregnancy
   C. Low levels of FSH in the first trimester
   D. High levels of GnRH throughout the pregnancy

8. Which of the following associations between the hormone and its role is FALSE?

   A. Estrogen—development of secondary sexual characteristics
   B. Progesterone—development and maintenance of endometrial walls
   C. LH—stimulate ovulation
   D. FSH—maturation of the ovarian follicles into the corpus luteum

9. Which of the following hormones is NOT derived from cholesterol?

   A. Aldosterone
   B. Testosterone
   C. Oxytocin
   D. Progesterone

10. Which of the following is TRUE regarding pancreatic somatostatin?

   A. Its secretion is increased by low blood glucose.
   B. It is always inhibitory.
   C. It is regulated by cortisol levels.
   D. It stimulates insulin and glucagon secretion.

11. Destruction of all beta cells in the pancreas would cause

   A. glucagon secretion to stop and a decrease in blood glucose.
   B. glucagon secretion to stop and an increase in blood glucose.
   C. insulin secretion to stop and an increase in blood glucose.
   D. insulin secretion to stop and a decrease in blood glucose.

12. Which of the following associations regarding aldosterone regulation is FALSE?

   A. Renin converts the plasma protein angiotensinogen to angiotensin I.
   B. Angiotensin I is converted to angiotensin II.
   C. Angiotensin II stimulates the adrenal cortex to secrete aldosterone.
   D. An increase in water reabsorption stimulates renin production.

13. A scientist discovers a new hormone that is relatively large in size and that triggers the conversion of ATP to cAMP. Which of the following best describes the type of hormone that was just discovered?

   A. Amino acid-derived hormone
   B. Peptide hormone
   C. Steroid hormone
   D. Tropic hormone

14. A patient presents to your office with muscle weakness, slowness in movement, and calcium deposits on his bones. A blood test reveals very low calcium levels in the blood. What is one treatment option for your patient?

   A. Increase calcitonin levels
   B. Increase PTH levels
   C. Increase mineralcorticoid levels
   D. Increase growth hormone levels

15. Oxytocin and vasopressin are

   A. produced and released by the hypothalamus.
   B. produced and released by the pituitary.
   C. produced by the hypothalamus and released by the pituitary.
   D. produced by the pituitary and released by the hypothalamus.

16. If the thymus gland is taken out in a three-year-old child, what problems will the child experience later in life?

   A. He will be prone to bacterial infections.
   B. He will be prone to viral and fungal infections.
   C. He will have dwarfism.
   D. He will have gigantism.

Small Group Questions

1. Many physiological parameters, such as blood Ca^{2+} concentration and glucose levels, are controlled by two hormones that have opposite effects. What is the advantage of achieving regulation in this manner instead of by using a single hormone that changes the parameters in one direction only?

2. At first glance, the signaling systems that involve cell surface receptors may appear complex and indirect, with their use of G proteins, second messengers, and often multiple stages of enzymes. What are the advantages of such seemingly complex response systems?

3. Discuss the sources and actions of parathyroid hormone and calcitonin in humans and describe the feedback mechanisms that control their release.

4. Suppose that two different organs, such as the liver and heart, are sensitive to a particular hormone. The cells in both organs have identical receptors for the hormone, and hormone-receptor binding produces the same intracellular second messenger in both organs. However, the hormone produces different effects in the two organs. Explain how this can occur.

5. The placenta secretes high levels of estradiol and progesterone during pregnancy. What would be the expected effect of these high hormone levels in the absence of pregnancy?

Explanations to Practice Questions

1. C

Let's take a look at each choice and eliminate the ones that correctly associate the hormone and its classification. Cortisol, along with cortisone, is a glucocorticoid secreted by the adrenal cortex. Aldosterone is a mineralcorticoid also secreted by the adrenal cortex. ADH, however, is not secreted by the adrenal cortex, but rather by the posterior pituitary, where it is stored after being synthesized by the hypothalamus. (C) is therefore the correct answer. Furthermore, ADH is a peptide hormone, not a steroid. For the sake of completion, we can confirm that androgens are cortical sex hormones also secreted by the adrenal cortex.

2. D

A hormone that directly stimulates its target organ is referred to as a direct hormone. Glancing at the answer choices, we notice that all of the hormones are secreted by the anterior pituitary gland. The direct hormones secreted by the anterior pituitary are growth hormone (GH), prolactin, and endorphins. From the given choices, only growth hormone is a direct hormone, which means that (D) is the correct answer. All of the other choices are tropic hormones.

3. A

The parathyroid glands secrete parathyroid hormone (PTH), a hormone whose function is to increase blood calcium levels. An increase in activity of the parathyroid glands would lead to an increase in PTH levels and, therefore, an increase in blood calcium levels (achieved mainly through an increase in the rate of bone resorption). (A) is thus the correct answer.

4. C

Growth hormone is a direct hormone secreted by the anterior pituitary. Among its many functions, the most important is the promotion of growth in bone and muscle.

An overproduction of growth hormone in children results in gigantism, whereas in adults it results in acromegaly (enlargement of the extremities of the face, such as the nose and ears). On the other hand, a deficiency of growth hormone results in dwarfism. From the answer choices, the only statement that is false is (C).

5. A

Estrogen levels increase right before ovulation, leading to a surge in LH, which stimulates the release of an egg (ovulation). Later, when the follicle develops into the corpus luteum, the levels of estrogen (and progesterone) increase to prepare for a possible pregnancy. The levels of estrogen are also high during pregnancy, when the placenta secretes high levels of estrogen and progesterone. (A) is therefore the correct answer.

6. B

Inflammation of the thyroid or iodine deficiency causes hypothyroidism in which the thyroid hormones are undersecreted or not secreted at all. Hypothyroidism in newborn infants is called cretinism and is characterized by mental retardation, short stature, and coarse facial features. (B) is therefore the correct answer.

7. D

During the first trimester of pregnancy, the corpus luteum is preserved by human chorionic gonadotropin (HCG); hence, progesterone and estrogen secretion by the corpus luteum are maintained during the first trimester. During the second trimester, HCG levels decline, but progesterone and estrogen levels rise since they are now secreted by the placenta itself. High levels of progesterone and estrogen inhibit GnRH secretion, thus preventing FSH and LH secretion and the onset of a new menstrual cycle. From the given choices, the correct answer is (D).

8. D

Since we are looking for a false association, we have to analyze each choice and eliminate the ones containing correct definitions of their respective hormones. Estrogen contributes to the development of secondary sexual characteristics, so (A) can be eliminated. The same applies to (B), since it is true that progesterone contributes to the development and maintenance of endometrial walls. (C) is also true, because LH stimulates ovulation in females. (D), on the other hand, is a false statement. FSH does stimulate the maturation of ovarian follicles. However, it is LH, not FSH, that stimulates the development of the corpus luteum from an ovarian follicle. (D) is therefore the correct answer.

9. C

Steroid hormones are derived from cholesterol. This characteristic makes them lipophillic and allows them to diffuse freely across cell membranes. Among them, we can find glucocorticoids (cortisol and cortisone), mineralcorticoids (aldosterone), and cortical sex hormones (androgens). Androgens include estrogen, progesterone, and testosterone. Thus, the only hormone from the given choices that is not derived from cholesterol is oxytocin, which is a peptide hormone. (C) is therefore the correct answer.

10. B

Let's quickly refresh our knowledge of somatostatin. Pancreatic somatostatin secretion is increased by high blood glucose or amino acid levels, leading to both decreased insulin and glucagon secretion. Somatostatin is also regulated by the levels of cholecystokinin (CCK) and growth hormone (GH). Somatostatin is always inhibitory regardless of where it acts. Based on this, (B) is the correct answer.

11. C

Our task in answering this question is twofold: We have first to determine what beta cells in the pancreas produce and, second, what would be the effect of stopping this hormone from being secreted. Because of the nature of the answer choices, we can eliminate half of them immediately: A cessation in glucagon secretion would lead to a decrease in blood glucose, whereas preventing insulin secretion would result in an increase in blood glucose. As such, we know for sure that (B) and (D) are incorrect. The beta cells in the pancreas produce and secrete insulin, as opposed to the alpha cells, which produce and secrete glucagon. Therefore, destruction of all beta cells in the pancreas would cause insulin secretion to stop, resulting in an increase in blood glucose levels. This is what occurs in type I diabetes. (C) is therefore the correct answer.

12. D

Let's begin with a quick review of aldosterone regulation, which is controlled by the renin-angiotensin system. When blood volume falls, the juxtaglomerular cells of the kidney produce renin, an enzyme that converts the plasma protein angiotensinogen to angiotensin I. Angiotensin I is then converted to angiotensin II by an enzyme in the lungs; angiotensin II ultimately stimulates the adrenal cortex to secrete aldosterone. Aldosterone helps to restore blood volume by increasing sodium reabsorption at the kidney, leading to an increase in water reabsorption. This removes the initial stimulus for renin production. Thus, (A), (B), and (C) correctly describe the renin-angiotensin system. (D) is false because it implies that there is a positive feedback rather than a negative feedback mechanism between the increase in water reabsorption and renin production. As such, (D) is the correct answer.

13. B

We know from the question stem that the newly discovered hormone functions as a first messenger, converting ATP to cAMP, which functions as a second messenger, triggering a signaling cascade in the cell. Hormones that act via secondary messengers and are relatively large in size (short peptides or complex polypeptides) are peptide hormones, as (B) indicates.

14. B

The question stem is basically telling us that the patient has too much calcitonin in his blood, as indicated by the low levels of calcium, the muscle weakness and slowness in movement, and the calcium deposits on his bones. The best way to treat this problem is by increasing the PTH levels in his blood. PTH raises blood calcium levels by stimulating calcium release from bone and decreasing calcium excretion in the kidneys. (B) is therefore the correct answer.

15.   C

Let's quickly review what we know about oxytocin and vasopressin. Oxytocin is produced by the hypothalamus and stored in the posterior pituitary; its primary function is to stimulate uterine contractions during labor and milk secretion during lactation. Vasopressin, also referred to as ADH, is made in the hypothalamus and stored in the posterior pituitary; its function is to increase water reabsorption in the kidneys. The only choice that correctly describes this is (C), the correct answer.

16.   B

This question is asking us to determine the role of the thymus in a three-year-old child. The thymus gland secretes hormones such as thymosin during childhood. Thymosin stimulates T-lymphocyte development and differentiation. The thymus atrophies by adulthood, after the immune system has fully developed. As such, removing the thymus gland in a child would leave him with undeveloped and undifferentiated T-cells, which would make him prone to viral and fungal infections. This condition could be lethal. (B) is therefore the correct answer.

13

The Nervous System

You may have heard the one about the frog that allowed itself to be boiled to death. The story goes that a frog will immediately jump out of a pot of already boiling water but will remain motionless if placed into cool water that is then heated to a boil very slowly. It's as if the frog's neurological system—its temperature and pain receptors—were unable to detect the increasing heat and the frog was completely unaware of the increasingly dangerous and ultimately deadly situation. Although the story has its origins in academic discussions of physiology published in the late 19th century (particularly one report of an experiment performed at Johns Hopkins University in 1882, in which a frog was boiled to death by raising the temperature by 0.12°C per minute), the supposed phenomenon has little scientific value today. We assure you that no National Institutes of Health–funded laboratories are slowly boiling frogs or other amphibians to their death (at least not for this particular objective). Rather, the story has taken on an almost allegorical significance, warning against everything from the slow encroachment of the police state or of communism to moral relativism and the slow descent of all civilization toward its ultimate destruction.

Let's not worry, for the moment at least, whether we are being sufficiently vigilant to prevent ourselves from being slowly boiled to death in a pot of political or moral evil. Let's focus on what those 19th-century scientists were investigating: namely, the nervous system of the frog. Although we were not in the lab working and observing alongside these scientists, we might imagine the questions they were asking and attempting to answer. *How does an organism sense its environment? What of its environment can an organism sense? How do organisms respond to the environment once they sense it? What are the thresholds for response?* And so on. These are fundamental questions about the nervous system, and more than 100 years since these experiments, we are still asking them. We certainly have learned much about the nervous system, its anatomical and functional divisions, the nature of the action potential, and the system's central importance for the coordination of nearly every other organ system, but there is much, much more that we do not know. It has become something of a cliché to say that the brain is the final frontier of human exploration and discovery. And yet, in a real sense, this is true.

The nervous system regulates the overall response of an organism to its environment. The human brain alone contains 100 billion neurons and 10 trillion synaptic connections: all of this in a three-pound organ protected by the skull. The nervous system is responsible for the integration of all the sensory information we receive each day—from recognizing the sound of the honking taxi driver to knowing the taste of pistachio ice cream to feeling the chill of the wind on our face. In addition, the nervous system is responsible for the control of all the muscular movement we described in Chapter 6 and glandular secretions, such as saliva (which is why your mouth becomes dry when you are nervous). In organisms such as humans, it is also capable of higher-level thinking and planning future goals. Its activities are coordinated through electrical and chemical messages. It truly is an amazing system. Let's get our synapses firing as we begin to probe carefully through the nervous system.

Neurons

STRUCTURE

Each neuron is specially designed to carry out its function. There are a variety of different types of neurons in the body, but they all share some features with which we should be familiar on Test Day. Let's take a look at Figure 13.1, which illustrates a prototypical neuron.

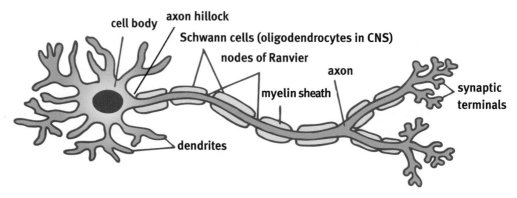

Figure 13.1

Starting on the left side of our diagram, we have the cell body. In the nervous system, we give this part of the cell a specialized name **(soma)**. The nucleus, endoplasmic reticulum, and ribosomes that we discussed in Chapter 1 are all located within the soma. As we move away from the cell body, we see many processes. The majority of these are **dendrites**. Dendrites are structures made to receive information. They transmit this information to the cell body, where it is integrated at the **axon hillock**, the enlargement at the beginning of the axon. We will see the importance of the axon hillock in action potential generation in a few pages. The axon hillock provides a connection between the cell body and the **axon**, which is a nerve fiber that is specialized to carry an electrical message. Most mammalian neurons are insulated by myelin; this is to prevent signal loss. We see the same concept in the power cords on our appliances; in addition to preventing us from electrocuting ourselves, the cord wrapping prevents the electricity running in the wires from escaping. The myelin has the added benefit of increasing the speed of conduction in axons. Myelin is produced by **oligodendrocytes** in the central nervous system and **Schwann cells** in the periphery. If we look closely at our diagram, we notice small breaks in the myelin sheath at regular intervals along the axon membrane. These exposed areas of axon membrane are termed **nodes of Ranvier** and are critical to proper signal conduction, as we will soon see. Finally, as we reach the end of the axon, we come to the **nerve terminal (synaptic bouton)**. This structure is enlarged and flattened to maximize neurotransmission to the next neuron and ensure proper production of neurotransmitter. Neurons are not physically connected to one another; rather, there is a slight space between two neurons. This space is known as the **synaptic cleft** or, simply, the **synapse**. Neurotransmitter released from the axon terminal traverses the synaptic cleft and binds to receptors on the second neuron. CEOs are much like neurons. They take in information from many sources (dendrites) and integrate it (axon hillock). Then, they carefully present a coordinated message (action potential traveling down the axon), which results in additional reports (neurotransmitters) distributed to division heads, directors, managers, and so on (muscles and glands), who are responsible for carrying out the company initiatives.

Real World

Sometimes the body mounts an immune response against its own myelin, leading to the destruction of this insulating substance (demyelination). Because myelin speeds the conduction of impulses along a neuron, the absence of myelin results in the slowing of information transfer. A common demyelinating disorder is multiple sclerosis (MS). In MS, the myelin of the brain and spinal cord is selectively targeted. Because so many different kinds of neurons are demyelinated, MS patients are riddled with a variety of symptoms such as weakness, lack of balance, vision problems, and incontinence.

[HOW IT WORKS]

MYELIN FORMATION

Long axons insulated with myelin carry signals between neurons faster than unmyelinated axons. Oligodendrocyte cells manufacture the fatty membrane and wrap the axon with 10 to 150 layers. Different factors can stimulate the myelination process; often astrocyte cells "listen in" on the signals traveling along axons and relay chemical messages to the oligodendrocytes. Below, a microscope shows axons in red being wrapped.

Neuron

Node of Ranvier

Astrocyte

Oligodendrocyte

Oligodendrocyte

Axon

Axon

Myelin sheath

Figure 13.2

FUNCTION

Now that we have the basic anatomy of the neuron, we can discuss the physiology that underlies neuronal signaling. Neurons use all-or-nothing messages called

Key Concept

There are many different types of neurons in the body. Not all of them have the same structure or even a complete set of axons and dendrites. What they share is the ability to signal chemically after electrical excitation.

action potentials to relay information to and from the central and peripheral nervous systems. This might include transmitting to our brain the words we are reading in the sentence, as well as sending the information to the areas of our central nervous system that process language. Action potentials cause the release of neurotransmitter into the synaptic cleft. Let's see how they work.

Resting Potential

All neurons exhibit a **resting membrane potential**. If we recall our electricity definitions, this means that there is a potential (voltage) difference between the inside of the neuron and the extracellular space. Usually, this is about –70 mV (the inside of the neuron is negative relative to the outside). We should think about how this gradient is set up. Certainly, if the system were left to its own devices, it would want to equilibrate to 0 mV. Neurons use selective permeability to ions and the **Na⁺/K⁺ ATPase** to maintain a negative internal environment (see Figure 13.3).

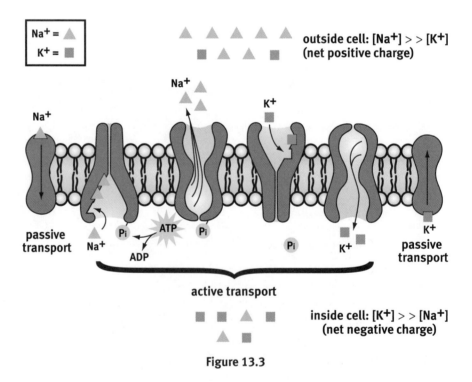

Figure 13.3

The neuron is like any other cell. It has a plasma membrane that is fairly impermeable to charged species. Remember that ions are unlikely to cross the nonpolar barrier, because it is energetically unfavorable. Inside of the neuron, $[K^+]$ is high and $[Na^+]$ is low. Outside of the neuron, $[Na^+]$ is high whereas $[K^+]$ is low. The negative resting potential is generated by both negatively charged proteins within the cell and the relatively greater permeability of the membrane to K^+ compared with Na^+. If K^+ is more permeable and its concentration is higher inside, it will diffuse down its gradient out of the cell. What does this mean in terms of charge movement? K^+ is positively charged, so its movement out of the cell results in a cell interior that is negative. Put another way, if we assume that the membrane starts at zero, and we take away a positive one $(0 - +1)$, we end up with a negative one on the inside of the cell. Na^+ cannot readily enter at rest, so the negative potential is maintained. We can see that the gradients and selective permeability we learned about in Chapter 1 have proven their importance in yet another organ system.

The Na^+/K^+ ATPase is important for restoring this gradient after action potentials have been fired. They transport three Na^+ out of the cell for every two K^+ into the cell at the expense of one ATP. Why is ATP necessary? Both Na^+ and K^+ are moved against their gradients by this process; thus, they qualify as active transport. Each time the pump works, it results in the inside of the cell becoming relatively more negative, as two positive charges are moved in for every three that are moved out.

Action Potential Initiation

When we learned about muscular contraction in Chapter 6, we said that it occurred in an all-or-none fashion. Either the fiber completely responded or not at all. We alluded to the fact that this response was ultimately due to the function of the neuron upon whose action muscle contraction depends. Because action potentials work in an all-or-none fashion, so too must muscles.

If we continue with the analogy of the CEO, we can understand that not all the information that she receives will be positive. Some may be negative, and she must determine, based on all the information, what the appropriate response for the company is. Similarly, neurons can receive excitatory and inhibitory input. The former type of input makes them more likely to fire an action potential, whereas the latter makes them less likely. As the information is integrated at the axon hillock, **depolarization** or **hyperpolarization** may occur. Inhibitory inputs cause hyperpolarization by making the cell more negative. Depolarization is caused by excitatory inputs and makes the cell less negative (relatively, more positive). If the axon hillock is depolarized to the **threshold value** (usually in the range of −55 to −40 mV), an action potential will be triggered.

The decision to initiate an action potential has been made, but how is it executed? Ion channels in the membrane open in response to the depolarization. Since they respond to voltage, they are known as **voltage-gated ion channels**. There are two types that are responsible for action potentials: Na^+ voltage-gated channels and K^+ voltage-gated channels. They are both present in each of the places we are about to discuss, but their activation is different (see Figure 13.4).

Bridge

Remember that the Na^+/K^+ ATPase isn't present only in neurons. We saw it earlier in red blood cells as a way to control cell tonicity. The Na^+/K^+ ATPase is able to make both an osmotic and electrogenic contribution to the cell.

Key Concept

Na^+ wants to go into the cell because it is more negative inside (electrical gradient) and because there is less Na^+ inside (chemical gradient).

Figure 13.4

First, the Na⁺ channels respond to the depolarization. Where was the concentration of Na⁺ higher? Outside. In addition, the inside of the cell is negative. Thus, there is a strong **electric** and **chemical (electrochemical) gradient** for sodium to move into the cell. This makes the cell potential become positive as a result of the sodium ion influx. Sodium channels then rapidly close when the membrane potential reaches about +35 mV. We now have a cell that is positive in the region where the channels just opened and closed. Take a look at Part 1 of Figure 13.5 to see this. The bracketed area is where sodium channels have opened. We can see that the cell is now positive on the inside.

The positive potential inside the cell is the trigger for the voltage-gated potassium channels to open. If we examine the area of the cell in question now (same part of Figure 13.5 as before), we see that it is positive inside. We also know that potassium is high inside the cell. Just as there was for sodium, there is now an electrical and chemical drive to move potassium. The only difference is that potassium will be driven out of the cell. The movement of positive charges out of the cell will result in restoration of the negative membrane potential. This process is known as **repolarization**. Often, the efflux of K⁺ will cause an overshoot of the resting membrane potential, and the membrane becomes more negative than that resting potential. We apply the term *hyperpolarization* to this situation.

Similar to what we observed in muscles, neurons exhibit **refractory periods**. During the **absolute** refractory period, no amount of stimulation will cause another action potential to occur. During the **relative** refractory period there must be greater than normal stimulation to cause an action potential, because the membrane is starting from a potential more negative than the resting value.

Impulse Propagation

All of the ion movements that we just discussed occurred only at the axon hillock. For a signal to be conveyed to another neuron, the action potential must travel down the axon and initiate neurotransmitter release. We term this movement **impulse propagation**. As the sodium from the axon hillock rushes in, it will cause depolarization in the regions surrounding it. This depolarization will result in the opening of sodium channels along the axon in a wavelike fashion. The depolarization of the membrane to +35 mV causes the sodium channels to slam shut just as the potassium channels begin to open. After the sodium depolarization wave, the potassium channels will cause a repolarization wave that resets the axon for the next action potential. Let's take another look at Figure 13.5 to see this drawn out.

Real World

A poison called tetrodotoxin (TTX) is found in the puffer fish, a delicacy in Japan. TTX blocks the voltage-gated Na^+ channels, thereby blocking neuronal transmission, and can rapidly cause death. For this reason, chefs who prepare puffer fish must be specially trained and licensed. If the fish is prepared correctly, you should experience only a slight numbing of your oral cavity.

Figure 13.5

In Part 1, we can see that sodium influx has led to depolarization of the bracketed area. In Part 2, the sodium has caused the opening of neighboring voltage-gated sodium channels, causing depolarization there. Meanwhile, the first set of sodium channels has closed, and the potassium channels have opened, causing repolarization. The action potential is propagated by the ordered opening and closing of these channels.

Looking at Part 2 of Figure 13.5, we should consider why the action potential doesn't move backward (back up the axon). It is because that region of the axon is refractory immediately after it has fired an action potential. The functional consequence of this is the one-way flow of information in neuronal axons.

The speed at which action potentials move depends on the length and cross-sectional area of the axon: The longer the axon, the higher the resistance and the slower the conduction. The greater effect, though, is based on the diameter of the axon. Greater diameters allow for faster propagation as they decrease resistance. Certainly there is a tradeoff for this, and mammalian organisms have developed myelin to cope with it. Myelin is an extraordinarily good insulator, preventing the loss of the electric signal. The insulation is so good that the membrane is only permeable to ion movement at the nodes of Ranvier. Thus, the signal hops from node to node. Transmission that occurs in this manner is referred to as **saltatory conduction** (from the Latin for "to jump").

Synapse

Our CEO is effective only if she has a company to run; our neuron is only useful if it has other cells to coordinate. The connection between two neurons is called a **synapse**. To make this clear, we label the terminal before the synapse (the neuron using its axon) the **presynaptic terminal** or **neuron** and the neuron receiving information through its dendrites the **postsynaptic terminal**. If a neuron signals to a gland or muscle, as we saw in Chapter 6, that cell is termed an **effector cell**. Most synapses are **chemical** in nature; they use small molecules referred to as **neurotransmitters** to send messages from one cell to the next (see Figure 13.6).

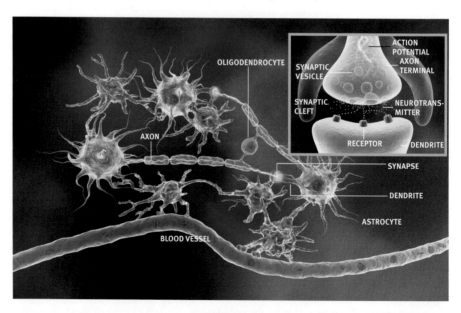

Figure 13.6

Neurons are like Boy Scouts: always prepared. At the nerve terminal, neurotransmitter is stored in membrane-bound vesicles. These vesicles wait for an action potential to come down the axon and depolarize the terminal membrane. They will then fuse with the presynaptic terminal and release the neurotransmitter into the synaptic cleft. This is an example of exocytosis, discussed in Chapter 1. Neurotransmitter release is calcium dependent.

Once released into the synapse, the neurotransmitter molecules diffuse across the cleft and bind to receptors on the postsynaptic membrane. This allows the message to be passed from one neuron to the next. As we stated earlier, neurons may be either inhibitory or excitatory; this distinction truly comes at the level of the neurotransmitter, when binding will result in either hyperpolarization or depolarization of the postsynaptic cell.

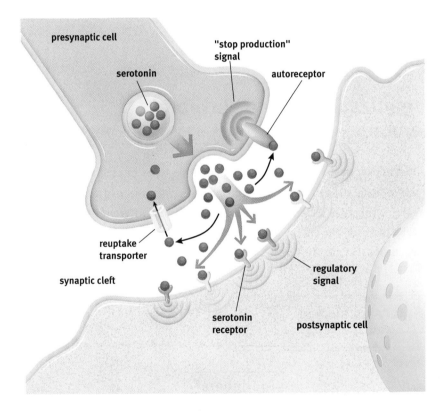

Figure 13.7

We don't want neurotransmission to continue indefinitely, so there must be a way to remove neurotransmitters from the synaptic cleft. In fact, there are several mechanisms, depending on the type of neurotransmitter involved. Some are broken down by enzymatic reactions (e.g., the action of acetylcholinesterase on acetylcholine, see Figure 13.8), some use **reuptake carriers** to be recycled into the presynaptic neuron (e.g., dopamine or serotonin as seen in Figure 13.7), and others may simply diffuse out of the area (e.g., nitric oxide).

Key Concept

It is critical to understand the difference between electrical and chemical transmission and that neurons use both. Within a neuron, electricity is used to pass messages in an all-or-nothing fashion. Between neurons, chemical molecules are used to pass messages in a modulated manner that depends on how much neurotransmitter is released.

Real World

Many common drugs (either in clinical use or street drugs) modify processes that occur in the synapse. For instance, cocaine acts by blocking neuronal reuptake carriers, thus prolonging the action of neurotransmitters in the synapse by preventing neurotransmitter re-entry into the nerve terminal. There are clinically useful drugs (e.g., used to treat glaucoma) that inhibit acetylcholinesterase, thereby elevating synaptic levels of acetylcholine. Nerve gases are extremely potent acetylcholinesterase inhibitors, which have been used in war and in terrorist activities. Nerve gas causes rapid death by preventing the action of skeletal muscle (most importantly, the diaphragm), leading to respiratory arrest.

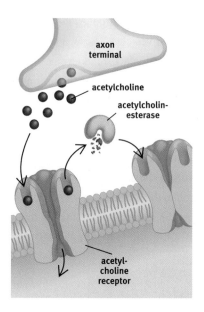

Figure 13.8

Organization of the Vertebrate Nervous System

★★★★☆

For the MCAT, we want to be able to describe the types of cells that make up the nervous system, as well as their interconnections. Neurons that carry information from the periphery to the brain or spinal cord are termed **afferent neurons**, whereas the cells that work in the opposite direction are **efferent neurons**. There are also **interneurons** that are only involved in local circuits. We will see examples of these in the next few pages, when we discuss reflex arcs.

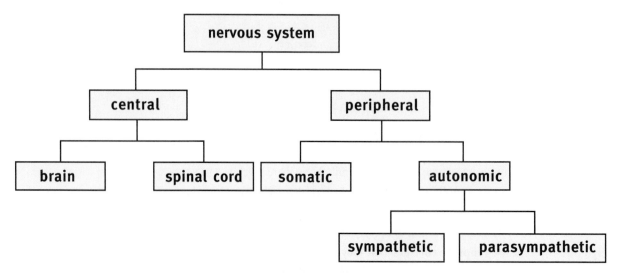

Figure 13.9

A single axon can carry only so much information, so the nervous system bundles many axons together into **nerves.** These nerves may be **sensory**, **motor**, or **mixed**. These terms refer to the type of information they carry. Mixed nerves carry both sensory and motor information. Much as the axons travel together, neuron cell bodies (somas) will also cluster. In the **peripheral nervous system**, these collections are known as **ganglia.** In the **central nervous system**, they are called **nuclei.** If we take a look at Figure 13.9, we can see the major divisions of the nervous system. The primary division is between the central (brain and spinal cord) and peripheral (all other structures) nervous systems. We will look at each system in turn.

CENTRAL NERVOUS SYSTEM

There are only two components to the central nervous system (CNS): the **brain** and the **spinal cord**.

Brain

The consistency of brain tissue is similar to that of gelatin. Since it is so delicate and vital for life, the brain is armored by the protective skull. It is responsible for integration of sensory information, coordination of motor movement, and cognition. The myelination that we saw around axons is also present in the brain. Its presence differentiates between **white matter**, consisting of unmyelinated axons, and **gray matter**, consisting of unmyelinated cell bodies and dendrites. We can divide the brain into the **forebrain**, the **midbrain**, and the **hindbrain** (see Figure 13.10).

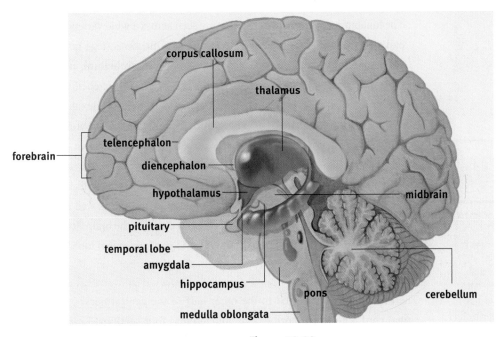

Figure 13.10

Forebrain

The forebrain is the most recently acquired part of the CNS in terms of evolutionary development. It is further broken down into the **telencephalon** and **diencephalon**. We can recognize the telencephalon from pictures of the brain. It consists of the left and right hemisphere. Each hemisphere can be further sectioned into the **frontal**, **parietal**, **occipital**, and **temporal** lobes. A large portion of the telencephalon is the **cerebral cortex**, a region of highly convoluted gray matter that can be seen on the surface of the brain. The cortex is responsible for the highest-level functioning in the nervous system, including creative thought and future planning. It also integrates sensory information and controls movement. Each hemisphere is independent; however, they do communicate through a large connection called the **corpus collosum**.

Nestled below and inside the telencephalon is the diencephalon. It consists of the thalamus and hypothalamus. We thoroughly discussed the hypothalamus in the previous chapter in relation to the endocrine system. The thalamus is the St. Louis of the nervous system; it functions as the gateway to the brain. All ascending sensory information is passed through the thalamus before being relayed to the cortex.

Midbrain

The midbrain serves as a relay point between more peripheral structures and the forebrain. It passes sensory and visual information to the forebrain, while receiving motor instructions from the forebrain and passing them to the hindbrain.

Hindbrain

The hindbrain contains structures that are seen across a wide variety of organisms and are responsible for many of the involuntary functions (e.g., respiration) that we have previously discussed. It is made up of the **cerebellum**, **pons**, and **medulla**, which together are referred to as the brainstem. The cerebellum is a quality control agent. It checks that the motor signal sent from the cortex is in agreement with the sensory information coming from the body. It is what prevents us from falling over when we trip on a sidewalk curb. It rapidly realizes that the motor signal to take a step was not successfully carried out, as we tripped. Instead of letting us fall on our faces, the cerebellum helps the cortex to adjust to the new situation so that we catch ourselves, preventing scrapes and bruises, as well as embarrassment! The medulla is the most highly conserved part of the brain. It is responsible for modulating ventilation rate, heart rate, and gastrointestinal tone.

Spinal Cord

The hindbrain is connected to the other half of the central nervous system, the spinal cord. The spinal cord can be divided into four sections. From the base of the skull to the coccyx, the divisions are **cervical**, **thoracic**, **lumbar**, and **sacral**. Almost all of the structures below the neck receive sensory and motor innervation

Real World

The injury that actor Christopher Reeve sustained was so devastating because he damaged his cord at the high cervical levels. Most of his spinal cord was essentially disconnected from his brain, and the communication between his body and his brain was severely compromised, producing a state of paralysis and a lack of sensation below the neck.

from the spinal cord. It is protected by the **vertebral column**, which, as it sounds, is a series of bones (vertebrae) that form a hollow column. The spinal cord runs through this column with nerves entering and exiting at each vertebra. In addition to integrating and distributing nerve signals for the brain, the spinal cord can participate in simple reflex arcs of its own. Like the brain, we can see both gray and white matter in the spinal cord cross section. The gray matter is deep to the white matter. As before, the white matter contains axons. In the spinal cord, these are the axons of motor and sensory neurons. The sensory neurons bring information in from the periphery and enter on the dorsal (back) side of the spinal cord. The cell bodies of these sensory neurons are found in the **dorsal root ganglia**. Motor neurons exit the spinal cord ventrally (see Figure 13.11).

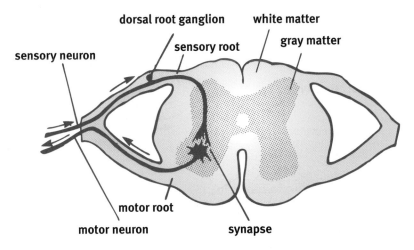

Figure 13.11

PERIPHERAL NERVOUS SYSTEM

The peripheral nervous system has a few more components, including 12 pairs of cranial nerves and 31 pairs of spinal nerves. Glancing back at Figure 13.9, we can see that we can divide peripheral innervation between the **somatic** (SNS) and **autonomic** nervous system (ANS). We have previously mentioned both of these divisions in relation to the musculoskeletal system.

Somatic Nervous System

The SNS is responsible for voluntary movement. We described the interface between the neuron and muscle as the neuromuscular junction. Release of acetylcholine from the nerve terminal onto the muscle leads to contraction (Chapter 6). The acetylcholine binding to its receptor on the muscle ultimately leads to muscle depolarization. The SNS is also responsible for providing us with reflexes, which are automatic. They do not require input or integration from the brain to function. There are two types of reflex arcs: **monosynaptic** and **polysynaptic**. Reflexes usually serve a protective purpose. For example, we'd pull our hand away from a hot stove before our brain processes that it is hot.

Monosynaptic

In a monosynaptic reflex arc, there is a single synapse between the sensory neuron that received the information and the motor neuron that responds. A classic example is the **knee-jerk** reflex (see Figure 13.12). When the patellar tendon is stretched, information travels up the sensory neuron to the spinal cord, where it interfaces with the motor neuron to contract the quadriceps muscle. The net result is a straightening of the leg, which lessens the tension on the patellar tendon. We should notice that the reflex is responding to a potentially dangerous situation. If the patellar tendon is stretched too far, it may tear, damaging the knee joint. This reflex helps to protect us.

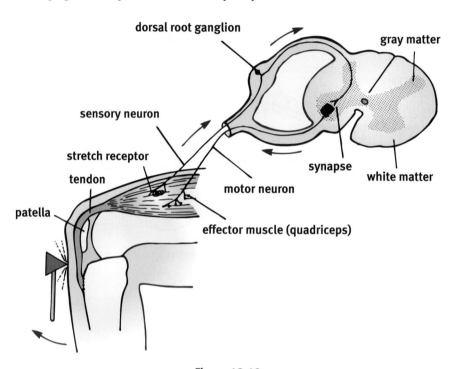

Figure 13.12

Polysynaptic

In a polysynaptic reflex arc, there is at least one interneuron between the sensory and motor neuron. A real-life example is your reaction to stepping on a tack, which involves the **withdrawal reflex**. The foot that steps on the tack will be stimulated to jerk up; this is a monosynaptic reflex. However, if we are to maintain our balance, we need our other foot to go down and plant itself on the ground. For this to occur, the motor neuron that controls the opposite (downward-moving) leg must be stimulated. Interneurons in the spinal cord provide the connection from the incoming sensory information on the leg being jerked up to the motor neuron for the supporting leg.

Autonomic Nervous System

We briefly mentioned the autonomic nervous system in several chapters, most recently in Chapter 12 on the endocrine system, when we described the "fight-or-flight" and "rest-and-digest" responses. Let's now take a look at the physical underpinnings of this system. The ANS is sometimes referred to as the involuntary nervous system, as it requires no conscious control. From Chapter 6, we know that cardiac and smooth muscle are both innervated by the autonomic nervous system. Smooth muscle is found throughout the body, including the blood vessels, the bronchi, the bladder, and the gastrointestinal tract. It is no surprise to us, then, that the autonomic nervous system exerts great control over blood pressure, ventilation dynamics, urination, and digestion.

The primary difference between the SNS and ANS is that the ANS is a two-neuron system. A motor neuron in the SNS goes directly to the muscle without synapsing. In the ANS, the neurons play a game of telephone; two neurons work in series to transmit messages. The first neuron is known as the **preganglionic neuron**, whereas the second is the **postganglionic neuron**. The preganglionic neuron's soma is in the CNS, whereas its axon travels to a ganglion in the PNS. Here, it synapses on the cell body of the postganglionic neuron, which then affects the target tissue (because it can be glandular, too).

Although the ANS can regulate each organ individually, it can also have coordinated effects. These can be divided into **sympathetic** and **parasympathetic**.

Sympathetic Nervous System

This is the part of the ANS that is responsible for "fight-or-flight." If our bothersome bear from previous chapters makes another surprise appearance, we would want to increase blood flow to the heart and skeletal muscle, while decreasing it to the GI tract and kidneys. In addition, increasing breathing rate and heart rate would ensure an adequate supply of oxygen to meet the demands of the rapidly contracting skeletal muscles. Finally, our pupils would dilate, so we could keep our eyes on that bear as we escaped. Preganglionic neurons use acetylcholine, whereas postganglionic neurons in the sympathetic nervous system use norepinephrine. Preganglionic sympathetic neurons can also cause the release of epinephrine from the adrenal medulla.

Parasympathetic Nervous System

The parasympathetic nervous system is the calm brother of the sympathetic nervous system. Once we get away from that bear, we can eat a nice pizza. We then would want increased blood flow to the organs of digestion and excretion with a concomitant decrease in flow to the skeletal muscle and heart. Moreover, since pizza eating is not a highly aerobic activity, heart rate and ventilation rate would decrease. The **vagus nerve**, which is one of the 12 cranial

Key Concept

The first neuron in the autonomic nervous system is called the preganglionic neuron, and the second is the postganglionic neuron.

Mnemonic

The ANS controls many functions within the body, but think in big picture terms. Autonomic means *automatic*. If it is a body function we don't have to think about, it probably has at least some autonomic input. From there, we can decide whether it is sympathetic (flight-or-fight) or parasympathetic (rest-and-digest).

nerves, is responsible for many of the parasympathetic effects in the thoracic and abdominal cavities. The parasympathetic nervous system uses acetylcholine as a neurotransmitter at both preganglionic and postganglionic neurons.

Special Senses

We have divided our discussion of neurons into sensory and motor. Sensory neurons come in three varieties: **interoceptors**, **proprioceptors**, and **exteroceptors**. The word root in each of them clues you in to what they monitor. Interoceptors monitor internal environment parameters, such as blood volume, blood pH, and partial pressure of CO_2 in the blood. Proprioceptors are important for our position sense. When we get up in the middle of the night to grab a cookie and glass of milk, proprioceptors help our brains grasp the relative position of our bodies in the dark. Exteroceptors are responsible for monitoring the external environment, such as light, sound, touch, taste, pain, and temperature. Furthermore, **nociceptors** sense pain and relay that information to the brain (see Figure 13.13).

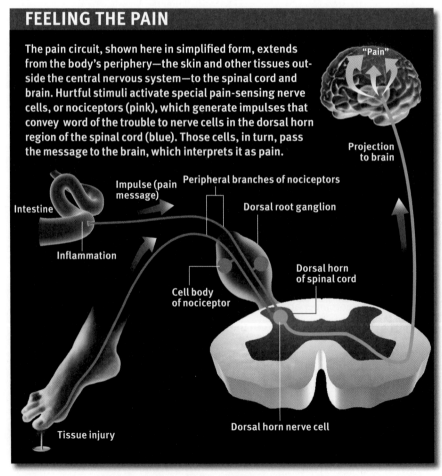

FEELING THE PAIN

The pain circuit, shown here in simplified form, extends from the body's periphery—the skin and other tissues outside the central nervous system—to the spinal cord and brain. Hurtful stimuli activate special pain-sensing nerve cells, or nociceptors (pink), which generate impulses that convey word of the trouble to nerve cells in the dorsal horn region of the spinal cord (blue). Those cells, in turn, pass the message to the brain, which interprets it as pain.

"Pain"

Projection to brain

Impulse (pain message)

Peripheral branches of nociceptors

Intestine

Dorsal root ganglion

Inflammation

Cell body of nociceptor

Dorsal horn of spinal cord

Tissue injury

Dorsal horn nerve cell

Figure 13.13

THE EYE

The eye is a specialized organ used to detect light (in the form of photons). Most of the exposed portion of the eye is covered by a thick layer known as the **sclera**, commonly known as the white of the eye. It does not cover the cornea. The eye is supplied with nutrients and oxygen by the **choroid**, which is directly beneath the sclera. The innermost layer of the eye is the **retina**, which contains the actual cells **(photoreceptors)** that transduce the light into electrical information the brain can process.

Looking at our own eyes, we know that the sclera is not continuous around the eye. In the front, there are several structures that allow light to pass into the eye and onto the retina. Light first passes through the **cornea**, a transparent structure that bends and focuses it. Light rays then move through the **pupil**. The muscular, pigmented **iris** can adjust the amount of light entering the eye by altering the diameter of the pupil; the more light available, the greater the degree of constriction. After the pupil, the light is passed through the **lens**, which does the final focusing. **Ciliary muscles** can adjust the thickness of the lens, which focuses the image on the retina (see Figure 13.14). Once light has been focused by these three structures, it will impinge on the photoreceptors of the retina and be turned into an electrical signal.

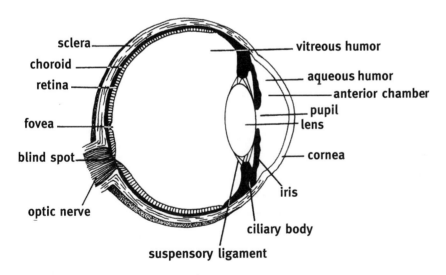

Figure 13.14

There are two main types of photoreceptors: **rods** and **cones**. Rods are responsible for transmission of black-and-white images and respond to low-intensity illumination. This makes them useful for night vision. Cones come in three varieties and manage color images. Each type of cone contains a pigment that absorbs a different wavelength of light; these wavelengths correspond to the colors red, green, and blue. Rods have only one pigment, **rhodopsin**, which explains their ability to respond only to black and white.

Real World

Color blindness is a result of lacking one, two, or three of these sets of cones. Total color blindness is most commonly due to a complete lack of cones.

Real World

Some people develop a plumbing problem in the eye and cannot adequately drain aqueous humor. This disease is called glaucoma. Because of the draining problem, pressure builds in the anterior chamber and is transmitted to the vitreous humor, leading to increased pressure on the optic nerve. If the pressure is not relieved, this condition can permanently damage the optic nerve and lead to blindness.

After excitation by light, the photoreceptors send a signal to the **bipolar cells**, which relay the information to the **retinal ganglion cells**. The axons of the ganglion cells bundle to form the **optic nerve**, which then exits the back of the eye. Because the optic nerve takes up space on the back of the eye, displacing photoreceptors, there is a **blind spot** at the site of exodus. Since we have two eyes, this is rarely a problem, as each eye compensates for the blind spot of the other.

The eye is filled with fluid to simplify the transmission of light to the retina. Aqueous humor is secreted near the iris at the base of the eye. It then travels to the anterior chamber, where it exits and eventually enters the venous blood.

THE EAR

The ear transduces sound waves (mechanical disturbances of pressure) into electrical signals that can be interpreted by the brain. In addition, it houses certain nerves that help coordinate balance.

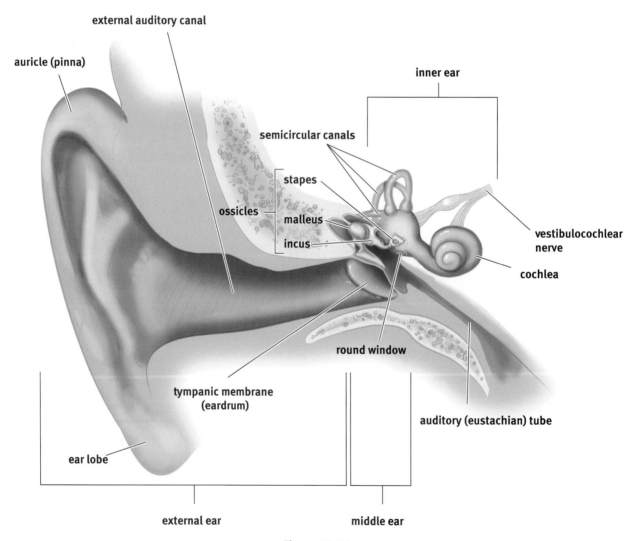

Figure 13.15

When listening to our favorite song on our MP3 players, quite a bit happens so that we hear the lyrics and the melody. The speaker generates longitudinal waves. The **outer ear**, which consists of the auricle and auditory canal, collects the waves and channels them to the **tympanic membrane**. The tympanic membrane is the beginning of the **middle ear**, which also includes the ossicles (**malleus, incus,** and **stapes**). The tympanic membrane vibrates due to sound waves pushing on it, and the ossicles move back and forth. These three bones then transmit the information through the **oval window** to the fluid-filled inner ear, which is made up of the **cochlea** and **semicircular canals**. The movement of the ossicles on the oval window creates fluid waves in the inner ear that depolarize the **hair cells** of the cochlea (see Figure 13.16). This is the transduction mechanism that generates an electrical signal the nervous system can interpret. The action potentials from the hair cells travel along the **auditory nerve to the brain** (see Figure 13.15).

Figure 13.16

The semicircular canals are important for balance. There are three per ear, one oriented in each plane (think x-, y-, and z-axes). The canals are filled with a fluid called **endolymph**, whose movement through the canals puts pressure on the hair cells inside. Because there is a canal in each dimension, the brain can integrate the signal from each canal and maintain balance, as well as interpret sudden acceleration and deceleration.

THE CHEMICAL SENSES

Taste and smell are the two chemical senses, so named because they take chemical molecules from the environment and turn them into electrical signals. This is termed **olfaction** and **gustatation** for smell and taste, respectively.

Taste

Taste receptors, or taste buds, are located on the tongue, soft palate, and epiglottis. Taste buds are composed of approximately 40 epithelial cells. The outer surface of a taste bud contains a taste pore, from which microvilli, or taste hairs, protrude. The receptor surfaces for taste are on the taste hairs. Interwoven around the taste buds is a network of nerve fibers that they stimulate. These neurons transmit gustatory information to the brainstem via three cranial nerves. There are four kinds of taste sensations: sour, salty, sweet, and bitter. Although most taste buds will respond to all four stimuli, they respond preferentially (i.e., at a lower threshold to one or two of them).

Smell

Olfactory receptors are found in the olfactory membrane, which lies in the upper part of the nostrils over a total area of about 5cm^2. The receptors are specialized neurons from which olfactory hairs, or cilia, project. These cilia form a dense mat in the upper nasal mucosa. When odorous substances enter the nasal cavity, they bind to receptors in the cilia, depolarizing the olfactory receptors. Axons from the olfactory receptors join to form the olfactory nerves. The olfactory nerves project directly to the olfactory bulbs in the base of the brain.

Conclusion

You should pat yourself on the back. All of the organ systems have been covered! Now let's examine that pat on the back. It required your sight to read the sentence instructing you to pat your back. The signal was then sent to the area of the brain that processes vision, which passed it off to the language centers. Once the meaning was understood, an impulse was sent along a motor neuron to cause your muscle to contract in such a way that you could actually pat yourself on the back. Then, sensory neurons told your brain that you had accomplished the action. Maybe you should get another pat on the back just for successfully going through all those connections! The nervous system is a highly integrated one; millions upon millions of cells allow for our appropriate interactions in the everyday world. If we dig even deeper to examine what else was going on during your back patting, we can understand that your

Real World

Have you ever gone into a room with a very strong smell that became hardly noticeable after a while? Olfactory receptors can be overpowered and, after constant stimulation, will desensitize to a given stimulus. This desensitization is a hallmark of much of the nervous system.

heart was beating and your lungs were drawing air. Even as your nervous system directed some of its attention and energy to accomplishing a specific task (patting your back), it never lost sight of the big picture: whole-body coordination of every organ system to maintain life. Congratulate your autonomic nervous system for doing such an excellent job. Hopefully you haven't tired your brain out by learning how it works! Let's move on to a more microscopic topic: genetics.

CONCEPTS TO REMEMBER

- ☐ The basic unit of the nervous system is the neuron, a polarized, electrically excitable cell.

- ☐ The resting potential of a neuron is established as a result of the chemical gradients of sodium and potassium ions, as well as their relative permeabilities to the membrane.

- ☐ An action potential requires rapid sodium influx followed by slower potassium efflux. Voltage-gated ion channels are responsible for allowing the ions to cross the plasma membrane.

- ☐ Depolarization of the nerve terminal will cause an influx of calcium ions, which leads to vesicle fusion and exocytosis of neurotransmitters.

- ☐ Neurotransmitter activity in the synaptic cleft may be terminated by degradation, reuptake, or diffusion out of the synapse.

- ☐ The central nervous system consists of the brain and spinal cord. The peripheral nervous system includes the 12 pairs of cranial nerves and 31 pairs of spinal nerves.

- ☐ Sensory information enters the spinal cord on the dorsal side, whereas motor signals leave from the ventral surface.

- ☐ The autonomic nervous system is responsible for involuntary actions, and the somatic nervous system is capable of carrying out voluntary movements.

- ☐ The autonomic nervous system may be further subdivided into two antagonists: the sympathetic and parasympathetic nervous system.

- ☐ The special senses (sight, hearing, smell, and taste) use special receptors to transmit the sensory information to the central nervous system.

Practice Questions

1. Resting membrane potential depends on

   A. the differential distribution of ions across the axon membrane.
   B. active transport.
   C. selective permeability.
   D. All of the above

2. All of the following are associated with the myelin sheath EXCEPT

   A. faster conduction of nervous impulses.
   B. nodes of Ranvier forming gaps along the axon.
   C. increased energy output for nervous impulse conduction.
   D. saltatory conduction of action potentials.

3. The all-or-none law states that

   A. all hyperpolarizing stimuli will be carried to the axon terminal without a decrease in size.
   B. the size of the action potential is proportional to the size of the stimulus that produced it.
   C. increasing the intensity of the depolarization increases the size of the impulse.
   D. once an action potential is triggered, an impulse of a given magnitude and speed is produced.

4. Which of the following would NOT be observed in a patient with a cerebellar lesion?

   A. Memory impairment
   B. Inability to balance
   C. Inability to coordinate hand and eye movements
   D. Inability to time rapid movements

5. By increasing the intensity of the stimulus, the action potential will

   A. increase in amplitude.
   B. increase in frequency.
   C. increase in speed.
   D. both (B) and (D).

6. Which of the following pairings is correct?

   A. Sensory nerves—afferent
   B. Motor nerves—afferent
   C. Sensory nerves—ventral
   D. Motor nerves—dorsal

7. When a sensory receptor receives a threshold stimulus, it will do all of the following EXCEPT

   A. become depolarized.
   B. transduce the stimulus to an action potential.
   C. inhibit the spread of the action potential to sensory neurons.
   D. cause the sensory neurons to send action potentials to the central nervous system.

8. Which of the following structures focuses light on the retina?

   A. Cornea
   B. Vitreous humor
   C. Lens
   D. both (A) and (C).

9. A specific disease affects only the rods present in a patient's retina. Which of the following will you most likely observe about the patient?

   A. He can no longer see colors.
   B. He can see very well in the dark.
   C. His levels of rhodopsin are almost nonexistent.
   D. He cannot detect more than one wavelength of light.

10. When the potential across the axon membrane is more negative than the normal resting potential, the neuron is said to be in a state of

    A. depolarization.
    B. hyperpolarization.
    C. repolarization.
    D. hypopolarization.

11. Which of the following statements concerning the somatic division of the peripheral nervous system is INCORRECT?

    A. Its pathways innervate skeletal muscles.
    B. Its pathways are usually voluntary.
    C. Some of its pathways are referred to as reflex arcs.
    D. Its pathways always involve three neurons.

12. In the ear, what structure transduces pressure waves to action potentials?

    A. Tympanic membrane
    B. Organ of Corti
    C. Oval window
    D. Semicircular canals

Small Group Questions

1. Tetraethylammonium (TEA) is a drug that blocks voltage-gated K^+ channels. What effect would TEA have on the action potentials produced by a neuron? If TEA could be applied selectively to a presynaptic neuron that releases an excitatory neurotransmitter, how would it alter the synaptic effect of that neurotransmitter on the postsynaptic cell?

2. The nerve gas sarin inhibits the enzyme acetylcholinesterase, which is normally present in the neuromuscular junction and is required to break down acetylcholine. Based on this information, what are the likely effects of this nerve gas on muscle function?

Explanations to Practice Questions

1. D

The polarization of the neuron at rest is the result of an uneven distribution of ions between the inside and outside of the cell. This difference is achieved through the active pumping of ions in and out of the neuron (e.g., Na^+/K^+ pump) and the selective permeability of the membrane, which allows only certain ions to cross. As such, (D) is the correct answer.

2. C

Let's quickly review the role of myelin in the nervous system. Myelin is a white, lipid-containing material surrounding the axons of many neurons in the central and peripheral nervous systems. Myelin is produced by glial cells (oligodendrocytes in the central nervous system and Schwann cells in the peripheral nervous system) and is arranged on the axon discontinuously. The gaps between the segments of myelin are called nodes of Ranvier. Myelin increases the conduction velocity by insulating segments of the axon so that the membrane is permeable to ions only at the nodes of Ranvier. Because of these nodes, the action potential jumps from node to node, a process known as saltatory conduction. Going back to the question, we can now safely select (C) as the correct answer. Myelin sheaths do not increase the energy output of nervous impulse conduction; rather, they speed conduction.

3. D

The action potential is often described as an all-or-none response. This means that whenever the threshold membrane potential is reached, an action potential with a consistent size and duration is produced. Neuronal information is coded by the frequency and number of action potentials, not the size of the action potential of the given answers, only (D) correctly describes the all-or-none response of a neuron.

4. A

A lesion in the cerebellum would affect some or all of its functions. A healthy cerebellum helps to modulate motor impulses initiated by the motor cortex and is important in the maintenance of balance, hand-eye coordination, and the timing of rapid movements. Generally, alcohol affects the cerebellum, so an intoxicated person transiently exhibits signs typical of a cerebellar lesion. From the given choices, only (A) does not describe an effect that would be produced from an impaired cerebellum. The hippocampus is the brain structure involved in memory. (A) is therefore the correct answer.

5. B

Neuronal information is coded by the frequency and number of action potentials, not the size of the action potential. Thus, increasing the intensity of the stimulus will increase the frequency of the action potential. The nervous system distinguishes a gentle touch versus a needle poke not by the magnitude of the action potential but rather by its frequency. (B) is therefore the correct answer.

6. A

Glancing at the answer choices, we notice that all of them are dealing with sensory or motor neurons, so let's quickly review these two categories. Sensory neurons bring information from the outside (skin, eyes, ears, etc.) to the nervous system, and they are therefore called afferent neurons. Additionally, sensory neurons synapse in the dorsal spinal cord. Motor neurons, on the other hand, take information from the nervous system to effector organs (e.g., muscles) and are therefore efferent. Also, they synapse in the ventral spinal cord. Based on this, we can safely select (A) as the correct answer.

7. C

Let's quickly review what happens when a sensory receptor receives a threshold stimulus. Since the stimulus is strong enough, we can assume that the receptor becomes depolarized, allowing it to transduce the stimulus to an action potential. The action potential will then be carried by sensory neurons to the central nervous system. Therefore, among the given choices, the only incorrect statement is found in (C). If a receptor is stimulated, it will promote the spread of the action potential to sensory neurons.

8. D

Light is focused on the retina by the cornea and the lens. The lens in the eye is a converging (convex) lens. The cornea also acts as a converging lens. As such, both the cornea and the lens help to focus light on the retina. (D) is thus the correct answer.

9. C

The rods detect low-intensity illumination and are important in night vision. The rod pigment, rhodopsin, absorbs one wavelength. If a patient's rods were affected, we would expect him to have a really difficult time seeing anything in the dark, and his levels of rhodopsin would drop sharply. The only choice that matches this prediction is (C), the correct answer.

10. B

When the potential across the axon membrane is more negative than the normal resting potential, the neuron is referred to as hyperpolarized. Hyperpolarization occurs right after an action potential and is caused by too much potassium exiting the neuron. (B) is therefore the correct answer.

11. D

The somatic division of the peripheral nervous system innervates skeletal muscles and is responsible for voluntary movement. Some of the pathways in this part of the nervous system are reflex arcs, which are reflexive responses to certain stimuli that involve only a sensory and a motor neuron. These neurons synapse in the spinal cord (they do not involve the brain). The pathways of the somatic division of the peripheral nervous system can involve two, three, or more neurons, depending on the type of signal. The correct answer therefore is (D).

12. B

The cochlea includes the organ of Corti, which contains specialized sensory cells called hair cells. Vibration of the ossicles exerts pressure on the fluid in the cochlea, stimulating the hair cells to transduce the pressure into action potentials, which travel via the auditory nerve to the brain for processing. (B) is therefore the correct answer.

Genetics

There is a saying: *The family that prays together, stays together*, implying that families united through religious or spiritual activity will experience less familial conflict and strife. For hundreds of years, European royalty practiced a notion at once quite similar and radically different, which we might characterize as, *The family that breeds together, leads together*. European royal families, for generations, have practiced what is known as royal intermarriage. For purposes of establishing or continuing political alliances, maintaining bloodline purity, or smoothing out diplomatic relations, marriages between and within royal families were arranged, resulting in such an interweaving of bloodlines that eventually most European royalty was (is) genetically related.

Such marriage unions led to rather severe restrictions on the gene pool—all the alleles represented in the royal family line(s). Offspring of parents who were also related to each other through blood lineage came to have greater similarities in their genotypes, and certain alleles became so frequent that their phenotypic expression became almost a hallmark of royal descent. For example, the House of Habsburg was perhaps the most infamous for its inbreeding practices, and members of this royal family bore the unmistakable mark of their restricted genes through a jaw malformation that even came to be known as the Habsburg lip. Medically termed *prognathism* (Greek for "forward jaw"), the condition is a misalignment of the upper and lower jaws (the maxilla and mandible, respectively). The Habsburg family portraits present individuals with prominent, forward-thrusting lower jaws and chins, characteristic of mandibular prognathism. The genetic condition has more than just aesthetic implications; it can lead to serious disfigurement and disability. Charles II of Spain suffered from the worst case of the Hapsburg lip on record; his lower jaw protruded so much further than his upper jaw that he was not able to chew his food.

Every physical characteristic of every living organism (and virus) is determined by a set of codes called genes. **Genes** are the heritable traits that can be passed on from one generation to the next. Coded for by DNA (the focus of our next chapter), they are organized onto **chromosomes**. We know from the ABO and Rh blood antigen system (Chapter 9) that there may be alternative forms of a gene. These different forms are known as **alleles**. Two final terms we should be familiar with are **genotype** and **phenotype**. Genotype is the actual allelic distribution of genes in an organism; phenotype is the outward appearance of an organism and depends on the genotype. How this control occurs will be a central theme of this chapter.

Mendelian Genetics ★★★★☆

A monk named Gregor Mendel developed several of the tenets of genetics in the 1860s based on his work with pea plants. By crossing only **true-breeding** plants

MCAT Expertise

The MCAT commonly tests the difference between genotype and phenotype. If we are given the genotype of an organism, we should be able to predict the phenotype. However, if we are given the phenotype, we cannot always predict the genotype because of the presence of dominant and recessive alleles.

(those whose offspring only ever have the same traits as the parents) with different traits, he was able to determine the laws of inheritance (see Figure 14.1).

Seeking Variation

MENDEL'S FACTORS: Early 20th-century scientists rediscovered the ideas of Gregor Mendel, who experimented with pea plants during the 1850s and 1860s to derive detailed laws of inheritance. Mendel posited the existence of discrete factors carrying trait information and observed that each individual would carry two copies—one from each parent—of a given factor. Although both were present, only one of the copies would dominate and produce the visible trait.

Figure 14.1

MENDEL'S FIRST LAW: LAW OF SEGREGATION

There are four basic tenets of Mendel's first law.

1. Genes exist in alternative forms (alleles).
2. An organism has two alleles for each gene, one inherited from each parent.
3. The two alleles segregate during meiosis, resulting in gametes that carry only one allele for any inherited trait.
4. If two alleles in an individual organism are different, only one will be fully expressed, and the other will be silent. The expressed allele is said to be **dominant**, the silent allele **recessive**.

In genetics problems, including those on the MCAT, dominant traits are assigned capital letters and recessive alleles are denoted by lowercase letters. If both copies of the allele are the same, that individual is said to be **homozygous.** If they are different, the individual is **heterozygous** for that trait.

Monohybrid Cross

A cross in which only one trait is being studied is said to be **monohybrid** (*mono–* means "one"). Gregor Mendel used pea plants with either purple or white flowers. The **parent** or **P generation** refers to the individuals being crossed; the offspring are the **filial** or **F generation**. The F distinction can be applied to multiple generations by using numeric subscripts. If we think of our grandparents as the P generation, then our parents are F_1, and we are F_2.

In Mendel's experiments, the purple flowers were determined to be homozygous dominant. This genotype can be designated as PP. The white flowers were homozygous recessive; their genotype would be written pp. When crossed, the genotype of the F_1 generation will be 100 percent Pp; we will show this graphically in a moment. What does this mean in terms of the color (phenotype) of our F_1 flowers? They will all be purple, because purple is dominant to white.

Punnett Square

For the MCAT, we will want to be able to draw and analyze a Punnett square, which is a diagram that predicts the relative genotypic and phenotypic frequencies that will result from a crossing of two individuals. The alleles of the two parents are arranged on the top and side of the square, with the genotypes of the progeny being represented at the intersection of these alleles (see Figure 14.2). The genotypes of the progeny will be the sum of the parental alleles.

MCAT Expertise

The ability to create and read Punnett squares is one of the most useful skills on the MCAT. One passage is commonly devoted to genetics and has questions that require the use of at least one Punnett square. Learn about them now for quick points on Test Day.

Parental: PP × pp

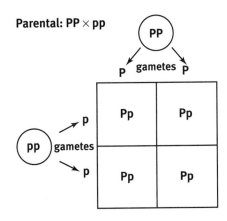

F_1 genotypes: 100% Pp (heterozygous)

F_1 phenotypes: 100% purple flowers

Figure 14.2

If the F_1 generation crosses with itself **(self-cross)**, the resulting offspring (F_2 generation) will be more phenotypically and genotypically diverse than their parents. First, note that the F_1 generation in Figure 14.2 is 100 percent Pp; all the flowers are purple heterozygotes. Now, if we take two of these individuals and cross them, we will get the Punnett square shown in Figure 14.3. The genotypic percentages will be 25 percent PP, 50 percent Pp, and 25 percent pp. Phenotypically, we get a 3:1 distribution, because both the homozygous dominant and heterozygous dominant will result in a purple-flowering plant. We should clearly notice that, unlike the F_1 generation in which the phenotype and genotype had the same percentages (100 percent) in the F_2 generation, there is a 1:2:1 distribution (homozygous dominant:heterozygous dominant:homozygous recessive) genotypically and a 3:1 distribution (purple:white) phenotypically. These ratios are, of course, theoretical and will not always hold true. They represent the probabilities of certain outcomes but not complete certainty. Usually, the more offspring a couple has, the closer their phenotypes will be to the expected ratios.

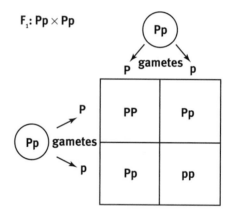

F_2 genotypes: 1:2:1; 1PP: 2Pp:1pp

F_2 phenotypes: 3:1; 3 purple:1 white

Figure 14.3

These ratios are standard Mendelian inheritance patterns that we should be familiar with for Test Day. Knowing them will save us time, translating into more questions answered and more points.

Test Cross

Monohybrid crosses are useful, but they aren't quite as interesting if we already know what the outcome should be, as we did above. After all, it's more exciting to be the detective on a case than to be a simple fact-checker. **Test crosses** allow us to be intrepid explorers. They are used to determine unknown genotypes. Let's take a look at Figure 14.4, then discuss how it works.

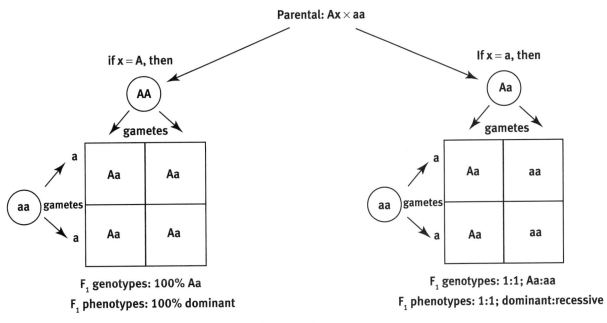

Figure 14.4

A fact that helps us with test crosses (and will help us on Test Day) is that only with a recessive phenotype (e.g., white flower) can we be sure of the genotype (pp). We cannot be sure if a dominant phenotype is heterozygous or homozygous, since both result in the same outcome. We can determine the genotype (and be good detectives) by crossing the unknown plant with a plant that has the recessive phenotype. If all the offspring (100%) are of the dominant phenotype, we would predict that the unknown parent is homozygous dominant for the trait (PP). If, instead, we get roughly a 1:1 distribution (50% purple and 50% white), we would expect that the unknown parent is heterozygous dominant (Pp). Since we are determining the genotype of the parent based on its offspring, test crosses are sometimes called **back crosses**. This makes sense, as we are working *back*ward.

MENDEL'S SECOND LAW: LAW OF INDEPENDENT ASSORTMENT

Dihybrid Cross

We can extend what we just learned to a situation in which we examine the inheritance of two genes using a **dihybrid cross** (*di–* means "two"). Mendel's **law of independent assortment** simply means that each gene's inheritance (assortment) is independent of (unrelated to) the inheritance of other genes.

Suppose you buy detergent so that you can do your laundry during your MCAT study session (multitasking is important!). While standing at the checkout line, you also decide to buy gum. The two purchases are entirely independent of each other. Buying detergent does not make you more or less likely to buy gum.

> **Key Concept**
>
> Can we think of why we wouldn't use a homozygous dominant organism for the test cross? It is because we wouldn't be able to tell the genotype of the test animal. Phenotypically, all of the offspring would be the same, because they would have at least one dominant allele from the homozygous dominant parent. Using a recessive individual allows us to work backward and determine genotype from phenotype (which isn't always possible).

We might say that these two purchasing decisions are unlinked. For genes that are **unlinked**, we can stick with Mendel and independent assortment. On the other hand, we will soon see cases in which genes are **linked** and the inheritance of one *does* affect the other.

Take a quick glance at Figure 14.5 before we walk through the details. The next few paragraphs will explain how the statistics for the genotypes and phenotypes are derived. We want to have these sorts of numbers memorized on Test Day to save us time.

MCAT Expertise

Much as we learned the common 3:1 distribution for a monohybrid cross, this 9:3:3:1 distribution is worth learning for dihybrid crosses. This quick fact will save you from drawing the Punnett square on Test Day.

Parental: **TTPP × ttpp**

F_1 genotypes: 100% **TtPp**

(self-cross) $F_1 \times F_1$: **TtPp × TtPp**

F_2 phenotypes: **9:3:3:1**

9 tall purple:3 tall white:3 dwarf purple:1 dwarf white

Figure 14.5

From Mendel's example, we will add another trait besides flower color: height. Recall from the monohybrid cross that purple was dominant to white. Similarly, the tall phenotype (T) is dominant to the dwarf one (t). As a quick check of our skills, what would the genotype of a short, white flowering plant be? ttpp. Remember that to generate the F_1 progeny, we crossed two true-breeding plants. Here, this would be one tall, purple plant (TTPP) and one dwarf, white plant (ttpp). Similar to what we saw with the monohybrid cross, all of the offspring will be the same: heterozygous tall, heterozygous purple plants (TtPp). The genotypes and phenotypes are both 100 percent for a certain plant type. Now we can have some fun. We can take the heterozygous progeny and cross them again. This is what we see in Figure 14.5. The result will be plants that distribute in a 9:3:3:1 phenotypic ratio (9 tall/purple:3 tall/white:3 dwarf/purple:1 dwarf/white), which is typical for a Mendelian dihybrid cross.

Statistical Analyses

Recall gametes from Chapter 4. Each pea plant in the F_1 generation is capable of producing four possible gametes, because the genes are independent of one another. The four gametes are **TP**, **Tp**, **tP**, and **tp**. We can calculate the given likelihood of a genotype in the progeny by multiplying the likelihood that one parent donated a specific gamete by the likelihood that the other parent donated a specific gamete. We multiply them because we are looking for the probability that *both* alleles will be incorporated.

If we wanted to generate a homozygous tall, homozygous purple plant (TTPP), we would need a TP from each parent. The likelihood of this is $\frac{1}{4}$ in each case. Multiplying these together, we get $\frac{1}{16}\left(\frac{1}{4} \times \frac{1}{4}\right)$. What does this mean to us? That 1 pea plant out of 16 will have this genotype (and the corresponding phenotype).

Let's look at a more interesting case. Say that we wanted to get a heterozygous purple, heterozygous tall plant. We could cross TP × tp, Tp × tP, tP × Tp, or tp × TP. Each of these would result in our desired genotype. We need to do the multiplication for each case. Every time, the likelihood of each gamete being selected is still $\frac{1}{4}$. We then multiply this by $\frac{1}{4}$, which is the chance of the desired allele from the other parent. As before, we get $\frac{1}{16}$; however, now we have 4 situations that could lead to this result. Since any of these combinations would work equally well, we sum these values $\frac{1}{16} + \frac{1}{16} + \frac{1}{16} + \frac{1}{16} = \frac{4}{16} = \frac{1}{4}$. Thus, $\frac{1}{4}$ of our plants will be heterozygous tall and heterozygous purple. We get $\frac{1}{4}$ as a result of the laws of statistics; we must sum the independent chances that we achieve the desired result. Like all statistical analyses, these rules work best with a large sample size.

Problem Solving

We may be asked on the MCAT to solve problems that involve crosses between organisms of known phenotype but unknown genotype. Let's walk through a hypothetical example now. Suppose that we have a tall, purple plant of unknown genotype crossed with a tall, white plant of unknown genotype. The offspring are 62 tall, purple plants; 59 tall, white plants; 20 dwarf, purple plants; and 21 dwarf, white plants. We would like to know the genotypes of the parents. On the MCAT, it is best to examine each trait separately and then assign the overall genotype.

> **Key Concept**
>
> Each trait assorts individually in a 3:1 ratio, as in a monohybrid cross. There are 9 purple, tall plants and 3 purple, dwarf plants for a total of 12 purples; and there are 3 white, tall plants and 1 white, dwarf plant for a total of 4 whites. Hence, the purple/white ratio is 12:4 = 3:1. Likewise, the tall/dwarf ratio is 3:1.

Let's start with color. We know the white plant will be pp, because white is recessive to purple. We also know that the other parent must be heterozygous for color, because there are white offspring in the F_1 generation. Thus, the other parent is Pp.

Now we can examine the height. Because there are dwarf offspring in the F_1 generation and both parents are phenotypically tall, they *must* both be heterozygous tall (Tt). If either (or both) were homozygous, all the progeny would be tall.

Thus, one parent is heterozygous purple and heterozygous tall, whereas the other is homozygous white and heterozygous tall.

We might consider that we could have analyzed this problem mathematically. An approximately 1:1 purple to white ratio exists (62 + 20 to 59 + 21), which is what we expect from crossing a heterozygous dominant trait (purple flower) with a homozygous recessive one (white flower). For height, we have a 3:1 tall to dwarf ratio (62 + 59 to 20 + 21); this is the standard distribution for a heterozygous organism crossed to another heterozygous individual. However, on the MCAT, we should be efficient and perform only the math that is required. It wasn't necessary here, and on Test Day, we could address a problem like this without actually crunching the numbers.

The Chromosomal Theory of Inheritance

As we previously mentioned, genes are organized in a linear fashion onto chromosomes. From Chapter 4, we should remember that **diploid** species have homologous pairs of chromosomes. One allele is located on one chromosome, whereas the other allele is located on the paired (homologous) chromosome.

SEGREGATION AND INDEPENDENT ASSORTMENT

Now that we have a firm grip of Mendel's laws (perhaps by the kinetochores), we should briefly review meiosis, as Mendel's laws are the functional consequence of it. Before meiosis I, cells undergo genome replication. The daughter DNA strand is held to the parent strand at the centromere. Together, they are known as sister chromatids. Homologous pairs of chromosomes line up during metaphase I and then separate during anaphase I. Recall that the name given to meiosis I is the **reductional division**, as cells are haploid afterward. Homologous pairs separate, although the sister chromatids remain attached until meiosis II. Since this is the step during which homologous chromosomes separate, independent assortment occurs during meiosis I.

NONINDEPENDENT ASSORTMENT AND GENETIC LINKAGE

Let's recall that our laundry detergent and gum example demonstrated independent purchases; buying one didn't cause you to buy the other. We will now take a look at nonindependent assortment of genes. Buying detergent may not make you purchase gum, but it does make it more likely that you will buy fabric softener because the two are typically located in the same aisle. Similarly, two genes that are closely related (in terms of distance from one another on a chromosome) may be inherited together.

Genetic linkage is a direct result of the organization of genes along chromosomes; linked genes are located on the same chromosome. During meiosis I, homologous chromosomes segregate into different cells. If two genes are located on the same chromosome, they tend to segregate together. The degree of genetic linkage can be tight and complete, with no recombinant phenotypes. Linkage can also be weak, for instance when the number of recombinants in the F_1 progeny approaches the number expected from independent assortment. Tightly linked genes recombine at a frequency close to 0 percent; weakly linked genes recombine at frequencies approaching 50 percent (i.e., the percentage expected from independent assortment).

RECOMBINATION FREQUENCIES: GENETIC MAPPING

Let's detail how we can determine the degree of linkage between two genes. We already stated that the frequency of recombination can range from 0 percent (completely linked) to 50 percent (completely unlinked). The process that leads to recombination is the physical exchange of DNA between homologous chromosomes that are paired during meiosis. This process is termed **crossing over** (Figure 14.6). Genes that were initially linked may be unlinked by crossing over. Of course, if recombination occurred between sister chromatids, no change in linkage frequency would be observed because sister chromatids are genetically identical.

MCAT Expertise

The 3:1 and 9:3:3:1 distributions that we learned for monohybrid and dihybrid crosses, respectively, work only if the genes are inherited independently (i.e., not linked). If they are linked, these ratios do not apply. However, don't fret. The MCAT is much more likely to ask you to determine *if* genes are linked rather than to calculate the exact numbers.

Figure 14.6

The distance between gene loci on a chromosome determines the degree of genetic linkage. The chance that a crossover and exchange event will occur between two points is generally directly proportional to the distance between the genes. In other

Bridge

Crossing over occurs when the homologous chromosomes pair up into tetrads during prophase I.

words, the further apart two genes are, the more likely it is that there will be a recombination event between them.

By analyzing **recombination frequencies**, we can construct a **genetic map**. A genetic map is a diagrammatic representation that shows the relative distance between the genes on a chromosome. By convention, one **map unit** corresponds to a 1 percent chance of recombination occurring. Thus, if we had two genes that were 25 map units apart, we would expect for 25 percent of the total gametes we examined to show recombination somewhere between these two genes. Recombination frequencies can be added in a crude approximation. For example, let's say we have genes XYZ that sit linearly on the chromosome. If we know the distance between X and Y, as well as the distance between Y and Z, the sum of these two numbers should provide us with the approximate recombination frequency for X and Z.

We can see a specific example illustrating this in Figure 14.7. We are shown that the recombination frequency of x and y is 8 percent. We draw this in Step 1 of the diagram. Now, we are told that the recombination frequency of X and z is 12 percent. As we see in Step 2 of Figure 14.7, z could be in either of two spots, since we haven't yet determined if the gene order is zxy or xyz. We'll need to use the distance between y and x as an arbiter. From the first two data points (x to y and x to z), they are either 20 map units (zxy orientation) or 4 map units apart change to (xyz orientation). Checking against what we have been given (yz is four map units), we conclude that xyz (or zyx) is the correct orientation in Step 3. These sorts of questions require a little bit of mental math, but if we know how to approach them, they will result in quick points on Test Day.

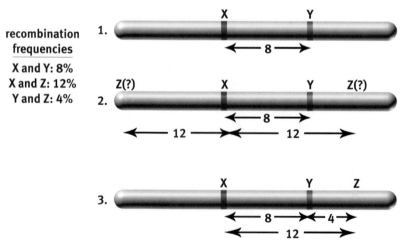

Figure 14.7. Chromosomes Map

Variations on Mendelian Genetics

Although it would certainly be nice if all systems followed Mendelian genetics, that isn't the case. We have actually already seen an exception with the ABO blood group system in Chapter 9. Mendelian genetics is based on the premise that there is a clear relationship between phenotype and genotype. We expect 100 percent of recessive phenotypes to have homozygous recessive genotypes; we also expect 100 percent of dominant phenotypes to be either heterozygous or homozygous dominant. In reality, we must be wary of four situations: **incomplete dominance**, **codominance**, **penetrance and expressivity**, and **inherited disorders**.

INCOMPLETE DOMINANCE

Our pea plant flowers were either white or purple, depending on the genotype. There was a clear 3:1 phenotypic ratio that we could predict in the F_2 generation; this proportion was based on the purple-coding allele being dominant to the white-coding allele. In some cases, however, neither allele is dominant (**incomplete dominance**); the resulting phenotype is a mixture of the two parental phenotypes. This occurs in another flower, the snapdragon, which has two alleles for color, red and white. We would expect the plants to be either red or white, depending on which allele is dominant. When we cross a homozygous red plant with a homozygous white plant, however, we get 100 percent pink plants in the F_1 generation. If we further self-cross these progeny, we find a 1:2:1 distribution (red to pink to white). If red were fully dominant, we would expect the Mendelian phenotype ratio of 3:1 (red to white). The pink color results from the combined effects of both alleles. See this data illustrated in Figure 14.8.

CODOMINANCE

Two conditions must be met for codominance to occur. First, there must be multiple coding alleles for a gene; second, more than one of these alleles must be dominant when expressed with a recessive allele. In situations of codominance, when two dominant alleles are both present, they will be expressed simultaneously. An important point to note is that the resulting phenotype is not an intermediate of the two alleles (incomplete dominance); it is, in fact, complete expression of both phenotypes.

When we studied the ABO blood system in Chapter 9, we were actually looking at a codominant system. Blood types A (I^A) and B (I^B) are both dominant to O (i). We can see that there are three coding alleles in the human population, but we know from Mendel's laws and our understanding of the chromosomal theory of inheritance that we will only have two alleles in any particular individual. People with type A blood have either $I^A I^A$ or $I^A i$ alleles; type B blood is the result of $I^B I^B$ or $I^B i$ alleles; type

Key Concept

Note that this 1:2:1 distribution for incomplete dominance is distinct from the 3:1 that we saw with classic monohybrid crosses.

Bridge

Type A individuals carry the A antigen on their RBCs and have circulating anti-B antibodies. Type B folks carry the B antigen and have circulating anti-A antibodies. Type O individuals have neither antigen and both antibodies. Type ABs have both antigens but neither antibody. That makes type O individuals universal donors and type AB individuals universal recipients.

snapdragons
R = allele for red flowers
r = allele for white flowers
Parental: RR × rr (red × white)

	R	R
r	Rr	Rr
r	Rr	Rr

F_1 genotypic ratio: 100% Rr
F_1 phenotypic ratio: 100% pink

F_1: Rr × Rr (pink × pink)

	R	r
R	RR	Rr
r	Rr	rr

F_1 genotypic ratio: 1RR:2Rr:1rr
F_2 phenotypic ratio: 1 red:2 pink:1 white

Figure 14.8

O blood only occurs with two recessive alleles ii. What happens when we combine the two codominant alleles? The genotype will be I^AI^B, and our individual will have type AB blood. We should emphasize that type AB blood is not an intermediate phenotype (what we would expect if A and B were incompletely dominant); instead, type AB blood is a fourth phenotype generated from the full expression of both the A and B alleles.

PENETRANCE AND EXPRESSIVITY

Penetrance and expressivity both reveal the complex interplay between genes and the environment. Penetrance of a genotype is defined as the number of individuals in the population carrying the allele who actually express the phenotype. Huntington's disease is an example of a disease that is not **fully penetrant**; it is an autosomal dominant disorder, yet 5 percent of people who have the dominant allele will not express symptoms of the disease. Diseases that exhibit this phenomenon may be further described by the degree of penetrance. We would say that Huntington's disease is **highly penetrant**, because 95 percent of individuals with the affected allele will exhibit disease symptoms.

A related, but distinct, concept is expressivity, which is defined as the varying expression of disease symptoms despite identical genotypes. Whereas penetrance is all or nothing in each individual (i.e., disease present or absent), expressivity is more of a gray area. The disease neurofibromatosis type 2 (NF2) is an autosomal dominant disease as a result of the mutation of the gene *merlin*. Interestingly, a range of phenotypes is associated with carrying the affected allele. Some patients are not affected at all, whereas others have debilitating tumors of the auditory nerve, which is needed for hearing and balance (Chapter 13). The disease shows variable expressivity because there is a range of presentations between none and severe. Although we don't need to remember these specific diseases for the MCAT, we should be able to recognize *penetrance* and *expressivity* when we see them in a question.

INHERITED DISORDERS

Recessive

If a condition is recessive, two copies of the recessive allele must be present for the disease phenotype to be present. Heterozygotes are **carriers** of the disease. The normal allele protects them from the affected one. Homozygous recessive individuals are usually the result of mating between two carriers. Offspring of these carriers will exhibit the expected 3:1 phenotypic ratio that we saw in our initial monohybrid cross earlier in the chapter. That is, one out of four children will be expected to have the disease.

Some recessive disorders, such as albinism, may be mild or have little functional consequence, whereas others may be **lethal**. An example of a more detrimental disease would be **cystic fibrosis** (CF). CF is caused by the deletion of a specific amino acid residue in a chloride channel. Individuals who are homozygous affected have problems with secretions like mucus and sweat. Their thick respiratory mucus predisposes them to infection with certain bacteria. Recessive diseases are capable of remaining in the gene pool, because carriers are not subject to the disease phenotype. CF heterozygotes have no problem in terms of secretions and will not be subject to natural selection on this basis.

The majority of recessive lethal gene mutations are **early acting**; that is, they cause death before the individual reproduces, usually during embryonic development or early childhood. We might expect these genes eventually to be selected against (Chapter 15); however, in several cases, it has been shown that carrying a mutation (but not being homozygous for it) may confer a survival advantage. For example, individuals who are heterozygous for sickle cell anemia exhibit natural resistance to malaria. The incidence of the sickle cell gene is significantly higher in individuals of African descent; it is hypothesized that this is due to malaria being pandemic in Africa, which places selective pressure on the sickle cell allele.

Dominant

Lethal alleles may also be dominant. In a dominant disease, only one copy of the allele is required for the phenotype to be expressed. An example of a dominant lethal disease is the Huntington's disease, which was discussed above. Because the effects of Huntington's disease gene aren't expressed until middle age, most of its victims have already had children by the time of diagnosis; assuming the other parent is normal, 50 percent of the children are predicted to inherit the Huntington's disease gene. This is an example of a **late-acting** mutation, because the lethality does not occur until the individual has passed on his or her genes.

SEX DETERMINATION

All of our previous discussion has concerned the **autosomes**. We will now turn our attention to the **sex chromosomes**. In sexually divergent species, a variety of mechanisms are responsible for determining sex. For the MCAT, we want to be experts on how this process occurs in mammals and, more specifically, humans. Humans have 22 pairs of autosomes and 1 pair of sex chromosomes. Females have two homologous X chromosomes, whereas males have an X and a Y chromosome (heterologous). Figures 14.9a and 14.9b show an X and Y chromosome, respectively.

Figure 14.9a

Figure 14.9b

During meiosis, these two chromosomes pair up for segregation purposes. We should know from Chapter 4 that these chromosomes will separate during meiosis I, which is when homologous pairs of autosomes part ways. The sex of a zygote is determined by the father, because the mother will always contribute an X chromosome. Approximately 50 percent of sperm contain the X chromosome and 50 percent contain the Y chromosome. The chances of being genotypically male (XY) or genotypically female (XX) are each 50 percent as shown in Figure 14.10.

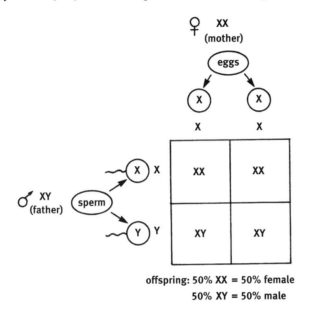

offspring: 50% XX = 50% female
50% XY = 50% male

Figure 14.10

SEX LINKAGE

Females have two X chromosomes and so may be heterozygous or homozygous for a genetic condition that is carried on the X chromosome. Males have only one X chromosome. If that chromosome has a mutation, the male will be affected. Such males are said to be **hemizygous**. Because there is never an extra X allele in males to compensate for a genetic mutation, **X-linked recessive** diseases appear much more commonly in males. We will use hemophilia as a model disease to look at sex-linked inheritance.

There are few X-linked dominant diseases and the Y chromosome is very small, so diseases of this sort aren't likely to be tested. However, if we were given a hypothetical situation on the MCAT involving a mutation on the Y chromosome, who would we predict to be affected? Males only. Moreover, if a man were affected, every one of his sons would have the disease, because he contributes his Y to each of them.

The ratios for sex-linked diseases depend on both parents. First, if the female is homozygous normal, none of the children will be affected. Why? All the sons will receive a normal X from the mother. Each daughter will receive a normal X as well. Because the diseases are recessive, it is irrelevant what the daughter receives from the father.

Let's now say that we have a carrier female and a normal male. This is shown in Figure 14.11a. First, we note that all of the daughters will be phenotypically normal (nonhemophiliac). They each receive a normal X from their father and so are protected from the disease. Genotypically, there is a 50:50 chance that they receive the affected allele from the mother. Thus, 50 percent of the daughters will be carriers, and the other 50 percent will be homozygous normal. Now for the sons. Each son gets a Y from the father, so the mother determines the presence of the disease. Like the daughters, there is a 50:50 chance of receiving each chromosome from the mother. Because the sons have only one X chromosome, they are either affected or normal; none of the sons can be carriers. We see that 50 percent will be hemophiliacs and 50 percent will be normal. Because there is an equal likelihood of having a male or female child, the overall distribution is 25 percent female homozygous normal (XX), 25 percent female heterozygous carrier (XX_h), 25 percent male normal (XY), and 25 percent male hemophiliac (X_hY).

a. Cross between a carrier female (X^hX) and a normal male (XY)

	X^h	X
X	X^hX	XX
Y	X^hY	XY

offspring
25% X^hX = 25% carrier female
25% XX = 25% normal female
25% X^hY = 25% hemophiliac male
25% XY = 25% normal male

b. Cross between a carrier female (X^hX) and a hemophiliac male (X^hY)

	X^h	X
X^h	X^hX^h	X^hX
Y	X^hY	XY

offspring
25% X^hX^h = 25% hemophiliac female
25% X^hX = 25% carrier female
25% X^hY = 25% hemophiliac male
25% XY = 25% normal male

Figure 14.11

Now let's examine what happens if we have a carrier mother and an affected father. This is diagrammed in Figure 14.11b. Starting with the daughters, we see that they will receive an affected allele from their father. The distribution of alleles from the

Key Concept

The male completely determines the sex of the child. This has certain implications for sex-linked diseases. Because they are usually on the X chromosome, a male cannot pass a sex-linked disease to his sons.

mother has not changed from above; however, as a result of the affected allele from the father, 50 percent of the daughters will be hemophiliacs, and 50 percent will be carriers. For the males, the analysis is the same as above because the father still only contributes the Y chromosome to his sons. Again, there is an equal likelihood of having a male or female child, so the overall distribution is 25 percent female homozygous affected ($X_h X_h$), 25 percent female heterozygous carrier (XX_h), 25 percent male normal (XY), and 25 percent male hemophiliac ($X_h Y$).

Pedigree Analysis

The ratios that we have determined throughout the chapter have depended on our ability to perform test crosses. Certainly, it would be unethical for scientists to perform these crosses on humans; instead, we use crosses that have already naturally occurred and analyze the outcomes. We diagram these crosses in **pedigrees**. When we see a pedigree on Test Day, we will need to remember its conventions. Males are represented by squares, and females are depicted with circles. If the shape is shaded, the individual is affected with the disease. Unshaded individuals are unaffected. If the disease in question is recessive, a carrier may (but will not always) be shown by half-shaded shape. For sex-linked traits, female carriers are always half-shaded if they have been identified as such.

Figure 14.12a shows the pedigree for an autosomal recessive trait and 14.12b for a sex-linked recessive trait. For practice, try to determine the genotypes of all the individuals shown.

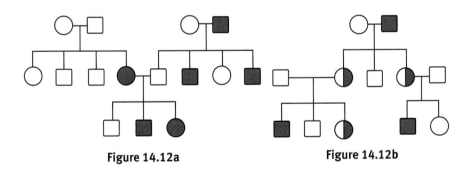

Figure 14.12a   Figure 14.12b

MCAT Expertise

When analyzing a pedigree, look for the recessive phenotype (because you will know the genotype) and work from there. If only males are affected, suspect sex linkage.

Chromosomal Aberrations

The proper segregation and assortment of genes depend on having both the correct number of chromosomes and chromosomes that are structurally normal. Failure to meet either of these criteria may result in genetic abnormalities in the offspring.

NUMERICAL ABNORMALITES

In humans, the diploid number is 46. Individuals with variations from this number are referred to as **aneuploid**. The most common cause for aneuploidy is **nondisjunction**. If during meiosis I homologous chromosomes, or during meiosis II sister chromatids, fail to separate, extra genetic material will be present in the gamete (see Figure 14.13). If we consider a secondary spermatocyte that fails to disjoin correctly for chromosome 21, we will get one gamete with two copies of chromosome 21 and one gamete with zero copies of chromosome 21. There will also be two normal gametes, each with one copy. Remember that the primary spermatocyte will have generated two secondary spermatocytes. If the other secondary spermatocyte does disjoin correctly, it will generate two gametes with normal genetic complements.

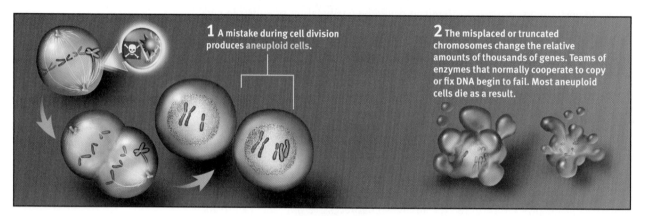

1 A mistake during cell division produces aneuploid cells.

2 The misplaced or truncated chromosomes change the relative amounts of thousands of genes. Teams of enzymes that normally cooperate to copy or fix DNA begin to fail. Most aneuploid cells die as a result.

Figure 14.13

If these sperm were to fuse with a genetically normal egg, there would be four possible results. Two out of four times, there would be no effect due to fusion with the normal haploid gametes. The diploid number would be restored. In one out of four cases, there would be an extra 21st chromosome ($2N + 1$). This is referred to as **trisomy**, more specifically trisomy 21, because that is the chromosome that is affected. The last gamete would result in **monosomy** ($2N - 1$), more accurately monosomy 21. Trisomy 21 results in Down syndrome.

Other than trisomy 21, aberrations in the number of autosomes usually result in spontaneous abortion before birth; however, the sex chromosomes are more resilient. Females may be born with a single X chromosome (**XO**); they are known as Turner syndrome females and are characterized by short stature, sterility, and few to no secondary female sexual characteristics. Females may also be born with an extra X chromosome (**XXX**) and are referred to as **metafemales** or **superfemales**. They may be mentally retarded and sterile. Males are also subject to extra sex chromosomes.

An **XXY** genotype **(Klinefelter male)** results in a tall male who develops breasts and undescended testes and is also usually sterile. Finally, some males may have an **XYY** genotype and may be taller than the average male. Generally, the presence of extra sex chromosomes is not incompatible with life.

CHROMOSOMAL BREAKAGE

Chromosomes may be damaged spontaneously or by environmental factors (e.g., X-rays, chemotherapeutic drugs). If a chromosome loses material, it has a **deletion**. The fragment that was lost may join to the homologous chromosome, resulting in a **duplication**, or it may join another chromosome, which leads to a **translocation**. If the genetic material finds its original home but reinserts itself in the opposite orientation, it has undergone an **inversion**. If these changes occur in the germ line cells, they may be passed on to the offspring. In fact, approximately 5 percent of Down syndrome cases result from a specific type of translocation (Robertsonian) rather than meiotic nondisjunction.

Real World

Chronic myeloid leukemia (CML) is associated with a specific chromosomal abnormality called the Philadelphia chromosome. The Philadelphia chromosome represents a reciprocal translocation from chromosome 22 to chromosome 9. The presence of the Philadelphia chromosome is a reliable marker for CML.

Conclusion

Genetics is a commonly tested topic with which we will want to be familiar for the MCAT. Mendel began the work of genetics by studying pea plants and showing the independent assortment of genes. We must understand the stereotypical ratios of monohybrid and dihybrid crosses. Ultimately, Mendel described the basics of genetics but was later corrected on several counts. Genes can be inherited together if they are linked, which depends on physical distance between the genes. In addition, allelic systems that show codominance, incomplete dominance, penetrance, or variable expressivity do not usually show a complete agreement between genotype and phenotype. In these cases, we must carefully analyze the genotypes to determine the deviations that are present. Furthermore, we described diseases as either dominant or recessive, depending on how many alleles were necessary to cause the phenotype. Sex-linked diseases are primarily due to mutations on the X-chromosome. They are usually inherited from the mother. Our final pages took us through alterations that could occur in chromosome structure or number. As we mentioned at the outset, genes (and therefore, chromosomes) are made of DNA. Our next chapter will examine nucleic acids and molecular genetics in great detail.

CONCEPTS TO REMEMBER

☐ Genes are the heritable units of organisms. They are composed of DNA and organized into chromosomes.

☐ Mendel's first law describes gene variants (alleles) and states that an individual carries two alleles for each gene. One of these alleles is inherited from each parent.

☐ Mendel expanded on his work by showing that genes are inherited independently of one another. That is to say, the segregation of one gene does not affect the segregation of another during gametogenesis.

☐ Genes may segregate together because of the degree of linkage between them; the physical distance between genes is directly related to the chance of recombination.

☐ Recombination can unlink genes by exchanging material between homologous chromosomes.

☐ Codominant systems, such as the ABO blood antigens, result from the existence of multiple alleles with at least two alleles being dominant to a third. The resulting phenotype is unique.

☐ In incomplete dominance, the resulting phenotype is an intermediate of the parents' phenotypes.

☐ Traits may be either recessive or dominant. A recessive trait requires two affected alleles for the phenotype to be expressed. A dominant trait requires only one.

☐ Sex-linked traits are primarily associated with the X chromosome and usually are recessive. Males are disproportionately affected.

☐ Variations in chromosomal number can result in disease. Aneuploidy of the sex chromosomes exhibits a milder disease course relative to aneuploidy of the autosomes.

Practice Questions

1. What is the gene order of linked genes A, B, C, and D, given the following recombination frequencies?

   freq AB: 6%   freq CD: 17%
   freq BC: 18%   freq AC: 12%
   freq AD: 5%   freq BD: 1%

   A. ACDB
   B. BDAC
   C. CBDA
   D. DBAC

2. In humans, the allele for black hair (B) is dominant to the allele to brown hair (b), and the allele for curly hair (C) is dominant to the allele for straight hair (c). When a person of unknown genotype is crossed against a straight-brown-haired individual, the phenotypic ratio is as follows:

   25% curly black hair
   25% straight black hair
   25% curly brown hair
   25% straight brown hair

   What is the genotype of the unknown parent?

   A. BbCC
   B. bbCc
   C. Bbcc
   D. BbCc

3. Which of the following is true concerning a sex-linked recessive disorder that is lethal in infancy?

   A. Females are unable to carry the gene.
   B. It will cause death in both males and females.
   C. It will cause death only in males.
   D. Male children of male carriers will be carriers.

4. Assuming classical Mendelian inheritance, how can one differentiate between a homozygous dominant individual and one who is heterozygous for the dominant trait?

   A. By crossing each individual with a known homozygous dominant and examining the offspring
   B. By crossing each individual with a known homozygous recessive and examining the offspring
   C. By crossing each individual with a known heterozygote and examining the offspring
   D. Both (B) and (C)

5. The distance between linked genes is directly proportional to

   A. the frequency of crossing over.
   B. the frequency of nonsense codons.
   C. the length of polypeptide chains.
   D. the ratio of AT:GC.

6. If a male hemophiliac (X^hY) is crossed with a female carrier of both color blindness and hemophilia (X^cX^h), what is the probability that a female child will be phenotypically normal?

   A. 0%
   B. 25%
   C. 50%
   D. Same as for a male child

7. If a test cross on a species of plants reveals the appearance of a recessive phenotype in the offspring, what must be true of the phenotypically dominant parent?

   A. It must be genotypically heterozygous.
   B. It must be genotypically homozygous.
   C. It could be either genotypically heterozygous or homozygous.
   D. It must have the same genotype as the testcross control parent.

8. Which of the following definitions is FALSE?

   A. Penetrance—the percentage of individuals in the population carrying the allele who actually express the phenotype associated with it
   B. Expressivity—the degree to which the phenotype associated with the genotype is expressed in the entire population
   C. Incomplete dominance—occurs when the phenotype of the heterozygote is an intermediate of the phenotypes of the homozygotes
   D. Codominance—occurs when multiple alleles exist for a given gene and more than one of them is dominant

9. In pea plants, the allele for round seeds (R) is dominant to the allele for wrinkled seeds (r), and the allele for yellow seeds (Y) is dominant to the allele for green seeds (y). A doubly heterozygous, round, yellow-seeded plant is crossed with a green, wrinkled-seeded plant. What percentage of the F_1 generation are recombinants?

   A. 0%
   B. 25%
   C. 50%
   D. 100%

Questions 10 to 12 are based on the pedigree below. The genotypes of individuals a, b, c, d, and e are unknown. (Shading is not indicated in these individuals.)

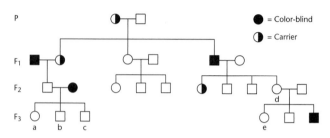

10. What are the genotypes of a, b, and c in the F_3 generation?

    A. X^cY, X^cX, and X^cX, respectively
    B. X^cX, X^cY, and X^cY, respectively
    C. X^cY, X^cX^c and X^cX^c, respectively
    D. X^cX^c, X^cY, and X^cY, respectively

11. What is the genotype of d in the F_2 generation?

    A. X^cX^c
    B. X^cX
    C. XX
    D. X^cY

12. What is the genotype of e in the F_3 generation?

    A. X^cX
    B. X^cX^c
    C. XX
    D. Either X^cX or XX

13. Which of the following definitions is INCORRECT?

    A. Trisomy—the zygote has three copies of a chromosome
    B. Nondisjunction—failure of homologous chromosomes or of sister chromatids to separate
    C. Translocation—the event by which a chromosomal fragment joins with its homologous chromosome
    D. Inversion—the event by which a chromosomal fragment joins with its original chromosome, but in reverse position

14. In a species of plants, a homozygous dominant red flower (RR) is crossed with a homozygous recessive yellow flower (rr). If the F_1 generation is self-crossed and the F_2 generation has a phenotype ratio of red:orange:yellow of 1:2:1, which event accounts for these results?

   A. Codominance
   B. Incomplete dominance
   C. Penetrance
   D. Expressivity

Small Group Questions

1. Why are lethal dominant alleles much less common than lethal recessive alleles?

2. Regarding hair color in rabbits, the B and b alleles are both dominant to w, but B is incompletely dominant to b. BB individuals have black hair, bb individuals have tan hair, and ww individuals have white. What would be the observed phenotypic ratios in the offspring of a Bb mother and a bw father?

Explanations to Practice Questions

1. B

This is a simple gene-mapping problem. Because there is a one-to-one correspondence between the frequency of recombination and the distance between genes on a chromosome, if we are given the frequencies, we can determine gene order. Remember that one map unit equals 1 percent recombination frequency. The easiest way to begin is to determine the two genes that are farthest apart (i.e., the genes that have the highest recombination frequency). In this case, genes B and C recombine with a frequency of 18 percent; this means that B and C are 18 map units apart on the chromosome:

The recombination frequency for C and D is 17%; C and D are 17 map units apart. D can either be 17 units to the right of C or 17 units to the left. To determine where D is, we need to look at the recombination frequency for B and D; if D were to the right of C, the BD frequency would be 18% + 17% = 35%. However, we are told that D is, in fact, 1 percent, indicating that D is to the left of C:

Now, we need to find out where A fits into the picture. The AC frequency is 12 percent; if A were 12 map units to the right of C, the AD frequency would be 17 + 12 = 29%. In fact, the AD frequency is 5%, indicating that A is 5 units to the right of D and 12 units to the left of C. The BD frequency + the AD frequency should equal the AB frequency, which is in fact the case: 1% + 5% = 6%.

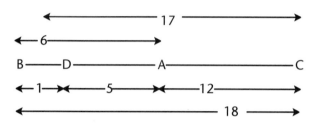

So the gene order is BDAC, choice (B). If we had drawn out the chromosome in the reverse order, CADB, that would have also been correct. However, since this is not one of the answer choices, we deduce that we should reverse CADB to BDAC.

2. D

In this dihybrid problem, a doubly recessive individual is crossed with an individual of unknown genotype; this is known as a test cross. The straight- and brown-haired individual has the genotype bbcc and can thus produce gametes of only one class, bc. Looking at the F_1 offspring, there is a 1:1:1:1 phenotypic ratio. The fact that both the recessive and dominant traits are present in the offspring means that the unknown parental genotype must contain both recessive alleles (b and c). The unknown parental genotype must therefore be BbCc. If you want to double-check the answer, you can work out the Punnett square for the cross BbCc × bbcc: BbCc can produce four different types of gametes, BC, Bc, bC, and bc, whereas bbcc can produce only bc gametes as previously mentioned. So the unknown parental genotype is BbCc, choice (D).

	BC	Bc	bC	bc
bc	BbCc	Bbcc	bbCc	bbcc
bc	BbCc	Bbcc	bbCc	bbcc
bc	BbCc	Bbcc	bbCc	bbcc
bc	BbCc	Bbcc	bbCc	bbcc
	↓	↓	↓	↓
	25% black curly	25% black straight	25% brown curly	25% brown straight

3. C

A sex-linked recessive gene is one that is carried on the X chromosome and can be passed only from fathers to daughters and from mothers to both sons and daughters. An early-acting, lethal, sex-linked recessive will kill all males in infancy, because males are XY and lack a dominant allele to mask the effects of the recessive lethal code. Males cannot be carriers of the lethal gene, as there will be no males of reproductive age with this gene to pass it on to offspring. Therefore, the gene will be inherited only from female carriers, who will pass the lethal gene to 50 percent of their offspring (all of their sons will die in infancy). A female can never be homozygous, because that would mean that she inherited one of the lethal alleles from her father—but that is impossible because all afflicted males die in infancy. Hence, there will be no female deaths as a result of the lethal allele. Thus choices (A), (B), and (D) can be ruled out. A cross between a female carrier and a normal male will produce 25 percent carrier daughters, 25 percent normal daughters, 25 percent homozygous sons (who will die in infancy), and 25 percent normal sons. So the correct answer is choice (C): All males with the early-acting sex-linked lethal recessive allele will die.

4. D

To differentiate between a homozygous dominant and a heterozygous dominant for a trait that exhibits classic dominant/recessive Mendelian inheritance, one must perform a cross that results in offspring that reveal the unknown parental genotype; this is known as a test cross. If we cross the homozygous dominant with a homozygous recessive, we will get 100 percent phenotypically dominant offspring; if we cross the heterozygous dominant with the homozygous recessive, we will get 50 percent phenotypically dominant and 50 percent phenotypically recessive offspring. Thus, using a homozygous recessive as a test crosser will allow us to distinguish between the two. We can also use a known heterozygote as the test crosser because when this is crossed with the homozygous dominant, 100 percent phenotypically dominant offspring are produced, and when it is crossed with the heterozygote, the phenotypic ratio of the offspring is 3:1 dominant:recessive. Hence, the correct answer is choice (D), because both choices (B) and (C) are viable options. Crossing both dominants with a known homozygous dominant, as in choice (A), will produce 100 percent phenotypically dominant offspring for both crosses, not allowing us to distinguish between the homozygote and the heterozygote.

5. A

Linked genes can recombine at frequencies between 0 and 50 percent to produce recombinants. The recombinant chromosomes arise through the physical exchange of DNA between homologous chromosomes paired during meiosis (during crossing over). The degree of genetic linkage is a measure of how far apart two genes are on the same chromosome. The probability of a crossover and exchange occurring between two points is generally directly proportional to the distance between the points. For example, pairs of genes that are far apart from each other on a chromosome have a higher probability of being separated during crossing over than pairs of genes that are located close to each other. Thus, the frequency of genetic recombination between two genes is related to the distance between them. Choice (A) is therefore the correct answer.

6. C

We are told that the female in this cross is a carrier of two sex-linked traits: color blindness and hemophilia. We are also told that the genes for these traits are not found on the same X chromosome, as indicated by her genotype, X^cX^h. Doing the cross, we obtain the following results:

	X^c	X^h
X^h	X^cX^h	X^hX^h
Y	X^cY	X^hY

Offspring

25% female hemophiliac
25% female carrier of both traits (phenotypically normal)
25% male hemophiliac
25% male color-blind

So of the female offspring, half, or 50 percent, will be phenotypically normal. Choice (C) is thus the correct answer.

7. A

Since homozygous recessive organisms always breed true (i.e., the genotype of the offspring can be predicted with 100 percent accuracy), they can be used to determine the genotype of another parent. In a process known as test cross or back cross, an organism with a dominant phenotype of unknown genotype (Ax) is crossed with a phenotypically recessive organism (genotype aa). In a test cross, the appearance of the recessive phenotype in the progeny indicates that the phenotypically dominant parent is genotypically heterozygous. Choice (A) is therefore the correct answer.

8. B

Glancing at the answer choices, we notice that we are tested on four basic definitions, so our task is to read each of them and cross out the ones that are correct. Penetrance is indeed the percentage of individuals in the population carrying the allele who actually express the phenotype associated with it, so choice (A) can be eliminated. Expressivity, however, is the degree to which the phenotype associated with the genotype is expressed in individuals who carry the gene. Since choice (B) talks about the entire population, rather than the individuals who are actual carriers, it is a false statement and, therefore, the correct answer. Just to confirm, choices (C) and (D) contain correct definitions about incomplete dominance and codominance, so they can be safely eliminated.

9. C

This is a basic dihybrid cross between a heterozygous, round, yellow-seeded plant (RrYy) and a green, wrinkled-seeded plant (rryy). RrYy produces four classes of gametes: RY, Ry, rY, and ry; rryy can produce only ry gametes. Here is the Punnett square:

	RY	Ry	rY	ry
ry	RrYy	Rryy	rrYy	rryy
ry	RrYy	Rryy	rrYy	rryy
ry	RrYy	Rryy	rrYy	rryy
ry	RrYy	Rryy	rrYy	rryy

The F_1 genotypic ratio is 1 RrYy:1 Rryy:1 rrYy:1 rryy. Phenotypically, the F_1 generation is one round yellow to one round green to one wrinkled yellow to one wrinkled green. Thus, 25 percent of the offspring are RrYy, which is one of the parental genotypes, and 25 percent of the offspring are rryy, which is the other parental genotype. Hence, 50 percent of the offspring have nonparental, or recombinant, genotypes.

10. B

Color blindness is a sex-linked recessive trait; females carrying the allele can pass it on to both sons and daughters, whereas males can pass it on only to their daughters. We are told that the genotypes of individuals a, b, c, d, and e on the pedigree are unknown. The parents of a, b, and c are a normal male (XY) and a color-blind female (X^cX^c). Using a Punnett square,

	X^c	X^c
X	X^cX	X^cX
Y	X^cY	X^cY

we see that all female offspring are carriers and all male offspring are color-blind. Therefore, a's genotype is X^cX, and b and c share the genotype X^cY.

11. B

The parents of d are a color-blind male (X^cY) and a normal female (XX). In the F_2 generation, d is a female. In such a mating, all daughters will be carriers because they inherit one of their Xs from their father, whose X chromosomes all have the trait for color blindness. Therefore, the genotype of d is X^cX, making choice (B) the correct answer.

12. D

To determine the genotype of e, we must first know the genotype of d. The parents of d are a color-blind male (X^cY) and a normal female (XX). In such a mating, all daughters will be carriers because they inherit one of their Xs from their father. Thus, e's parents are a carrier female (X^cX) and a normal male (XY). Using a Punnett square,

	X^c	X
X	X^cX	XX
Y	X^cY	XY

we see that 50 percent of daughters are carriers and 50 percent are normal. Hence, the genotype of e is unknown; it could be either X^cX or XX, making choice (D) the correct answer.

13. C

Glancing at the answer choices, we notice that they all test us on our knowledge of chromosomal aberrations. Let's quickly go through each choice, eliminating the ones containing correct definitions.

Trisomy can be thought of as a type of nondisjunction that results in the zygote having three copies of a chromosome; a typical example is Down syndrome, which of-

ten has a trisomy of chromosome 21. Choice (A) can be therefore crossed out. Nondisjunction is indeed the failure of homologous chromosomes to separate during meiosis I or of sister chromatids to separate during meiosis II; we can eliminate choice (B) as well. Choice (C) is incorrect; in translocation, the chromosomal fragment joins with a nonhomologous chromosome; if the fragment joins with its homologous chromosome, the event is referred to as duplication. Choice (C) must be the answer we want. We can quickly verify that choice (D) contains the correct definition of inversion, and indeed, it does.

14. B

Some progeny in the second generation are apparently blends of the parental phenotypes. The orange color is the result of the combined effects of the red and yellow heterozygotes. An allele is incompletely dominant if the phenotype of the heterozygote is an intermediate of the phenotypes of the homozygotes. Choice (B) is therefore the correct answer.

15

Molecular Genetics

In the world of molecular genetics, the devil truly is in the details. Seemingly small changes to the genetic code can result in disastrous, life-altering, life-threatening, even life-incompatible alterations to protein structure and function. As protein function necessarily depends on protein structure, protein structure necessarily depends upon the genetic code. One of the clearest examples of this—and a clear example of the dire results of even the smallest errors in the genetic system—is the molecular basis for the pathophysiology of sickle cell disease, also called sickle cell anemia. A disease most prevalent in people of tropical or subtropical origin, sickle cell anemia is a genetic disorder that results in abnormally shaped red blood cells. Rather than having the normal flexible biconcavity, these red blood cells assume a shape that is rigid and sickle shaped (like the curved blade used to cut tall grasses).

Sickle cell disease is caused by a point mutation in the gene for the β-globin chain of hemoglobin. In this particular mutation, a thymine nucleotide is substituted for an adenine nucleotide, resulting in the substitution of valine for glutamic acid at the sixth position from the amino terminus of the β-globin chain. Individuals with sickle cell disease are homozygous for the mutated allele, which is autosomal recessive. The substitution of a nonpolar amino acid for an acidic (charged) amino acid has no effect on the secondary, tertiary, and even quaternary structure of hemoglobin: Under normal physiological conditions, this is a totally benign mutation! However, under low-oxygen conditions, the deoxy form of hemoglobin exposes a hydrophobic patch on the protein with which the nonpolar valine residue can interact by way of hydrophobic interactions. These interactions cause the hemoglobin molecules (called hemoglobin S, for the sickle cell mutation) to aggregate and form precipitates that distort the shape of the red blood cell and decrease its elasticity.

Under conditions of low oxygen tension, the aggregation of hemoglobin and the resulting shape change lead to damage of the erythrocyte membrane. Repeated sickling causes accumulated membrane damage and significantly decreased elasticity. These damaged cells do not return to their normal shape even after oxygen levels have been restored. When these abnormally shaped cells pass into the microvasculature (i.e., the capillaries), they can get stuck, blocking off blood supply to the tissue and causing ischemic tissue damage and high levels of pain.

The last chapter introduced us to genes as the fundamental units of heredity. We briefly noted that they are composed of **deoxyribonucleic acid (DNA)**. We saw that for traits to be inherited, the genes that code for the traits must be passed from one generation of individuals to the next. This ultimately means that the genetic code itself (DNA) must be transmitted. Each cell in the human body contains the complete blueprint for all the proteins that are necessary for life and that make each person unique. In Chapter 4, we noted that DNA replication is critical for cell division and reproduction. The self-replicating nature of DNA, and its ability to direct protein production, form the central dogma of molecular genetics (see Figure 15.1). This chapter will take us through the complete process from DNA to RNA to protein and, in some cases (e.g., retroviruses), backward from RNA to DNA and ultimately to protein (see Figure 15.1). We will primarily examine the eukaryotic mechanisms of gene replication, although a review of some bacterial and viral genetics is included for Test Day completeness.

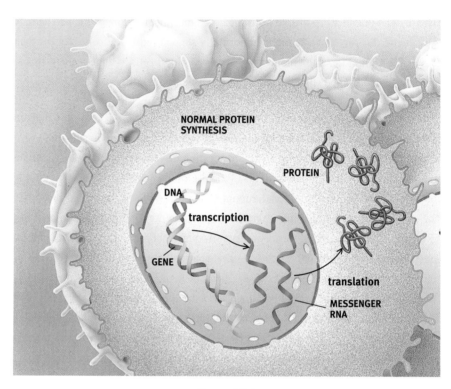

Figure 15.1

Key Concept

This central dogma is key to doing well on the MCAT biology section. The MCAT has become increasingly focused on molecular genetics—of which this theory forms the core. Also, keep in mind that some viruses (retroviruses, including HIV) use RNA as their genetic material, which is then turned back into DNA in a process called reverse transcription.

DNA ★★★★☆

Like many other biological molecules that we have examined, DNA is a polymer. Its basic unit is a **nucleotide**, which has three basic parts: a **deoxyribose sugar**, a **nitrogenous base**, and a **phosphate group** (see Figure 15.2). The sugar forms the core to which the other two components are bound. There are four nitrogenous bases in two categories: **cytosine** and **thymine** are single-ringed **pyrimidines**, whereas **adenine** and **guanine** are double-ringed **purines**. Take a glance at the sidebar for a quick way to remember this distinction on Test Day.

Mnemonic

If you have trouble remembering which bases are purines and which are pyrimidines, just think CUT the PIE. Cytosine, Uracil, and Thymine are PYrimidines. Adenine and Guanine are purines (PURe As GOLD).

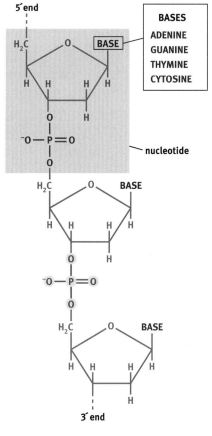

Figure 15.2

DNA nucleotides may be combined to form **polynucleotides**. The ordering and bonding between them is regular. The deoxyribose sugar has both a 3′-OH and a 5′-OH group. It gets the name *deoxy–* because the 2′ position has an –H rather than an –OH. The 3′ group is bound to the 5′ group of the next sugar. The three-dimensional structure of DNA has the chain formed by the sugars and phosphates, with the nitrogenous bases being put off to the side. This has important functional consequences, which we will see momentarily.

Looking at Figure 15.3, we can see several features of DNA. First, two linear molecules are wound together in a spiral orientation, making it a **double-stranded helix**. The sugar phosphate chain that we mentioned in the last paragraph is oriented to the outside of the helix, whereas the nitrogenous bases are forced into the middle of the DNA molecule. This allows for base pairing through hydrogen bonding of the side chains, giving greater stability to the overall molecule. A pairs with T, forming two hydrogen bonds and C with G, making three hydrogen bonds. Note that a pyrimidine pairs with a purine in each case.

Key Concept

Because of complementary base pairing in DNA, the amount of A will equal the amount of T, and G will equal C in double-stranded organisms. Also, because G is triple-bonded to C, the higher the G/C content of DNA, the more tightly bound the two strands will be.

Key Concept

If A–T forms two hydrogen bonds and C–G forms three hydrogen bonds, what does this mean about the relative stability of DNA strands that are A/T-rich versus those that are C/G-rich? Because H-bonds are *inter*molecular interactions, you can use heat to melt the two strands of DNA apart. This is the basis of the polymerase chain reaction. This A/T versus C/G ratio tells us how high this temperature needs to be, with more C/G requiring a higher temperature.

Figure 15.3

Key Concept

One of the most common MCAT topics tested is the 5′→3′ nature of DNA. This may be in the form of a discrete or passage-based question. It may be on transcription, translation, or general base pairing. The bottom line is that DNA and RNA work in a 5′→3′ direction. This fact is likely to earn you a quick point on Test Day.

We can see in Figure 15.3 that the two strands are **antiparallel**; that is, one strand has a **5′→3′ polarity**, whereas its complementary strand has a **3′→5′ polarity**. The directionality of DNA is one of its most important features; the enzymes that replicate and transcribe DNA can only move 5′→3′. We will discuss the functional consequences of this shortly. The 5′ end of DNA has an –OH or phosphate group bound to the number 5 carbon of the terminal sugar, while the 3′ end has a –OH on the number 3 sugar (see Figure 15.4). The combination of all these properties gives us the **Watson-Crick model** of DNA.

Watson, Crick, and Wilkins (another one of their colleagues) were awarded the 1962 Nobel Prize in Physiology or Medicine for their discovery of DNA, along with the elucidation of its structure and significance. It was revealed later that Rosalind Franklin was actually the scientist who had created the X-ray images of DNA used by Watson and Crick. Unfortunately, she had died by the time this information became public.

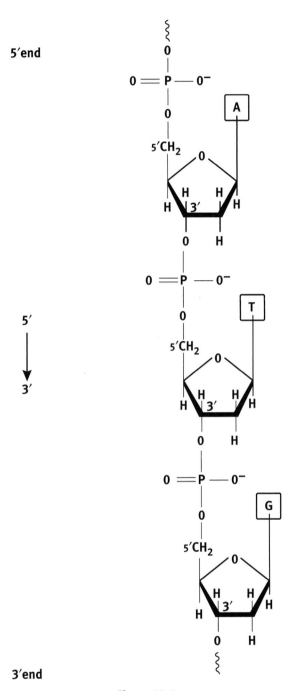

5'end

5'

3'

3'end

Figure 15.4

DNA REPLICATION (EUKARYOTIC)

For both reproduction and replacement purposes, cells must be able to replicate the genome. We will focus on eukaryotes for the MCAT, although prokaryotes use a similar process.

Semiconservative Replication

parent strands

daughter strands

Figure 15.5

Chapter 4 introduced us to the idea that DNA undergoes **semiconservative replication**. Each new helix contains a strand from the parent DNA molecule and a newly synthesized strand (see Figure 15.5). Because the DNA helix is tightly bound together, the helix must first unwind to allow replication to occur. This allows each of the parent strands to act as a template for generation of a daughter strand. In the days before printing presses, monks used to carry out the same process with ancient tomes. They would copy a book from an existing manuscript (parent strand), generating a new one (daughter strand). As with DNA, this would allow for further dissemination of the material contained in the books. This process also ensures that each of the new helices is identical.

Origin of Replication

The human genome has about 3 billion base pairs; it is truly amazing to think that all of those base pairs are in every single one of our cells (with the exception of gametes, which have half the genetic complement). Because there are so many bases, DNA unwinds in multiple places to allow for efficient replication to occur. Each of these points is named an **origin of replication** (see Figure 15.6). The generation of new DNA proceeds in both directions, creating **replication forks**, so named because each looks like a fork in the road.

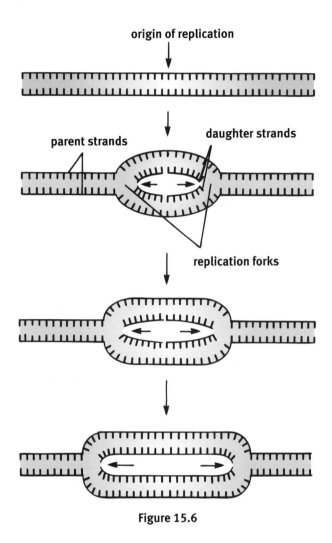

origin of replication

parent strands   daughter strands

replication forks

Figure 15.6

Unwinding and Initiation

Now that we know where the helix dissociates, we can describe the enzymes that carry this process out. **Helicase** unwinds the helix, generating single-stranded regions of DNA. DNA isn't particularly fond of being unwound; recall that we described the hydrogen bonding that occurs between the two strands. To keep the two strands from reassociating, **single-strand binding proteins** (SSB) enter and stabilize the single strands. Think of two large magnets; we have to work to pull them apart, just as helicase has to pull apart the two strands of the DNA helix. And if we don't keep them apart, they will reassociate. As helicase unwinds DNA, it causes positive supercoiling that strains the DNA helix. So **DNA gyrase** (a topoisomerase) relieves overwound DNA by introducing negative supercoils. We can illustrate supercoiling by thinking of the old-fashioned cord between the phone and the handset. It has coils in it already; however, as we know from experience, the cord may wrap around itself further. These coils are known as **supercoils**.

Bridge

Remember that bacteria have topoisomerases as well. Some of our antibiotics poison these as their mechanism of actions. Because the topoisomerases of bacteria are somewhat different from ours, we aren't hurt. We also use topoisomerase poisons in cancer treatment. In this case, we want to stop cell division, so we prevent DNA replication (which is required for cell division) by keeping it from unwinding.

DNA polymerase is the enzyme responsible for adding the individual nucleotides to the growing strand. However, it won't work unless it recognizes where to begin. It requires an RNA **primer**, which is several nucleotides long. **Primase** (an RNA polymerase) is the enzyme that generates the RNA primer. When children learn to read, they must first understand the alphabet and may use a reading primer to learn. DNA polymerase needs the RNA primer to understand how to generate the new strand. The first nucleotide of the sequence binds to the 3′ end of the primer chain.

Synthesis

As we mentioned already, synthesis occurs in the 5′→3′ direction. A number of different enzymes, collectively referred to as **DNA polymerases**, catalyze this process. Helicase moves forward, unwinding the DNA helix. SSBs bind to prevent reassociation, and DNA gyrase introduces negative supercoils to prevent torsional strain on the helix. Free nucleotide triphosphates (in the 5′ position) pair with the parent strand, and DNA polymerases cut the phosphodiester linkage to incorporate the new base. Free pyrophosphate (PP$_i$) is also generated.

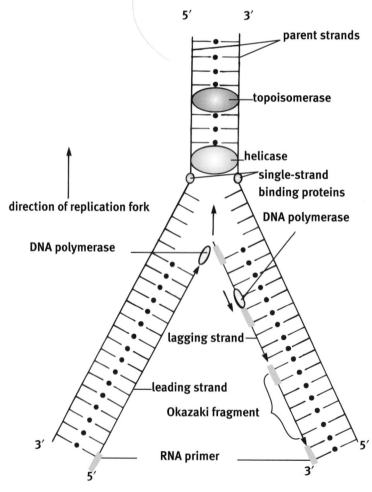

Figure 15.7

Due to the directionality of DNA polymerase, certain constraints arise. Remember that the two strands of the helix are antiparallel to each other. In each replication, there will be a 3′→5′ strand whose complement will be coded 5′→3′. This presents no problem to the DNA polymerase, which can form the complement strand, known as the **leading strand**, in a continuous fashion. The complementary parent strand at the replication fork will have a 5′→3′ polarity. If DNA polymerase were to sit down directly and work, it would necessarily have to produce the daughter strand in the 3′→5′ direction, because it would have to read the parent strand 5′→3′. We already know that DNA polymerase cannot do this. How do we solve this problem? DNA polymerase can only produce daughter strand DNA in the 5′→3′ direction, so small sections known as **Okazaki fragments** (around 1,000 base pairs) are produced at a time. The primer is introduced as far forward as possible, and then instead of working forward toward the point of the replication fork (which occurs in the leading strand), DNA polymerase works back toward the origin of replication. This strand is known as the **lagging strand**. Since the replication fork is moving in the other direction, synthesis occurs piecemeal so that the ultimate direction of replication is the same and both new strands can be generated at the same time. To be clear, the leading strand is produced continuously 5′→3′. The lagging strand is produced discontinuously through the formation of Okazaki fragments, which are produced 5′→3′. The summation of Okazaki fragments is in the 3′→5′ direction. The small gaps between the Okazaki fragments are also filled with nucleotides, and the sugar phosphate backbone is added by **DNA ligase** (see Figure 15.7).

RNA ★★★★☆☆

Ribonucleic acid (RNA) is similar to DNA in many ways, with three major exceptions. It uses ribose instead of deoxyribose as a sugar, it is usually **single stranded**, and the base uracil replaces thymine (see Figure 15.8). There are multiple types of RNA, each of which has different functions. RNA is found in both the nucleus and the cytoplasm, where it participates in **transcription** and **translation**, respectively. We will discuss four types of RNA: **mRNA**, **tRNA**, **rRNA**, and **hnRNA**. The name of each type clues us in to its function.

> **Key Concept**
>
> As we said before, replication is subject to the 5′→3′ rule. This means that one strand, the lagging, is synthesized discontinuously. In the past, the MCAT has used this fact to ask which strand is more likely to be subject to errors. Not surprisingly, it is the lagging strand, as the replication machinery has to hop on and off more often.

> **Key Concept**
>
> DNA:
> • Double stranded
> • Sugar = deoxyribose.
> • Base pairing: A/T, G/C
> • Found in nucleus only.
>
> RNA:
> • Single stranded
> • Sugar = ribose.
> • Base pairing: A/U, G/C
> • Found in nucleus and cytoplasm.

Figure 15.8

MESSENGER RNA (mRNA)

Messenger RNA is created during transcription. It carries the genetic message from the nucleus to the cytoplasm so that it can be translated into a protein. In eukaryotes, mRNA is **monocistronic**, meaning that each mRNA molecule translates into only one product. In prokaryotes, particularly bacteria, messages may be **polycistronic**, and different proteins can be formed by starting translation at different positions on the mRNA.

TRANSFER RNA (tRNA)

Once the message arrives at the ribosome, amino acids must be linked into the nascent polypeptide chain. tRNA, found in the cytoplasm, carries out this function. There are 20 amino acids, each of which is selected by a different **codon**, so there is a different tRNA for each amino acid.

RIBOSOMAL RNA (rRNA)

Ribosomal RNA is synthesized in the nucleolus. It forms an integral part of the ribosomes that are used for protein assembly in the cytoplasm.

HETEROGENEOUS NUCLEAR RNA (hnRNA)

We will soon describe how mRNA is generated. Its immediate precursor is heterogeneous nuclear RNA, which is larger and includes riboproteins in its structure.

Protein Synthesis (Eukaryotic)   ★★★★☆

TRANSCRIPTION

Although the DNA contains the actual coding sequence for a protein, the machinery to generate that protein is in the cytoplasm. DNA cannot leave the nucleus, as it will be quickly degraded, so it must use RNA to transmit its message. The encoding of mRNA is known as **transcription**.

Figure 15.9

Transcription begins in a manner analogous to DNA replication (see Figure 15.9). We must unwind the DNA helix so that we can access the gene of interest. However, we use only one strand to generate the growing RNA molecule. This template strand is also called the **antisense strand**, because its nucleotide sequence is antiparallel and complementary to the RNA strand produced from it. Like DNA replication, this process can only occur in the 5′→3′ direction; it is catalyzed by **RNA polymerase**. Base pairing is the same as that in DNA with the exception that uracil substitutes for thymine in the RNA chain. We might wonder how the transcription machinery knows where to begin work, as there are 3 billion base pairs in the genome and over 30,000 genes. Specialized DNA regions known as **promoters** signal where to begin transcription. There are also **termination sequences**, which signal RNA polymerase to dissociate from DNA, thereby stopping transcription. The DNA double helix re-forms, and the newly formed RNA is hnRNA (pre-mRNA).

POST-TRANSCRIPTIONAL PROCESSING

CLASSIC GENE EXPRESSION
A DNA sequence is transcribed into a single-stranded copy made of RNA. Cellular machinery then "splices" this primary transcript: Introns—each of which is defined by distinctive nucleotide sequences at its beginning and end, known, respectively, as the 5′ (five-prime) and 3′ (three-prime) splice sites—are removed and discarded while exons are joined into an mRNA version of the gene that will be translated into a protein by the cell.

Figure 15.10

Key Concept

The MCAT commonly tests what is necessary for a piece of RNA to become a message. The RNA that is synthesized from the DNA must be processed in three ways: (1) a 5′ guanosyl cap must be added, (2) a poly-A tail must be added, and (3) introns must be removed. Failure to complete these steps will result in degradation of the pre-mRNA.

Key Concept

Each codon represents only one amino acid; however, most amino acids are represented by multiple codons.

Key Concept

The degeneracy of the code accounts for the fact that a mutation in DNA does not always result in an altered protein. A mutation within an intron will also not change the protein product because introns are cleaved out of the mRNA transcript and never translated into protein. The genetic code is mostly degenerate for amino acids that are commonly used. Amino acids such as glycine and proline, which are necessary to make collagen, are completely redundant at the third position, whereas those amino acids that are used less commonly may have only one or two coding sequences.

Before an hnRNA strand can leave the nucleus, it must undergo three processes to become a messenger RNA that is capable of interacting with the ribosomal subunits in the cytoplasm (see Figure 15.10). First, a 5′-guanosyl cap must be added to stabilize the starting end of the transcript. Second, we need to put a poly-adenine (poly-A) tail on to protect the 3′ end of our message. The last piece of the puzzle is to remove the **introns**. Eukaryotic genes contain coding **(exons)** and noncoding **(introns)** regions. We want our message to include only the coding regions so that the proper protein will be made. The processing of hnRNA to mRNA occurs in the nucleus. You can think of introns as the commercials in a television show. If you were to tape the show in that antiquated VCR your friends make fun of, you might choose to pause recording during the commercials so that only the show itself (exons) gets taped.

THE GENETIC CODE

We know that DNA and RNA share the same language; they both code using nitrogenous bases. Proteins are made of amino acids, which are not nitrogenous bases. We use the genetic code as a Rosetta Stone to advance from an RNA-coded message to a protein during translation.

There are four letters in the genetic alphabet (A, C, T/U, and G) and 20 words (amino acids) in the protein language. The different nucleotide letters can be put together to form words (e.g., ACC). These mRNA words are then translated into the words of amino acids, the language of proteins (e.g., ACC corresponds to threonine). If each nucleotide word consisted of only two nucleotides, the maximum number of words that could be formed would be 16 (4^2). However, since there are 20 naturally occurring amino acids (i.e., 20 words in the protein language), 16 nucleotide words would be insufficient. Using three genetic letters to form each word, however, would be sufficient. With three nucleotides, we can make 64 words (4^3). As you will immediately recognize, there is actually an excess of genetic words. This is the **degeneracy** or **redundancy** of the genetic code. There are multiple three-letter nucleotide words that can code for the same amino acid. This **triplet** word is known as a **codon** (see Figure 15.11). With few exceptions, the genetic code is universal.

NATURE'S CODE

IF A GENE SEQUENCE is a "sentence" describing a protein, then its basic units are three-letter "words," or "codons," each of which translates into one of 20 amino acids or a "stop translating" signal. Cellular machinery transcribes DNA genes into RNA versions—whose nucleotide building blocks are represented by the letters A, C, G, and U—and then translates the RNA genes, codon by codon, into a corresponding amino acid sequence. Nature's exact amino acid definitions (*below*) were worked out during the early 1960s. But the significance of patterns in the code would not be fully appreciated for several decades.

SYNONYMS AND SIMILARITIES

Many of the 64 possible three-letter codons specify the same amino acid, providing alternative ways for genes to spell out most proteins. These synonymous codons tend to differ by just a single letter, usually the last, forming a pattern of blocks. Codons for amino acids with similar affinities for water also tend to differ by their last letter, and codons sharing the same first letter often code for amino acids that are products or precursors of one another. These features, as it turns out, are crucial to the survival of all organisms and may even help speed their evolution.

Second Nucleotide Position

First Nucleotide Position	U	C	A	G
U	UUU Phenylalanine UUC Phenylalanine UUA Leucine UUG Leucine	UCU Serine UCC Serine UCA Serine UCG Serine	UAU Tyrosine UAC Tyrosine UAA STOP UAG STOP	UGU Cysteine UGC Cysteine UGA STOP UGG Tryptophan
C	CUU Leucine CUC Leucine CUA Leucine CUG Leucine	CCU Proline CCC Proline CCA Proline CCG Proline	CAU Histidine CAC Histidine CAA Glutamine CAG Glutamine	CGU Arginine CGC Arginine CGA Arginine CGG Arginine
A	AUU Isoleucine AUC Isoleucine AUA Isoleucine AUG Methionine	ACU Threonine ACC Threonine ACA Threonine ACG Threonine	AAU Asparagine AAC Asparagine AAA Lysine AAG Lysine	AGU Serine AGC Serine AGA Arginine AGG Arginine
G	GUU Valine GUC Valine GUA Valine GUG Valine	GCU Alanine GCC Alanine GCA Alanine GCG Alanine	GAU Aspartate GAC Aspartate GAA Glutamate GAG Glutamate	GGU Glycine GGC Glycine GGA Glycine GGG Glycine

Figure 15.11

TRANSLATION

Now that we have a proper RNA message in the cytoplasm and we understand the system of conversion from genetic words (codons) to protein words (amino acids), we can put together a protein sentence. This process is known as **translation**. Translation requires the mRNA, tRNA, ribosomes, amino acids, and energy.

tRNA

The genetic code tells us which amino acid and codon go together, but it doesn't actually do the heavy lifting. It is up to tRNA to shuttle the correct amino acid to

Bridge

We can think of DNA as being responsible for genotype and proteins as being responsible for phenotype.

the ribosome when it is needed. To do this, tRNA needs to be able to recognize both the codon and the amino acid that it is carrying. This is reflected in tRNA's three-dimensional structure. On one end, there are nucleotides that are complementary to the codon; they are known as the **anticodon**. On the opposite pole of the molecule, tRNA is bound to the amino acid that corresponds to the codon in question. Each tRNA has a CCA nucleotide sequence where the amino acid binds. We might wonder how the tRNA knows which amino acid to select if the CCA sequence is conserved between all tRNAs. Each tRNA has a helper **tRNA synthetase**, an enzyme that binds the amino acid to the tRNA using GTP. The result is an **aminoacyl-tRNA complex**.

Ribosomes

Way back in Chapter 1, we referred to ribosomes as the factories of the cell. Now we are going to see them in action. Ribosomes are composed of two subunits, each of which is made up of ribosomal proteins and rRNA. There is a large and small subunit, and they only bind together during protein synthesis. The purpose of the ribosome is to take the actual message and the charged aminoacyl-tRNA complex to generate the protein. To do so, they have three binding sites. One is for the mRNA; the other two are for the tRNA. The binding sites for tRNA are the **A site**, which holds the aminoacyl-tRNA complex, and the **P site**, which binds to the tRNA attached to the growing polypeptide chain.

Polypeptide Synthesis

Once we have all the requisite components, we can actually make a protein. This process can be divided into three stages: **initiation**, **elongation**, and **termination**. As we describe each step, let's look at Figure 15.12 to help us follow the intricacies.

Initiation

Synthesis begins with mRNA seeking out a small ribosome. They bind in the presence of **initiation factors**, and the small ribosome slides along the mRNA until it reaches a start codon (AUG). The initiation aminoacyl-tRNA complex, **methionine tRNA** (with the anticodon 5′-CAU-3′), base pairs with the start codon. At this point, the large ribosomal subunit joins the complex, completing the ribosome. The tRNA is in the **P site** at this point, because it is a part (and the only part) of the growing polypeptide chain.

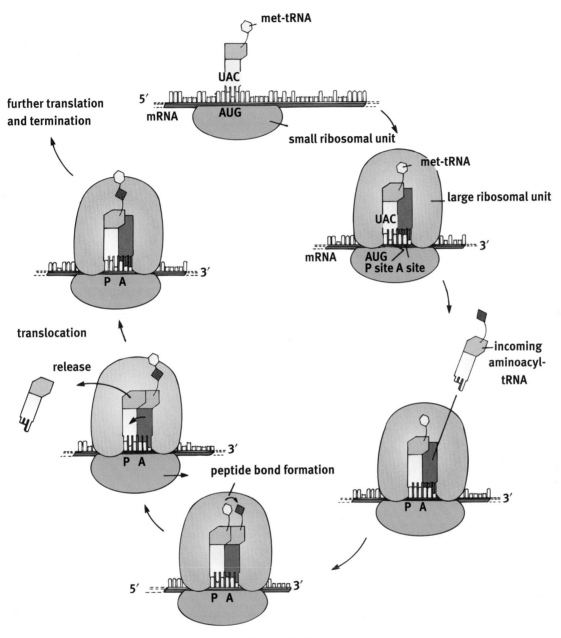

Figure 15.12

Elongation

Once the complex has been formed, the ribosome can slide along the mRNA, adding new amino acids as it goes. Hydrogen bonds form between the mRNA codon in the A site and the complementary tRNA anticodon. This fills the A site. We now have a charged aminoacyl-tRNA in both the A site and the P site. The enzyme, **peptidyl transferase**, uses the energy that was stored in the amino-acyl-tRNA complex when the amino acid was loaded (remember, this was from

Key Concept

$5' \rightarrow 3'$

DNA→DNA = replication: New DNA synthesized in $5' \rightarrow 3'$.

DNA→RNA = transcription: New RNA synthesized in $5' \rightarrow 3'$ direction.

RNA→protein = translation: mRNA read in $5' \rightarrow 3'$ direction.

Mnemonic

Transcription sounds like *transcribe*. When we transcribe information, we use the same language to write it down. This is like DNA to RNA. *Translation* is exactly what it says; we are changing the language. Protein translation changes the language from nucleotides to amino acids.

Bridge

PTM are a great way for a peptide to know where it is targeted. Cells have many compartmentalized structures and functions to carry out. PTM often are the way in which proteins are correctly sorted within the cell.

Real World

Post-translational modifications are often important for proper protein functioning. For example, several of the blood-clotting factors, including prothrombin, require post-translational carboxylation of some of their glutamic acid residues in order to function properly. Interestingly enough, vitamin K is required as a cofactor in these carboxylation reactions. For this reason, vitamin K deficiency will result in a bleeding disorder.

GTP) to catalyze the formation of a peptide bond. The aminoacyl-tRNA used for this is the one in the P site. The bond is made between the single amino acid in the A site and the methionine in the P site. Now the tRNA in the P site is free, and there is still an aminoacyl-tRNA in the A site. This aminoacyl-tRNA has its own amino acid, which is now bound to a methionine. **Translocation** is necessary to add the next amino acid residue. The ribosomal assembly slides in a $5' \rightarrow 3'$ direction along the mRNA. This moves the next codon into place in the A site. At the same time, the uncharged tRNA in the P site is expelled, and the aminoacyl-tRNA that is carrying our nascent chain moved from the A site to P site. The process is ready to begin again with an empty A site (see Figure 15.12).

Termination

Translation has its own set of stop signs. If the codon in the A site is UGA, UAA, or UAG, it is known as a **termination codon**. Instead of a new aminoacyl–tRNA binding to the A site, a protein called **release factor** binds to the termination codon, causing a water molecule to be added to the polypeptide chain. The polypeptide chain will then be released from the tRNA in the P site, and the two ribosomal subunits will dissociate. To save time, as well as increase the amount of protein that may be made from a single transcript, several ribosomes may translate a message at the same time. This is known as a **polyribosome**.

POST-TRANSLATIONAL MODIFICATIONS (PTM)

The new polypeptide is subject to modification just as hnRNA was after transcription. It will fold into a secondary structure based on the lowest energy conformation. Often during this process, the polypeptide will be cleaved or have sugars added to it. We saw an example of this in Chapter 12 with insulin, which is cleaved from a larger peptide to its active form. Other modifications include phosphorylation, carboxylation, and methylation.

MUTATIONS

We mentioned mutations briefly in the previous chapter as a way to increase genetic diversity (at the always present risk of killing the organism). Let's take a glance at the types of mutations and how they occur. They may be classified as **base pair mutations**, **base pair insertions**, or **base pair deletions**. Base pair mutations are also called **point mutations**, whereas insertions and deletions are both also known as **frameshift mutations**.

Types of Mutations

Point Mutations

A point mutation occurs at a single nucleotide residue. Depending on where it is in the genome, it may have no effect at all (perhaps if it is in a noncoding region) or a highly detrimental effect (sickle cell anemia). Even if the mutation occurs in a coding region, it may still have no effect. Such mutations are termed **silent mutations**. Looking back at the genetic code chart, can we think of why such mutations exist? It is because the genetic code is degenerate. For example, the amino acid glycine requires only the first two nucleotides of the codon to ensure that it is inserted into the polypeptide chain. The final nucleotide could be A, C, U, or G, so a "mutation" in this position would be irrelevant. Thus, a mutation at this nucleotide position will have no effect. Changes in either the second or first nucleotide can be more detrimental. A point mutation at the first or second position in the codon may result in a **missense mutation** in which one amino acid is substituted for another.

Key Concept

Silent mutations are a result of the degeneracy of the genetic code. It makes sense that those amino acids that are used most commonly are redundant. That way, if the third position gets changed, no effect will be seen in the organism.

Real World

A **nonsense mutation** is a mutation that produces a premature termination of the polypeptide chain by changing one of the codons to a stop codon. Nonsense mutations can have disastrous effects. Thalassemia is a genetic disease in which erythrocytes are produced with little or no functional hemoglobin, leading to severe anemia. Thalassemia can be caused by a variety of different mutations: Point mutations can change a codon into a stop codon, and frameshift mutations (insertions and deletions) can introduce a stop codon in the altered reading frame.

Figure 15.13

Sickle cell anemia results from the mutation of the second nucleotide in the codon resulting in a GUG instead of a GAG (see Figure 15.13). The resultant hemoglobin S (mutant hemoglobin) is generated with a valine instead of a glutamic acid. Figure 15.14 shows red blood cells affected with sickle cell anemia. Notice that the classic biconcave shape is no longer present, all due to a single amino acid swap.

Figure 15.14

Frameshift Mutations

Codons consist of three nucleotides; this is referred to as the **reading frame**. Insertion or deletion of nucleotides will shift the reading frame, usually resulting in either changes in the amino acid sequence or premature truncation of the protein (due to the generation of a nonsense mutation). The effects are usually much more serious than a base pair substitution. For example, cystic fibrosis is caused by a frameshift mutation that results in the loss of a phenyl-alanine at position 508 in the polypeptide chain, resulting in a defective chloride ion channel. The disease is characterized by infertility, increased incidence of bacterial infections, and decreased life span.

Mutagenesis

New mutations may be introduced in a variety of ways. DNA polymerase is subject to making mistakes, albeit at a very low rate. In addition, ionizing radiation, such as ultraviolet rays from the sun, can damage DNA (see Figure 15.15). DNA is also capable of damaging itself. Elements known as **transposons** can remove and insert themselves into the genome. If they insert in the middle of a coding sequence, the gene will be disrupted.

How Sunlight Can Cause a Permanent Mutation

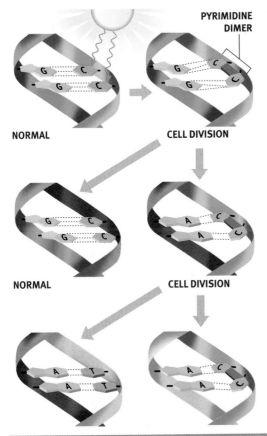

PYRIMIDINE DIMER

NORMAL

CELL DIVISION

NORMAL

CELL DIVISION

ULTRAVIOLET LIGHT can break chemical bonds in adjacent pyrimidine bases, often at a point on the DNA strand where two cytosines (C) occur. New bonds then form (red), linking the disrupted bases together in a so-called pyrimidine dimer.

REPLICATION requires that a cell separate the paired DNA strands (green and blue), each of which is used as a template to construct a new strand (purple) by mating guanine (G) with cytosine and adenine (A) with thymine (T). The strand unaffected by sunlight produces normal DNA (left), but the strand containing the pyrimidine dimer pairs disturbed Cs with As instead of matching them properly with G s.

CONTINUED REPLICATION repeats the error, mating the dimer once more with a pair of As (right). On the opposite strand (left), these As are matched with Ts, creating a genetic mutation. The dimer may eventually be eliminated by "excision repair," but the C-to-T mutation is permanent. When such a mutation falls within a cancer-related gene, the cell becomes prone to malignancy.

Figure 15.15

Key Concept

Remember, a mutation will be inherited only if it occurs in the germ (sex) cell line. Mutations limited to somatic cells will not be passed on to the next generation. They may, however, have an important role in the development of tumors.

Viral Genetics

★★★★☆☆

Viral genomes come in a variety of shapes and sizes (see Figure 15.16). Some are made of only a few genes, whereas others have several hundred. In addition, they may be made of either DNA or RNA, and they may be single or double stranded. Viruses are specific in terms of host selection and may even be cell-specific within that host. For example, herpes simplex type 1 infects only neurons.

Single-Strand
RNA Virus

human immunodeficiency virus
(causes AIDS)

Double-Strand
RNA Virus

retrovirus
(pathogen of plants
and animals)

Single-Strand
DNA Virus

inovirus
(pathogen
of bacteria)

Double-Strand
DNA Viruses

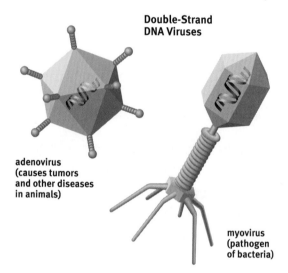

adenovirus
(causes tumors
and other diseases
in animals)

myovirus
(pathogen
of bacteria)

Figure 15.16

INFECTION OF HOST CELL

We know from Chapter 1 that viruses cannot reproduce on their own, violating a key tenet of the Cell Theory. Instead, they must invade a host cell and hijack its machinery. Viruses may only infect cells that have receptors that recognize the viruses' protein coat **(capsid)**. Otherwise, the cell is essentially invisible to the virus. Depending on the virus, different amounts of material will be inserted into the cells. Viruses such as HIV fuse and completely insert, whereas bacteriophages only insert the genetic material, leaving their capsids outside.

GENOME REPLICATION AND TRANSCRIPTION

DNA-Containing Viruses

The DNA-containing viruses have it a bit simpler than the RNA-containing ones. Because their genome is DNA, just like that of the cells, they can enter the nucleus and make use of the DNA and RNA polymerases found there without extra work. A few DNA viruses carry out replication in the cytoplasm. These viruses must bring with them their own DNA and RNA polymerases because the host's are restricted to the nucleus, which these particular viruses never enter.

RNA-Containing Viruses

When the viral genome is RNA, the process is slightly different and occurs in the cytoplasm. Our cells do not have enzymes to replicate RNA. Some viruses will bring **RNA replicase** with them. Others will wait for the enzyme to be translated from their own genome, which acts as mRNA for this purpose.

A special subclass of RNA viruses is known as **retroviruses**. These viruses create a DNA copy from RNA using an enzyme called **reverse transcriptase**. It is called reverse transcriptase because it creates DNA from RNA rather than the other way around (normal transcription). These viruses then integrate the newly synthesized DNA into the host genome. This is clever, because the host will then transcribe and translate the DNA as if it were its own. Moreover, the only way to remove the offending virus genome from the cell now is to kill the cell. This is one reason why diseases such as HIV are particularly difficult to treat. Figure 15.17 shows the integration of HIV into the genome.

A SELF-COPYING COMMANDO

Efforts to devise vaccines and new treatments for HIV depend on knowledge of the virus's life cycle. HIV invades host cells and commandeers their machinery to make more copies of itself. First, a protein called Envelope on the virus must bind to CD4 and CCR5 proteins on the cell surface (*1*). As the virus fuses with the cell, it empties its contents into the cytoplasm (*2*). A viral enzyme, reverse transcriptase, then copies the virus's RNA genome into double-stranded DNA (*3*), often making errors that generate diversity in the virus copies. Another viral enzyme,

integrase, inserts the copy into the host DNA (*4*). Cell machinery transcribes the viral genes back into RNA (including RNA that can serve as templates for proteins) that travels to the cytoplasm, where ribosomes produce the encoded proteins (*5*). Viral RNA and proteins then move toward the cell membrane, where they gather into a budding virus particle (*6*). In the immature new virus copy, the HIV protease enzyme modifies viral protein chains, enabling the particles, or "virions," to mature into a form that is ready to infect a new cell (*7*).

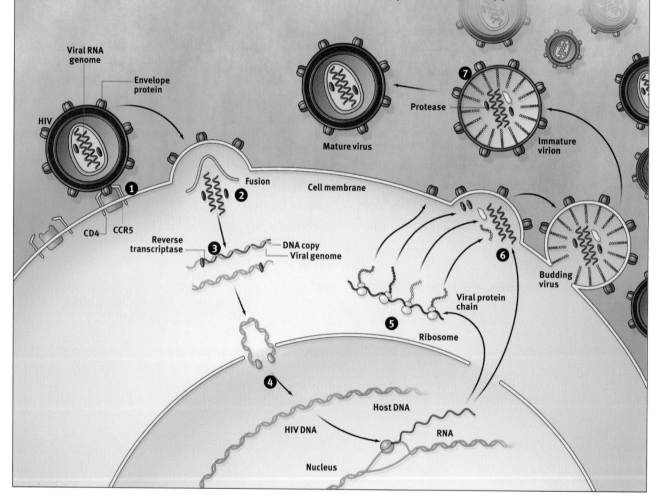

Figure 15.17

TRANSLATION AND PROGENY ASSEMBLY

Using the ribosomes, tRNA, amino acids, and enzymes of the host, the transcribed genes are now translated into protein. These proteins are usually structural and allow for creation of new viral particles (**virions**). A single virus may create hundred or thousands of new virions.

PROGENY RELEASE

Viral progeny may be released in two ways. The host cell may lyse as a result of being filled with viral particles. The viral invasion may also initiate apoptosis (cell suicide) and in the process release viral progeny. Cell lysis commonly happens when a large number of virions are formed in the cell. The disadvantage of this for the virus is that it cannot continue to use the cell for its life cycle. When a virus instead leaves the cell by fusing with its plasma membrane, the process is known as **extrusion**. It is similar to budding and allows the virus to keep the host cell alive. A virus in this state is said to be in a **productive cycle** (see Figure 15.18).

host cell membrane

viral progeny

Figure 15.18

BACTERIOPHAGE

Bacteriophages are viruses that specifically target bacteria. As mentioned earlier, they simply insert their DNA, while keeping their viral envelopes and other structures outside the cell, by boring a hole in the bacterial surface. Depending on growth conditions and the specific phage, the virus may enter a **lytic** or **lysogenic** cycle (see Figure 15.19). These two phases are similar to the lysis and productive cycle that we saw previously.

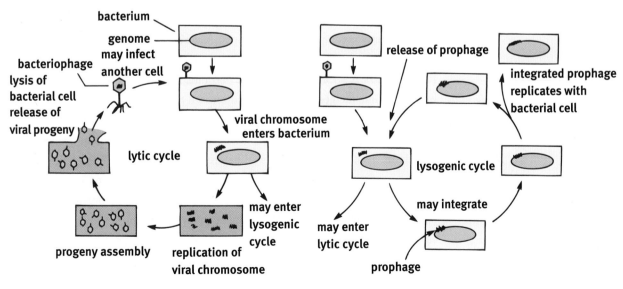

Figure 15.19

Lytic Cycle

During a lytic cycle, the virus makes maximal use of the cell's machinery with little regard to damaging the cell. Once the host is swollen like a balloon with new virions, the cell lyses, and other bacteria can be infected. Bacteria in the lytic phase are termed **virulent**.

Lysogenic Cycle

In the event that the virus does not lyse the bacteria, it may integrate into the host genome as a provirus. One of the clever aspects to this system is that as the bacteria reproduces, so will the virus, because it is a part of the host's genome. Although the virus may remain indefinitely integrated into the host genome, at some point, environmental factors (radiation, light, or chemicals) will cause the provirus to leave the genome and revert to a lytic cycle (see Figure 15.19). Although phages seem quite deadly to bacteria (and make no mistake, they can be), there may be some benefit to having them integrated in the lysogenic cycle. Infection with one strain of phage generally makes the bacteria less susceptible to other phages (superinfection). Since the provirus is relatively innocuous, there may be some evolutionary advantage to this association.

Bacterial Genetics

BACTERIAL GENOME

Our last set of organisms to consider are bacteria. Remember from Chapter 1 that bacteria are prokaryotes. They are single-celled organisms containing a circular DNA genome and no membrane-bound organelles. The genome localizes to the nucleoid region of the cell.

Many bacteria contain extrachromosomal material known as **plasmids**. We mentioned these in Chapter 1 as a way for bacteria to gain antibiotic resistance (see Figure 15.20). A specialized subset of plasmids known as **episomes** is capable of integrating into the genome. When we discussed transcription and translation in eukaryotes, we noted that they were separate events. This distinction is in both time and space. Transcription occurs in the nucleus, whereas translation occurs in the cytoplasm. Transcription occurs well before translation, because the hnRNA must be processed and translocated to the cytoplasm before translation occurs. This is not the case in bacteria. Because there are no membrane-bound organelles, the two processes are not physically separate. In fact, they occur almost simultaneously. Recall that we saw that eukaryotic mRNA is monocistronic, meaning each mRNA can code only for one protein. Bacteria may produce polycistronic messages in which multiple proteins are coded in the same mRNA molecule.

REPLICATION

Because the bacterial chromosome is a single circular molecule, containing far fewer genes than eukaryotic chromosomes, bacteria do not need as many origins of replication. In fact, they have only one. Replication occurs in both directions at the rate of approximately 500 bases per second. A commonly used laboratory strain of *E. coli* only has about 4.5 million base pairs (compared with 3 billion in humans), so it doesn't take long for the entire genome to be duplicated.

GENETIC VARIANCE

In Chapter 4, we described the details of sexual and asexual reproduction. Under favorable growth conditions, bacteria utilize binary fission, a method of asexual reproduction, to increase their numbers rapidly. What was the important consequence of this? Each daughter cell would be genetically identical. We showed that sexual reproduction would allow for greater genetic diversity, which helps species survive less-than-ideal situations by introducing new, potentially advantageous phenotypes. Bacteria have three mechanisms to increase genetic diversity: **transformation**, **conjugation**, and **transduction**.

Transformation

Transformation results from the integration of a foreign chromosome fragment (plasmid) into the host genome. The result is a bacterium that is genetically unique from the cell that it just was and any daughter cells that it produced before adding the plasmid to its genome.

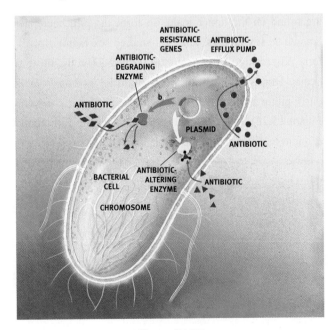

Figure 15.20

Real World

Resistance to antimicrobial drugs is a serious problem in the field of medical therapeutics. Typically, one or several genes for antibiotic resistance are located on plasmids, which can be transferred either by a conjugation-like mechanism or by the process of viral transduction. For example, penicillins contain a ß-lactam ring, which is necessary for activity, and bacterial genes encoding a ß-lactamase (also called penicillinase) have been identified on bacterial plasmids. ß-lactamase will inactivate penicillin and thus confer penicillin resistance to the bacteria that acquired the plasmid. A new type of drug, called a ß-lactamase inhibitor (e.g., clavulanic acid), has been added to penicillin drugs to re-establish sensitivity of the bacteria to the drug. Augmentin, a combination of ampicillin (a type of penicillin) and clavulanic acid, is frequently prescribed to combat resistance to ampicillin.

Conjugation

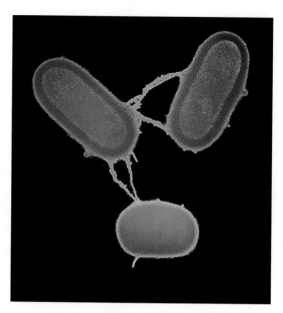

Figure 15.21

Conjugation is the bacterial form of mating (sexual reproduction). It involves two cells forming a **cytoplasmic bridge** between them that allows for the transfer of genetic material (see Figure 15.21). The transfer is one way, from the **donor male (+)** to the **recipient female (−)**. The bridge is made from appendages called **sex pili** that are found on the donor male. To form the pili, bacteria must contain plasmids known as **sex factors**. The best-studied sex factor is the F factor in *E. coli*. Bacteria possessing this plasmid are termed F+ cells; those without it are called F− cells. During conjugation between an F+ and an F− cell, the F+ cell replicates its F factor and donates the copy to the recipient, converting it to an F+ cell (see Figure 15.22). Plasmids that do not induce pili formation may transfer into the recipient cell along with the sex factor.

Figure 15.22

The sex factor is a plasmid, but through processes such as transformation, it can become integrated into the host genome. In this case, when conjugation occurs, the entire genome replicates since it now contains the sex factor. The donor cell will then attempt to transfer its entire genome into the recipient. Usually the bridge collapses before the full DNA sequence can be moved. Cells that have undergone this change are referred to by the abbreviation **Hfr** for high frequency of recombination.

Transduction

Figure 15.23

Transduction is an accidental method of genetic recombination, but this doesn't mean that it isn't useful. When bacteriophages integrate into the host genome, they do not always perfectly excise. In fact, they may be removed from the circular chromosome and take whole bacterial genes with them. These bacterial genes will then be packaged along with the viral genome, since the cellular machinery doesn't distinguish between them. The phage can then go infect a new bacterium, and when it integrates into the genome, the new host bacterium will receive the new gene (see Figure 15.24).

Figure 15.24

GENE REGULATION

Unlike eukaryotes, which separate their biochemical functions into distinct compartments (and thereby add a level of control), prokaryotes use regulation primarily at the transcriptional level to regulate metabolism.

In prokaryotes (and eukaryotes, as well), the ability to transcribe a gene is based on RNA polymerase's access to the genome. **Operons** direct this process. They are made up of **structural genes**, an **operator gene**, and a **promoter gene** (Figure 15.25).

Starting from the right side of Figure 15.25, we can identify each of these. The structural gene codes for the protein of interest—for example, lactase, an enzyme that digests the disaccharide lactose. Next is the operator site. It consists of a nontranscribable region of DNA that is capable of binding a repressor protein. The promoter site is similar in function to that seen in eukaryotes: It provides a place for RNA polymerase to bind. The sequence farthest to the left codes for a protein known as the **repressor**. This protein can bind to the operator sequence and acts as a roadblock. RNA polymerase cannot get from the promoter to the structural gene because the operator region has a giant repressor in the way.

Key Concept

Although bacteria are much simpler organisms and their genomes are different (smaller, circular, and no introns), they are still subject to levels of control. Gene regulation is critical to all organisms' survival; for example, cancer (simply defined as unregulated cell division) is caused by a loss of genetic regulation of cell division.

These systems come in two flavors: **inducible** and **repressible**. Inducible systems require the presence of a compound known as an **inducer** to cause transcription of the structural gene. Repressible systems are the opposite. They are constantly transcribing unless a **corepresssor** is present. Let's take a look at each system in more detail.

Inducible Systems

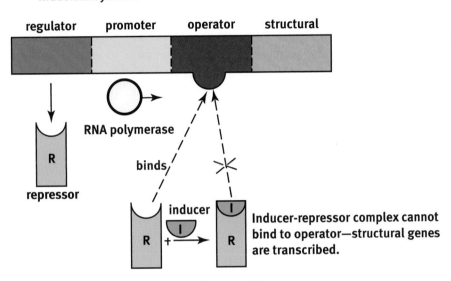

Figure 15.25

In these systems, the repressor is always made. It binds tightly to the operator sequence and thereby prevents transcription of the structural genes. To remove the block, an inducer must bind the repressor protein so that RNA polymerase can move down the gene. Inducible systems operate on a principle analogous to competitive feedback for enzyme activity. As we raise the level of inducer high, most of the repressor will be bound to it, rather than the operator sequence. This system is useful because it allows gene products to be produced only when they are needed. An example is the *lac* operon, which codes for enzymes that allow a bacterium to digest lactose in place of glucose (see Figure 15.26). Because this is more energetically expensive, bacteria use this option only when lactose is high and glucose is low. Thus, the correct genes are induced by the situation.

Figure 15.26

Key Concept

What sort of systems would you want to be inducible? Why make a system inducible at all? Recall that gene expression (from transcription to the final protein product) is energetically expensive. Any cell looks to do it at a minimum level of energy expenditure while maintaining maximal output. Inducible systems in bacteria are one way to do this by preventing gene expression when it is unnecessary.

Repressible Systems

Serving as the antithesis to inducible systems, repressible systems allow constant production of a protein product. In contrast to the inducible system, the repressor made by the regulator region is inactive until it binds to a corepressor. The complex can then bind to the operator region and prevent further transcription. Repressible systems behave on the principle of negative feedback. Often the final structural product can serve as a corepressor. Thus, as its levels get higher, it can bind the repressor, and the complex will attach to the operator region to prevent further transcription of the same gene. An example is the *trp* operon (see Figure 15.27). Bacteria produce the amino acid tryptophan under a repressible system. When tryptophan is high in the local environment, there is no need to make it internally. Tryptophan serves as a corepressor and binds with the repressor as a complex to the operator, thereby preventing the bacteria from making its own tryptophan, which would be energetically wasteful.

Figure 15.27

Conclusion

Molecular genetics is the field of science that underlies the Mendelian genetics that we learned in Chapter 14. Mendelian genetics allows us to predict that a flower would be tall and purple, and molecular genetics helps us figure out how those traits are coded for. Additionally, we should make the connection that, in order for genetic traits to be passed on in any organism, the genome must be replicated. This chapter has shown us how that can be done in eukaryotes, bacteria, and viruses. DNA's structure is critical to this process because it provides the genome with stability to last over the lifetime of the organism. Shorter-lived messages make use of RNA. To make these shorter-lived messages into proteins, we need our trusty genetic code, which serves as a translator between the language of nitrogenous bases and amino acids. Without transcription and translation, DNA can do little more than store the genome. It is the transformation of the genetic code into proteins that allows cells to go about their business. We have examined mutations, which can result in changes to the amino acid sequence and, ultimately, the structure and function of proteins. These changes in the DNA are the molecular basis by which evolution occurs. The next, and final, chapter will review the key concepts of evolution.

CONCEPTS TO REMEMBER

☐ DNA is deoxyribonucleic acid. It is a double-stranded, antiparallel double helix that exhibits base pairing between complementary nitrogenous bases. Its purpose is to store the genome.

☐ RNA is ribonucleic acid. It substitutes ribose for deoxyribose and uracil for thymine. It is usually single stranded and exists in the forms of mRNA, tRNA, rRNA, and hnRNA.

☐ Replication of the genome requires enzymes to separate the strands (helicase) and insert the appropriate complementary bases (DNA polymerase) in a $5' \rightarrow 3'$ manner.

☐ Generation of a eukaryotic mRNA from an hnRNA requires addition of a 5'-guanosyl cap and 3'-poly-A tail. Introns must also be spliced out.

☐ The genetic code is degenerate. Multiple codons may code for the same amino acid. This is one of the mechanisms by which silent mutations occur.

☐ Translation consists of three phases: initiation, elongation, and termination. The initiation and termination steps have specific codons to signify them.

☐ Post-translational modifications may include addition of covalent moieties (e.g., methylation, carboxylation, glycosylation). In addition, large peptides may be cleaved before they are active.

☐ Viral genomes are more diverse than the genomes of cellular organisms. They may be single or double stranded; they may also be made of DNA or RNA.

☐ Bacteria may use transduction, conjugation, and transformation to increase genetic diversity.

☐ Bacteria use inducible and repressible systems to control gene expression at the transcriptional level.

Practice Questions

1. In the DNA of a fruit fly (*Drosophila melanogaster*), 20 percent of the bases are cytosines. What percent are adenines?

   A. 20%
   B. 30%
   C. 40%
   D. 60%

2. In a single strand of a nucleic acid, nucleotides are linked by

   A. hydrogen bonds.
   B. phosphodiester bonds.
   C. ionic bonds.
   D. van der Waals forces.

3. What role does peptidyl transferase play in protein synthesis?

   A. It transports the initiator aminoacyl-tRNA complex.
   B. It helps the ribosome to advance three nucleotides along the mRNA in the 5′ to 3′ direction.
   C. It holds the protein in its tertiary structure.
   D. It catalyzes the formation of a peptide bond.

4. Which stage of protein synthesis does NOT require energy?

   A. Initiation
   B. Elongation
   C. Termination
   D. All of the above require energy.

5. Topoisomerases are enzymes involved in

   A. DNA replication.
   B. DNA transcription.
   C. RNA processing.
   D. RNA translation.

6. You have just sequenced a piece of DNA that reads as follows:

   5′—TCTTTGAGACATCC—3′

   What would be the base sequence in the mRNA transcribed from this DNA?

   A. 5′-AGAAACUCUGUAGG-3′
   B. 5′-GGAUGUCUCAAAGA-3′
   C. 5′-AGAAACTCTGTAGG-3′
   D. 5′-GGATGTCTCAAAGA-3′

7. Which of the following statements regarding differences between DNA and RNA is FALSE?

   A. DNA is double stranded, whereas RNA is single stranded.
   B. DNA uses the nitrogenous base thymine; RNA has uracil.
   C. The sugar in DNA is deoxyribose; the sugar in RNA is ribose.
   D. DNA strands replicate in a 5′ to 3′ direction, whereas RNA is synthesized in a 3′ to 5′ direction.

8. When trypsin converts chymotrypsinogen to chymotrypsin, some molecules of chymotrypsin bind to a repressor, which in turn binds to the operator and prevents further transcription of trypsin. To which gene regulation system is this process most similar?

   A. Transduction
   B. *lac* operon
   C. *trp* operon
   D. Lysogenic cycle

9. Which of the following DNA sequences would have the highest melting temperature?

   A. CGCAACCATGCG
   B. CGCAATAATACA
   C. CGTAATAATACA
   D. CATAACAAATCA

10. Chemical analysis of some viral DNA has given the following results: 20 percent of the bases are adenines, 35 percent are thymines, 15 percent are cytosines, and 30 percent are guanines. What must be true of this DNA?

    A. It is in the process of being transcribed into mRNA.
    B. It is mitochondrial DNA.
    C. It is single stranded.
    D. It is in the S stage of the cell life cycle.

11. Herpes is a virus that enters the human body and remains dormant in the nervous system until it produces an outbreak, without any particular reason. Which of the following statements correctly describes herpes?

    A. While it remains dormant in the nervous system, the virus is in its lysogenic cycle.
    B. During an outbreak, the virus is in the lytic cycle.
    C. Herpes integrates itself into the DNA of the cell.
    D. All of the above.

12. What does a polycistronic mRNA do?

    A. It contains a large number of cytosine bases.
    B. It is translated to a protein that contains many cysteine amino acids.
    C. It codes for more than one polypeptide.
    D. It is translated to a protein involved in polycystic fibrosis.

13. Resistance to antibiotics is a well-recognized medical problem. What mechanisms account for a bacterium's ability to increase its genetic variability and thus adapt itself to different antibiotics?

    A. Binary fission
    B. Conjugation
    C. Transduction
    D. Both (B) and (C)

Small Group Questions

1. Many point mutations do not have an effect on the gene product. What are two possible explanations for this observation?

2. Why does DNA molecule with a high G-C content have a higher boiling point?

3. Why might a virus prefer to enter a lysogenic versus a lytic cycle?

Explanations to Practice Questions

1. B

If 20 percent of the bases are cytosines, 20 percent of the bases must also be guanines because they base-pair. The remaining 60 percent $(100 - 20 - 20 = 60)$ of bases are adenines and thymines. Again, because of complementary base pairing, 30 percent must be adenines and 30 percent thymines. (B) is the correct answer.

2. B

Nucleotides bond together to form polynucleotides. The 3′ hydroxyl group of one nucleotide's sugar joins the 5′ hydroxyl group of the adjacent nucleotide's sugar by a phosphodiester bond. (B) is therefore the correct answer.

3. D

Peptidyl transferase is an enzyme that catalyzes the formation of a peptide bond between the amino acid attached to the tRNA in the A site and the one attached to the tRNA in the P site. (D) is therefore the correct answer.

4. D

All three stages of protein synthesis (initiation, elongation, and termination) require a large amount of energy, making (D) the correct answer.

5. A

Topoisomerases, such as DNA gyrase, are involved in DNA replication. DNA gyrase is a type of topoisomerase that enhances the action of helicase enzymes by the introduction of negative supercoils into the DNA molecule. These negative supercoils facilitate DNA replication by keeping the strands separated and untangled.

6. B

To answer this question correctly, we must remember that mRNA will be antiparallel to DNA. Our answer should be 5′ to 3′ mRNA, with the 5′ end complementary to DNA's 3′ end. Thus, the desired mRNA strand will be 5′-GGAUGUCUCAAAGA-3′, which matches with (B).

7. D

Since we are looking for the false statement, we have to read every choice and eliminate those that are true. Let's quickly review the main differences between DNA and RNA. DNA is double stranded, with a deoxyribose sugar and the nitrogenous bases A, T, C, and G. RNA, on the other hand, is usually single stranded, with a ribose sugar and the bases A, U, C, and G. (A), (B), and (C) all state correct differences between DNA and RNA. (D) is incorrect because both DNA replication and RNA synthesis proceed in a 5′ to 3′ direction. (D) is therefore the correct answer.

8. C

The question stem is basically telling us that the end product of an enzyme-catalyzed reaction binds to a repressor, which in turn binds to the operator to prevent further transcription of the enzyme. This is a repressible system of gene regulation similar to *trp* operon, in which transcription is the norm as long as there is no corepressor present. The corepressor (in this case, chymotrypsin) binds to the repressor, forming a complex that binds to the operator and prevents transcription. (C) is therefore the correct answer.

9. A

The melting temperature of DNA is the temperature at which a DNA double helix separates into two single strands. To do this, the hydrogen bonds linking the base pairs must be broken. Cytosine binds to guanine by three hydrogen bonds, whereas adenine binds to thymine with two hydrogen bonds. The amount of heat needed to disrupt the bonding is proportional to the number of bonds. Thus, the more C and G present in a DNA segment, the higher the melting point. Therefore, (A) has the highest melting temperature, and (D) has the lowest. (A) is therefore the correct answer.

10. C

The main conclusion we can draw from the information given in the question stem is that the percentages of C and G are not equal and the percentages of A and T are also not equal. The only explanation for this is that the DNA is single stranded, as (C) indicates.

11. D

Viruses can exist in either the lytic or lysogenic cycle; they may even switch between them throughout their lifetime. During the lytic cycle, the virus's DNA takes control of the host cell's genetic machinery, manufacturing numerous progeny. In the end, the host cell bursts (lyses) and releases new virions, each capable of infecting other cells. In the lysogenic cycle, viral DNA is integrated into the host cell's genome, where it can remain dormant for days or years. Either spontaneously or as a result of environmental circumstances, the provirus can re-emerge and enter a lytic cycle. Thus, all of the answer choices correctly describe the herpes virus, making (D) the correct answer.

12. C

The term *polycistronic* refers to prokaryotic mRNA and its ability to code for more than one polypeptide (usually a group of related proteins). (C) is therefore the correct answer.

13. D

Bacterial cells reproduce by binary fission, an asexual process in which the progeny is identical to the parent. However, several mechanisms exist to allow for genetic variance within a population: transformation, conjugation, and transduction. Transformation is the process by which a foreign chromosome fragment is incorporated into the bacterial chromosome via recombination, creating new inheritable genetic combinations. Conjugation can be described as a sexual mating in bacteria; it is the transfer of genetic material between two bacteria that are temporarily joined. Transduction occurs when fragments of the bacterial chromosome accidentally become packaged into viral progeny produced during a viral infection. (D) is therefore the correct answer.

Evolution

We've done it! We have made it to the final chapter in our Biology Review Notes. Our final topic, evolution, is quite fitting. **Evolution** is the process of adaptation and change leading to genetic diversity and new life forms. It may be accomplished by **natural selection**, **mutation**, **genetic drift**, and **genetic shift**. Certainly over the course of reading these few hundred pages, you have evolved as a critical thinker and test taker. You have become an expert in the MCAT Biological Sciences and have emerged a new species of test taker who is meaner, leaner, and all the more ready to go out and earn a 15 on the Biological Sciences section of the MCAT. Before you can do that, though, you need to finish this chapter! It will cover different hypotheses that have been suggested to explain evolution, as well as empirical observations to support them. Evolution is a theory; it is only as good as the evidence behind it. Let's examine that evidence.

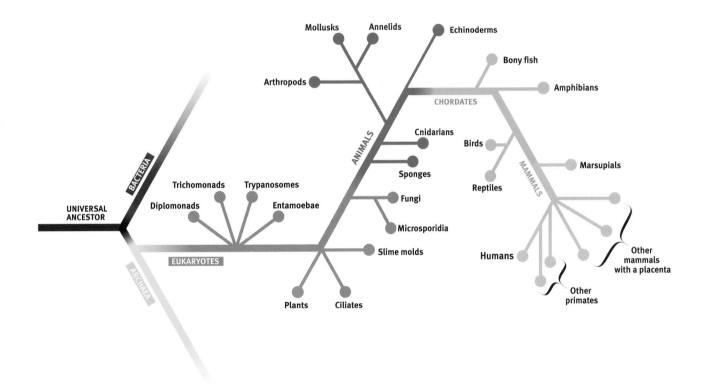

Figure 16.1

Theories of Evolution ★★★★★☆

The development of evolutionary thought has a relatively short history; the first theories suggesting that new species may arise from older ones were proposed in the 19th century. Significant "evolution" of these evolutionary theories has occurred since then. We will examine four of the major contributions to the field.

LAMARCK'S INHERITANCE OF ACQUIRED CHARACTERISTICS THEORY

One of the earliest (and eventually disproven) theories of evolution was that of Jean Baptiste Lamarck. He proposed that the concept of **use and disuse** was behind the generation of newer species from older ones. Organs that were used extensively would develop, whereas those that were not used would atrophy. This would suggest, for example, that the diminutive size of the human appendix is due to its relative disuse by our evolutionary forebears. These changes were termed **acquired characteristics** by Lamarck and were proposed to underlie the emergence of new, more complex species. Lamarck is best remembered for having the first organized approach to evolution. We now know that his theory was incorrect because traits are inherited, not acquired. This makes for an interesting concept in MCAT terms, as we must recognize that Lamarck's ideas, although testable, are spurious.

DARWIN'S NATURAL SELECTION THEORY

Darwin published *On the Origin of Species*, his masterwork, in 1859. In it, he detailed a mechanism for evolution that had several main tenets.

1. Organisms produce offspring, few of which survive to reproductive maturity.
2. Chance variations within individuals in a population may be **inheritable**. If these variations give an organism a slight survival advantage, they are termed **favorable**.
3. Individuals with a greater preponderance of these favorable variations are more likely to survive to reproductive age and produce offspring; the overall result will be an increase in these traits in future generations. This process is known as **natural selection**. Over long periods of time, aggregations of these favorable traits will result in the separation of organisms into distinct species. **Fitness** is defined as the reproductive success of an individual. Reproductive success is directly related to the relative genetic contribution of an individual to the next generation.

Darwin's theory was ultimately proven to be correct in many ways, though not completely. Carrying our appendix example forward, Darwin would suggest that having a small appendix is somehow favorable, leading to the current anatomical state of affairs. The elucidation of the larger field of genetics in the 20th century led to refinements and the currently accepted theory known as **neo-Darwinism** or the **modern synthesis**.

NEODARWINISM (THE MODERN SYNTHESIS)

Once scientists proved that genes ultimately changed due to mutation or recombination (Chapter 14), Darwin's theory was updated to the current form. When mutation or recombination results in a change that is favorable to the organism's survival, that change is more likely to pass on to the next generation; the opposite is also true. This

Key Concept

If we see any hint of the buzz phrases *use and disuse* or *inheritance of acquired characteristics* on Test Day, think Lamarck. And don't forget—Lamarck was wrong!

Key Concept

Evolution is not equivalent to natural selection. The MCAT likes to test your ability to understand that natural selection is simply a *mechanism* for evolution. Natural selection is equivalent to *survival of the fittest*.

Key Concept

Natural selection:

- Chance variations occur as a result of mutation and recombination.
- If the variation is "selected for" by the environment, that individual will be more "fit" and more likely to survive to reproductive age.
- Survival of the fittest leads to an increase of those favorable genes in the gene pool.

process is termed **differential reproduction**. After time, those traits passed on by the more successful organisms will become pervasive in the **gene pool**. The gene pool is the sum total of all genes from all individuals in the population at a given time. Because it is the gene pool that changes over time, we must be careful to say that populations, not individuals or species, evolve.

PUNCTUATED EQUILIBRIUM

One final theory to consider was proposed as a result of research into the fossil record. Upon examination, it was discovered that little evolution within a lineage of related forms would occur for long periods of time, followed by a massive burst. Niles Eldredge and Stephen Jay Gould proposed the theory of punctuated equilibrium to explain this in 1972. In contrast to Darwin's theory, punctuated equilibrium suggests that changes in species occur in rapid bursts rather than evenly over time. An example with which we might be familiar is that of the dinosaurs. When examining rock layers, we find many dinosaur fossils are present until the Cretaceous-Tertiary Boundary, about 65 million years ago. After this, there are none, but there is a relative flourishing of mammalian species. Dinosaurs did not disappear gradually from the face of the earth; rather, there was a massive catastrophic event that fundamentally altered the course of their evolution.

> **MCAT Expertise**
>
> Keep in mind that evolution is a theory—not a fact. The kinds of passages that are likely to include evolution are persuasive argument types. Be sure to think about how the passage information we are given on Test Day would fit within a given mechanism or concept (e.g., punctuated equilibrium).

Evidence of Evolution ★★★☆☆☆

As our sidebar pointed out, evolution is a theory that explains the origins of species. The theory of evolution functions in the same way that the theory of gravity functions to explain the behavior of mass: a scientific hypothesis supported by evidence and observation. The evidence that underlies it comes from a wide variety of scientific disciplines, including **paleontology**, **biogeography**, **comparative anatomy**, **comparative embryology**, and **molecular biology**.

PALEONTOLOGY

You may remember paleontology from when you learned about dinosaurs in middle school. Certainly, it is a wider field than that, encompassing the study of the complete fossil record. Using radioactive dating that employs some of the same principles we saw with autoradiography in Chapter 1, scientists are able to determine a fossil's age. By relating the ages of different fossils to their anatomies and relative abundances, paleontologists can determine the chronological succession of species in the fossil record.

BIOGEOGRAPHY

Evolution is an interesting phenomenon because it does not occur equally in all places around the globe. Darwin made many of his observations in the Galapagos Islands, which contain a number of unique flora and fauna. On one island, he found that the species present were more similar to those on the mainland than the organisms found on the other islands. He hypothesized that these animals and plants must have migrated to the island and then evolved in isolation from one another, thereby leading to species **divergence**.

COMPARATIVE ANATOMY

By comparing similar structures between species, it is possible to determine the degree of evolutionary similarity between them. **Homologous structures** are similar in structure and share a common evolutionary origin, even if they don't have a similar appearance, shape, or form. If we were to look at a bat, we initially might think that its wings are different from our arms. However, both are forearm structures that are common among mammals. So, too, are whales' flippers, which evolved from the homologous structural precursor in the common ancestor of mammals.

Analogous structures serve a common purpose but evolved separately in each species. Whereas we know that most birds and insects are capable of flight, their wings are analogous, not homologous. The species in each group that was capable of flight benefited (by way of natural selection) from this ability and developed unique mechanisms to achieve flight over time. Bird wings and bee wings serve a similar purpose but are not related in origin through evolutionary development from a common ancestor.

Finally, **vestigial structures** may be present in organisms. These are remnants of organs that have lost their ancestral function. Humans have a coccyx, commonly referred to as the tailbone. Animals with tails use them for balance. Humans walk upright, and the structure has been lost. The appendix (Figure 16.2) is sometimes debated but is often considered vestigial because its presence is not necessary for life. When inflamed, it is removed in a routine procedure known as an appendectomy.

Figure 16.2

COMPARATIVE EMBRYOLOGY

We used model organisms such as sea urchins, in Chapter 5, to understand human embryology. We were really doing comparative embryology at that point. By analyzing similarities between the embryos of different species, we can get a greater insight into evolutionary patterns. For example, the coccyx that we mentioned in the last paragraph as vestigial is actually present as a tail for about four weeks during human embryogenesis. Another example would be gills, which are present in all chordates (a group that includes fish, birds, and humans) during embryogenesis.

MOLECULAR BIOLOGY

As we saw in Chapter 15, DNA is capable of undergoing changes by mutation. By comparing the DNA sequence between different species, scientists can predict the degree of similarity between two organisms. For example, the chimpanzee shares over 95 percent of its genome with humans, whereas the mouse shares only about 85 percent. As species become more taxonomically distant, the amount of shared genome will decrease. One way of indirectly comparing DNA sequences is by comparing protein structures. Figure 16.3 shows how differences in protein structure indicated when new species originated.

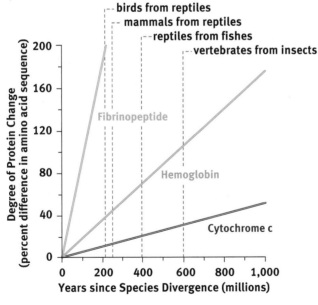

Figure 16.3

Genetic Basis of Evolution

If evolution works by selecting those variations that are more favorable, we must have a method to generate those differences at the level of the genome. This can be accomplished through mutations, random base changes in the DNA sequence, and recombination, novel genetic combinations that result from sexual reproduction and crossing over.

HARDY-WEINBERG EQUILIBRIUM

How often an allele appears in a population is known as the **gene frequency**. For example, in your college biology course, the number of people with alleles for type A blood, divided by the total number of blood type alleles in the class, would be the gene frequency for type A blood in this group of people. Evolution results from changes in these gene frequencies in reproducing populations over time. When the gene frequencies of a population are not changing, the gene pool is stable, and no evolution is occurring. Five criteria must be met for this to be true.

1. The population is very large.
2. There are no mutations that affect the gene pool.
3. Mating between individuals in the population is random.
4. There is no net migration of individuals into or out of the population.
5. The genes in the population are all equally successful at reproducing.

Provided all these conditions are met, we can state that the population is in **Hardy-Weinberg equilibrium** and use a pair of equations to predict the allelic and phenotypic frequencies.

Let us define a gene as having only two possible alleles, T and t. Further, we will say that p is the frequency of the dominant allele T and q is the frequency of the recessive allele t. There are only two possible choices at the gene locus, so $p + q = 1$, because the combined frequency of the alleles must total 100 percent. We can square both sides of the equation to get $(p + q)^2 = 1^2$. Expanding the binomial on the left, we derive a second equation:

$$p^2 + 2pq + q^2 = 1$$

Where p^2 = frequency of TT (dominant homozygotes)

$2pq$ = frequency of Tt (heterozygotes)

q^2 = frequency of tt (recessive homozygotes)

We should be aware that each equation provides us with different information. The first tells us about the frequency of *alleles* in the population, whereas the second provides information about the frequency of a *phenotype* in the population. Both are useful pieces of information. We should also be aware that there will always be two times as many alleles in the population as there are individuals; this is because each person has two alleles. For example, if we have 100 people in the sample, there would be 200 alleles.

These equations can be used to show that if microevolution is not occurring in a population (guaranteed by the previous conditions), the gene frequencies will remain constant from generation to generation. We will show this in the example below.

Let's say that we have a population in which the frequency for the gene for tallness, T, is 0.80. This means that q is 0.20 by subtraction. Setting up our F_1 cross below for two heterozygotes, we can see the results of such a mating.

	$p = 0.80$	$q = 0.20$
$p = 0.80$	$p^2 = 0.64$ TT = 64%	$pq = 0.16$ Tt = 16%
$q = 0.20$	$pq = 0.16$ Tt = 16%	$q^2 = 0.04$ tt = 4%

We see that we get 64 percent homozygous tall, 32 percent heterozygous tall, and 4 percent homozygous short. These are the phenotypic frequencies. To calculate the gene frequencies, we need to look at the next table.

> 64% TT = 64% T allele + 0% t allele
> 32% Tt = 16% T allele + 16% t allele
> 4% tt = 0% T allele + 4% t allele
> ———————————————————
> Gene frequencies = 80% T allele + 20% t allele

Notice that the gene frequencies are unchanged compared to the parent generation. T is still 0.80 and t is still 0.20. Species in Hardy-Weinberg equilibrium will exhibit this property.

MICROEVOLUTION

In all populations, eventually one or more of the tenets will be violated. After all, mutations in the human genome are introduced about once every 10 million base pairs during DNA replication. This alone would be enough to upset Hardy-Weinberg equilibrium, which is more a theoretical model than an assessment of real-world situations. There are five agents of microevolutionary change that we need to define briefly.

Key Concept

Hardy-Weinberg equations allow you to find two pieces of information: first, the relative frequency of genes in a population and, second, the frequency of a given phenotype in the population. Be sure to remember on Test Day that there will be twice as many genes as individuals in a population—because each individual has two autosomal copies of each gene.

Natural Selection

Genotypes with favorable variations are selected through natural selection, and the frequency of favorable genes increases within the gene pool. If a bird has a mutation that causes its wings to be more efficient, it will have more energy to contribute instead to reproduction. Thus, it will produce more offspring, and this trait will be selected for.

Mutation

Gene mutations change allele frequencies in a population, shifting gene equilibria.

Assortive Mating

If mates are not randomly chosen but, rather, selected according to criteria such as phenotype and proximity, the relative genotype ratios will be affected and will depart from the predictions of the Hardy-Weinberg equilibrium. On the average, allele frequencies in the gene pool remain unchanged. An example of this can be seen with Tay-Sachs disease, which is a recessive lysosomal storage disorder. The frequency of carriers in the general population is 1 in 300, meaning a random mating would only result in a 1 in 360,000 chance of having a child afflicted with the disease ($1/300 \times 1/300 \times \frac{1}{4}$). Remember that we have to multiply by $\frac{1}{4}$ because two heterozygotes only have a 1 in 4 chance of having an affected child. In the Ashkenazi Jewish population, the carrier rate is much higher, 1 in 30. If these individuals select mating partners within their ethnic group, they have a 1 in 3,600 chance of having an affected child. The chances are 100-fold greater owing to assortive mating.

Genetic Drift

Genetic drift refers to changes in the composition of the gene pool due to chance. Genetic drift tends to be more pronounced in small populations, where it is sometimes called the founder effect. This can happen when a small population of a species finds itself in reproductive isolation from other populations as a result of natural barriers or catastrophic events.

Gene Flow

Migration of individuals between populations will result in a loss or gain of genes and, thus, change the composition of a population's gene pool.

Modes of Natural Selection ★★★☆☆

Whereas the previous section discussed several mechanisms for microevolution, which deals with changes in a population over a short period of time (tens to hundreds of years), natural selection is the only method capable of generating stable evolutionary changes over long periods of time (thousands to millions of years).

It may occur as **stabilizing selection**, **directional selection**, or **disruptive selection** (see Figure 16.4).

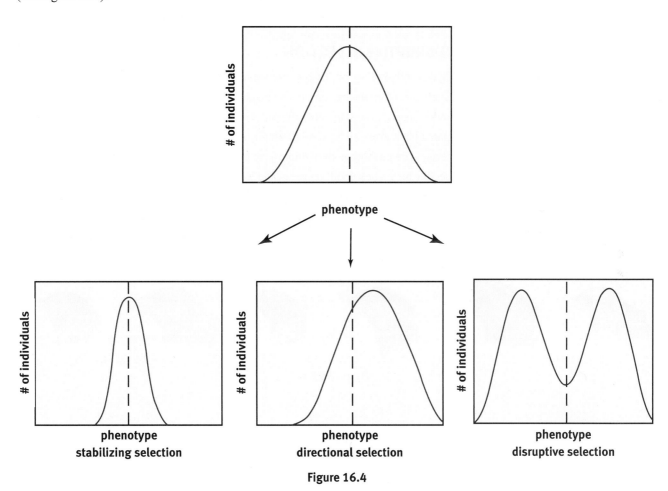

Figure 16.4

STABILIZING SELECTION

Stabilizing selections work to keep phenotypes within a specific range by eliminating extremes. For instance, human birth weight is maintained within a narrow band by stabilizing selection. Fetuses that weigh too little may not be healthy enough to survive, and fetuses that weigh too much can experience trauma during delivery through the relatively narrow birth canal. In addition, the larger the fetus, the more resources it requires from the mother. For all of these reasons, it is advantageous to keep birth weights within a narrow range.

DIRECTIONAL SELECTION

Adaptive pressure leads to the emergence and dominance of an initially extreme phenotype. If we have a heterogeneous plate of bacteria, very few may have resistance to antibiotics. If we then treat the plate with ampicillin (a type of antibiotic), only those colonies that exhibit resistance will survive. A new standard phenotype

MCAT Expertise

Natural selection is a theory. Each of these forms of selection would be pressured for by a different environment. On the MCAT, remember to consider why a particular situation might engender stabilizing selection versus disruptive selection.

emerges as a result of differential survivorship. Natural selection is the history of differential survivorship over time. The emergence of mosquitoes resistant to DDT, a type of pesticide, is attributed to directional selection.

DISRUPTIVE SELECTION

In disruptive selection, both extreme phenotypes are selected over the norm. When Darwin studied finches on the Galapagos islands, he noted that although there were many species, they arguably all had a common ancestor. However, when he compared beak sizes, they were all either large or small. No animals exhibited the intermediate phenotype of medium-size beaks. Darwin hypothesized that the sizes of seeds (the finches' food) on the island led to this effect. Seeds were either quite large or fairly small, requiring a large or small beak, respectively. Thus, if the original ancestor had a medium-size beak, over time, the animals with slightly larger or smaller beaks would be selected for.

Figure 16.5

Altruistic Behavior ★★★☆☆

Darwin's theory is not without exceptions. It has been observed in several species, including many insect species such as bees and ants, that certain individuals will endure sacrifices to benefit others. These social insects have large castes of workers that are sterile but work for the benefit of the whole colony, including the sexually reproducing insects. Such selfless behavior is termed **altruistic**.

Some attempted to explain this phenomenon by proposing group selection, suggesting that there was a gene that led certain individuals within the population not to reproduce. Can we see the flaw in this theory? How would the gene that coded for decreased or no reproduction be passed on? It couldn't; if its whole purpose was to prevent reproduction, it would be exterminated from the gene pool immediately, because it would have no way to be passed to future generations.

A related theory to group selection is **kin selection**, which suggests that organisms will behave altruistically if they are closely related to successfully reproducing organisms. This would explain our social insect example above, because the workers are related to the fertile queen of the colony. This theory is consistent with neo-Darwinism. **Inclusive fitness** refers to the number of alleles that an individual passes on to the next generation, even if only indirectly through altruistic behavior.

Speciation

Speciation is defined as the emergence of new species, a group of individuals who can interbreed freely with each other but not with members of other species. If we took two groups of the same species and separated them geographically for a long period of time, different evolutionary pressures would lead to different adaptive selections. If enough time passed, the changes would be sufficient to lead to **reproductive isolation**. We would now consider the two groups separate species. Reproductive isolation may occur either prezygotically or postzygotically. Prezygotic mechanisms prevent formation of the zygote completely; postzygotic mechanisms allow for gamete fusion but yield either inviable or sterile offspring. Mules are an example of postzygotic reproductive isolation. Although a horse and donkey can produce a viable mule, the mule will be sterile and thus unable to contribute to a self-perpetuating mule lineage.

PREZYGOTIC ISOLATING MECHANISMS

Temporal Isolation
Two species may breed during different seasons or times of the day, thus preventing interbreeding.

Ecological Isolation
Two species living in the same territory but in different habitats. They rarely meet and, therefore, rarely mate.

Behavioral Isolation
Members of two species are not sexually attracted to each other because of differences in such things as pheromones (chemical signals) and courtship displays.

Reproductive Isolation
The genitalia of two species are incompatible, so interbreeding cannot occur.

Gametic Isolation
Intercourse can occur, but fertilization cannot.

POSTZYGOTIC ISOLATING MECHANISMS

Hybrid Inviability
Genetic incompatibilities between two species abort hybrid zygote development, even if fertilization does occur.

Hybrid Sterility

Hybrid offspring are sterile and thus incapable of producing functional gametes.

Hybrid Breakdown

First-generation hybrids are viable and fertile, but second-generation hybrid offspring are inviable and/or infertile. The potential for hybrid breakdown exists whenever closely related but reproductively isolated species are introduced to each other, and it occurs more in plants than in animals.

Adaptive Radiation

When a single ancestral species gives rise to a number of different species, **adaptive radiation** has occurred. Each species diverges to the point that it is able to occupy a unique ecological **niche**. Going back to the finches we mentioned previously, they exhibit adaptive radiation because the single ancestor led to 13 distinct species, each of which has a specific environmental role that is not filled by another species. What would be the benefit of such rapid evolution? It decreases competition for limited resources.

Patterns of Evolution

When we look at similarities between two species, we must be careful to determine whether those similarities are due to sharing a common ancestor or sharing a common environment with the same evolutionary pressures. When analyzing species this way, three patterns of evolution emerge: **convergent evolution**, **divergent evolution**, and **parallel evolution** (see Figure 16.6).

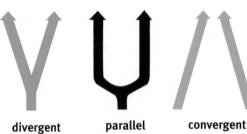

Figure 16.6

CONVERGENT EVOLUTION

Convergent evolution refers to the independent development of similar characteristics in two or more lineages not sharing a recent common ancestor. For example, fish and dolphins have come to resemble one another physically, although they belong to different classes of vertebrates. They evolved certain similar features in adapting to the conditions of aquatic life.

DIVERGENT EVOLUTION

Divergent evolution refers to the independent development of dissimilar characteristics in two or more lineages sharing common ancestry. For example, seals and cats are both mammals belonging to the order Carnivora, yet they differ markedly in general appearance. These two species live in very different environments and adapted to different selection pressures while evolving.

PARALLEL EVOLUTION

Parallel evolution refers to the process whereby related species evolve in similar ways for a long period of time in response to analogous environmental selection pressures.

Origin of Life ★★★★☆☆

Although we have discussed some very simple organisms, we have not suggested how life began. The earliest evidence of life appears in stromatolites, the trace evidence of photosynthetic bacteria, which have been dated to about 3.5 billion years ago. These organisms were primitive prokaryotes. In the 1920s, Oparin and Haldane proposed a mechanism for the origin of life, which was tested in the 1950s by Stanley Miller.

Oparin and Haldane suggested that the conditions of early earth favored the creation of organic molecules, such as simple amino acids. The very early planet contained high amounts of carbon, hydrogen, and nitrogen along with lesser amounts of oxygen. The mixture of these atoms in the seas has been termed **primordial soup**. It was hypothesized that with massive energy input from many sources, including the sun, lightning, radioactive decay, and volcanic activity, bonds formed between these atoms. Miller carried out an experiment in which he mixed these gases and exposed them to an electrical discharge. At the end of a week, many simple amino acids were found in the reaction apparatus. Further experimentation led to creation of all 20 amino acids, lipids, and all 5 of the nitrogenous bases of DNA and RNA (see Figure 16.7).

FORMATION OF ORGANIC MOLECULES

The Original Origin-of-Life Experiment

In the early 1950s, Stanley L. Miller, working in the laboratory of Harold C. Urey at the University of Chicago, did the first experiment designed to clarify the chemical reactions that occurred on the primitive earth (*left*). In the flask at the bottom, he created an "ocean" of water, which he heated, forcing water vapor to circulate (*arrows*) through the apparatus. The flask at the top contained an "atmosphere" consisting of methane (CH_4), ammonia (NH_3), hydrogen (H_2), and the circulating water vapor. Next he exposed the gases to a continuous electrical discharge ("lightning"), causing the gases to interact. Water-soluble products of those reactions then passed through a condenser and dissolved in the mock ocean. The experiment yielded many amino acids and enabled Miller to explain how they had formed. For instance, glycine appeared after reactions in the atmosphere produced simple compounds—formaldehyde and hydrogen cyanide—that participated in the set of reactions shown below. Years after this experiment, a meteorite that struck near Murchison, Australia, was shown to contain a number of the same amino acids that Miller had identified (*table*) and in roughly the same relative amounts (*dots*); those found in proteins are highlighted in blue. Such coincidences lent credence to the idea that Miller's protocol approximated the chemistry of the prebiotic earth. However, more recent findings have cast some doubt on that conclusion.

HOW GLYCINE FORMED

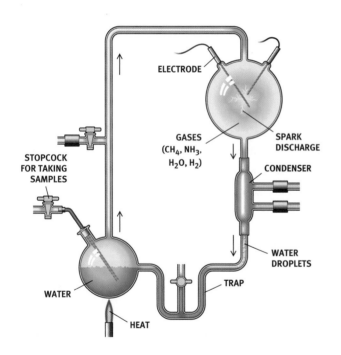

AMINO ACID	MURCHISON METEORITE	DISCHARGE EXPERIMENT
GLYCINE	• • • •	• • • •
ALANINE	• • • •	• • • •
α-AMINO-*N*-BUTYRIC ACID	• • •	• • • •
α-AMINOISOBUTYRIC ACID	• • • •	• •
VALINE	• • •	• •
NORVALINE	• • •	• • •
ISOVALINE	• •	• •
PROLINE	• • •	•
PIPECOLIC ACID	•	‹
ASPARTIC ACID	• • •	• • •
GLUTAMIC ACID	• • •	• •
β-ALANINE	• •	• •
β-AMINO-*N*-BUTYRIC ACID	•	•
β-AMINOISOBUTYRIC ACID	•	•
γ-AMINOBUTYRIC ACID	•	• •
SARCOSINE	• •	• • •
N-ETHYLGLYCINE	• •	• • •
N-METHYLALANINE	• •	• •

Figure 16.7

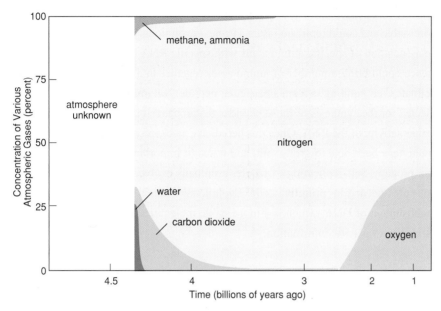

ATMOSPHERIC COMPOSITION, shown by the relative concentration of various gases, has been greatly influenced by life on the earth. The early atmosphere had fairly high concentrations of water and carbon dioxide and, some experts believe, methane, ammonia, and nitrogen. After the emergence of living organisms, the oxygen that is so vital to our survival became more plentiful. Today carbon dioxide, methane, and water exist only in trace amounts in the atmosphere.

Figure 16.8

FORMATION OF PROTOBIONTS

In laboratory experiments, abiotically produced polymers in an aqueous solution were found to assemble spontaneously into tiny proteinaceous droplets called microspheres. These microspheres had a selectively permeable membrane that separated them from their surroundings and maintained an independent internal environment. Colloidal droplets called coacervates had been formed in Oparin's laboratory from a solution of polypeptides, nucleic acids, and polysaccharides. They are capable of carrying out enzymatic activity within their membrane if enzymes and substrate are present. Although microspheres and coacervates have some properties characteristic of life, they are not living cells. The collection of organic polymers that are believed to have been the primitive ancestors of living cells are called *protobionts*.

FORMATION OF GENETIC MATERIAL

These hypothetical protobionts had the ability to grow in size and divide but did not have a way of transmitting information to the next generation. The evolution of genetic material is difficult to map out, but it is believed that short strands of RNA were the first molecules capable of self-replication and of storing and transmitting information from one generation to the next. Experiments in the laboratory have shown that free bases can align with their complementary bases on a short RNA sequence and bind together, creating a new short RNA chain. Natural selection probably favored RNA sequences whose three-dimensional conformations were more stable and could replicate faster. The next evolutionary step may have involved the association of specific amino acids with specific RNA bases. Thus, an RNA sequence could bring a number of amino acids together in a particular sequence and facilitate their bonding to form a particular peptide. Natural selection may also have selected for the synthesis of those peptides that enhanced the replication and/or the further activity of the RNA. Once this hereditary mechanism developed, protobionts would have been able to grow, split, and transmit important genetic information to their progeny. Self-replicating molecules eventually evolved to code for many of the molecules needed by primitive cells. Evolutionary trends then led to the eventual establishment of DNA, which is a more stable molecule than RNA, as the primary warehouse of genetic information.

Conclusion

Our final chapter in the review of biology for the MCAT has been a journey through the relatively short history of the development of the theory of evolution. We have reviewed one of the earliest theories, Lamarck's "use and disuse"; Darwin's theory of natural selection; and the modern neo-Darwinian theory founded on the understanding of molecular genetics. We noted the vast body of evidence supporting evolution, including findings in paleontology, biogeography, comparative anatomy, comparative embryology, and molecular biology. The genetic basis of evolution explains both macro- and microevolutionary development, which can result in speciation and subspeciation, respectively. Within the realm of microevolution, the MCAT will expect you to be able to analyze allelic frequencies in genetically stable populations using the Hardy-Weinberg equations. We reviewed the key concepts of natural selection and patterns of macroevolution. Finally, we discussed an important theory on the origin of life and the development of organic molecules that became the basis for RNA and DNA.

Although our time together has been brief, we would like to congratulate you on a job well done completing these review notes. The MCAT is an exam that requires you to be an expert on a great deal of content. It is our sincere hope that these pages have illuminated you. As you continue your studies approaching Test Day, return to these chapters when you are feeling a little unsure of a topic; let them be your constant guide to the highest-yield material for the MCAT. We hope that we have accomplished our goal of reviewing the biology content clearly and concisely. Furthermore, we hope that we have been able to assure you of your ability to perform well on the MCAT. Your success on the exam is based on the hard work you invest now. You can be sure that your time and effort will pay off in points on Test Day. Finally, we hope that we have been able to help you enjoy the learning process. We know and understand that this is not an easy test for which to prepare. We know that it is not always fun. We know that it can be frustrating, stressful, and anxiety provoking. But we also know that the art and science of medicine is your passion. Biology—and physics and chemistry—is the foundation upon which your future medical practice is built. What could be more fun and more rewarding than the opportunity to prove yourself intellectually capable of success in your passionate pursuit of excellence in the medical sciences? We wish you all the best on your MCAT and in your future career as a physician!

CONCEPTS TO REMEMBER

- ☐ Evolution is the process of adaptation and change leading to genetic diversity and new life forms.

- ☐ Lamarck wrongly suggested that evolution occurred by increased or decreased use of a structure.

- ☐ Darwin's theory of natural selection in its modern synthesis is capable of explaining much of the evolutionary record. Natural selection states that those organisms with more favorable traits will have greater reproductive success, thereby leading to those traits being expressed to a greater degree in the next generation.

- ☐ Punctuated equilibrium is an alternative theory of evolution stating that evolution occurs in rapid bursts rather than gradually over time.

- ☐ Hardy-Weinberg equilibrium can be used to predict phenotypic and allelic frequencies in a nonevolving population.

- ☐ Whereas microevolution may occur by many mechanisms, long-term evolutionary changes may be carried out only by natural selection. Natural selection may be classified as stabilizing, directional, or disruptive selection based on the new species deviation from the original normative standard.

- ☐ Altruistic behavior benefits one individual at the direct reproductive expense of another.

- ☐ Evolution may be described as convergent, divergent, or parallel.

- ☐ Experimental evidence from Stanley Miller demonstrates that the primordial environment of the earth was sufficient to create the organic molecules necessary for life.

- ☐ RNA is thought to be the first molecule capable of passing genetic information on to the next generation.

Practice Questions

1. Which of the following statements is INCORRECT regarding inheritance of traits?

   A. A mutation due to excessive amounts of ultraviolet light occurs in an unfertilized egg; this will affect the child who is born from that egg.
   B. The muscular strength gained by a weight lifter during his lifetime is inherited by his children.
   C. A green-feathered bird that survived all of the predators in the forest will pass on the green feather genes to its offspring.
   D. A flower with tasty nectar that is eaten by a butterfly is more likely to pass on its delicious genes through the pollen spread by the butterfly than one that is not tasty.

2. Which of the following statements is FALSE based on Darwin's theory of evolution?

   A. Natural selection is the driving force of evolution.
   B. Favorable genetic variations become more and more common in individuals throughout their lives.
   C. Natural selection drives organisms to live in groups and ultimately become distinct species.
   D. Fitness is measured in terms of reproductive success.

3. Which of the following is NOT a necessary condition for the Hardy-Weinberg equilibrium?

   A. Large population size
   B. No mutations
   C. Monogamous mating partners
   D. No net migration into or out of the population

4. As the climate got colder during the Ice Age, a particular species of mammal evolved a thicker layer of fur. This is an example of what kind of selection?

   A. Stabilizing selection
   B. Directional selection
   C. Disruptive selection
   D. Speciation

5. At what point are two populations descending from the same ancestral stock considered separate species?

   A. When they can no longer produce viable, fertile offspring
   B. When they look significantly different from each other
   C. When they can interbreed successfully and produce offspring
   D. When their habitats are separated by a significantly large distance so that they cannot meet

6. In a nonevolving population, there are two alleles, R and r, which code for the same trait. The frequency of R is 30 percent. What are the frequencies of all the possible genotypes?

   A. 49% RR, 42% Rr, 9% rr
   B. 30% RR, 21% Rr, 70% rr
   C. 0.09% RR, 0.42% Rr, 0.49% rr
   D. 9% RR, 42% Rr, 49% rr

7. As the ocean became saltier, whales and fish independently evolved mechanisms to maintain the concentration of salt in their bodies; this can be explained by

    A. divergent evolution.
    B. parallel evolution.
    C. convergent evolution.
    D. analogous evolution.

8. In a particular Hardy-Weinberg population, there are only two eye colors: brown and blue. Of the population, 36 percent has blue eyes, the recessive trait. What percentage of the population is heterozygous for brown eyes?

    A. 24%
    B. 48%
    C. 60%
    D. 64%

9. In a certain population, 64 percent of individuals are homozygous for curly hair (CC). The gene for curly hair is dominant to the gene for straight hair, c. What percentage of the population has curly hair?

    A. 4%
    B. 32%
    C. 64%
    D. 96%

10. Which of the following was NOT a belief of Darwin's?

    A. Evolution of species occurs gradually and evenly over time.
    B. There is a struggle for survival among organisms.
    C. Genetic mutation and recombination are the driving forces of evolution.
    D. Those individuals with fitter variants will survive and reproduce.

11. The proposed primordial soup was composed of organic precursor molecules formed by interactions between all the following gases EXCEPT

    A. oxygen and hydrogen.
    B. helium.
    C. nitrogen.
    D. carbon.

12. Microspheres can be characterized by all of the following statements EXCEPT

    A. they are composed of tiny, abiotically produced proteinaceous droplets.
    B. they are also known as colloidal droplets called coacervates.
    C. they have a selectively permeable membrane.
    D. they have an internal chemical environment distinct from that of their surroundings.

Small Group Questions

1. Why is it incorrect to regard evolution as progressive (i.e., proceeding from lowest or simplest to highest or most complex)?

2. Adaptive radiation results when an ancestral species gives rise to many descendants, which are adapted to different parts of the environment. How would scenarios for adaptive radiation differ if speciation occurred allopatrically (different ranges) versus sympatrically (overlapping ranges)?

3. Typically, r-selected species produce many offspring, each of which has a relatively low probability of surviving to adulthood. On the other hand, k-selected species invest more heavily in fewer offspring, each of which has a relatively high probability of surviving to adulthood. In the scientific literature, r-selected species are occasionally referred to as "opportunistic," whereas k-selected species are described as in "equilibrium." Using natural selction, explain the advantage of each.

4. Can Hardy-Weinberg equilibrium be achieved in nature? Why or why not?

Explanations to Practice Questions

1. B

To find the correct answer, we have to read each choice in part and eliminate the ones that fit with the modern-day theories of inheritance. Basically, any statement that will argue that acquired characteristics are passed on to the offspring will be incorrect. Based on this, we can tell right away that (B) is incorrect because the muscular strength is an acquired characteristic and thus cannot be transmitted to the offspring. Lamarck argued that a giraffe that stretches its neck to reach for high trees will produce offspring with longer necks, but modern evolutionary theories proved this argument to be incorrect. (B) therefore is the correct answer.

2. B

Darwin's theory of natural selection, in a nutshell, argues that chance variations in our genes occur thanks to mutation and recombination; further if the variation helps the individual survive to reproductive age and produce many offspring, the variation of the fit individual will be transmitted to the next generation. The survival of the fittest leads to an increase of those favorable genes in the gene pool. Basically, Darwin strongly believed that, as (A) states, natural selection is the driving force of evolution and that the fitness of an individual is measured in terms of reproductive success, as (D) states. Through natural selection, organisms become separated in groups, depending on how adapted they are to a particular environment, and these groups eventually separate to the point of becoming distinct species. Thus, based on Darwin's theory, (B) is the false statement. The theory of natural selection applies to a population of organisms, not to a particular individual. As such, favorable genetic variations become more and more common from generation to generation, not during the lifetime of an individual. In fact, the chance mutations

an individual organism accumulates over its life span are more likely to be harmful than helpful. (B) is therefore the correct answer.

3. C

The Hardy-Weinberg equilibrium exists in certain ideal conditions that, when satisfied, allow one to calculate the gene frequencies within a population. The Hardy-Weinberg equation can be applied only under these five conditions: (1) the population is very large; (2) there are no mutations that affect the gene pool; (3) mating between individuals in the population is random; (4) there is no net migration of individuals into or out of the population; (5) the genes in the population are all equally successful at reproduction. Thus, from the given choices, only (C) is false. Monogamy is not a necessary condition for the Hardy-Weinberg equilibrium to be applied, making (C) the correct answer.

4. B

The situation described in the question stem is an example of directional selection. In directional selection, the phenotypic norm of a particular species shifts toward an extreme to adapt to a selective pressure, such as an increasingly colder environment. Only those individuals with a thicker layer of fur were able to survive during the Ice Age, thus shifting the phenotypic norm. (B) is the correct answer.

5. A

Two populations are considered separate species when they can no longer interbreed and produce viable, fertile offspring. (A) is therefore the correct answer.

6. D

Let's use the information provided by the question stem to set up our equations.

We are told that the frequency of R equals 30%, and as such, $p = 0.30$. The frequency of the recessive gene $r = 100\% - 30\% = 70\%$; thus, $q = 0.70$. The frequency of the genotypes, according to the Hardy-Weinberg equilibrium, is $p^2 + 2pq + q^2 = 1$, where $p^2 = $ RR, $2pq = $ Rr, and $q^2 = $ rr. We can now calculate the frequencies of all the possible genotypes:

$$p^2 = (0.3)^2 = 0.09 = 9\% \text{ RR}$$

$$2pq = 2(0.3)(0.7) = 0.42 = 42\% \text{ Rr}$$

$$q^2 = (0.7)^2 = 0.49 = 49\% \text{ rr}$$

Choice (D) matches our results and is therefore the correct answer.

7. C

When two or more lineages not sharing a recent common ancestor independently developed similar characteristics, a convergent evolution is said to have taken place. Whales and fish do not share a recent common ancestor; whales are mammals, but fish are not. Since they independently developed a similar mechanism to maintain the concentration of salt in their bodies, convergent evolution must have occurred. (C) is therefore the correct answer.

8. B

Using the information given to use in the question stem, we can determine that the percentage of the population with blue eyes (genotype = bb) = 36% = q^2 = 0.36; therefore, $q = 0.6$. Since this is a Hardy-Weinberg population, we can assume that $p + q = 1$, so $p = 1 - 0.6 = 4$. The frequency of heterozygous brown eyes is therefore $2pq = 2(0.4)(0.6) = 0.48$. So 48% of the population is heterozygous for brown eyes, making (B) the correct answer.

9. D

We can assume that this is a Hardy-Weinberg population since we are not told otherwise. Let us denote P the frequency of the dominant allele (C) and q the frequency of the recessive allele (c). The CC frequency is 64%, which means that $p^2 = 0.64$, or $p = 0.80$. Since $p + q = 1$, $q = 1 - 0.80 = 0.20$. The problem asks for the percentage of the

population with curly hair; this includes both homozygous and heterozygotes (CC and Cc). The genotype frequencies can be found using the equation $p^2 + 2pq + q^2$.

$$CC = p^2 = (0.8)^2 = 0.64 = 64\% \text{ homozygous curly}$$

$$Cc = 2pq = 2(0.8)(0.2) = 0.32 = 32\% \text{ heterozygous curly}$$

$$Cc = q^2 = (0.20)^2 = 0.04 = 4\% \text{ straight hair}$$

Therefore, the percentage of the population with curly hair is $64\% + 32\% = 96\%$, making (D) the correct answer.

10. C

Darwin's main argument was that natural selection is the driving force of evolution. He argued that chance variations occur thanks to mutations and recombination. If the variation is selected for by the environment, that individual will be more fit and more likely to survive to reproductive age. Survival of the fittest leads to an increase of those favorable genes in the gene pool. Based on this, (C) is the correct answer, because it does not match Darwin's beliefs regarding evolution.

11. B

According to Oparin and Haldane, the conditions during the early years of earth's existence favored the abiotic synthesis of organic molecules. Carbon, hydrogen, nitrogen, and small amounts of oxygen present in the atmosphere and seas bonded together in various ways and accumulated, forming a primordial soup. Thus, out of the answer choices, the molecule that did not participate in the formation of the precursor molecules was helium, (B).

12. B

In laboratory experiments, abiotically produced polymers in an aqueous solution can spontaneously assemble into tiny proteinaceous droplets called microspheres. These microspheres have selectively permeable membranes and their internal chemical environment is distinct from that of their surroundings. Colloidal droplets are called coacervates. Thus, from the given choices, the one that does not describe microspheres is (B), the correct answer.

High-Yield Problem Solving Guide for Biology

High-Yield MCAT Review

This is a **High-Yield Questions section**. These questions tackle the most frequently tested topics found on the MCAT. For each type of problem, you will be provided with a stepwise technique for solving the question and key directional points on how to solve for the MCAT specifically.

At the end of each topic, you will find a "Takeaways" box, which gives a concise summary of the problem-solving approach, and a "Things to Watch Out For" box, which points out any caveats to the approach discussed above that usually lead to wrong answer choices. Finally, there is a "Similar Questions" box at the end so you can test your ability to apply the stepwise technique to analogous questions.

We're confident that this guide can help you achieve your goals of MCAT success and admission into medical school!

Good luck!

Key Concepts

Chapter 1

Hypertonic solution

Hypotonic solution

Sodium potassium pump

Osmosis

The sodium potassium pump is an ATPase that pumps 3 Na$^+$ out of the cell and 2 K$^+$ into the cell for each ATP hydrolyzed. Cells can use the pump to help maintain cell volume. What would most likely happen to the rate of ATP consumption if a cell were moved to a hypertonic environment?

1) Determine the relationship between two solutions to predict the flow of water.

A hypertonic environment means that the environment is more concentrated than the cell is. Note that you can similarly express this condition by stating that the cell is hypotonic to the environment. A hypotonic solution is one that is less concentrated than the solution to which it is being compared.

The cell is being moved into a hypertonic environment, which means that the environment is more concentrated with solutes than the interior of the cell. Thus, we can predict that water will flow out of the cell.

Takeaways

Questions that involve osmosis are usually combined with other biology topics (particularly kidney function) to create a multistep solution. The key is to have a solid understanding of what *hypertonic* and *hypotonic* mean and how the terms can be used interchangeably to describe the same state.

Things to Watch Out For

Some students presume that the scenario presented will eventually return to equilibrium and may actually predict that ATP consumption will decrease and then increase. However, the question stem does not speak of a return to equilibrium. Be wary of trying to read too much into the question.

2) Given the flow of water, determine how the biological function in the question will be affected.

Water will flow out of the cell, thus decreasing cell volume. To counter this effect, ATP consumption will decrease to maintain cell volume.

The sodium potassium pump moves in two potassium ions as it moves out three sodium ions. The net effect is to decrease cell solute concentration as the cell loses one ion per each pump. The pump is dependent upon ATP consumption; therefore, relative to its current rate of ATP consumption, an increase in consumption will decrease cell volume, whereas a decrease in consumption will increase cell volume.

Similar Questions

1) Antidiuretic hormone (ADH) directly increases the ability of the blood to reabsorb water from the nephron. If an individual's blood becomes hypotonic with respect to the filtrate, would ADH secretion increase or decrease?

2) The reabsorption of water from the filtrate increases as the concentration of the interstitial fluid increases. Using the terms *hypertonic* and *hypo-osmotic*, describe the relationship between the interstitial fluid and the filtrate as well as the relationship between the filtrate and the interstitial fluid.

3) Alcohol and caffeine block the activity of ADH, a hormone that increases the ability of the blood to reabsorb water from the filtrate. An individual drinks a large coffee in the morning, and when he goes to the restroom finds that his urine is nearly colorless. Was the urine produced hypotonic, isotonic, or hypertonic to the blood?

Fetal Circulation

Fetal lungs are supplied with only enough blood to nourish the lung tissue itself because fetal lungs do not function prior to birth. Obstruction of which fetal structure would cause an increase in blood supply to fetal lungs?

1) Identify the unique structures involved in fetal circulation.

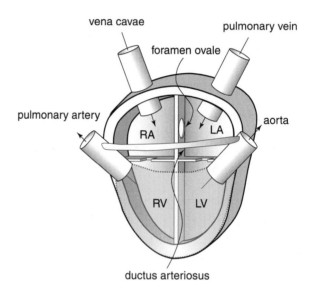

Fetal circulation differs from adult circulation in several important ways. The major difference is that in fetal circulation, blood is oxygenated in the placenta because, as the question states, fetal lungs are nonfunctional before birth. The fetal circulatory route contains three shunts that divert blood flow away from the developing fetal liver and lungs. The umbilical vein carries oxygenated blood from the placenta to the fetus. The blood bypasses the fetal liver by way of a shunt called the ductus venosus before converging with the inferior vena cava. The inferior and superior vena cavae return deoxygenated blood to the right atrium. Because the oxygenated blood from the umbilical vein mixes with the deoxygenated blood of the vena cavae, the blood entering the right atrium is only partially oxygenated. Most of this blood bypasses the pulmonary circulation and enters the left atrium directly from the right atrium by way of the foramen ovale, a shunt that diverts blood away from the right ventricle and pulmonary artery. The remaining blood in the right atrium empties into the right ventricle and is pumped to the lungs via the pulmonary artery. Most of this blood is shunted directly from the pulmonary artery to the aorta via the ductus arteriosus, diverting even more blood away from the fetal lungs.

2) Examine the normal flow of blood to fetal lungs.

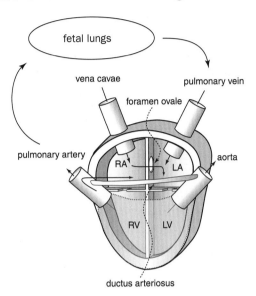

In the fetus, the pulmonary arteries carry oxygenated blood to the lungs, though this blood is by no means saturated with oxygen. The blood that is delivered to the lungs is further deoxygenated there because the blood unloads its oxygen to the fetal lungs, which need it for proper development. Remember, gas exchange does not occur in the fetal lungs—it occurs in the placenta. The deoxygenated blood then returns to the left atrium via pulmonary veins. Despite the fact that this blood mixes with the partially oxygenated blood that crossed over from the right atrium (via the foramen ovale) before being pumped into the systemic circulation by the left ventricle, the blood delivered via the aorta has an even lower partial pressure of oxygen than the blood that was delivered to the lungs. Deoxygenated blood is returned to the placenta via the umbilical arteries.

3) Determine which structure is most critical in bypassing fetal lungs.
The ductus arteriosus and foramen ovale shunt blood from the pulmonary arteries to the systemic circulation, bypassing the lungs. Obstruction of either structure would cause an increase in blood supply to the fetal lungs, because all of the blood pumped into the pulmonary arteries by the right ventricle would then have to flow through the lungs—there would be no place else for it to go.

Remember: There are three important shunts that divert blood flow in the fetus: the ductus venosus, the foramen ovale, and the ductus arteriosus.

Key Concepts

Chapter 7

Digestive enzymes

Pancreatic enzymes

Pancreas

Duodenum

Gastric acid

Takeaways

Having a good understanding of the normal digestive system provides a strong basis for evaluating the effects of abnormalities that may occur within the system.

Things to Watch Out For

An acidic duodenal pH will affect the functioning ability of all of the pancreatic enzymes, but protein absorption can still occur because proteins are digested in the stomach. Carbohydrate digestion does not rely on pancreatic secretions. Absorption can still occur because carbohydrates begin digestion in the mouth and continue to be broken down by maltase and sucrase in the intestinal brush border.

Digestive System

In the gastric phase of digestion, food in the stomach, particularly the presence of amino acids and peptides, causes G cells to secrete gastrin, which in turn stimulates parietal cells. Gastrin secretion is normally inhibited once acidic chyme, with a pH less than 3, reaches the duodenum. What physiological condition would be the result of a gastrin-secreting tumor?

1) Determine the role of gastrin in the stomach.

According to the question stem, gastrin stimulates parietal cells when food is present in the stomach. Parietal cells secrete HCl, and therefore gastrin is a physiological agonist of HCl secretion. Once the chyme reaches a certain acidity (pH < 3) and moves into the small intestine, gastrin secretion is inhibited and therefore HCl secretion is decreased.

2) Determine the role of HCl in the stomach.

In the stomach, HCl is necessary for the proper function of pepsin because the proper pH for pepsin is between 1 and 3.

3) Examine what occurs when acidic chyme reaches the small intestine.

Once the chyme moves into the small intestine, the pH needs to be increased to reach the optimal pH (≈ 8) for pancreatic proteases and lipases. Therefore, gastrin release is inhibited, and the pancreas is stimulated to secrete bicarbonate to neutralize the acid. The pancreas also releases hydrolytic enzymes, such as amylase, trypsinogen, chymotrypsinogen, and pancreatic lipases.

4) Examine the effect of a gastrin-secreting tumor.

A gastrin-secreting tumor will secrete gastrin at all times and will not be inhibited by normal feedback mechanisms, such as the presence of chyme in the small intestine. This gastrin will continually stimulate parietal cells to produce HCl. This excess of acid will move with the chyme into the small intestine. Normal amounts of bicarbonate will be released; however, this is not enough to neutralize such an excess of HCl.

5) Determine the effects of an acidic environment in the small intestine.

Pancreatic juices require a less acidic environment than do stomach enzymes. If the environment in the small intestine is too acidic, then pancreatic secretions will be unable to function normally. While proteins and carbohydrates are partially digested before they reach the small intestine, fats do not begin digestion until they reach the duodenum. If pancreatic lipases are unable to function due to an excessively acidic environment, they will not be able to digest lipids. This hypersecretion of gastrin will lower the pH of the duodenum so that pancreatic lipases are inactivated. This will result in the malabsorption of lipids, also known as steatorrhea.

Remember: *The pH levels of the stomach and the small intestine affect the ability of enzymes to function properly.*

Similar Questions

1) A patient with a peptic ulcer takes a large overdose of antacid. This would affect the activity of what enzyme?

2) Pancreatic ductal cells secrete bicarbonate, which is moved into the intestinal lumen. What would be the physiological results if these ductal cells were destroyed by an autoimmune disorder?

3) Pancreatitis is a disease that prevents the pancreas from being able to produce adequate amounts of lipase enzymes. What will be the physiological results of this disease?

Key Concepts

Chapter 8

Respiratory system

Alveoli

Oxygen exchange

Physiological dead space

Anatomical dead space

Alveolar dead space

Takeaways

The respiratory system is intimately linked to the circulatory system. Oxygen is delivered to tissues, and CO_2 is removed from tissues and ultimately removed from the lungs through capillaries.

Things to Watch Out For

Under resting conditions, alveolar oxygen equilibrates with the arterial blood of the pulmonary capillary. This is considered a perfusion-limited exchange. Under conditions of exercise, the partial pressures of oxygen do not equilibrate along the length of the pulmonary capillary and the partial pressure gradient is maintained.

Respiratory System

The volume of the lungs that does not participate in gas exchange is considered physiological dead space. There are two types of dead space that are seen at rest: anatomical and alveolar. Anatomical dead space is in the conducting areas, such as the mouth and trachea, where oxygen enters the respiratory system but does not contact alveoli. Alveolar dead space is the area in the alveoli that does contact air but lacks sufficient circulation to participate in gas exchange. How can physiological dead space be reduced?

1) Examine each type of dead space separately.

Anatomical dead space refers to the air that remains in the mouth and trachea with every breath. Because the size and length of the mouth and trachea are set and relatively unchangeable, it is unlikely that physiological dead space can be decreased through the anatomical dead space.

Alveolar dead space involves alveoli that contact air but do not participate in gas exchange. Because the alveoli are normal, they are capable of participating in gas exchange under the right conditions; therefore, alveolar dead space can be reduced.

---

2) Review the method of gas exchange at the tissues and in the lungs.

In the normal lung, O_2 will diffuse from alveolar air into the pulmonary capillary. When the partial pressures of O_2 in alveolar air and capillary blood equilibrate, the diffusion stops. Normally this occurs before the blood in the pulmonary capillary passes out of the lungs and is considered perfusion-limited gas exchange. This O_2 is bound to hemoglobin and is taken and released to the tissues. CO_2 is produced by the tissues and diffuses into capillary blood, where it is carried to the lungs as HCO_3^-. At the lungs, the reaction is reversed, and CO_2 is exhaled.

---

3) Determine why some alveoli do not participate in gas exchange.

There is not sufficient blood flow through the capillaries of these "dead space" alveoli to induce them to participate in gas exchange. There must be blood flow for gas exchange to occur.

---

4) Determine how to increase blood flow through the lungs.

If pulmonary blood flow were increased, then more alveoli would be perfused with blood and would therefore participate in gas exchange. Increasing pulmonary blood flow would require increasing the output of the right ventricle. Cardiac output increases during exercise because there is an increased heart rate and increased venous return due to skeletal muscle activity. Therefore, exercise would increase the amount of pulmonary blood flow. This increased flow of blood through the lungs would recruit more alveoli for gas exchange and, therefore, reduce alveolar and physiological dead space.

Remember: Gas exchange occurs between alveolar air and the pulmonary capillaries. To increase the number of alveoli being used for gas exchange, the amount of pulmonary blood available for gas exchange must also be increased.

Similar Questions

1) What is the result if blood flow to the left lung is completely blocked by a pulmonary embolism?

2) If an area of the lung is not ventilated due to an obstruction, what is the partial pressure of oxygen (Po_2) of the pulmonary capillary in that area?

3) At what point will the diffusion of air from the alveoli to the capillary stop?

Key Concepts

Chapter 9

Circulation

Cardiac circulation

Cardiac oxygen consumption

Blood volume

Circulation

Increased O_2 consumption in the left ventricle coupled with left ventricular hypertrophy and a heart murmur is most likely the result of what condition, and what symptoms would be seen in a patient with this condition?

1) Examine the reasons for increased O_2 consumption in the heart.

O_2 consumption in the heart increases when there is increased afterload (or increased aortic pressure), increased heart rate, increased contractility, and/or increased size of the heart.

2) Examine the reasons for left ventricular hypertrophy.

Left ventricular hypertrophy is the abnormal enlargement of the muscle of the left ventricle. This thickening occurs when the left ventricle has to work harder to generate enough force to overcome greater pressure as it is pumping (greater afterload).

3) Review the flow of blood through the heart.

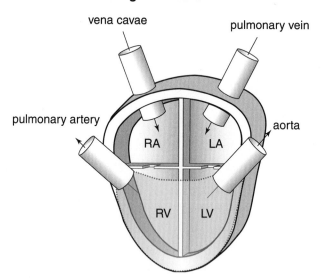

Takeaways

It's important to be able to integrate knowledge from different areas, in this case O_2 consumption, blood flow, and the pathway of the heart, when examining a question.

Blood travels into the right atrium through the vena cava. It moves through the tricuspid valve into the right ventricle and is then passed into the pulmonary artery, which carries it to the lungs. After leaving the lungs, blood travels through the pulmonary vein to the left atrium, then through the mitral valve into the left ventricle. The left ventricle pumps blood through the aortic valve into the aorta.

4) Determine the cause of the heart murmur.

Heart murmurs result from turbulent blood flow through the heart, particularly through the valves. Deformities of a valve will cause blood flow through the valve to become turbulent and create a heart murmur.

5) Determine the cause of the left ventricular hypertrophy and the increased O_2 consumption.

The left ventricle thickens and uses more oxygen because it cannot easily pump the blood through the aortic valve into the aorta. Stenosis is a condition in which the leaves of a heart valve adhere to each other, decreasing the volume of blood flow through the valve. Therefore, a stenotic aortic valve would make pumping blood through the aortic valve more difficult and lead to increased O_2 consumption and left ventricular hypertrophy.

6) Determine the effects of decreased blood flow due to aortic stenosis.

If less blood can be pumped from the left ventricle into the aorta, the ability to supply the body with blood will be reduced. This can cause blood to back up into the lungs and cause shortness of breath, especially with activity, as well as chest pain. Also, because less blood is going out to the body, weakness can result; further, because less blood is going to the brain, fainting is a symptom of aortic stenosis.

Remember: *Knowing the pathway that blood takes through the heart is essential!*

Similar Questions

1) Where would a patient diagnosed with stenosis of the mitral valve experience the greatest increase in blood pressure?

2) If a tracer substance were injected into a patient's superior vena cava, which structure would it reach last before leaving the heart?

3) The decrease in the number of pulmonary capillaries due to the loss of functional lung tissue will most likely result in a pressure overload. Where will this overload occur?

Key Concepts

Chapter 9

Oxygen dissociation curve

Arterial blood saturation

Venous blood saturation

Right/left shift

Bohr effect

Normal Oxygen Dissociation Curve

How does the oxygen dissociation curve of arterial blood differ from the curve for venous blood, and what accounts for this difference?

1) Review the normal oxygen dissociation curve.

The oxygen dissociation curve shows the percent saturation of hemoglobin as a function of the partial pressure of O_2 (P_{O_2}). At $P_{O_2} = 100$ mm Hg, hemoglobin saturation is 100 percent, which means that four oxygen molecules are bound to the hemoglobin. At $P_{O_2} = 40$ mm Hg, hemoglobin is 80 percent saturated, and at $P_{O_2} = 25$ mm Hg, hemoglobin is 50 percent saturated with oxygen molecules. The cooperative binding of O_2, meaning the binding of the first O_2 molecule, facilitates the binding of the next and results in a sigmoidal, or S-shaped, curve.

Takeaways

It is important to understand how to read the oxygen dissociation curve and how changes in the curve equate to changes in the affinity of hemoglobin for oxygen. Increases in P_{CO_2}, decreases in pH, and increases in temperature shift the curve to the right. The opposite—a decrease in P_{CO_2}, an increase in pH, or a decrease in temperature—shifts the curve to the left.

2) Examine how arterial blood differs from venous blood.

Things to Watch Out For

Right shifts of the curve are more common, but don't forget the factors that shift the curve to the left.

After blood passes through the lungs and into the arteries, the hemoglobin is 100 percent saturated with oxygen. The tissues of the body produce CO_2 as waste. The increase in CO_2 at the tissues decreases the pH of the tissues. Increases in CO_2 or decreases in pH decrease the affinity of hemoglobin for oxygen and cause the curve to shift slightly to the right, increasing the Po_2 and facilitating the unloading of O_2 at the tissues. The tissues keep Po_2 low by consuming O_2 for aerobic metabolism, so that the O_2 diffusion gradient is maintained. In arterial blood, the hemoglobin saturation at 40 mm Hg is 80 percent, but in venous blood, the Hb saturation at 40 mm Hg is 75 percent. Therefore, about 5 percent more oxygen is released. This right shift of the curve is known as the Bohr effect. An increase in temperature also causes a right shift.

At the lungs, alveolar gas has a Po_2 of 100 mm Hg. O_2 diffuses from the alveolar air into the capillaries. O_2 is bound very tightly to hemoglobin because at a Po_2 of 100 mm Hg, hemoglobin has a very high affinity for O_2. This maintains the partial pressure gradients and facilitates the diffusion of oxygen into the blood.

Similar Questions

1) How is the P_{50} of venous blood different from that of arterial blood?

2) How will the fetal oxygen dissociation curve differ from that of an adult?

3) How will arterial Po_2 be affected by living at a high altitude?

Key Concepts

Chapter 9

Oxygen dissociation curve

Carbon monoxide

Hemoglobin

Left shift

Abnormal Oxygen Dissociation Curve

Carbon monoxide (CO) binding to hemoglobin occurs in competition with oxygen (O_2) to hemoglobin binding; hemoglobin's affinity for CO is over 200 times its affinity for O_2. However, the binding of CO at one site increases the affinity for O_2 at the remaining sites. Draw the oxygen dissociation curve for CO poisoning, measuring hemoglobin oxygen content (in units of mL O_2/dL) on the vertical axis.

1) Visualize the normal oxygen dissociation curve.

The oxygen dissociation curve shows the percent saturation of hemoglobin as a function of the partial pressure of O_2 (P_{O_2}). At $P_{O_2} = 100$ mm Hg, hemoglobin saturation is 100 percent, which means that four oxygen molecules are bound to the hemoglobin. At $P_{O_2} = 40$ mm Hg, hemoglobin is 80 percent saturated and at $P_{O_2} = 25$ mm Hg, hemoglobin is 50 percent saturated with oxygen molecules. The cooperative binding of O_2, meaning the binding of the first O_2 molecule, facilitates the binding of the next and results in a sigmoidal, or S-shaped, curve.

Takeaways

Be familiar with the concepts of P_{O_2} and P_{CO_2}, what factors change their values, and how they are represented graphically.

2) Examine the effect that CO binding has on O_2 binding.

The question stem states that CO competes with O_2 when binding hemoglobin. Because hemoglobin affinity is 200 times greater for CO than for O_2, hemoglobin will preferentially bind CO first on a hemoglobin molecule. This will decrease the amount of O_2 that can bind to hemoglobin and, therefore, decrease the amount of O_2 that is in the blood.

3) Determine the effect that CO binding will have on the oxygen dissociation curve.

The question stem also states that the binding of CO increases hemoglobin affinity for O_2 at the remaining sites. Any physiological factor (i.e., decreased Pco_2, increased pH, or decreased temperature) that increases the affinity of hemoglobin for oxygen has the effect of shifting the curve to the left. Any physiological factor (i.e., increased Pco_2, decreased pH, or increased temperature) that decreases the affinity of hemoglobin for oxygen has the effect of shifting the curve to the right. The right shift is known as the Bohr effect. However, in this case, the affinity of hemoglobin for oxygen is increased, and there will be a left shift in the oxygen dissociation curve. It is this left shift that makes CO poisoning so deadly; with CO bound to hemoglobin, the O_2 molecules are bound so tightly that they cannot be off-loaded at the tissues, and thus asphyxia occurs.

Remember: The oxygen dissociation curve can be shifted to the left or to the right based on physiological conditions.

Similar Questions

1) How will exercise affect the oxygen dissociation curve?

2) What type of physical reaction would high Pco_2 cause?

3) What would the oxygen dissociation curve look like in a patient with metabolic alkalosis?

Lymphatic System

Approximately 20 L/day of fluid filters across capillaries. Reabsorption across capillaries is approximately 16 L/day, so the excess fluid must be returned to circulation by the lymphatic system. Lymphatic vessels are attached to the underlying connective tissue by fine filaments. What purpose do these filaments serve?

1) Examine the structure of lymph vessels.

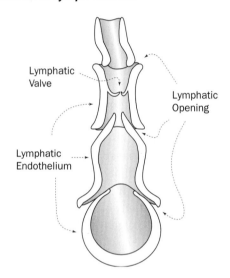

Lymphatic Valve

Lymphatic Opening

Lymphatic Endothelium

Takeaways

The lymphatic system plays a very important role in returning fluid, cells, and proteins back to the blood stream, but it relies on the movement of skeletal muscles to accomplish this role.

Lymphatic vessels have very thin walls that lack the smooth muscle that is found in arteries. Lymph vessels contain valves that ensure the unidirectional flow of lymph through the vessels. Filtrate from blood vessels, including cells and protein that have moved into the interstitial fluid compartment, is picked up by the lymphatic vessels. Lymphatic vessels called lacteals absorb fats from the gastrointestinal tract. The filtrate is moved through the system of lymphatic vessels, passing through lymph nodes where foreign particles are destroyed and removed. It rejoins blood circulation at the thoracic duct and superior vena cava.

2) Determine how interstitial fluid moves through lymph vessels.

Because lymphatic vessels do not have smooth muscle in their walls, they must rely on outside forces to move the lymph fluid through the vessels. The movement of skeletal muscles around the lymphatic vessels aids in moving lymph along, and their one-way valves prevent backflow of this fluid.

3) Determine how interstitial fluid enters lymphatic vessels.

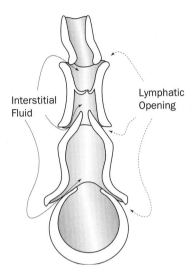

Interstitial Fluid

Lymphatic Opening

Capillaries have tight junctions between their endothelial cells. These tight junctions prevent unregulated passage of solutes in and out of the capillary lumen. Lymphatic vessels do not possess these tight junctions but rather have openings through which the interstitial fluid, complete with cells and proteins, can pass into the vessel. Because the lymph vessels are attached by fine filaments to their underlying connective tissue, skeletal muscle contraction will pull on these filaments and distort the lymphatic vessel. This distortion causes spaces to open between the endothelial cells of the vessel and allows the interstitial fluid to enter.

Remember: Lymphatic vessels differ from blood vessels in that they lack smooth muscle around the vessel and lack tight junctions between endothelial cells.

Similar Questions

1) If a patient's lymphatic channels have been obstructed by the spread of malignant tumors, what will result?

2) What physiological conditions can contribute to excess fluid in the interstitial space?

3) How does the lymphatic system return interstitial proteins to the blood?

Key Concepts

Chapter 11

Plasma osmolarity

Filtrate osmolarity

ADH

Aldosterone

Water reabsorption

A student discovers that drinking diet caffeinated soda results in a significant increase in urine volume and frequency. What are the physiological factors driving this phenomenon?

1) Identify the relevant kidney function affected: filtration, secretion, and/or reabsorption.

Excessive urine output means that there is a failure to reabsorb water from the nephron. Thus, the problem is at the reabsorption level.

Renal failure relating to filtration usually results in irregular plasma osmolarity (i.e., the urea concentration is too high, or the albumin concentration is too low). Secretion plays a critical role in maintaining blood pH, K^+ concentration in blood, and nitrogenous waste concentration in the filtrate. Reabsorption also affects filtrate concentration, as essential substances such as glucose, salts, and blood are returned to the blood.

2) Identify the role of plasma osmolarity and ADH.

Caffeine (as well as alcohol) inhibits ADH activity, thus decreasing water reabsorption activity from the collecting duct. Presuming the solution is isotonic to the blood, no change in plasma osmolarity is expected.

ADH works directly on the collecting duct by increasing its permeability to water; thus, a decrease in ADH levels will lead to a decrease in water reabsorption. ADH secretion is triggered by a sustained increase in plasma osmolarity. Note that if the solution is hypertonic to the blood plasma, osmolarity increases momentarily, but water from the interstitial fluid will move in to stem the increase (notice that the end result leads to an increase in arterial pressure).

3) Identify the role of blood pressure, renin, and aldosterone.

Ingestion of a large volume of soda increases arterial pressure, leading to a decrease in renin and aldosterone and, therefore, a decrease in water reabsorption.

Recall that aldosterone increases sodium reabsorption, and because water follows sodium on its way out of the tubules of the nephron, it also increases water reabsorption. Keep in mind that aldosterone is regulated by renin, which is secreted when blood pressure is low.

Takeaways

Questions related to the nephron appear in varying contexts. The key is to isolate the relevant component of the kidney function being tested and then to tease apart which particular step(s) above (i.e., filtrate osmolarity) are being affected.

4) Identify the role of filtrate osmolarity.

An abnormally high filtrate osmolarity will decrease the osmotic gradient between the tubule and the interstitial fluid, causing a drop in water reabsorption levels.

Diet sodas substitute Nutrasweet® for sugar, but unlike glucose, the Nutrasweet® cannot be reabsorbed back into the blood from the nephron—hence the high filtrate osmolarity. Even if you did not know that Nutrasweet® cannot be reabsorbed from the nephron, it is imperative to recognize the role that filtrate osmolarity can play in water reabsorption. Recall that with diabetes mellitus, a similar mechanism is at play: Due to the high glucose concentration, not all of the sugar is reabsorbed from the nephron, leading to an abnormally high filtrate concentration, less water reabsorption, and ultimately the excretion of urine with glucose.

Things to Watch Out For

The function of the kidney is to produce urine hypertonic to the blood, but in the situation described above, the urine produced is likely to be hypotonic to the blood. Alcohol consumption produces similar physiological effects. However, frequent urination does not always mean that the urine is hypotonic to the blood. Patients who excrete protein in their urine (filtration failure) have low levels of blood osmolarity, and thus there is a low level of water reabsorption. Therefore, the urine produced will still be hypertonic to the blood.

Similar Questions

1) A patient has been found to have insufficient levels of ADH. What symptoms would be prevalent?

2) Diabetics who fail to take insulin experience dehydration. What are the physiological factors driving this phenomenon?

3) A patient with renal failure has nephrons that lack the ability to actively secrete or reabsorb any substances. What type of actions can the kidney still perform?

Key Concepts

Chapter 11

Starling forces

Capillary filtration

Plasma proteins

Glomerular capillaries

Takeaways

As blood flows through a capillary, fluid that is lost at the arterial end is reabsorbed at the venule end when normal blood proteins are present. Changes in Starling forces alter the conditions where capillaries are present. An increase in capillary hydrostatic pressure or an increase in interstitial oncotic pressure will lead to capillary filtration. An increase in capillary oncotic pressure or interstitial hydrostatic pressure will oppose capillary filtration.

Things to Watch Out For

Remember that proteins act as a solute and water will flow to the areas of higher solute concentration.

Starling Forces

A patient with kidney disease has extensive damage to the glomerular capillaries. These capillaries have become permeable to plasma proteins. What symptoms will this patient have as a result of this kidney damage?

1) Determine the effect of glomerular capillaries that are permeable to proteins.

Glomerular capillaries do not normally allow the passage of plasma proteins or red blood cells. If the capillaries are damaged so that plasma proteins enter the renal tubule, these proteins will be lost because they cannot be reabsorbed along the tubule.

2) Examine the forces at work on capillaries.

The relationship of the different forces at work in the capillaries is explained by Starling forces as follows. Capillary hydrostatic pressure (P_c) is blood pressure, and it is the major force in capillary filtration. Osmotic pressure is the major force that keeps fluid from leaving the capillaries and is considered the oncotic pressure (π_c) of the plasma proteins. The interstitial fluid also has hydrostatic pressure (P_i), which opposes filtration out of the capillary. The proteins of the interstitial fluid exert oncotic pressure (π_i) and tend to favor filtration out of the capillary. To recap in simpler terms, the blood pressure in the capillary tries to force fluid out the capillary, whereas the pressure of the fluid in the interstitial space tries to hold the fluid in the capillary. The proteins in the interstitial space try to "suck" fluid out of the capillary, whereas the proteins in the blood try to hold the fluid in the capillary.

When blood enters the arterial end of a capillary, the P_c pressure acts to force fluids to leave the capillary and enter the interstitial space. This loss of fluid along the capillary increases the concentration of the solute, or proteins, in the blood. This increase in oncotic pressure "pulls" fluid back into the capillary at the venous end. Any fluid that is not returned to the capillary is generally picked up by the lymphatic system.

3) Determine the effect when proteins are lost from the blood.

The loss of plasma proteins will cause a drop in oncotic pressure in the blood. As a result, water that leaves the arteriole end of the capillary will not be reabsorbed at the venule end. Fluid in large quantities cannot be picked up by the lymphatic system, so this fluid will remain in the interstitial space and back up in the extremities, a condition known as edema. The failure of fluid to be reabsorbed from the interstitial space also leads to a large drop in blood volume and therefore blood pressure.

Similar Questions

1) What factors increase the loss of fluid to the interstitial space at the arterial end of a capillary?

2) What physiological conditions can increase capillary oncotic pressure?

3) What symptoms will patients with inadequate lymphatic function have?

Menstrual Cycle

During the follicular phase of the menstrual cycle, a dominant follicle is produced that secretes estrogen. If this follicle produces normal amounts of estrogen during the early days of its maturity but declines in estrogen production by day 10 of the menstrual cycle, what would be the result?

1) Visualize the menstrual cycle, focusing on the follicular phase.

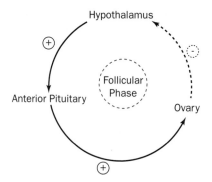

In the follicular phase, the hypothalamus secretes GnRH, which acts on the anterior pituitary to promote the release of FSH. FSH acts on the ovary and promotes the development of several ovarian follicles. The mature follicle begins secreting estrogen.

2) Determine the normal role of estrogen up until day 10.

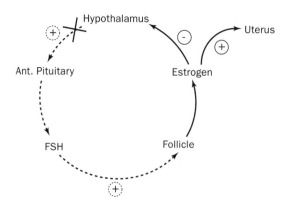

Estrogen has both positive and negative feedback effects in the menstrual cycle. Early in the follicular phase, the estrogen acts on the uterus, causing vascularization of the uterine wall. It also acts in a negative feedback loop to inhibit the release of FSH from the anterior pituitary in order to prevent the development of multiple eggs. Because the question stem states that early levels of estrogen are normal, vascularization of the uterus and inhibition of FSH will both occur normally.

Things to Watch Out For

Estrogen has both negative and positive feedback effects on FSH and LH at different times in the menstrual cycle. Remember that estrogen levels fall dramatically after the LH surge but rise again during the luteal phase. During this phase, however, both estrogen and progesterone are now produced by the corpus luteum, and both have a negative feedback effect.

3) Determine the normal role of estrogen after day 10.

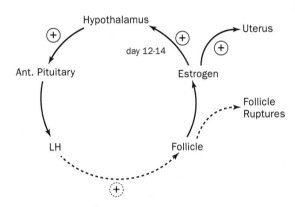

The question also states that estrogen levels decline after day 10. Now focus on the role of estrogen after day 10. Estrogen levels increase rapidly around day 12 of the cycle, and this burst of estrogen has a positive feedback effect on the secretion of FSH and LH. This results in the LH surge. The LH surge is responsible for ovulation, or the release of an egg.

Similar Questions

1) At what point in the follicular phase is FSH inhibited?

2) What are the actions of estrogen in the follicular phase of the menstrual cycle?

3) How can ovulation during the menstrual cycle be prevented?

4) Examine the consequence a decrease in estrogen after day 10.

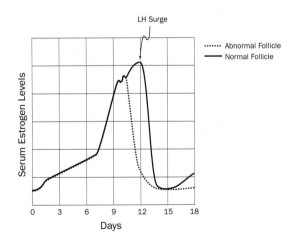

Therefore, if estrogen levels decrease after day 10 rather than increase as they normally should, there will be no ovulation.

Key Concepts

Chapter 13

Action potentials

Depolarization

Refractory periods

Action Potential

A nerve action potential is depicted below. If during the action potential, a stimulus were to be applied as indicated by the arrow, what would result?

1) Visualize the graph of the action potential.

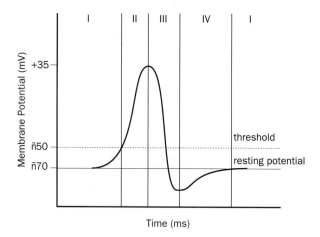

Takeaways

It is important to understand each stage of the action potential, including which gates are open or closed and which ions are flowing.

Region I—The cell is at rest and all gates are closed.

Region II—Depolarization: Sodium gates are open, and sodium flows into the cell, moving the membrane towards the sodium equilibrium potential.

Region III—Repolarization: Sodium gates close, and potassium gates open, moving the cell closer to the potassium equilibrium potential.

Region IV—Hyperpolarization: All gates are closed, and the cell is ready to undergo another action potential, but the distance to the threshold is farther so it is harder to stimulate the cell. This is known as the relative refractory period.

2) Review the characteristics of the action potential.
Action potentials propagate by the spread of currents to adjacent membranes; they are considered "all-or-nothing" because once threshold is reached, an action potential will continue. During an action potential (regions II and III), no other action potential can be elicited, no matter how large the stimulus. This is known as the absolute refractory period.

3) Evaluate the region in which the new stimulus is being applied.
The new stimulus being applied to the action potential occurs during repolarization. This is also during the absolute refractory period, a time during which no new action potentials can be elicited. Therefore, the new stimulus will not produce a new action potential.

Remember: Action potentials are all-or-nothing. Once one begins, it will continue, and a new action potential cannot be stimulated until after the absolute refractory period.

Similar Questions

1) At what point in the action potential is sodium closest to its electrochemical equilibrium?

2) What forces can increase the speed of an action potential?

3) How can an action potential be inhibited?

Key Concepts

Chapter 14

Penetrance

Genotype

Phenotype

Probability

Classical Genetics—Probability & Penetrance

Dystonia is a syndrome of involuntary spasms and sustained contractions of the muscles. One form of the disease is childhood dystonia, in which dystonia begins in the leg or foot and eventually spreads to involve the entire body. If one parent has this type of dystonia, while the other parent has no alleles for the disease, a child of those parents has a 50 percent chance of having the genotype for the disease. Given that the gene's penetrance is 40 percent, if a man with the disease (his mother was homozygous recessive) and a woman with no alleles for the disease have two children, what is the probability that both children will be healthy?

1) Identify the inheritance pattern.

No generation is skipped, and gender does not matter; thus, dystonia is an autosomal, dominant trait.

Whether it is presented in a pedigree diagram or indirectly given in the question stem, the inheritance pattern should be identified quickly. In the question stem above, we are told that if just one parent has the disease, there is at least a 50 percent chance he or she will pass it on to a child; thus, the trait must be dominant. The probabilities cited in the question stem are independent of the gender of the parent or the child; thus, sex-linked inheritance is ruled out.

Takeaways

After identifying the pattern of inheritance for the gene and the genotypes of the parental generation, set up the Punnet square to aid in the calculations of the probability questions posed. Unless otherwise stated, it is safe to assume that the penetrance of a gene in a given question is 100 percent.

2) Identify the relevant genotypes to set up the Punnet square.

Because the man is afflicted with the disease, and we have determined that the disease is autosomal dominant, he must be homozygous (DD) for the trait or heterozygous (Dd). Because his mother was homozygous recessive (dd), he must be heterozygous for the disease, as he received one recessive allele from his mother. The woman has no alleles for the disease and thus must be homozygous recessive (dd).

	D	d
d	Dd	dd
d	Dd	dd

The relevant genotypes may vary depending on the question. In this question, the relevant genotypes are those of the parents because we are interested in the probability of conceiving a healthy child.

3) Use the Punnet square to calculate the probability for each event.

The probability that the couple will bear two healthy children is $(80\%)^2 = 64\%$.

There is a 50 percent chance that a child will be homozygous recessive (healthy) and a 50 percent chance that the child will inherit the genotype for the disease. However, because penetrance is only 40 percent, there is only a 20 percent $(50\% \times 40\%)$ chance of the child actually expressing the disease. Therefore, there is an 80 percent chance that the child will be healthy.

Recall that penetrance is the dependence of an organism's phenotype on the genotype. One hundred percent penetrance signifies no environmental effects, whereas 0 percent penetrance signifies no genetic influence of a particular gene on a physical trait. Here, we have 40 percent penetrance, which means that only 40 percent of the heterozygotes will actually suffer from childhood dystonia.

Remember: To find the probabilities of both events occurring, multiply the probabilities of each event.

Things to Watch Out For

Beware of tricky probability questions. One typical trap is as follows: A disease is expressed in individuals who are homozygous recessive for the gene. Given parents who are both heterozygotes, what is the probability that a healthy child will be homozygous dominant? The Punnet square indicates 25 percent, but the trick is that we know the child is healthy; thus, there are only three possible outcomes—not four. Therefore, the probability is $1/3$ instead of $1/4$.

Similar Questions

1) The phenotype of an individual is known, but her genotype is not. Given a pedigree, could you determine the probability that she is homozygous dominant for this trait?

2) If normal parents have a color-blind son, what is the probability that he inherited the gene for color blindness from his mother? What is the probability that he inherited the gene from his father?

3) A woman with blood genotype B marries a man with blood genotype A. What is the chance that their first child will have blood type B? What is the chance that their first and second children will have blood type B?

Key Concepts

Chapter 15

Transcription

Antisense strand

Sense strand

DNA Transcription

An RNA strand with the sequence 5′-GACTGAUCAGACTA-3′ was erroneously created when a mutant RNA polymerase substituted a thymine for the second cysteine when it encountered a GG in the reading frame of the DNA. What is the antisense strand of the DNA from which this RNA was transcribed? (Assume that "GA" is not in the antisense strand.)

Takeaways

When solving any transcription problems, follow these rules:

- G pairs with C and T pairs with A.
- In RNA, T is replaced with U.
- The sense strand of the DNA = the transcribed hnRNA with U replacing T.
- The antisense strand and the sense strand are complements of each other.

1) Determine the correct primary structure of RNA.
We can substitute CC for CT in the fragment to produce the correct sequence of RNA:

5′-GACCGAUCAGACCA-3′.

In this case, when C precedes T, we know that it is due to the mutant polymerase. The first G in the DNA sequence GG will correctly have been transcribed as C, but the second G will have been incorrectly transcribed as T, yielding CT instead of CC.

Things to Watch Out For

Note that the sequence described above is for problems that ask for DNA sequence from RNA sequence. In problems that ask for RNA sequence from DNA sequence, perform step 3 first, followed by step 2 and then step 1.

Be careful to maintain the correct polarity in every step of the problem. The newly synthesized strand is built in the 5′ to 3′ direction, and the reading frame is read in the 3′ to 5′ direction.

2) Determine the sense strand.
We can simply replace the uracils with thymines to get the following sense strand:

5′-GACCGATCAGACCA-3′.

Transcription always proceeds in the 5′ to 3′ direction starting at the 3′ end of the antisense strand. The RNA corresponds to the sense strand (minus any introns that were spliced out—in this problem we will assume there were no introns).

We are working backwards, going from RNA to DNA. The RNA produced represents the sense strand with the thymines replaced by uracil.

3) Determine the antisense strand.
   5′-GACCGATCAGACCA-3′ → sense strand
   3′-CTGGCTAGTCTGGT-5′ → antisense strand

The antisense strand of DNA is the complement of the sense strand of DNA. We can determine the sense strand by remembering that G pairs with C, that T pairs with A, and that the antisense strand is antiparallel to the sense strand (meaning that the 3′ end of the sense strand will line up with the 5′ end of the antisense strand and vice versa).

Similar Questions

1) What is the base sequence of the mRNA produced from the following sense strand of DNA: 3'-TAGGGTACGTACCTA-5'?

2) What are the possible primary structures of mRNA produced from the antisense strand 3'-GAATACCAGTAGTATTTGCCGATGACTAGTTAGCCGTTAGC-5' after splicing by a splisosome that makes blunt-end cuts between GG in the sequence 5'-CGGC-3'?

DNA Replication

The following molecule of DNA is replicated using two cycles of PCR in the presence of N^{15}-labeled guanine. What percentage of the DNA strands will contain the labeled guanine in both strands (sense and antisense strands)?

5' – CATACTGATCATCTAGCGTATGCGT-3'
3' – GTATGACTAGTAGATCGCATACGCA-5'

1) Determine what happens after the first round of replication.

DNA replication is semiconservative, which means that for every strand of original DNA, one new strand of DNA is synthesized as its new complement.

Our templates for this first round of replication are these:

5' – CATACTGATCATCTAGCGTATGCGT – 3'
3' – GTATGACTAGTAGATCGCATACGCA – 5'

Neither of these original strands contains the labeled guanine. So the first round of replication gives us this:

5' – CATACTGATCATCTAGCGTATGCGT – 3'
3' – GTATGACTAGTAGATCGCATACGCA – 5'*

and

5' – CATACTGATCATCTAGCGTATGCGT – 3'*
3' – GTATGACTAGTAGATCGCATACGCA – 5'

where the * marks strands containing the labeled guanine.

The original strand with the 5' to 3' polarity at the site of replication will be the lagging strand, because nucleotides can only be added in the 5' to 3' direction. Primase lays down a new primer to which DNA polymerase can bind in intervals of about 500 nucleotides so that its new complementary strand can be created in short fragments called Okazaki fragments. The primer for these Okazaki fragments is RNA and is replaced with DNA before ligase joins the short fragments together. This process eliminates the need to create the replicate strand in the 3' to 5' direction.

2) Determine what happens after the second round of replication.

Our templates for the second round of replication are as follows:

5' – CATACTGATCATCTAGCGTATGCGT – 3'
3' – GTATGACTAGTAGATCGCATACGCA – 5'*

and

    5′ − CATACTGATCATCTAGCGTATGCGT − 3′
    3′ − GTATGACTAGTAGATCGCATACGCA − 5′*

So this second round of replication gives us this:

    5′ − CATACTGATCATCTAGCGTATGCGT − 3′
    3′ − GTATGACTAGTAGATCGCATACGCA − 5′*

and

    5′ − CATACTGATCATCTAGCGTATGCGT − 3′*
    3′ − GTATGACTAGTAGATCGCATACGCA − 5′*

and

    5′ − CATACTGATCATCTAGCGTATGCGT − 3′*
    3′ − GTATGACTAGTAGATCGCATACGCA − 5′*

and

    5′ − CATACTGATCATCTAGCGTATGCGT − 3′*
    3′ − GTATGACTAGTAGATCGCATACGCA − 5′

with the asterisks again indicating strands containing labeled guanine.

In the second round of replication, the new strands from the first round of replication are used as templates to create newer strands.

Things to Watch Out For

Be careful in noting the polarity of the strands. Remember that DNA is always synthesized in the 5′ to 3′ direction.

3) Determine the percentage of DNA molecules that only have "new" strands.
Of the double-stranded DNA molecules, 50 percent will have both strands with the labeled N^{15} guanine.

After two rounds of replication, the middle two double-stranded DNA molecules have both strands labeled with the N^{15} guanine, whereas the outer two double strands of DNA still maintain one original strand.

Similar Questions

1) What is the product after 5′-ACGAGCTATGCTACTATATG-3′ goes through two rounds of replication?

2) A molecule of DNA is replicated using three cycles of PCR in the presence of N^{15}-labeled nuclei acids. What percentage of the newly formed DNA will contain an unlabeled strand?

Hardy-Weinberg

The gene for gigantism is known to be on a recessive allele. The dominant allele for the same gene codes for a normal phenotype. In North Carolina, 9 people out of a sample of 10,000 were found to have gigantism phenotypes, whereas the rest had normal phenotypes. Assuming Hardy-Weinberg equilibrium, calculate the frequency of the recessive and dominant alleles as well as the number of heterozygotes in the population.

1) Solve for the frequency of the recessive allele.
gigantism = homozgygous recessive = gg = q^2
$q^2 = 9/10,000 = 0.0009$
$q = 0.03$
Recessive allele frequency = 3%

Refer back to the Hardy-Weinberg equation:

$p^2 + 2pq + q^2 = 1$

Because gigantism will only emerge with a recessive genotype, it will be represented as gg. From the Hardy-Weinberg equation, the recessive genotype is depicted as q^2. By taking the square root of q^2 we get the frequency of the recessive gigantism allele or 0.03.

---

2) Solve for the frequency of the dominant allele.
$p + q = 1$
$p = 1 - q$
$1 - 0.03 = 0.97$
Dominant allele frequency = 97%

The frequency of the dominant allele plus the recessive allele equals 1. To solve for the frequency of the dominant allele, you subtract the recessive allele frequency from 1.

---

3) Solve for the heterozygous population.

$2pq$ = frequency of heterozygotes

$Gg = 2(0.97) \times (0.03)$

$Gg = 0.058$ or about 6%

$0.058 \times 10,000 = 580$ people

To find the heterozygous population, we need to use the heterozygous portion of the Hardy-Weinberg equation. Plugging in $2pq$ gives us the frequency of the heterozygous genotype.

Things to Watch Out For

There are five circumstances in which the Hardy-Weinberg law may fail to apply. These five are mutation, gene migration, genetic drift, nonrandom mating, and natural selection.

Similar Questions

1) Suppose a similar survey was done in New York. However, this time they found 90 people with gigantism out of a survey of 200,000 people. Calculate the same parameters with the new survey.

2) An allele x occurs with a frequency of 0.8 in a wolf pack population. Give the frequencies of the genotypes XX, Xx, and xx.

3) If the homozygous recessive frequency of a certain allele is 16 percent, determine the percentage of phonetically normal individuals.

Art Credits for Biology

Figure 1.1—Image credited to Bryan Christie Design. From Working Knowledge: Lab Tests by Mark Fischetti. Copyright © 2002 by Scientific American, Inc. All rights reserved.

Figure 1.3a—Image credited to Eye of Science/Photo Researchers, Inc. From The Challenge of Antibiotic Resistance by Stuart B. Levy. Copyright © 1998 by Scientific American, Inc. All rights reserved.

Figure 1.3b—Image credited to E. Gray/Photo Researchers, Inc. From The Challenge of Antibiotic Resistance by Stuart B. Levy. Copyright © 1998 by Scientific American, Inc. All rights reserved.

Figure 1.4—Image credited to Jeff Johnson Hybrid Medical Animation/Photo Researchers, Inc. From The Once and Future Nanomachine by George M. Whitesides. Copyright © 2001 by Scientific American, Inc. All rights reserved.

Figure 1.7—Image created by Jeff Johnson Hybrid Medical Animation/Photo Researchers, Inc. From Sweet Medicines by Thomas Maeder. Copyright © 2002 by Scientific American, Inc. All rights reserved.

Figure 1.8. Image credited to Jeff Johnson Hybrid Medical Animation/Photo Researchers, Inc. From The Once and Future Nanomachine by George M. Whitesides. Copyright © 2001 by Scientific American, Inc. All rights reserved.

Figure 1.9—Image credited to Tomo Narashima. From Budding Vesicles in Living Cells by James E. Rothman and Lelio Orci. Copyright © 1996 by Scientific American, Inc. All rights reserved.

Figure 1.10—Image credited to Dana Burns Pizer and Tomo Narashima. From Caloric Restriction and Aging by Richard Weindruch. Copyright © 1996 by Scientific American, Inc. All rights reserved.

Figure 1.11—Image credited to Christoph Blumrich. From Uprooting the Tree of Life by W. Ford Doolittle. Copyright © 2000 by Scientific American, Inc. All rights reserved.

Figure 1.12 (Cell surface illustration)—Image credited to Ryota Matsuura, Robert Ezzell, and Donald E. Ingber. From The Architecture of Life by Donald E. Ingber. Copyright © 1998 by Scientific American, Inc. All rights reserved.

Figure 1.12 (MF, MT, IF illustrations)—Images credited to Laurie Grace. From The Architecture of Life by Donald E. Ingber. Copyright © 1998 by Scientific American, Inc. All rights reserved.

Figure 1.12 (MF and MT photographs)—Images credited to Donald E. Ingber. From The Architecture of Life by Donald E. Ingber. Copyright © 1998 by Scientific American, Inc. All rights reserved.

Figure 1.12 (IF photograph)—Image credited to Robert D. Goldman, Northwestern University Medical School. From The Architecture of Life by Donald E. Ingber. Copyright © 1998 by Scientific American, Inc. All rights reserved.

Figure 1.16—Image credited to Daniela Naomi Molnar. From Are Aliens Among Us? by Paul Davies. Copyright © 2007 by Scientific American, Inc. All rights reserved.

Figure 2.2—Image credited to Michael Goodman. From Drugs by Design by Charles E. Bugg, William M. Carson and John A. Montgomery. Copyright © 1993 by Scientific American, Inc. All rights reserved.

Figure 3.7—Image credited to Dana Burns Pizer and Tomo Narashima. From Caloric Restriction and Aging by Richard Weindruch. Copyright © 1996 by Scientific American, Inc. All rights reserved.

Figure 3.8—Image credited to Tomo Narashima. From The 1997 Nobel Prizes in Science, The Mechanism of Life by Staff Editor. Copyright © 1998 by Scientific American, Inc. All rights reserved.

Figure 4.1—Image credited to Dimitry Schidlovsky. From How Cancer Arises by Robert A. Weinberg. Copyright © 1996 by Scientific American, Inc. All rights reserved.

Figure 4.4. Image credited to Dimitry Schidlovsky. From The Centrosome by David M. Glover, Cayetano Gonzalez and Jordan W. Raff. Copyright © 1993 by Scientific American, Inc. All rights reserved.

Sidebar Page 80—Image credited to Lucy Reading—Ikkanda. From The Real Life of Pseudogenes by Mark Gerstein and Deyou Zheng. Copyright © 2006 by Scientific American, Inc. All rights reserved.

Figure 4.10—Image credited to Tomo Narashima. From Future Contraceptives by Nancy J. Alexander. Copyright © 1995 by Scientific American, Inc. All rights reserved.

Figure 4.12.—Image credited to Tomo Narashima. From Mother Nature's Menders by Mike May. Copyright © 2000 by Scientific American, Inc. All rights reserved.

Chapter 5 Cover—Image credited to Bradley R. Smith. From Visualizing Human Embryos by Bradley R. Smith. Copyright © 1999 by Scientific American, Inc. All rights reserved.

Figure 5.1—Image credited to Gamma Presse. From Blastomere Blowup by Charles Q. Choi. Copyright © 2006 by Scientific American, Inc. All rights reserved.

Figure 5.2—Image credited to Jason Burns/Phototake. From Embryonic Stem Cells for Medicine by Roger A. Pederson. Copyright © 1999 by Scientific American, Inc. All rights reserved.

Figure 5.5—Image credited to Andrew Swift. From The Stem Cell Challenge by Robert Lanza and Nadia Rosenthal. Copyright © 2004 by Scientific American, Inc. All rights reserved.

Chapter 6 Cover—Image credited to Aaron Goodman. From Regrowing Human Limbs by Ken Muneoka, Manjong Han, and David M. Gardiner. Copyright © 2008 by Scientific American, Inc. All rights reserved.

Figure 6.1—Image credited to John Gurche. From Food for Thought by William Leonard. Copyright © 2002 by Scientific American, Inc. All rights reserved.

Figure 7.3—Image credited to Biomedial Imaging Unit/Southhampton General Hospital/Photo Researchers, Inc. From Bugs and Drugs by Gunjan Sinha. Copyright © 2005 by Scientific American, Inc. All rights reserved.

Figure 7.4—Image credited to Jeff Johnson Hybrid Medical Animation/Photo Researchers, Inc. From Atherosclerosis: The New View by Peter Libby. Copyright © 2002 by Scientific American, Inc. All rights reserved.

Chapter 9 Cover—Image credited to Jeff Johnson Hybrid Medical Animation. From Atherosclerosis: The New View by Peter Libby. Copyright © 2002 by Scientific American, Inc. All rights reserved.

Figure 9.2—Image credited to Roberto Osti. From Surgical Treatments of Cardiac Arrhythmias by Alden H. Harken. Copyright © 1993 by Scientific American, Inc. All rights reserved.

Sidebar Page 192—Image credited to Roberto Osti. From Surgical Treatments of Cardiac Arrhythmias by Alden H. Harken. Copyright © 1993 by Scientific American, Inc. All rights reserved.

Figure 9.6 (illustration and chart). Image credited to Johnny Johnson; Source: Biology, by Neil Campbell. From The Search for Blood Substitutes by Mary L. Nucci and Abraham Abuchowski. Copyright © 1998 by Scientific American, Inc. All rights reserved.

Figure 9.6 (erythrocytes)—Images credited to Dr. Dennis Kunkel/Phototake. From The Search for Blood Substitutes by Mary L. Nucci and Abraham Abuchowski. Copyright © 1998 by Scientific American, Inc. All rights reserved.

Figure 15.13—Image credited to Dr. Gopal Murti/Photo Researchers, Inc. From Founder Mutations by Dennis Drayna. Copyright © 2005 by Scientific American, Inc. All rights reserved.

Figure 15.14—Image credited to Laurie Grace. From Sunlight and Skin Cancer by David J. Leffell and Douglas E. Brash. Copyright © 1996 by Scientific American, Inc. All rights reserved.

Figure 15.15—Image credited to Jared Schneidman Design. From Viral Quasispecies by Manfred Eigen. Copyright © 1992 by Scientific American, Inc. All rights reserved.

Figure 15.16—Image credited to Tami Tolpa. From The Vaccine Search Goes On by David I. Watkins. Copyright © 2008 by Scientific American, Inc. All rights reserved.

Figure 15.19—Image credited to Tomo Narashima. From The Challenge of Antibiotic Resistance by Stuart B. Levy. Copyright © 1998 by Scientific American, Inc. All rights reserved.

Figure 15.20—Image credited to Dr. L. Caro/Photo Researchers, Inc. From Bacterial Gene Swapping in Nature by Robert V. Miller. Copyright © 1998 by Scientific American, Inc. All rights reserved.

Figure 15.21—Image credited to Sally Bensusen. From Bacterial Gene Swapping in Nature by Robert V. Miller. Copyright © 1998 by Scientific American, Inc. All rights reserved.

Figure 15.22—Image credited to Eye of Science/Photo Researchers, Inc. From Bacterial Gene Swapping in Nature by Robert V. Miller. Copyright © 1998 by Scientific American, Inc. All rights reserved.

Figure 15.23—Image credited to Sally Bensusen. From Bacterial Gene Swapping in Nature by Robert V. Miller. Copyright © 1998 by Scientific American, Inc. All rights reserved.

Figure 15.25—Image credited to Tami Tolpa. From The Power of Riboswitches by Jeffrey E. Barrick and Ronald R. Breaker. Copyright © 2007 by Scientific American, Inc. All rights reserved.

Chapter 16 Cover—Image credited to Sean McCabe; Sources: Daniel Sambraus, Pascal Goetgheluck, Bio Photo Associates. From Traces of a Distant Past by Gary Stix. Copyright © 2008 by Scientific American, Inc. All rights reserved.

Figure 16.1—Image credited to Bryan Christie Design. From Deciphering the Code of Life by Francis S. Collins and Karin G. Jegalian. Copyright © 1999 by Scientific American, Inc. All rights reserved.

Figure 16.2—Image credited to Craig Kiefer. From Evolution and the Origins of Disease by Randolph M. Nesse and George C. Williams. Copyright © 1998 by Scientific American, Inc. All rights reserved.

Figure 16.3—Image credited to Cleo Vilett. From 15 Answers to Creationist Nonsense by John Rennie. Copyright © 2002 by Scientific American, Inc. All rights reserved.

Figure 16.5—Image credited to Patricia J. Wynne. From 15 Answers to Creationist Nonsense by John Rennie. Copyright © 2002 by Scientific American, Inc. All rights reserved.

Figure 16.7—Image credited to Jared Schneidman Design. From The Origin of Life on Earth by Leslie E. Orgel. Copyright © 1994 by Scientific American, Inc. All rights reserved.

Figure 16.8- Image credited to Ian Worpole. From The Evolution of the Earth by Claude J. Allegre and Stephen H. Schneider. Copyright ©1994 by Scientific American, Inc. All rights reserved.

Part II
Practice Sections

INSTRUCTIONS FOR TAKING THE PRACTICE SECTIONS

Before taking each Practice Section, find a quiet place where you can work uninterrupted. Take a maximum of 70 minutes per section (52 questions) to get accustomed to the length and scope.

Keep in mind that the actual MCAT will not feature a section made up of Biology questions alone, but rather a Biological Sciences section made up of both Biology and Organic Chemistry questions. Use the following three sections to hone your Biology skills.

Good luck!

Practice Section 1

Time—70 minutes

QUESTIONS 1–52

Directions: Most of the questions in the following Biology Practice Section are organized into groups, with a descriptive passage preceding each group of questions. Study the passage, then select the single best answer to the question in each group. Some of the questions are not based on a descriptive passage; you must also select the best answer to these questions. If you are unsure of the best answer, eliminate the choices that you know are incorrect, then select an answer from the choices that remain.

PASSAGE I (QUESTIONS 1–7)

Certain species of hermit crabs inhabit gastropod shells for protection from predators and the environment. Studies have shown that crabs have the ability to take advantage of chemical cues emitted by gastropod flesh, not only informing them that the original shell occupant is dead, but also guiding and orienting the crab to the shell's location at a great range (Diaz et al. 1995). Factors influencing shell choice include size (Blackstone 1985), structural integrity (Rotjan et al. 2004), and material. A 1995 study by Diaz et al. showed that at closer distances, crabs also rely heavily on visual cues to locate a shell and gauge its quality. They showed specifically that crabs employ visual assessment of shell shape, in delicate combination with shell color and chemical cues, in choosing a shell. Crabs presented with a choice of silhouettes favored horizontal rectangle shapes, exhibiting distaste for vertical diamond shapes. Furthermore, crabs presented with single silhouettes had difficulty orienting to suboptimal shell shapes such as triangles, but easily oriented to optimal shell shapes, such as horizontal diamonds (Diaz et al. 1995).

An experiment was designed by behavioral ecology students to examine the effect of color on hermit crab shell choice. They believed that hermit crabs would prefer shells that offer a camouflage advantage and designed an experiment to test the hypothesis that hermit crab shell choice is influenced by color.

In the first control experiment, 50 hermit crabs were presented with a choice between shells with a clear coat of paint or no paint. The shells were set on a background of natural black rocks. In the second experiment, 50 hermit crabs were presented with a choice between shells with a pink coat of paint or a clear coat of paint, set on a background of pink colored rocks. In the third experiment, 50 hermit crabs were presented with a choice between shells with a pink coat of paint and a clear coat of paint, set on a background of natural black rock.

Crabs were deshelled two hours in advance and placed in heated tanks prior to the experiment. The shells, all originally black, were painted immediately before use and allowed to dry for roughly 10 minutes before the experiment began.

The following morning, the shell choice of each crab was recorded. A crab was recorded as choosing a particular shell only if it was physically inside of it at the time of observation.

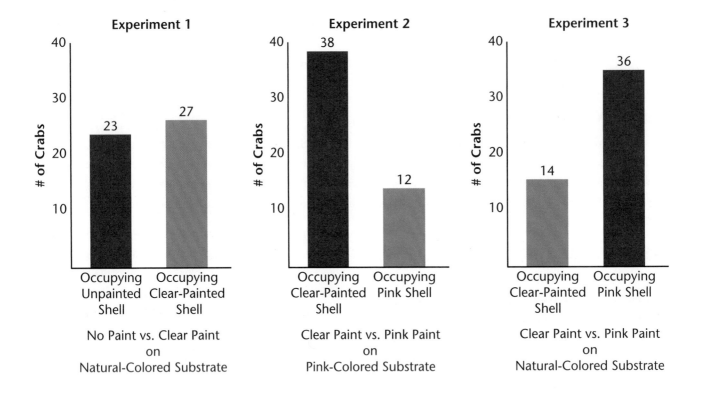

1. Which of the following would be a reasonable null hypothesis for this experiment?

    A. Hermit crabs do not show preference for shells based on color.
    B. Hermit crabs prefer shells most similar in color to their environment.
    C. Hermit crabs prefer shells different in color to their environment.
    D. Hermit crabs always prefer darker-colored shells.

2. Which of the following is not a legitimate concern over the experiment setup?

    A. Shell sizes were not identical.
    B. Shells were not identical distances away from the subject crabs.
    C. The pink paint released olfactory signals.
    D. The pink paint darkened after drying.

3. Based on the data, which of the following conclusions is MOST likely to be true?

A. Hermit crabs show a preference for color.
B. Hermit crabs always prefer black shells.
C. Hermit crabs always prefer pink shells.
D. Hermit crabs prefer black shells because their natural environment is black rock.

4. Which of the following statements is LEAST likely to explain the data?

A. Hermit crabs communicate to one another visually.
B. Hermit crabs' natural environment is light-colored.
C. Hermit crabs' natural predators are all color-blind.
D. Natural selection favors hermit crabs that stand out in their environment.

5. Based on the data, what evolutionary forces could be at play on these hermit crabs in an environment with many areas of pure pink rocks and many areas of pure black rocks?

A. Disruptive selection
B. Directional selection
C. Both A and B
D. Neither A nor B because null hypothesis is true

6. A hypothetical population of 89 black-shelled hermit crabs was discovered in the red sands of Jordan's Wadi Rum desert. Hermit crabs are not native to this region and experts believe they were introduced to the environment by South American tourists. Scientists began tracking this unique population of crabs in 1992. By 2007, only four crabs remained. These findings

A. strongly call into question the hypothesis that shell color affects hermit crab shell choice.
B. do not call into question the validity of the hypothesis that shell color affects hermit crab shell choice.
C. strongly support the hypothesis that shell color affects hermit crab shell choice.
D. are invalid because the hermit crabs are not native to Jordan.

7. The species of hermit crab used in the experiment and a second species of hermit crab are monophyletic. This second species is color-blind. Which of the following scenarios is most likely?

A. These two species of hermit crabs do not share a common ancestor.
B. Color-blindness is an analogous trait between the two species.
C. This second species of hermit crab was influenced by evolutionary pressures of the founder effect.
D. Color-blindness is a homologous trait between these two species.

PASSAGE II (QUESTIONS 8–17)

Cystic fibrosis is a serious genetic disorder causing fibrotic lesions of the pancreas, obstruction of the lungs with thick mucus, and reproductive and intestinal problems. The severity of the respiratory obstruction due to mucus can range from mild difficulty to serious problems that sharply decrease life span. The most common form of the disease results from the loss of three nucleotides coding for the amino acid phenylalanine. The pedigree of an affected family is presented below:

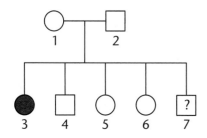

A researcher interested in identifying genotypes of each family member assayed polymorphisms revealed through the variation in length of restriction fragments containing the locus for cystic fibrosis. DNA of each family member was obtained from blood samples. Then, under specific conditions, DNA was digested by restriction enzymes, which recognize specific DNA sequences. The lengths of the DNA fragments were compared through gel electrophoresis. In gel electrophoresis, DNA fragments migrate through the gel. Smaller fragments move faster than larger ones, and thus separate based on their size. The gel is shown below, with the DNA fragments moving from the top toward the bottom of the page:

8. According to the pedigree, the disease alleles of the gene are most likely

    A. codominant.
    B. X-linked.
    C. recessive.
    D. dominant.

9. If male 7 from the pedigree marries a female carrier, the probability of their having a healthy noncarrier child is

    A. 0 percent.
    B. 25 percent.
    C. 50 percent.
    D. 75 percent.

10. According to the passage, what can be concluded about the expressivity of the disease?

    A. The expressivity is homogeneous in the population.
    B. Expressivity varies.
    C. Expressivity approaches 90 percent.
    D. There is not enough information to make a decision.

11. It can be inferred from the passage that a mutation leading to the most common form of cystic fibrosis can be classified as a(n)

    A. deletion.
    B. nondisjunction.
    C. inversion.
    D. insertion.

12. Based on the polymorphisms of DNA fragments, family member 7 is most likely

    I. heterozygous.
    II. homozygous recessive.
    III. homozygous dominant.
    A. I only
    B. II only
    C. I or II
    D. I or III

13. Which family member is not carrying the disease allele?

  A. 1
  B. 4
  C. 6
  D. 7

14. According to the passage, when compared to the fragment with the normal allele, the speed of movement through the gel of DNA fragment containing the disease allele would be

  A. slower, as the disease allele fragment is larger.
  B. slower, as the disease allele fragment is shorter.
  C. faster, as the disease allele fragment is larger.
  D. faster, as the disease allele fragment is shorter.

15. According to its functional significance, cystic fibrosis mutation can be referred to as

  A. missense.
  B. nonsense.
  C. silent.
  D. None of the above

16. The researcher later used the restriction fragment length polymorphism method described to assay 100 members of the U.S. population for cystic fibrosis. One person had the disorder. Identify the observed frequency of the disease allele.

  A. 0.01
  B. 0.1
  C. 1
  D. 0.9

17. Family member 5 marries a carrier of the cystic fibrosis allele. On average, what proportion of their children will be affected?

  A. ¼
  B. ¾
  C. ½
  D. 0

QUESTIONS 18 THROUGH 21 ARE NOT BASED ON A DESCRIPTIVE PASSAGE.

18. Young patients after an untreated throat infection with streptococci bacteria can develop rheumatic heart disease later in life. Studies have shown that the heart disease affects primarily the mitral valve whose surface cells have proteins similar to a surface protein common to many strains of streptococcal bacteria.

Based solely on the information above, what class of disease best describes rheumatic heart disease?

  A. Congenital endocrine abnormality such as type I diabetes
  B. Hypersensitivity reaction such as an autoimmune disease
  C. Allergic reaction such as a bee sting
  D. Congenital structural abnormality of the heart such as a patent foramen ovale

19. The activation of phosphofructokinase-1 by glucagon-mediated increase in PKA activity is an example of what type of modulation of protein activity?

  A. Competitive antagonism
  B. Synergism
  C. Noncompetitive antagonism
  D. Allosteric activation

20. What is the purpose of hexokinase?

    A. Phosphorylate glucose-6-phosphate to glucose-1, 6-bisphosphate

    B. Phosphorylate glucose-6-phosphate to fructose-1, 6-bisphosphate

    C. Isomerize glucose-6-phosphate to fructose-6-phosphate

    D. Phosphorylate glucose to glucose-6-phosphate

21. Both oxalacetate and acetyl-CoA can be generated from pyruvate. Which of the following ratios, if greater than one, would favor the production of pyruvate from oxalacetate and acetyl-CoA, rather than the usual 'forward' reaction?

    A. Carbon dioxide/oxygen

    B. FAD/FADH2

    C. Glycogen/glucose

    D. Glucose/fructose-1, 6-bisphosphate

PASSAGE III (QUESTIONS 22–28)

The electron transport chain (ETC) is the site of the final process in aerobic glucose catabolism where most of the ATP is produced. The ETC is comprised of a series of carrier proteins that pass electrons along the inner membrane of mitochondria. The carrier proteins are embedded in the inner membrane. Each carrier is first reduced when it accepts electrons, and then oxidized as it passes electrons along to the next carrier. In the figure below, steps 1 through 6 show ETC carriers starting with NAD^+ (nicotinamide adenine dinucleotide) and ending with molecular oxygen.

The passage of electrons along the ETC does not in itself explain ATP production. The chemiosmotic hypothesis is used to tie electron transport with phosphorylation. According to this theory, as electrons are passed from carrier to carrier in the chain, protons (H^+) are pumped across the impermeable inner mitochondrial membrane into the intermembrane space, building up the electrical and pH gradients. The energy of the gradient is responsible for ATP production. When a specific gradient is reached, accumulated protons pass through the transmembrane enzyme complex ATP-synthase from intermembrane space back into the mitochondrial matrix, dissipating the gradient and making ATP.

The fact that the highly specific order of the carriers and their oxidation is tied with phosphorylation makes the final ATP synthesis fully susceptible to any interruptions along the chain. Some of the currently identified blockers and their sites of action are listed in the table below:

Inhibitors	Site blocked
Rotenone	Step 2 of ETC
Antimycin A	Step 4 of ETC
Sodium azide	Step 6 of ETC
Cyanide	Step 6 of ETC
Carbon monoxide	Step 6 of ETC
Oligomycin	Inhibits ATP synthase
2,4-dinitrophenol	↑ Permeability of inner mitochondrial membrane

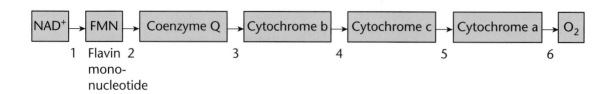

NAD⁺ → FMN → Coenzyme Q → Cytochrome b → Cytochrome c → Cytochrome a → O₂

1   Flavin   2   3   4   5   6
      mono-
      nucleotide

22. According to the chemiosmotic hypothesis described in the passage, the electrical and pH gradients developed across the inner mitochondrial membrane can be described as having

    A. more positive charge and higher pH in the intermembrane space than in the matrix.

    B. more negative charge and lower pH in the intermembrane space than in the matrix.

    C. more negative charge and higher pH in the intermembrane space than in the matrix.

    D. more positive charge and lower pH in the intermembrane space than in the matrix.

23. Applying the information from the previous table, in cells treated with antimycin A, all of the following can be expected EXCEPT

    A. oxygen remains the final acceptor of electrons.

    B. the proton gradient is decreased.

    C. ATP synthesis is decreased.

    D. cytochrome b is fully reduced.

24. While testing an unknown electron transport chain inhibitor, a researcher measured a high proton gradient while no ATP synthesis could be detected. Using the information in the previous table, what could be the unknown inhibitor?

    A. 2,4-dinitrophenol

    B. Antimycin A

    C. Rotenone

    D. Oligomycin

25. Application of which of the following inhibitors will prevent electrons from reaching oxygen?

    I. Oligomycin

    II. Rotenone and antimycin A

    III. Cyanide and carbon monoxide

    A. I only

    B. II and III only

    C. II only

    D. I, II, and III

26. It can be inferred from the passage that the higher permeability of inner mitochondrial membrane due to 2,4-dinitrophenol most likely results in

    A. more protons accumulated in the intermembrane space, increasing the electric gradient.

    B. protons escaping the intermembrane space, decreasing the electric gradient.

    C. more ATP produced by ATP synthase.

    D. oxygen leaving the mitochondria.

27. It can be inferred from the passage that the mitochondrial matrix contains

    A. ATP synthase.

    B. ADPs.

    C. phosphates.

    D. ADPs and phosphates.

28. A researcher is interested in isolating fully reduced cytochrome a. All of the following inhibitors can be used for this purpose EXCEPT

    A. cyanide.

    B. sodium azide.

    C. rotenone.

    D. carbon monoxide.

PASSAGE IV (QUESTIONS 29–32)

The pathophysiology of asthma involves the inflammatory cascade and constriction of bronchiole airways. Treatment of asthma requires the use of several medications in combination. Traditional treatment of asthma involves use of a beta agonist to decrease the amount of bronchiole constriction that decreases the size of the airway. Additional treatments include corticosteroids to reduce inflammation, and anti-cholinergic medication to decrease the amount of parasympathetic stimulation to the respiratory system. Newer medications block the leukotriene pathway that contributes to the inflammatory cascade. Other medications block IgE-mediated histamine release that can trigger an asthma attack.

Many of the medications used to treat asthma are delivered directly to the lungs by inhalers. The effectiveness of the medication is directly related to the amount of medication that is present in the lungs. If the inhaler is used incorrectly, more of the medication will end up in the back of the throat instead of within the lung tissue.

In an effort to determine the best inhaler for treating asthma, a scientist used three different drug delivery devices to deliver a radiolabeled bronchodilator directly to the lungs. Patients were then imaged with a PET scanner to determine how much of the radiolabeled medication had been delivered directly to the lung. This technique of radiolabeling a medication for delivery is analogous to radiolabeling a monoclonal antibody that is being used for cancer treatment. The monoclonal antibody will hone to the cancer cells and block receptors crucial to the functioning of the tumor mass, while the radioactivity that is delivered will caused apoptosis and necrosis of the cancer mass. The direct use of radiolabeling, for drug delivery or treatment, has become very popular because imaging technology is sophisticated enough to detect where radioactivity is present.

The scientist delivered a set amount of radiolabeled bronchodilator to 11 asthma patients using three different inhalers. The amount of radioactivity (in Bq/unit of lung tissue) detected was as follows:

	Inhaler A	Inhaler B	Inhaler C
Subject 1	6	9	15
Subject 2	10	7	0
Subject 3	18	3	3
Subject 4	6	11	0
Subject 5	6	4	5
Subject 6	9	7	8
Subject 7	3	9	2
Subject 8	0	2	5
Subject 9	7	1	12
Subject 10	4	0	8
Subject 11	9	0	7

29. What additional variable could have affected the results?

   A. Presence of pre-existing lung disease beyond asthma
   B. Tidal volume
   C. Sex
   D. Zero order kinetics of bronchodilators

30. IgE is traditionally associated with which of the following immunocytes?

   A. Neutrophil
   B. Basophil
   C. T-lymphocyte
   D. Mast cells

31. Anticholinergic medication during an asthma attack is appropriate because

    A. the parasympathetic response encourages exercise.

    B. there is reduced blood flow to the lungs during exercise.

    C. sympathetic drive encourages bronchodilation.

    D. parasympathetic drive encourages bronchoconstriction.

32. Which inhaler, on average, was most effective in delivering bronchodilator to the lungs?

    A. A

    B. B

    C. C

    D. They were all equally effective.

QUESTIONS 33 THROUGH 35 ARE NOT BASED ON A DESCRIPTIVE PASSAGE.

33. Those with abetalipoproteinemia exhibit, among other things, low levels of chylomicrons in their bloodstream. Which of the following symptoms is likely caused by this metabolic disorder?

    A. Diarrhea or excessive watery stool

    B. Steatorrhea or excessive fat in the stool

    C. Hyperlipidemia or excessive fat in the blood stream

    D. Hypertriglyceridemia or elevated levels of triglycerides in the blood stream

34. Which of the following DNA replication errors would be expected to have the LEAST severe consequence?

    A. $A \rightarrow T$

    B. $A \rightarrow G$

    C. $A \rightarrow C$

    D. $A \rightarrow U$

35. The discovery of which of the following enzymes challenged the central dogma of molecular biology and why?

    A. Reverse transcriptase, because transcription was thought to be unidirectional only from DNA to RNA

    B. Reverse transcriptase, because transcription was thought to be unidirectional only from 5′ to 3′ and never 3′ to 5′

    C. Integrase, because the central dogma did not account for movement of DNA within the chromosome

    D. Integrase, because the central dogma did not account for the existence of DNA outside of the nucleus

PASSAGE V (QUESTIONS 36–41)

Sheryl Williams, a 45-year-old real estate agent comes to your office as a new patient. She states up front that she's extremely busy and that she is pressed for time. Her only reason for being there is for health insurance purposes; she claims there is nothing wrong with her. With that in mind, you proceed with your history-taking and physical exam. You have only just started when the patient grimaces and clutches her stomach. She asks you how much longer the exam would be.

You realize this is not typical behavior, and begin to question the patient further. She states that the pain will gradually subside within the next few hours. She says she's been having these episodes for the past few months, and thinks they must be hunger pains. Because food can worsen the pain, she has cut back on her caloric intake. As a result, she has lost weight, which she considers a good thing. You ask about other symptoms she may have, and after some consideration, she tells you that she feels bloated a lot. She mentions in passing that she has been having frequent diarrhea, and she noticed that her feces have started to look a bit oily. She wonders if she should cut back on eating fatty foods.

You sense that these are more than just hunger pains and inform Sheryl of your concerns. She agrees to further testing. You order a serum gastrin level test, secretin stimulation test, endoscopy, and abdominal CT. The test results come back indicating highly elevated serum gastrin levels. Endoscopy shows multiple small ulcers in the distal duodenum, and CT shows a small mass on the head of the pancreas.

36. The mass is determined to be a gastrinoma (a gastrin secreting tumor). The patient undergoes surgery and the tumor is removed. How does gastrin affect H^+ secretion?

   A. Activates the cholecystokinin-B (CCKB) receptor
   B. Activates H2 receptors
   C. Activates the muscarinic (M3) receptor
   D. Activates somatostatin

37. The patient noted that her feces appeared "oily." When there is fat in the stool, this condition is called steatorrhea. This could be an indication of malabsorption of dietary lipids. How does the patient's condition affect her ability to absorb lipids?

   A. Inhibition of the liver to produce bile salts
   B. Inactivation of pancreatic enzymes
   C. Autoimmune reaction to gluten
   D. Facilitating intestinal colonization by flagellated bacterium

38. Which of the following substances does not stimulate H^+ secretion by gastric parietal cells?

   A. GIP
   B. Ach
   C. Histamine
   D. Gastrin

39. Gastrin is secreted from G cells located in the antrum of the stomach. One function of gastrin is to

   A. promote fat digestion and absorption.
   B. inhibit gastric emptying.
   C. promote secretion of pancreatic and biliary HCO_3^-.
   D. stimulate gastric mucosa growth.

40. The patient stated that she had been experiencing frequent diarrhea, and that the feces appeared to be oily. Why would someone with Zollinger-Ellison syndrome have frequent episodes of diarrhea?

   A. Decreased ability of the large intestine to absorb water and compact feces
   B. Increased parasympathetic stimulation
   C. Overproduction of motilin by M cells of the small intestine in conjunction with oversecretion of gastrin by G cells
   D. Malabsorption due to villi blunting

41. In Zollinger-Ellison syndrome, proper regulation over gastrin production and H^+ secretion is lost. Normally, what type of physiologic control is exhibited once the proper gastric pH is reached?

   A. Baroreceptor (pressure-regulated)
   B. Positive feedback control
   C. Negative feedback regulated
   D. Pulsatile regulation

PASSAGE VI (QUESTIONS 42–46)

Estrogen is a hormone that is very important in the female (and to a lesser extent, male) reproductive cycle and for other body structures, particularly promoting healthy bone and muscle. However, estrogen has also been implicated with many types of gynecological cancers, particularly breast cancer. Scientists have found that an ideal way to target this cancer is through targeting the enzyme-catalyzed production of estrogen. Aromatase is an enzyme in the cytochrome 450 family that catalyzes the conversion of testosterone to estrogen. This enzyme is found primarily in the brain, gonads, and adipose (fat) tissue. The first figure shows a generalized reaction coordinate under standard conditions.

Reaction Coordinate for Estrogen Production

The next figure shows the Michaelis-Menten model for aromatase in the adipose (breast tissue) of a healthy woman under standard conditions.[1]

Michaelis-Menten Model of Aromatase

42. What is the overall change in the free energy (ΔG) of the *catalyzed* reaction?

   A. 70 kJ/mol

   B. 45 kJ/mol

   C. 35 kJ/mol

   D. 0 kJ/mol

43. By approximately what percentage does aromatase lower the activation energy of the reaction?

   A. 0%

   B. 33%

   C. 66%

   D. 100%

44. Studies have found that aromatase activity is high in obese individuals, yet in animal models, those lacking aromatase are obese. What is the best explanation for this?

   A. At high concentrations of fat tissue, the aromatase reaction rate increases past the V_{max} in a nonobese individual.

   B. The reaction's product serves to inhibit aromatase when it is present at high levels.

   C. The enzyme requires a higher activation energy to successfully complete the reaction in the obese individual.

   D. The enzyme structure changes in obese individuals, and the wrong substrate is being catalyzed by the reaction.

---

[1]Kagawa N., H. Hori, M.R. Waterman, and S. Yoshioka, "Characterization of Stable Human Aromatase Expressed in *E. coli*," *Steroids* 69, no. 4 (2004): 235–43.

The table below shows several types of aromatase inhibitors used in the treatment of breast cancer:[2]

Prescription Aromatase Inhibitors

Drug	Mechanism	Notes
Formestane	Suicidal	Injection only
Exemestane	Suicidal	Androgen steroid; similar effect to competitive inhibitors
Letrozole	Competitive	Approved in US
Fadrozole	Competitive	Approved in Japan only; less weight gain
Anastrozole	Competitive	Approved in US

45. What type of regulation mechanism does letrozole use?

A. Allosteric inhibition

B. Allosteric activation

C. Feedback inhibition

D. None of the above

46. 'Male menopause' is characterized by unusually low androgen levels. How can androgen levels be increased in an affected man?

A. Aromatase activation

B. Aromatase inhibition

C. Artificial injection of aromatase from female cells

D. None—aromatase has no effect in men

PASSAGE VII (QUESTIONS 47–52)

Diabetes mellitus (DM) is a metabolic disease affecting blood sugar that results from defects in insulin secretion. It is relatively common, affecting 23.6 million people in the United States, 8 percent of the U.S. population.[3] Type I, or juvenile diabetes, occurs when the body does not produce any insulin at all. Type II, often called adult-onset diabetes (though children can be affected as well), occurs when the body is resistant to normal levels of insulin that are produced, and is often diagnosed in adulthood.

While diabetes does have some genetic influence, its incidence is often combined with other risk factors such as age and obesity. However, there are two rare forms of diabetes that are entirely due to genetics. Maturity-onset diabetes of the young (MODY) is a monogenic form that accounts for 1–5 percent of diabetes cases in the United States. MODY is an autosomal dominant condition. There are several varieties, but each of them is due to mutations in single genes which lead to insufficient insulin production in the body. MODY is usually diagnosed when patients are in their twenties. Like type II diabetes, MODY can be controlled without artificial insulin, and for otherwise healthy individuals, symptoms may not become apparent until later in life.

Another rare genetic form of type II diabetes is maternally inherited diabetes and deafness (MIDD), which accounts for ~1 percent of diabetes cases. MIDD is transmitted maternally through the mitochondrial DNA (mtDNA). Like MODY, MIDD is usually diagnosed at a younger age than type II diabetes, and is not associated with obesity or other typical risk factors. Unlike MODY, MIDD requires artificial insulin to control blood sugar.

The following pedigree is from an isolated rural community in the southern United States over four generations. It is unique in that the family has presented with the MODY, MIDD, and traditional forms of type II diabetes.[4]

---

[2] Buzdar, A.U. "Endocrine Therapy for Breast Cancer." In *Breast Cancer*, by K.K. Hunt and J. Mendelsohn, eds. *MD Anderson Cancer Series*. Houston, TX: University of Texas Press, 2001.

[3] American Diabetes Association. Total Prevalence of Diabetes & Pre-Diabetes. http://www.diabetes.org/diabetes-statistics/prevalence.jsp

[4] Adapted from C. Cervin et al., "Cosegregation of MIDD and MODY in a Pedigree: Functional and Clinical Consequences." *Diabetes* 53 (2004): 1894–1899.

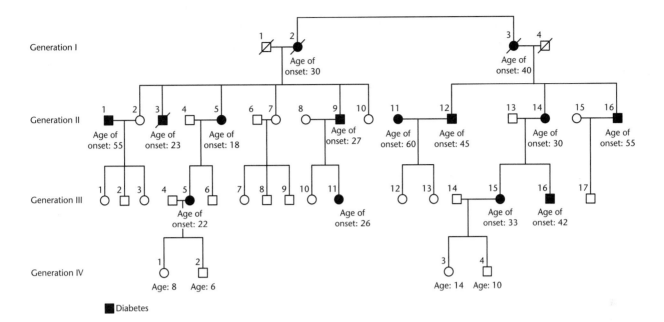

Generation I

Generation II

Generation III

Generation IV

■ Diabetes

47. The two sisters in generation I of this pedigree both have diabetes. What are their likely genotypes? (capital letter = dominant allele, lowercase letter = recessive allele)

A. MM, MM

B. Mm, Mm

C. Mm, mm

D. None of the above

48. Based on the available information, what forms of diabetes could individual II-1 present with?

   I. Type I diabetes

  II. Type II diabetes

 III. MODY

 IV. MIDD

A. I or III only

B. II or IV only

C. III or IV only

D. I, II, III, or IV

49. What is the likelihood that individual IV-2 (the six-year-old boy) will develop diabetes before age 40?

A. 0%

B. 25%

C. 50%

D. 75%

50. What is the likelihood that individuals III-12 and III-13 will both develop diabetes before age 40, assuming their mother has type II diabetes?

A. 0%

B. 12.5%

C. 25%

D. 50%

51. If the penetrance of the MODY allele is 85 percent, what is the likelihood that all of the nondiabetic children of individuals I-1 and I-2 are actually heterozygotes?

A. 0.3%

B. 2.25%

C. 15%

D. 85%

52. A form of MODY called atypical diabetes mellitus (ADM), which has been identified only in African-American and some Asian populations, is characterized by initial need for insulin that eventually gives way to type II diabetic symptoms. If individual III-17 was to marry a heterozygote for ADM, what is the likelihood that their child would inherit a permanently insulin-dependent form of diabetes?

A. 0%

B. 25%

C. 50%

D. 100%

Practice Section 2

Time—70 minutes

QUESTIONS 1–52

Directions: Most of the questions in the following Biology Practice Section are organized into groups, with a descriptive passage preceding each group of questions. Study the passage, then select the single best answer to the question in each group. Some of the questions are not based on a descriptive passage; you must also select the best answer to these questions. If you are unsure of the best answer, eliminate the choices that you know are incorrect, then select an answer from the choices that remain.

PASSAGE I (QUESTIONS 1–7)

Human immune deficiency virus (HIV) is responsible for over 2 million deaths annually worldwide and over 40,000 new infections each year in the United States. The current approach to treatment for HIV infections consists of highly active antiretroviral therapy (HAART), a combination of three to four antiretroviral drugs. Some early therapeutics focused on the inhibition of reverse transcription and consisted of two drug classes: nucleotide/nucleoside reverse-transcriptase inhibitors (NRTIs) and nonnucleoside reverse transcriptase inhibitors (nNRTIs). NRTIs generally mimic nucleic acids and terminate chain elongation. nNRTIs generally bind to a nonactive site on reverse transcriptase to cause a conformational change that interferes with transcription.

As a student interested in the molecular genetics of infectious diseases, you decide to set up an experiment examining three antiretroviral drugs (drugs A, B, and C) that target the reverse transcriptase enzyme. You culture recombinant CD4+ T cells (one of the major targets of HIV) and infect them with HIV. You then either expose them to plain cell culture media or one of three antiretroviral drugs. After 24 hours, you process cells and measure the levels of viral RNA and reverse transcriptase activity. Your results (as compared to the control group) are shown below:

	Viral RNA Concentration	Reverse Transcriptase Activity
Drug A	↓	↔
Drug B	↓	↔
Drug C	↓	↓
Drug D	↔	↔

1. The purpose of this experiment was most likely to

   A. test the efficacy of four new antiretroviral drugs.
   B. contrast the different mechanisms of antiretroviral drugs.
   C. test a new line of recombinant T cells as models for human infection.
   D. test the reliability over time of new assays.

2. If the mechanism of drug A was related to its ability to mimic the nucleotide adenine and terminate the addition of further nucleotides to the nascent DNA strand, with which parent strand base would it pair with in reverse transcription?

   A. Thymine
   B. Guanine
   C. Uracil
   D. Cytosine

3. Given the results of the experiment, what is a possible mechanism for drug C?

   A. Binding and inhibition of viral elongation factor activity
   B. Binding and inhibition of reverse transcriptase activity
   C. Inhibition of viral entry into host cells
   D. Early DNA chain termination during reverse transcription

4. The experiment described in the passage was performed on drug D, a drug recently approved by the FDA to treat HIV. The results of the experiment show no change in viral RNA products or the reverse transcriptase activity. Which of the following best explains these results?

   A. Poor sample quality of drug D
   B. Drug D's mode of action is not related to reverse transcription
   C. Drug D is quickly metabolized to an inactive form by the host cell
   D. Drug D has no effect on the virus

5. As described in the above passage, the action of non-nucleotide reverse transcriptase inhibitors is most similar to which of the following?

   I. Competitive inhibitor
   II. Noncompetitive inhibitor

   A. I
   B. II
   C. I and II
   D. Neither I nor II

6. Based on the information in the passage, which of the following is TRUE of nucleotide/nucleoside reverse transcriptase inhibitors?

   A. They cause early termination of translation.
   B. They are noncompetitive inhibitors of reverse transcriptase.
   C. They cannot be removed after incorporation into the virus DNA.
   D. They bind a site separate from the active enzymatic site on reverse transcriptase.

7. After cell entry and reverse transcription, HIV can become a latent provirus, inserting itself into the host genome. During this stage, where in the cell is viral DNA normally found?

A. Lysosome
B. Cytoplasm
C. Nucleus
D. Storage vesicles

PASSAGE II (QUESTIONS 8–17)

Teratology is the branch of science that focuses on the causes, mechanisms, and patterns associated with abnormal embryological development. Until the 1940s, it was believed that human embryos were protected from environmental agents such as drugs and viruses. It was thought that barriers such as the fetal membranes and the mother's abdominal and uterine walls provided sufficient protection for the developing fetus.

Then, in the 1940s, well-documented cases were being reported about certain drugs and viruses that were producing severe anatomic deformities and even fetal death. For simplicity's sake, the causes of congenital anatomic anomalies are divided into genetic factors and environmental factors. But research has shown that many of the common congenital anomalies are caused by multifactorial inheritance.

The causes of human congenital anomalies or birth defects break down into the following categories:

50–60% unknown etiology
20–25% multifactorial inheritance
7–10% environmental agents
7–8% mutant genes
6–7% chromosomal abnormalities

8. In the 1950s and 1960s, thalidomide was popularly prescribed to pregnant women suffering from morning sickness and difficulty sleeping. The drug was never tested with that population, and after it had caused hundreds of birth defects, it was withdrawn. In general, what is considered to be the most critical stage of fetal development?

A. Third trimester
B. Embryonic stage
C. Fertilization
D. Fetal stage

9. Nondisjunction refers to when chromosomal DNA does not separate appropriately, which can result in gametes containing either more or less than the standard amount of genetic material. Which of the following disorders is due to nondisjunction?

A. Cystic fibrosis
B. Sickle cell disease
C. Down syndrome
D. Polycythemia vera

10. A newborn is presented to you with a huge mass located at the anal region, which you recognize as a sacrococcygeal teratoma. You know that is the persistence of the primitive streak, formed from the

A. hypoblast.
B. prochordal plate.
C. epiblast.
D. exocoelomic membrane.

11. A four year-old girl presents with five days of total blindness. There was no history of trauma, and intracranial pressure is normal. An MRI is taken and reveals a large suprasellar mass compressing upon the lateral ventricles and pituitary fossa. Urgent surgery is performed and her eyesight is eventually recovered. This tumor was most likely which of the following?

A. Medulloblastoma

B. Craniopharyngioma

C. Glioblastoma multiforme

D. Optic nerve glioma

12. Which abdominal wall defect does not involve the umbilical cord?

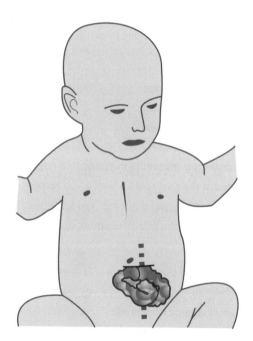

A. Myeloschisis

B. Omphalocele

C. Meckel diverticulum

D. Gastroschisis

13. A young couple comes to your office with concerns about miscarriage. They have heard stories about how a person can suddenly lose her pregnancy, and they want to know as much as they can about the subject. They mention something about extra chromosomes and want to know what that means. Which of the following karyotypes represents triploidy?

A. 47 XXX

B. 48 XXX

C. 69 XXX

D. 92 XXXX

14. An often-seen complication of pregnancy is that of a fertilized ovum implanting itself in tissue other than the uterine wall. There are multiple sites where this may occur, but the most common site for an ectopic pregnancy is

A. isthmic.

B. cornual.

C. ampullary.

D. abdominal.

15. You meet with a young couple that has been trying to get pregnant for the past year without success. During your initial workup, the woman states that she has a history of PID (pelvic inflammatory disorder) and wants to know if that could be the reason. What is the most common cause of PID?

A. Syphillis

B. Human papilloma virus

C. Chlamydia

D. Herpes

16. The physician is worried that the fetus may be suffering from fetal erythroblastosis, a disease caused by

  A. rubella.
  B. point mutation of the beta-globin chain of hemoglobin.
  C. CFTR gene mutation.
  D. anti-Rh antibodies.

17. The usual result of an oocyte fertilized by two sperm is

  A. dizygotic twins.
  B. partial mole.
  C. normal pregnancy.
  D. fetal gigantism.

QUESTIONS 18 THROUGH 21 ARE NOT BASED ON A DESCRIPTIVE PASSAGE.

18. Recent studies have shown that viruses can make many DNA and/or RNA transcripts from the same genomic strand of either DNA or RNA, each of which has different frames. Which of the following organisms uses a process in translation that is MOST similar to this?

  A. Eukaryote
  B. Prokaryote
  C. Both of the above
  D. Neither of the above

19. Although many classes of bacteria exhibit antibiotic resistance, researchers have noted that more classes of Gram-negative bacteria have antibiotic resistance than gram positive. What is the unique structural feature of Gram-negative bacteria which MOST LIKELY contributes to this phenomenon?

  A. Capsid
  B. Membrane-bound organelles
  C. Inner cell wall
  D. Outer cell wall

20. The lumen of the nuclear membrane is continuous with what organelle?

  A. Nucleolus
  B. Endoplasmic reticulum
  C. Golgi apparatus
  D. Ribosome

21. Which type of cell releases glucagon?

  A. Beta cell
  B. Alpha cell
  C. Plasma cell
  D. Delta cell

PASSAGE III (QUESTIONS 22–31)

The female menstrual cycle is a synchronized set of events that results in the ovulation of a solitary follicle and ensures that the uterus is prepared to receive an embryo. The cycle is controlled by gonadotropin-releasing hormone (GnRH) released by the hypothalamus. The pituitary gonadotropins secrete luteinizing hormone (LH) and follicle stimulating hormone (FSH) that dictate menstruation.

The cycle is divided into three main phases. The beginning of phase 1 is typically taken to be the first day of menses. In this phase, the failure to achieve fertilization after ovulation causes the uterine lining to be discharged. Simultaneously, new tertiary follicles begin to develop. In phase 2, the follicles continue to grow. As they enlarge, they secrete increasing amounts of estradiol, which stimulates endometrial growth in preparation of implantation. Moderately high estradiol levels inhibit GnRH secretion by the hypothalamus, while very high levels of estradiol stimulate GnRH secretion. When estradiol levels reach a certain threshold, positive feedback causes LH secretion to surge. The LH surge causes meiosis to resume in the oocyte of the largest follicle, and ultimately results in ovulation at the beginning of phase 3. The corpus luteum is also formed in this phase, which secretes estradiol and progesterone. The combination of these two hormones in high concentration maintains the uterine wall, and serves as a negative feedback loop in LH production. If fertilization does not occur, the ovum begins to disintegrate, typically 24 hours after ovulation but occasionally as late as 72 hours after ovulation. In contrast, male sperm can typically survive inside a woman's reproductive tract for 72 to 96 hours.

22. Which of the following is NOT a phase of menstruation?

  A. Destructive
  B. Secretory
  C. Gestational
  D. Proliferative

23. Below is an image of a menstrual cycle. How many ova does this woman produce per year?

  A. 11
  B. 12
  C. 13
  D. 14

24. The corpus luteum is

  A. the disintegrated ovum, when fertilization fails to occur.
  B. the product of ovum and sperm fertilization.
  C. the follicle before ovulation occurs.
  D. the follicle following ovulation.

25. Which of the following conditions would NOT contribute to infertility?

  A. Extremely low levels of body fat
  B. Abnormally high levels of progesterone
  C. Abnormally low levels of estrogen
  D. Abnormally short luteal cycles coupled with long follicular cycles

26. The combination birth control pill is a mixture of estradiol and progesterone taken to prevent pregnancy. This drug affects a woman's menstrual flow by

  A. making it lighter, through mimicking the circulating levels of progesterone and estradiol during pregnancy, preventing the proliferative uterine phase.
  B. making it lighter, through mimicking the surge of FSH and LH right before ovulation, preventing the proliferative uterine phase.
  C. making it heavier, through mimicking the circulating levels of progesterone and estradiol during pregnancy, stimulating the proliferative uterine phase.
  D. making it heavier, through mimicking the surge of FSH and LH right before ovulation, stimulating the proliferative uterine phase.

27. Which of the following is NOT contained in menstrual discharge?

A. Blood
B. Cells previously lining the vagina
C. Stratum functionalis
D. Zygote

28. At the beginning of the follicular phase, circulating estradiol levels are low. However, by the midfollicular phase, estradiol has reached moderately-high circulating levels. Which of the following is TRUE of the follicular phase?

A. FSH levels are lower just before the midpoint of the follicular phase than at the beginning.
B. FSH levels are lower at the midpoint of the follicular phase than at the end.
C. FSH levels see a decline at about the midpoint of the follicular phase.
D. FSH levels are held constant throughout the menstrual cycle via a complex mechanism of positive and negative feedback loops.

29. Which of the following graphs accurately depicts the relationship between FSH and estradiol in the follicular phase?

A.

B.

C.

D.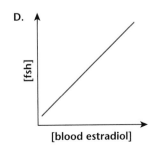

30. Studies have shown that a combination of estradiol and progesterone causes release of FSH and LH before ovulation, yet a combination of estradiol and progesterone inhibits release of FSH and LH after ovulation. Which of the following is TRUE?

A. Very low estradiol and very high progesterone levels cause the FSH and LH surges that lead to ovulation.
B. Very high estradiol and very low progesterone levels suppress FSH and LH production after ovulation.
C. Very high estradiol and very low progesterone levels cause the FSH and LH surges that lead to ovulation. The opposite conditions contribute to FSH and LH suppression after ovulation.
D. Both A and B

31. There is a 0.3 to 0.5° Celsius rise in basal body temperature immediately after ovulation during a woman's menstrual cycle. If a couple wanted to use the basal body temperature method as a form of birth control, which of the following minimum considerations should they follow? Assume a cycle of 28 days according to the following chart.

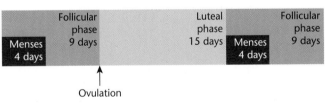

A. Only have sexual intercourse during a 21-day timespan, starting three days after the basal temperature rise
B. Only have sexual intercourse during a 12-day timespan, starting three days after the basal temperature rise
C. Only have sexual intercourse during a 21-day timespan, starting 14 days after the basal temperature rise
D. Only have sexual intercourse during a 12-day timespan, starting 14 days after the basal temperature rise

PASSAGE IV (QUESTIONS 32–38)

Mitochondrial inheritance disorders are a particular family of diseases that are passed from mother to child. All are related to a group of underlying mutations affecting mitochondrial functioning. Because mitochondria are found in all human cells, these mitochondrial defects can affect any tissue in the body. Disease presentations include muscle weakness, strokes, epilepsy, or heart failure.

Mitochondria are the only cellular organelles, aside from the nucleus, that contain their own DNA, known as mitochondrial DNA (or mtDNA). mtDNA is inherited from the mother. Mutations in mtDNA can affect energy production within cells and therefore lead to disease. Tissues that consume the most energy are maximally affected by defective mitochondria.

As part of a laboratory experiment you isolate the mtDNA of several families who have known mitochondrial inheritance disorders. From each family you isolate gene X, a commonly mutated mitochondrial gene involved in oxidative phosphorylation. You then analyze the genes via gel electrophoresis, including a negative control of gene X from a healthy individual.

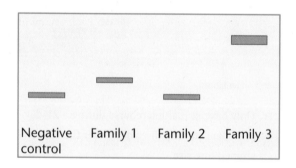

32. Given the results regarding the control gene and the gene from family 2, which of the following explains the presence of a mitochondrial inheritance disorder in family 2?

    I.   Mutation of another vital mitochondrial gene in family 2
    II. Point mutation in gene X of family 2
    III. No genetic mutations in family 2

    A. I
    B. II
    C. III
    D. I and II

33. On further investigation, it is found that gene X produces a transmembrane protein. Taking this into account, along with the information in the passage, what is the most likely location of this protein in the cell?

    A. Outer mitochondrial membrane
    B. Nuclear membrane
    C. Inner mitochondrial membrane
    D. Non-membrane-bound protein in the mitochondrial matrix

34. If we assume that a specific mitochondrial inheritance disorder affects the ability of the electron transport chain to donate electrons to oxygen, the most likely compound to increase in someone with this disorder is

    A. lactic acid.
    B. phospholipids.
    C. alanine.
    D. carbon dioxide.

35. According to the passage, mitochondrial inheritance disorders have

A. multiple genotypes and multiple phenotypes.
B. one genotype with multiple phenotypes.
C. multiple genotypes with one phenotype.
D. one genotype with one phenotype.

36. Consider a scenario where scientists have just discovered a mitochondrial inheritance disorder that does not obey the traditional maternal inheritance pattern. It is found to be due to a mutation in the nuclear DNA of the cell. Which of the following explains how a mutation in nuclear DNA could cause a disease with similar presentation to a mitochondrial inheritance disorder?

A. Mitochondrial DNA can recombine with nuclear DNA.
B. All the genes needed for mitochondrial function are located in nuclear DNA.
C. Certain nuclear DNA products are transported to the mitochondria where they play a vital role in mitochondrial function.
D. All the genes needed for mitochondrial function are located in the mitochondrial DNA.

37. The family tree below depicts the inheritance of MELAS (mitochondrial encephalomyopathy, lactic acidosis, and strokelike episodes), a mitochondrial inheritance disorder.

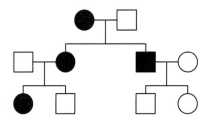

Which of the following contributes to this inheritance pattern?

I. Maternal inheritance pattern of mitochondria
II. Mitochondria possess their own separate genome
III. Sperm cell mitochondria contribute to ova during fertilization

A. I
B. II
C. I and II
D. I, II, and III

38. Which of the following statements is TRUE of mitochondrial DNA and eukaryotic nuclear DNA?

A. Mitochondria and nuclear DNA each encode for their own ribosomes.
B. Mitochondrial DNA and nuclear DNA are always circular.
C. Mitochondrial DNA and nuclear DNA have the same pattern of inheritance.
D. Mitochondrial DNA and nuclear DNA often recombine during cell division.

QUESTIONS 39 THROUGH 41 ARE NOT BASED ON A DESCRIPTIVE PASSAGE.

39. Which of the following enzymes decomposes polysaccharides into maltose?

A. Amylase

B. Lipase

C. Trypsinogen

D. Pepsin

40. Which of the following mutations in an RNA codon would be expected to produce the LEAST severe result?

A. AAA → AGA

B. AAA → AAG

C. AAA → GAA

D. AAA → AAT

41. What is the genetic basis for the statement, "Males drive evolution"?

A. Genes from males are dominant to those expressed by females.

B. Genes from males have been exposed to more positive selection than those of females.

C. Gametogenesis in the male produces four unique sperm cells whereas in the female it produces only one ovum.

D. Males can procreate for a longer time than females and thus a male has a larger contribution to the next generation's genes than a female.

PASSAGE V (QUESTIONS 42–48)

Epilepsy affects approximately 100 million people living in the world and afflicts all nationalities indiscriminately. Seizures are the symptoms of this disease and may vary greatly in type and degree. These seizures result from sudden excessive electrical discharges of neurons in any number of areas in the brain, manifesting in different ways such as disturbances of movement, loss of vision, loss of hearing, and abrupt changes in mood. Although epilepsy is one of the oldest conditions known to man, much is still unknown about the disorder. In the elderly, epilepsy is more likely caused by an underlying brain disease or may be the result of brain trauma. Still, there are many people, especially adolescents and infants, for whom the cause of epilepsy is unknown. In these cases, the most commonly accepted theory is that there is an imbalance of neurotransmitters, which causes a lower threshold for convulsions. The following are two controversial proposed mechanisms—not mutually exclusive of each other—for how epilepsy develops from a normal, healthy brain.

The kindling model is one proposed mechanism by which epileptogenesis may occur. In the kindling model, seizures begin to occur spontaneously after repeated subconvulsive stimuli. Typically, the model is used in research to induce epilepsy in various research animals. This is done through very low, usually electrical stimulation of the brain. After a prolonged period of such stimulation, the animals would start to convulse due to voltage sensitization. This sensitization may last for as long as 12 weeks after discontinuation of stimuli.

Excitotoxicity is another proposed mechanism by which epileptogenesis may occur. The process revolves around the actions of certain endogenous excitotoxins, including glutamate, a prominent excitatory neurotransmitter. Glutamate is known to cause apoptosis when left in the synaptic cleft in elevated concentrations via overactivation of NMDA receptors. Brain trauma may actually initiate this mechanism by causing ischemia, which is defined as a restriction in blood supply to particular areas, which then through a cascade of events causes an elevated accumulation of glutamate at the synapse.

42. Based on the passage, which of the two mechanisms would be supported by a finding that carbamazepine, an anticonvulsive medication commonly used to treat epilepsy, was found to stabilize the inactivated state of the voltage-gated sodium channels responsible for action potential propagation?

A. Excitotoxicity

B. Kindling model

C. Both of the mechanisms can be supported.

D. Neither of the mechanisms can possibly be supported.

43. Which of the following accurately describes the differences between the previous two models of epileptogenesis?

A. The kindling model, unlike the excitotoxicity model, concerns primarily processes at the synapse.

B. The kindling model, unlike the excitotoxicity model, does not involve the use of chemical stimulation.

C. Excitotoxicity is concerned with a possible chemical process by which epileptogenesis occurs, whereas the kindling model is mainly concerned with a possible electrical process by which epileptogenesis occurs.

D. Both models are essentially the same.

44. Assuming you accept the excitotoxicity view of epileptogenesis, which of the following methods would BEST treat acute seizure activity in a patient with extremely elevated concentration of glutamate?

A. Extracellular administration of an enzyme, which degrades glutamate

B. Increasing vesicle release into the synaptic clefts in the brain

C. Lowering the threshold stimulus for action potentials to occur in the brain

D. A and C

45. Glutamate is known to be the major excitatory neurotransmitter in mammals. Glutamate does NOT

A. depend on its receptors in whether it will be excitatory or inhibitory.

B. become released into the synaptic cleft by vesicles.

C. mediate epileptogenesis via its receptors.

D. All of the above

46. Based on the given information, which of the following is a plausible mechanism by which trauma to the brain results in epilepsy?

A. Ischemia depletes metabolic nutrients necessary for production of uptake carriers.

B. Trauma agitates the synaptic cleft, which increases the movement and activity of neurotransmitters.

C. Trauma causes increased action potentials.

D. A and C

47. Which of the following phenomena could plausibly explain the kindling model?

A. The phenomenon that an action potential may not occur if the threshold stimulus is reached very slowly

B. The existence of a time period after an action potential has been initiated in which no stimulus could possibly create another action potential

C. The existence of a time period after action potential initiation during which only an abnormally large stimulus could create another action potential

D. None of the above is plausible.

48. Which of the following could possibly explain an abrupt loss of balance in someone with elevated levels of glutamate in his brain?

A. Trauma to the cerebellum

B. Trauma to the thalamus

C. Trauma to the hypothalamus

D. Trauma to the brainstem

PASSAGE VI (QUESTIONS 49–52)

The human body is made up of approximately 60 percent water, with the percentage varying based on the fat content of the individual. In general, lean muscle contains about 75 percent water, while adipose tissue contains only 14 percent water. Therefore, athletes who have very low concentrations of body fat have particularly high water content and need to be adequately hydrated. However, for athletes in high-endurance events such as marathon runners, excessive water concentration can actually be harmful, and sometimes fatal, as evidenced by the death of a 28-year-old female runner in the Boston Marathon in 2002 from hyponatremic encephalopathy.

Figure 1 shows sodium and potassium concentrations in a normal cell and serum. The normal sodium concentration in the blood is ~140 mEq/L.[5] Hyponatremia is a disorder caused by abnormally low sodium concentration in the blood (below 130 mEq/L). For high-endurance athletes, sodium concentration can be rapidly diluted by drinking excess water. When this occurs in brain cells, it causes brain swelling, sometimes leading to coma or death.

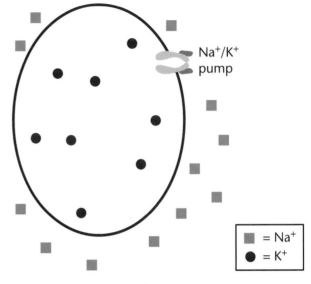

Figure 1

49. Given the information in Figure 1, what is the ratio of the H_2O concentration inside the cell to the concentration outside the cell, respectively?

A. 1:1

B. 2:3

C. 3:1

D. 3:2

50. What molecule is required to control the balance of sodium and water within a cell?

A. NaCl

B. Glucose

C. ATP

D. Urea

---

[5] Ackerman, G. L. Serum Sodium. In Walker, K. H., Hall, W. D., and Hurst, J. W. (Eds.), Clinical Methods: The history, physical, and laboratory examinations. Butterworth, 1990. Retrieved from http://www.ncbi.nlm.nih.gov/bookshelf/br.fcgi?book=cm&part=A5466

51. Hyponatremic encephalopathy has particularly severe consequences for women, as evidenced by the sole death in the Boston Marathon. What is the most likely explanation for this?

    A. Women consume more water during strenuous exercise than men.

    B. Women have a smaller brain mass than men do, so the same amount of cell deaths yields a higher proportion of lost brain capacity.

    C. Sex hormones impair brain cell adaptation to excess water levels.

    D. Vasopressin is present at high levels in affected women.

52. While intravenous sodium is necessary to reverse the effects of hyponatremia, doing so too rapidly can cause a serious problem in the myelin sheath. What part of the neuron does myelin insulate?

    A. Nucleus

    B. Synapse

    C. Axon

    D. Node of Ranvier

Practice Section 3

Time—70 minutes

QUESTIONS 1–52

Directions: Most of the questions in the following Biology Practice Section are organized into groups, with a descriptive passage preceding each group of questions. Study the passage, then select the single best answer to the question in each group. Some of the questions are not based on a descriptive passage; you must also select the best answer to these questions. If you are unsure of the best answer, eliminate the choices that you know are incorrect, then select an answer from the choices that remain.

PASSAGE I (QUESTIONS 1–8)

To function properly, many enzymes require certain ranges of physical conditions. One such enzyme, tyrosinase (also known as catechol oxidase), is responsible for coloration in the skin and hair of several animal species. There are several metabolic pathways involved in coloration that are mediated by this enzyme. For example, tyrosinase converts the amino acid tyrosine into melanin in pigment-producing cells but in other cells, oxidizes catechol to become the yellow benzoquinone.

Tyrosinase is responsible for coloration in Himalayan rabbits. To understand its functioning within certain temperature ranges, an experiment was performed on the rabbits at varying temperatures. Three groups of rabbits were raised at three different temperatures. The results in the following table show the percentage of individuals of each group exhibiting a type of fur coloration:

	% Dark	% Medium	% Light
32°C Group	1	7	92
28°C Group	6	85	9
10°C Group	90	8	2

The study concluded that tyrosinase is thermolabile, meaning that it functions best at certain temperatures.

However, in humans, skin coloration, long thought to be due to tyrosinase activity, has been shown to act independent of temperature variations. While melanin synthesis pathways are mediated by tyrosinase at several stages, the extent of its role in determining skin pigmentation is unclear. Results from several studies with human epidermal cell cultures show a high correlation between melanin concentration and tyrosinase activity. This would indicate that tyrosinase levels determine skin coloration.

Other data contradict this finding. Results from several immunotitration experiments and Western immunoblots show no statistical differences between the actual numbers of tyrosinase molecules among tissue sample groups and different levels of melanin concentrations.

Thus, two alternate, opposing hypotheses are currently accepted:

- Hypothesis 1: Tyrosinase levels determine skin color because of a high correlation between the melanin concentration and tyrosinase activity.
- Hypothesis 2: Tyrosinase levels do not determine skin color because of findings from immunotitration experiments and Western immunoblots.

1. What further data would best support hypothesis 2 without refuting the results of hypothesis 1?

   A. Post-translational alterations in tyrosinase to change its activity levels differ with varying melanin levels.

   B. Genetic alterations in tyrosinase to change its activity levels differ with varying melanin levels.

   C. Tyrosinase activity varies with temperature in most animal species, but not in humans.

   D. Melanin concentration and skin coloration are not positively correlated with each other.

2. From the passage, one could logically infer that the metabolic activity of tyrosinase in Himalayan rabbits is

   A. least active in cooler climates.

   B. independent of body temperature.

   C. inactive at or below cooler, arctic temperatures.

   D. more active at cooler body temperatures.

3. Based on the data presented in the passage, which region of the rabbit is likely to be dark in color at 25°C?

   A. Chest

   B. Dorsal

   C. Limb

   D. Ventral

4. Which portion of tyrosinase is most important in terms of its overall functioning?

   A. Active site

   B. Allosteric site

   C. Substrate site

   D. Enzyme-substrate complex

5. What level of structural organization of tyrosinase is first and most importantly affected by temperature changes?

   A. 0°

   B. 1°

   C. 2°

   D. 3°

[Source: Journal of Investigative Dermatology (1993) 100, 806–811; doi:10.1111/1747.ep12476630. Role of Tyrosinase as the Determinant of Pigmentation in Cultured Human Melanocytes. Ken Iozumi, George E Hoganson, Raffaele Pennella, Mark A Everett and Bryan B Fuller].

6. If a future study were conducted on chemical activity in melanin-producing cells, which finding would best support hypothesis 2 while accepting the results of hypothesis 1?

    A. Gene epistasis in melanin-producing cells
    B. Allosteric interactions with tyrosinase
    C. Transcriptional variations within melanin producing cells
    D. Elevated pH changes within cell organelles

7. Based on findings from the passage, what is TRUE about the thermolability of tyrosinase between 10°C and 35°C?

    A. Its active site is completely denatured at 10°C.
    B. Its active site is partially denatured at 10°C.
    C. Its allosteric site is completely denatured at 25°C.
    D. Its allosteric site is completely denatured at 35°C.

8. What other physical factors might likely determine tyrosinase activity?

    A. pH
    B. Pressure
    C. Both of the above
    D. Neither of the above

PASSAGE II (QUESTIONS 9–16)

Renal clearance (C) of a particular solute is given by the equation:

$$C = (U \times V)/P$$

U is the concentration of the solute in the urine, and V is the urine flow rate. P is the concentration of the solute in the blood.

The general definition for filtration fraction (FF) is defined as the percentage of blood plasma that filters through the glomerulus. Filtration fraction is given by the equation:

$$FF = GFR/RPF$$

GFR is the glomerular filtration rate and RPF is the renal plasma flow. The glomerular filtration rate is equal to the clearance of inulin, a polysaccharide that is neither secreted nor reabsorbed. RPF is approximately equal to the clearance of p-aminohippuric acid (PAH).

In standard clinical practice, plasma creatinine concentration (P_{cr}) is used to measure glomerular function. Creatinine is an inert product of creatine metabolism and is produced at a constant rate by muscle tissue. Creatinine is almost exclusively excreted by the kidney and enters the kidney via filtration through the glomerulus. The production rate of creatinine (Cr_{Prod}) is given by the equation:

$$P_{cr} \times GFR = Cr_{Prod}$$

Rearranged, the same equation gives us the plasma creatinine concentration, which is:

$$P_{cr} = Cr_{Prod}/GFR$$

Plasma Creatinine as an Index for GFR

9. Which of the following MUST be true when GFR = C?

   A. The solute is neither secreted nor reabsorbed.
   B. The solute is inulin.
   C. Glucose is reabsorbed from the proximal convoluted tubules.
   D. All of the above

10. Which of the following is TRUE when C < GFR?

   A. Reabsorption of the solute has occurred
   B. Secretion of the solute has occurred.
   C. Both of the above
   D. None of the above

11. Which of the following MUST be assumed when using inulin to measure glomerular filtration rate?

   A. The filtered concentration of inulin is exactly the same as the plasma concentration.
   B. Inulin increases the rate of filtration.
   C. Inulin lowers renal plasma flow.
   D. Inulin lowers renal blood flow.

12. Which of the following statements of inulin is most likely true?

   A. It is bigger than an erythrocyte.
   B. It is bigger than albumin.
   C. It is bigger than glucose.
   D. None of the above

13. No known solute is completely filtered from the blood after a single pass through the glomerular apparatus. PAH is most likely

   A. bigger than an erythrocyte.
   B. bigger than albumin.
   C. both filtered and secreted by the kidney.
   D. None of the above

14. Which of the following is TRUE when C > GFR?

   A. The solute is being secreted into the tubules of the nephron.
   B. There is more filtration than clearance occurring.
   C. The solute is being resabsorbed from the tubules of the nephron.
   D. None of the above

15. A patient has a plasma creatinine concentration of 4 mg/dL. Her clearance of PAH is 550 mL/min. Approximately what percent of plasma is filtered by the patient's kidneys per minute?

   A. 5.5%
   B. 7.5%
   C. 10%
   D. 14.5%

16. Which of the following statement describes renal blood flow in relation to PAH clearance?

   A. It is greater
   B. It is less
   C. It is equal
   D. It is indeterminable

PASSAGE III (QUESTIONS 17–23)

Interferons are molecules produced by leukocytes and fibroblasts in response to viral infections. When a virus enters a cell and begins replication, it also stimulates transcription of antiviral genes in the infected cell, which are translated and released. These antiviral genes are responsible for the protective effect of interferons in widespread viral infections. This is thought to occur by prevention of viral RNA translation thereby blocking viral protein synthesis. A set of interferons secreted by T cells, gamma-interferons, also potentiate phagocytosis towards virally infected cells of the body.

17. The following are the results of an experiment to test interferon production in response to various pathogens.

Bacteria	+
Viruses	+++
Fungi	–
Protozoa	–

What is the most likely explanation for these findings?

A. Fungi and protozoa are generally extracellular pathogens.
B. Variation in the structure of bacterial cell walls
C. Differences between prokaryotic and eukaryotic life cycles
D. Locomotive properties of bacteria and protozoa

18. The following are the results of an experiment where interferon was added to plates of virally infected cells two hours after initial inoculation with high titers of a virus. The control represents a plate of virally infected cells before and two hours after addition of culture medium. Which of the following patterns of growth would be expected in the control group, assuming the virus is cytolytic?

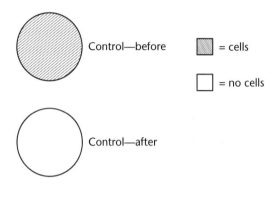

Control—before   ▨ = cells
Control—after   ☐ = no cells

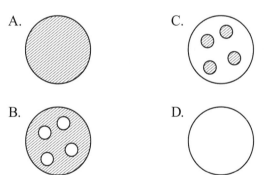

A.   C.

B.   D.

19. Which of the following findings on microscopy would provide proof that interferons inhibited viral RNA synthesis?

A. Lack of a viral envelope

B. Lack of the viral cytopathic effect

C. Lack of viral penetration into the nucleus

D. Lack of viral capsid protein

20. Gamma interferon, synthesized by T lymphocytes, stimulates the humoral immune system to fight viral infections. Which of the following findings would provide evidence that the humoral immune system has been recruited?

A. Increased phagocytosis of virally infected cells

B. Increased inflammation at the site of viral entry

C. Increased concentration of B lymphocytes at the site of viral entry

D. Increased concentration of immunoglobulins at the site of viral entry

21. Cytotoxic T cells are capable of killing virally infected cells via a number of ways. Interferon production by cytotoxic T cells leads to which of the following?

A. Involvement of immunoglobulins

B. Release of cytolytic enzymes

C. Use of intracellular machinery to break down infectious particles

D. Recruitment of macrophages to the site of infection

22. People born without a thymus would have which of the following laboratory derangements?

A. Low lymphocyte count

B. Low immunoglobulin titer

C. High immunoglobulin titer

D. High interferon concentrations

23. Certain diseases affecting tissue perfusion can have a profound effect on the efficiency of the immune system. Poor oxygen delivery would hamper which of the following immunoprotective events?

A. Antigen presentation by natural killer cells

B. Respiratory burst by macrophages

C. Antibody production by B cells

D. T cell maturation in the thymus

QUESTIONS 24 THOUGH 36 ARE NOT BASED ON A DESCRIPTIVE PASSAGE.

24. Which of the following describes the central reaction of a Western blot?

A. Insertional mutagenesis

B. Nucleotide template-directed polymerization

C. Plasmid-driven transcription

D. Nucleotide hybridization

25. Which of the following is an assumption of the Hardy-Weinberg model?

A. Mating between populations occurs at a set rate.

B. Mutation occurs at a set frequency.

C. Positive selection for certain genotypes occurs but does not eliminate any genes.

D. The population being studied is large and stable.

26. Angiotensin DIRECTLY causes the release of which of the following from the adrenal cortex?

A. Renin

B. Aldosterone

C. Calcitonin

D. Thyroxine

27. Cystic fibrosis is a genetic disorder inherited through an autosomal recessive gene.

If a male heterozygous carrier and a female heterozygous carrier have a female child who is homozygous for the diseased trait, what is the chance that a second child will develop cystic fibrosis?

A. 0%
B. 12.5%
C. 25%
D. 75%

28. Given the principle of independent assortment, how many unique gametes could be produced from the genotype AaBbCc?

A. 4
B. 6
C. 8
D. 12

29. Some types of mammals have especially long loops of Henle that maintain a steep osmotic gradient. This adaptation enables the organism to

A. excrete urine of higher osmolarity.
B. secrete less solute across the membrane into the renal tubule.
C. produce urine that is isotonic to body fluids.
D. reabsorb more blood proteins such as albumin.

30. Mice are administered a drug that inhibits endocytosis. Then, they are intravenously infused with a substance that is found to accumulate rapidly inside cells. This substance is most likely a

A. steroid hormone.
B. polypeptide.
C. second messenger.
D. glucose analog.

31. The lung is a more common site for primary tuberculosis than the duodenum because

A. the mycobacterium that causes tuberculosis cannot survive in organs other than the lungs.
B. the lung has a more readily available supply of oxygen than does the alimentary canal.
C. the bile salts present in the small intestine destroy the tubercle bacilli.
D. the low pH of the digestive secretions in the stomach kills mycobacteria before they enter the duodenum.

32. An MRI scan of a child's brain reveals a tumor growing on her posterior pituitary gland. Which of the following symptoms might have predicted this finding?

A. Hypertension
B. Increased plasma calcium levels
C. Decreased plasma calcium levels
D. Precocious puberty

33. A researcher investigates the cells involved in bone formation and resorption. From which of the following types of cells are osteoclasts most likely to be differentiated?

A. Red blood cells
B. Fibroblasts
C. Plasma cells
D. Macrophages

34. Many runners find that smoking cigarettes decreases their speed and endurance. This finding is due to all of the following effects of nicotine EXCEPT

A. constriction of the terminal bronchioles of the lungs.
B. increase in surfactant secretion by type II alveolar epithelial cells.
C. swelling of the epithelial linings.
D. paralysis of the cilia on the surfaces of respiratory epithelial cells.

35. Which of the following structures is found in bacterial cells?

  A. Ribosome

  B. Mitochondrion

  C. Golgi apparatus

  D. Nuclear membrane

36. One type of DNA mutation that can occur as a result of environmental toxin exposure is a deletion, in which one or more nucleotides are deleted during the replication of the cell's genome. However, in mutations in which three base pairs are deleted, the mutated gene often codes for a relatively normal protein. This is likely due to

  A. the fact that most DNA mutations have no effect on cellular function.

  B. codons' ability to expand in size to fill the gaps created by base-pair deletions.

  C. retention of the original reading frame.

  D. occurrence of a back-mutation.

PASSAGE IV (QUESTIONS 37–46)

Erythropoietin (EPO) is a hormone synthesized in the kidney that is responsible for stimulating red blood cell production. Therapeutically, it is used to treat severe anemia as seen in kidney disease and cancer. However, recently it has gained notoriety as a performance-enhancing drug capable of providing the user with additional oxygen carrying capacity. Because intense aerobic training stimulates endogenous production of EPO, absolute levels are not helpful in determining whether or not an athlete has used it for doping. Current methods of detecting exogenous EPO administration extort the aberrant glycosylation of the recombinant form of EPO.

Although erythropoeisis can be stimulated by EPO, production of effective red blood cells is dependent on the availability of iron in the body. Iron is an ion integrated into the heme molecule. Formed heme molecules negatively feedback on the rate-limiting step of heme synthesis.

Endogenous EPO production is regulated by oxygen levels sensed by the kidneys. Adequate oxygen levels allow for hydroxylation and thus inactivation of hypoxia-inducible factor (HIF), a transcription factor of EPO found in kidney cells.

37. In the healthy human adult, erythropoeisis occurs in which of the following locations?

  I. Liver

  II. Spleen

  III. Skull

  A. I only

  B. II only

  C. III only

  D. I and III

38. The kidney is also involved in the processing of which of the following substances?

  A. Folic acid

  B. Vitamin D

  C. Vitamin K

  D. Riboflavin

39. Which of the following laboratory findings would you expect in a patient with chronic kidney disease who is unable to produce adequate EPO levels?

  A. Larger than normal (macrocytic) red blood cells

  B. Smaller than normal (microcytic) red blood cells

  C. Normal sized (normocytic) red blood cells

  D. Fragments of red blood cells (schistocytes)

40. Which of the following laboratory techniques would be most useful for distinguishing exogenous from endogenous EPO?

A. Northern blot
B. Peripheral smear
C. Spectrophotometry
D. Enzyme-linked immunoabsorbant assay (ELISA)

41. The following data were obtained in a mouse population exposed to varying levels of oxygen. Biologically active HIF was measured by ELISA. Red blood cell percentage by volume was measured by centrifuging a blood sample and comparing the volume of sediment to the total volume of the sample.

The most likely explanation for the shape of the curve at low oxygen levels in the graph above is

A. insensitivity of ELISA to high levels of HIF.
B. exhaustion of iron stores in chronic low oxygen states.
C. impairment of HIF transcription secondary to chronic low oxygen states.
D. red blood cell clumping.

42. Genetic mutations resulting in insuppressable HIF would directly result in

A. abnormally high numbers of red blood cells.
B. abnormally low numbers of red blood cells.
C. abnormally high levels of EPO at elevated oxygen concentrations.
D. abnormally low levels of EPO at elevated oxygen concentrations.

43. Which of the following properties of the red blood cell allows it to complete its course through the circulation?

A. Lack of a nucleus
B. Lack of protein production
C. Lack of a structural protein network
D. Lack of cholesterol in the cell membrane

44. According to the passage, HIF acts at which of the following steps?

Hypoxia $\xrightarrow{\text{A}}$ EPO $\xrightarrow{\text{B}}$ Erythropoiesis $\xrightarrow{\text{D}}$ RBC

Heme precurors $\xrightarrow{\text{C}}$ Heme↑

A. Hypoxia → EPO
B. EPO → Erythropoiesis
C. Heme precursors → Heme↑
D. Erythropoiesis → RBC

45. Epinephrine works systemically to shunt blood to the skeletal muscles, brain, and heart away from nonessential organs such as the stomach, intestines, and kidneys. One would expect which of the following responses to a prolonged administration of epinephrine?

A. Increase in EPO production
B. Accelerated gastric emptying
C. Decrease in renin secretion
D. Increased endogenous catecholamine production

46. In order to bind oxygen, the iron contained in heme needs to be retained in the Fe^{2+} state. Which of the following enzymes is likely responsible for returning Fe^{3+} to its most efficient oxygen-binding state?

A. Catalase

B. Enolase

C. Reductase

D. Oxidase

PASSAGE V (QUESTIONS 47–52)

Bones break when subjected to forces greater than their mechanical strength to bear force. Whether a bone will fracture under a given load depends on both the inherent strength of the bone and the magnitude of the force. Materials such as bone whose mechanical properties are dependent on the loading rate of an applied force are said to be viscoelastic. The viscoelasticity of bone is important clinically because when force is applied at low speeds, bone is weak, and when force is applied at higher speeds, bone is stronger.

Bone fractures are a common occurrence. They are important to note and treat not only because they are painful and debilitating, but also because they may reflect underlying medical disease such as an endocrine disorder or cancer.

Bone healing is divided into primary and secondary processes. Primary healing requires precise reapproximation of the fracture ends, and rarely occurs naturally. It requires rigid immobilization of the fracture and compression of the cortices of the bone together. Primary bone healing is simply the deposition of new bone across the fracture by osteoblasts. This new bone integrates into the two opposing sides through tunnels created by osteoclasts called *cutting cones*. There will be local bone resorption and eventual recreation of normal bone structure. In secondary bone healing, the body first produces a mass of cartilage scar that is subsequently transformed to bone by matrix deposition and calcification.

In addition to serving as the framework of the body, bone is the main storage depot for calcium and phosphorus. A full 99 percent of calcium in the body is stored as hydroxyapatite in the bone. In a typical 24-hour period, 500 mg of calcium is released by the bone and 500 mg is replaced by osteoblast formation of new bone. Like calcium, phosphorus is stored in the body primarily in the bone, although nearly 100 g is present in the extracellular fluid, approximately 10 times the amount of extra-skeletal calcium. The primary circulating factors that affect calcium balance are PTH, vitamin D, calcitonin, and calcium. PTH is released by the parathyroid in response to low calcium levels and acts directly on osteoblasts, which stimulate osteoclasts to promote the release of calcium. Vitamin D must be made active by enzymatic steps in the liver and the kidney. The liver will hydroxylate vitamin D at position 25; the kidney will then add a hydroxyl group at position 24 or 1. An addition to position 24 will be an inactive form, while an addition at 1 will be an active form of vitamin D to work on calcium reabsorption in the body. Vitamin D will act at the kidney to promote reabsorption of calcium from glomerular filtrate and at the intestine to promote absorption directly from the gut.

47. Why might bone development be hampered in cloudy climates?

A. Poor development of the periosteum

B. Less sunlight to produce vitamin C from endogenous precursors

C. Barometric pressure changes increase the likelihood of a break

D. Less sunlight to produce vitamin D from endogenous precursors

48. Bone loss would result from overactivity of which of the following cells?

A. Osteoblasts

B. Osteoclasts

C. T lymphocytes

D. B lymphocytes

49. It can be inferred from the passage that the majority of bone healing occurs by

A. endochondral ossification.

B. membranous ossification.

C. primary healing.

D. secondary healing.

50. A patient who has had her thyroid removed complains of nausea, tetany, numbness, and tingling around her lips. Excess of what mineral most likely contributes to these symptoms?

A. PTH

B. Calcitonin

C. Phosphorus

D. Calcium

51. Vitamin D is stored in which of the following?

A. Interstitial fluid

B. Fat

C. Muscle

D. Liver

52. T and B cells are both developed in the bone, but T cells mature in which of the following?

A. Liver

B. Spleen

C. Thymus

D. Thyroid

Answers and Explanations

Practice Section 1

ANSWER KEY

1.	A	19.	D	36.	A
2.	D	20.	D	37.	B
3.	A	21.	A	38.	A
4.	C	22.	D	39.	D
5.	C	23.	A	40.	D
6.	B	24.	D	41.	C
7.	C	25.	B	42.	C
8.	C	26.	B	43.	B
9.	A	27.	D	44.	B
10.	B	28.	C	45.	D
11.	A	29.	A	46.	B
12.	B	30.	D	47.	D
13.	B	31.	D	48.	B
14.	D	32.	A	49.	C
15.	D	33.	B	50.	A
16.	B	34.	B	51.	A
17.	A	35.	A	52.	A
18.	B				

PASSAGE I

1. A

The null hypothesis is a hypothesis designed such that if it is refuted, then the the alternate hypothesis (the hypothesis the experimenters are testing) is supported. As it says in the passage, the experimenters' hypothesis is that hermit crab shell choice is influenced by color. (B), (C), and (D) all present null hypotheses that if rejected, do not validate

the experimenters' hypothesis. If (B) is shown to be false, hermit crabs could prefer shells with the starkest color difference from their environment, and thus would still display color preference. If (C) is shown to be false, hermit crabs could prefer shells with the least color difference from their environment, and thus would still display color preference. If (D) is shown to be false, hermit crabs could prefer lighter-colored shells in certain instances, in which case color preference would still be an influence.

2. D

If the pink paint darkened after it was applied to the shells, this would not nullify the hypothesis that hermit crabs show shell preference based on color cues. There is still a color difference between the unpainted shells and the dark pink shells.

3. A

According to the data, the hermit crabs choose the unpainted black shells when on a background of pink rocks, and pink shells when on a naturally black-colored substrate. This could be due to any number of reasons, but the experimental data only implies that hermit crabs demonstrate a preference for color when choosing shells, not why that preference exists. We can eliminate (B) and (C) because neither statement was supported by all experiments. Furthermore, data from Experiment 3 directly contradicts (D). Only (A) was supported by the data from these experiments.

4. C

(A), (B), and (D) present scenarios in which the visual cue—color—would affect hermit crab reproductive success. (C), however, presents a scenario in which color does not confer any advantage or disadvantage. Because hermit crabs show a preference for certain colors in the experiment, this suggests that certain colors confer reproductive advantages.

5. C

The experiment shows that crabs prefer dark-colored shells on white substrate, suggesting some kind of reproductive advantage for dark-colored shells in this environment. One would therefore expect evolutionary forces to select for crabs with dark shells in an environment of pure-white rocks, moving crabs in the direction of dark shells. Based on the experiment, one would also expect evolutionary forces to select for crabs with white shells in an environment of pure-black rocks. As evolutionary forces push the hermit crabs to fill different environmental niches, you will see selection in two opposite directions, also known as disruptive selection.

6. B

These findings do not strongly support the hypothesis that shell color affects hermit crab shell choice because the findings do not offer any indication as to why the crab population died out. Nor are the crabs in this population presented with a choice between differently-colored environments or shells. These findings do not conflict with the hypothesis either. Again, no evidence of preference or indifference to shell color is presented. Finally, the fact that the hermit crabs are not native to Jordan may suggest that the environment was likely suboptimal in many ways. However, it does not invalidate the hypothesis that hermit crabs use color to help choose new shells.

7. C

Because these two species of hermit crabs are monophyletic, they share a common ancestor. As the species of hermit crabs used in the experiment show a strong prefer-

ence for shells based on color, we can conclude that they are not colorblind. The trait must have arisen spontaneously in the second hermit crab species, or it must have been lost spontaneously in the first. In either case, because the trait is not shared between the two species, it can be neither analogous (a trait shared due to parallel evolutionary forces) nor homologous (a shared trait that arose from shared genetic lines). (C), then, could be possible. The founder effect refers to new selective pressures affecting a population introduced to a new environment, which cause it to deviate from the rest of the species.

PASSAGE II

8. C

The disease allele is most likely recessive. While neither parent expresses the condition, one of the children is affected. In a dominant condition, one parent (at least) would need to be affected. There is no information in the text or pedigree to suggest codominance or a sex-linked trait. In the case of X-linked recessive inheritance, males are generally affected and that is not seen in this case.

9. A

If male 7, who is affected, marries a carrier, 50 percent of offspring would be affected and 50 percent would be carriers. A healthy noncarrier child cannot be born. It can be seen that male 7 is affected looking at the gel analysis. Male 7 has the same marker as an affected female 3 and no other marker to be heterozygous. It also makes sense as a smaller fragment with disease allele (due to deletion) migrates faster through the gel.

10. B

Expressivity, a term that refers to the degree of disease severity observed in affected individuals, varies according to the passage. It is mentioned that while some patients have mild respiratory difficulties, others have serious problems.

11. A

A mutation leading to cystic fibrosis can be classified as a deletion, as it results in a loss of three nucleotides. Inversion

(C) would not change the number of nucleotides and would only affect their sequence. Insertion (D) would increase the number of nucleotides. Nondisjunction (B) refers to a failure of chromosomes to separate during meiosis; it does not deal with nucleotides.

12. B

Male 7 is homozygous recessive according to the gel electrophoresis results.

13. B

The fourth member alone is neither affected nor carrying a disease allele. On the gel, he has a larger fragment which migrated more slowly than the disease allele-containing fragment. It is the only fragment present, pointing to a homozygous condition.

14. D

A DNA fragment containing the disease allele would be shorter due to the deletion leading to cystic fibrosis; thus, it would move faster through the gel.

15. D

A mutation responsible for cystic fibrosis results in a deletion of three nucleotides. A nonsense mutation (B) introduces a stop code prematurely into the DNA sequence. A missense mutation (A) replaces one nucleotide with another, changing the peptide sequence of the encoded protein. A silent mutation (C) changes one of the nucleotides without affecting the type of amino acid in a sequence.

16. B

The frequency of the disease genotype is 1/100. The frequency of the disease allele, according to the Hardy-Weinberg principle, is the square root of 1/100 or 0.1.

17. A

Family member 5 is a carrier, as she has two types of DNA fragments: one for the wild type and one for the mutant allele. If member 5 marries another carrier, ¼ of their offspring on average will be affected.

QUESTIONS 18–21

18. B

(A) is a misuse of a detail; both rheumatic fever and type I diabetes occur initially in young populations, but co-occurence does not imply a similar etiology. (C) is a distortion; the specific hypersensitivity mechanism that causes rheumatic fever is cross-reactivity, where the immune system mistakes a body tissue for a foreign substance because they look similar. In an allergic reaction, the body has a response against a foreign substance that is too severe. In (D), although rheumatic fever causes a structural problem in the heart, the type of lesion mentioned in the passage occurs after infection, not at birth.

19. D

The question is intended to distract you with enzyme names that might seem intimidating. Nevertheless, the concept is simple: A kinase, when activated, phosphorylates its substrate. If the substrate is a metabolic enzyme, then this phosphorylation will take place at an allosteric site. Because this action activates PFK-1, the indicated process is an example of allosteric activation. (A) and (C) are wrong because the process causes an activation or agonistic effect, not an inactivation or antagonistic effect. Synergism (B) would require more than one enzyme with the same substrate to be present. This question presents two enzymes with different substrates.

20. D

The suffix *kinase* indicates that the function of the enzyme is to phosphorylate not isomerizes, thus eliminating (C). (A) is wrong because the indicated reaction does not occur. (B) is wrong because the indicated conversion would require two enzymes: an isomerase to convert glucose to fructose and a kinase to add the second phosphate group.

21. A

This question tests your ability to paraphrase the question and see the concept through the details. A good paraphrase is: Under what conditions does the breakdown of glucose stop with glycolysis and not proceed to form intermediates of the Krebs cycle? Since oxygen is the final electron acceptor of the electron transport chain, one could predict that low levels of oxygen would prevent aerobic metabolism. This is true and the accumulated pyruvate is converted to lactate under such conditions. (B) indicates a high concentration of oxidized substrates, implying an abundance of oxygen. (C) is wrong because while this would signal for an increase in the rate of glycolysis, it gives no information as to the oxygen levels of the cell and thus the ability of the cell to proceed into aerobic respiration. (D) is wrong because low levels of fructose-1,6-bisphosphate initiate the signal for gluconeogenesis, a separate metabolic pathway.

PASSAGE III

22. D

The passage describes that protons (H^+) are pumped across inner mitochondrial membrane into the intermembrane space making the intermembrane space more positive when compared to the matrix. pH drops in the intermembrane space as the proton concentration increases when compared to the matrix of mitochondria. (A) and (B) are only half right, and (C) is opposite the correct answer.

23. A

You're asked to choose one of the results that cannot be observed upon administration of antimycin A. According to the table, antimycin A blocks step 4 of the electron transport chain. The first figure shows that blocking step 4 will prevent the passage of electrons from cytochrome b to cytochrome c in the electron transport chain. As electrons don't travel further than cytochrome b, oxygen cannot remain the final acceptor of electrons (step 6 of ETC) and the transport is stopped at step 4 (choice A). (B) is wrong, as antimycin A indeed decreases the proton gradient, because when electrons travel only part of the transport chain less protons are pumped to the mitochondrial intermembrane space. This can be inferred from the passage that describes the buildup of proton gradient as electrons are passed from carrier to carrier. (C) is wrong. ATP synthesis is indeed stopped as the electrons never reach the final acceptor oxygen and the gradient would be lower than needed for ATP synthesis. This is inferred from the passage that mentions the specific gradient required. (D) is wrong as cytochrome b is indeed fully reduced and it can no longer pass its electrons to cytochrome c.

24. D

You're asked to use information in the passage and figures to determine which of the inhibitors will stop ATP synthesis without affecting the proton gradient. The table shows that oligomycin blocks the action of ATP synthase, which is responsible for ATP production. At the same time, as oligomycin does not affect any of the carriers in the chain, the electron gradient would be established and could not be dissipated as ATP synthase does not work (D). Choices (B) and (C) are wrong because both inhibitors interfere with electron transport along the chain, making the proton gradient less, even though ATP synthesis will come to a halt. (A) is wrong as 2,4-dinitrophenol makes the inner mitochondrial membrane more permeable to protons that can escape from the intermembrane space back into the matrix without building up the gradient.

25. B

The question asks you to identify inhibitors that will interfere with the transport of electrons along the chain so that the final electron acceptor oxygen cannot receive electrons. Inhibitors listed in items II and III alone will interfere with the electron transport chain, while oligomycin does not disrupt the chain of carriers and blocks ATP synthase directly.

26. B

The question asks you to suggest what happens when the permeability of the inner mitochondrial membrane is increased. As the passage addresses the importance of building up a proton gradient across impermeable inner membrane, it can be inferred that if protons are allowed to pass, they will escape the intermembrane space—thus, decreasing the gradient. For (C), a lower proton gradient would decrease ATP synthesis, not increase ATP production.

27. D

The passage explains that, as protons pass through the ATP synthase into the mitochondrial matrix, ATP is made. As ADP and phosphates are needed for ATP production, it makes sense that they would be present in mitochondrial matrix. (A) is wrong because, as per the passage, ATP synthase is a transmembrane enzyme complex and embedded into the membrane, and thus not in the mitochondrial matrix.

28. C

Rotenone will not produce a fully reduced cytochrome a, as rotenone disrupts step 2 of ETC and electrons don't go beyond FMN, leaving cytochrome a oxidized. (A), (B), and (D) interfere with step 6 preventing cytochrome a from passing its electrons to oxygen. Thus cytochrome a would be left fully oxidized.

PASSAGE IV

29. A

The presence of pre-existing lung disease could have a negative effect on the inspiratory reserve volume of the individuals in the study. A patient with asthma, an obstructive pulmonary disease, an asbestosis, or a restrictive lung disease would likely have different inspiratory reserve volumes. Tidal volume should not impact this experiment because the amount of drug delivered is the same in each case; we look for radioactivity, not a concentration-dependent phenomenon. Sex will make no difference; male lungs would generally be larger, but the measurements are made per unit of lung tissue. Bronchodilators with zero order kinetics are metabolized independently of their concentration. Because these medications are delivered directly to the lungs and do not undergo metabolism before contacting their target tissue, the kinetics of metabolism will have no bearing on the results.

30. D

IgE is formed as a result of exposure to an allergen. The first time the allergen is present, the body will form IgE, but there will be no signs of allergy. IgE circulates and 'docks' or 'connects' to mast cells via the Fc region of the antibody. When the antibody comes in contact again with its antigen, a conformation change takes place in the antibody and the mast cell degranulates, resulting in histamine release and contributing to asthma attack.

31. D

The key to this question is knowing that acetylcholine is the primary neurotransmitter of the parasympathetic response. During the parasympathetic response, the body is relaxed, the heart rate decreases, and blood flow to the gut is increased. Remember parasympathetic is to 'rest and digest.' The sympathetic response, in contrast, comes into play when being chased by a tiger. The body will need great airflow to support running away. An asthma attack, then, is the opposite of a sympathetic response; it causes relative bronchoconstriction. The use of an anticholinergic medication will promote the sympathetic system to open the airways.

32. A

This question just requires summing the values for each column. The largest total will be the most effective, on average, at delivering medication to the lungs.

QUESTIONS 33–35

33. B

Chylomicrons transport fats from the intestines to the circulation. With that, one can predict that with low levels of chlyomicrons, the lipids will not enter circulation (eliminating (C) and (D)) but will pass out with the stool. While diarrhea (A) is always possible in a metabolic disorder, it is not specific to abetalipoproteinemia.

34. B

Replication errors are the least severe if chemical class of the base isn't changed. That is, a mutation from a purine to a purine is less severe than a mutation from a purine to a pyrimidine. Using this, we can predict that (B) is the correct answer since (A) and (C) involve the change from a purine, A, to a pyrimidine, C or T. (D) is wrong for two reasons: first is, again, a purine change, and second, uracil is found only in RNA. Its inclusion in a strand of DNA would indicate a serious replication error.

35. A

The central dogma of molecular biology is that the genetic information contained in DNA is first transcribed to RNA and then translated to a linear sequence of amino acids which comprise the primary structure of a protein. The central dogma does not make claims to the details of transcription, as (B) suggests only that is transferred information between DNA and RNA; nor does it tell of the flow of information or the organelle subserving this function, as in choices (C) and (D).

PASSAGE V

36. A

Gastrin, usually secreted by G cells in the antrum of the stomach, stimulates the cholecystokinin-B (CCKb) receptor, which then stimulates the parietal cells to secrete H^+, as (A) describes. Activating the receptors in either (B) or (C) would stimulate H^+ production, but activating H2 and M3 receptors requires histamine and acetylcholine, respectively. (D) is misleading: somatostatin inhibits, not promotes, H^+ secretion.

37. B

There are a few ways that Zollinger-Ellison syndrome can cause malabsorption of dietary lipids. One way is inactivation of pancreatic enzymes. Pancreatic enzymes are inactivated at acidic pH. With the overproduction of H^+ caused by an oversecretion of gastrin, pancreatic enzymes are inactivated, causing impairment of dietary lipid absorption. (A) is wrong, as Zollinger-Ellison syndrome does not affect the liver's ability to create bile salts. Celiac disease is an autoimmune disease of the small intestine in reaction to gluten which eliminates (C). (D) is referring to one of the major causes of peptic ulcer disease (PUD), *H. pylori*, a flagellated bacteria associated with duodenal and gastric ulcers.

38. A

Only (A) does not stimulate H^+ secretion: Gastric inhibitory peptide, or GIP, causes pancreatic beta cells to secrete insulin, as well as inhibits H^+ secretion in the stomach. Acetylcholine (ACh), histamine, and gastrin [(B), (C), and (D)] all bind to different receptors on parietal cells, all three leading to an increase in H^+ secretion. ACh is released from the vagus nerves, histamine is released from mastlike cells in the gastric mucosa, and gastrin is released from G cells in the stomach's antrum.

39. D

Gastrin has two main functions: first, to stimulate H^+ secretion by gastric parietal cells, and second, to stimulate gastric mucosa growth. Gastrin is secreted by G cells located in the antrum of the stomach, and its secretion is stimulated when food is ingested, or by local vagal reflexes. (A) and (B) refer to functions of cholecystokinin (CCK), while (C) refers to a function of secretin.

40. D

In some cases of Zollinger-Ellison syndrome, diarrhea may be the only presenting symptom. This results from an oversecretion of gastrin and gastric acid production. The high acid content damages intestinal villi, leading to malabsorption and frequent diarrhea.

41. C

The physiologic control of gastrin, the gastric G cells, are under negative feedback control. Once the gastric contents have been properly acidified, gastrin secretion is inhibited. But in Zollinger-Ellison syndrome, the tumor does not respond to gastric pH and gastrin is produced regardless.

PASSAGE VI

42. C

The free energy of the reaction is the same whether it is catalyzed or uncatalyzed. It is the difference between the starting energy (here 45 kJ/mol) and the final reaction energy (here 10 kJ/mol), yielding 35 kJ/mol. (A) is the uncatalyzed activation energy—final energy. (B) is the catalyzed activation energy—final energy. (D) is wrong because the final energy is much lower than the initial value.

43. B

The activation energy for the uncatalyzed reaction is 80 kJ/mol, and the catalyzed is 55 kJ/mol. $80 - 55 = 25$, and $25/85 \sim 32\%$. (A) is wrong because the enzyme by definition lowers the activation energy some amount. (C) is wrong because the activation energy required is still 66% of what it was originally; it only went down 33%. (D) is wrong because there is still clearly some activation energy required for the reaction to occur.

44. B

Estrogen is associated with conversion from fat to muscle, and therefore some of it is necessary in the body. In people with high fat content, however, the estrogen cannot 'keep up,' and its efficacy is reduced. (A) is wrong because velocity can never be higher than V_{max} in any individual. (C) is wrong because the aromatase is just as active (i.e., requires same activation energy) as in a healthy person, but is working over many more cells. (D) is wrong because changing the structure of the enzyme (e.g., via exogenous chemicals, or through denaturation) is unlikely to have it catalyze different reactions, and the passage doesn't suggest that aromatase is promiscuous (non-specific).

45. D

The table dictates that letrozole is a competitive inhibitor of aromatase. Competitive inhibitors have a strong affinity for the active site of the enzyme they inhibit, and bind there reversibly through non-covalent interactions. Allosteric sites refer to sites on the enzyme other than the active site, so both (A) and (B) are incorrect. (C) is wrong because there is no feedback from the product (estrogen) in this type of inhibition.

46. B

Aromatase inhibition will decrease estrogen production, and therefore increase androgen availability. (A) is wrong because as the enzyme converts androgen to estrogen, activating aromatase will lead to even lower androgen counts.

(C) is wrong because men do naturally have some aromatase in their bodies, and for the same reason as (A), androgen counts would decrease with artificial injection. (D) is wrong because aromatase (and the estrogen it produces) does affect men (by increasing libido, for instance) as well as women.

PASSAGE VII

47. D

Since three of I-2's six children have early-onset diabetes, she's likely passing on either MIDD or MODY. Because III-11 has early-onset diabetes inherited from her father, I-2 must be heterozygous for MODY (Mm). I-3 can only have MIDD, both because of the relatively late onset of diabetes in her genetic line, as well as the only inheritance to Generation III being matrilineal (through II-14). Given that each of the genotypes listed are autosomal, and thus do not describe mtDNA, (A), (B), and (C) are wrong.

48. B

The individual could present with type II diabetes or MIDD. The age of onset means that the individual could not present with type I (juvenile) diabetes. Type II is the most likely option given his age, but MIDD is also possible; we do not have any information on his mother, and as a male he would not pass on the disease to his children. II-1 may also have an allele for MODY: there is a 1 in 8 chance a heterozygote and a homozygous recessive could have three children that do not present with the disease. However, each of the answer choices containing III are wrong for other reasons: (A) and (D) include type I diabetes, and (C) omits type II diabetes.

49. C

This requires the determination that the MODY form of diabetes is present on the bloodline containing individual IV-2, and that it has autosomal dominant inheritance (stated in the passage introduction). This means that the mother, who has the disease, is heterozygous (homozygous dominant is extremely rare for such diseases, but this can be confirmed to not be the case by looking at the previous generations). With this deduction, a Punnett square could be made as follows.

Mother

Father	M	m
m	Mm	mm
m	Mm	mm

From this, the answer is clearly 50 percent. (A) would require both parents to be homozygous recessive, and this is not the case since the mother had early-onset diabetes. (B) is typical of autosomal *recessive* conditions, and the passage said that MODY is autosomal dominant. (D) requires both parents to be heterozygous, and in this case the father would also have diabetes.

50. A

These two individuals have no risk of developing a genetically-inherited form of diabetes (the only types that come before age 40). Their father has MIDD, but since this disease is mitochondrial and thus passed matrilineally, it will not be passed through him. The mother can be assumed to have type II diabetes, due to the late age of occurrence. (B) would have assumed that both offspring would have had a 25 percent chance of getting the disease, as is typical with autosomal recessive. (C) would have assumed both offspring had a 50 percent chance of developing the disease, as would have been the case with autosomal dominant. (D) is simply the chance of one individual getting it if it had been autosomal dominant.

51. A

Penetrance is the likelihood that a certain genotype will express the phenotype. There are three nondiabetic offspring in Generation II. If each of these offspring fall within the 15 percent chance of nonpenetrance, the overall probability of this happening is $(.15)^3 = 0.03$. (B) is $(.15)^2$, which would be for only two of the offspring. (C) is the chance that *any one* of the nondiabetic children is a carrier. (D) is the rate of penetrance for those who have diabetes.

52. A

ADM is a form of MODY, so we can assume that it, too, is an autosomal dominant trait. In addition, the question stem states that ADM is not permanently insulin-dependent. MIDD is, but because the individual's father has MIDD, it will not be passed on to him through mitochondrial DNA. Therefore, the individual has no chance of developing insulin-dependent diabetes (and a 50 percent chance of developing ADM). (B) is the likelihood if one of the conditions was autosomal recessive. (C) would be correct if looking at the risk of developing any kind of diabetes. (D) is the chance if the mother, not the father, had MIDD.

Practice Section 2

ANSWER KEY

1.	B	19.	D	37.	C
2.	C	20.	B	38.	A
3.	B	21.	B	39.	A
4.	B	22.	C	40.	B
5.	B	23.	C	41.	C
6.	C	24.	D	42.	B
7.	C	25.	D	43.	C
8.	B	26.	A	44.	A
9.	C	27.	D	45.	A
10.	C	28.	B	46.	A
11.	A	29.	A	47.	D
12.	D	30.	C	48.	A
13.	C	31.	A	49.	B
14.	C	32.	D	50.	C
15.	C	33.	C	51.	D
16.	D	34.	A	52.	C
17.	B	35.	A		
18.	A	36.	C		

PASSAGE I

1. B

The goal of this experiment, mentioned in the context of the two major classes of antiretroviral drugs that target reverse transcriptase, is to compare the two different mechanisms by which they act.

2. C

This question is asking which nucleotide pairs with adenine. The trick is to recognize that the parent strand in this case is RNA. Therefore, an adenine nucleotide (DNA) will pair with a uracil (RNA).

3. B

Drug C decreases the activity of the reverse transcriptase. This result, along with the information provided in the passage about drug mechanisms, means (B) is a possible mechanism (nonnucleoside reverse transcriptase inhibitor). (D) describes the mechanism of a nucleotide/nucleoside reverse transcriptase inhibitor, which based on the information in the passage, does not affect reverse transcriptase activity. (A) and (C) would not have any effect on reverse transcriptase activity.

4. B

The assay described in the passage is used to evaluate drugs that target reverse transcriptase. It is likely that drugs with other targets will not have an effect on the same variables as those examined in the assay used. Drug D is FDA approved and therefore the sample quality is unlikely to be at fault, and it should have an effect on the virus [(A), (C), and (D)].

5. B

Competitive inhibitors bind to the same active site that the substrate binds to, preventing the binding of the substrate. Noncompetitive inhibitors bind to the enzyme at a different site than the enzyme's active site. Given the description provided in the passage, non-nucleotide reverse transcriptase inhibitors act as noncompetitive inhibitors of reverse transcriptase.

6. C

As described in the passage, the mechanism of nucleoside/nucleotide reverse transcriptase inhibitors involves the early termination of transcription after their incorporation into the daughter DNA strand, implying that they cannot be removed. They do not affect translation (A). They are competitive inhibitors of reverse transcriptase (B). They act at the active site of reverse transcriptase (D).

7. C

Once a retrovirus integrates its DNA into the host DNA, it is called a provirus until its viral mRNA is transcribed. By definition, the viral DNA will be found in the nucleus.

PASSAGE II

8. B

The most critical (and susceptible) stage of fetal development is considered to be the embryonic stage (weeks 3–8), when all organ morphogenesis is occurring. If the drug was ingested during fertizilation (C), the likely outcome would be termination of pregnancy before implantation. The later weeks (A) and (D) are considered less critical because all the organ systems have been formed.

9. C

Down syndrome is the excess of genetic code on the 21st chromosome. A typical human's karyotype is either 46 XY (typical male) or 46 XX (typical female). There are many ways for this to occur, via either a complete extra chromosome [trisomy 21 (47, XX, +21)] or a portion of one due to translocations. About 95 percent of Down syndrome is due to trisomy 21; in the majority of cases, nondisjunction occurs with the maternal gamete. Cystic fibrosis (A) is caused by a mutation in the CFTR (cystic fibrosis transmembrane conductance regulator) gene. Sickle cell disease (B) is an inherited blood disorder whereby red blood cells contain an abnormal type of hemoglobin. Polycythemia vera (D), a myeloproliferative disorder, is considered to be due to a mutation of the JAK2 protein, thereby allowing for unregulated control of blood cell production.

10. C

The first sign of gastrulation is the formation of the primitive streak, which arises from (C) epiblast cells, not (A) hypoblast cells. During normal embryonic development, the primitive streak will diminish in size and eventually become an insignificant structure that ultimately disappears by the end of the fourth week. But sometimes the remnants will persist and give rise to a sacrococcygeal teratoma. This is the most common tumor in newborns and most often occurs in females. Most of the tumors are benign, diagnosed on routine antenatal ultrasonography, and surgically removed. The prochordal plate (B) is composed of hypoblast cells that fused with epiblast cells to form a circular, midline thickening, and will be the future site of the mouth. The yolk sac is formed from a portion of the exocoelomic cavity (D), which is formed in part from hypoblast cells and the inner surface of the cytotrophoblast.

11. A

Medulloblastoma is a highly malignant primary brain tumor that originates in the cerebellum or posterior fossa. It manifests with increased intracranial pressure due to blockage of the fourth ventrcile. Craniopharyngioma (B) is a slow-growing tumor that develops from Rathke's pouch. It is the most common supratentorial tumor in childhood. The tumor may enlarge and compress the optic chiasm, resulting in blindness. Glioblastoma multiforme (C) is the most common primary brain tumor in adults. It is a rapidly growing, highly destructive tumor with death occurring within months. The tumor is associates with necrotic tissue because the tumor grows faster than new blood vessels can be developed to provide nourishment for the tumor cells. Optic nerve glioma (D) is the most common primary neoplasm of the optic nerve. Often diagnosed during childhood, about 10 percent of cases occur in association with neurofibromatosis type I. It is a tumor of the visual system and has been known to involve the optic nerve, optic chiasm, and/or optic tract.

12. D

Gastroschisis is a result of a defect lateral to the median plane of the anterior abdominal wall. This defect allows the intestines and sometimes other organs to develop outside the fetal abdomen without involving the umbilical cord. No parietal peritoneum covers the organs. Omphalocele (B) is an anterior abdominal defect that does involve the umbilical cord. During the eighth week of development, the fetal midgut undergoes a physiologic umbilical herniation, in which the organs extend out into the extraembryonic celom, occupying the proximal segment of the umbilical cord. It is believed that an omphalocele occurs when the bowel fails to return into the abdomen. Meckel diverticulum (C) is a small outpouching of the small intestine that is present at birth. It is the vestigial remnant of the omphalomesenteric duct (vitelline duct) and is considered to be the most common gastrointestinal tract malformation. Myeloschisis (A) is considered to be the most severe form of spina bifida. The spinal cord in this area remains open due to lack of complete neural tube fusion.

13. C

Triploidy is an abnormal chromosomal condition usually resulting from fertilization of an oocyte by two sperm (dispermy). Most triploid fetuses are aborted spontaneously or are stillborns, and some die shortly after birth. (A) and (B) are aneuploidy, and (D) is tetraploidy.

14. C

An ectopic pregnancy occurs when the blastocyst implants within an abnormal location. Oftentimes, the woman has a history of endometriosis or pelvic inflammatory disease. The most common site is the ampulla portion of the fallopian tube (80–90%), isthmic (5–10%); cornual (1–2%), abdominal (1–2%), and cervix (less than 1%).

15. C

Pelvic inflammatory disease/disorder (PID) is a general term applied to inflammation of the female reproductive system (uterus, fallopian tube, and/or ovaries) that has progressed to scarring and adhesions to nearby tissues and organs. PID is often associated with STDs (sexually transmitted diseases). With each episode of infection, the chance of infertility increases. (C), Chlamydia trachomatis and Neisseria gonorrhoeae are considered the leading causes of PID. Patients testing positive for one are often tested for the other, as the two are often both present. Syphillis (A) is an STD caused by the spirochete, Treponema pallidum. Untreated syphilis can lead to systemic dissemination and damage—especially of the heart, brain, eyes, and bones—and has even been fatal in some. Human papilloma virus (HPV) (B) is considered to be the most common sexually transmitted disease in the United States. There are over 100 subtypes and some are known to cause cancer, primarily cervical, anal, vulvar, and penile cancers. Herpes (D) simplex virus (HSV) type 1 (HSV-1) and type 2 (HSV-2) are known to cause herpes simplex. Although in the past genital herpes was considered to have been caused by HSV-2, the rate of genital HSV-1 infections has increased dramatically. Typical manifestations are painfully inflamed papules and vesicles on the outer genital surface, as well as the inner thigh, buttocks, or anus.

16. D

Fetal erythroblastosis (aka hemolytic disease of the newborn) occurs when small amounts of fetal blood pass through the placental membrane and enters the maternal blood. If the mother is Rh negative, and the fetus is Rh positive, the mother may have anti-Rh IgG antibodies which will enter fetal circulation and attack fetal red blood cells. If severe, the infant may be stillborn or die shortly after birth. Rubella (aka German measles) (A) is caused by the rubella virus. The disease is usually mild in children and adults, but if a mother is infected within the first 20 weeks of pregnancy, the child may be born with congenital rubella syndrome (CRS), and that can lead to developmental deafness, blindness, congenital heart defects, and even infant death. Sickle cell anemia occurs when there is a point mutation on the beta-globin chain of hemoglobin (B), when glutamic acid is substituted by valine. This causes red blood cells to lose their elasticity and become sickle-shaped during low oxygen conditions. Cystic fibrosis is caused by mutation of

the CFTR (cystic fibrosis transmembrane conductance regulator) gene (C). This gene produces a chloride ion channel that is issential in sweat glands, digestive juices, and mucus production.

17. B

A partial hydatidiform mole usually results from an oocyte fertilized by two sperm. Most partial moles are triploid (contain three chromosome sets). The embryo usually dies, and the chorionic villi form into cystic swellings which resemble bunches of grapes. The moles will produce an abnormally high amount of human chorionic gonadotropin. Dizygotic twins (A) are the result of fertilization of two oocytes. The two zygotes may be of the same or different sexes.

QUESTIONS 18–21

18. A

Translation refers to the production of protein from mRNA. Though the conversion of DNA to RNA is discussed, the idea here is that one initial piece of information can give rise to multiple secondary pieces. This happens in eukaryotes through alternative splicing, where exons from one transcribed RNA strand can be spliced in multiple ways to make multiple mRNA products coding for different proteins. (B) and (C) are incorrect, because prokaryotic DNA is monocistronic. Although in transcription prokaryotes do have multiple reading frames (as do eukaryotes), this is not true in translation; their genes are organized in an operon and thus groups of proteins are produced en masse on one mRNA transcript in tandem fashion.

19. D

Gram-negative bacteria do not take up the gram stain because they have an outer cell wall which impedes the movement of any polar or large substance into the periplasmic space. This could also be a barrier to drugs. Capsids (A) are found in viruses, not bacteria. Bacteria are prokaryotes and thus have no membrane-bound organelles (B). All bacteria have an inner cell wall (C).

20. B

Only the endoplasmic reticulum is directly connected to the space between the inner and outer nuclear membranes. The nucleolus (A) resides in the nucleus. Neither (C) nor (D) is continuous with the nucleus.

21. B

This is a straight recall question. Plasma cells (C) do not secrete hormones; they function in the immune system. Beta cells of the islets of Langerhans in the pancreas secrete insulin. Delta cells in the gastric antrum, intestine, and pancreas secrete somatostatin.

PASSAGE III

22. C

The destructive phase (A) is another name for the menstrual phase. It is named as such because during this period, the uterine lining is destroyed and discarded. The secretory phase (B) is another name for the luteal phase. It is named as such because during this period, many hormones are secreted. The gestational phase (C) does not exist. Gestation refers to the period in which a woman carries an embryo in her womb. As menstruation refers to the cycle of events which lead up to gestation, it does not logically follow that one of its phases would occur during gestation. (You may be thinking of the name *pregestational phase*, which is another name for the luteal phase.) The proliferative phase (D) is another name for the follicular phase. It is called as such because during this period, follicules and the endometrium proliferate.

23. C

The passage tells us that the female menstrual cycle is a set of events which leads to ovulation. Ovulation is the release of ova into the uterus for fertilization. The chart shows us that the woman's menstrual cycle is 28 days long. This means that in a 365-day year, she would undergo 365/28 = 13 full menstrual cycles.

24. D

If fertilization fails to occur, the ovum is distentegrated through menses (A). It does not become the corpus luteum.

The product of ovum and sperm fertilization is a zygote. The follicle before ovulation occurs is a follicle. It goes through different stages such as tertiary follicle and then Graafian follicle. What remains of the follicle following ovulation becomes the corpus luteum.

25. D

One would expect the conditions in (D) to increase the proportion of time a woman is susceptible to pregnancy, and in so doing, indirectly increase fertility. As for (A), about one-third of estrogen comes from fat. One needs very high levels of estradiol (an estrogen) to stimulate the LH surge necessary of ovulation. This is also why anorexic women often experience secondary ammenorhea. Progesterone (B) is actually used as a form of birth control. Low levels of estrogen (C) would exacerbate infertility, as explained in (A).

26. A

By mimicking the levels of progesterone and estradiol in the body during pregnancy, the combination pill stops the proliferative (follicular) phase, preventing both menses and ovulation.

27. D

The zygote is what is formed after the egg's fertilization by the sperm. If fertilization occurs, menses is prevented from occurring. Blood (A) is contained in menstrual discharge as a result of broken blood vessels in the endometrium. As the endometrium exits the body, it sloughs off some of the cells lining the vagina (B). The stratum functionalis (C) is the outer layer of the endometrium, and is the layer that is discharged.

28. B

FSH is inhibited by high estradiol levels. Estradiol levels increase until the midpoint of the follicular phase, and FSH increases until that time as well. FSH dips at the midpoint as a result of high levels of estradiol secreted by large follicles, inhibiting GnRH. GnRH from the hypothalamus controls FSH secretion by the pituitary.

29. A

In the beginning of the follicular phase, estradiol levels are low, and FSH and LH secretion is high due to the absence of negative feedback by estradiol on FSH and LH production. At about the middle of the follicular phase, estradiol levels are moderately high and begin to exert negative feedback on FSH and LH production. By the end of the follicular phase, very high estradiol levels are present, and at very high concentrations, estradiol stimulates FSH and LH production, resulting in an LH surge.

30. C

If you refer to the figure in the passage, you will see that (C) is true. The relationship between estradiol and progesterone levels controls gonadotropin release. Before the FSH and LH surge, there is high estradiol but low progesterone. After ovulation, there is high progesterone but low estradiol.

31. A

To prevent pregnancy, the couple needs to limit coitus in a way that prevents viable sperm from coming in contact with a viable ovum. We know from the passage that ova can remain viable for up to three days after ovulation (ovum disintegration typically begins 24 hours after ovulation but can begin as late as 72 hours later). We also know that male sperm can stay viable in the female reproductive tract for up to four days. A woman with the given menstrual cycle should limit coitus to the time span starting three days after the basal temperature rise, and ending 21 days later (four days before ovulation), or choice (A).

PASSAGE IV

32. D

The experiment shows that the size of gene X in family 2 and the control group is the same. It is possible that there was a point mutation in gene X that affected its functional capability yet not the length of the gene. In mammals mtDNA encodes for 37 genes, so it is possible that the mtDNA mutation in family 2 affects one of the other genes. We know from the passage that family 2 has the clinical presentation of mitochondrial inheritance disorder, so item III is wrong. Items I and II are correct.

33. C

Since we know from the passage that gene X plays a role in aerobic respiration, we can predict the location of the gene X product. All proteins that play a role in aerobic respiration reside in the inner mitochondrial membrane and mitochondrial matrix. Because we know that the protein is a transmembrane protein, we can assume it is found in the inner membrane and not as a free protein in the matrix (D).

34. A

This question tests your ability to synthesize information from the passage with your knowledge about aerobic respiration. When oxygen is unavailable to accept electrons, pyruvate acts as the electron acceptor, forming lactic acid. It is unlikely that dysfunctions of aerobic respiration would cause an increase in phospholipids, alanine, or carbon dioxide.

35. A

As described in the passage and the subsequent experiment, mitochondrial inheritance disorders can take on multiple phenotypes (the visible appearance of a disease) and can be due to different mutations (different genotypes).

36. C

If a mitochondrial disorder were to be caused by a mutation in nuclear DNA, the mitochondria must rely somewhat on certain gene products from nuclear DNA. (A) is factually incorrect: mitochondrial DNA does not recombine with nuclear DNA. However, mitochondria are the only nonnuclear organelle to possess their own DNA (B). However, mitochondria are only semi-autonomous and do not encode all their necessary genes in the mitochondrial DNA (D).

37. C

Based on the passage and family tree illustration, we know that mitochondrial inheritance disorders have maternal inheritance of a mitochondrial genome that is separate from the nuclear genome. Maternal inheritance occurs because sperm cell mitochondria do not contribute to ova during fertilization. Items I, II, and III are correct.

38. A

Mitochondria have their own ribosomes separate from those made in the nucleus. Mitochondrial DNA is circular, but nuclear DNA is often found as linear chromosomes, thus (B) is incorrect. mtDNA has maternal inheritance, whereas there are maternal and paternal inputs in nuclear DNA inheritance, so (C) is incorrect. (D) is implausible: mtDNA is held within the mitochondrion (specifically, within the matrix), and thus cannot access nuclear DNA to recombine with it.

QUESTIONS 39–41

39. A

Lipase (B) breaks down fats, which are a different chemical class from polyscccharides. Pepsin (D) is a hormone, not an enzyme. Trypsinogen (C) is a zymogen, not a hormone. The rationale for eliminating these answer choices is guided by the prediction, garnered from the question stem, that the answer must be an enzyme which is specific for starches.

40. B

With regard to RNA mutations, there are three important things to remember. First, like in DNA, changes within the same base group of nucleotides (i.e., from purine to purine, or pyrimidine to pyrimidine) produce less severe mutations than changes between groups (i.e., from purine to pyrimidine, or vice versa). Second, remember that changes to the third nucleotide of any codon (also known as the "wobble position") is usually the least prone to result in adverse consequences, due to the structure of the tRNA-mRNA interface. Finally, with questions focusing on RNA, eliminate any answer choice that includes T, as RNA replaces it with U. Using this knowledge, (B) is correct because the mutation is both in the wobble position and changes a purine for a purine. (A) and (C) are wrong because the change is not in the wobble position. (D) is wrong because, although the mutation is in the wobble position, AAT is not a valid RNA codon (AAU would be).

41. C

This question tests your ability to critically evaluate what some consider an inflammatory statement. (A) and (B) have no basis in genetics. (D) assumes that a longer time for procreation will result in increased progeny. (C) is true because male gametes have more genetic variation than female gametes and thus have a higher chance of containing a mutation encoding a sexually advantageous trait.

PASSAGE V

42. B

The voltage-gated sodium channels that are affected by carbamazepine are very likely to be implicated as a mediator for a kindling-like mechanism which is voltage-dependant in action. The sodium channel activity does not necessarily support excitotoxicity, which is based on the toxicity of certain neurotransmitters in the synapse.

43. C

Excitotoxicity, not the kindling model, deals primarily with the toxicity of neurotransmitters that are found at the synapse, so (A) is wrong. Moreover, even though lots of sub-threshold potentials are shot and culminate at the synapse (leading to excitability of downstream neurons), (A) is wrong because the excitotoxicity model does deal with processes at the synapse. Since the passage does not specify whether the kindling model does not use chemical stimulation to cause sensitization, (B) is also wrong.

44. A

In light of the excitotoxicity view, extracellular administration of an enzyme which degrades glutamate (A) is a suitable method for normal treatment of a chronically epileptic patient. (B) would exacerbate seizures, as per the excitotoxicity hypothesis, and lowering the action potential threshold stimulus is related to the kindling model, and thus we can eliminate (C) and (D).

45. A

The question asks for the one false statement. Glutamate, as per the passage, is an excitatory neurotransmitter, so (A) is false. However, (B) is accurate: as a neurotransmitter, it is packaged in and released from synaptic vesicles into the synaptic cleft. We can also eliminate (C), as the statement is supported by the excitotoxicity model in the passage. Since only one choice is false, we must also eliminate (D).

46. A

By cutting off blood flow, metabolic nutrients for the maintenance and production of various enzymes and carriers are impaired. Nothing in the passage leads you to believe reasonably that trauma to the brain would cause an increase in Brownian motion of neurotransmitters (B). Nor does the passage suggest any impact on action potential propagation (C) by trauma to the brain.

47. D

(A) is not plausible because the kindling model does not gradually increase the stimulus; moreover, the "epileptic threshold" is lowered, whereas the threshold stimulus is raised in accommodation. (B) and (C) are concerned as well with a raising of the threshold, and in the case of absolute refractory period, to an infinitely high one.

48. A

The cerebellum is responsible for balance.

PASSAGE VI

49. B

The Na^+/K^+-ATPase (or sodium-potassium pump) transports three sodium ions out of the cell for every two potassium ions it transports inside. Given that the figure only accounts for the pump and the solutes it transports, the relative concentration of water inside the cell must reflect the ratio the pump establishes. Thus, the ratio of water inside the cell to outside the cell must be 2:3, or choice (B). This could also be inferred from counting the 8 K^+ ions in the cell, and the 12 Na^+ ions outside of the cell.

50. C

ATP is the energy source for the sodium-potassium pump, which is necessary to control the sodium level in the cell. (B) is misleading, because while table salt would form Na^+ ions, it isn't strictly necessary to establish or maintain the sodium/water balance. Both (C) and (D) could serve as solutes, but neither plays a role in the model described in the passage; moreover, (D)'s main function is to package nitrogen for excretion.

51. D

Vasopressin is released when the body is dehydrated and causes the body to conserve water. It also controls the menstrual cycle and is highest at the time of ovulation. Vasopressin interferes with the sodium-potassium pump, causing a "misinforming" such that the body thinks it is dehydrated when there's actually an excess of water. There is no evidence that women consume any more water than men (A); in fact, it is likely that they consume less because they sweat less. Brain mass (B) is determined by size, not gender (children do have a higher likelihood of hyponatremia for this reason, however). Although estrogen (C) does contribute to water storage, testosterone (another sex hormone also found in women) can actually block the effect of vasopressin.

52. C

The myelin sheath is a dielectric material composed of lipids and proteins, produced by Schwann cells (in the PNS) or oligodendrocytes (in the CNS) to insulate the axon. The nucleus is in the cell body, not the axon, so choice (A) is incorrect. The synapse is the cleft between neurons, and is not associated with myelin so we can eliminate (B). Meanwhile, nodes of Ranvier are the gaps between myelinated sections of an axon, thus, (D) is incorrect.

Practice Section 3

ANSWER KEY

1.	A	19.	D	36.	C
2.	D	20.	E	37.	C
3.	C	21.	D	38.	B
4.	A	22.	A	39.	C
5.	D	23.	B	40.	D
6.	B	24.	D	41.	B
7.	B	25.	D	42.	C
8.	A	26.	B	43.	A
9.	D	27.	C	44.	A
10.	A	28.	C	45.	A
11.	A	29.	A	46.	C
12.	C	30.	A	47.	D
13.	C	31.	D	48.	B
14.	A	32.	A	49.	D
15.	A	33.	D	50.	D
16.	A	34.	B	51.	B
17.	A	35.	A	52.	C
18.	D				

PASSAGE I

1. A

(A) allows both hypotheses 1 and 2 to be valid and their data accepted. Tyrosinase levels are not correlated with melanin levels; they are correlated with melanin levels and thus skin color. A logical synthesis of the two hypotheses would be that somehow after translation of the gene for tyrosinase, the actual enzyme's activity is changed to become more active to produce darker colorations. Gene alterations (B) would mean gene products would correlate with melanin synthesis—that gene product could only be tyrosinase. (C) bears no relation to the relevance of the hypotheses.

2. D

The table shows that the cooler temperature correlates with more active melanin production and hence, tyrosinase

activity level. A lower temperature (A) means more activity. The table shows varying activity levels with different group temperatures (B). A small percentage of coloration is detected at 5° (C).

3. C

The limb is the coolest region of the body, since it is the farthest from the body's core. Thus, it will have the highest activity rate at lower temperatures based on the passage results.

4. A

The active site (A) is the most involved and important area in the activity of any enzyme. The other areas are either not as involved or not real areas of an enzyme.

5. D

While temperature can affect secondary, tertiary, and quaternary structure, the active site of most enzymes is formed from the tertiary (three dimensional, non-covalent-bonded structure) and quaternary (multi-unit structure of proteins) structure. There is no zeroth-level organization in proteins, so (A) is incorrect. Primary organization (B) refers to the covalent-bonded, amino acid sequence, and will not be affected by temperature.

6. B

An allosteric inhibitor (B) would alter enzymatic activity after translation of the gene and the activity level of tyrosinase. (A) and (C) apply to tyrosinase levels and would refute hypothesis 1 because it is pre-translational. (D) is simply about pH, which is an unknown variable based upon the passage.

7. B

There is some coloration at 10°C indicating some level of activity (B). There is no complete denaturing at any level (A) and (D). Choice (C) is a distracter because an allosteric site would enhance enzymatic activity if it were denatured, but in this case, activity is only moderate at 25°C so it's less plausible than (B).

8. A

pH is often a factor regulating enzymatic activity. Pressure is not generally an issue in living systems' enzymatic metabolism.

PASSAGE II

9. D

The passage states that the glomerular filtration rate is equal to the clearance of inulin, which is neither secreted nor reabsorbed. Glucose is normally always reabsorbed from the proximal convoluted tubules.

10. A

Less of the solute has been excreted than has entered the Bowman's capsule.

11. A

GFR is best approximated by a solute that is neither secreted nor reabsorbed in the nephron.

12. C

Inulin is a polysaccharide, as the passage states. Inulin would not be able to filter into the Bowman's capsule if it were bigger than an erythrocyte (red blood cell) or albumin (A) and (B), both of which cannot be filtered.

13. C

Approximately 90 percent of PAH which enters the kidneys, whether via the glomerular apparatus or nephron vasculature, is excreted. (A) and (B) are wrong because PAH would not be able to be filtered through the glomerulus if it were bigger than an erythrocyte and albumin.

14. A

Clearance is a measurement of the excretion flow rate and GFR is a flow rate measurement of all the volume of fluid, including the solute, which filters through all the glomeruli in the body.

15. A

PAH clearance is equal to RPF, and if you look at the graph, a plasma creatinine concentration of 4 mg/dL corresponds to about 30 mL/min. Thus, using the filtration fraction equation (FF = GFR/RPF), the answer is 30 mL/min divided by 550 mL/min, or approximately 5.5%.

16. A

PAH is equal to RPF, and if one remembers that plasma is a component of blood, renal blood flow should be greater than renal plasma flow.

PASSAGE III

17. A

Interferons are messenger proteins that cause upregulation of anti-infective genes in other cells. This means that the antiviral properties of interferons can be utilized only on pathogens located within the cell, such as viruses and a few bacteria. They have no effect on typical extracellular pathogens such as fungi and protozoa.

18. D

Interferon works to protect cells that have yet to be virally infected or which have yet to undergo viral uncoating inside the cell. Addition of interferon at this point in time would not be protective to the cells on the plate, and would thus cause the cytotoxic effect to clear the plate of viable cells.

19. D

Viral RNA is needed to produce proteins vital to viral proliferation, which includes the capsid protein. The viral envelope is obtained as the virus buds off of the infected cell and is not synthesized by genetic material contained in the virus. The cytotoxic burst is not a characteristic of every virus's replication cycle. Some viruses carry their own nucleic acid polymerase and thus do not need to penetrate the nucleus. The genetic material of the virus can be DNA or RNA; thus, the virus's inability to infect is not specific to the inhibition of viral RNA.

20. D

Stimulation of humoral, or B cell immunity, requires presentation of antigens to B cells, which then form antibodies specific to those antigens. Inflammation, phagocytosis, and histamine are mechanisms used by the non-specific and/or cell-mediated immune system. B lymphocytes may or may not be activated, depending on if they carry the immunoglobulin specific to the antigen being presented. Therefore, the most specific indication of B cell activation is the presence of immunoglobulins.

21. D

Cytotoxic T cells eliminate infected cells in three main ways: first, direct cytotoxicity via granzymes (B), second, indirect cytotoxicity via the FAS/FAS-L pathway (C), and third, interferon production, stimulating phagocytosis of the infected cell (D). Immunoglobulin production is a hallmark of the humoral immune system (A).

22. A

Recall that the thymus is the maturation site for T cells, the predominant lymphocyte in the bloodstream. Without this maturation process, T lymphocytes are quickly removed from circulation.

23. B

Oxygen is required for the synthesis of digestive enzymes used by macrophages. Poor perfusion leading to chronically hypoxic tissue tends to result in macrophages with a diminished ability to phagocytize foreign material and present antigens to stimulate the B cell response.

QUESTIONS 24–29

24. D

Insertional mutagenesis (A) describes site-directed mutagenesis. Nucleotide template-directed polymerization (B) describes the polymerase chain reaction (PCR). Plasmid-driven transcription (C) describes the creation of a knock-in mutant. This is a straight recall question.

25. D

This question requires that you recall the assumptions of the Hardy-Weinberg model. Rather than predicting an answer outright, it is easier to scan the answer choices and eliminate those that are not tenets of the model. (A) is a distortion because mating between distinct populations would introduce new genes into the pool and thus change the frequency of alleles in a population. However, you could be fooled by the phrase "set rate," which implies stability. (B) and (C) directly contradict the HW model.

26. B

This question requires you to reason through the renin-angiotensin-aldosterone (RAS) system. Renin is secreted by the juxtaglomerular apparatus (JGA) in response to low vascular volume (and hence low blood pressure). This causes the release of angiotensin, which, after conversion by angiotensin-converting enzyme (ACE) to angiotensin II in the lungs, causes the release of aldosterone from the zona glomerulosa of the adrenal cortex. (A) causes the release of angiotensin. (C) is released in response to high serum calcium levels. (D) is released in response to TSH.

27. C

The genotype of the first child is unrelated to the odds of the second child having a given genotype. Using a Punnett square, with C as the normal gene and c as the gene for cystic fibrosis, the chances of the child inheriting the cc genotype, and thus having the disease, are 25 percent.

28. C

The formula for determining the number of genetically unique gametes for a given genotype with two possible alleles at each gene is 2^n, where $n = 3$. Therefore, there are a total of eight possible gametes.

29. A

Here you must know the role of the loop of Henle in the nephron. The question stem states that it maintains the osmotic gradient. It therefore allows the urine to become more concentrated, or hypertonic to the blood. (B) is wrong because a steeper osmotic gradient would allow more solute to be secreted, not less. (C) is wrong because urine should be hypertonic to body fluids, to allow the body to clear waste without becoming dehydrated. (D) is wrong because the loop of Henle does not reabsorb blood proteins. In fact, blood proteins should not pass through the glomerulus at all; they are too large and their negative charge prohibits glomerular filtration.

QUESTIONS 30–36

30.   A

(A) is correct because steroids are lipid-based and will pass into the cell readily. (B) is incorrect because peptides are generally negatively charged and thus would not move across the phospholipid membrane. (C) is incorrect because second messengers are molecules that work within the cell in response to activation from substance that bind to the cell membrane, rather than themselves originating from outside the cell. (D) is incorrect because glucose is a hydrophilic substance and a glucose analog would be unlikely to pass readily across the plasma membrane without a glucose transporter molecule.

31.   D

(A) is incorrect because there is no reason that the lungs would be uniquely suited to support the growth of mycobacteria. (B) is incorrect because although the lungs are the site for oxygen exchange, the digestive tract also has sufficient oxygen to support aerobic bacterial growth, such as the bacteria that causes stomach ulcers. (C) is incorrect because the bile salts are involved in fat emulsification, and would not likely prohibit bacterial growth. (D) is correct because it explains why the digestive tract is inhospitable to bacterial growth: most bacteria will not survive in the low pH of the stomach.

32.   A

The question requires you to know that vasopressin (ADH) and oxytocin are the hormones released by the posterior pituitary gland. Because vasopressin increases fluid retention, a tumor causing increased vasopressin release could lead to hypertension. Plasma calcium levels are increased and decreased by parathyroid hormone and calcitonin, respectively, which are not related to the posterior pituitary, and thus (B) and (C) are incorrect. (D), precocious puberty, can be triggered by a tumor forming on the anterior pituitary gland, which releases FSH and LH, but not the posterior gland.

33.   D

To answer this question, you need to know that osteoclasts are responsible for reabsorbing bone into the blood. (D), the macrophage, is a cell type that is also responsible for engulfing substances (such as infectious materials). Of (A), (B), and (C), red blood cells supply oxygen to the tissues, fibroblasts compose connective tissue and skin, and plasma cells produce antibodies as part of the immune response, but none of these cell types have roles in physiology analogous to that of an osteoclast.

34.   B

(A) is incorrect because bronchiole constriction would decrease gas exchange, thus contributing to decreased running performance. (B) is correct because increased surfactant would facilitate gas exchange by reducing surface tension on the alveoli, not reduce it. (C) is incorrect because swollen epithelial linings would make it more difficult for gas exchange to occur. (D) is incorrect because these cilia normally beat continuously to remove excess fluids and foreign debris from the respiratory tract.

35.   A

The question relies on your knowledge of the differences between prokaryotes and eukaryotes. Even if you do not remember which of the structures are found in prokaryotes such as bacteria, you can predict the answer based on your knowledge that prokaryotes lack membrane-bound organelles. Ribosomes lack membranes, so choice (A) is correct. (B), the mitochondrion, has the inner and outer membranes crucial to the electron transport chain. (C), the

Golgi apparatus, has a single membrane. (D), the nuclear membrane, would not be present in a prokaryote because it lacks a nucleus.

36. C

The question asks how coding for a functional protein could be retained in the presence of a genetic mutation. (C) is correct because codons consist of three base pairs. If three base pairs were deleted, the reading frame would be conserved and a polypeptide would be created lacking one amino acid but otherwise normal; function might be retained. (A) is incorrect because mutations in DNA actually give rise to a wide array of illnesses. (B) is incorrect because codons are always the same size and would not expand to fill a gap; furthermore, there would be no physical gap to fill because the codons would still be linked normally in the DNA strand. (D) is incorrect because back mutations resulting in restored function are extremely rare.

PASSAGE IV

37. C

The bone marrow of centrally located bones such as the skull, sternum, vertebrae, and pelvis is primarily where hematopoiesis is located. The liver and spleen are sites of red cell production in the fetus, and occasionally in children and adults if the bone marrow is unable to keep up with demand for new red blood cells.

38. B

The kidney is the site of hydroxylation of vitamin D precursors into the most biologically active form, 1,25-dihydroxycholecalciferol. Folic acid and riboflavin (Vitamin B_2) are supplied by diet. Vitamin K is obtained from dietary sources as well as from the normal flora present in the large intestine.

39. C

EPO stimulates red blood cell formation in the bone marrow and is also thought to promote longevity of the red blood cell once it leaves the bone marrow. Thus, lack of EPO would not result in abnormally sized or shaped cells unless an iron deficiency were also present. Schistocytes are the remnants of destroyed red blood cells in the circulation.

40. D

ELISA utilizes labeled antibodies which can be formulated to almost any moiety, including the manufactured sugars attached to exogenous EPO. Northern and Western blots are tests of RNA and protein expression, respectively. A peripheral smear would be used to examine the relative shapes and sized of blood cells. Spectrophotometry would not be sensitive in a blood sample.

41. B

Heme synthesis is dependent on iron stores in the body. Oxygen carrying capacity of red blood cells is dependent on the concentration of heme. Thus, at chronically low states of oxygen, the body eventually loses the ability to compensate due to exhaustion of iron stores. At low oxygen states, one would expect elevated amounts of HIF, which the data confirms. Clumping of red blood cells would cause an increase in the expected red blood cell percentage.

42. C

The key to this question is the phrase "directly result in." If a mutation rendered HIF unable to be suppressed, the direct result would be the production of EPO regardless of oxygenation. Because EPO stimulates production and enhances longevity of RBCs, (A) is tempting. However, this is not the direct result of the mutation, but the result of elevated EPO. (B) is the opposite of the secondary result of this mutation, and (D) is the opposite of the direct result of insuppressible HIF.

43. A

Red blood cells are anuclear—therefore, they do not reproduce by binary fission nor make proteins once they are matured and released into the bloodstream. The lack of a nucleus makes the cell particularly bendable, and thus able to navigate narrow capillaries. The structural proteins of the red blood cell allow it to fold down upon itself without losing its functional capacity to carry oxygen. The red blood cell membrane contains both cholesterol for structural stability and proteins to allow interactions with endothelial cells in capillaries.

44. A

HIF is active in its nonhydroxylated state to act as a transcription factor for EPO. The effect of EPO on erythropoiesis is mediated by the EPO receptor in the bone marrow. Heme precursors (amino acids and pyroxidine) become heme by a process dependent on iron stores. Increased red blood cell production leads to tissue oxygenation by improved oxygen carrying capacity of the blood per volume.

45. A

Epinephrine preferentially shunts blood away from the digestive and filtration systems of the body toward systems that facilitate escape from danger. The blood vessels supplying the kidneys vasoconstrict, thus exposing them to lower levels of oxygenated blood. In addition to increased EPO production, renin secretion also increases, as the vasoconstriction of the renal arterioles causes a sensation of volume depletion to the cells of the kidney. Epinephrine is normally regulated with a negative feedback mechanism. Prolonged exposure to exogenous epinephrine would shut down the body's normal production of it.

46. C

Methemoglobin reductase is responsible for converting Fe^{3+} back to Fe^{2+} in order to bind to oxygen. Fe^{3+} incorporated into heme is seen in 1–2 percent of molecules in a healthy individual. This percentage can increase with certain blood cell or metabolic diseases, leading to a chronic hypoxic state. The pneumonic OIL RIG (oxidation is loss, reduction is gain) can be used to remember how charges change.

PASSAGE V

47. D

Vitamin D is an important part of bone development. It can be synthesized from a precursor that is found in the skin. This precursor gets hydroxylated in the liver and again in the kidneys to become active. Vitamin D then acts at the kidney and intestine to increase reabsorption and absorption of calcium respectively. The development of the periosteum (A) will not be affected by a decrease in sunlight. Vitamin C (B) is important to the hydroxylation and cross-linking of collagen fibrils, not for bone development. Slight changes in barometric pressure (C) will not impact bone development.

48. B

Osteoclasts are responsible for breaking down bone so it can be remodeled or so calcium can be released into the serum. Osteoclast function is opposed by osteoblasts which lay down bone matrix that is subsequently calcified (remember osteoBlast Builds). Overactivity of osteoclasts will cause bone loss, known clinically as osteoporosis. Overactivity of T and B cells [(C) and (D)] can cause a variety of problems including autoimmunity, leukemia, and hypergammaglobulinemia, but will not directly contribute to bone loss.

49. D

Secondary healing is responsible for most of bone healing. It involves the presence of a large hematoma that forms at the site of a bone break. This hematoma becomes a callus, which is subsequently vascularized. Collagen is laid down by mesechymal cells that migrate to the callus from the periosteum and surrounding soft tissue. Over time, the collagen that is laid down is replaced by calcified bone. Primary healing (C) is the direct deposition of bone at the site of a fracture without the step of collagen deposition that is subsequently replaced by bone. Moreover, the passage states that primary healing rarely happens, due to the need for precise alignment of the fracture ends. Membranous ossification (B) is a process of bone development that is responsible for the development of flat bones like the pelvis and bones of the cranium. In these instances, no collagen skeleton is present before bone is produced. Endochondral ossification (A) involves the deposition of collagen. (A) and (B) are processes of embryologic bone development, not bone healing.

50. D

Calcium is crucial to the functioning of the nervous system, as well as for muscle contraction. One of the hormones produced by the thyroid is calcitonin, which downregulates blood calcium levels via inhibiting osteoclast activity and Ca^{++} absorption in the small intestine. This patient likely suffers from hypercalcemia, or elevated blood calcium levels. Be careful when reading the questions: neither (A) nor (B) are minerals. Blood phosphorus levels (D) are regulated by the parathyroid glands (through PTH), not the thyroid.

51. B

Vitamin D is one of four fat-soluble vitamins; A, K, and E are also stored in the fat. The other common vitamins are water-soluble and are lost in the urine if they aren't used at the time of ingestion.

52. C

The thymus is an organ in the neck which is very active during development and childhood. T cells in the thymus undergo a process of clonal deletion; if, for example a T cell "recognizes" or seeks to attack antigens naturally present on body tissues, that T cell will be eliminated by the thymus so it does not proliferate and go into the body to attack "self" tissues. Clonal deletion may lead to autoimmune attacks, in which T cells attack body tissue that they believe is foreign material; the problem is that the T cells think the foreign material must be neutralized and removed from the body.

Glossary

Abductor A muscle that moves a limb away from the center of a body. Compare *adductor*.

Absorption The process by which substances are taken up into, or across, tissues (e.g., from the intestinal lumen into the blood).

Acetylcholine A neurotransmitter found throughout the nervous system (e.g., somatic motor neurons, preganglionic parasympathetic and sympathetic nerves, and postganglionic parasympathetic nerves). It is metabolized by acetylcholinesterase.

Acrosome The large vesicle at the head of a sperm cell containing enzymes that degrade the ovum cell membrane to allow fertilization.

Actin A protein found in the cytoskeleton and muscle cells; it is the principal constituent of the thin filament.

Action potential An abrupt change in the membrane potential of a nerve or muscle caused by changes in membrane ionic permeability. Results in conduction of an impulse in nerves or contraction in muscles.

Active immunity An immune response (antibody production or cellular immunity) acquired in response to exposure to an antigen.

Active site Substrate-binding region of an enzyme.

Active transport The use of energy to move a substance across a membrane against a concentration gradient.

Adaptation The development of characteristics that enable an organism to survive and reproduce in its habitat.

Adaptive radiation The evolutionary process by which one species gives rise to several species, each specialized for different environments.

Adductor A muscle that moves a limb toward the center of a body. Compare *abductor*.

Adenine A purine base present in DNA and RNA; it forms hydrogen bonds with thymine and uracil.

Adenosine triphosphate A nucleotide molecule consisting of adenine, ribose, and three phosphate moieties. The outer two phosphates are bound by high-energy bonds. ATP plays a central role in energy exchange in biological systems. (Adenosine diphosphate [ADP] contains two phosphate groups and one high-energy bond.)

Adipose Refers to fatty tissue, fat-storing tissue, or fat within cells.

Adrenaline (Epinephrine) A hormone synthesized by the adrenal medulla; it stimulates the fight-or-flight response. It is also a neurotransmitter in the sympathetic nervous system.

Adrenocorticotropic hormone (ACTH) A hormone secreted by the anterior pituitary that stimulates hormone production in the adrenal cortex.

Aerobic Refers to a biological process that occurs in the presence of molecular oxygen (O_2) or to organisms that cannot live without molecular oxygen. Compare *anaerobic*.

Afferent (sensory) neuron A neuron that picks up impulses from sensory receptors and transmits them toward the central nervous system.

Allantois One of four embryonic membranes, it contains the growing embryo's waste products.

Allele Alternative forms of the same gene coding for a particular trait. Alleles segregate during meiosis.

Alveolus Basic functional unit of the lung; a tiny sac specialized for passive gas exchange between the lungs and the blood.

Amino acids The building blocks of proteins, each containing an amino group, a carboxylic acid group, and a side chain (or R-group) attached to the alpha carbon.

Amnion The innermost fluid-filled embryonic membrane; it forms a protective sac surrounding the embryos of birds, reptiles, and mammals.

Amylase An enzyme found in saliva and pancreatic juices that hydrolyzes starch to maltose. Also known as ptyalin, diastase, or amylopsin.

Anabolism The process by which complex molecules (macromolecules) are synthesized from simple ones.

Anaerobic Refers to a biological process that can occur without oxygen or to organisms that can live without molecular oxygen. Compare *aerobic*.

Analogous structures Structures that are similar in function but of different evolutionary origins (e.g., whale flippers and fish fins).

Anaphase The stage of mitosis or meiosis characterized by the migration of chromatids or homologous chromosomes to opposite poles of the dividing cell.

Androgen Any male sex hormone (e.g., testosterone and dihydrotestosterone).

Anterior Front of an organism. Compare *posterior*.

Antibiotic Substance that kills or inhibits the growth of bacteria or fungi (usually by disrupting cell wall assembly or by binding to ribosomes, thus inhibiting protein synthesis).

Antibody (Immunoglobulin) Immune or protective protein evoked by the presence of foreign substances (antigens) in the body. Each antibody binds to a specific antigen in an immune response.

Anticodon The three-nucleotide sequence on tRNA that is complementary to the mRNA codon.

Antidiuretic hormone (ADH, vasopressin) A hormone synthesized by the hypothalamus; it inhibits urine excretion by increasing water reabsorption in the kidneys.

Archenteron The central cavity in the gastrula stage of embryological development; it is lined by endoderm and ultimately gives rise to the adult digestive tract.

Asexual reproduction Any reproductive process that does not involve the fusion of gametes (i.e., budding).

Atrioventricular node (AV node) A small mass of nodal tissue that serves as an electrical bridge between the atria and the ventricles; located in the lower portion of the wall that separates the atria.

Autosome Any chromosome other than the sex chromosomes.

Axon The long fiber of a neuron; it conducts impulses away from the cell body toward the synapse.

Bacillus Rod-shaped bacterium. Compare *coccus*.

Bacteriophage A virus that invades bacteria and sometimes uses bacterial RNA and ribosomes to self-replicate. See *transduction*.

Bile A solution of salts, pigments, and cholesterol produced by the liver and stored in the gall bladder; it emulsifies large fat droplets when secreted into the small intestine via the bile duct.

Binary fission A type of asexual reproduction characteristic of prokaryotes in which there is equal nuclear and cytoplasmic division.

Blastocoel The fluid-filled central cavity of the blastula.

Blastopore Opening of the archenteron to the external environment in the gastrula stage of embryonic development.

Blastula The early embryonic stage during which the embryo is a hollow, fluid-filled sphere of undifferentiated cells.

Bowman's capsule The cuplike structure of the nephron; it collects the glomerular filtrate and channels it into the proximal convoluted tubule.

Budding A type of asexual reproduction in which the offspring starts out as an outgrowth of the parent that subsequently splits off to exist as an independent organism.

Bundle of His Part of the conducting system of the heart; it carries impulses from the AV node to the ventricles.

Calcitonin A polypeptide hormone secreted by the thyroid; it causes the deposition of calcium and phosphate in bones and thus lowers their concentrations in the blood.

cAMP See *cyclic adenosine monophosphate.*

Cartilage A firm, elastic, translucent connective tissue produced by cells called chondrocytes.

Catabolism The chemical breakdown of complex substances (macromolecules) to yield simpler substances and energy.

Catalyst A substance that speeds up a chemical reaction by lowering the activation energy without being altered or consumed during the reaction.

Cecum A cavity open at one end, such as the blind pouch (diverticulum) at the junction of the large and small intestines.

Central nervous system (CNS) The brain and spinal cord. Compare *peripheral nervous system.*

Centriole A small organelle in the cytoplasm of animal cells; it organizes the spindle apparatus during mitosis or meiosis.

Centromere The area of a chromosome at which sister chromatids are joined; it is also the point of attachment to the spindle fiber during mitosis and meiosis.

Cerebellum The section of the mammalian hindbrain that controls muscle coordination and equilibrium.

Cerebral cortex The outer layer of the forebrain, consisting of gray matter; it is the site of higher cognitive functions in humans. Neurons of the cerebral cortex initiate voluntary muscle action and constitute the final reception area for sensory impulses.

Chiasmata Site at which crossing over occurs between homologous chromosomes during meiosis.

Chondrocyte A differentiated cartilage cell that synthesizes cartilage matrix.

Chromatid Each of the two chromosomal strands formed by DNA replication in the S phase of the cell cycle; held together by the centromere.

Chromosome A filamentous body found within the nucleus of a cell composed of DNA and proteins (histone and nonhistone) and containing the cell's genetic information.

Circadian rhythm A behavioral pattern based on a 24-hour cycle.

Citric acid cycle See *Krebs cycle.*

Cleavage A series of mitotic divisions of the zygote immediately following fertilization, resulting in progressively smaller cells with increased nucleus-to-cytoplasm ratios.

Coccus Spherically shaped bacterium. Compare *bacillus.*

Cochlea The coiled tube that comprises the auditory sensory organ of the inner ear.

Codominance (Incomplete dominance) A genetic effect in which the phenotype of a heterozygote is a reflection of both alleles at a particular locus. Compare *dominant, recessive.*

Codon A three-base sequence on an mRNA strand; it codes for a specific tRNA anticodon and thus for a specific amino acid.

Coenocytic Cells consisting of many nuclei housed within the same cytoplasm (i.e., skeletal muscle tissue).

Coenzyme An organic cofactor required for enzyme activity.

Cofactor Nonprotein molecules required by many enzymes for activity.

Colon The large intestine.

Conjugation The temporary joining of two organisms via a tube called a pilus, through which genetic material is exchanged; a form of sexual reproduction used by bacteria, fungi, algae, and protozoans.

Connective tissue Animal tissue composed of cells lying in an extracellular proteinaceous network, which supports, connects, and/or surrounds the organs and structures of the body.

Convergent evolution The process by which unrelated organisms living in a similar environment develop analogous structures.

Cornea The thin, transparent layer that covers the front of the eye.

Corpus callosum A thick bundle of nerve fibers that connects the two cerebral hemispheres.

Corpus luteum The remnant of the ovarian follicle, which after ovulation continues to secrete progesterone. Its degeneration leads to menstruation; maintains uterine lining during pregnancy.

Cortex The external layer found in many organs of the body, including the brain, adrenal glands, and kidney.

Crossing over The exchange of genetic material between homologous chromosomes during meiosis.

Cyclic adenosine monophosphate (cAMP) An intracellular participant in one of the mechanisms of hormonal action; synthesized from ATP by adenylate cyclase. Also referred to as a "second messenger."

Cytochromes Iron-containing proteins that function in the electron transport chain in mitochondria and in photophosphorylation in chloroplasts.

Cytokinesis The division and distribution of parent cell cytoplasm to the two daughter cells during mitotic and meiotic cell division.

Cytoplasm The fluid and solutes within a cell membrane, external to the nucleus and cellular organelles.

Cytosine A pyrimidine base found in nucleic acids; it hydrogen-bonds with guanine.

Deletion A type of genetic mutation in which one of the bases in the DNA template is deleted during replication.

Dendrite The portion of a neuron that receives stimuli and conveys them toward the cell body.

Deoxyribose The five-carbon cyclic (pentose) sugar found in DNA.

Dermis The layer of skin cells under the epidermis. Contains sweat glands, hair follicles, fat, and blood vessels.

Diastole The period of relaxation of cardiac muscle during which the atrioventricular valves open and the ventricles fill with blood. Compare *systole*.

Diencephalon Posterior forebrain containing the thalamus and hypothalamus.

Differentiation The process by which unspecialized cells become specialized. Involves selective transcription of the genome.

Diffusion The flow of molecules from a region of high concentration to a region of low concentration as dictated by the laws of thermodynamics.

Digestion The breakdown of macromolecular nutrient material via mechanical and chemical means to simple molecular building blocks; this facilitates absorption.

Diploid (2*N*) Having two chromosomes of each type per cell. Compare *haploid*.

Disaccharide A sugar composed of two monosaccharide units.

Divergent evolution A process of change whereby organisms with a common ancestor evolve dissimilar structures (e.g., dolphin flippers and human arms).

DNA (Deoxyribonucleic acid) Nucleic acid composed of monomers consisting of the five-carbon sugar deoxyribose, a phosphate group, and a nitrogenous base (adenine, cytosine, guanine, or thymine); contains the cell's genetic information.

Dominant Refers to an allele in a diploid cell whose phenotypic effect is the same in both homozygotes and heterozygotes. Compare *codominance, recessive*.

Dorsal Situated towards the back of an organism.

Duodenum First segment of the small intestine; the contents of the stomach and the pancreatic and bile ducts empty into it. Site of digestion and some absorption.

Ectoderm Outermost embryonic germ layer; it gives rise to the skin and nervous system. Compare *mesoderm, endoderm.*

Effector An organ, muscle, or gland used by an organism to respond to a stimulus.

Efferent (motor) neuron A neuron that transmits nervous impulses from the spinal cord to an effector.

Electron transport chain The chain of cytochromes in mitochondria that transfers electrons from NADH to oxygen with the release of energy, which is then used to synthesize ATP via oxidative phosphorylation.

Embryo The early developmental stage of an organism. In humans, the term refers to the first two months after fertilization. Compare *fetus.*

Endocrine Refers to ductless glands that produce or secrete hormones.

Endoderm Innermost embryonic germ layer; it later gives rise to the linings of the alimentary canal and of the digestive and respiratory organs. Compare *ectoderm, mesoderm.*

Endoplasmic reticulum Membrane-bound channels in the cytoplasm that transport proteins and lipids to various parts of the cell.

Endotherms (Homeotherms) Organisms that maintain a constant internal temperature.

Enzyme A protein that catalyzes a biochemical reaction.

Epidermis The outermost layer of the skin.

Epididymis The coiled tube in which sperm gains motility and is stored after its production in the testes.

Epiglottis The small flap of cartilage covering the glottis during swallowing.

Epinephrine See *adrenalin.*

Epithelium The cellular layer that covers internal and external surfaces.

Erythrocyte Red blood cell; a biconcave, disk-shaped cell that contains hemoglobin and has no nucleus.

Esophagus Portion of the alimentary canal connecting the pharynx and the stomach.

Estrogen Female sex hormone that stimulates the development of secondary sexual characteristics and is secreted by the ovarian follicle.

Estrous cycle The regular changes in the behavior and physiology of a female mammal throughout her fertile life.

Eukaryote A unicellular or multicellular organism composed of cells that contain a membrane-bound nucleus and other membrane-bound organelles. Compare *prokaryote.*

Evolution The changes in the gene pool from one generation to the next caused by mutation, nonrandom mating, natural selection, and genetic drift.

Excretion The release of metabolic wastes by an organism.

Exocrine glands Glands that release their secretions into ducts (e.g., the liver, sweat glands).

Extensor A muscle used in the straightening of a limb. Compare *flexor.*

F_1 generation The first generation of offspring from a cross-fertilization of individuals.

F_2 generation The offspring from the cross-fertilization of individuals from the F_1 generation.

Facultative anaerobes Prokaryotes that can exist with or without oxygen.

Fallopian tube See *oviduct.*

Feedback inhibition The process by which the concentration of a product or intermediate in a metabolic pathway inhibits the pathway that led to its formation.

Fermentation Catabolism of macromolecules in the absence of oxygen.

Fertilization Fusion of the nuclei of two gametes.

Fetus A developing organism that has passed the early developmental stages. In humans, the term refers to an embryo from the third month of pregnancy until birth. Compare *embryo*.

Fibrin The insoluble protein that forms the bulk of a blood clot.

Fight-or-flight response An organism's reaction to danger, which includes increased heartbeat, pupil dilation, increased respiration, constriction of the peripheral blood vessels, and reduced digestive activity. It is stimulated by adrenalin release and by innervation of the sympathetic nervous system.

Filtration In the nephron, the process by which blood plasma is forced (under high pressure) out of the glomerulus into Bowman's capsule. Also, a process used to separate and purify aqueous solutions.

Fixation The process of preparing tissues for microscopic examination.

Flagellum A microscopic, whiplike filament that functions in locomotion of sperm cells and some unicellular organisms; composed of microtubules.

Flexor A muscle used in the bending of a limb. Compare *extensor*.

Follicle The set of cells surrounding a developing or mature ovum. Secretes

nutrients and estrogen and atrophies into the corpus luteum after ovulation.

Follicle-stimulating hormone (FSH) The anterior pituitary hormone that stimulates the maturation of ovarian follicles and spermatogenesis.

Fovea An area in the center of the retina containing the greatest concentration of cones and, therefore, the area of sharpest vision.

Gamete Sperm or ovum; a cell that has half the number of chromosomes of a somatic cell (haploid) and can fuse with another gamete to form a zygote.

Ganglion A mass of neuron cell bodies; ganglia integrate and coordinate impulses.

Gastrin A hormone released by the pyloric mucosa of the stomach when food enters the stomach. Stimulates the secretion of gastric juices.

Gastrula The embryonic stage characterized by the presence of endoderm, ectoderm, the blastocoel, and the archenteron. The early gastrula is two layered; later a third layer, the mesoderm, develops.

Gene The basic unit of heredity; a region on a chromosome that codes for a specific product.

Gene flow The movement of alleles into and out of a population's gene pool.

Gene pool All of the alleles for every gene in every individual in a given population.

Genetic code The system of nucleotide triplets (codons) in DNA and RNA that codes for individual amino acids.

Genetic drift Variations in the gene pool caused by chance.

Genome An organism's complete set of chromosomes.

Genotype The genetic composition of an entire organism or reference to a particular trait.

Genus A taxon of closely related species.

Glomerulus The network of capillaries encapsulated by Bowman's capsule. Acts as a filter for blood entering the nephron.

Glottis The opening to the trachea.

Glucagon A hormone produced in the alpha cells of the pancreas that increases the concentration of blood glucose.

Glycogen The principal storage form of glucose in animals.

Glycolysis The anaerobic catabolism of glucose to pyruvic acid.

Golgi bodies Organelles that play a role in the packaging and secretion of proteins and other molecules produced intracellularly.

Gonad Ovary or testis; the reproductive organ in which gametes are produced.

Gray matter Any region in the central nervous system that consists largely of neuron cell bodies, dendrites, and synapses. Compare *white matter*.

Guanine A purine base present in DNA and RNA; it forms hydrogen bonds with cytosine.

Haploid (*N*) Having only one of each type of chromosome per cell. Compare *diploid*.

Hardy-Weinberg law States that gene ratios and allelic frequencies remain constant through the generations in a nonevolving population.

Haversian system The structural unit of compact bone. Consists of a hard, inorganic matrix surrounding a central canal.

Hemoglobin Iron-containing protein found in red blood cells that binds O_2 and transports it throughout the body.

Hepatic Of or pertaining to the liver.

Heterotrophic An organism that requires preformed organic nutrients because it cannot form them from inorganic precursors.

Heterozygous Having two different alleles for a particular trait. Compare *homozygous*.

Histone Structural protein found in eukaryotic chromosomes.

Homeostasis Maintenance of a stable internal physiological environment in an organism.

Homologous chromosomes Chromosomes in a diploid cell that carry corresponding genes for the same traits at corresponding loci.

Homologous structures Structures that are similar in function and are of the same evolutionary origin.

Homozygous Having two identical alleles for a given trait. Compare *heterozygous*.

Hormones Chemical messengers secreted by cells of one part of the body and carried by the bloodstream to cells elsewhere in the body, where they regulate biochemical activity.

Hybrid The resultant offspring of a cross (mating) either between two different gene types or between two different species.

Hydrolysis The breaking apart of a molecule by the addition of water.

Hyperplasia An increase in the number of cells in a tissue or organ.

Hypertonic solution A solution that, when compared to another, has a greater concentration of solute particles and, consequently, a greater osmotic concentration. Compare *hypotonic solution, isotonic solution*.

Hypertrophy An increase in the size of individual cells within a given site or tissue.

Hyphae Branched filaments of a fungus.

Hypothalamus The region of the vertebrate forebrain that controls the autonomic nervous system and is the control center for hunger, thirst, body temperature, and other visceral functions. Also secretes factors that stimulate or inhibit pituitary secretions.

Hypotonic solution A solution that, when compared to another, has a lower concentration of solute particles and, consequently, a lower osmotic concentration. Compare *hypertonic solution, isotonic solutions*.

Ileum The terminal portion of the small intestine.

Immune reaction The process by which the body defends itself in response to an antigen (e.g., the production of antibodies).

Immunoglobulin See *antibody*.

Incomplete dominance See *codominance*.

In situ At the site of (origin).

In vitro In a test tube or in culture.

In vivo In a living organism.

Independent assortment Unlinked genes within a primary germ cell separate randomly during gametogenesis (see *Mendel's second law*).

Induction The initiation of cell differentiation in a developing embryo due to the influence of other cells.

Insulin A hormone produced by the beta cells in the pancreas that lowers blood glucose concentration.

Interneuron A neuron that has its cell body and nerve terminals confined to one specific area.

Interphase The stage between successive nuclear divisions; it is divided into the G_1, S, and G_2 stages. Cell growth and DNA replication occur during interphase.

Inversion A chromosomal mutation in which a section of a chromosome breaks off, flips over, and then reattaches in its original spot.

Invertebrate An animal that does not possess a backbone. Compare *vertebrate*.

Iris The part of the eye that contracts or dilates to regulate the amount of light passing through the pupil.

Isolation Mechanism that prevents genetic exchange between individuals of different species or populations.

Isotonic solution A solution that, when compared to another, has the same concentration of solute particles and, consequently, the same osmotic concentration. Compare *hypertonic solution, hypotonic solution*.

Jejunum The middle portion of the small intestine.

Kidney Vertebrate organ that regulates water and salt concentration in the blood and is responsible for urine formation.

Krebs cycle (citric acid cycle, TCA cycle) A metabolic pathway used in cellular respiration in which acetyl CoA combines with oxaloacetic acid to form citric acid, which then undergoes a series of reactions to yield NADH, FADH, ATP, and CO_2. Occurs in aerobes.

Latent period The short interval between the application of a stimulus to a muscle and the contraction of the muscle.

Leukocyte White blood cell; the four principal types of leukocytes are granulocytes, macrophages, monocytes, and lymphocytes.

Ligament Connective tissue that joins two bones.

Linkage Tendency for certain alleles to be inherited together due to proximity on the same chromosome.

Lipases Enzymes that specifically cleave the bonds of lipids.

Lipids A group of molecules that are insoluble in water but are soluble in a variety of organic solvents: oils, waxes, fats, steroids, glycolipids, phospholipids.

Locus In genetics, an area or region of a chromosome.

Loop of Henle The U-shaped section of a mammalian nephron.

Lumen The opening within a tube or a sac.

Luteinizing hormone (LH) A hormone secreted by the anterior pituitary. In females, it transforms a follicle into a corpus luteum and triggers ovulation. In males, it stimulates testosterone secretion.

Lymph Clear tissue fluid derived from blood plasma and transported through lymph vessels to the lymphatic ducts, which empty into the circulatory system.

Lymphocyte A type of white blood cell involved in an organism's immune response.

Lysogenic cycle (Lysogeny) Bacteriophage infection involving the integration of viral DNA into the bacterial genome without disrupting or destroying the host. The virus may subsequently re-emerge and enter a lytic cycle.

Lysosome A membrane-bound organelle that stores hydrolytic enzymes.

Lytic cycle Bacteriophage infection involving the destruction (lysis) of the host bacterium.

Macrophage A phagocytic white blood cell.

Marsupial A mammal with a ventral pouch in which its young develop after birth.

Medulla The internal section of an organ (e.g., the adrenal glands and the kidney); the medulla oblongata of the mammalian hindbrain.

Medulla oblongata The part of the brainstem closest to the spinal cord. It controls functions such as breathing and heartbeat.

Meiosis A process of cell division in which two successive nuclear divisions produce four haploid gametes from one diploid germ cell. Compare *mitosis*.

Mendel's first law Alleles segregate during meiosis.

Mendel's second law Alleles of unlinked genes independently assort during meiosis.

Meninges The three membranes that envelop the brain and spinal cord: the dura mater, arachnoid, and pia mater.

Menstruation The shedding of the uterine lining that occurs every four weeks in a nonpregnant, sexually mature human female.

Mesoderm The middle embryonic germ layer; it gives rise to the muscular, skeletal, urogenital, and circulatory systems. Compare *ectoderm, endoderm*.

Messenger RNA (mRNA) This class of RNA is the product of the transcription process and acts as a template for the synthesis of polypeptides (translation).

Metabolism The sum of all biochemical reactions that occur in an organism.

Metamorphosis Transformation of an immature animal into an adult; change in the form of an organ or structure.

Metaphase The stage of mitosis or meiosis during which single chromosomes or tetrads line up on the central axis of the dividing cell and become attached to spindle fibers.

Metencephalon The anterior portion of the hindbrain of vertebrates; it includes the cerebellum and the pons.

Microtubule A small, hollow tube composed of two types of protein subunits; serves numerous functions in the cell (e.g., microtubules comprise the internal structures of cilia and flagella).

Mitochondria Membrane-bound cellular organelles in which the reactions of aerobic respiration and ATP synthesis occur.

Mitosis Cellular division that results in the formation of two daughter cells that are genetically identical to each other and to the parent cell. Compare *meiosis*.

Monocyte A white blood cell that transforms into a macrophage in the presence of foreign invaders.

Monosaccharide A sugar consisting of one monomer (e.g., glucose, fructose, or galactose). See also *disaccharide*.

Morphogenesis The development of structure and form in an organism.

Morula The solid ball of cells that results from the early stages of cleavage in an embryo.

Motor neuron See *efferent neuron*.

Mucosa The type of epithelial tissue that lines moist body cavities; a mucous membrane.

Mutagen An agent, either chemical or physical, that can cause mutations.

Mutation An inheritable change in the genetic composition of an organism.

Mycelium A collection of filamentous hyphae that makes up a fungus.

Myelin The white, lipid-containing material surrounding the axons of many neurons in the central and peripheral nervous systems.

Myoglobin Heme-containing protein that binds molecular oxygen in muscle cells.

Myosin A protein found in muscle cells that functions in muscle contraction. Myosin fibers are also called thick filaments

NAD (Nicotinamide adenine dinucleotide) A coenzyme that functions in cell respiration.

NADH The reduced form of NAD.

NADP⁺/NADPH (Nicotinamide adenine dinucleotide phosphate). An electron acceptor/donator system that functions, primarily, in biosynthetic processes.

Natural selection An ongoing evolutionary process resulting in changes in gene frequencies. It leads to the differential development of different phenotypes in a population.

Negative feedback See *feedback inhibition*.

Nephron The functional unit of the vertebrate kidney.

Nerve A bundle of nerve fibers.

Nerve impulse The self-propagating change in electric potential across the axon membrane.

Neural tube Embryonic hollow tube that subsequently gives rise to the central nervous system.

Neuron A cell that conducts electrical impulses; the functional unit of the nervous system.

Neurotransmitter A chemical agent released into the synaptic cleft by the synaptic bouton of a neuron. Binds to receptor sites on postsynaptic neurons or effector membranes to alter activity.

Niche The role of a given organism within the environment, including its interactions with other organisms and with the physical environment.

Nitrogen fixation Incorporation of atmospheric nitrogen into inorganic nitrogen compounds. Performed by bacteria.

Nodes of Ranvier Points on a myelinated axon that are not covered by myelin.

Nondisjunction Failure of homologous chromosomes to separate during meiosis.

Noradrenaline *See norepinephrine.*

Norepinephrine A hormone secreted by the adrenal medulla that stimulates the fight-or-flight response; also a neurotransmitter.

Notochord A supportive rod running just ventral to the neural tube in lower chordates and in vertebrate embryos.

Nuclear membrane Double membrane enveloping the nucleus, interrupted periodically by pores; found in eukaryotic cells only.

Nucleic acid Polymer of nucleotides (e.g., DNA and RNA).

Nucleoid The region in prokaryotic cells where the chromosome is located.

Nucleolus Dense body visible in a nondividing nucleus. Site of ribosomal RNA synthesis.

Nucleosome Packaging unit of DNA in eukaryotic cells consisting of DNA and histone proteins complexed together.

Nucleotide An organic molecule composed of three subunits: a five-carbon sugar, a phosphate group, and a purine or a pyrimidine (nitrogenous base). The basic subunits of DNA and RNA.

Nucleus The eukaryotic membrane-bound organelle that contains the cell's chromosomes.

Oocyte An undifferentiated cell that undergoes meiosis to produce an egg cell (ovum).

Oogenesis Gametogenesis in the ovary leading to the formation of mature ova.

Operator A site on DNA that interacts with a repressor protein, regulating transcription of an operon.

Operon A segment of DNA consisting of a promoter, operator, and structural genes. The structural genes code for products of a specific biochemical pathway; their transcription is regulated by a repressor protein.

Organ A body part composed of a group of tissues that form a functional and structural unit.

Organelle Any specialized cytoplasmic structure.

Osmosis The diffusion of water across a semipermeable membrane from a region of low solute concentration to a region of high solute concentration.

Ovary The female egg-producing gonad.

Oviduct (Fallopian tube) The tube leading from the outer extremity of the ovary to the uterus; generally, the site of fertilization.

Ovulation The release of the mature ovum from the ovarian follicle.

Ovum The female gamete; egg cell.

Oxidation The loss of electrons or hydrogen from an atom, ion, or molecule; the addition of oxygen to an atom, ion, or molecule.

Oxidative phosphorylation The synthesis of ATP using the energy released from the reactions of the electron transport chain.

Oxygen debt The amount of oxygen needed to reconvert lactic acid to pyruvate following strenuous exercise of muscle tissue.

Pancreas A gland that secretes digestive enzymes into the duodenum via a duct and synthesizes and secretes the hormones insulin, glucagon, and somatostatin; located between the stomach and the duodenum.

Parasympathetic nervous system The subdivision of the autonomic nervous system involved in rest or homeostasis; it is antagonistic to the sympathetic nervous system.

Parathyroids Two pairs of glands located on the thyroid that secrete hormones that regulate calcium and phosphorous metabolism.

Parthenogenesis A form of asexual reproduction yielding progeny

without fertilization of the ovum by spermatozoa.

Passive immunity Immunity conferred by the transfer or injection of previously formed antibodies.

Passive transport The movement of a substance across a membrane without the expenditure of energy.

Patella The bone of the kneecap.

Pathogen A disease-causing agent.

Pepsin A stomach enzyme that cleaves peptide bonds of proteins.

Peptide bond The bond between two amino acids that results from a condensation reaction between the carboxyl end of one amino acid and the amino end of the other.

Peripheral nervous system Includes all neurons outside the central nervous system, including sensory and motor neurons; it is subdivided into somatic and autonomic nervous systems. Compare *central nervous system*.

Peristalsis Rhythmic waves of muscular contraction that move a substance through a tube (e.g., food through the digestive tract).

Peritoneum Membrane lining of the abdomen and pelvis that also covers the visceral organs.

Permeable Allowing solutes to pass through; a term usually applied to biological membranes.

Phagocytosis A type of endocytosis in which large particles are engulfed by a cell.

Phenotype The physical manifestation of an organism's genotype.

Phylogeny The evolutionary history of related organisms.

Physiology The study of the life processes of plants or animals.

Pinocytosis A type of endocytosis in which small particles or liquid are engulfed by a cell.

Pituitary The bilobed endocrine gland that lies just below the hypothalamus; because many of its hormones regulate other endocrine glands, it is known as the "master gland."

Placenta The structure formed by the wall of the uterus and the chorion of the embryo containing a network of capillaries through which exchange between maternal and fetal circulation occurs.

Plasma The fluid component of blood containing dissolved solutes, minus the red blood cells.

Plasma cells Derived from B-lymphocytes; have the ability to produce and secrete antibodies.

Platelets Small, enucleated disk-shaped blood cells that play an important role in blood clotting.

Polar body A small, nonfunctional haploid cell created during oogenesis.

Polypeptide A polymer composed of many amino acids linked together by peptide bonds.

Polyploid A cell or an organism that has more than two alleles per trait.

Polyribosome A group of ribosomes attached to a strand of mRNA, simultaneously translating it.

Population A group of organisms of the same species living together in a given location.

Portal system A circuit of blood in which there are two capillary beds in tandem connected by an artery or vein.

Posterior Pertaining to the rear, or tail end. Compare *anterior*.

Potential An electrical difference or gradient between two points or structures (e.g., across axon membranes).

Progesterone A hormone secreted by the corpus luteum and the placenta; it prepares the uterine wall for implantation and maintains the thickened wall during pregnancy.

Prokaryote Cell lacking a nuclear membrane and membrane-bound organelles, such as a bacterium. Compare *eurkaryote*.

Promoter A specific site on the DNA strand to which RNA polymerase attaches to initiate operon transcription.

Prophase The stage of mitosis or meiosis during which the DNA strands condense to form visible chromosomes;

during prophase I of meiosis, homologous chromosomes align.

Prostate A gland in the mammalian male that secretes alkaline seminal fluid.

Prosthetic group A nonpolypeptide unit tightly bound to an enzyme that is essential for that enzyme's activity.

Proteins Complex organic polymers of amino acids linked together by peptide bonds.

Proximal Closer to some point of reference, that point usually being the midline of the body (e.g., the elbow is proximal to the hand).

Purines Double-ringed nitrogenous bases such as adenine and guanine.

Purkinje fibers The terminal fibers of the heart's conducting system; located in the walls of ventricles.

Pyloric sphincter The valve that regulates the flow of chyme from the stomach into the small intestine.

Pyrimidines Single-ringed nitrogenous bases such as cytosine, thymine, and uracil.

Recessive An allele that does not express its phenotype in the presence of a dominant allele. Compare *codominance, dominant.*

Recombination New gene combinations achieved by sexual reproduction or crossing over in eukaryotes and by transformation, transduction, or conjugation in prokaryotes.

Reduction The process whereby an atom, ion, or molecule gains electrons or hydrogens; the loss of oxygen from an atom, ion, or molecule.

Reflex An involuntary nervous pathway consisting of sensory neurons, interneurons, motor neurons, and effectors; it occurs in response to a specific stimulus.

Refractory period The period of time following an action potential during which the neuron is incapable of depolarization.

Regeneration A type of asexual reproduction in which an organism replaces lost body parts.

Releasing hormones Proteins synthesized and secreted by the hypothalamus that stimulate the pituitary to synthesize and release its hormones.

Renal Of or pertaining to the kidneys.

Repressor In an operon, the protein that prevents attachment of RNA polymerase to the promoter by binding to the operator. It is coded for by the regulator.

Respiration (1) Cellular respiration: The series of oxygen-requiring biochemical reactions that lead to ATP synthesis. (2) External respiration: The inhalation and exhalation of gases and their exchange at a respiratory surface.

Resting potential The electrical potential of a neuron at rest, approximately 70mV across the axon membrane.

Retina The innermost tissue layer of the eye; the sensory cells (rods and cones) are located there.

Retrovirus An RNA virus that contains the enzyme reverse transcriptase, which transcribes RNA into DNA.

Rh factor An antigen on a red blood cell whose presence or absence is indicated by a + or –, respectively, in blood type notation.

Ribosome Organelle composed of RNA and protein; it translates mRNA during polypeptide synthesis.

RNA (Ribonucleic acid) Nucleic acid composed of monomers consisting of the five-carbon sugar ribose, a phosphate group, and a nitrogenous base (adenine, guanine, cytosine, or uracil); functions in protein synthesis.

Sarcolemma Muscle cell membrane capable of propagating action potentials.

Sarcomere The functional contractile unit of striated muscle.

Sarcoplasmic reticulum The endoplasmic reticulum of a muscle cell; it envelops myofibrils.

Selection pressure A force, resulting from natural selection parameters, that causes changes within the gene pool of a population.

Semen Fluid released during ejaculation consisting of sperm cells suspended in seminal fluid.

Seminal vesicle A gland found in mammalian males that produces seminal fluid.

Sensory neuron See *afferent neuron.*

Sex-linked gene A gene located only on a sex chromosome; such genes exhibit different inheritance patterns in males and females.

Sexual reproduction Any reproductive process that involves the fusion of gametes resulting in the passage of combined genetic information to offspring.

Sinoatrial node (SA node, pacemaker) A group of cells on the surface of the right atrium of the heart; it initiates and controls cardiac muscle contraction.

Somatic cells Autosomal cells; all cells in the body except germ cells and gametes.

Species A taxonomic classification applied to organisms of common ancestry who possess the ability to produce fertile offspring.

Sperm The mature male gamete or sex cell.

Spermatogenesis Gametogenesis in the testes leading to sperm formation.

Sphincter A ring-shaped muscle that closes and opens a tube (e.g., the pyloric sphincter).

Spindle A structure within dividing cells composed of microtubules; it is involved in the separation of chromosomes during mitosis and meiosis.

Spore An asexual reproductive cell that can endure extreme environmental conditions and develop into an adult organism when conditions become favorable.

Stem cells Nondifferentiated, rapidly dividing cells in the marrow of long bones that differentiate into red and white blood cells.

Steroids Four-ringed organic lipid molecules that make up many hormones and vitamins.

Stimulus Any change in an organism's internal or external environment that changes the organism's activity.

Sympathetic nervous system The subdivision of the autonomic nervous system that produces the "fight-or-flight" response. Compare *parasympathetic nervous system.*

Synapse The junction between two neurons into which neurotransmitters are released.

Synapsis The pairing of homologous chromosomes during prophase I of meiosis.

Syngamy The union of gametes.

Systole The period of heart contraction during which the ventricles contract and pump blood into the aorta and pulmonary arteries. Compare *diastole.*

Taxonomy The classification of organisms according to their evolutionary relationships.

TCA cycle See *Krebs cycle.*

Telencephalon Anterior portion of the forebrain.

Telophase The final stage of mitosis or meiosis during which the chromosomes uncoil, nuclear membranes reform, and cytokinesis occurs.

Template A molecule that directs the synthesis of another molecule by acting as a model or pattern (e.g., mRNA is the template for protein synthesis).

Tendon A fibrous connective tissue that connects a bone to a muscle.

Test cross A cross between an organism showing a dominant trait and an organism showing a recessive trait to determine whether the former organism is homozygous or heterozygous for that trait.

Testis The male sperm-producing organ; also secretes testosterone.

Tetanus Sustained muscle contraction that results from continuous stimulation.

Tetrad A pair of homologous chromosomes synapsing during prophase I of meoisis. Each chromosome consists of two sister chromatids; thus, each tetrad consists of four chromatids.

Thalamus The relay center between the brainstem and the cerebral cortex; located in the posterior part of the forebrain.

Thoracic duct The lymphatic vessel that empties lymph into the bloodstream.

Threshold The lowest magnitude of stimulus strength that will induce a response.

Thrombin An enzyme that participates in blood clotting; it converts fibrinogen into fibrin.

Thymine A pyrimidine present in DNA but not in RNA; it forms hydrogen bonds with adenine.

Thymus A ductless gland in the upper chest region of vertebrates; it functions in the development of the immune system.

Thyroid A vertebrate endocrine gland located in the neck; it synthesizes thyroxine.

Thyroxine A hormone produced and released by the thyroid that regulates metabolic rate.

Tissue A mass of similar cells and support structures organized into a functional unit.

Tonus A continuous state of muscle contraction.

Trachea The tube that connects the pharynx to the bronchi; the windpipe.

Transcription The synthesis of RNA molecules from a DNA template.

Transduction The transposition of genetic material from one organism to another by a virus. See *bacteriaphage.*

Transfer RNA (tRNA) RNA molecules that bind to specific amino acids and carry them to ribosome/mRNA complexes during protein synthesis.

Transformation Uptake and incorporation of "naked" DNA by a recipient bacterial cell.

Translation The process by which protein synthesis is directed by an mRNA nucleotide sequence.

Uracil A pyrimidine found in RNA but not DNA; it forms hydrogen bonds with adenine.

Urea A nitrogenous waste product produced in the liver from ammonia and CO_2.

Ureter The duct that carries urine from the kidneys to the bladder.

Urethra The tube that leads from the bladder to the exterior.

Urine Liquid waste resulting from the filtration, reabsorption, and secretion of filtrate in the nephron.

Uterus Organ in the mammalian female reproductive system that is the site of embryonic development.

Vaccine A solution of fractionated, dead, or attenuated live pathogenic material that is introduced into an individual for the purpose of stimulating a primary immune response or "boosting" a previously produced anamnestic state.

Vacuole A membrane-bound organelle in which water-soluble nutrients and wastes are stored.

Vagus nerve The tenth cranial nerve; it innervates the pharynx, larynx, heart, lungs, and abdominal viscera. Responsible for maintaining homeostatic activity.

Vas deferens The tube carrying sperm from the testis to the urethra in mammalian males.

Vasopressin See *antidiuretic hormone.*

Vena cavae Two large veins, the superior vena cava and the inferior vena cava, that return deoxygenated blood from the periphery to the heart (right atrium).

Ventral Pertaining to the undersurface or front surface of an organism.

Ventricles The chambers of the heart that pump blood into pulmonary and systemic circulation.

Vertebrate Member of phylum chordata possessing a backbone composed of vertebrae (member of subphylum vertebrata). Compare *invertebrate.*

Vestigial Referring to an organ or limb that has no apparent function now but was functional at some time in the organism's evolutionary past.

Villus A small projection from the wall of the small intestine that increases the surface area for digestion and absorption.

Virus A tiny, organism-like particle composed of protein-encased nucleic acid; viruses are obligate parasites.

Vitamin An organic nutrient that an organism cannot produce itself and that is required by the organism in small amounts to aid in proper metabolic functioning; vitamins often function as cofactors for enzymes.

White matter The portion of the central nervous system consisting primarily of myelinated axons. Compare *gray matter.*

Wild type A genetics term for the phenotype characteristic of the majority of individuals in a particular species.

X chromosome The female sex chromosome.

Y chromosome The male sex chromosome.

Zygote The diploid ($2N$) cell that results from the fusion of two haploid (N) gametes.

Zymogen An inactive enzyme precursor that is converted into an active enzyme.

Index